THE
CHAMPAGNE
GUIDE

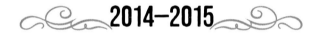

2014–2015

For Henri Krug

Published in 2013 by Hardie Grant Books

Hardie Grant Books (Australia)
Ground Floor, Building 1
658 Church Street
Richmond, Victoria 3121
www.hardiegrant.com.au

Hardie Grant Books (UK)
Dudley House, North Suite
34–35 Southampton Street
London WC2E 7HF
www.hardiegrant.co.uk

A Cataloguing-in-Publication entry is available from the catalogue of the
National Library of Australia at www.nla.gov.au
The Champagne Guide 2014–2015
ISBN 9781742705415

Publisher: Fran Berry
Project Editor: Hannah Koelmeyer
Editor: Katri Hilden
Design Manager: Heather Menzies
Text design: Clare O'Loughlin
Cover design: Aileen Lord
Design: Susanne Geppert
Photographer: Tyson Stelzer
Production: Todd Rechner

Colour reproduction by Splitting Image Colour Studio
Printed in China by 1010 Printing International Limited

THE DEFINITIVE GUIDE TO THE CHAMPAGNE REGION

THE
CHAMPAGNE
GUIDE

2014–2015

'THE BEST GUIDE EVER PUBLISHED ON CHAMPAGNE'
— *Huon Hooke, Sydney Morning Herald*

TYSON STELZER

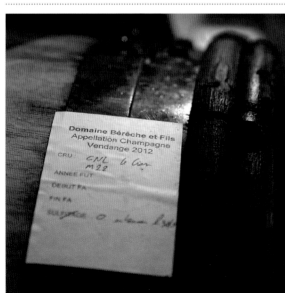
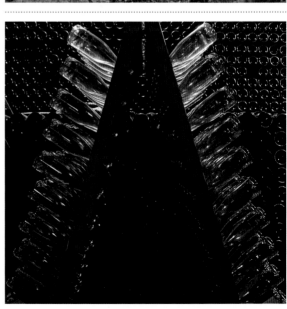

Contents

OPPOSITE, CLOCKWISE FROM TOP LEFT: *Grand cru pinot noir ripening in Mailly-Champagne; the historic street sign of Vilmart, the leading grower in Rilly-la-Montagne; pruning grand cru chardonnay in Oger in winter 2013; riddling rosé at Le Brun-Servenay in Avize; vintage 2012 maturing in barrel at Bérèche in Craon de Ludes; grand cru chardonnay ripening in the cool summer of 2011 in Le Mesnil-sur-Oger.*

ON THIN ICE

A dramatic midwinter night descends on an ancient northern village. Icy gusts race off the Montagne de Reims, howl through the narrow cobblestone streets of Rilly-la-Montagne and disappear into vines clinging to the slopes below. The clock strikes midnight and the temperature plummets to nine degrees below zero. A blizzard whips up, spiralling around corners, battering pointed rooftops and blasting a whitewash of snow at vines outfacing the elements. Then, as quickly as it came, everything falls into tranquil silence. The last, lingering snowflakes dance in slow motion before completing a perfect white veil over one of Champagne's oldest wine villages.

THERE'S AN EERIE CALM TO THE STILLNESS OF THIS place. The streets are deserted tonight. Safely tucked away behind thick stone walls, tired bodies thaw in warm beds. At dawn, frozen feet will crunch along countless rows of vines, heaving giant, rusted wheelbarrows ablaze with this year's prunings, bringing what warmth they can to numb fingers, shaping vines for a harvest that will not come to life for eight months.

Vines stand in lifeless silence in the frigid darkness, sullen under star and sky, speechless in the deathly cold. A rabbit darts up a row, hopeful for green shoots. It will find no life in this frozen landscape for at least two months, yet even these dormant days play their part in the life cycle of this foreboding place. The cold kills oïdium, lurking in the soil to pounce at the first opportunity in spring, with the menacing power to destroy a harvest.

And so the cycle of the seasons has gone for centuries. There is a timelessness to this place. Vines have thrived around Rilly-la-Montagne, on the foothills of one of the highest points of the Montagne de Reims, for 1500 years, and probably much longer. As the snow settles tonight, the twinkling lights of the ancient city of Reims come into view, winking across the plains below. This is a sacred city, the spiritual capital of France, the birthplace of the monarchy, where its kings were crowned for eight centuries, now the world's spiritual home of sparkling wine.

Deep below, cavernous chambers hewn into solid chalk by Roman hands in the 3rd century are home to a billion bottles, tiny glass tombs buried in the silence of the earth, in blissful ignorance of the snowstorm above.

Cramant, the mightiest grand cru of the Côte des Blancs, catches the pale midwinter sun from under its shroud of white snow.

The lazy sun will show its pale face for the first time in two weeks tomorrow, lurking limpid above the Montagne, reserving its energy for another day when it will reluctantly bring a new vintage to life in one of the coldest wine regions on the planet. The vivid colours of warmer days have long faded to bleak browns and stark greys. Vast plains and gentle slopes are transformed by brilliant snow white, etched with the dark lines of meticulously pruned vines.

This winter wonderland evokes joyful childhood memories of white Christmases, of magical storybook scenes of quaint villages clinging to the edges of an ancient Montagne, pinpointed by fairytale steeples reaching out of rooftops perfectly iced by a blizzard's fury. Bathed in soft, golden, angelic light, it's easy to imagine everything is perfect in this blissful panorama. The truth for Champagne is a very different story.

Rilly-la-Montagne stands as a sentinel to the sweep of history, never lifting its gaze from the remarkable drama that has played out on the fields below over four millennia. Champagne has always been a flashpoint of tension. Attila the Hun was defeated here in the Catalonic Field Battle in the 5th century, it was here that the Knights Templar was founded in the 12th century, crusades planned in the 13th, Napoleon fought the Russians in the 19th, and bitter conflict ensued in the First and Second World Wars. The fight today is a different one, as vignerons battle earth and sky in the ultimate quest to nurture grapes to ripeness.

'It is very difficult to grow wines in this terroir — we have so many wars!' exclaims Veuve Clicquot Chef de Cave Dominique Demarville. A struggle with the elements is a day-to-day battle in this land where climates collide and leave their indelible stamp on a vintage. Of all the fabled winegrowing slopes on the planet, none are more formidable than these for ripening grapes. The average annual temperature here is an icy 10°C. In February 1985, it plummeted to −22°C, killing vines. Louis Roederer Chef de Cave, Jean-Baptiste Lécaillon, refers to a tension between continental and oceanic weather. 'The balance of oceanic push and continental neutrality is the story of Champagne and the diversity of our climate,' he says.

The drama of this story is intensifying. In June 2012, one of the most ferocious hailstorms in the history of Champagne battered the village of Urville, leaving a corridor of destruction in its wake like a typhoon, stripping vines bare of leaves and fruit. In 15 minutes, more than half the vines of the village were obliterated. Damage was estimated at 130%, as the entire 2012 crop was lost and likely one-third of 2013.

Such is the adventure, and such is the menace, of growing grapes in Champagne.

'In Champagne we have two advantages: bad weather and bad soils!' quips Pol Roger's Managing Director Laurent d'Harcourt. Champagne's landscape below the ground is just as wild as that above. While limestone is considered the holy grail of the greatest chardonnay and pinot noir, this stark, lifeless, infertile chalk stone is a harsh environment in which to implant any living thing. 'It is amazing that people have the passion to continue to make wines in this region,' Demarville reflects.

The magic of Champagne is alive in this cruel place, not in spite of its tough soil and dismal climate, but because of it. If this were some idyllic, sun-drenched haven, there would be no sparkling wine at all. Champagne would be just a northerly outpost of Burgundy, celebrated for nothing more than chardonnay and pinot noir.

There is a romance to Champagne quite unlike any other wine land on earth. Contrary to everything hopeful marketers would have us believe, this is not a romance of glamorous estates, illustrious histories, elaborate packaging, fabricated prestige, gushing rhetoric, stratospheric pricing, flirtations with royalty, sightings with supermodels, or websites with more animated glitz that you can point a cursor at. It's a romance that goes beyond the bubbles, beyond the atmosphere of ancient chalk cellars and chalk-infused vineyards gracing gentle slopes, beyond even a people as dignified and determined as the champagnes they devote their lives to raising. The real romance of champagne is a tough love. It's about a desperate struggle to root vines into stark white stone. About grappling for survival in the most harrowing wine-growing climate on the planet. And about transforming an insipidly austere and unpalatably acidic juice into the most celebrated beverage in the world.

This is the real story of Champagne. It's a tale lost behind guarded brands and marketing frippery. It's time the true Champagne is brought out from ancient caverns and into the gentle light of day. Again this year I have scoured Champagne, clambering up vineyard slopes, exploring cellars, tasting from tank, barrel and bottle to discover a place of more intricate detail and wildly contrasting extremes than I have ever imagined. I have again fought my way through the froth and bubble of the most overmarketed wine region in the world to unearth the truth behind every champagne in this guide. All that counts here is taste, and the places, procedures and people that bring it to life. This book gets under the surface of Champagne to unearth the terroirs, the grapes, the craft and the hands that make the wine in your glass smell, taste and bubble like no other on the planet.

The stark truth of this place is far more gripping than even the most clever marketing campaign can fabricate, a tale of tension between earth and sky, played out in full cinematic drama every year. Of all my weeks in Champagne, in summer and winter, all but a few days have been dank, sodden days of misty mornings, sullen grey skies and unrelenting rain. My photos throughout this book are as much an attempt to capture the real Champagne as my words. This is not a land painted in vibrant pastel hues and vivid colours, but of autumn and winter shades of brown and grey, and the glistening, crystalline white of bitter cold.

Tonight, twilight comes early. Even in the dead of winter, movements of the heavenly bodies illuminate the personalities of each Champagne terroir. Under a blanket of white, one by one the majestic slopes bid fare-well to the lazy sun as it is subsumed by the horizon. When most vineyards lurk in long shadows, the beacons of the southern slopes of the Montagne de Reims glow golden in the winter twilight, like giant solar traps watching every movement of the pale northern sun, recording every detail of the season in tiny buds deep within the wood of every vine. Even now, the majesty of these grand slopes and their generous wines is as clear as daylight.

On the northern slopes of the Montagne, the twi-light has faded in Rilly-la-Montagne. The sun has retired, never mustering the energy to melt its icy shroud today. Weary feet crunch home, leaving barrows smouldering between rows of vines. Night sets in and all is still. But sky and soil are never silent in Champagne. Another season has dawned and the vine has begun transcribing its dramatic story in the record of its fruits.

The Champagne Guide

BIENVENUE!
Welcome to the most up-to-date Champagne Guide

There's a dazzling world of champagne to be discovered. Never have a greater variety of styles, wider diversity of brands or more exquisite quality emerged from the source of the finest fizz on earth. Champagne offers more options than ever to add sparkle to your occasion, your cuisine, your mood and your taste. It's a thrilling chase to find just the right bottle, but it can be a daunting task, too. This guide will take the guesswork out of your next bottle of bubbles.

EVERY BOTTLE OF CHAMPAGNE HAS ITS OWN STORY. Its story shapes its personality. The complexities of champagne growing and production create more intricately detailed characters than any other wine. Yet most Champagne brands offer very little insight into the personality of the house and its cuvées. This book dares to get under the surface of this vast and complex place to uncover the character of every champagne worthy of your attention.

The intricate personality of a bottle of champagne is shaped by its house style, vintages, grape varieties, reserve wines, winemaking techniques, Chef de Cave preferences, maturation time, dosage, time since disgorgement and, of course, the terroir of the vineyards themselves. In the following pages, you'll discover not just what these things mean but, most importantly, how they smell, taste and feel in more than 500 champagnes from close to 100 houses, all of which have been tasted recently.

An understanding of a champagne's personality will guide you to identify the styles that most appeal to your palate, and then to discover new and exciting champagnes in a similar shape. It will help you to hone in on the best time and place to serve them, the most suitable cuisines to match, and, most importantly, point you towards the very best that Champagne has to offer, for every taste and every budget.

UP-TO-THE MOMENT GUIDE
Champagne is a fast-moving target, and an up-to-the-minute guide to the champagnes to drink this year is just as critical as it is for any other wine. This is why this book is very different to every other champagne

guide. Time is everything in the development of champagne, and the landscape of the wines on the shelves is changing rapidly. Since my last edition, new vintages have landed and non-vintages have rolled on to new blends. Non-vintage champagne is always based on one or two years, and even the most skilful blender with the greatest depth of reserve wines remains at the mercy of the raw materials presented by an ever more temperamental mother nature. Successive batches are never the same, particularly evident this year, with the distinctive 2008 vintage base almost always superior to 2007 and 2009.

On occasions when last year's vintage is still current, I've retasted the wine and written an all-new review. I'm amazed how quickly some have blossomed, and others have wilted.

Champagne is the most intricately complex of all wines to craft, and hence to assess. Every bottle has two lives, one relying on the sustaining presence of the lees prior to disgorgement, and the other in more rapid development post-disgorgement. Its evolution is not only a question of years since vintage, but also years, months and even weeks since disgorgement. A non-vintage champagne disgorged three months ago will present a different impression of its dosage than the same wine disgorged nine months ago. A rosé disgorged in time for Christmas 2013 will be much fresher than the 2012 release. And a vintage wine shipped this year has spent a year longer on lees than the same vintage shipped last year, and will present a different personality accordingly. Furthermore, different disgorgements are often based upon subtly different blends, if not completely different base wines altogether. Many houses tweak the dosage, with later disgorgements typically receiving less sugar.

This presents a dilemma in communicating meaningful guidance on each cuvée, prompting me to compile this book unlike any other champagne guide. Every champagne featured here was tasted recently, almost exclusively in the first half of 2013. Not all champagnes travel as confidently as others, and the concerns I raised last year regarding storage, care of handling and timely arrival into export markets have only exacerbated in my tastings this year, so I have earnestly sought to retaste as many wines outside Champagne as possible, in some cases in as many as four different places.

This has all led me to a bold step which may be unprecedented in champagne publishing: inclusion not only of disgorgement date, base vintage and location of tasting, but also of different scores for the same cuvée when these details change. A complex undertaking, but I'm convinced there's no other way to fairly interpret champagne for its markets across the globe.

I have resisted the temptation to publish drinking windows. The complexities of champagne ageing pre- and post-disgorgement confound any guidance that I could offer. A late-disgorged champagne freshly plucked from a very cold chalk cellar under the house where it was made will always tell a very different tale to the same wine disgorged and shipped decades ago and kept far away under different conditions.

I've recently admired champagnes from seven decades, and marvelled at the freshness of recently disgorged old bottles, but any attempt to extrapolate this to the lifespan of early-disgorged wines is tricky. I have instead noted champagnes with the potential to age, and those coming to the end of their life.

INTERNATIONAL GUIDE

Publishing a true international champagne guide to this level of detail, featuring only recently tasted, current disgorgements, has again proved a monumental undertaking. The pace of change in the champagne landscape this year is nothing short of astounding, and champagne lovers the world over are thirsty for fresh guidance. The increasing international interest in this publication prompted a welcome offer from Hardie Grant to publish this edition, and offer global distribution.

This could not come at a more important time. In 2012, Champagne shipped more bottles outside the European Union than ever before. As the economic instability of Europe intensifies, Champagne is focusing on growing its exports to countries like the US,

Japan, Australia and China. Strong double-digit growth in champagne consumption was again shown by Japan, Australia and China in 2012. Dom Pérignon Chef de Cave Richard Geoffroy describes this as the year champagne really started to explode in China. For Veuve Clicquot's Dominique Demarville, the crisis in Europe is an opportunity for Champagne to reassess itself and expand its markets across Asia.

As champagne better establishes itself around the world, misconceptions abound. The sweeping generalisations of popular rhetoric that characterise our thinking about modern wine, for good and for bad, hold less weight in Champagne than perhaps anywhere else. It is not strictly true that grower producers are good and négociant houses are bad, parallel imports are inferior, low dosage is best, small growers are more attentive than large ones, low yields are better than high, organics and biodynamics always out-perform traditional viticulture, mid-slopes are superior to high and low sites, deep roots instil more minerality than shallow, grand cru is better than premier cru, Côte des Blancs is good and the Aube is bad, natural corks are best, or that chardonnay ages long and pinot meunier does not.

Such questions cut to the core of the present and future of Champagne, and there is much to be unearthed about each in the coming pages. Champagne is a profoundly complex place, and if you catch just a glimpse of its vivid detail, this book has achieved its goal.

To guarantee that you're up to speed with the very latest in Champagne, I've updated all 95 champagne producers, dropped a few lesser estates and added more than 20 important players. Commentary on the current state of play in the region has been fully updated and expanded. With a massive 70% more content than the last edition, I've crammed in as many houses and reviews as I can. There simply aren't enough pages to include everything, so for the first time you'll find four additional houses, more than 40 cuvées and a chapter on Champagne's best restaurants at www.champagneguide.com.au.

By request, I've also included pronunciations of the name of every house and grower. If in doubt, set Google Translate's 'Listen' feature to 'French'.

A new era in champagne has arrived, and there has never been a better time to raise a glass to discover the intricate personality of the most celebrated beverage on earth. Get ready to sparkle.

Cumières, one of Champagne's 319 villages, rising in prominence as its growers capture the character of its sunny slopes.

Using this guide

*C*hasing the best fizz that money can buy? Bienvenue! Your glass is about to froth over. You'll be astounded at what Champagne has to offer if you know what to look for this year, and the following pages will guarantee you don't miss a thing. Even in the lowest price bracket, I've found 10 champagnes worthy of a gold medal in a wine show — twice as many as last year.

What do my scores mean?

Points are a quick way to highlight the best champagnes in each category. It seems a travesty to reduce the grand complexities of champagne to a number, but scores are offered for those who find them useful. Broadly, anything less than 85 is faulty, less than 90 is sound but unexciting, and 91 is where all the real fun begins. A 94 point champagne has impeccable purity and immaculate balance — a gold medal in a wine show. Beyond, it's not greater concentration of flavour, more obvious fruit or more clever winemaking tricks that set it apart. True greatness is declared by something more profound: the inimitable stamp of place — 'terroir' to the French, articulated most eloquently in length of finish and palate texture. Persistence of aftertaste and depth of mineral character to distinguish the very finest champagnes.

100 The pinnacle of character, balance and persistence. This year, less than 1% of champagnes tasted scored 100 points. Sadly, they're all ear-splittingly expensive.

99 Almost perfection (20 on the 20 point scale). Less than 1% of champagnes tasted.

98 An exceedingly rare calibre of world-class distinction. Less than 3% of champagnes tasted. The prestige cuvées of the top houses tend to rule this territory.

97 More than exceptional; 4% of champagnes tasted. Look out for one $$$ cuvée in the stratosphere this year.

96 Exceptional. Top gold or trophy standard in a wine show (19/20); 8% of champagnes tasted. There's something for everyone here this year.

95 Offering an edge that pushes beyond excellent. 16% of champagnes tasted.

94 Excellent champagne that I love. Gold medal in a wine show (18.5/20). 18% of champagnes tasted. Look out for ten $ cuvées.

93 Almost excellent; 11% of champagnes tasted.

92 A very good wine that characterises its place and variety; 11% of champagnes tasted.

91 Better than good, offering an edge of distinction. Silver medal (17/20); 7% of champagnes tasted. With more than 425 champagnes at 91 or above this year, why drink anything less?

90 A good wine that I like; 4% of champagnes tasted. Only buy if it's cheap.

89 Better than sound and almost good; 4% of champagnes tasted.

88 Sound. Worth buying if it's cheap. Bronze medal standard (15.5/20); 3% of champagnes tasted.

87 Almost sound; 3% of champagnes tasted.

86 Simple and ordinary. Less than 1% of champagnes tasted.

85 Ordinary and boring, though without notable faults (14/20); 1% of champagnes tasted.

84 Borderline faulty. Less than 1% of champagnes tasted.

83 Faulty. Less than 1% of champagnes tasted. Caution!

82 Distinctly faulty (12/20). Less than 1% of champagnes tasted.

81 Exceedingly faulty. Less than 1% of champagnes tasted. Stand well clear.

80 Horrid. Less than 1% of champagnes tasted. You've been warned.

See page 350 for a full list of wines by score

The Champagne Guide

Price

WHETHER YOU'RE ON THE HUNT FOR A BARGAIN OR A DECADENT SPLURGE, THIS GUIDE WILL HELP YOU FIND THE right bottle in no time. Each cuvée is price-coded to indicate what you can expect to pay in an average retail store. Champagne is one of the most readily-discounted wines on the shelves, so shop around and you're sure to find the big brands on special. Back-vintage champagnes not currently available are listed without indication of price.

	Euros (France)	Great British Pounds	US Dollars	Australian Dollars	Hong Kong Dollars	Singapore Dollars
$	‹€25	‹£30	‹$50	‹$60	‹$400	‹$80
$$	€25–50	£30–50	$50–80	$60–100	$400–550	$80–140
$$$	€51–65	£51–65	$81–100	$101–150	$551–650	$141–160
$$$$	€66–140	£66–130	$101–200	$151–300	$651–1100	$161–250
$$$$$	›€140	›£130	›$200	›$300	›$1100	›$250

PAST VINTAGES

Champagne is capable of maturing magnificently. Alongside current releases, this guide features past and future vintages tasted recently. This reflects the various vintages available in different markets, puts an estate's cuvées in a historical context, and provides an insight into the potential of its most age-worthy vintages. We can all envy those who might have an old bottle or two lurking in the cellar, and perhaps be enticed to lay one down for a decade or two ourselves.

Three editions of this book now in print, each featuring fresh tastings, provide an accumulating catalogue of successive releases. I've resisted the temptation to create a hulking archive of every champagne I've ever tasted, preferring to offer a relevant, up-to-date snapshot of champagnes just as you'll find them this year.

CHAMPAGNE VINTAGES

The tumultuous climate of Champagne makes the stamp of the season more dramatic than in any other wine region. Champagne has seen two decades of wild vintage fluctuations, recording two of its finest seasons ever in 1996 and 2008, and two of its most challenging in 2001 and 2003.

There's a disconcerting trend in Champagne to release vintage wines more often. While some Chef de Caves argue that a progressive warming of the climate has rendered more seasons capable of standing alone, I am increasingly unconvinced of the merits of warm seasons like 2001, 2003 and 2005. Many houses and growers were ambitious in releasing vintage wines from 2003 and 2005. We have now entered an era in which greater consumer discernment is necessary in selecting vintages. There are notable exceptions highlighted throughout this guide, but the general rule for the first decade of the new millennium is to stick with the even years. Here's my ranking of the past two decades of Champagne vintages, from best to worse.

The great vintages: 1996, 2008, 2012, 2002, 1995, 1998. The good vintages: 2000, 2004, 1999, 2006, 2007, 2009. The poor vintages: 2005, 2010, 1997, 2011, 2003, 2001.

Storm clouds over Fleury-la-Rivière just before vintage 2011. Champagne's wild climate produces dramatic vintage variations.

ON THE HOUSE

*T*he Best Champagnes of the Year lists on the following pages highlight the most important wines in this book. These are the finest fizzes that money can buy this year, the most reliable bargains, the most pristine big blends, the most sought-after growers, the most sublime rosés, the most brilliant blanc de blancs, the most balanced low-dosage champagnes, and the upper reaches of the stratosphere of prestige.

THE CHAMPAGNE GUIDE 2014–2015 HALL OF HONOUR acknowledges the finest houses of the year. A house is only as worthy as its current cuvées, so its rating is based exclusively on the quality of its wines in the market this year, not on past performance or museum wines. History and reputation count for nothing if current wines don't live up to expectation. Underperforming houses do not deserve your attention nor mine, so unless a house scores at least 5 out of 10, it does not score at all.

Roughly, to rate 10 out of 10, the entry non-vintage cuvée of the house would typically score 95/100, vintage cuvées around 96, and prestige cuvées 97.

To attain 5 out of 10, these numbers drop to 91, 93 and 94 respectively.

There is a prudent saying in Champagne that if you make a good brut NV, you are a good house. The entry-level cuvées that comprise the majority of the house's production bear a strong weighting in its rating.

The watering of the barrels in the courtyard of the fabled house of Krug, the most luxurious and decadent of all champagnes.

HALL OF HONOUR

The Champagne Guide
• 2014–2015 •

The Best Champagnes of the Year

❧ Under $ ❧

AGRAPART & FILS 7 CRUS BRUT NV
$ ● 94 POINTS ● PAGE 55

AGRAPART & FILS TERROIRS BLANC DE BLANCS GRAND CRU EXTRA BRUT NV
$ ● 94 POINTS ● PAGE 55

CAMILLE SAVÈS CARTE BLANCHE BRUT NV
$ ● 94 POINTS ● PAGE 91

L. BÉNARD-PITOIS BRUT NATURE NV
$ ● 94 POINTS ● PAGE 217

L. BÉNARD-PITOIS BRUT RÉSERVE NV
$ ● 94 POINTS ● PAGE 216

LANSON ROSE LABEL BRUT ROSÉ NV
$ ● 94 POINTS ● PAGE 227

LENOBLE CUVÉE INTENSE BRUT NATURE DOSAGE ZÉRO NV
$ ● 94 POINTS ● PAGE 248

LENOBLE CUVÉE INTENSE NV
$ ● 94 POINTS ● PAGE 248

PHILIPPONNAT ROYALE RÉSERVE BRUT NV
$ ● 94 POINTS ● PAGE 283

TARLANT ZERO BRUT NATURE NV
$ ● 94 POINTS ● PAGE 327

J. DUMANGIN FILS BRUT 17 NV
$ ● 93 POINTS ● PAGE 182

J. DUMANGIN FILS GRANDE RÉSERVE BRUT NV
$ ● 93 POINTS ● PAGE 183

J. DUMANGIN FILS BRUT PREMIER CRU ROSÉ NV
$ ● 93 POINTS ● PAGE 183

LAHERTE FRÈRES BLANC DE BLANCS ULTRADITION NV
$ ● 93 POINTS ● PAGE 221

LANSON BLACK LABEL BRUT NV
$ ● 93 POINTS ● PAGE 227

PIERRE GIMONNET & FILS BRUT IER CRU CUIS BLANC DE BLANCS NV
$ ● 93 POINTS ● PAGE 289

PIERRE GIMONNET & FILS BRUT SELECTION BELLES ANNEES IER CRU BLANC DE BLANCS NV
$ ● 93 POINTS ● PAGE 289

TARLANT BRUT RESERVE NV
$ ● 93 POINTS ● PAGE 326

❧ Under $$ ❧

ANDRÉ CLOUET BRUT MILLESIME 2008
$$ ● 96 POINTS ● PAGE 63

BOLLINGER SPECIAL CUVÉE BRUT NV
$$ ● 96 POINTS ● PAGE 89

DE SOUSA CUVÉE 3A EXTRA BRUT NV
$$ ● 96 POINTS ● PAGE 108

ERIC RODEZ CUVÉE MILLÉSIME 2004
$$ ● 96 POINTS ● PAGE 141

GEORGES LAVAL CUMIÈRES PREMIER CRU BRUT NV
$$ ● 96 POINTS ● PAGE 166

JACQUESSON CUVÉE NO 736 EXTRA BRUT NV
$$ ● 96 POINTS ● PAGE 199

BILLECART-SALMON BRUT RÉSERVE NV
$$ ● 95 POINTS ● PAGE 79

ERIC RODEZ CUVÉE BLANC DE NOIRS NV
$$ ● 95 POINTS ● PAGE 140

GASTON CHIQUET CUVÉE OR BRUT MILLÉSIMÉ 2004
$$ ● 95 POINTS ● PAGE 155

GATINOIS GRAND CRU BRUT RÉSERVE NV
$$ ● 95 POINTS ● PAGE 157

GATINOIS GRAND CRU BRUT MILLÉSIMÉ 2006
$$ ● 95 POINTS ● PAGE 158

J. LASSALLE CUVÉE ANGÉLINE PREMIER CRU BRUT 2007
$$ ● 95 POINTS ● PAGE 187

LAHERTE FRÈRES LES VIGNES D'AUTREFOIS 2008
$$ ● 95 POINTS ● PAGE 222

LANSON BRUT VINTAGE GOLD LABEL 2002
$$ ● 95 POINTS ● PAGE 228

LE BRUN-SERVENAY BRUT MILLÉSIME VIEILLES VIGNES 2004
$$ ● 95 POINTS ● PAGE 243

NAPOLÉON BRUT VINTAGE 1998
$$ ● 95 POINTS ● PAGE 267

PASCAL DOQUET PREMIER CRU VERTUS 2004
$$ ● 95 POINTS ● PAGE 272

PAUL BARA BOUZY BRUT RÉSERVE NV
$$ ● 95 POINTS ● PAGE 274

TARLANT CUVÉE LOUIS NV
$$ ● 95 POINTS ● PAGE 329

❧ Under $$$ ❧

ANDRÉ CLOUET 1911 NV
$$$ ● 96 POINTS ● PAGE 63

BILLECART-SALMON CUVÉE SOUS BOIS BRUT NV
$$$ ● 96 POINTS ● PAGE 81

EMMANUEL BROCHET EXTRA BRUT PREMIER CRU MILLESIME 2006
$$$ ● 96 POINTS ● PAGE 137

GOSSET GRAND MILLÉSIME BRUT 2004
$$$ ● 96 POINTS ● PAGE 171

J. LASSALLE SPECIAL CLUB BRUT 2004
$$$ ● 96 POINTS ● PAGE 187

PAUL BARA SPECIAL CLUB 2004
$$$ ● 96 POINTS ● PAGE 275

PAUL BARA SPECIAL CLUB ROSÉ 2006 $$$ ● 96 POINTS ● PAGE 276

POL ROGER BRUT VINTAGE 2002
$$$ ● 96 POINTS ● PAGE 305

BÉRÈCHE ET FILS VALLÉE DE LA MARNE RIVE GAUCHE NV
$$$ ● 95 POINTS ● PAGE 74

The Champagne Guide

CHARLES HEIDSIECK MILLESIME
BRUT 2000
$$$ ● 95 POINTS ● PAGE 98

EGLY-OURIET LES VIGNES DE
VRIGNY PREMIER CRU BRUT NV
$$$ ● 95 POINTS ● PAGE 134

ERIC RODEZ CUVÉE DES GRANDS
VINTAGES NV
$$$ ● 95 POINTS ● PAGE 141

JACQUES PICARD ART DE VIGNE
BRUT MILLESIME 2002
$$$ ● 95 POINTS ● PAGE 193

LANSON EXTRA AGE BRUT NV
$$$ ● 95 POINTS ● PAGE 229

LAURENT-PERRIER MILLESIME 2002
$$$ ● 95 POINTS ● PAGE 239

PAUL DÉTHUNE CUVÉE PRESTIGE
BRUT NV
$$$ ● 95 POINTS ● PAGE 278

TAITTINGER CUVÉE BRUT
MILLÉSIME 2004
$$$ ● 95 POINTS ● PAGE 321

VILMART & CIE GRAND CELLIER
D'OR BRUT PREMIER CRU 2007
$$$ ● 95 POINTS ● PAGE 346

Under $$$$

BILLECART-SALMON CUVÉE
NICOLAS FRANÇOIS
BILLECART 2002
$$$$ ● 99 POINTS ● PAGE 82

BILLECART-SALMON CUVÉE
ELISABETH SALMON BRUT
ROSÉ 2002
$$$$ ● 98 POINTS ● PAGE 83

BILLECART-SALMON CUVÉE
NICOLAS FRANÇOIS BILLECART
2000
$$$$ ● 98 POINTS ● PAGE 83

DE SOUSA CUVÉE DES CAUDALIES
BRUT ROSÉ NV
$$$$ ● 98 POINTS ● PAGE 109

BILLECART-SALMON BLANC DE
BLANCS BRUT 1999
$$$$ ● 97 POINTS ● PAGE 82

BOLLINGER LA GRANDE ANNÉE
BRUT 2002
$$$$ ● 97 POINTS ● PAGE 90

CHARLES HEIDSIECK BLANC DES
MILLÉNAIRES 1995
$$$$ ● 97 POINTS ● PAGE 99

DEUTZ CUVÉE WILLIAM DEUTZ
ROSÉ MILLÉSIME 2002
$$$$ ● 97 POINTS ● PAGE 115

GOSSET CUVÉE CELEBRIS BLANC DE
BLANCS EXTRA BRUT NV
$$$$ ● 97 POINTS ● PAGE 172

GOSSET CUVÉE CELEBRIS EXTRA
BRUT VINTAGE 1998
$$$$ ● 97 POINTS ● PAGE 172

KRUG GRANDE CUVÉE NV
$$$$ ● 97 POINTS ● PAGE 211

LAURENT-PERRIER GRAND
SIÈCLE NV
$$$$ ● 97 POINTS ● PAGE 240

POL ROGER SIR WINSTON
CHURCHILL 2000
$$$$ ● 97 POINTS ● PAGE 306

VEUVE CLICQUOT LA GRANDE
DAME BRUT 2004
$$$$ ● 97 POINTS ● PAGE 337

BOLLINGER LA GRANDE ANNÉE
BRUT 2004
$$$$ ● 96 POINTS ● PAGE 90

DEUTZ CUVÉE WILLIAM DEUTZ
BRUT MILLÉSIME 1999
$$$$ ● 96 POINTS ● PAGE 115

DEUTZ CUVÉE WILLIAM DEUTZ
BRUT MILLÉSIME 2000
$$$$ ● 96 POINTS ● PAGE 115

DUVAL-LEROY FEMME DE
CHAMPAGNE 2000
$$$$ ● 96 POINTS ● PAGE 132

JACQUES SELOSSE V.O. GRAND
CRU BLANC DE BLANCS EXTRA
BRUT NV
$$$$ ● 96 POINTS ● PAGE 195

JACQUESSON MILLÉSIME 2000
$$$$ ● 96 POINTS ● PAGE 200

LANSON NOBLE CUVÉE BRUT
MILLÉSIMÉ 2000
$$$$ ● 96 POINTS ● PAGE 230

VILMART & CIE COEUR DE CUVÉE
PREMIER CRU 2002
$$$$ ● 96 POINTS ● PAGE 347

Under $$$$$

BILLECART-SALMON LE CLOS
SAINT-HILAIRE 1998
$$$$$ ● 100 POINTS ● PAGE 84

DOM PÉRIGNON
OENOTHÈQUE 1996
$$$$$ ● 100 POINTS ● PAGE 125

KRUG CLOS DU MESNIL 2000
$$$$$ ● 100 POINTS ● PAGE 213

KRUG CLOS D'AMBONNAY 1998
$$$$$ ● 100 POINTS ● PAGE 214

BILLECART-SALMON GRANDE
CUVÉE 1998
$$$$$ ● 99 POINTS ● PAGE 84

KRUG VINTAGE 1998
$$$$$ ● 99 POINTS ● PAGE 212

DOM PÉRIGNON 2004
$$$$$ ● 98 POINTS ● PAGE 124

JACQUESSON AŸ VAUZELLE TERME
RECOLTE BRUT 2002
$$$$$ ● 98 POINTS ● PAGE 202

KRUG VINTAGE 2000
$$$$$ ● 98 POINTS ● PAGE 212

KRUG ROSÉ BRUT NV
$$$$$ ● 98 POINTS ● PAGE 213

TAITTINGER COMTES
DE CHAMPAGNE BLANC DE
BLANCS 2002
$$$$$ ● 98 POINTS ● PAGE 322

TAITTINGER COMTES
DE CHAMPAGNE BLANC DE
BLANCS 2004
$$$$$ ● 98 POINTS ● PAGE 322

DOM PÉRIGNON ROSÉ 2000
$$$$$ ● 97 POINTS ● PAGE 125

JACQUESSON DIZY CORNE
BAUTRAY RÉCOLTE BRUT 2002
$$$$$ ● 97 POINTS ● PAGE 199

LOUIS ROEDERER CRISTAL
ROSÉ 2004
$$$$$ ● 97 POINTS ● PAGE 257

SALON CUVÉE S BLANC DE BLANCS
1999
$$$$$ ● 97 POINTS ● PAGE 315

VEUVE CLICQUOT CAVE PRIVÉE
BRUT 1990
$$$$$ ● 97 POINTS ● PAGE 338

VEUVE CLICQUOT CAVE PRIVÉE
ROSÉ 1979
$$$$$ ● 97 POINTS ● PAGE 339

VEUVE CLICQUOT LA GRANDE
DAME ROSÉ 2004
$$$$$ ● 97 POINTS ● PAGE 337

The Best Blanc de Blancs Champagnes of the Year $$-$$$

PIERRE PÉTERS CUVÉE SPÉCIALE BLANC DE BLANCS LES CHÉTILLONS 2004
$$$ • 97 POINTS • PAGE 297

PIERRE GIMONNET & FILS SPECIAL CLUB BLANC DE BLANCS 2005
$$ • 96 POINTS • PAGE 292

DE SOUSA CUVÉE DES CAUDALIES BLANC DE BLANCS GRAND CRU NV
$$$ • 96 POINTS • PAGE 108

PASCAL DOQUET VIELLES VIGNES LE MESNIL-SUR-OGER BLANC DE BLANCS 2002
$$$ • 96 POINTS • PAGE 273

PIERRE GIMONNET & FILS MILLESIME DE COLLECTION BLANC DE BLANCS 2005
$$$ • 96 POINTS • PAGE 292

PIERRE PÉTERS CUVÉE SPÉCIALE BLANC DE BLANCS LES CHÉTILLONS 2006
$$$ • 96 POINTS • PAGE 296

POL ROGER BLANC DE BLANCS 2002
$$$ • 96 POINTS • PAGE 305

DE SOUSA GRAND CRU RÉSERVE BLANC DE BLANCS BRUT NV
$$ • 95 POINTS • PAGE 107

GASTON CHIQUET BLANC DE BLANCS D'AŸ NV
$$ • 95 POINTS • PAGE 154

LE MESNIL BLANC DE BLANCS 2004
$$ • 95 POINTS • PAGE 246

PIERRE GIMONNET & FILS GASTRONOME 1ER CRU BLANC DE BLANCS CUVÉE 2008
$$ • 95 POINTS • PAGE 289

PIERRE PÉTERS CUVÉE LA RÉSERVE OUBLIÉE BLANC DE BLANCS BRUT NV
$$ • 95 POINTS • PAGE 296

DELAMOTTE BLANC DE BLANCS 2002
$$$ • 95 POINTS • PAGE 111

DEUTZ BLANC DE BLANCS 2007
$$$ • 95 POINTS • PAGE 113

GODMÉ PÈRE & FILS LES ALLOUETTES SAINT BETS CHARDONNAY BRUT MILLÉSIME 2004
$$$ • 95 POINTS • PAGE 168

LENOBLE CUVÉE GENTILHOMME GRAND CRU BLANC DE BLANCS MILLÉSIME 2006
$$$ • 95 POINTS • PAGE 250

PASCAL DOQUET LE MESNIL-SUR-OGER BLANC DE BLANCS BRUT NV
$$$ • 95 POINTS • PAGE 273

PASCAL DOQUET LE MESNIL-SUR-OGER BLANC DE BLANCS COEUR DE TERROIR BRUT 2002
$$$ • 95 POINTS • PAGE 273

PIERRE PÉTERS CUVÉE SPÉCIALE BLANC DE BLANCS LES CHÉTILLONS 2005
$$$ • 95 POINTS • PAGE 297

RUINART BLANC DE BLANCS BRUT NV
$$$ • 95 POINTS • PAGE 312

The Best Rosé Champagnes of the Year $$-$$$

BOLLINGER ROSÉ BRUT NV
$$ • 96 POINTS • PAGE 89

DEUTZ BRUT ROSÉ MILLÉSIME 2008
$$$ • 96 POINTS • PAGE 114

LARMANDIER-BERNIER ROSÉ DE SAIGNÉE PREMIER CRU EXTRA BRUT NV
$$$ • 96 POINTS • PAGE 234

LOUIS ROEDERER BRUT ROSÉ 2008
$$$ • 96 POINTS • PAGE 255

PAUL BARA SPECIAL CLUB ROSÉ 2006
$$$ • 96 POINTS • PAGE 276

ANDRÉ CLOUET BRUT ROSÉ NV
$$ • 95 POINTS • PAGE 63

ERIC RODEZ CUVÉE ROSÉ NV
$$ • 95 POINTS • PAGE 141

FLEURY PÈRE & FILS ROSÉ DE SAIGNÉE BRUT NV
$$ • 95 POINTS • PAGE 146

GATINOIS GRAND CRU BRUT ROSÉ NV
$$ • 95 POINTS • PAGE 158

L. BÉNARD-PITOIS BRUT ROSÉ NV
$$ • 95 POINTS • PAGE 217

PIERRE PÉTERS CUVÉE ROSÉ FOR ALBANE BRUT NV
$$ • 95 POINTS • PAGE 296

EGLY-OURIET GRAND CRU BRUT ROSÉ NV
$$$ • 95 POINTS • PAGE 134

GOSSET GRAND ROSÉ BRUT NV
$$$ • 95 POINTS • PAGE 171

JACQUESSON DIZY TERRES ROUGES ROSÉ RÉCOLTE EXTRA BRUT 2007
$$$ • 95 POINTS • PAGE 200

LAURENT-PERRIER CUVÉE ROSÉ BRUT NV
$$$ • 95 POINTS • PAGE 239

LOUIS ROEDERER BRUT ROSÉ 2007
$$$ • 95 POINTS • PAGE 255

POL ROGER ROSÉ 2004
$$$ • 95 POINTS • PAGE 305

RUINART BRUT ROSÉ NV
$$$ • 95 POINTS • PAGE 313

The Best Low-Dosage Champagnes of the Year $$-$$$

LARMANDIER-BERNIER TERRE DE VERTUS PREMIER CRU BLANC DE BLANCS NON-DOSÉ 2008
$$$ • 96 POINTS • PAGE 234

ANDRÉ CLOUET SILVER BRUT NATURE NV
$$ • 95 POINTS • PAGE 62

CHARTOGNE-TAILLET LES ORIZEAUX EXTRA BRUT 2008
$$ • 95 POINTS • PAGE 103

LARMANDIER-BERNIER LONGITUDE BLANC DE BLANCS PREMIER CRU EXTRA BRUT NV
$$ • 95 POINTS • PAGE 233

VEUVE FOURNY & FILS CUVÉE R DE VVE FOURNY & FILS VERTUS EXTRA BRUT NV
$$ • 95 POINTS • PAGE 344

VEUVE FOURNY & FILS CUVÉE BLANC DE BLANCS VERTUS PREMIER CRU VINTAGE EXTRA BRUT 2006
$$ • 95 POINTS • PAGE 344

DUVAL-LEROY BLANC DE BLANCS BRUT NATURE 2002
$$$ • 95 POINTS • PAGE 130

ERIC RODEZ CUVÉE ZÉRO DOSAGE NV
$$ • 95 POINTS • PAGE 140

AGRAPART & FILS MINÉRAL BLANC DE BLANCS GRAND CRU EXTRA BRUT 2006
$$$ • 95 POINTS • PAGE 56

J.L. VERGNON BLANC DE BLANCS CONFIDENCE BRUT NATURE MILLÉSIME 2008
$$$ • 95 POINTS • PAGE 190

LARMANDIER-BERNIER TERRE DE VERTUS PREMIER CRU BLANC DE BLANCS NON-DOSÉ 2007
$$$ • 95 POINTS • PAGE 234

BILLECART-SALMON EXTRA BRUT NV
$$ • 94 POINTS • PAGE 79

CHARTOGNE-TAILLET CHEMIN DE REIMS EXTRA BRUT
$$ • 94 POINTS • PAGE 102

EMMANUEL BROCHET LE MONT BENOIT EXTRA BRUT NV
$$ • 94 POINTS • PAGE 137

LARMANDIER-BERNIER LATITUDE BLANC DE BLANCS À VERTUS EXTRA BRUT NV
$$ • 94 POINTS • PAGE 233

POL ROGER PURE BRUT NATURE NV
$$ • 94 POINTS • PAGE 304

TARLANT BRUT PRESTIGE EXTRA BRUT 2000
$$ • 94 POINTS • PAGE 327

VEUVE FOURNY & FILS CUVÉE BLANC DE BLANCS VERTUS PREMIER CRU BRUT NATURE NV
$$ • 94 POINTS • PAGE 343

The village of Aÿ, on the southern slopes of the Montagne de Reims, source of some of Champagne's finest pinot noir.

DOWN TO EARTH
The lay of the land

Of all the great wine lands of the world, the lay of the land in Champagne reflects less of the glamour and the drama of its fruits than perhaps any other. This is agricultural turf in plain clothes. On a small range of hills rising less than impressively from a chalk plain 145 kilometres north-east of Paris lies the patchwork of 33,500 hectares of vineyards that is Champagne. Too exposed to wind and rain and not sufficiently blessed by the sun, there is no chance of ripening grapes on the flatter land here, which is instead planted to mundane harvests of cereal crops, sugar beet and carrots. 'If we were only 20 kilometres south we would be growing corn or wheat,' Jacquesson's Jean-Hervé Chiquet told me from his family estate in Dizy, in the precise centre of Champagne.

AND YET THIS SAME LAND SENDS A SHIVER DOWN MY spine every time I come close. By some miracle, its drab hillsides produce fruits that thousands of winegrowers around the globe strive desperately to emulate, yet none have equalled.

Austere and impoverished soft white chalk is Champagne's secret, a remnant of an ancient seabed. Cool, damp cellars are easily hewn from it, and the score marks of their Roman creators are still visible 17 centuries later. Its true blessing is espoused in the vineyards, bestowing its fruits with crystalline minerality, reflecting and storing heat and retaining moisture — a perfectly regulated vine humidifier.

The lay of the land in Champagne is intricate and complex, and each individual village and vineyard has its own personality. Such is the irregularity of the climate in one of the planet's most marginal wine-growing regions that but a handful of sites are capable of delivering consistent fruits with the propensity to stand alone. Even in the heart of Champagne, the quality and character of each vineyard varies wildly.

Champagne comprises five districts: the Montagne de Reims, Vallée de la Marne and Côte des Blancs (together making up The Marne, the heart of Champagne), Côte de Sézanne and Côte des Bar (Aube).

THE MONTAGNE DE REIMS

The 'Montagne de Reims' is no mountain, more a wooded hillock, rising to an unimpressive 180 metres above the surrounding plains and just 275 metres above sea level. Yet even this elevation is sufficient to orientate some of Champagne's mightiest vineyards. The vines of the Montagne de Reims follow the slope of a hillside topped with dense forest, in a backward 'C' formation from Villers-Allerand on the northern slopes, reaching a crescendo in the thundering grand crus of Bouzy and Ambonnay in the south. Pinot noir is king here, and nowhere in Champagne produces pinot noir equal to the great chalky sites of the Montagne de Reims. There are also substantial plantings of pinot meunier, and chardonnay is on the rise.

The 'Petite Montagne' is a north-western extension of the Montagne de Reims, extending from Sermiers to north of Reims itself, nurturing Champagne's most northerly vineyards on soils of sand and clay, well suited to pinot meunier.

The Montagne de Reims' finest villages are Bouzy, Ambonnay and Verzenay.

CÔTE DES BLANCS

Chardonnay is left largely to the 'Côte des Blancs', 96% of which is planted to the variety, the remainder largely pinot noir in the commune of Vertus in the south.

This region has again put forward a large proportion of highlights in this year's guide. With dramatic slopes, warmer days and thinner topsoils making chalk more accessible than anywhere else in the region, the Côte des Blancs produces Champagne's most regular fruit, and its most reliable, exhilarating and mineral-infused wines. This is why many are sold

unblended as blanc de blancs. These can be among the most searingly structured and long-lived wines of Champagne. There is perhaps no village in Champagne capable of standing alone as confidently as Le Mesnil-sur-Oger in the heart of the Côte des Blancs.

The Côte des Blancs' finest villages are Cramant, Avize, Oger, Le Mesnil-sur-Oger and Vertus.

VALLÉE DE LA MARNE

More than half of the 'Vallée de la Marne' is planted to pinot meunier, although pinot noir plantings are on the increase. The south-facing sites towards its eastern end rival the great grand crus of the Montagne de Reims. In its cooler western reaches of more clay soils, neither pinot noir nor chardonnay will ripen at all. This is exclusively the territory of the easier to grow and ripen pinot meunier.

The Vallée de la Marne's finest villages are Aÿ and Mareuil-sur-Aÿ.

CÔTE DE SÉZANNE

The 'Côte de Sézanne' is a little way south of the Côte des Blancs and shares the same south-east orientation and dominance of chardonnay. Its soils are heavier and its wines more rustic.

CÔTE DES BAR

More than 100 kilometres to the south-east of the Côte des Blancs, the outpost of 'Aube' (Côte des Bar) is closer to Burgundy than to Reims.

Pinot noir is the principal grape here, comprising four-fifths of the region's plantings, producing vigorous and more rustic wines. Planted largely during the late 1980s, vine maturity is now in step with the rest of the region and the Aube has enjoyed significant increases in quality in recent years.

The Côte des Bar's finest villages are Celles-sur-Ource, Les Riceys and Urville.

Le Mesnil-sur-Oger, the Côte des Blancs' most confident grand cru and source of some of Champagne's finest chardonnay.

The Marne

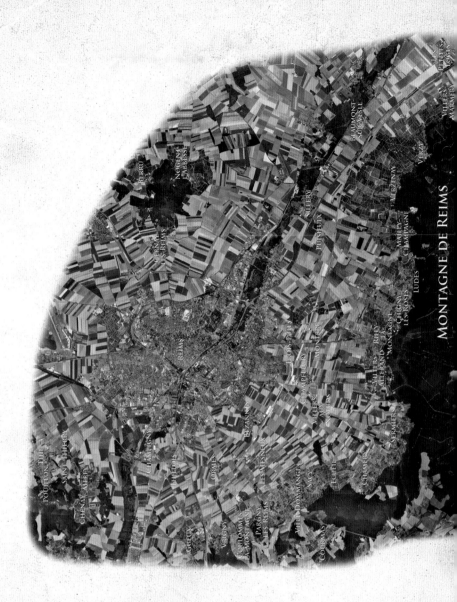

VALLÉE DE LA MARNE

CÔTE DES BLANCS

N

VINEYARDS

FOREST

GENERAL AGRICULTURE

URBAN

VILLAGE/CITY

0 1 2 3 4 5 6 7 8 9 10KM

THE CHEF IN THE CELLAR
How champagne is made

*C*hampagne must be the most successfully processed creation in all of agricultural history, through a convoluted, painstaking method designed expressly to transform an insipidly austere and undrinkably acidic juice into the most celebrated beverage in the world. Every element of the champagne process is geared towards making its searing acidity less challenging — bubbles, yeast, chaptalisation, dosage, blending and ageing. The genius of champagne production calls on more tricks than any other wine style to create flavour, complexity and balance. The traditional method by which this is achieved is known as Méthode Traditionnelle.

PRESSING
HOW CAN WHITE WINE BE MADE FROM THE RED PINOT noir and pinot meunier grapes? The secret is careful, selective harvesting and immediate, gentle pressing, to avoid staining the clear juice of these dark-skinned grapes. All grapes in Champagne are handpicked and gently pressed nearby as whole bunches in four-tonne lots. By law, only the first 2550 litres of juice from every four tonnes of grapes may be used. On current yields, this equates to an average production of 10,000 bottles per hectare.

The *coeur de la cuvée*, the 'heart of the cuvée', is the middle of the pressing, yielding the purest juice.

The *tailles* — coarser, inferior juice that flows last from the press — is used in varying levels according to the house style, and rarely at all in the finest cuvées.

SETTLING
Débourbage is the settling of solids and impurities from the must (pressed grape juice), allowing clear juice to be drawn off from the top.

This process is taken to another level by the houses of Billecart-Salmon and Pol Roger, who perform a second settling of the must at cold temperature, producing particularly exquisite and fresh champagnes.

FIRST FERMENTATION
The 'alcoholic' fermentation of champagne takes place in stainless steel tanks. Traditional oak barrels are coming back into vogue for fermentation and/or maturation, to increase suppleness, texture, power and complexity. Most champagne producers 'chaptalise'

prior to fermentation by adding sugar or concentrated grape juice to increase the alcoholic strength. Some makers 'inoculate' the ferment with cultured yeasts, while others rely on wild yeasts.

MALOLACTIC FERMENTATION
Malolactic fermentation converts tart 'malic' (green apple) acid into softer 'lactic' (dairy) acid. This process is practised by most houses to soften their wines. Notable exceptions include Gosset, Lanson and Salon.

With the advent of warmer vintages, an increasing number of houses are experimenting with blocking malolactic fermentation.

ASSEMBLAGE
Skilful blending is Champagne's answer to its erratic seasons. Challenging vintages are handled by blending wines from different vineyards, different vintages (reserve wines) and different grapes.

Champagne is usually a blend of chardonnay (for structure, elegance and finesse), pinot noir (for perfume, body and richness) and pinot meunier (for plump fruitiness). Blanc de blancs ('white wine from white grapes') is usually chardonnay and blanc de noirs ('white wine from red grapes') usually pinot noir/meunier.

The key distinguishing factor between champagne houses lies in the cuvée — the blend created in assembling different wines. There is no skill in the winemaking world that I envy more than that of the Chef de Cave in blending a fine champagne.

'It is as if we have to make a cake,' explains Louis Roederer's Mary Roche. 'The recipe changes every year because the ingredients change with the season, but the cake must remain the same.' This is further confounded by the number of ingredients. Bollinger Special Cuvée NV is a blend of an incredible 240 base wines, spanning three varieties and two vintages, plus at least five older reserve wines.

Perhaps the most profound challenge of all lies in blending a wine now that must be consistent with the house style when it emerges from the cellar in two, five or eight years' time. It is little wonder the French call the blender the 'Chef de Cave'.

It is the blend more than anything that determines the non-vintage house style, from the rich concentration of Krug and Bollinger, to the delicate finesse of Pol Roger and Billecart-Salmon.

Reserve wines (for NV blends)

Non-vintage wines are deepened by a portion of older vintage 'reserve' wines stored in tank, barrel or bottle. These are crucial for maintaining consistency in Champagne's wildly fluctuating seasons.

Tirage

Prior to bottling, a 'liqueur de tirage' of sugar and wine is added (see 'Second fermentation', further down).

Bottling

Wines are bottled and sealed under crown seal, or occasionally cork. They may be filtered and cold stabilised at this time to remove any solids.

Second fermentation

The sugar added to champagne prior to bottling induces a secondary fermentation in the bottle known as the 'prise de mousse'. Under the pressure of a sealed bottle, the carbon dioxide produced dissolves in the wine, creating sparkling wine. The finer the still wine and the cooler the cellar in which this fermentation occurs, the smaller the bubbles. Larger bottles ferment more slowly — one reason why magnums are superior and half bottles are inferior to standard bottles. A finer bead is an indicator of quality.

Sparkling wine is a phenomenon only of recent centuries. It first came about in the 16th and 17th centuries, when fermentation of the grapes harvested in late autumn would stop as soon as the icy northern winter set in. The still champagne would be shipped to England and bottled. With the warmth of spring came a re-fermentation in bottle, and sparkling wine was born. It remains a point of contention between the French and the English to this day as to which nationality first put the bubble in champagne.

The truth, perhaps, is that neither should take credit for what was effectively a rather fortuitous accident!

Maturation

Acidity is the key to champagne, but its astringency makes these wines unapproachable in their youth. The mellowing, softening effect of age is crucial to the champagne style. Dead yeast cells ('lees') from the second fermentation remain in the bottle and contribute subtly to champagne's complexity. The longer this process of 'autolysis' persists the better, improving mouthfeel and longevity, and adding biscuity, bready nuances to the flavour profile.

The mandatory minimum in champagne is 15 months for non-vintage and three years for vintage wines, but reputable producers always far exceed these minima, typically ageing non-vintage cuvées 3–4 years, vintage cuvées 7–8 years, and prestige cuvées sometimes 10 years or more.

Riddling (remuage)

In the early 19th century, Antoine Müller, cellar master of the widow Clicquot (Veuve Clicquot), invented a method of cleaning the wine of the sediment created when it ferments in bottle without losing its bubbles. A wooden desk ('pupitre') pierced with holes holds the mature bottles sideways. Each bottle is given a quarter-rotation every day, and slowly tilted from horizontal to upside down. The lees sediment collects in the neck of the bottle. This process of 'remuage' is performed by a 'riddler', who can turn 50,000–60,000 bottles every day!

In modern times, the riddling process has been taken over by gyropalettes in most champagne houses. These giant robotic arms slowly rotate large cages of bottles. The effect is the same, perhaps even more consistent, albeit without the romance.

A gyro can riddle a cage of bottles in as little as three days, but many estates use a longer cycle of a week or more.

Disgorgement (dégorgement)

After riddling, the sediment is settled on the inside of the cork or crown cap. The neck of the bottle is then frozen, the cap released, and the plug of sediment shot out ('dégorgement' in French), leaving perfectly clear wine behind.

Dosage (the final addition)

To replace the volume lost through disgorgement, the bottled is topped up with sweetened wine ('liqueur d'expédition') and a new cork is inserted.

'Zero dosage' champagnes are topped up with dry wine. See page 47 for dosage trends.

MAKING ROSÉ CHAMPAGNE

Rosé champagne is made in the same manner as white champagne, with a subtle difference. Colour is achieved in one of three ways.

Most commonly, a 'blending method' ('rosé d'assemblage') is used, in which a tiny quantity of pinot noir or pinot meunier made as a table wine is added (often only 5–10%, but sometimes as much as 20%). A rapid increase in demand for rosé has recently put pressure on supplies of quality red wine for blending in Champagne.

The 'Saignée' method adds free-run juice from just-crushed red grapes, producing the finest, palest wines. A 'limited maceration' method produces darker, heavier wines through a quick soak on red grape skins.

Rosé production is tricky, not only in marrying champagne's acidity with red wine tannin, but in determining the desired depth of colour long before

it is set. Yeast is a highly effective fining agent, leaching colour during both primary and secondary fermentations.

Rosé now accounts for 10% of champagne production — a massive explosion from some 3% just 15 years ago. On average, it's priced around 30% above its white counterparts. The Champenois justify this on the basis that it costs more to produce red wine than white in Champagne. I'm not convinced. Old vines are required and yields must be kept low to ensure sufficient ripeness, but this does not equate to such a premium in production costs.

Even if the cost of producing red wine to make rosé were as high as double that of the base white wine, an addition of 10% in the blend only increases the total cost of production by 10%. And then there are absurd extremes. Ruinart's prestige Dom Ruinart Rosé is identical to its Dom Ruinart but for an addition of 15% pinot noir. However, its price is more than double, meaning that the house values its pinot noir at a preposterous €2000 per 750mL!

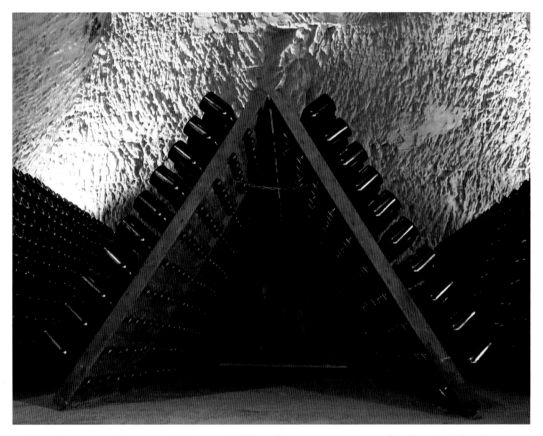

Riddling racks in Taittinger's crayères, with the score marks of their 4th century Roman creators still visible in the chalk walls.

The Champagne Guide

CHALK IT UP
Terroir, Minerality, Organics and Biodynamics

*T*o contemporary France, the answer to the industrialisation and brand-driven mentality of the modern wine world is to endeavour to express every nuance of terroir in its full detail. Its greatest wine producers are striving to reduce yields, sorting fruit fastidiously to remove imperfections, and working with purposeful inaction in the winery. Place of origin is everything, brand, to most, is nothing, and no vintage is ever the same.

IN THIS FRANCE, CHAMPAGNE IS THE PRECISE ANTI-thesis. Its very success has been built not just on ignoring these aspirations but, in some cases, on purposely, boldly, and at times necessarily, turning them completely upside down. Here, brands rule and blending of varieties, vineyards and even vintages is the norm. Fruit sorting is rare, high yields are not, and the influence of the maker to mould a wine into a consistent style is paramount.

Some 78% of champagne is made by large merchant houses and cooperatives, and the top five houses account for almost one-third of this. Many purchase fruit from a large number of growers, and because pressing takes place at numerous press centres across the region, most are not able to check individual fruit parcels, and many are not even able to oversee the pressing itself — arguably the most important stage of champagne production for quality and freshness. There is often no reward for fruit of higher ripeness than the legal minimum of 8.5% potential alcohol. And there is no incentive for low yields, so few growers are prepared to risk pruning and green harvesting to reduce yields in a region with such a precarious climate. As a result, Champagne has the biggest problem of excess yields in all of France. One-third of Champagne is not fully picked each year, and most growers either break the legal yield limit and sell it on a thriving black market, or leave the excess fruit on the vines for the birds to eat.

But change is coming, and Champagne is increasingly defined by an ever more intricate diversity. More grower producers are arising with the daring to keep yields under close scrutiny, and to coax terroir from individual plots, even to bottle single-vineyard, single-vintage wines.

Driving along the D9 at the bottom of the slope of the Côte des Blancs, with fairytale spires of grand cru villages flashing by, less than a kilometre apart, you could be on the RN74 skirting the legendary villages of Burgundy's Côte des Nuits. Here, as there, every vineyard is unique in exposition, slope and soil. Never have I seen the Champenois more determined to express the detail of some 84,000 individual vineyards and 275,000 individual plots. Rows of tiny, gleaming, new stainless steel tanks and little barrels line the walls of many a 'cuverie', from the smallest estate to many large houses. Vinifying every parcel separately is now the norm, even if it is ultimately destined for a larger blend.

'My father said if you have a chance to vinify a wine on its own you will express more of its personality,' Olivier Krug told me. 'The more individuality you get, the more precise you can be with selection choices.' An astonishing philosophy for Krug, a house that gathers more than 200 parcels every vintage, and blends 10 vintages into every non-vintage wine.

The detail of Champagne has never been painted with a finer brush. From the tiniest grower tending single rows of vines to the small-batch philosophy of the most fanatical large house, the contrasting colours of champagne are sparkling more vividly than ever. Most sensibly maintain that Champagne's greatest strength lies in its vast matrix of blending permutations, in a region boasting very few sites truly capable of flying solo with any degree of complexity and consistency. Even one of the most celebrated exceptions, Krug's Clos du Mesnil, prompted numerous calls of complaint to the house on its first release, claiming that they were crazy to release a single-site champagne.

Change comes slowly here.

Didier Gimonnet of Pierre Gimonnet & Fils speaks as intricately about terroir as anyone I've met in Champagne. 'Our champagnes have a personality because of the vineyards they come from,' he says. 'All the styles depend only on the terroir. When I present the house I always say that I'm not a winemaker, just an interpreter of the terroir.'

These words could have come from any Burgundian. But at this point his philosophy takes a dramatic divergence as he introduces a word I had not heard before. A word which encapsulates the essence that distinguishes Champagne from practically every other terroir-focused wine land on earth.

'I am against monoterroir,' he says. 'My focus is on very polished blends and combining the qualities of different terroirs to produce complexities.'

Monoterroir. Have we for too long defined the elusive ideal of terroir too narrowly and dismissed champagne on account of the brush of the blender? In Champagne, perhaps the truest expression of terroir is found in the blend?

Ancient sea life fossilised in Jérôme Prévost's soils in Gueux define the mineral texture of his champagnes.

WHAT LIES BELOW – MINERALITY

Minerality is a strong candidate for the most elusive concept in wine tasting. Misconceptions abound.

It's regarded by some to be an intangible character in wine, by others as an absence of fruit, an attempt to describe any element that isn't fruity, even as the kerosene notes of mature riesling or other aromatic whites.

Minerality is categorically none of these things. Minerality is the texture and mouthfeel of a wine derived from its soil. It is every bit as tangible as acidity or tannin, albeit more elusive to measure and define.

The signature of minerality is articulated in champagne more eloquently than any other wine. Minerality lifts a champagne off the two-dimensional page of aroma and flavour, inflating it into a three-dimensional, life-sized form of texture and feeling.

In the village of Avize, Pascal Agrapart describes the minerality of one of his most distinctive vineyards as reminiscent of blackboard chalk dust from his school days. Champagne is very much more than fruit and acid, sugar and bubbles. Minerality adds a structural intensity and a textural perspective, fine-grained in the Côte des Blancs, and more coarse in the Côte des Bar.

And it has another dimension, one of mineral personality. There are terroirs of Champagne of savoury minerality, of spicy minerality, of salty liquorice mineral texture in Vertus, of neutral minerality in the Montagne de Reims and, most pronounced of all, terroirs of the Côte des Blancs of salty minerality that heave and froth with the very waves of the sea that deposited its chalk subsoils millennia ago. Not with the fresh coastal seaspray hints of Bordeaux or Jerez but here, more than 200 kilometres from any sea, resonating with an ocean that receded 55 million years prior. Drinking champagne is not only a modern history lesson in recent vintages, villages and family backgrounds, but an ancient historical encounter with the very geology of the continent itself. Could a wine capture anything more profound?

The French put it better than we do. '*L'eau de roche ou le sel de la terre*' — 'the water of the rock (crystal) or the salt of the earth' — says fanatical terroirist Anselme Selosse of Jacques Selosse, whose roots are embedded as firmly in the bedrock of Avize as anyone in Champagne. 'In its purity, its transparency, its specificity, a great wine of terroir can only be of *l'eau de roche*,' he says.

In nearby Le Mesnil-sur-Oger, grower Rodolphe Péters speaks of minerality of 'ocean flavours, oyster shells and sea salt.' His Le Mesnil vineyard Les Chétillons embodies this as dramatically as any in Champagne. Bottle after bottle that he opens demonstrates that over three decades of maturity and changes of winemaker, flavours evolve, intensity builds and bubbles fade, but minerality remains transfixed. 'It is a stake, it remains for a very long time,' he declares.

Minerality is the timeless fingerprint of the land. Acidity and sugar give voice to the vagaries of sun and sky, fruit derives its identity from the grape variety, but minerality speaks of a much more ancient origin, the soil itself, snapped into sharp focus in a cold climate. When we speak of terroir in its highest order we speak of cool places. The patchwork of Burgundy, riesling slopes of Germany, chalk of Sancerre, grand crus of Alsace, rolling hills of Barolo. Its expression in the fields of the southern Rhône, Provence, even the noble plains of Bordeaux, shares nothing of the same precision. The icy touch of Champagne, the coldest of all, awakens the soil and gives it birth in its fruits.

CAPTURING MINERALITY

Hanging on the wall of the tiny cellar of Georges Laval in Cumières is an unlikely but profoundly revealing display. Two skeletons of old vines, one with strong, thick roots plunging vertically downward, the other from a neighbouring vineyard on the same soil planted at a similar time, with but a thin 'afro' of surface roots.

Vincent Laval's father started growing organic vines in 1971, placing him among the first in Champagne to do so. He had planted the vine with deep roots organically, while the other was from a vineyard managed traditionally, later purchased by the Lavals. Vincent ripped out the purchased vines and replanted organically, for reasons starkly apparent in this display.

It's a similar story at Chartogne-Taillet in the little village of Merfy, where Alexandre Chartogne pulled out a traditionally managed vineyard with shallow roots in 2007, after conducting in-depth studies of microbiological activity and vine root growth. 'When I arrived in 2006 I wanted to see the soil life, so I dug channels in the soil to examine how the roots reacted,' he explains. 'I discovered that different microorganisms act at different depths, and when the soil is aerated and not compacted they act at all levels. Herbicides have the effect of killing microorganisms in the top two layers and so the roots of the vines go sideways, rather than downwards to produce terroir wines.'

Scientists remain puzzled as to how wines can present textures reminiscent of their subsoils, since the relevant elements are never detected in the grapes or wines by analysis, and are rarely soluble in water. I recently put the question to Dr Emmanuel Bourguignon, who works closely with his father, leading Burgundian soil scientist, Claude Bourguignon.

'We still do not yet really know how minerality is transferred from the soil to the wine, but there are several theories,' he responded. 'My father is currently working on the role of the microbes in the soil and the way in which enzymes play a part in their activity. Particular minerals in the soil activate certain enzymes.'

Anselme Selosse, who employs Bourguignon as a soil consultant, describes the bedrock on which the vines are planted as the interface between terroir and plant. Rarely soluble, its dissolution is due largely to the work of microorganisms acting at the interface between soil and rock, transforming the rock salt into a soluble form that is able to be absorbed by the roots.

In the same village, the eponymous wines of Erick de Sousa express brilliant minerality. 'I was certified organic in 2010 to encourage the vines to draw deeply from the trace elements specific to each terroir,' he says. 'Our old vines have deep roots that plunge 35–40 metres into the chalk to obtain minerality.'

For Rodolphe Péters in the shallow soils of nearby Le Mesnil, the key to the profound mineral expression in his Pierre Péters wines is not about deep roots at all. 'I speak with friends about the roots going deep here in the Côte des Blancs, and they insist that you need the roots to go deep, but I say, "It is bullshit!"' he emphasises. 'The interface between the topsoil and the deep soil is where you find all the available minerality, and here in Le Mesnil it is right here, between 10 and 30 centimetres from the surface.' He adds that it is very different in the Montagne de Reims, where the topsoil might be 1.5 or 2 metres deep, and hence deep roots are crucial for accessing minerality.

Deep roots or not, the secrets of unlocking minerality are similar across Champagne. Aeration of the soil is crucial, and many growers, small and large, are ploughing vineyards, often with a horse, to reduce soil compaction. In many sites, this is still experimental, and the outcome is uncertain; this is not a procedure whose results can be analysed short-term. Bollinger has used horses to plough one-tenth of its estate vineyards for two years, just to see what the result will be. Others are more convinced. 'I avoid even walking in the vineyard, because this risks crushing the chalk,' Péters explains. Across the region, grasses are planted in the mid-rows of some vineyards to encourage organic life and provide competition, driving surface roots down to the interface between topsoil and chalk.

Composting and avoidance of pesticide and herbicide are practised by the most diligent to further encourage microbial life, although this does not always equate to organic or biodynamic certification. 'I want to keep the soil alive with organics, but I can't achieve this using certified organics,' explains Péters.

'Every five years I analyse the soils in selected plots and find them full of the copper of our grandfathers' treatments. But we have stronger diseases like mildew and oïdium now. My father says that he never had to protect the vineyard from mildew like we have in the past decade. So I can't be restrained to organic treatments. My philosophy is to follow the best procedures of the best of all philosophies.'

BIODYNAMICS: THE HOLY GRAIL?

Champagne has long been notorious for its over-reliance on chemicals in its vineyards. When growers Anselme Selosse and Pierre Larmandier expressed interest in purchasing a vineyard in Vertus in 2002, the agent was surprised that both showed such interest in the way the vines had been tended, without the use of herbicides, having never seen buyers interested in this before. Things are changing, and a concerted push towards more environmentally friendly practices has seen Champagne halve its chemical treatments in the past 15 years.

Despite the region's best efforts, its erratic climate makes practising biodynamics or even organics a nail-biting pursuit. The biggest menace is disease, a challenge to manage under organic or biodynamic regimes, which do not permit the systematic fungicide sprays traditionally relied upon in this wet climate.

There are grumbles in Champagne that some have jumped on the biodynamics bandwagon without certification, and continue to purchase fruit that is not grown biodynamically. More sensible growers have embraced the best of organic and biodynamic practice for reasons other than marketing. While some have embraced full certification, every site is different in Champagne, and a number of the region's top growers have found success with partial adoption.

Louis Roederer manages Champagne's biggest bio-dynamic regime by an order of magnitude, although certification is not the goal. 'We see it as just one means of achieving terroir expression,' says Chef de Cave Jean-Baptiste Lécaillon. Over the past decade, the house has converted more than 60 hectares to biodynamics, and its fruit has already shown greater ripeness, more acidity and more accentuated salty minerality. It has found that a different approach is necessary in each region of Champagne. 'There are some years in which biodynamics is much better, and some years in which it is not so effective,' he explains. In 2012, Lécaillon reported losses of 30–50% in some plots, and greater under biodynamics than traditional viticulture. 'It involves so much risk,' he says. 'Biodynamics removes all the safety of chemicals, and if it's not done properly, you can really get caught quickly.'

Brothers Charles-Henry and Emmanuel Fourny know this well. In the mid-1990s, they conducted bio-dynamic trials, forsaking synthetic chemicals in two parcels in their Veuve Fourny estate in Vertus. The wild spread of mildew necessitated weekly sprayings with copper sulphate, permitted under biodynamics despite its toxicity and detrimental effect on the soil and vine growth. Much of the crop was lost, and the brothers returned to non-toxic synthetic products with a regime of grass in the mid-rows and pheromones to reduce insect breeding.

'If there are no grapes it is difficult!' exclaims Pascal Agrapart in Avize. 'I prefer to have grapes to make wines!' With vineyards 20 kilometres apart in seven villages, he has difficulty getting between his vines by tractor to practise an organic regime. 'I don't want to have certification because I want to be able to plough the soil when I can, and use chemicals when I need to.'

Leading Cumières grower Jean-Baptiste Geoffroy describes his approach as 'bio-logical' rather than 'bio-dynamic.' He pays focused attention to the health of the soil through ploughing under the vines, planting of natural grasses in the mid-rows and avoidance of herbicides, but explains that a fully organic approach does not make good sense here. 'When we have 25 milli-metres of rain, I must spray very quickly,' he points out, 'but after 20 millimetres of rain in Cumières it isn't possible to get a tractor into the vineyards. It's very steep and the thick layer of clay makes it very muddy. In Chouilly, by comparison, you can have 50 milli-metres and get in the next day.' Such practicalities dictate the use of inorganic chemicals here.

Some question whether a biological approach is all it's cracked up to be. 'The CIVC [Champagne's regulatory, supervisory and promotional body] is conducting a lot of experiments with sustainable and biological vineyards,' explains Ruinart Chef de Cave Frédéric Panaïotis. 'In 2012 they sprayed their biological vineyards with organic sprays seven times, and their sustainable vineyard with systematic sprays twice. Which is more natural? And some are using a horse to tend vines. But is this biologically responsible, considering the land that's used to keep a horse, the amount of grass they eat and the methane they produce? We need to take a big picture view.'

In the little village of Gueux, the intuitive Jérôme Prévost makes deeply terroir-driven wines on a tiny scale without herbicides, but he is adamant that his is not a biodynamic approach. 'Making wine isn't like cooking, but biodynamics is too much like a recipe,' he maintains.

'Every plot of land is different and you have to work with emotion and sensation to understand nature, not read about it from a book. You have to go out in the vines and feel the sun and the wind; to have all of your senses attuned; to taste with your eyes and your ears.'

The Champagne Guide

Bubble, bubble, toil and trouble
Is global warming the end for Champagne?

I f you believed all the commentary, you'd have to conclude that the Champagne we know and love is all but doomed. Global demand is pushing volumes up and quality down. The financial crisis has pushed prices down to unsustainable levels. The boundaries of the region are poised to swell into lesser lands. And global warming spells Armageddon for the region that has built a wine style around its cold climate.

HOTTING UP

FROM THE 1950S TO THE 1980S, THE AVERAGE TEMP-erature of Champagne's growing season was a steady 14.3°C. In the 1990s, this increased to 15°C.

What of the 2000s? Could it have risen by the same amount again, to 15.7°C? Surely not double, to 16.4°C? Wrong. The latest 10-year average in Champagne has shot up to a whopping 16.6°C.

What effect on viticulture? Ripeness levels in Champagne have risen, in spite of an increase of 50% in yields. Acidity has dropped and pH has risen. For the technocrats, natural alcohol has jumped to 9.9% over the past decade, from 9.6% over the previous 30 years, total acidity has dropped from 13.5g/L to 11.38g/L (tartaric), and pH has risen from 3.05 to 3.10. These numbers do not spell good news for Champagne.

'There is a major effect of global warming in Champagne. It is a fact,' declares Dom Pérignon Chef de Cave, Richard Geoffroy. 'And it's been around for longer than you think. We've been looking at the data and the crucial point of inflection was in the mid-80s.' Harvest is now three weeks earlier than when Napoléon Chef de Cave Jean-Philippe Moulin arrived in Champagne in 1977. 'A century ago, Hautvillers would have three months of snow, and all the kids would toboggan in the vineyards,' Moulin told me, as we surveyed the snowless village in the middle of the unseasonably warm winter of 2013.

The last typical harvest in Champagne was in 1988, with every season since delivering greater rich-ness and less minerality, according to Patrick Le Brun at Le Brun-Servenay in Avize. In Mareuil-sur-Aÿ, Laurent Bénard of L. Bénard-Pitois is also concerned by declining acidity and mineral expression. 'We have too much sun in summer and the growing season is too short,' he reports. 'My parents never harvested in August, even in the hot season of 1976, but I have harvested in August in 2003, 2007 and 2011.'

'The year 2003 was the perfect description of a nightmare!' says Veuve Clicquot Winemaking Development Director, Cyril Brun, who rushed back from his honeymoon in Australia and drove straight from the airport to the vineyard in the wake of Champagne's hottest summer in history. 'Even in warmer years like 1985 and 1976, we still had a much better balance than in 2003. July and August burnt the acid out of the grapes.'

Champagne had more defined seasons 20 years ago, and it's more difficult to produce flavour ripeness without high sugar levels today, reports Didier Gimonnet of Pierre Gimonnet & Fils in Cuis. 'I believe that Champagne's extreme climate is essential for the vines to suffer a little in order to produce typicity of champagne character,' he says. 'Without this, our wines are rich and smooth, but this is not the style of champagne.'

Not everyone in Champagne is convinced. Krug winemaker Julie Cavil points out that the hot seasons at the beginning of the 1990s, 1976 and 1949 were all declared vintages and that Champagne hasn't experi-enced exclusively warmer vintages this decade. The talented and well-travelled grower producer Gilles Dumangin agrees. 'I can see nothing now to indicate the climate is changing,' he says. He recalls years when he was young when the climate was very cool, and speaks of seasons when his father, Jacky, was young when it was very hot. 'This is the climate, it goes up and down. It's nothing more than microclimate changes.'

Storm warning

Temperature rise in itself is not the big concern in Champagne's changing climate. The real problem is that the weather is becoming more extreme and more unpredictable. Winters are now longer, wetter and warmer; summers are shorter, hotter and more erratic. There's more rainfall, changed rainfall patterns and more violent storms, hail and frost. Humidity is on the rise, as are strong winds. And 2011 served up the entire onslaught. After a challenging season of spring heatwave, wet summer and intermittent hail storms, the season culminated in the second-earliest harvest since 1822. This all equates to more pests and diseases, more risk of exposure to spring frosts and summer heat, and more danger from severe rot.

In 2012, the Côte des Bar was savaged by one of the worst hailstorms in Champagne history. At Fleury Père & Fils in Courteron, Jean-Sebastien Fleury missed the hail but copped everything else: multiple frosts, rains disrupting flowering, mildew, then a cold summer followed by scorching heat of 41°C. 'It was a very unusual season, with the worst conditions you could have,' he reports. In nearby Bar-sur-Seine, Devaux Chef de Cave, Michel Parisot, suffered the same fate. 'Some years are warmer and some years are not,' he says. 'But the change we've seen in the past decade is that storms are always more violent now.'

Much has been written on the changing face of Champagne, and the conclusion has not been optimistic: Champagne as we know it is in dire trouble.

Warming to climate change

Many in Champagne have a different idea. 'I think global warming has been favourable for Champagne until now,' suggests Laurent d'Harcourt, Managing Director for Pol Roger, who sees the quality of champagne on the rise across the region.

'We have global warming, but we needed some in Champagne! The growing conditions, the weather, the days of sunshine are ideal, better than they've ever been.' He qualifies this by adding, 'We don't want it to be too much warmer. If we have a lot of 2003s, it will be a big concern!'

Richard Geoffroy is embarrassed to agree that global warming has so far been for the better in Champagne, suggesting that it has lifted the lesser vintages. G.H. Mumm Chef de Cave Didier Mariotti credits this improved consistency for an increase in the quality of non-vintage blends across the region.

In Avize, Pascal Agrapart is happy that harvest dates have moved forward to September, allowing greater flexibility to hold off and harvest later than an October harvest permits. 'In Champagne, climate change is more a good opportunity than a risk,' agrees Veuve Clicquot Chef de Cave, Dominique Demarville.

Play it cool

Demarville has used this opportunity to prepare for warmer vintages. In response to decreasing acid levels, he has begun experimenting with blocking malolactic fermentation to sustain levels of malic acidity in some parcels destined for reserve wines and vintage cuvées. Many houses in Champagne are now trialling non-malolactic parcels.

Greater inconsistency of seasons increases the urgency to keep large stocks of reserve wines. 'If you look at the last four harvests, 2008 was exceptional, with high acidity and lots of structure, 2009 was ripe, with low acidity, 2010 was dilute, and 2011 was very inconsistent,' Demarville points out. 'If you don't have sufficient stocks of reserve wines, you can't make great non-vintage champagne.'

Others have embraced the richer fruit delivered by warmer seasons as an opportunity to increase the use of oak for fermentation and maturation. No doubt this notable trend in Champagne over the past decade has been encouraged in part by the region's changing climate.

Climate change will increasingly impact the way champagne is made. There's much that can be done in the vineyards, too. 'We have spent 100 years trying to capture more sunshine, and that could be changed tomorrow!' points out Ruinart Chef de Cave, Frédéric Panaïotis. 'There is a lot that can be done to cope with temperature increases of up to 1.5°C across the growing season, without changing the fruit profile.' His biggest concern is ensuring a sufficiently long ripening season, which could be achieved using trellising systems to reduce exposure.

Warmer vintages call for greater discernment in when to harvest. 'When I began here in 1987, it was very simple: if we had more than 10% potential alcohol and less than 8g/L of acidity, it was good to harvest,' recalls Gimonnet. 'Now we must change the criteria to determine the date of harvest, looking at the maturity of the pips and skins and the taste of the juice, to avoid herbaceous flavours.'

Vineyard practices are also being modified to encourage balance in erratic seasons. At Veuve Clicquot, grasses introduced in the vineyards create surface competition and drive roots deeper, providing more consistent water supply, retaining acidity in warmer seasons. 'When the roots are on the surface, they pump water and produce dilution when it rains,' Demarville explains. Thus deep roots increase consistency in both wet and dry seasons.

These practices give Demarville confidence for the future. 'So many things have happened in Champagne over the past century, and we will adapt again,' he says.

'We will adapt our winegrowing and our winemaking to ensure that we can continue to make champagnes of elegance and minerality. I don't think climate change will change the style of champagne.'

WHAT TO BELIEVE?

Should we believe the doomsayers or the marketers, or let the wines speak for themselves? Even in the rollercoaster of recent vintages, there are signs of hope for Champagne's future. The 2008 harvest is the most resounding evidence that Champagne is still able to pull off all its old tricks — a vintage of classic finesse and tightly-clenched acidity that looks set to rival anything of the past two decades. For all the inconsistencies of 2011, Demarville upholds the season as evidence that Champagne is still capable of producing strong acidity. And, most recently, the 2012 vins clairs of some houses could rank this vintage ahead of 2002. For Laurent Champs at Vilmart & Cie, the wonderful acidities of 2012 surpass even the great 1996.

The present and the future of Champagne hinge on the quality of the 309 million bottles it churns out every year. There are growers and houses in Champagne who are raising their game in the wake of global warming, through stringent standards and carefully managed yields in the vineyard, and fanatical attention to detail in the winery. Those who don't subscribe to such philosophies will likely fall by the wayside.

For this, Champagne will only be a better place. The challenges presented by the coming decades in Champagne look set to widen the gap between those who really care, and those who are only out to make a quick buck. The contrast, it seems, is already stark.

For now, it appears Champagne is far from losing its sparkle. Yet.

A storm descends on Mutigny on the eve of vintage 2011. Champagne's climate is becoming increasingly tumultuous.

Has the bubble burst?
Yields, boundaries and classification

Champagne is gearing up to mushroom. Production is bulging at the seams and houses are scurrying to find ways of meeting anticipated demand from China and India. In 2008, after four years of escalating exports, a preliminary proposal was accepted for the inclusion of 40 more villages in the region. What do spiralling yields, expanding boundaries and an antiquated cru classification mean for the future of Champagne?

CHAMPAGNE SALES HIT AN ALL-TIME RECORD OF 338.7 million bottles in 2007, then temporarily softened almost 30% because of the global financial crisis in 2009. By 2011, total sales were back to 323 million, dampened slightly by the crisis in Europe to 309 million in 2012. This reprieve can only be temporary, and Champagne is contemplating how long it will be before global demand exceeds production.

Authorities have already taken one step towards anticipating this demand, increasing the allowed maximum yield to 15.5 tonnes per hectare between 2007 and 2011 (cut back to 9.7 tonnes to address oversupply due to the financial crisis in 2009).

'The problem with champagne is that every grower considers the maximum yield permitted by the appellation to be an economic minimum,' admits Jacquesson's Jean-Hervé Chiquet. 'About 90% of growers harvest the maximum permitted by the appellation, plus whatever remains on the vines.' Some unscrupulous growers have even purchased vineyards in the Côte des Bar, with no intention to ever harvest. They instead cheat the system by using the allocation of these vines to increase yields in the Côte des Blancs.

Dedicated growers are working painstakingly to achieve balanced crops. For Jacquesson, planting cover crops in the mid-rows is important for controlling yields. 'Until recent environmental priorities became prominent, significantly less than 1% of Champagne growers practised this,' Chiquet notes. 'Some years ago, the head of the local union was interviewed in our local paper about organic viticulture and said he's only interested if it doesn't have an effect on the maximum appellation of the region. And so they make the yield the first priority, and everything else comes next.'

The question of rising yields is a touchy topic in Champagne. Over the past decade, yields have swollen to an average of nearly 100 hectolitres (hL) per hectare, from less than 60hL over the 30 years prior. A few years ago, some grand cru villages announced averages of 130hL. These are massive crop loads by any standard. Bordeaux yields just 50hL/hectare. Even France's lowliest *vins de table* are not permitted yields as high as Champagne.

In Champagne, 15.5 tonnes equates to a maximum pressing of 9880 litres per hectare, or 98.8 hL. 'In Vertus, you are considered a bad grower if you do not produce 100hL/hectare,' reveals attentive grower Pierre Larmandier, who limits his yields for his Larmandier-Bernier wines to 60–70hL. 'People produce too much in the Côte des Blancs, and the big houses just buy everything.'

Respected grower Eric Rodez produces just 30–40% of the permitted yield, to give voice to the minerality of his Ambonnay vineyards. He speaks of yields in the region rising from five tonnes per hectare in 1950, six in 1960, eight in 1970, 10 in 1980, 12 in 1990 and 14 today. 'It's crazy!' he says. 'Why always more?'

Most of the time 100hL/hectare is excessive, but the solution is not as simple as a sweeping reduction in yields. Some of Champagne's better vintages — like 1982, 1990 and 2004 — have typically been high-yielding years. Low yields mean higher alcohol, and greater fruit intensity and concentration, but these are not qualities on which Champagne's finest wines are built. We do well not to blindly cheer Champagne into a winegrowing mould simply because it works for the table wines of warmer regions.

The Champagne Guide

'We're not trying to make Alsacian riesling or white Burgundy at 14 degrees alcohol!' Antoine Roland-Billecart of Billecart-Salmon points out. Balance is the key. 'You can make good wines but not great wines with high yields in Champagne,' adds Chiquet.

Celebrated Cuis grower Didier Gimonnet values finesse and elegance above concentration. 'We have never elaborated a great vintage here with less than 50hL/hectare,' he says. 'It is impossible to have balance at this level.' He lists 1982, 1983 and 2004 as high-yielding vintages of very good balance.

'In 2004 we had huge yields, averaging above 100hL/hectare across the domain,' he recalls. The exceptionally warm 2003 season built up reserves in the vines, ripening an unusually large number of bunches. Gimonnet points to a sufficiently high yield as crucial to achieve Champagne's classic balance of sugar and acidity at harvest, expressing surprise that flavour and minerality are not diluted.

'One would expect that high yields would mean less minerality, but in 2004 we had both,' he says. 'The terroir of Champagne is extraordinary — high yield with great expression of terroir!' Exceptional years aside, Gimonnet proposes 75hL/hectare as the ideal target to maintain proper balance in Champagne. This equates to 10,000 bottles per hectare.

Too many lesser growers overshoot this target too often. Champagne of finesse and balance depends upon carefully managed yields. 'My grandfather always told me you should take what mother nature gives you, and that's it,' says Roland-Billecart, who admits this ideal only works in some years. He plants grasses in mid-rows to reduce yields to 70hL/hectare. 'We want consistency of ripeness without too much concentration, maintaining freshness and acidity.' In some places, much lower yields are targeted: Billecart's famed single-hectare Clos Saint Hilaire is green harvested (crop thinned) to just 10 small bunches per vine, yielding a miniscule 40hL/hectare.

It's dangerous to generalise, because ideal yields in Champagne depend heavily on site, season and vines. In Merfy, north of Reims, Alexandre Chartogne green harvests to an average of 60hL/hectare and as little as just 20hL/hectare in his oldest vines. 'When I worked in Avize, I was amazed at the quality of grapes in the vineyards between 60 and 90hL/hectare,' he reports. 'The wines in barrel were perfect, and I wondered how they could achieve this from such yields.'

In nearby Le Mesnil-sur-Oger, the priority of Rodolphe Péters is to capture the brilliant mineral terroir of the village, and for him this means reading the balance of the season. He explains, '9–10g/L of acidity and 10–11% potential alcohol is ideal, but I need to make a choice, because some years I need just 9.5% for freshness, while other years I can let the fruit ripen to 10.5% or 11%.' He adds, 'The fashion now is small production, ripeness and high maturity, but Champagne was not built on these. It was built on a comfortable balance in the grapes and a comfortable level of production, and we need to stay true to our foundation.'

Any discussion of yield without reference to planting density only tells part of the story. 'We have no more grapes per plant at 75hL/hectare than they have at 50hL in the Médoc (Bordeaux), because we have 8000 plants per hectare while they have 5500,' points out Gimonnet. The average density across the region is currently 7600, but some are slowly replanting at 10,000. Pierre Larmandier explains that with a greater density of vines, it's possible to extract more minerals per square metre of soil. 'Others talk about square metres of leaves determining quality, but I care about grapes per square metre of soil,' he says.

One celebrated small grower, who I cannot name for fear the authorities will be on his doorstep, told me of a historical density prior to phylloxera in the late 1800s of 30,000–40,000 plants per hectare, with just four bunches per vine, producing the same yields per hectare as vines today that carry three to four times the crop load. In an attempt to revive the old-fashioned approach, he recently planted a vineyard at more than 20,000 vines per hectare, but was refused appellation status for exceeding the maximum permitted density.

Greater density of planting does not always correlate with quality. 'My grandfather planted at more than 12,000 vines per hectare, but I have an old vineyard planted at less than 4000 producing the

Pierre Larmandier checks chardonnay grapes before harvest 2011.

same yields, and it's one of my best vineyards,' says another grower, who must also be kept anonymous because low densities are illegal, too.

EXPANDING BOUNDARIES

If spiralling yields are not the solution for Champagne to meet future demand, perhaps more vineyard area is?

Under the proposed expansion of the region, individual plots are currently being examined for their suitability for grape growing, primarily in the Côte des Bar and Vitry-le-François, to the south-east of Chalons-sur-Marne. It will likely not be until 2018 that all the results are assessed and new boundaries are laid. The financial crises of recent years have taken the pressure off supply, allowing timelines to be relaxed, with the earliest vineyard plantings not expected until 2020, and the first wines some years later.

What to make of all this? You only have to look as far as German riesling in the 1970s and 1980s, and bulk Aussie 'critter' wines and New Zealand sauvignon blanc in the past decade, to understand the dire repercussions of volume-based decisions. Heaven forbid that Champagne follows this same sordid spiral.

In addition to the current 319 villages and 33,500 hectares of Champagne, Taittinger President, Pierre-Emmanuel Taittinger, estimates there may be between 1200 and 5000 hectares of land suitable for quality champagne production in the proposed 40 new villages. But will Champagne's growth be restrained to such sensible proportions? The short-term economic imperative is a powerful motivator. Land values for those who win this lottery are expected to rise from €5000 to €1 million per hectare. Not to mention political pressure from those champagne houses that stand to benefit the most.

Quality vineyard land in Champagne rarely comes up for sale, and when it does is exorbitantly priced. The family of Duval-Leroy Sales Manager Michel Brismontier were swamped with hundreds of offers at €1 million a hectare for their 3–4 hectare family estate in 2011. 'There is now no relationship between the cost of land and the return on the vineyard,' notes Pierre Larmandier, who is still repaying a 2002 vineyard purchase in premier cru Vertus. It has since doubled in value, appreciating at the rate of a house in Paris.

Grand cru Côte des Blancs is now selling for €2 million a hectare. It's estimated it would take more than 40 years to realise return on this investment. 'It's very rare to find land in the heart of a grand cru, so whenever there's an offer, there's always high demand,' says Didier Gimonnet in Cuis, who hasn't seen value since his last purchase in 2008.

Pressure is escalating as houses employ aggressive tactics to secure grape supply. In June 2012, Louis Vuitton-Moët Hennessy placed ads in local newspapers, announcing it would pay 4% more for its grapes in the 2012 vintage, then door-knocked growers with enticing incentive offers. Grape prices in Champagne have risen by 3–5% annually in recent years, pushing grand cru Côte des Blancs chardonnay to €6 a kilogram. Something has to give.

The biggest champagne brands have the most to gain from the region's expansion, and small growers have the most to lose. Small growers have driven much of Champagne's recent quality improvement, and surely any change in the AOC should encourage and not discourage this? Throw open any well-established industry to new players without a quality imperative and watch the mayhem that unfolds.

It's perhaps comforting that there is more concern over Champagne's expanding boundaries outside the region than within. In my conversations with growers and houses, from the smallest to the very largest, I have been surprised by the level of enthusiastic support for Champagne's expansion. There's certainly much debate and argument yet to come before anything is resolved, but to date there has been a stark contrast with the first mapping of Champagne's limits a century ago. In April 1911, Marne growers protested the inclusion of the outer districts by torching the cellars of Aÿ merchants suspected of purchasing grapes from elsewhere.

This is now a question of 'when' rather than 'if'. 'Everyone in Champagne agrees that the region needs to expand,' says Veuve Clicquot's Cyril Brun. 'Who knows what the Chinese and Indian markets will be like in 20 years' time? Some people want the pace of change to be fast, others want it to be slow.'

Pol Roger's Laurent d'Harcourt believes the expansion of the appellation has been well studied. 'The Champagne region did not grow between 1950 and 2010, and yet its production increased from 30 million to more than 300 million bottles,' he says.

Proponents argue that the proposed additions are situated in gaps inside, rather than outside, the perimeter of existing Champagne regions. 'There is still huge potential for land that has been unexploited,' points out Brun, 'sections between vineyards with the same soils and exposure, which have not borne grapes for centuries.' It was once equally profitable to grow carrots as it was to grow grapes in Champagne. No longer, and no surprise that everyone wants a slice of the booming champagne business.

Brun raises the question of who will be behind the exploitation of that land. 'They are likely to be farmers

who have been growing corn or other agriculture, with an attitude that higher yields are best,' he suggests. 'Consequently, we expect the quality to be acceptable at first, but not spectacular. In time, they will need to be coached by more experienced growers to produce quality fruit.' He suggests this would be good news in the long term, though not in the medium term.

Many unknowns remain. Will land owners speculate on their newly zoned real estate to make a quick profit? And just how long will it be before stability is finally regained in the region? It's not too late for Champagne to get this right, if quality is championed ahead of volume. But if the region is truly serious about increasing quality, there's more to be done than just rigorous assessments of new lands.

ANTIQUATED CRU CLASSIFICATION

In Champagne's appellation system, vineyard classification is based around the 'échelle des crus' — a crude village-by-village growth system established in 1919. Seventeen villages are designated 'grand cru', and 41 'premier cru'. If a village is rated grand cru, so is every vineyard in its bounds, and fetches a price accordingly. Such simplification is clearly nonsensical.

Pierre Gimonnet is one of the Côte des Blancs' most fastidious growers and thoughtful blenders, controlling 28 hectares of largely old vines, mainly in the heart of Cuis, Cramant, Chouilly, Oger and Vertus. 'We have 12 grand cru vineyards, but we have no grand cru blends, because the wines are better balanced when they're blended with premier crus,' explains Didier Gimonnet. This deprives him of the right to label his wines 'grand cru' and command grand cru prices.

'I am going to be politically incorrect,' he warns. 'There are 319 villages in Champagne, but the best wines come from just 20 or 30 and no more. Within these villages, you need to be in the heart of the terroir. Cramant, for instance, is grand cru, but only 150 hectares of its 230 hectares produce exceptional wine. Cuis is premier cru and it is not a great terroir for exceptional cuvées, but there are a few hectares here which are of good quality.' Another famous grower suggests the 80 hectares around Mont Aigu are the only reason Chouilly's 420 hectares are rated grand cru.

This is equally true in the premier cru village of Vertus. 'Of course, the grand crus are the best places on average,' explains Pierre Larmandier. 'But my best sites in Vertus are better than the worst in Cramant.'

At a time of crisis in the region in 1992, the large houses called in a group of young winegrowers, chaired by Pierre Larmandier and Jérôme Prévost. The two presented their approach in the vineyard and proposed a system of paying for grapes according to quality and not just volume. The proposal was written off on the insistence that there was no way of measuring quality. Their case for a more precise classification was dismissed as a scandal. 'In the end, we were fed up as no one understood, so we decided to make our own champagne instead,' Larmandier reports. Thus began two of champagne's most celebrated growers.

The designations of premier cru and grand cru are historically based on convenience for the houses, who might purchase fruit from 20 or 30 growers in the same village, at the same price. 'The problem of Champagne is that the grower is the exception,' Larmandier laments. 'The big houses and cooperatives are not interested in going further with a classification, so we're wasting our time because we are only very small.'

It's about time Champagne woke up to the reality that its 19,000 growers are no longer the exception, with more than one-quarter now producing champagne of their own. And it's not only the small growers on lesser crus who are blatantly ignoring champagne's antiquated vineyard classification.

Billecart-Salmon's single-hectare Clos Saint-Hilaire produces one of Champagne's finest blanc de noirs from the premier cru village of Mareuil-sur-Aÿ. 'So what if it isn't grand cru?' says Antoine Roland-Billecart. 'Sometimes it's better to have an old vine in a premier cru.' In the neighbouring village of Aÿ, Bollinger agrees, with its glorious flagships La Grande Année and La Grande Année Rosé each containing a portion of premier cru fruit.

The idea permeates all the way to the top. Krug is another prestige cuvée not made from 100% grand cru vineyards. Instead, all of its wines are blind tasted and the house makes its own classification every vintage. No wonder Billecart-Salmon, Bollinger, Krug, Pierre Gimonnet and Larmandier-Bernier, spanning the full spectrum of style and price, make some of the finest wines in Champagne today.

Even Champagne's largest players are joining the chorus of support. 'I have a dream,' Veuve Clicquot's Chef de Cave, Dominique Demarville, tells me. 'I hope that one day we will pay for grapes according to quality, not according to volume and vineyard designation.'

If Champagne were to give due respect to its growers and its finest houses, and seriously look at its existing territory, it would radically revise its crude village-by-village cru system and assess each and every vineyard in its own right — just like its neighbours, Burgundy and Alsace. I am told such a reassessment will never happen. It seems the credibility of Champagne's cru status will remain in tatters.

FIZZERS
Corked, stale and lightstruck

Champagne as a region is currently facing dire quality challenges on many levels. But when it comes to drinking champagne this year, there is a looming monster that diminishes all of the region's other woes into insignificance: the gross inconsistency in the condition in which champagne reaches the consumer. The number of corked, stale and lightstruck champagnes on the shelves this year is appalling.

TWO YEARS AGO I RAISED THE ALARM ON CHAMPAGNES arriving in the market out of condition, reporting one bottle in 10 on the shelves to be faulty. This year's findings are downright scandalous.

A champagne's condition depends on the consistency of the closure, transportation, storage and selling cycle. Flaws in these stages lead variously to cork taint, flavour scalping, oxidation, staleness and the phenomenon dubbed 'lightstruck'. Each of these is quantifiable, well understood and has a demonstrated solution. Some in Champagne have implemented change, with excellent results. The continued refusal of other champagne producers and their overseas agents to acknowledge these concerns is the single most significant factor impeding the quality of champagne today.

Champagne is an exceedingly fragile beverage, and it distresses me that you may not find the wines in this book to be in the same condition that I experienced them. It's prudent to be keenly aware of the inconsistencies that plague champagnes so that you can immediately recognise and reject any bottle that's out of condition.

This is why I've mentioned every faulty bottle I've encountered throughout this guide. The detail with which I've described the aromas, flavours, textures and styles of each cuvée is not only to point you to champagnes that match your taste, or to entice you to find these characters in your own sipping, but to offer a benchmark that equips you to identify a faulty champagne. I am but one voice in a country that drinks less than 2% of champagne's annual production. Change will not be effected unless consumers send a loud message that we do not accept champagne that is corked, oxidised, stale or lightstruck, and we will

continue to return it and request replacement bottles until such time as these problems are finally resolved.

This call led my inaugural *Champagne Guide* to be hailed as 'bold', 'politically incorrect', 'lacking diplomacy', even 'rude'. There are more superlatives and more high scores in this current edition than any publication I've written — credit where credit is due. But all is not perfect in paradise, and there are too few voices in the world holding one of the most expensive and celebrated of all wine styles accountable for quality and consistency. I am answerable to one person only, and that is you, and the assurance that you can always drink the best champagne that money can buy.

Hundreds of tastings, conversations and visits over recent years have only reinforced my resolve. I will continue to raise these concerns with those for whom they are most pertinent in Champagne. And I will continue to keep them prominent in the wider conscience of the wine world. Not for criticism's sake, but because I am confident that Champagne can and will be a much better place with due attention to several small but crucial details.

CORKED
I have been witness to many catastrophic closure disasters over the years, but one event in 2013 topped them all. I have the privilege of consulting on the champagne selection for a large, high-profile Australian company. We were recently offered the entire production of 25,000 bottles of a 13-year-old vintage prestige cuvée by one of the largest and most famous champagne houses. Were it not for the events that ensued, it would have been featured in this book with a $$$$ price tag and score of 96 points.

The first sample bottle was cork tainted, as were the third and fourth, prompting a massive sampling of bottles from every pallet when the first container landed. Of 62 bottles opened, 13 were cork tainted — an appalling 21%. On reporting back to France, the house immediately initiated its own tests of the same vintage and found an even higher 25% cork tainted. Alarmed and apologetic, it promptly recalled the entire production, never to be released. More than €4 million worth of top champagne down the drain. Perhaps most disconcertingly, virtually no distributor, retailer or restaurant has the capability to batch test any champagne in this way. Had this shipment been sold to anyone else, more than 5000 very expensive cork tainted bottles would most likely have gone undetected before reaching the consumer.

Cork taint is imparted randomly by natural corks, giving a mouldy, 'wet cardboard' or 'wet dog' character to champagne. It suppresses fruit and shortens the length of finish. In its most subtle form, it may simply have a slight dulling effect on the bouquet and palate.

Across my tastings for this book this year, I've encountered cork taint in one in 15 bottles sealed with natural cork, and a further one in 30 has been oxidised, while a second bottle of the same cuvée has been sound. Add these two figures together, and one in 10 bottles sealed with a natural cork went straight down the sink. Bottles sealed with a DIAM closure (read on) accounted for one-sixth of the champagnes I opened, and showed zero cork taint and a similar oxidation rate of around one in 30.

These figures are based only on variant bottles where a second bottle was sound, so do not include oxidation or premature development where multiple bottles were affected due to transportation, storage or an untimely sales cycle. For consistency, I have based these figures only on bottles I opened myself, since I didn't always see the cork when others opened bottles. These results therefore don't include, for instance, my Dom Pérignon tasting with Richard Geoffroy, in which two of six bottles were corked, my tastings at the Australian Wine Research Institute in Adelaide, in which one of two bottles of Dom Pérignon Oenothèque 1996 was corked, or my masterclasses around Australia, in which 10 out of 20 bottles of Dom Pérignon 2003 were rejected due to cork taint or oxidation. To be fair, I have counted only one of the 13 bottles corked in the fiasco recounted earlier. Accounting for these exceptions, my one in 10 fault rate is perhaps conservative.

Across tastings of some 100 champagne brands this year, the cork taint I encountered plagued eight brands, with two (Veuve Clicquot and Moutard) showing cork taint in more than one bottle. Is cork taint specific to particular brands or bottling lines? It seems not, since it appeared for only two of these seven brands in my tastings last year (Veuve Clicquot and Dom Pérignon). Both these houses tell me they are diligent in batch testing corks prior to bottling.

If champagne producers are rigorous in batch testing and rejecting every shipment that shows greater than 2–3% taint (as they claim to be), why are we seeing two to three times this level of cork-tainted champagne in the market? I put this question to the Chef de Cave of the house afflicted with 21% cork taint, and was impressed with his frank response. Over a long conversation, he explained that 200 corks are batch tested from every shipment of 400,000– 500,000 corks. If three out of 200 are badly tainted or seven have minor taint, the batch is rejected. This should therefore equate to less than 3.5% cork taint in any batch. The house has also investigated other sources of cork taint, even testing the air in the winery, the bottling line and disgorgement lines every second year, finding no traces of airborne cork taint. He claims that he personally finds just one bottle in 1000 tainted, and sometimes less.

The house ultimately traced this cork taint to the cork liners used behind crown caps in its cellar, since replaced with more reliable synthetic liners. If only the same could be achieved with corks in finished bottles. Thousands of bottles I've opened attest that Champagne's attempts to keep out sinister corks are clearly not working. Border security is failing, and one in 15 planes are going down.

Champagne disagrees with my one in 15 (6.5%) cork taint finding, but I can only report the numbers as I've found them this year, which, incidentally, are consistent with my tastings over the past three years, and anecdotally equivalent to those of other independent critics in different parts of the world. Champagne's regulatory, supervisory and promotional body, the CIVC, will not commit to a figure, but a number of houses stand by 2% after rigorous batch testing.

This rabbit hole goes deep. 'Cork suppliers are well aware of batches afflicted with higher levels of taint and mix these through good batches to maintain acceptable averages,' I was informed by a former head of the CIVC Research & Development unit, and long-standing Chef de Cave for several significant houses. 'Most houses use 1.5% cork taint as the threshold for rejecting a batch of corks, but the lower the rate demanded, the better the corks supplied.' Perhaps this explains in part why three-quarters of the cork-tainted bottles I encounter are from medium to large houses.

DIAM is the only cork product guaranteed free from cork taint.

Whatever the reason, Champagne has a monumental cork problem. Take the bottle back if it's corked and request a replacement. Champagne houses will not demand lower rates of taint from their suppliers unless their consumers demand it. If you and I put up with corked champagne, so will they.

But what if that special bottle has been popped to propose to your love, to celebrate your wedding night or to toast your lifetime achievement? You can replace the bottle, but can you replace the moment? One bottle in 10. Those are abominable odds. If I knew of any other premium product with a failure rate like that I'd never buy it. Ever.

PERFORMING SEALS: CROWN CAPS

When I visit most champagne houses, I hear of little imperative to address this cork crisis. But with each passing year, a growing band of some of the finest houses and growers are pursuing more reliable closures.

The crown cap is the best seal for champagne, as a billion bottles in Champagne's cellars attest. Ruinart Chef de Cave, Frédéric Panaïotis, spent years working in the CIVC's technical department studying closure alternatives. He found 4% cork taint could be reduced to 2% with rigorous sampling and batch control. 'Crown cap is the only reliable solution,' he says. 'We don't want to use it, but we will if we have to.'

In 2004, Nicolas Chiquet of Gaston Chiquet disgorged a 2001 blanc de blancs as a trial under two different natural corks, DIAM and crown caps. 'Every time I do the tasting I prefer the caps,' he reports.

Didier Gimonnet of Pierre Gimonnet keeps champagnes for private consumption under caps. 'After five or six years, we prefer the wines under crown caps,' he says. 'For quality, freshness and purity, I am sure caps are the best closures. It's incredible that we devote so much time and energy to create the best champagnes we can, and at the end of the process we insert a cork, which completely changes the evolution of the wine and could destroy it completely!'

Some in Champagne favour the character that cork brings to the ageing process. Dom Pérignon ages its Oenothèques and Bollinger ages its reserve and vintage wines under natural cork pre-disgorgement. Bollinger Chef de Cave Mathieu Kauffmann suggests that champagne does not age reliably under crown seal for longer than five years. This was addressed by more reliable liners for crown seals in the mid-1990s. Liners are now available with a wide range of porosities, permitting selection according to the desired ageing.

The challenge for champagne under crown cap is aesthetic, not technical. 'It's absolutely impossible to sell champagnes with caps in the European market as it's simply not the tradition,' Gimonnet emphasises.

It's also currently illegal under Champagne's rules, though the CIVC is at liberty to change this. 'There is not much specified in the regulations regarding closure, except that the vintage should appear on the side of the cork inside the bottle,' Panaïotis explains. 'So it could be printed on the inside of the crown seal.'

Champagne's reluctance to change its rules is based on perceived consumer reaction. Perhaps the market should make this decision, not the gatekeepers.

THE DIAM REVOLUTION

The alternative that's gaining traction is Mytik DIAM, now sealing close to one in six champagnes — some 50 million of 309 million bottles sold in 2012. A brand of champagne closure made by Oeneo, DIAM is moulded from granulated fragments of cork which have been treated to extract cork taint and some 150 other molecules that might produce 'off' characters.

DIAM is a significant improvement on natural cork, more consistent in maintaining freshness, and the only cork product guaranteed to be free of cork taint. I have never encountered cork taint in a genuine DIAM, though in comparative tastings with still wines, I've often noted a slight muting effect on the aromatics of the bouquet and palate, but not nearly as acute as that of natural cork.

Champagne also holds its pressure more consistently under DIAM, which is rated to lose 0.7–1.3 cubic centimetres of gas per day, compared with traditional corks of 0.5–2.5. It provides a more consistent physical seal than natural cork, and trials at Bollinger have confirmed a lower rate of oxygen interchange in DIAM than natural cork (too low for Bollinger's ageing under cork pre-disgorgement, but a good sign for DIAM's performance post-disgorgement). It generally more reliably protects champagne from oxidation, though I've encountered a couple of exceptions showing random oxidation this year, both traced to incorrectly inserted DIAMs.

Purity-focused Vertus grower Veuve Fourny switched its entire range to DIAM in 2006. 'We compared 20 bottles of our Blanc de Blancs under DIAM with 20 bottles of the same wine bottled under natural cork for five years,' Emmanuel Fourny reports. 'All the DIAMs were similar, fresh and with pure fruit. The others were more evolved and each bottle had a different personality. Using a normal cork is like Russian roulette!' In the five years since, the company has not once sent its standard letter in reply to complaints regarding cork faults. 'It's a kind of revolution in Champagne,' Fourny says.

Billecart's Australian agent reported an immediate drop in returned bottles when DIAM was introduced on the company's non-vintage wines in 2006. Testing is currently underway on the ageing of its vintage wines under DIAM.

DIAM holds freshness more reliably than natural cork. In Le Mesnil-sur-Oger, Rodolphe Péters of Pierre Péters switched to DIAM in his non-vintage cuvées after trialling it and two natural corks (Amorim and Subir Tap) in a 2001 vintage blanc de blancs disgorged in early 2008. 'We tasted the wines over a year before deciding to use DIAM, and even after six months we observed differences,' he clarifies. 'The Amorim was more smoky and nutty, the Subir Tap more honeyed, and the DIAM cleaner, closed and more reductive.'

Péters opened samples for me in early 2013. The Subir Tap showed overt development, stripped and contracted; the Amorim (his preference in this tasting), showed more approachability, with oxidative development drawing out more rounded, honeyed, nutty notes, while retaining fresh citrus fruits. The DIAM, my preference, showed less development, upholding more primary lemon citrus fruit expression, better length and a hint of reductive character. 'If your wine has good structure it has more resilience to shipping and storage under DIAM than the same wine under cork,' he says. 'When I taste my wine in very far markets like Japan or the west coast of the US, it still tastes like my wine when it is sealed with DIAM.'

Nicolas Chiquet, at Gaston Chiquet in Dizy, is fanatical about preserving the character of his fruit, and now uses DIAM in every cuvée. 'It is a huge advantage!' he exclaims. 'Natural cork gives variation between bottles, but I want regularity. Every bottle is

very regular under DIAM because the oxygen ingress is very consistent and there is no cork taint.'

Even long after disgorgement, DIAM is hailed for retaining consistency. 'Since using it, I can now open bottles four or five years after disgorgement and they are absolutely identical,' reports Gilles Dumangin, of J. Dumangin Fils.

Champagne houses and growers report three reasons for reluctance to switch to DIAM. The first is that it is aesthetically not as attractive as a natural cork — an argument I find puzzling, since even natural corks are moulded from fragments. Houses that have made the change do not report aesthetics to be a concern. Since switching four years ago, Devaux has sold some 1.8 million bottles under DIAM, and received just two complaints from customers related to its appearance. French consumers are the most resistant to the closure for aesthetic reasons, prompting G.H. Mumm to launch DIAM only in Australia and New Zealand in 2012. 'France is not as ready as the New World to receive it,' reports Chef de Cave Didier Mariotti. 'But if you can guarantee no more cork problems, I don't know why we're waiting!'

The second reason for reluctance is an uneasiness in committing to a single supplier, preferring to spread risk across a range of cork companies. Understandable, given the notorious performance of natural corks of late. However, it seems counterintuitive to favour a selection of unreliable corks over a single product known to be more reliable. This surely increases the risk rather than decreasing it.

Third, and most significant, not everyone in Champagne is favourable to the slowing of development by decreased oxygen ingress through DIAM closures. 'Our trials have revealed that DIAM doesn't produce the same evolution in bottle, so it doesn't develop the way we would expect,' reports Taittinger Deputy General Manager, Damien Le Sueur. In response, Mytik has recently released a new DIAM branded 'Access' with greater permeability, permitting 1–1.8 cubic centimetres of gas loss per day, in the middle of the range for a natural cork, but with greater consistency. Veuve Clicquot has launched trials, with results pending.

On the back of DIAM's success, some 25 other similar-looking 'technological' corks have been launched by other brands, claiming to be taint-free. Contrary to their claims, without DIAM's cork-taint extraction process, these granulated closures often increase the incidence of cork taint. I've witnessed this on a number of occasions, including four cork-tainted bottles in a row recently. Gilles Dumangin reports

90–95% taint in some of these products, as well as higher rates of oxidation.

The A-team of producers using DIAM on at least one cuvée includes Ayala, Besserat de Bellefon, Billecart-Salmon, Canard-Duchêne, Chanoine, Claude Carré, Collet, Devaux, De Saint Gall, De Telmont, Duperrey, Ernest Rapeneau, Eustache Deschamps, G.H. Mumm, Gaston Chiquet, Gauthier, Gobillard, Gosset, Haton, Henri Maire, Henriot, J. Dumangin Fils, Jacquart, Laherte Frères, Lanson, Le Mesnil, Martel, Mercier, Moët & Chandon, Napoléon, Pascal Doquet, Paul Louis Martin, Perrier-Jouët, Philippe Gonet, Pierre Gimonnet, Pierre Moncuit, Pierre Péters, Pommery, Roland Champion, Taittinger, Tribaut-Schloesser, Veuve A. Devaux and Veuve Fourny.

It's about time more champagne houses offered a reliable closure on those 309 million bottles that leave their cellars annually. At 6.5%, that's more than 20 million bottles of corked champagne down the sink every year. Champagne makes an average of €14.15 for every bottle it ships, bringing the total bill for cork taint to €284 million annually. Add random oxidation and it jumps to €440 million. The average shelf price of the corked champagnes I opened this year was €90. At this rate, the value runs into the billions.

Freshen up, Champagne!

Beware of stale and fruit-flat champagnes. Too many bottles lose freshness from sealing faults, poor transportation, bad storage conditions or simply sitting on the shelves too long.

Bollinger uses a computerised system on its bottling line to check for cork-seal defects and rejects 3–4%. (If only it could detect cork taint, too!) When I visited the bottling line, a full cart was stacked 10-high with rejects destined to be used as liquor. Over a year, 20,000 bottles pass through that cart. Only five such detection systems are in use in Champagne. For everyone else, that cart of rejects trundles off to market.

Champagne rosé is a sensitive soul. Across my tastings, no champagne style varies more around the world, from one disgorgement to the next, or one year to the next. Rosé champagne loses its freshness, character and appeal more quickly than white champagne post-disgorgement, and because it's often bottled in clear glass, it's also more susceptible to lightstruck degradation (see page 44). Even at the very top end, vintage rosé possesses a lower resilience to the effects of oxidation as it ages in bottle.

In 2010, I reported Ruinart Brut Rosé NV to be disappointingly stale and fruit-flat. When Chef de Cave Frédéric Panaïotis visited Brisbane in 2011 to host a tasting for discerning media and trade he responded, 'You must have tasted the disgorgement from the 2005 base, a poor vintage that has developed quickly. We will taste the lovely, fresh 2007 base today.'

When the rosé was served, it tasted fruit-flat and simple, though not as stale as last year. 'This looks like the 2006 base to me!' he apologised, as he quickly whisked everyone's glasses away. 'It's lacking fruit character.' He recorded the bottle code to decipher later. If the maker himself can't distinguish a tired, old disgorgement until it's opened, what chance do the rest of us have?

'My position for non-vintage champagne is that I don't want the disgorgement date on the bottle,' Panaïotis defended. 'Probably only 5% of consumers are interested in this information, and printing the date will only confuse others, who might read it as a use-by date.' This seems a hollow excuse. There's no way to decipher the bottling code, either. 'If it could be deciphered, it would no longer be a code,' he dismissed. Instead, Panaïotis suggests writing down the code and emailing Ruinart for the base vintage.

When I sent a request for the disgorgement dates and base vintages for Moët & Chandon's non-vintage wines in 2011, the response came back from the Moët Hennessy agent that, 'These are all NON VINTAGE, hence do not have a vintage base year.' Finally, after three weeks and a dozen emails backwards and forwards, the base year and disgorgement were confirmed by Chef de Cave Benoît Gouez himself. In response to the same question, Laurent Perrier outright refuses to disclose disgorgement dates and base vintages.

Champagne could resolve this ridiculous state of affairs in a heartbeat by printing disgorgement dates on every bottle. Many smaller producers are doing this, and it's all the more helpful for medium and large houses, who usually disgorge in successive batches, each of which is subtly different, and who are more likely to have older disgorgements lingering in some markets.

'The date of disgorgement is very important, because a bottle will taste very different six months after disgorgement than it will two years after,' explains Didier Gimonnet. The disgorgement date communicates a world of information, stamping the bottle with an indelible time reference, the only clue to its age, to locating a fresh bottle and avoiding a stale one, to finding a similar bottle if you like it, or giving it a wide berth if you don't. Collectors are increasingly ageing non-vintage wines like Krug Grande Cuvée and Laurent-Perrier Grand Siècle, and a disgorgement date would provide a means of managing these collections. Armed with a little knowledge from this book, the disgorgement date is your insight into the base vintage of a non-vintage blend and all the information that goes with this. Disclosure of disgorgement dates on every bottle removes ambiguity.

It also keeps importers and retailers accountable to timely movement of stock. Without this, some will keep slowly trickling disgorgements into the market that should have been consumed years ago. But for some, even a disgorgement date on every bottle is insufficient discouragement. Ayala's Australian agent assured me they would address the problem after reading my grumbles about stale, old, 2006 disgorged bottles of Ayala Rosé Majeur Brut NV in 2010. In August 2011, I was dismayed to be poured the same disgorgement by the agent at a trade tasting. The March 2011 disgorgement was current in France at the time, making the Australian stock five years too old. A promised fresh sample never came. If stale old bottles still linger in warehouses, how many more lurk on retail shelves?

Some champagne producers print disgorgement dates only at the request of their agents in particular markets, offering a lazy excuse to remove accountability for timely stock turnover. Surely it's in the interests of every house to protect its reputation by ensuring outdated stock can be easily identified in every market? It's an opportunity every house owes its customers, but precious few deliver.

Antoine Roland-Billecart looking for a fresh old champagne.

Last year, Veuve Clicquot could not tell me with certainty the base vintages of the non-vintage cuvées I tasted. Chef de Cave Dominique Demarville admits the biggest challenge in printing disgorgement dates lies in managing the logistics on the labelling line. If Lanson and Ayala can do it, surely Clicquot can, too. 'I'm all for transparency and if I can put the disgorgement date on the label I will,' he says. 'We're working on it, and I cross my fingers that we'll have it in the next few years.' Until then, the three-digit number on every Clicquot cork is the disgorgement date. The first two digits are the year and the third digit is the bimester (e.g. 114 is July/August 2011).

G.H. Mumm Chef de Cave Didier Mariotti tastes every cuvée from each warehouse in most export markets every six months, and checks the disgorgement date of cuvées in every restaurant he visits. 'You can work hard on the blend, ageing and disgorgement, and if you don't focus on the supply chain you can destroy everything,' he reveals. Mumm prints disgorgement dates only on its Brut Selection for the French market, but Mariotti believes it's always best to disclose the disgorgement date. To this end, he's following Krug's lead in introducing a bottle code to unlock information for the consumer.

In 2012, Krug introduced an ingenious ID code above the barcode of every bottle. Using this code, Krug.com reveals the season and year in which the bottle was shipped, the number of years over which it has aged, the blend and the vintage story for vintage wines, and the number of wines and each of the vintages in non-vintage blends. It's a discrete little code that won't confuse anyone, but for those in the know, it also reveals the disgorgement date on the spot, since the first three digits are the trimester (first digit) and year (second and third digits) of disgorgement.

Smaller growers are leading the way in transparent disclosure of information on every bottle. On each of his eponymous labels, Jean-Baptiste Geoffroy displays vintages, varieties, dosage and date of disgorgement — a laudable commitment for a small grower who disgorges every 2–3 months and tweaks the dosage for each disgorgement. In Chigny-les-Roses, Gilles Dumangin disgorges every shipment to order, and each back label not only declares disgorgement date, blend and dosage, but also features a unique QR code to unlock a wealth of information, including vineyards, food matches, reviews and importer's details.

I have again done everything possible to feature the freshest, most recent disgorgements in this guide. The huge inconsistency in champagne prompted me to call in two samples of every bottle. The rate at which I reached for backups was alarming. Those smaller producers and occasional medium-sized houses who print the disgorgement date clearly on every bottle do their customers an important service by giving them the opportunity to find a fresh bottle. If you encounter a bottle that seems stale, without a date to guide you, there is another clue.

The expansion of the cork after it's removed gives an indication of the length of time elapsed since disgorgement. The more it swells back to its original cylindrical form, the more recent the disgorgement. The base of a very young cork will eventually swell back to almost the same diameter as the top. A very old cork will not swell at all. Unfortunately, this is an imprecise art, since the variability of cork means that even corks disgorged on the same day will swell by varying amounts. DIAMs are more consistent.

Until every bottle leaving Champagne is printed with its disgorgement date: consumer, beware! Take back your bubbles if it's not up to scratch. If it's corked, the replacement will be on form (fingers crossed), but if it's stale, order something else.

LIGHTSTRUCK

There is another factor that plagues champagne freshness. Did you know that if you leave a bottle in the light it might taste like onions? 'Lightstruck' is the name wine scientists give to the menacing effect of degradation of wine exposed to ultraviolet light from fluorescent lamps and, worse, sunlight.

Black bottles are best, though very rare; dark green bottles partly solve the problem, naturally filtering 92% of ultraviolet light (equivalent to SPF15 sunscreen), but white flint (clear) glass blocks just a tiny fraction. Louis Roederer recently switched to brown bottles for its vintage wines because they up the UV protection to 97% (SPF30).

When Ruinart Chef de Cave Frédéric Panaïotis opened a bottle of Blanc de Blancs for me at the house this year, it didn't look right, lacking freshness and aromatics and tasting vegetal. It was eventually ascertained that this clear bottle had been left on a desk in an office for a few days. A replacement from the same batch was pristine.

Artificial light can produce discernible changes in wine bottled in clear glass within just a few hours. In extreme cases, champagne will even deteriorate in a glass which has been pre-poured and left on a sunny table for just a few minutes. For champagne, the problem is exacerbated because long lees ageing makes Méthode Traditionnelle wines particularly susceptible to 'lightstruck' degradation. Fruit esters (like citrus aromas) are diminished, and reductive characters (sulphur, cabbage, corn, garlic, onion, gherkin, bacon, gunsmoke, burnt rubber) are produced.

There is no wine more susceptible to lightstruck degradation than champagne in clear glass bottles, which makes rosé particularly vulnerable. Some bottles are lightstruck and others are simply too old, affected by less than ideal storage conditions, or a combination of all three. It's often difficult to ascertain which effect is the prime culprit, but it is telling that a high proportion of the stale champagnes that I open are in clear glass bottles.

'A clear bottle is nice because you can see the wine, but if it is left on the shelf too long, it is a disaster!' exclaims Dominique Demarville. 'For me, light is more dangerous for champagne than the cork or the temperature.' For this reason, he continues to bottle Veuve Clicquot rosé in green bottles. There is not yet a clear glass treatment to block UV light for champagne, as there is for beer, because it's a different wavelength of light that troubles champagne. Panaïotis is working on a solution for clear bottles, but reports that there are no possibilities on the horizon. In the meantime, he's now printing warnings on the packaging. The week before I visited, his boss requested Ruinart Rosé in a clear bottle. Panaïotis' response was, 'No way!'

How do you avoid a lightstruck wine? Some champagne houses ship clear bottles in cellophane wrap for protection. This is even more effective than dark bottles, so be sure to keep the bottle in its wrap until the moment you serve it. (One step more sophisticated, Gilles Dumangin sells his top rosé in a protective cotton bag!) Never buy a clear glass bottle of champagne that's been sitting on the shelf or in an illuminated fridge unless it's sealed in its box, cellophane or bag.

The Champenois use yellow lights with no ultraviolet in their cellars to avoid lightstruck wines. It's time the same was considered around the world. Where this isn't always possible, champagnes displayed without a protective covering should be shielded behind a sheet of Perspex or UV-tinted glass. Research on lightstruck remains ongoing, and some of the best in the world has been conducted by the Australian Wine Research Institute. Google 'AWRI lightstruck'.

The only way Champagne will take its troubles with faulty bottles seriously is if we as consumers send Champagne and its agents a clear message that we will not tolerate expensive bottles that are out of condition. It is imperative that every bottle that's old, stale, corked or clearly lacking in freshness is returned.

Do your bit, and change will come.

The Champagne Guide

HOUSE RULES
The grower vs house fallacy

The stark distinction drawn around the world between Champagne négociant houses, cooperatives and grower producers is perplexing. Champagne drinkers who pop only the household names of the big brands miss an important dimension of the great diversity of champagne's finest offerings. Those who hunt fanatically for nothing but small growers miss an equally exciting experience. The very notion of imposing such a division undermines the complex and diverse relationships between champagne brands and the vineyards from which they are sourced. In Champagne itself, there is no such segregation, and its very suggestion is vigorously dismissed by both sides.

'IT'S VERY EASY TO HAVE AN "US AND THEM" APPROACH — but this is not in the spirit of Champagne,' says celebrated Vertus grower producer Pierre Larmandier, who recently changed importers in the United States for his Larmandier-Bernier label over such discussion.

'We think it's just absurd that there's a "growers versus houses" mentality in the market,' agrees Christian Holthausen, former Communications Director for the houses of Piper and Charles Heidsieck. 'We all eat and drink together!' Even the very term 'grower producer' is challenged. 'From where do they think we pull our grapes?' Holthausen exclaims.

Philosophically, some of Champagne's finest grower producers align themselves more closely with particular houses. 'It is not because we are small that we make good wine — some houses make distinguished wine, and even the biggest houses can be very good,' says Larmandier. He includes the house of Jacquesson in his tasting association with Jacques Selosse, Egly-Ouriet and Jérôme Prévost, and points out that there are many small growers in his zone of the Côte des Blancs who produce 'ordinary wines'.

The complexities of ownership and management of vineyards do not align with such a simple segregation of producers. The champagne appellation labels of 'négociant-manipulant' (one who purchases grapes), and 'récoltant-manipulant' (one who makes wine from estate vineyards), do not distinguish, for example, vines managed under lease arrangements. Billecart-Salmon owns just 14 hectares, but manages a further 65 hectares on lease. 'We do everything from pruning through to harvest,' explains Antoine Roland-Billecart,

'and this is very important, as it enables us to conduct the vineyards the way we want and yield 70hL/hectare rather than 90.' He highlights the great advantage in purchasing fruit in excess of the requirements of the house, permitting inferior parcels to be onsold, crucial for maintaining exemplary quality.

The discussion of vineyard ownership is further convoluted by the many Champagne estates divided among family through succession and inheritance.

The average Champagne grower now owns less than 0.7ha. In the little village of Chavot, the small, seventh-generation producer Laherte Frères is registered as a négociant-manipulant but, this is merely a formality. A récoltant-manipulant may purchase just 5% before it is designated a négociant. The estate buys from 10 hectares in 75 parcels across 10 nearby villages, all owned and tended by members of the immediate family. Half of the holdings are managed biodynamically; the remainder essentially organically. The oldest vines have been cultivated by different generations of the family for some 70 years, but now reside under different ownership in the eyes of the law. For all intents and purposes, the estate is a grower producer.

At the other extreme, within some larger houses, there is good argument that distinction should be made even for individual cuvées. Louis Roederer's non-vintage blends include 45% négociant fruit, but its vintage wines are assembled exclusively from estate sources. 'For the vintage wines, I do not say Roederer is a champagne house,' says Chef de Cave Jean-Baptiste Lécaillon. 'We are three growers, one in Montagne de Reims, one in Vallée de la Marne and one in Côte des Blancs.'

Any suggestion of distinguishing growers and négociants on size is equally shaky. The legendary négociant house of Salon produces less than 80,000 bottles in a worthy vintage. Exemplary grower producer Pierre Gimonnet produces more than thrice this volume every year.

And the complexities compound. In the village of Chigny-les-Roses, Gilles Dumangin owns three hectares of vineyards under his J. Dumangin brand, and buys from his parents' three hectares and a further nine. He oversees the staff who manage his vineyards in the same manner as he oversees his other growers. 'Would I produce better wines if I grew all the grapes myself?' he asks. 'No. I'd do everything exactly the same.'

What's in a name? More outside Champagne than inside, it seems. 'There is too much hype about the récoltant-manipulant,' Dumangin suggests. 'Because I am a négociant as well as a grower, I am excluded from grower producer tastings for a large UK publication and from some French articles. The important competition Concours Général Agricole de Paris does not accept any entry from négociants, even if they can prove it is made only from their own fruit.'

In response, Dumangin has recently registered a second company as a récoltant-manipulant in order to access these prejudiced channels. Such exclusivity seems out of place in a region that warmly celebrates its own diversity. 'A lot of growers are producing their own wines, which is just fantastic because it produces such a diversity of styles!' rejoices Roland-Billecart. 'The growers are becoming more and more important, which is good for Champagne.'

Ruinart Chef de Cave Frédéric Panaïotis says he's happy to see growers commanding good prices and good reputations, as this is ultimately helpful for the houses and for the region.

The lines in Champagne are blurring. 'Once upon a time, the houses did not own vineyards,' explains Pol Roger Managing Director, Laurent d'Harcourt. 'Now they're becoming more like growers. Meanwhile, growers are sourcing from many villages rather than just their own, and becoming more like houses. Many cooperatives now have their own brands and are acting as négociants.'

Champagne's tangled web of vineyard ownership and management runs deep and wide, but there is a much simpler and more substantive reason why market-imposed biases for or against négociants or growers are out of place. In a blind tasting, no characteristic or quality indicator distinguishes the great houses from the great growers. To exclude any would be to lose a colour from the remarkable and intricate tapestry that is Champagne.

It is equally true that there are both under-performing houses and growers. 'For me, quality is not a question of size,' declares Veuve Clicquot Chef de Cave Dominique Demarville. 'There are growers making exceptional champagnes and some doing a very bad job, and it's the same with the champagne houses.'

Dumangin proposes that the number of houses producing good wines is a higher proportion than the number of grower producers. Jean-Hervé Chiquet of Jacquesson suggests that of Champagne's 5000 growers who make their own wine, less than 100 are top growers. 'There are more and more top growers all the time, though still only a small number,' he says.

This book makes no attempt to segregate champagne producers as houses, cooperatives or grower producers. Instead, the focus is the detail and distinctiveness of each, highlighting a uniqueness that transcends simplistic classification and its intrinsically unfair prejudices.

I enjoy the grand spectacle of a pulsating stadium of U2 proportions, and equally appreciate the intimacy of my favourite local funk band in an eclectic jazz club. It would do both an injustice to suggest that one is somehow a more authentic experience. The musical world is a richer place for the coexistence of both. So, too, is the world of champagne for its growers, houses and cooperatives.

The 13th century church amid the vines of Chavot.

Just a spoonful of sugar

The searing levels of acidity inherent in grapes grown in Champagne's bitterly cold climate scream out for a little sweetness to temper their impact. In the final stage of the champagne process, the bottle is topped up with 'dosage' — usually a mixture of wine and sugar syrup. Over the centuries, dosage levels have gradually lowered, and in recent years the catch cry seems to have become 'how low can you go?' Is progressively lower dosage really the most delightful way for champagne?

THERE WAS GREAT ANTICIPATION WHEN THE WORLD'S oldest champagne was found in a shipwreck in the depths of the Baltic Sea in 2010. When the first 1820s bottle surfaced, the drop in pressure popped the cork and the divers immediately raised a glass to celebrate their discovery, expressing surprise to find it very sweet. Two hundred years ago, champagne was as sweet as dessert wine today, in an attempt to make it palatable within 12 months of harvest to meet increasing demand. Sometimes as much as 330g/L of sugar was added — sweeter than most Sauternes, and more than twice the sweetness of Coca-Cola!

Well ahead of its time, the house of Perrier-Jouët shipped its 1846 vintage to London with no added sugar, and it was quickly written off as too severe, or 'brute'-like. The style slowly gained favour over a generation, and in 1876 the term 'brut' was officially introduced for dry champagne.

'The most brilliant idea of the centuries has been to make champagne an apéritif instead of a dessert wine! A genius idea!' exclaims Veuve Clicquot Chef de Cave, Dominique Demarville. 'If we were still a dessert wine, we would be nothing.'

Until recently, to qualify as 'brut', champagne required less than 15g/L of sweetness — a little less than a teaspoon of sugar in a cup of coffee. This has now been lowered to a maximum of 12g/L.

'Extra brut' requires less than 6g/L, and 'brut nature' or 'brut zero' less than 3g/L, since even wines of zero dosage usually have a touch of sweetness remaining from fermentation.

Antoine Roland-Billecart of Billecart-Salmon likens dosage to makeup. 'If there are no problems and you want to show the real character of the wine, you don't need a high dosage,' he points out. 'The significant decrease in dosage over the past decade has been very important in allowing the fruit to show to its full capacity, rather than masked with sugar.'

We should all raise a glass to celebrate Champagne's low-sugar diet, and to many of the region's most fanatical houses and growers who have progressively lowered dosage as their wines have become ever finer. Sweetness can mask many evils, and for too long Champagne has notoriously bolstered inferior fruit with excessive sugar.

Champagne's sweet dreams may be a thing of the past, but has it all gone too far?

'Zero dosage' is all the rage, and the intent of the 'Coke Zero' movement of the wine world is certainly noble — but trouble brews when popularity comes before good sense. French writers and bloggers are pushing zero-dosage hard, and too many champagne brands have merrily joined the parade simply because it's the thing to do. Dogmatically slashing dosage to zero purely for the sake of branding is self-defeating.

'We're going to see more and more wines with lower dosage, but dosage is crucial for balance,' points out Demarville. 'Many are simply releasing their brut NV without dosage, but to make it well it must be a special blend.'

A carefully tweaked low dosage is not designed to make a wine taste sweet. In tastings of the same champagne with 5g/L alongside the same wine with zero, I am astounded by the effect of just a spoonful of sugar in an entire bottle. Floral aromas are lifted, palate is softened and more harmonious, fruit is more expressive and, in the most delightful way, it doesn't taste sweet. Mary Poppins might have been onto something.

Champagne's most progressive makers carefully tweak the dosage of every cuvée, every year, to create a precise balance. Sometimes zero dosage is the right answer, but we do well to resist becoming so caught up in the fanfare that we miss the many excellent brut and extra brut wines on the shelves. The majority of champagne's most refined wines this year have a dosage of 4–8g/L.

The wines of Pierre Gimonnet are among Champagne's most pure and precise and find a balance with dosage levels in this range. When Didier Gimonnet was encouraged to introduce a zero-dosage wine by his US importer in 2011, he refused on the spot. 'This is not my philosophy!' he replied. 'We want to make wines which are very well balanced.'

Some houses have made the mistake of simply releasing their standard cuvée without any dosage, usually with thin, insipid results. Only the most fanatical houses can pull this off successfully. When François Domi blended Billecart-Salmon's Extra Brut,

he started with the Brut Réserve and experimented with dosages of 0–8g/L, settling on zero for 'the best expression of delicacy, finesse and elegance'.

More often, the most balanced zero-dosage wines are custom-built from the ground up. When Pol Roger blends its Pure Brut it avoids components with high acidity, favouring those with more floral aromas, producing a wine even more refined than its beloved Brut Réserve.

Has the 'no added sugar' campaign of Champagne run its full course?

With warmer vintages to contend with, will chaptalisation by the addition of sugar prior to fermentation be the next thing to go?

And just what would a diver think if a zero-dosage champagne were to surface in 200 years?

Winter at Moët's Mont Aigu lodge in Chouilly. Champagne tempers its bitterly cold climate with a touch of sweetness.

The Champagne Guide

Shades of grey in a parallel universe

To buy or not to buy parallel imported champagne?

The face of Champagne is changing rapidly, not only with the maelstrom of changing climate and the refinement of its finest minds.

Champagne is a luxury international commodity, highly vulnerable to the gusty winds of economic change that characterise the contemporary world. Currency fluctuations have smoothed the seas for the trading of champagnes from an ever more diverse variety of sources. The result is record low prices. It's hard to go past the tantalising discounts we've seen on familiar champagne brands in recent years. But are they a safe buy?

'Parallel' or 'grey' imports are brought in by parties other than the usual agent, typically via a third-party country. There's nothing new about this practice, but the rate at which parallels are moving between markets is on the rise.

Traditional importers are naturally up in arms about such exploitation of brands they've spent years building in their country. But for the champagne lover, increased availability and more competitive pricing can only be a good thing.

Or can it? Champagne is one of the most fragile of all wine styles, quickly deteriorating under adverse storage or transportation conditions, even losing freshness simply sitting on a shelf. Adding another port to an already long journey from the far side of the planet — not to mention an indeterminate period in a foreign warehouse or wharf under dubious conditions — can only exacerbate Champagne's already monumental problem of inconsistent freshness.

Or so traditional importers would have us believe.

What's the truth? I recently resolved to find out for myself, purchasing each of the seven champagnes that Australian wine retailer Kemenys was parallel importing, and selling at discounts of up to 46% less than usual pricing, from the entry-level Lanson Black Label Brut NV, to the prestige Bollinger La Grande Année. I lined these up alongside the same wines purchased from their longstanding importers, and served each of the seven pairs blind to six experienced palates (two Masters of Wine, two retailers, another wine writer and myself).

The consensus fell four votes to two in favour of the parallel imported bottles (the seventh vote was tied), though in most cases we were splitting hairs. It was concluded that any variation resulting from different importers was effectively indiscernible compared with cork variation, different batches and varying times since disgorgement. In tracing the history of the seven parallel imported bottles, all had come to Australia via the UK or the Netherlands. Three were fresher (more recently disgorged) than the traditional imports, two less fresh, and two effectively the same.

It's impossible to make global generalisations based on just seven bottles from one source, but this exercise certainly serves to demonstrate that nothing is black and white in the world of grey imports. I have since learnt that my tasting was perhaps a best-case scenario, since Kemenys is rigorous in shipping and storing only under climate-controlled conditions, and conducts its own comparative tastings to ensure the champagnes it sources are as fresh as any other. Not all parallel importers show the same discretion — and neither, for that matter, do all traditional importers.

It's rarely possible to identify a parallel-imported champagne from the bottle. Best to develop a relationship with a trusted retailer prepared to stand by the provenance of every bottle they sell, and to guarantee to replace any not up to scratch. Some importers welcome you to buy direct, offering first access to small-grower champagnes that may never reach the shelves. Get on their lists for regular offers at prices that often leave the large-house markdowns for dead. Don't be lured only by big discounts on household brands. Some growers offer outstanding value at full price, and I've highlighted these throughout the following pages.

Awash with bubbles
How to serve champagne

Champagne glasses

Using decent glassware is essential for fully appreciating wine, and all the more for champagne.

How important? 'We worked with wine glass company Riedel for more than a year to develop a glass which was ideal for Krug Grande Cuvée,' Olivier Krug told me. 'They proposed 26 glasses and I would take them home to try with my wife until very late at night!'

The more I visit and taste with the Champenois, the more I appreciate the way a large glass draws a champagne out of itself. Champagne holds its bead longest in an elongated glass, but don't select one so narrow that you can't get your nose in to appreciate the bouquet. 'It's not just about the bubbles. Champagne is a wine, not just scenery!' says Duval-Leroy Sales Manager Michel Brismontier, who serves champagne in normal wine glasses rather than flutes.

The Champenois prefer slightly wider glasses than typical champagne flutes, to allow their finest cuvées sufficient space to open out. Think halfway between a flute and a fine white wine glass. All good glasses curve in slightly at the top. The finer the glass, the better they look at the table, and the less the champagne will warm up when you pour it. Cut, engraved or coloured glasses make it harder to appreciate the wine's appearance.

My favourite champagne glass is the Riedel Vinum XL Champagne. This is the largest glass I've found, with a bowl of white wine glass proportions that draws down into the stem sufficiently to produce a focused stream of bubbles. Moët & Chandon use these as their tasting glass and tell me they were designed in the 1960s. They'll set you back as much as a bottle of non-vintage champagne (each!), making for an expensive but worthwhile investment in champagne enjoyment.

My second-favourite glass is one-fifth of the price. The Luigi Bormioli Magnifico Flute is very nearly as large as the Riedel and almost as fine. If you can't find these, grab a medium-sized white wine glass over a champagne flute for any serious bottle of fizz.

The traditional flat champagne 'coupe' glasses are now practically unheard of in Champagne, except in historical ceremony. They are inferior because the large surface area evaporates both bead and aroma rapidly. The wide, flanged rim means that the wine is spilled to the sides of the tongue, where sensitivity to acidity is heightened.

It's paramount that there is not the slightest residue of detergent in the glass, as this will instantly destroy the mousse (bubbles) and the taste. Riedel recommends washing under warm water without detergent, and polishing with microfibre towels. Never dry a glass by holding the base and twisting the bowl, as this may snap the stem.

Serving temperature

'The temperature of service is very important,' emphasises Oliver Krug, who admits to being obsessed with the quality of service. 'We may work for 10 or 20 years to create Grande Cuvée, ship in the best refrigerated container, and then you might be served the first Krug of your life in a stupid flute as cold as ice and you miss 99% of the pleasure and the message!'

Antoine Roland-Billecart of Billecart-Salmon says wine is like a human being in the cold. 'Put yourself out in the snow and you won't show anything either, you'll be all covered up!' he says. 'Three degrees breaks everything in champagne. It should be served at cellar temperature, and never below eight degrees.' Cellar temperature for the Champenois means 10°C.

Champagne is often served much too cold. Poured at fridge temperature, it will taste flavourless and acidic. The only exceptions are particularly sweet styles, which are best toned down with a stern chill. In general, the finer the wine, the warmer I tend to serve it. The Champenois suggest 8–10°C for non-vintage and rosé styles, and 10–12°C for vintage and prestige wines.

If you're pulling a bottle out of a climate-controlled cellar, it will need to be cooled a little further, so pop it in the fridge for half an hour. If it's at room temperature to start with, 3–4 hours in the fridge or 15 minutes in an ice bucket might be in order. On a warm day, serve champagne a touch cooler, as it will soon warm up.

Always hold a champagne glass by its base or stem, to avoid warming the wine in your hand. This will also reduce the likelihood of any aromas on your hands interfering with its delicate bouquet.

AGE AND CELLARING

Twenty-year-old champagne is one of my favourite indulgences, and a particularly good vintage wine or prestige cuvée will comfortably go the distance. Generally, aim to drink vintage champagnes between eight and 15 years after vintage, and non-vintage wines within five years. Most entry-level NVs have little to gain from bottle ageing, but exceptions are noted throughout this guide. Late-disgorged vintages are held on lees in the cellar and can improve over many decades, disgorged shortly prior to release.

Late-disgorged champagne is generally best consumed within a few years of disgorgement, as it doesn't tend to cellar confidently post-disgorgement. 'Disgorgement is a shock for a wine, like a human going into surgery,' explains Antoine Roland-Billecart. 'When you're young, you recover much better. When an old champagne is disgorged, it may oxidise.' This is why Billecart disgorges its museum stock at the same time as its standard releases. Different houses have different philosophies, and there are always exceptions. I've tasted very old late-disgorged bottles that have held up magnificently five years after disgorgement.

Champagne spends the first years of its life in a dark, humid, chalk cellar under Champagne at a constant temperature of 8–10°C, so it will get a rude shock if it's thrust into a warmer environment. Champagne is highly fussy when it comes to proper cellaring conditions and, unless you live somewhere particularly cold, if you don't have a climate-controlled cellar, err on the side of caution and drink it within a few years.

Champagne in clear glass bottles is remarkably light-sensitive, so keep it in the dark at all times. If it comes in a box, bag or cellophane wrap, keep it covered until you serve it. See page 44 for more on the effects of light on champagne.

HOW TO OPEN A BOTTLE OF BUBBLY

Opening a champagne bottle is pretty easy, but some people make such a fuss about it that they end up stuffing it up altogether. There are a few basic points to grasp before spraying your friends with fizz.

First, ensure that nobody has shaken the bottle before you get hold of it (not funny!). Always have a target glass nearby to pour the first gush into, but not too close (I inadvertently shot the bowl clean off one of those expensive Riedels with a stray cork!). Check the firing range for chandeliers and unsuspecting passers-by and re-aim if necessary.

Remove the capsule using the pull-tab, if it has one. Hold the bottle at 45 degrees and remove the cage with six half-turns of the wire, keeping your thumb firmly over the end of the cork, in case it attempts to fire out of the bottle. Some prefer to loosen the cage and leave it on the cork, which is sometimes unavoidable if the cork starts to edge its way out.

Twist the bottle (not the cork) slowly and ease the cork out gently. If you encounter a stubborn, young cork, use a clean tea towel to improve your grip. When the cork is almost out, tilt it sideways to release the gas slowly. It should make a gentle hiss, not an ostentatious pop. This is important, as it maintains the maximum bead (bubbles) in the wine and reduces the risk of a dramatic gush.

HOW TO POUR CHAMPAGNE

Check that the wine tastes right, then pour half a glass for each drinker, topping them up after the 'mousse' has subsided. You can choose to tilt the glass to minimise frothing — I do. Sparkling wine is the only style where you can break the rule of never more than half-filling a glass, but do leave sufficient room for your nose so you can appreciate the bouquet!

The Champenois sometimes recommend decanting champagne. This does offer some advantages in encouraging older or more robust champagnes to open up, but I have never been successful without losing most of the bubbles.

A large glass can draw a champagne like Salon out of itself.

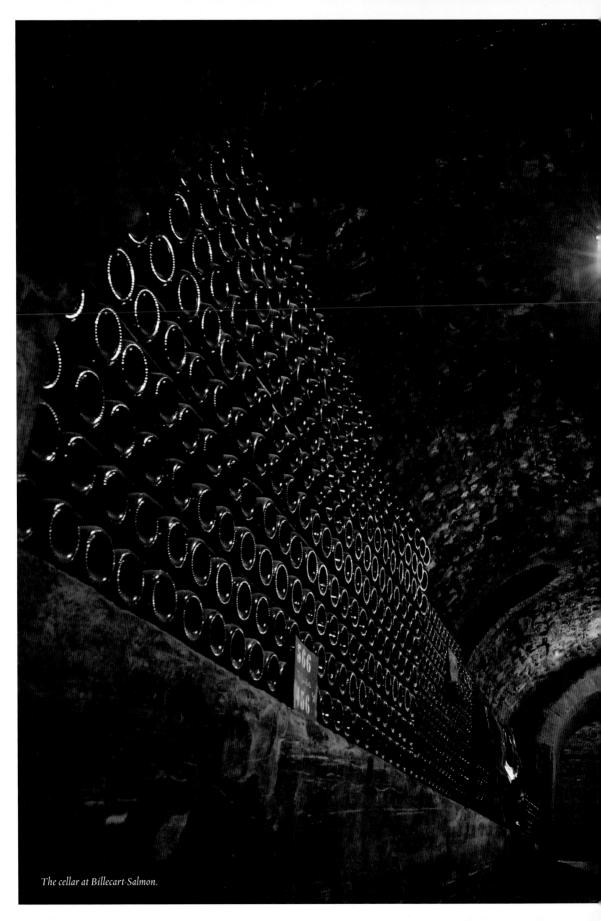

The cellar at Billecart-Salmon.

AGRAPART & FILS

(A-gra-pah e feess)

7/10

57 AVENUE JEAN JAURÈS 51190 AVIZE
www.champagne-agrapart.com

'If we have good grapes we have good wines,' is Pascal Agrapart's refreshing philosophy. While many others rigidly pursue regimes in the vineyard and winery because that's the way it's always been done, or is the latest fad, the ethos and practice of Agrapart are quite the antithesis. This fanatical Avize grower upholds practices not far from organics or biodynamics, yet has never sought certification under either, preferring to maintain the freedom to listen sensitively to the rhythm of the seasons and respond to the benefit of his vines. His restless pursuit of a detailed expression of place is articulated in the purity and crystalline mineral expression of his wines.

IN CHAMPAGNE IT IS A RARE CLAIM TO BE THE FOURTH generation to produce champagne from one's own vineyards. Yet Pascal and brother Fabrice Agrapart do so not with a staid reliance on the ways of their forebears, but with a progressive and at times courageous sense of spontaneity.

Inspired by Burgundy to make wines of character true to their place, Agrapart upholds terroir as being more important than variety. Chardonnay comprises 95% of almost 10 hectares of enviable estate plantings, mainly in the grand crus of Avize, Oger, Cramant and Oiry, divided across 62 plots of vines of an impressive average age of 40 years — some more than 65 years.

Every effort is focused on encouraging the roots of these old vines into the mother rock to draw out the mineral character of each site. Vineyard management is painstakingly eco-friendly, with no chemical pesticides or herbicides used. Vineyards are ploughed to break up surface roots, aerate the soil and maintain microbial life, while organic fertilisers, compost and manure are adapted according to soil analyses.

Pascal Agrapart upholds that '25% of the wine is made by the soil and 25% by the weather', and points out that the microclimates are very different in each of his parcels. This poses a greater challenge to an organic regime than would a single site.

'I don't want to have certification because I want to be able to plough the soil when I can, and use chemicals when I need to,' he says. The disease threat of the wet 2012 vintage necessitated chemical treatments.

Agrapart works his 1959 vines in his 'La Fosse' vineyard in Avize only by hand and horse, and he's more down-to-earth about this than anyone else I've met in Champagne. 'There is no compacting of the soil, and perhaps there is more oxygen and microbial life, and perhaps the roots go deeper, and perhaps there is more minerality in the wine. Perhaps, perhaps! Perhaps it is better — and perhaps it's just sentimental!'

Each winemaking element is designed to preserve the detail of the vineyard. Sensitive, intelligent use of large, old oak for vinification, and ageing of finer parcels for vintage wines and non-vintage reserves is not for woody flavour, but oxidation — for Agrapart, 'oxidation is not the enemy of wine'. He buys five-year-old barrels from Burgundy and the Loire and maintains them until they're very old. Larger 600-litre puncheons are favoured, for a higher ratio of wine to wood.

Wild yeasts from the vineyards further draw out the character of each site. Full malolactic fermentation is encouraged, for stability, balance and evolution of the wine, which he suggests removes the need for sterile filtration and high levels of sulphur dioxide preservative. The results are usually clean and precise, but occasionally the vintage cuvées display a savoury character that could reflect low levels of brettanomyces infection.

The energy of Agrapart's grand cru chardonnay vineyards and the endurance injected through barrel fermentation make these very long-lived cuvées that appreciate extended lees ageing prior to release. Ageing a minimum of three years for non-vintage and seven for vintage cuvées necessitates a stock of 360,000 bottles to sustain an annual production of 90,000. This is a significant production for hand-riddling, but the hands-on approach of the estate is maintained.

Most of Agrapart's seven cuvées are blanc de blancs, with a little pinot in his entry wine, and a single-field blend of six grape varieties. Low dosages are used throughout, which he suggests reduces the importance of ageing the wine between disgorgement and release. On the basis of the integration of 7 Crus, disgorged just two weeks prior to my tasting, he may be on to something. While disgorgement dates aren't printed on back labels, they're easy to decode from the cork. The number is the year of disgorgement, and the letter is the month (A for January, B for February, and so on).

Agrapart's wines are characterful, deeply mineral expressions of their terroirs, given articulate voice through a diligent hands-on approach to every detail.

AGRAPART & FILS 7 CRUS BRUT NV • $

94 points • TASTED IN AVIZE

A blend of equal parts of 2010 from young vines aged 20–40 years in lesser sites, and 2009 from good parcels; 25% of 2009 components matured in barrels; 90% chardonnay and an increasing percentage of pinot noir (now 10%) from Avize, Oger, Oiry, Cramant, Avenay Val d'Or, Bergères-lès-Vertus and Mardeuil; full malolactic fermentation; aged 3 years on lees; 7g/L dosage

Agrapart's precision and attention to detail is proclaimed from the very first cuvée, an accurate and incisive citrus-charged style of textural presence and great persistence. Delightful grapefruit spice and lemon zest are accented with hints of clove, a soft, creamy bead, and excellent chalk mineral character. A very fresh disgorgement, just two weeks old when I tasted it, yet already beautifully integrated.

AGRAPART & FILS TERROIRS BLANC DE BLANCS GRAND CRU EXTRA BRUT NV • $

94 points • TASTED IN AVIZE

A classification of better parcels than 7 Crus; 20–40-year-old vines in Avize, Oger, Cramant and Oiry; equal portions of 2009 and 2008; 25% of 2008 component matured in barrels; full malolactic fermentation; aged 4 years on lees; low dosage of 5g/L

A seamlessly crafted blanc de blancs of enticing purity and approachability, singing with pristine lemon blossom, white peach and lemon zest. The palate is creamy and textural, embedded deep in grand cru chalk soils, with grapefruit rind crunch and elegant notes of anise lingering seamlessly through a dry finish.

AGRAPART & FILS COMPLANTÉE GRAND CRU EXTRA BRUT 2008 • $$

94 points • TASTED IN AVIZE

A blend of co-planted pinot noir, pinot meunier, pinot blanc, arbane, petit meslier and chardonnay from young vines planted in 2002; vinified in oak barrels; full malolactic fermentation; aged on lees under cork; unfiltered; low dosage of 5g/L; just 600 bottles produced

Agrapart is the first to admit that from such young vines, subsequent vintages (of 1300 bottles each) are stronger than this young release, but this is nonetheless a fascinating wine that shows great potential. If nothing else, its ability to let the village speak clearly and express its fine undercurrent of chalky Avize minerality, through the untrained voice of such young vines, is impressive in itself. More than this, it's a wine of great fruit complexity and expression, showcasing the full sweep of its six varieties, spanning everything from ripe pear, white stone fruits, lemon and lime, to tropical nuances and hints of exotic spice. It finishes short and simple, but give these vines some proper age, stand back, and behold.

AGRAPART & FILS MINÉRAL BLANC DE BLANCS GRAND CRU EXTRA BRUT 2006 • $$$

95 points • TASTED IN AVIZE

A 50/50 blend of 40-year-old vines from nearby parcels in Avize and Cramant; Avize vinified in tank, Cramant in old oak barrels; full malolactic fermentation; no filtration; 5 years on yeast lees; low dosage of 3–4g/L

Appropriately named, Minéral bores deep into the hard white chalk very close to the surface of these two vineyards, lingering very long with finely poised chalk minerality. It's a delightfully expressive wine that hits high notes of wonderful freshness and purity, within a style of reverberating concentration, substance and creamy, textural mouthfeel. White nectarine leads out, layered with honey, brioche and nougat, finishing with hints of nutmeg. Pascal Agrapart describes it as a vertical wine with dark acidity, but to me the acidity is as fresh and bright as daylight, with a softness of early morning light filtered through fine mist.

AGRAPART & FILS L'AVIZOISE BLANC DE BLANCS GRAND CRU EXTRA BRUT 2005 • $$$$

94 points • TASTED IN ADELAIDE

From 55-year-old vines in two parcels on the best slopes of Avize; made exclusively in old oak barrels; full malolactic fermentation; aged on lees under natural cork for 5 years; unfiltered; low dosage of 3–4g/L

Just 600–800 metres from the parcels that comprise Minéral, but here expressing a very different personality of clay soils over chalk, which manifest themselves in a pronounced, taut mineral expression and an edgy and fresh persona of grapefruit and lemon zest. An impressively defined 2005, balanced with the creamy, nutty influence of oak, finishing taut and cut.

AGRAPART & FILS L'AVIZOISE BLANC DE BLANCS GRAND CRU EXTRA BRUT 2006 • $$$$

89 points • TASTED IN AVIZE

Lacking the pristine control of the 2004 or even the 2005, this vintage carries a hint of savoury charcuterie complexity, which may reflect some funky barrel character. This is a powerfully rich blanc de blancs with real breadth of exotic fruits and succulent white stone fruits, though lacking a little in freshness and vivacity. It finishes drying and textural.

AGRAPART & FILS VÉNUS BLANC DE BLANCS GRAND CRU BRUT NATURE 2006 • $$$$

94 points • TASTED IN AVIZE

'La Fosse', a single 1959 planting of just one-third of one hectare on chalk in Avize; tended only by hand and horse; made exclusively in old oak barrels; full malolactic fermentation; unfiltered; aged on lees under natural cork for 5 years; zero dosage

Pascal Agrapart describes the minerality of Vénus as reminiscent of the chalk dust from the blackboard when he was at school. Breathe deep: the intensity of the chalk minerality of this cuvée is something to behold. Its mouthfeel and texture are somehow elevated through the savoury, layered complexity and softening influence of barrel maturation and cork ageing, like the high notes of the strings of an orchestra are propelled by the rumbling depths of the percussion and horns. Vénus is more about textural precision and mineral persistence than it is about layered complexity of pear and apple fruits, preserved lemon and mixed spice. A savoury and intellectual cuvée, a philharmonic experience rather than a mosh pit encounter.

AGRAPART & FILS EXPÉRIENCE BLANC DE BLANCS GRAND CRU BRUT NATURE NV • $$$$

87 points • TASTED IN AVIZE

2007 and 2008 vintages; no chaptalisation; wild yeast for both first and second fermentations; vinified in barrel; aged on cork; full malolactic fermentation; zero dosage

Agrapart has pushed the boundaries to the extreme in Expérience, and then pushed them further still, in pursuit of champagne with nothing added but the juice of grapes and a tiny dose of sulphur dioxide. It's a blend of equal parts of the parcels that comprise l'Avizoise and Minéral, though Agrapart admits that it's purposely less fresh than either. For my palate, the philosophy is more noble than its execution. This is a developed and savoury champagne, to the point of being dried out. The fruit has already contracted into its secondary phase, lacking expression and vivacity, finishing firmly textured and hard, with wood spice notes and a short aftertaste. It seems it's been stripped of the character of its place in favour of an idealistic regime.

ALAIN THIÉNOT

(Ah-la Tea-e-noh)

---

4 RUE JOSEPH-CUGNOT 51500 TAISSY
www.thienot.com

CHAMPAGNE
THIÉNOT
REIMS.FRANCE

Since establishing his eponymous house in Taissy in 1985, former broker Alain Thiénot has acquired a formidable empire encompassing champagne houses Canard-Duchêne, Joseph Perrier and Marie Stuart, and several Bordeaux châteaux. This small house of 350,000 bottles annually remains a family affair, and is the proud custodian of 27 hectares of estate vineyards in the Montagne de Reims, Côte des Blancs and Sézanne, supplying an impressive three-quarters of its needs. Use of oak has been abandoned to better express each cuvée's terroir. A number of cuvées display off-putting reductive characters this year (see website for details).

ALAIN THIÉNOT BRUT NV • $$

85 points • DISGORGED FIRST QUARTER OF 2012 • TASTED IN BRISBANE

2009 vintage with 20% reserve wines; 45% chardonnay, 35% pinot noir and 20% pinot meunier from across the Montagne de Reims; 8g/L dosage

A distinctly reductive wine of gherkin, fennel and toasty characters. Subtle white fruits, grapefruit and preserved lemon quiver in the background. It finishes short and thin, with balanced dosage. A second bottle displayed light cork taint.

ALAIN THIÉNOT BRUT ROSÉ NV • $$$

90 points • DISGORGED FIRST QUARTER OF 2012 • TASTED IN BRISBANE

2009 vintage with 30% reserve wines from 2008 and 2007; 45% pinot noir, 35% chardonnay and 20% pinot meunier from across the Montagne de Reims; 7% red wines from old vines; 8g/L dosage

A light, soft, creamy and fruity rosé with a pale salmon hue and an elegant aroma of rosehip, white cherry and strawberry hull. The palate has a creamy bead and a subtle homemade ice cream feel. Its fruit presence lacks detail and definition, though it's clean and fresh, with well-managed interplay between dosage and acidity.

ALFRED GRATIEN

(Al-fre Gra-shah)

5/10

30 RUE MAURICE CERVEAUX 51201 EPERNAY
www.alfredgratien.com

CHAMPAGNE
PRODUIT EN FRANCE
ALFRED GRATIEN
Epernay

lfred Gratien is a small house producing never more than 300,000 bottles annually, with a long history of making wines of complexity. Its champagnes are made in a rigorously classical way, with the first fermentation and at least six months of ageing taking place exclusively in small 228-litre neutral barriques, previously used four times in Chablis. Reserve wines are stored in large oak barrels. Malolactic fermentation is systematically avoided, to ensure that the champagne retains its original character, maintaining freshness as it ages and preserving the aroma of the grapes and the land from which they came.

ALFRED GRATIEN WAS ACQUIRED BY THE HENKELL & Co group in 2004, retaining its 65 growers from which grapes are sourced, and contributing a new cuverie for storage and blending of the young wines. Since 2007, the new owners have wisely left the house in the hands of young Nicolas Jaeger, the fourth generation of the Jaeger family to serve as Chef de Cave of the house.

Gratien's non-vintage cuvées are deeply complex wines that retain a zingy freshness, thanks to lively malic acidity, softened gently by a minimum of three years bottle ageing. Its vintage cuvées are a real step up, always a majority of chardonnay, and typically from the Côte des Blancs' greatest grand crus. With full barrel vinification and no malolactic fermentation, these are long-ageing styles that can be quite abrupt and challenging in their youth. These are not champagnes for the uninitiated.

Vintage wines are aged under natural cork, which Jaeger claims assists in preventing oxidation and enhancing tertiary aromas, complexity and firmness. I find it somewhat counter-intuitive that a philosophy aimed at retaining the purity of the wine through the use of old oak and the avoidance of malolactic fermentation is prepared to submit it to the vagaries of natural cork for ageing in the cellar, increasing the likelihood of cork taint and other variabilities associated with cork.

Bollinger manages to pull this off without mishap, but the frequency with which I reached for replacement Gratien bottles in my tastings this year was alarming.

Alfred Gratien Cuvée Brut Classique NV • $$

92 points • Disgorged June 2012 • Tasted in Brisbane

46% chardonnay, 29% pinot noir, 25% pinot meunier; aged at least 4 years in the cellars; no malolactic fermentation; 9g/L dosage

A medium straw hue reflects barrel maturation and long bottle ageing. The bouquet is lively and exact, with freshly cut pear, lemon zest, orange pulp and subtle mixed spice. The taut twang of malic acidity neatly juxtaposes the creaminess of barrel fermentation and the nuttiness of three years bottle age. It leads out fresh and citrus-accented and concludes complex and fleshy, with dried peach, fresh fig and a backbone of racy malic acidity.

Alfred Gratien Cuvée Brut Classique Rosé NV • $$

92 points • Tasted in Brisbane

41% chardonnay, 34% pinot noir, 25% pinot meunier with pinot noir still red wine; no malolactic fermentation; 8g/L dosage

A vibrant rosé of medium salmon crimson hue, a celebration of strawberries, red cherries and tangy plums. Well-managed oak maturation lends a savoury overtone of wood spice, even hints of cigar box, which marry with lively red fruits to give a tomato-like impression, while maintaining zingy freshness thanks to a tense blade of malic acidity cutting through from start to finish.

Alfred Gratien Brut Millesime 1999 • $$$

94 points • Disgorged February 2012 • Tasted in Brisbane

63% chardonnay, 17% pinot noir, 20% pinot meunier; aged a minimum of 7 years, but in this case closer to 12 years; natural cork used for second fermentation; no malolactic fermentation; 8g/L dosage

Barrel maturation and a glorious 12 years cellaring have blessed it with a glowing, medium straw hue and generous aromas of baked fig, poached pear, butter on toast, honey, glacé peach and wood spice. The palate is wonderfully creamy, gliding with the polished integration of a decade of maturation, yet retaining the lemon zest crunch of malic acidity on a long, poised finish. The first bottle was overpowered by cork wood notes; the second, pristine.

Alfred Gratien Cuvée Paradis Brut NV • $$$$

91 points • Disgorged March 2012 • Tasted in Brisbane

65% chardonnay, 35% pinot noir; strangely, never vintage labelled, but always from a single year, which is sadly not disclosed; 8g/L dosage

Two contrasting personalities jostle for position, one of bitter grapefruit and a taut lemon juice cut, the other of toasty, savoury development, struggling to find harmony, which may or may not come with cellaring. The taut firmness of malic acidity contrasts with an impression of dill in the presence of oxidative fermentation in old barrels, for an assertive yet invigorating result. The first bottle was distinctly woody, with a savoury, oxidative harshness that lent a vinegary note to the finish; the second was sound. Strictly for seasoned champagne drinkers.

The Champagne Guide

ANDRÉ CLOUET

(An-dray Cloo-ay)

9/10

8 RUE GAMBETTA 51150 BOUZY

Bouzy and Ambonnay are the epicentre of pinot noir in Champagne, and the Clouet family is the privileged custodian of eight hectares of estate vines in the best middle slopes of both villages. These are rich and concentrated expressions of pinot noir, wines of deep complexity, multi-faceted interest and engaging character, yet with remarkable restraint and sense of control. Recent tastings confirm my impression that this small and relatively unknown grower ranks high among Champagne's finest practitioners of pinot noir — and represents one of the best value of all.

WHEN I FIRST MET YOUNG CHEF DE CAVE JEAN-François Clouet, he didn't show me through his winery or cellars, didn't walk me through rows of vines, or even pour his champagnes. He took me to the top of the vineyards, on the edge of the forest overlooking Bouzy, and recounted the remarkable sweep of history that had played out in view of this place over two millennia: Attila the Hun, the Catalonic Field Battle, the birth of the monarchy, the crusades and the Templars. 'To understand Champagne you need to understand its political history,' he said.

For Clouet's family, that history began here in 1492, and his family still resides in the house his ancestors built in Bouzy in 1741. 'My family was making wine in Champagne at the same time Dom Pérignon was starring!' he exclaimed. This history lives on, not only in the spectacular labels designed by Jean-François' great-grandfather in 1911 (harking back to the family's printer heritage, making books for the king since 1491),

but in a traditional approach in the vineyards. 'I like the idea of the work of human hands in pruning, performing the same actions as my grandfather and even the Romans, who planted vines here 2000 years ago.'

For a family so deeply rooted in Champagne history, there is a distinctly modern twist to Jean-François' approach. It is his goal that someday none of his champagnes will have any dosage at all, an ideal that he correctly describes as revolutionary.

'Not to be snobby or arrogant, but I have a real sense that a zero-dosage wine from a single village can really showcase the pedigree of the village,' he suggests. 'You have to be an extremely good winemaker to make zero-dosage champagne. It's like a woman with no makeup.' And if anyone can do it anywhere, Jean-François can in Bouzy and Ambonnay. To this end, for some years he has experimented with using Sauternes barriques from Château Doisy Daëne for alcoholic fermentation. 'It gives the illusion of the wine being sweet, when it is not sweet at all!' he claims. The result, to my astonishment, is quite magnificent.

When Clouet began working on the estate 10 years ago, he took note of those embarking on organic and biodynamic regimes. 'Biodynamics and organics look good on paper,' he says, 'but my idea is that it is simply important to take care of the ground by hand without the use of herbicides.' Stringent sorting during harvest maintains freshness and purity in his cuvées.

Clouet's focus remains resolutely on pinot noir, which comprises 100% of every cuvée except his Millesime, a 50/50 blend of pinot noir and chardonnay. 'I am frustrated with the idea of blending from everywhere!' he exclaims. 'I love pure pinot noir! No makeup and no compromise!'

Clouet is fascinated by the geological history of his soils, and makes it his goal to express the minerality of pure chalk in his wines. 'Fantastic minerality and low dosage are important for good pinot noir,' he claims. His cuvées receive low dosages of 6g/L.

As seriously as he takes his responsibilities, Clouet doesn't take himself too seriously, and likens his wines to independent films. 'I love Hollywood movies, but sometimes I want to watch something independent. Winemaking in Champagne is the same,' he says. 'One is not better than the other. Dom Pérignon and Pol Roger are fantastic, with all the action of James Bond in *Skyfall*, but sometimes I have a taste for something else.'

His bubblies offer that something else, without the Hollywood budget, yet with pyrotechnics of their own.

ANDRÉ CLOUET SILVER BRUT NATURE NV • $$

95 points • TASTED IN BOUZY

100% Bouzy and Ambonnay pinot noir from 2009 and 2008; Grande Réserve with zero dosage; 30% fermented in Sauternes barriques

Jean-François Clouet's zero-dosage ideal is realised with magnificent clarity here. Such is the concentration and richness of his pinot noir that it has absolutely no need for any sweetness. The bouquet is delightfully fresh, lifted, pure and expressive, with lemon zest, yellow mirabelle plums and red apple fruits. The palate follows impeccably, showcasing the concentration of Bouzy with exceptional purity and focus. Its barrel work blends impeccably, contributing nuances of nougat, brioche and honey. Succulent yellow summer fruits pull seamlessly into a crunchy finish of red apple and lemon zest, concluding long and refined, with refreshingly taut acidity and soft, chalky minerality. Classic Bouzy of the finest order.

ANDRÉ CLOUET GRANDE RÉSERVE BLANC DE NOIRS BRUT NV • $$

94 points • TASTED IN BOUZY

100% Bouzy and Ambonnay pinot noir; 6g/L dosage

Release after release, year after year, I have always marvelled at the lemon blossom freshness that Clouet manages to capture in pinot noir from two of Champagne's most powerful terroirs. Here it is again, in a captivating interplay of fleshy mirabelle plums, white peaches, crunchy golden delicious apples, and even a hint of pepper. Wild honey and mixed spice join the maelstrom along the way, gliding obediently into a well-defined finish of soft minerality and integrated dosage.

André Clouet Brut Rosé NV • $$

95 points • Tasted in Bouzy

100% Bouzy and Ambonnay pinot noir; 2010 base vintage; 10% Bouzy red wine; 6g/L dosage

'I say 10% of the blend is from my blood!' declares Jean-François Clouet, who has changed the style of his family's rosé to a fresher and more direct mood, not so soft, aiming for the lively impression of malic acidity, even though it goes through full malolactic fermentation. The result is a rosé that epitomises elegance and focus, in the midst of the generous red fruits that characterise Bouzy and Ambonnay. This cuvée encapsulates that wonderful talent of pinot noir to build and rise on the finish, opening to wonderful characters of perfumed rosehip, pink pepper and pomegranate. An undercurrent of fine, chalk mineral texture, accurate line and persevering length define a pristine and enticingly priced rosé.

André Clouet Brut Millesime 2008 • $$

96 points • Tasted in Bouzy

50% pinot noir and 50% chardonnay from Bouzy and Ambonnay; 6g/L dosage

A great vintage for a top producer in one of pinot noir's finest villages, this is a champagne that captures finesse and poise, framing them in deep-set concentration; the signature of Bouzy and Ambonnay. Fleshy white summer fruits, pear and grapefruit zest of considerable depth open out to notes of brioche and nougat, honed with chardonnay's precision, finishing long and focused. The depth of chardonnay's mineral expression, painted in the vivid colours of 2008, takes this cuvée to another level, with an ever-present undercurrent that froths with well-defined, finely chalky texture.

André Clouet 1911 NV • $$$

96 points • Tasted in Bouzy

A magnificent recipe: 100% pinot noir from Clouet's 10 best plots, dubbed by Jean-François 'the golden square of Bouzy'; 50% 2002 fermented in Sauternes barriques; 50% solera of reserve wines; full malolactic fermentation; a symbolic production of just 1911 bottles; 6g/L dosage

Clouet's flagship is a radiant, golden silk-satin ballgown of ravishing complexity and breathtaking grace, a delicate high-heeled balancing act of refreshing poise in the midst of profound concentration. Its richness ventures to champagne's outer limits of succulent white fruits of all kinds, grilled pineapple, honey and great complexity of brioche, nougat and butter. Celebrating a generous 50% reserve from solera, its rumbling maturity is proclaimed in hints of butterscotch, coffee beans and smouldering hearth. Just when you fear it's all too much to behold, the vibrant energy of its 2002 base swoops into a finish defined by well-poised acidity and softly mineral, fine chalk texture. It holds its posture of tall, slender magnificence for minutes without ever dropping its determined gaze.

ANDRÉ JACQUART

(An-dray Zhah-khah)

6/10

63 AVE DE BAMMENTAL 51130 VERTUS
www.a-jacquart-fils.com

ANDRÉ JACQUART

Merging the family estates of fifth-generation growers, brother and sister Marie and Benoît Doyard, in 2004, blessed André Jacquart with enviable vineyard holdings of 16 hectares of chardonnay in the great Côte des Blancs terroirs of Mesnil-sur-Oger and Vertus, three hectares of pinot noir in the Aube and four in the Aisne. A move from Le Mesnil to Vertus, the purchase of two new presses and 200 barrels in the same year, and the estate was reborn. In a laudable and unusual move for Champagne, production has been reduced by almost one-third since then, in pursuit of quality.

MARIE AND BENOÎT, GRANDCHILDREN OF ANDRÉ Jacquart, use just half of the family's holdings for their own wines, exclusively from vines with an average age of more than 40 years in their best sites in Le Mesnil-sur-Oger and Vertus.

Vineyards are managed sustainably, with a focus on organic viticulture and the use of biodegradable inputs. Yields are restricted by de-budding to around two-thirds of the permitted levels, and several pickings are performed in each site to select only ripe grapes.

This level of ripeness allows malolactic ferment-ation to be blocked across all cuvées, which in turn calls for softening through barrel fermentation and long ageing. Fermentation takes place in both stainless steel tanks and barrels aged 2–6 years. Wines in barrel are fermented by natural yeasts and aged in barrel for 5–8 months. Non-vintage cuvées are aged a minimum of four years on lees, and vintage cuvées at least five years. Both are aged a further 12 months post-disgorgement, prior to release — significantly longer than most in Champagne.

André Jacquart's champagnes are wines of impressively accurate fruit, well-defined terroir expression, and vivid mineral personality. Even barrel work and long ageing are insufficient to tame the bold combination of 100% Le Mesnil and Vertus chardonnay, full malic acidity and low dosage of typically just 3–4g/L, making these quite edgy and assertive wines.

These are not crowd-pleasing champagnes, but styles that will stretch and delight the well-seasoned champagne enthusiast.

André Jacquart Brut Expérience Blanc de Blancs 1er Cru NV • $$

98 points • Tasted in Brisbane

2006 vintage with reserves of 2005 and 2004; 60% Vertus, 40% Le Mesnil-sur-Oger; 40% barrel fermented in 4-year-old Burgundy barrels; low dosage of 4g/L

Rigorous attention to low yields and ripe fruit is announced right from the bouquet of the very first wine of the estate, proclaiming a gorgeous richness of succulent fruit presence, layers of juicy white summer fruits and mixed spice intrigue. The palate contrasts the tension of Vertus chardonnay with the depth and power of Le Mesnil-sur-Oger, creating a blanc de blancs that is at once fresh and tangy with grapefruit crunch, and succulent and fleshy with white peach depth. Its barrel fermentation builds texture and suppleness, accenting subtle toasted almond notes without adding woody overtones. Low dosage is elegantly integrated, framing lively malic acidity as the highlight of a long finish.

André Jacquart Mesnil Experience Blanc de Blancs Grand Cru NV • $$$

92 points • Tasted in Brisbane

Base vintage 2006, though not declared as a vintage cuvée; 100% Le Mesnil-sur-Oger chardonnay; 70% fermented in fourth-use oak; aged on lees for 60 months; low dosage of 4g/L

The intensity and focus of Le Mesnil-sur-Oger chardonnay holds forth with considerable confidence. Tight grapefruit, lemon zest and crunchy pear carry with linear determination, depth and breadth through the palate, with a subtle note of green olives in the background, a character Le Mesnil is more likely to develop with considerable age, but perhaps barrel work has drawn it out sooner here? A tightly honed acid profile underlines salty minerality, uniting with wood work to build a well-textured mouthfeel, accented by a fine, creamy bead. Savoury barrel nuances in concert with tense acidity lend a sour astringent note to the finish.

André Jacquart Experience Millésime Le Mesnil-sur-Oger Blanc de Blancs Grand Cru 2006 • $$$

94 points • Tasted in Brisbane

50+-year-old vines in the best southern lieux-dits of Le Mesnil-sur-Oger; 100% barrel fermented in third-use oak, aged on lees for more than 60 months; low dosage of 3g/L

This is an intricately and intelligently assembled Le Mesnil-sur-Oger of considerable impact, with oak and fruit carrying each other forth with persistence and effortless line. The concentration and vivacity of Le Mesnil are celebrated in vibrant grapefruit zest and lemon juice, set against a backdrop of inimitable Le Mesnil salty chalk mineral structure. Barrel fermentation contributes a wood spice character, accenting hints of fennel and green olive, amplifying notes of nutmeg and anise and rounding out the assertive structure of young Le Mesnil chardonnay, building back palate generosity while retaining its sour malic acidity.

AYALA

(Eye-yah-lah)

5/10

2 BLVD DU NORD BP36 51160 AŸ

www.champagne-ayala.fr

CHAMPAGNE

AYALA

DEPUIS 1860 à AY

ig changes are at hand at Ayala, and its wines are beginning to shine. When I visited Ayala's grand premises, the historic Château d'Aÿ, and met its head, Hervé Augustin, sporting his distinctive bow tie in the vibrant red of the brand, he was quick to admit that the house had been left sleeping until it was purchased by Bollinger in 2005. No longer.

NICOLAS KLYM HAS OVERSEEN AYALA'S CELLAR FOR MORE than 30 years, but there has never been an evolution in the style more pronounced than during the past eight.

This is no label-deep makeover, but runs to the core of the house style. Refreshingly, their average dosage has been lowered from 11g/L of sweetness to just 7g/L. To distinguish it from the pinot-dominant style of Bollinger, the percentage of chardonnay in the key wine of the house, Ayala Brut Majeur, has been raised from 25–30% to 40%. And, again in contrast to its stable mate, every cuvée is vinified in stainless steel tanks, in a quest for minerality, purity and freshness.

Ayala lays claim to less than five hectares of vineyards of its own, but this is somewhat misleading, as it continues to access fruit from the original 40 hectares retained by its previous owners. It is also in the fortunate position of sharing vineyard sources with Bollinger — a share that it claims is very easy, thanks to Ayala's strong reliance on chardonnay.

Ayala is a medium-sized house with an annual production of 700,000 bottles, and a medium-term aspiration to increase this to 1 million. There are currently 2.5–3 million bottles in its cellars, where non-vintage wines spend 30 months on lees, vintage wines six years, and prestige wines up to 10. Perle d'Ayala wines are aged under natural cork said to produce a wine more resilient to the effects of oxygen during ageing. Like Bollinger, this necessitates hand disgorgement, and every bottle must be checked for taint. All wines undergo full malolactic fermentation.

Ayala's long history with dry wines began in 1870, just a decade after the house was founded, with the release of a champagne of 22g/L residual (in a market of typically 100–150g/L). The house claims to have produced the first zero-dosage champagne, though it will have to argue this with Perrier-Jouët, which shipped its 1846 vintage to London without adding sugar. Ayala's success with this style in recent times is uncontested, with its Brut Nature Zero Dosage finding tremendous popularity by the glass in London.

Ayala's noble practice of printing the disgorgement date on the back of each bottle gives consumers a chance to identify a fresh disgorgement before purchase — an opportunity precious few champagne houses deliver.

Ayala Brut Majeur NV • $$

92 points • Disgorged April 2012 • Tasted in Brisbane
93 points • Disgorged October 2011 • Tasted in Adelaide

40% chardonnay, 40% pinot noir, 20% pinot meunier; 30 months on lees; 7g/L dosage

I've never seen Brut Majeur more wonderfully lemon fresh, pristine and refined than its October 2011 disgorgement, thanks to the brilliantly refined 2008 base vintage, with 2007 reserves. A more recent April 2012 disgorgement of 2009 and 2008 misses tension and lemon zest top notes. Nonetheless, a refreshing, fruity and primary aperitif in the modern Ayala style. Elegant front-palate chardonnay proclaims Ayala's regime of improvement, flowing into well-composed, honeyed, ripe fruit persistence. Fine, mineral structure interplays with subtle dosage and lemon zest crunch to achieve balance and clean purity.

Ayala Brut Nature Zero Dosage NV • $$

90 points • Disgorged October 2011 • Tasted in Brisbane

This is Brut Majeur, sans dosage, a fascinating study in the effect of sweetness. I've always preferred the low dosage to the no-dosage, which is often less fresh in Australia than in France and the UK. The zero-dosage style possesses less resilience to ageing, lending biscuit notes and a touch of dry aggressiveness to the finish. Nonetheless, its lively citrus fruit and lemon blossom style is upheld admirably on its clean, tense finish. A bracing yet well-composed Brut Nature for the well-seasoned champagne aficionado.

Ayala Blanc de Blancs Brut 2004 • $$$

93 points • Disgorged March 2011 • Tasted in Brisbane
50% Le Mesnil-sur-Oger, 20% Cramant, 25% Chouilly; 6 years on lees, 7g/L dosage

The same disgorgement I tasted on the eve of its release in mid-2011 in Aÿ has really come into its own two years later. Almost a decade of maturity has built biscuity, toasty complexity and nuances of honey and nougat, while upholding its primary white fruits of fresh lemon, yellow mirabelle plums and ripe white peach. Its acid line remains energetic and will confidently sustain it for some years yet.

Ayala Perle d'Ayala Brut Millesime 2002 • $$$$

92 points • Tasted in Brisbane
The same composition as the Blanc de Blancs (50% Le Mesnil-sur-Oger, 20% Cramant, 25% Chouilly) plus 20% Aÿ pinot noir; aged on natural cork; 6g/L dosage

Perle 2002 has been kicking around for a couple of years now, gaining a medium straw-yellow hue and quite an exotic personality of honeydew and star fruit. Its chardonnay-led white fruit profile is building generosity and plump richness, beginning to broaden out into a biscuity finish of toasty, nutty, nougat complexity. It's ready to drink right away, retaining a creamy, succulent and silky feel to its soft finish. Anything it has lost in vibrancy is more than compensated for in layered complexity.

BARONS DE ROTHSCHILD

(Bah-roh de Roths-shield)

5/10

2 RUE CAMILLE LENOIR 51100 REIMS
www.champagne-bdr.com

CHAMPAGNE
BARONS DE ROTHSCHILD
PRODUCE OF FRANCE

The biggest challenge facing the launch of a new champagne brand lies in securing premium grapes. It takes a family as well connected as the Rothschilds to build a Champagne house around chardonnay from the grand crus and premier crus of the Côte des Blancs. In less than a decade, their well-crafted set of young, fruity wines has set a precedent for what can be achieved from a standing start, even in this highly competitive region.

WHEN THE ROTHSCHILDS OF THE FABLED BORDEAUX Château Lafite, Château Mouton and Château Clarke united to establish their own Champagne house, it was the first time the three competing branches of the family had worked together in 160 years. They began scoping out fruit sources in 2003, and by 2005 had secured an impressive portfolio of long-term contracts with growers, giving access to 20 hectares of vineyards, largely in Le Mesnil-sur-Oger, Oger and Cramant.

This has since quadrupled to 82 hectares from more than 45 growers managing more than 90% premier cru and grand cru vineyards. This is more than the 60 hectares required for the production of the house, permitting a selection of the best, and sale of the rest.

BdR has ascribed its deep, rapid infiltration of the Côte des Blancs to its network of relationships through the Rothschild family and the strategic placement of its winery in Vertus. A princely €10 million was invested in Caves de Vertus, retaining the underground cellar and rebuilding the winery. Jean Philippe Moulin was employed as winemaker in 2007, bringing a wealth of experience with chardonnay from his years at Ruinart.

Moulin's focus rests resolutely on cool fermentation exclusively in small stainless steel tanks, although there has been some experimentation with barrel ferment-ation for a yet-to-be-released 2006 grand cru blanc de blancs prestige cuvée. A high proportion of chardonnay across all cuvées calls for long ageing, with whites resting on their lees for four years, and rosés for three.

Small amounts of pinot meunier have been removed from the blends to emphasise the longer-ageing char-donnay and pinot noir. The dosage has been lowered from 7–8g/L on first release in 2009, to 5–6g/L today.

Last year BdR sold 250,000 bottles in 49 count-ries, and now holds close to 2.7 million bottles in its cellar. Two-thirds are Brut NV, with the remainder evenly split between Blanc de Blancs and Rosé.

Lovers of champagne, the family remains the big-gest client. Every dinner for each brand in the portfolio begins and ends with champagne.

The Champagne Guide

BARONS DE ROTHSCHILD BRUT NV • $$$

92 points • DISGORGED JUNE 2012 • TASTED IN BRISBANE

2007 base with at least 40% of reserves from 2006 and 2005; 60% chardonnay, 40% pinot noir; aged 4 years on lees; 6g/L dosage

'It's a war to buy grapes in Champagne, and especially in the Côte des Blancs,' says BdR CEO and Managing Director Frédéric Mairesse. The success of the house in establishing its chardonnay supply has built a Brut NV of high-tensile acid structure. Primary grapefruit juice and lemon zest accent a well-measured and expressively fruity style. Notes of roast nuts, toast, wild honey and clove have increased as the wine has aged in bottle, bringing complexity to an impressively balanced finish of lingering fruit character.

BARONS DE ROTHSCHILD BLANC DE BLANCS NV • $$$

92 points • DISGORGED MARCH 2012 • TASTED IN BRISBANE

2007 base with reserves of 2006 and 2005; grand cru Côte des Blancs from Le Mesnil-sur-Oger, Oger, Avize and Cramant; some bâtonnage (lees stirring) in tank; aged 4 years on lees in bottle

It's difficult to distinguish BdR's Blanc de Blancs bottle from its Brut, varying only by the name on the neck foil, but there's no mistaking this cuvée in the glass. It's a generous and ripe blanc de blancs, with preserved lemon becoming succulent white peach and honey, even grilled pineapple. Fruit ripeness and dosage unite in a concentrated finish, with slowly evolving notes of roast nut and wild honey more pronounced in recent tastings. In the midst of its generosity, well-structured acidity brings finesse and harmony to a long finish of soft, gentle, lingering minerality.

BARONS DE ROTHSCHILD ROSÉ NV • $$$

90 points • DISGORGED JUNE 2012 • TASTED IN BRISBANE

2008 base with reserves of 2007 and 2006; the base is the Blanc de Blancs; 85% chardonnay from Cramant, Le Mesnil-sur-Oger, Avize and Oger; 15% Verzenay pinot noir red wine; aged 3 years on lees

Such is the dominance of chardonnay in BdR's rosé that Mairesse dubs it 'pink chardonnay'. Blanc de blancs is stained with red wine from five hectares of Verzenay pinot noir, made in-house using a purpose-built winery. Yields are decreased between 25% and 40%, and fruit is vinified using the same sorting table and small tanks as Lafite and Mouton.

Six months can be a long time in the world of champagne rosé, and already the refreshing strawberry and red cherry fruits of youth are beginning to subside. There is now a copper tint to its medium salmon hue, and its dried fruit and mixed spice complexity is becoming toasty and nutty, with suggestions of gingernut biscuits, even the first signs of gaminess. Nonetheless, it retains the vibrancy of its acidity, which sustains secondary red berry fruits on a long finish, harmonising seamlessly with low dosage and a soft, creamy bead.

BENOÎT LAHAYE

(Bur-nwah La-ay)

7/10

33 RUE JEANNE D'ARC 51150 BOUZY

A BOUZY

BENOÎT LAHAYE
CHAMPAGNE
GRAND CRU

*O*nly the most daring and fastidious growers practise a certified biodynamic regime in a climate as erratic as Champagne's. Benoît Lahaye is among the more thoughtful of these, an advocate of natural winegrowing from the beginning. After taking responsibility for the family estate in 1993, he ceased systematic herbicides the very next year and progressively introduced cover crops to encourage competition and prevent erosion. Lahaye achieved full organic certification in 2007, and biodynamic in 2010. He didn't stop there, attempting to reduce soil compaction by introducing a horse to work the vines. He thanks such techniques for higher ripeness and natural acid retention.

In the heart of the pinot noir epicentre of Bouzy, Lahaye's 4.8-hectare estate is planted to 88% pinot noir: three hectares in Bouzy, one next door in Ambonnay, and tiny parcels in Tauxières-Mutry and Voipreux. It has only been since 1996 that Lahaye has bottled his own champagnes, today producing just 50,000 bottles annually.

Lahaye's natural, minimalist, intuitive approach extends to the cellar. Since 2012, all base wines have been fermented in 205-litre barriques of average age four years. Natural yeasts are used for every ferment, with malolactic fermentation blocked or allowed, according to the parcel and the season. Vintage wines are aged under cork or crown seal, with corks favoured for more structured seasons and capsules for more expansive vintages. Lahaye has progressively decreased dosage, with Brut NV released as both brut and brut nature.

BENOÎT LAHAYE BLANC DE NOIRS NV • $$

94 points • DISGORGED JANUARY 2013 • TASTED IN BOUZY

Aged at least 24 months on lees; 5/gL dosage

A seamless assemblage of fruit and barrel complexity marries the expressive, grapey, youthful generosity of guava, star fruits, poached strawberries, red apples and succulent stone fruits with the depth and intrigue of clove spice. Pure and lively, with soft, grapefruit-like acidity and an undercurrent of chalky minerality.

BÉRÈCHE ET FILS

(Bair-aysh e Feess)

LE CRAON DE LUDES 51500 LUDES
www.champagne-bereche-et-fils.com

GRAND VIN DE CHAMPAGNE

Bérêche & Fils

PROPRIÉTAIRES DE VIGNES

Young brothers Raphaël and Vincent Bérèche exemplify an enthusiastic and talented new generation that is transforming some of Champagne's smaller, longstanding estates. Working alongside their father, Jean-Pierre, the brothers represent the fifth generation of the family to grow and make champagnes with a very real sense of purity and craftsmanship. They are rightfully celebrated among the leading minds of Champagne's young generation, and their extensive range of current cuvées is proof of their talent, with recent tastings from barrel and bottle showcasing the dramatic leap forward in the Bérèche style since the duo took the lead.

WHILE MANY WOULD UPHOLD ADHERENCE TO REGIMES of organic or biodynamic certification as the holy grail of viticulture, Champagne's tumultuous climate makes such ideals in many sites infeasible at best.

After a few hours in Bérèche's cellars on the edge of the forest above Craon de Ludes, I was left with the overwhelming impression that if there's any philosophy in force in the vines and wines of Bérèche, it's one of intuitive sensitivity and good sense.

'We take a bit of this and a bit of that,' Raphaël declares unassumedly. 'We work in an organic way, but if there is too much rain in July and disease breaks out, we use a systemic chemical and then continue with our organic approach.' He's the first to admit Champagne is a difficult place to attempt to control everything, particularly in an estate as far-flung as this.

Until 1950, Bérèche managed just 2.5 hectares in Ludes. Holdings have since grown to a total of 9.5 hectares of mature vines, averaging 38 years of age.

Vineyards are centred around Ludes and neighbouring Chigny-les-Roses, and extend as far as Trépail in the eastern Montagne de Reims, Ormes west of Reims, and Mareuil-le-Port and Festigny in the Vallée de la Marne.

Raphaël emphasises the importance of managing all the vines themselves, to control yields. The modest production of 85,000 bottles from 9.5 hectares reflects particularly low yields. 'One problem of Champagne is that the yields are sometimes too high,' he admits. His brother Vincent has managed the vineyards since 2008, achieving balanced vines and fully mature fruit by maintaining yields of just 60–65hL/hectare — less than two-thirds the regional average. 'If we have higher yields, we need to put more products on the vines and there is a greater risk of disease,' Raphaël explains. 'It's like me — if I ate at [nearby restaurant] Le Grand Cerf every day I would die in two weeks!'

Bérèche encourages balance in his vines through spontaneous grass grown in the mid-rows, ploughed

Raphaël Bérèche uses traditional, labour-intensive techniques in the cellar to maintain fruit precision.

and requires chemicals to clean. Slightly larger and older 300-litre Burgundy barrels are preferred to Champagne's traditional 205-litre barrels; their more subtle influence on the wine maintains fruit precision.

Wines are matured for extended periods in both barrels and tanks prior to bottling. Ageing on lees with a little bâtonnage allows the wines to become slightly reductive, providing protection from oxidation, even with only very small additions of sulphur dioxide. A low-sulphur regime is a priority for Bérèche, with small additions to maintain freshness only on the press and after fermentation, and none at bottling or disgorgement. Bérèche prizes low pH, dissolved carbon dioxide gas and sugar in the dosage ahead of sulphur dioxide for preserving freshness. This seems to work most of the time, although I have occasionally noted funky barrel notes in some cuvées.

Even with such low sulphur levels, Bérèche has no trouble fully blocking malolactic fermentation, thanks to very cold (8°C) cellars at the top of Craon de Ludes. 'Historically, Champagne did not have malolactic fermentation,' Raphaël points out. 'This was only introduced in the 1980s, to make it easier to drink, and to reduce the time in the cellar.'

Bérèche is working to increase the time each cuvée is aged, with a new cellar under the house to increase capacity for reserve wines. Its Reflet d'Antan Brut NV cuvée was withdrawn for a full year to change the release cycle, providing an extra year of age. With the exception of the entry Brut NV and Extra Brut NV, all cuvées are aged on cork instead of crown seal, to increase oxygen interactaction and produce a more creamy bead and a more open, characterful and complex wine, with a more logical coherence of nose and palate.

Cork ageing necessitates hand disgorgement, and it takes two people to taste and disgorge 1200 bottles a day. A traditional liqueur d'expédition is used in place of grape concentrate, at very low levels of dosage, so as to faithfully preserve tension and minerality in the wines. Raphaël highlights that even 2–3g/L of dosage is important for ageing, and does not regard his Extra Brut NV as a style to age for more than five years. Back labels of all cuvées are impressively informative, disclosing dosage, disgorgement date and base vintage.

The wines of Bérèche are vinous champagnes of dry complexity. Even as young vins clairs, these are wines generously expressive of both ripe fruit intensity and the mineral signature of their sites. Assertive malic acidity, barrel fermentation and low dosage conspire to make some cuvées more than a little aggressive. These are not champagnes for the timid, but they will confidently keep fanatics enthralled.

every month during the warmer months. 'If we mowed we'd have too much grass and it would be like a soccer field!' he quips. Herbicide has been eliminated since Raphaël began in 2004. He believes this is the most important treatment to avoid, for the sake of the pH and acidity of the finished wines.

Biodynamics has been trialled since 2007 on a three-hectare plot in front of the house, as a test for the whole estate, but Raphaël admits that it's easier to manage nearby than 40 kilometres away in Festigny. 'We are just nine people and 9.5 hectares, so it's very important that we don't lose our crop!' he says.

Bérèche's simple and natural approach in the vineyard carries into the cellar, where labour-intensive, traditional techniques are favoured, from first fermentation to disgorgement. An intuitive approach provides flexibility in responding to the seasons. While long, slow, natural primary fermentations are the goal, in 2004 the fermentations ran too long, so were energised with commercial yeasts. He likes the idea of yeasts from the domaine and the grape, but admits that they're really derived from the cellar and barrels.

Fermentation is equally divided between oak barrels and old enamel-lined concrete tanks. 'Enamelled tanks are not as aesthetic in the cellar as stainless steel, but they're better for the wine,' he affirms, pointing out that stainless steel creates more reductive wines

The Champagne Guide

BÉRÈCHE ET FILS CAMPANIA REMENSIS NV • $$$

93 points • DISGORGED OCTOBER 2012 • TASTED IN CRAON DE LUDES

2009 base vintage; no malolactic fermentation; 3g/L dosage

A brand new cuvée that I've never seen anywhere but Bérèche's cellar, this is a very restrained rosé of lovely texture and structure. Raphaël is critical of saignée rosé for its heaviness, instead crafting this as a blend with a very small addition of red wine. Its colour is medium crimson, surprisingly deep for a rosé as elegant and refreshing as this, and a credit to his method of blending in black glasses to judge the addition of red wine on nose and palate rather than colour. It's fresh and taut, with gorgeous notes of red apple, red cherry and strawberry hull. Tight malic acidity and low dosage accentuate chalky mineral texture, while lingering red cherry pinot character is apparently reinforced by ageing under cork.

BÉRÈCHE ET FILS BRUT RÉSERVE NV • $$

94 points • DISGORGED OCTOBER 2012 • TASTED IN CRAON DE LUDES
95 points • DISGORGED JUNE 2012 • TASTED IN BRISBANE

2010 base vintage with 30% reserves from 2009 and 2008; 35% pinot noir, 35% chardonnay, 30% pinot meunier; 20% fermented in old barrels, the remainder in enamel-lined tanks; aged at least 24 months; no malolactic fermentation; dosage 8g/L; reserve wines from a perpetual reserve commenced in 1985, with two-thirds of each demi-muid removed as the reserve each year, providing a depth of complexity while maintaining chalky freshness in the reserves

Bérèche admits aspiring to richness, finesse, freshness and chalk minerality with this cuvée, and pulls it off with impeccable precision in this young blend. Wonderful ripeness of rounded yellow fruits and figs contrasts with the freshness of lemon zest, fine, chalky minerality and the taut structure of malic acidity, settling into a calm balance of internal harmony. I loved it three months after disgorgement and I adored it nine months after, when its perfume unravelled to rose petal high notes, fresh strawberry hull and white cherries. It lingers long, fragrant and pristine, a grand celebration of the unbridled joy of youth.

BÉRÈCHE ET FILS LES BEAUX REGARDS CHARDONNAY BRUT NATURE NV • $$$

93 points • DISGORGED NOVEMBER 2012 • TASTED IN CRAON DE LUDES

2009 vintage declared on back label; no malolactic fermentation; 4000 bottles; 2g/L dosage here, though usually released with zero dosage

A beautifully concentrated blanc de blancs of preserved lemon, apple, mixed spice and white peach fruit, hinting at almond and vanilla. Malic acidity gives a taut, honed edge to the finish, balanced by its generosity of fruit and spice. Tasted just two months after disgorgement, this is a young champagne of great potential that will benefit from at least another six months to settle into itself.

BÉRÈCHE ET FILS VALLÉE DE LA MARNE RIVE GAUCHE NV • $$$

95 points • 2009 VINTAGE DISGORGED OCTOBER 2012 WITH DOSAGE 2G/L
• TASTED IN CRAON DE LUDES

93 points • 2008 VINTAGE DISGORGED OCTOBER 2011 WITH DOSAGE 3G/L
• TASTED IN BRISBANE

A new cuvée of pure pinot meunier from the family's best parcel of old vines in the Vallée de la Marne, planted in 1969; vinified in 350–600-litre barrels; aged on lees in barrel for 8 months and under cork at least 30 months; no malolactic fermentation; 1800 bottles

The 2009 vintage base is a delightful expression of meunier, with wonderful and surprising focus and freshness. A fantastic nose of alluring red cherries, yellow mirabelle plums, mixed spice, figs and understated exotics pre-empts a palate of purity and definition, held intricately in place by fine, malic acidity and refined, understated chalk texture. Lemony malic acidity draws the finish out very long. Even 18 months after disgorgement, the energy and tension of the 2008 vintage base leaves its components sitting more disjointed than the young 2009, with taut malic acidity a touch firm in closing. This is a vintage to mature for at least a few more years, and it may well prove to long outlive meunier's usually modest expectations.

BÉRÈCHE ET FILS VIEILLE VIGNES SELECTIONNEES 2005 • $$$

93 points • DISGORGED JUNE 2012 • TASTED IN CRAON DE LUDES

40% pinot noir, 40% chardonnay, 20% pinot meunier; vinified in tank; 6g/L dosage

Much has progressed at Bérèche since this more classic style of the past was made. Nonetheless, it's a pretty good take on the challenging 2005 season. Yes, it's ripe and, yes, it's slightly dried out on the finish — as 2005 tends to be — but its malic acidity keeps it bright and highlights its soft, fine, mineral texture. There's wonderful fruit intensity of yellow summer fruits, praline, nougat, roast nuts, mixed spice and honey, finishing creamy and persistent.

BÉRÊCHE ET FILS COTEAUX CHAMPENOIS 2011 • $$

91 points • TASTED IN CRAON DE LUDES

100% pinot meunier; full malolactic fermentation; no sulphur; two barrels

Still white champagne is extremely rare, and this is intended to be a fun drink to enjoy young, rather than something too serious. Gorgeous spice and lovely mirabelle plum fruit shows off the breadth and personality of pinot meunier. Oak lends structure and nutty texture, and there are butter and butterscotch notes from malolactic fermentation. A fascinating and well-made wine.

BÉRÈCHE ET FILS REFLET D'ANTAN BRUT NV • $$$

92 points • 2008 VINTAGE BASE, DISGORGED OCTOBER 2012 WITH 7G/L DOSAGE
• TASTED IN CRAON DE LUDES

93 points • 2007 VINTAGE BASE, DISGORGED SEPTEMBER 2011 WITH 6G/L DOSAGE
• TASTED IN BRISBANE

The reserve wine for the Brut NV from perpetual reserve (see above); one-third of each of the three varieties from Ludes and Chigny-les-Roses; no malolactic fermentation; aged on cork a minimum of 3 years

A champagne that prizes expression of character above comfortable appeal, uniting the multi-layered savoury complexity of barrel work with the succulence of ripe yellow summer fruits, the spice of ginger and the bite of grapefruit zest. Its wood work accentuates a salty, savoury edge of oyster shell and green olives, verging on smoky nuances in the midst of a sour lemon, malic acid finish. The salty mineral character builds to great presence on the finish amid well-toned fruit, finishing dry and linear, with considerable carry; powerful yet never heavy or imposing. I noted a hint of savoury, charcuterie barrel funk and a touch of drying astringency in the 2008 base.

BÉRÈCHE ET FILS LE CRAN LUDES PREMIER CRU 2005 • $$$$

91 points • DISGORGED JUNE 2011 • TASTED IN BRISBANE

55% chardonnay, 40% pinot noir, 5% pinot meunier; 100% barrel fermented in 205-litre, 228-litre and 500-litre barrels of 30% new oak; aged on lees for 8 months and under cork a minimum of 60 months; no malolactic fermentation; 2g/L dosage

Rich and ripe with grilled pineapple and succulent ripe peach, verging on overripe to the point of compost suggestions. For all that, the structure is well balanced, with crunchy grapefruit notes and bright malic acidity, finishing with well-controlled phenolic grip that harmonises with subtle toasty notes of new barrels. It concludes creamy and persistent, with lingering salty minerality. The bad-tempered 2005 vintage has handled barrel fermentation and maturation reasonably well here.

BÉRÈCHE ET FILS INSTANT ROSÉ NO 1 BRUT NATURE 2006

94 points • DISGORGED LATE 2009 • TASTED IN CRAON DE LUDES

55% chardonnay, 40% pinot meunier, 5% pinot noir; from two parcels of Le Cran in Ludes, 6% red wine from Ormes; aged 8 months in barrel and 30 months under natural cork; no malolactic fermentation; zero dosage; tiny production of 895 bottles

Raphaël describes his first blended rosé as a learning exercise for creating Campania Remensis. His aspires to a light colour and serious aroma, both of which he has nailed here. Its freshness is quite a revelation for a rosé of this age, with a perfumed lift and an enticing core of cherry fruits of consummate finesse and purity, accented with cherry kernel notes and structured with beautifully fine, textural tannins and vibrant acidity.

BILLECART-SALMON

(Bill-khah Sal-moh)

10/10

40 RUE CARNOT BP8 51160 MAREUIL-SUR-AŸ
www.champagne-billecart.fr

The art of crafting elegant, graceful champagne requires the most exacting skill. Sweetness, richness and breadth cover all manner of sins in champagne, but a wine in its unadorned, raw nakedness reveals even the slightest blemish for all to see. The mark of Billecart is made not by the heavy footfall of concentration, power and presence, but rather by the fairy touch of delicacy and crystal-clear fidelity. Every one of its dozen cuvées articulately speaks the house philosophy of 'respecting the integrity of the fruit, freshness and acidity'.

ON THE SURFACE, THERE APPEARS LITTLE TO DISTIN-guish the fruit sources of this medium-sized house in Mareuil-sur-Aÿ. Vineyard holdings are small, servicing a 1.7 million bottle annual production with just 14 hectares of estate vines and more than 300 hectares of bought fruit. How does Billecart maintain such transcendental standards in every one of its cuvées?

Antoine Roland-Billecart, who manages the house with his brother François, answers this question with a refreshingly frank honesty. 'We are not very focused on marketing,' he begins in impeccable English. 'Vini-fication is the key for us, and all the rest is bullshit.'

Even in the desperately youthful state of 2012 vins clairs still wines, the pinpoint clarity of the house is breathtaking. Chardonnay sings with lemon blossom, crisp as dawn air; a pinot meunier from Charly-sur-Marne is as perfumed as pristine young riesling; and a pinot meunier from Leuvrigny maintains freshness, even after fermentation in 10-year-old barrels.

Such elegant delicacy places Billecart dizzyingly high among Champagne's finest houses, but also infuses its cuvées with an inherent fragility, rendering them parti-cularly vulnerable to imperfections in closure, transportation or storage. In recent tastings, I've encountered an alarming 30% of bottles not quite as fresh as they should be, particularly among non-vintage cuvées. I've noted imperfect bottles in my reviews that follow as an aid in the unfortunate task of identifying a faulty bottle. Without disgorgement dates indicated on bottles, it's difficult to ascertain the age of non-vintage cuvées, but be sure to ask for fresh stock that hasn't lingered on retail shelves.

It's encouraging to see all non-vintage cuvées under DIAM closures this year, as many of my concerns have been traceable to natural corks.

Billecart's vintage wines can be coiled up tight in their youth and appreciate plenty of time to open up in a large glass.

The Champagne Guide

Over many hours of visits and intensive tastings with Antoine and Cellar Master François Domi, an enlightening picture emerges, illuminating some 11 spheres that account for the astounding performance of Billecart-Salmon.

LONGSTANDING FAMILY MANAGEMENT

Although not exclusively owned by the family, Billecart has been under family management since it was founded in 1818. The family still lives on site, and there is a long-visioned continuity at play. The eighth generation of the family, Nicolas Roland-Billecart, came on board alongside his father François, uncle Antoine and grandfather Jean in 2010.

'My father turns 90 next March and we are very lucky that he still joins us for every tasting,' Antoine reflects. 'He began working in wine when he was 16 and has over 70 harvests in his memory. His experience of terroir is so great that he can comment on the effect of every parcel in a blend and challenge us to consider what a wine will be like in 20 years. "This sample won't last, and in 15 years you're going to cry!" he tells us. He has such experience that he can feel a vintage by smelling and tasting the musts, building the blend in his mind before we even taste it.'

HANDS-ON VINEYARD MANAGEMENT

'It's easy to work for a company that is searching for quality as the goal across the whole process,' François Domi says. Starting with the fruit. 'The best grapes on the best terroirs are expensive, but this is our priority.'

Billecart's production has trebled since 20 years ago. When François Roland-Billecart took charge at that time, the house enjoyed solid contracts with longstanding growers in the best sites. Sensing the changing dynamic as growers increasingly held their best fruit for their own champagnes, he set about acquiring vineyards centred around Mareuil-sur-Aÿ. In 2004, the family sold a 45% share in the firm to a Reims-based financier, and in so doing secured access to an additional 80 hectares of grand cru fruit.

Today, the company also manages 65 hectares under lease arrangement, taking full control, from pruning to harvest. 'This is very important,' explains Antoine, 'because it enables us to conduct the vineyard the way we want, yielding 70hL per hectare rather than 85–90, ensuring consistent ripeness and balanced concentration and acidity.'

In vineyards under company control, there has been a return to a more natural way of growing vines and promoting soil health through an absence of pesticides and herbicides. All growers are encouraged to grow grasses in the mid-rows to limit yields. A generational approach to farming, rather than a full biodynamic regime, is the aspiration.

PARCEL SELECTION

Even at a modest 70hL/hectare, Billecart's output is tiny for an estate sourcing from 320 hectares. Antoine considers the flexibility of sourcing grapes from many growers to be strategic, permitting vinification of 140% of production every year, with lesser parcels sold as still wines, or declassified to Billecart's second label, Charles Le Bel.

'It is our strategy to source more grapes than we need — a directive our father passed on to us a long time ago,' Antoine explains. 'It's a good financial model that allows us to be very selective and sell any parcel that doesn't work for our cuvées.'

METICULOUS PRODUCTION REGIME

The precision of Billecart is proclaimed in a squeaky-clean winery. Each element of its meticulous production is geared towards capturing every nuance in the fruit. Billecart presses half the fruit it purchases and uses a pneumatic press for larger parcels, because it's more gentle than the traditional press. One hundred 40hL tanks and some 450 barrels maintain individual control over every one of 280 parcels.

'We have to be very precise, increasing quality by being overly selective, keeping what we want and getting rid of what we don't want to keep,' explains Antoine. A massive new blending tank was commissioned in 2009 to lower the risk of oxidation and increase the consistency of the blends.

COLD SETTLING AND COOL FERMENTS

Perhaps Billecart's most revolutionary technique is its practice of double débourbage. After the standard clarification process to settle out solids, the juice is settled a second time at 4°C for a minimum of 48 hours. The house pioneered this technique of cold settling in Champagne in 1952, inspired by the brothers' maternal grandfather's experience in brewing beer. At this temperature, the coarser lees are removed without risk of oxidation, delivering pristine juice for fermentation. The process is expensive and time-consuming. 'Most of our colleagues thought we were crazy!' admits Antoine.

The juice is then brought up to just 13°C — never more than 14°C — for the primary fermentation. (All 100 tanks are individually temperature controlled, and the barrel hall is regulated to below 16°C.) At this temperature, cultured yeasts from the natural yeasts of nearby villages take 3–4 weeks to complete fermentation. Such cool, long ferments are crucial for retaining greater freshness and delicacy than a standard champagne ferment of one week at 20°C.

All parcels for non-vintage blends pass through malolactic fermentation, but for vintage wines this is dependent upon the season. For Antoine, 'respecting the style of the vintage is more important than anything else', and winemaking is adapted each year to suit.

INCREASING USE OF OAK

When Antoine comes to work every day he asks himself what can be done to improve vinification within the house style. As a devotee of Krug Clos du Mesnil — he openly volunteers the inaugural vintage as his favourite blanc de blancs of all time — it's no surprise Billecart has increased the use of oak barrels for fermentation since 1996. Fifty barrels in that year became 80 in 1997. A new barrel room now houses almost 450 barrels and two new large oak foudres.

Old barrels, having seen six or seven vintages in Burgundy, are used for the fermentation of all grand cru fruit, and bâtonnage is conducted weekly, according to taste. Barrels currently range from five to 15 years of age. The goal at Billecart, as always, is to encourage subtle complexity rather than overt character.

LOW DOSAGE

Antoine considers a decrease in dosage over the past decade as crucial in allowing the fruit to show its full character. 'It is like makeup,' he proposes. 'You don't need it if there is no problem, and you want to show the real character of the wines.' Dosage levels are low: typically 8g/L in non-vintage wines, and around just 4g/L in vintage wines. This places the vintage wines firmly in 'Extra Brut' (extra dry) territory. Any more sweetness might play havoc with such delicate styles.

DIFFERENT LIQUEUR FOR EVERY DOSAGE

The final nuance comes at disgorgement: every cuvée has a different liqueur at Billecart. Domi conducts many tastings with different dosages, from wines aged in barrel and those in tank, to determine which best suits each wine. A different liqueur is used for every disgorgement, so completely different liqueurs can be chosen for the start, the middle and the end of a cuvée.

'The wine is in a constant state of evolution,' explains Antoine, 'so it might be better, for instance, to freshen it with more chardonnay than pinot noir.'

Such is the fanatical attention to every detail that it took almost a year to find the right dosage for Blanc de Blancs Brut 1999. 'We weren't happy with it, so we

Billecart's increasing use of oak builds subtle complexity.

waited and simply didn't release it,' Antoine recalls. 'We were working on grand cru parcels, but then I said, "Forget grand crus, we need something more comfortable." So we tried Bergères-les-Vertus with 3% reserve wine and of that, 1% 1998 barrel-fermented chardonnay. Then we tried eight, seven, six, five, four, three and two grams per litre of sweetness and settled on 5.5.' Such is the way of Billecart.

LONG AGEING

Billecart's non-vintage wines are aged for 3–4 years, and its millésime collection a minimum 8–10 years (the 2002 Cuvée Nicolas François Billecart was released in 2013). Slow sales in 2012 permitted the Brut Réserve NV to now be released after 36 months in the cellar, rather than the 24 months of recent years.

SUPERIOR CLOSURE

Finally, and crucially, all non-vintage wines except blanc de blancs have been sealed with DIAM cork since 2006. DIAM is not perfect, but it is demonstrably superior to natural cork. Billecart's Australian agent reported an immediate drop in returned bottles as soon as DIAM was introduced. Billecart is currently five years into a 10-year trial of ageing of vintage wines under DIAM. I look forward to the day when Billecart's top wines are entrusted to a reliable closure.

THE GENIUS OF FRANÇOIS DOMI

Alongside the enthusiastic energy of Antoine Roland-Billecart, François Domi is the quietly spoken and reflective genius. He started in the lab at Billecart as an oenologist almost 30 years ago and describes himself today as part of the furniture. His unassuming manner means his name is never listed among Champagne's rock stars, but his greatest hits of the past two decades surely place him at the top of the charts.

Billecart-Salmon Brut NV • $$

92 points • Disgorged 19 December 2011 • Tasted in Brisbane

2007 base; 80% chardonnay, 20% pinot noir; DIAM closure; 300,000–350,000 bottles annually

The subtle omission of 'Réserve' from the label is easy to miss, but this is not the entry Billecart we all know and love. Reserved largely for airlines, this is the same wine as Billecart's second label, Charles Le Bel. In stark contrast to the Réserve, the blend is led boldly by chardonnay, with a higher proportion of tailles in the blend. It's normally released younger than the Réserve, so, ironically, it contains a higher proportion of reserve wines, though here there's a full four years between base vintage and disgorgement, making for a more toasty, juicy, rounded style of succulent white peach and almond notes. It's less refined and precise than the Réserve, but its more curvaceous shape is well-suited to flying. For a second label, it's well made and easy to enjoy.

Billecart-Salmon Brut Réserve NV • $$

95 points • 2010 vintage base • Disgorged April 2013 • Tasted in Mareuil-sur-Aÿ

95 points • 2009 vintage base • Disgorged May 2012 • Tasted in Brisbane, Melbourne
    and Mareuil-sur-Aÿ

35% reserves; 40% pinot meunier, 35% pinot noir, 25% chardonnay; 9g/L dosage; DIAM closure; around 1 million bottles annually

Billecart is royalty among the readily available entry NVs. After the enchanting 2008 base last year, I braced myself for a dip in the 2009 and 2010, but the consistency remains rock solid, a credit to impressive levels of reserve wines.

Brut Réserve is a captivating contradiction, dressing one of Champagne's higher representations of pinot meunier in one of the most delicate and graceful of attires. It glides onto the stage and sings with the pristine signature of the house, energising the red apple, berry and strawberry fruits of pinot meunier with a breathtakingly refined melody of pure lemon blossom and lemon meringue, in a dazzling display of fine, chalk minerality and understated, fragrant elegance. A slight increase in dosage reflects Billecart's intuitive approach to each disgorgement, not a trend toward sweetness.

All but one bottle I've opened this year has been pristine (one developed, pungent, oxidised, maderised bottle fell victim to an imperfectly inserted DIAM). The effortless, understated purity of Billecart can even leave the unsuspecting wondering what the fuss is all about, but wait for the second sip and the orchestra will strike up and lift your mood in an instant.

Billecart-Salmon Extra Brut NV • $$

94 points • Disgorged 31 January 2012 • Tasted in Brisbane and Mareuil-sur-Aÿ

2007 base vintage; 40% pinot meunier, 35% pinot noir, 25% chardonnay; zero dosage; DIAM closure

One of the most refined zero-dosage champagnes, built on the same base as Brut Réserve — but crucially, not simply a zero-dosage version of the same. It's older, with an extra year on lees — 'not so it has more fat', explains Antoine, 'but so it is more rounded, with less angles'. The liqueur in the dosage is different, too, with 5mL of reserve wines contributing volume, structure and persistence. The 2006 chardonnay lends nuances of wax and butter-like silkiness to a honed focus of flint and crisp lemon zest. It's clean, fresh and pristine 18 months after disgorgement, proclaiming Billecart's refreshing clarity in a brittle shell of bone-shaking purity and citrus minerality.

BILLECART-SALMON DEMI-SEC NV • $$

92 points • Disgorged November 2011 • Tasted in Brisbane

2008 base vintage; 40% pinot meunier, 35% pinot noir, 25% chardonnay; 40g/L dosage

The third in Billecart's Brut Réserve trilogy, with a dosage right in the middle of champagne's demi-sec spectrum, from 32g/L to 50g/L. Again one of the most refreshing and well-crafted sweet champagnes on the shelves this year, the same base as the Brut Réserve charges it with the acidity and poise to handle its honeyed sweetness. This transforms the clean fruit precision that defines Billecart into candied citrus, lemon drops and glacé figs, with a creamy, sweet finish, well toned by balanced acidity. Well executed, but nothing on the clean purity of Brut Réserve.

BILLECART-SALMON BRUT BLANC DE BLANCS GRAND CRU NV • $$$

95 points • 2008 base vintage • Disgorged January 2013 • Blend of Le Mesnil-sur-Oger, Avize, Chouily and Cramant • Tasted in Mareuil-sur-Aÿ

89 points • 2005 vintage base • Disgorged 10 September 2010 • Blend of Avize, Cramant, Le Mesnil-sur-Oger, Oger and Chouily • Tasted in Brisbane

Partial malolactic fermentation to retain 2g/L of malic acidity; 8g/L dosage; DIAM closure

'In your dreams,' responded Jean Roland-Billecart when his son Antoine proposed a non-vintage blanc de blancs. 'We don't have sufficient quantity of chardonnay, but if you find the grapes to produce it, go ahead.' And find them he did. Not just anywhere, but in the five grand crus of the Côte des Blancs, and in 1997 Billecart made its first non-vintage blanc de blancs. The arresting 2008 vintage makes for a beautifully pristine blanc de blancs. Elegantly understated lemon and grapefruit evolve to anise, highlighted by struck flint. The tense structure and energetic tang of the season heighten wonderful mineral expression. By contrast, the 2005 vintage base is showing premature development, clutching its chalk mineral spine for dear life.

BILLECART-SALMON BRUT ROSÉ NV • $$$

94 points • Disgorged October 2012 • Tasted in Adelaide and Brisbane

2008 vintage base; 40% chardonnay, 30% pinot noir, 30% pinot meunier; just 7–8% pinot noir red wine from Mareuil-sur-Aÿ, more for aromatic effect than colour; 9g/L dosage; DIAM closure

The utter restraint of Billecart places delicate rosés very close to its heart, dubbed internally 'champagne rosé' rather than 'rosé champagne'. Antoine delights in recalling a tasting in which he poured the wine in black glasses for sommeliers. Not one identified it as a rosé. 'When my grandfather began producing rosés in the early 1960s, most thought it a fanciful, artificial wine that lacked purity,' he recalls. 'He persevered, convinced it would have its place. Those sceptics are now making their own!' The wonderfully energetic 2008 base defines a restrained and elegantly pretty rosé of pale salmon hue and very subtle strawberry hull and white cherry fruit. Delightfully understated and elegantly persistent, it carries with grace and poise amidst a taut profile of refined acidity and soft mineral presence. This cuvée is at its best in its youth. Older disgorgements have quickly evolved to a pale orange hue and astringent orange rind flavours.

The Champagne Guide

BILLECART-SALMON CUVÉE SOUS BOIS BRUT NV • $$$

95 points • 2008 VINTAGE BASE • DISGORGED NOVEMBER 2012 • MALOLACTIC
FERMENTATION ON PINOT MEUNIER ONLY. TASTED IN MAREUIL-SUR-AŸ

95 points • 2006 VINTAGE BASE • DISGORGED FEBRUARY 2012 • NO MALOLACTIC
FERMENTATION • TASTED IN ADELAIDE AND BRISBANE

One-third of each of the champagne varieties; one-third reserve wines from the previous
two harvests, which Antoine describes as 'the fourth third so it doesn't fit in the bottle!';
fully oak-fermented below 16°C; aged on lees in barrel with bâtonnage (lees stirring) for
6 months; 7g/L dosage; DIAM closure

Sous bois is as distinctive for Billecart as its bold, modern label. Billecart is constantly
experimenting, and occasionally something emerges from its trials for all to behold. 'With
the diversity of Champagne's regions and the rise of the growers, it's increasingly important
for us to produce more interesting, small-production wines,' points out Antoine. Sous bois is
literally 'under wood', inspired by oak-fermented parcels destined for Billecart's top cuvées.
The precision of the 2008 season has brought this blend closer to its aspiration — fresher,
tighter, more elegant, ultimately more 'Billecart' than the grand complexity and fullness of the
inaugural 2006 base, with its flamboyant spectacle of swirls of butterscotch. The 2008 exalts
the crunchy strawberry hull and fresh white cherries of its pinot core, intricately interwoven
with the spice, toast and creamy texture of oak, without ever becoming oaky. It sings with
classic Billecart precision, while basking in the richness of barrel fermentation, silky and
alluring, confronting and commanding, all at once. Don't serve it too cold, and give it lots
of air in a large glass.

BILLECART-SALMON EXTRA BRUT VINTAGE 2004 • $$$

95 points • DISGORGED JANUARY 2013 • TASTED IN MAREUIL-SUR-AŸ

70% pinot noir, 30% chardonnay; one-third fermented in 5-year-old barrels to add interest; 3g/L dosage

Deemed of insufficient interest for Cuvée Nicolas François Billecart, 2004 gave birth to a new cuvée. It's barely
moved in three years, retaining youthful precision of fresh lemon and grapefruit, slowly evolving to preserved
lemon and brioche. Subtle reductive character is manifested in notes of gunpowder, lingering on a finish of
chalk mineral texture and low-flying, streamlined persistence. The first bottle opened was cork-tainted.

BILLECART-SALMON BLANC DE BLANCS BRUT 2004 • $$$$

98 points • DISGORGED JANUARY 2013 • TASTED IN MAREUIL-SUR-AŸ

Blend of grapes from Le Mesnil-sur-Oger, Avize and Cramant; 15% fermented in barrels; mid-2014 release

BdB 2004 makes a monumental declaration: from Billecart's proud position in the heart of pinot territory,
this house is masterful in its command of the finest chardonnay crus. Shy and reserved a year before release, it
takes some hours to unravel and reveal its stately magnificence. At almost a decade of age, its exacting, youthful
freshness of lemon and white peach is breathtakingly elegant, yet innately intense. Subtle oak structure gently
coaxes out notes of almond, nougat and subtle toasty complexity, building creamy texture and accenting
dazzling chalk minerality. Grand longevity.

BILLECART-SALMON BLANC DE BLANCS BRUT 1999 • $$$$

97 points • DISGORGED 2 APRIL 2012 • TASTED IN MAREUIL-SUR-AŸ AND BRISBANE

The Côte des Blancs' finest grand crus: the finesse of Chouilly, the power of Avize and Cramant, the structure and longevity of Le Mesnil-sur-Oger and Oger; every parcel vinified separately to retain character; 5.5g/L dosage

Billecart's 1999 BdB has uncoiled with astounding conviction over the past two years, revealing a magnificence and beguiling transparency that even its 12-year-old self could not anticipate. It's evolving slowly and assuredly, reaching that magic point where rising layers of buttery, toasted almonds, brioche, subtle vanilla and freshly baked butter cake burst forth. Primary lemon and white peach are still alive after 14 years, sustained by vibrant, lemon zest acidity. The fabled chalk terroirs of the Côte des Blancs' A-list reach out with their inimitable, mouth-filling chalk minerality, in a revelation of intricately, epically intertwined complexity, silky and creamy, yet absolute sheer precision at every moment. Not an iota of detail is lost in its incredible finish. It's right at the top of its arc, but such is its freshness, who can say what surprises may yet be in store?

BILLECART-SALMON CUVÉE NICOLAS FRANÇOIS
BILLECART 2002 • $$$$

99 points • DISGORGED OCTOBER 2012 • TASTED IN MAREUIL-SUR-AŸ

60% Montagne de Reims pinot noir, 40% Côte des Blancs chardonnay; 18% barrel-fermented in old oak casks; no malolactic fermentation; 4g/L dosage; 50,000 bottles

Some champagnes volunteer their life story within seconds of first introductions, like overworked movie trailers that leave you fully convinced you've seen the film. Others churn in your consciousness for days, slowly unravelling their story long after the credits have rolled. My first introduction to NFB 2002 was four months before its release, when it emerged, blinking, into the stark daylight of Mareuil-sur-Aÿ from the depths of Billecart's cellars. It squirmed, shocked, uncomfortable at first, then began to play an exhilarating script that held me captivated for a full half hour. As always, the greatness of Billecart is proclaimed not by impact or power, but by slowly rising complexity and profound chalk mineral presence. A hint of struck flint reduction makes way for the icy brightness of grapefruit zest, lemon, white peach, then the warmth of figs, and later, yellow summer fruits. A decade in the cellar has set down layers of toast and nuts, even wood spice. Refreshing acidity takes time to uncoil, and minerality rises slowly, super fine, confident and taut, surging on the finish in a cascade of chalk that lingers, undeterred, for minutes. There is nothing overt or glamorous about NFB 2002, yet its delightful poise and intricate craftsmanship clearly proclaim one of the great Billecarts of the modern era, taming the exuberance of 2002 with exacting skill.

This is a champagne with many characters and subplots to reveal, to be enjoyed slowly in the presence of the most intimate company — and ideally not until it has rested at least another decade in the darkness.

The Champagne Guide

BILLECART-SALMON CUVÉE NICOLAS FRANÇOIS BILLECART 2000 • $$$$

98 points • DISGORGED 3 APRIL 2012 • TASTED IN MAREUIL-SUR-AŸ AND BRISBANE

60% Montagne de Reims pinot noir, 40% Côte des Blancs chardonnay; vinified partially in old oak casks; no malolactic fermentation; 4g/L dosage

This is developing much slower than anyone anticipated of the harrowing 2000 vintage, including its maker, François Domi. Such is the endurance of this cuvée that it has not diminished at all since I first reviewed it in 2008 and named it Wine of the Year in the inaugural edition of *The Champagne Guide*. As of 2000, Grande Cuvée is no more, so Billecart's finest grand cru fruit is now reserved for NFB. It's barely moved in five years, a wine of wonderful volume within a frame of restrained mineral expression and pinpoint clarity, with pinot's authority controlled by chardonnay's tone. Malic acidity cracks the controlling whip, energising fresh, youthful notes of lemon, grapefruit, even lime, flowing seamlessly into those warm, yellow late-summer fruits, becoming bees wax, warm hearth, butter and mixed spice. A whiff of struck flint adds another dimension, finishing with great power of chalk mineral texture. One of the greatest 2000s, drinking majestically now and who knows for how long? The bottle I tasted in Australia was slightly dulled, but such is the Russian roulette of natural cork.

BILLECART-SALMON CUVÉE ELISABETH SALMON BRUT ROSÉ 2002 • $$$$

98 points • DISGORGED 16 FEBRUARY 2012 • TASTED IN MAREUIL-SUR-AŸ AND BRISBANE

50% chardonnay, 50% pinot noir; 8g/L dosage

Simultaneously capturing euphoric freshness, refined elegance and exacting fruit definition is one of the finest skills of Champagne's winemakers, and nowhere is this more challenging than in the tightrope balance of long-aged rosé. In the sublime 2002 season, Billecart has achieved the seemingly impossible and conjured a rosé both larger and lighter than life. True to her name, Elisabeth Salmon radiates a gorgeous, ethereal, pale-salmon hue. In a display of intricately coiled, ultra-pristine detail, dainty red cherry, crunchy pomegranate, lifted rose petal and wild strawberry fruit burst forth in clear peals like church bells, dissolving into vapour-like lightness. Nuances of struck flint, cherry kernel, even a wisp of fresh coffee bean and dark chocolate, cascade into a marvellous flow of crunchy white cherry definition, charged with a core of tightly clenched, energetically coiled acidity. Mineral presence is a marvel, chalk-dust fine and magnificently intertwined with the most sophisticated fruit. A breathtaking rosé of the utmost finesse and character, projecting a fruit presence and unbroken line of mesmerising persistence. Elisabeth Salmon 2002 is not only one of the finest rosé champagnes this year, it ranks high among the greatest of the modern era.

BILLECART-SALMON GRANDE CUVÉE 1998 • $$$$$

99 points • DISGORGED 4 NOVEMBER 2011 • TASTED IN BRISBANE

60% pinot noir, 40% chardonnay; 4g/L dosage

Grande Cuvée is no more, but one of the great champagnes of recent times has not gone quietly into the night. Its final vintage just keeps getting better, returning for yet another rousing encore this year. At a full 15 years of age, Grande Cuvée has grown into an iridescent gleam of yellow straw. Its core of white fruits of all kinds remains rock solid, supported by thick orchestral scoring of toasty complexity and reductive, flinty gunpowder. Tightly wound and enchantingly focused, it unravels in freeze-frame slow motion to reveal delicate layers of nuance, all the while tightly hugging rails of crystalline-pure acidity. It rises on the finish with outstretched magnificence, an epiphany of relentless persistence underlined by consummately fine-spun, deep-set textural presence that froths and foams with sea-salt minerality. Billecart's resolve to redirect its top fruit to Nicolas François Billecart, at one-third of the price, is certainly noble, but Grande Cuvée will forever be missed. Farewell, old friend.

BILLECART-SALMON LE CLOS SAINT-HILAIRE 1998 • $$$$$

100 points • DISGORGED 17 FEBRUARY 2011 • TASTED IN BRISBANE

1 hectare clos in Mareuil-sur-Aÿ; planted exclusively to pinot noir since 1964; yielding a minuscule 40–45hL/hectare, less than one bottle per vine; harvested in two passes at full ripeness; two cuvées vinified in situ; fully fermented in oak; zero dosage; just 3500–7500 bottles, only in top vintages

Le Clos Saint-Hilaire has no right to its profound echelon. It is but a premier cru vineyard, although this is perhaps more a reflection on the inadequacies of an oversimplified cru system. More significantly, in soil — deeper and less chalky than, for instance, the Clos des Goisses at the other end of the village — and in aspect (due east, far from the sought-after south-facing orientation), it has no claims to greatness. It is but a flat expanse beside the press house in the village. The genius of François Domi and the painstaking attention to detail of Billecart must play a dramatic role here. I could not name another wine at this level, of any variety, anywhere in the world, of which the same could be said.

Alongside Krug Clos d'Ambonnay, Billecart Le Clos Saint-Hilaire is the king of blanc de noirs. It was conceived as Antoine and François Roland-Billecart stood on the wall of the clos late one night during harvest in 1995. With plenty of red wine in stock for rosé, they decided they could afford to put this pinot noir in the cellar for a decade to see how it looked on its own.

Le Clos Saint-Hilaire's third release is a towering masterpiece, remarkable at 15 years of age not only for retaining profound mineral clarity and impeccable freshness in the midst of unfathomable complexity, but for a sheer persistence that elevates it to a level above virtually every other champagne. Its precision is as bright as daylight, bursting with sheer magnificence of pristine cherries. Flickers of gunpowder reduction announce intrigue, quickly vaporising to reveal spellbinding purity of pristine red and black fruits, the epitome of pinot noir character and refinement. Then its light begins to dim to a soft-focus twilight of dark mystery, revealing deeper tones of plum cake, cherry liqueur, mixed spice, vanilla pod and dark chocolate. Brilliant acidity pierces its gentle calm like pinpoint starlight illuminating a soft landscape of understated yet deeply-penetrating and mouth-engulfing mineral texture.

To stand in this place and behold Le Clos Saint-Hilaire is a time-stopping experience that will stir the depths of your soul. Its twilight won't fade for at least another 15 years.

The Champagne Guide

BOIZEL

(Bwah-zel)

46 AVENUE DE CHAMPAGNE 51200 EPERNAY
www.boizel.com

Evelyne Roques-Boizel is the fifth generation to head Boizel. Seven hectares of estate vineyards are complemented with long-term contracts with growers in about 50 villages, boosted in 1994 after an injection of funds from the Lanson-BCC group. Boizel's clean, fruity style is achieved through fermentation in stainless steel vats at 18°C, full malolactic fermentation and long ageing of non-vintage cuvées of at least three years. Vintage wines are aged between five and seven years, after a small proportion of vinification in barrel.

BOIZEL BRUT RÉSERVE NV • $$

90 points • DISGORGED JULY 2012 • TASTED IN BRISBANE

70% 2008, 15% 2007, 15% 2006; 55% pinot noir, 30% chardonnay, 15% pinot meunier from 30 villages, largely premier crus; 350,000 bottles annually; 9g/L dosage

Boizel's entry wine is a pale, fresh and fruity champagne with a bouquet of lemon zest, white peach and honey. The palate is lively and primary, charged with zesty citrus fruits and classic, fresh 2008 acid definition. It finishes clean, precise, short and crisp, with well-integrated dosage.

BOIZEL BRUT ROSÉ NV • $$

89 points • DISGORGED APRIL 2011 • TASTED IN BRISBANE

80% 2007, 20% 2006; 50% pinot noir (including 8% red wine from Cumières and Les Riceys), 30% pinot meunier, 20% chardonnay; 60,000 bottles annually; 8g/L dosage

This wine was already almost two years post-disgorgement before it reached me, dulling its salmon hue with a distinct bronze tint. Secondary red berries have lost their vibrant lift, becoming toasty and honeyed, with a suggestion of mixed spice. A bruised red apple tiredness on the finish suggests it's probably seen better days. Nonetheless, its acidity remains crisp, its dosage well integrated and its secondary complexity will appeal to some.

BOLLINGER

(Boh-lahn-zhay)

20 BOULEVARD DU MARÉCHAL DE LATTRE DE TASSIGNY 51160 AŸ
www.champagne-bollinger.com

CHAMPAGNE
BOLLINGER
MAISON FONDÉE EN 1829

It's another world at Bollinger. Take everything you know about large champagne houses, the way champagne tastes, the way it's fermented, the way it's aged, even the ownership of the vineyards and the companies, and brace yourself for a very different story at Bollinger. I've met with the good Bollinger folk many times in recent years in Australia and in their illustrious maison in Aÿ, and on every occasion I have been astounded by the pace of change. If Bollinger wasn't your style five years ago, come hither! With the trajectory of Special Cuvée intersecting with the sublime 2008 vintage, there's never been a better time to bask in the glory of this legendary house. These are ravishing champagnes that now rank high among the very best of the region. James Bond, you've finally got it right.

'I DID NOT WANT TO MAKE A REVOLUTION OF CHANGE,' Bollinger's quietly insightful Chef de Cave Mathieu Kauffmann told me recently. 'A journalist asked me 10 years ago what I wanted to change and I said, "Nothing!"' Kauffmann's humility is refreshing, but the truth is much more exciting: Bollinger has been transformed since he commenced in 2001.

The Bollinger house style has long been a love-it-or-hate-it champagne, oft maligned for the aldehydes that can develop as a result of oxidation during barrel ageing. Oxidation during fermentation is positive, but prior to fermentation it suppresses fruit, and post-fermentation it dulls the wine. The priority now is to suppress oxidation, creating fresher and less aldehydic wines. 'It is all the small details that have refined the style,' Kauffmann reveals. And it has to be, for to create champagnes of such grandeur, exacting attention must be applied to every element of the process.

There are 10 facets that set Bollinger apart among Champagne houses, beginning in the vineyards.

ESTATE VINEYARDS

Bollinger is a champagne of cathedral proportions: massive, impacting and magnificent. Its weight derives foremost from estate-grown pinot noir. Every cuvée has a minimum of 60% pinot noir, and an impressive two-thirds of the grapes come from estate vineyards. (The only other house boasting such proportions is Louis Roederer.) Centred around Aÿ, Champagne's pinot noir epicentre, Bollinger's mighty 163 hectares comprise 85% grand cru and premier cru vineyards.

'When we buy grapes, we see them,' emphasises Kauffmann. This is why the house favours Aÿ and the nearby villages of Louvois, Mareuil-sur-Aÿ, Verzy and Verzenay. 'We only buy grapes from the Marne, not because others are inferior, but because it's easier to assess grapes nearby,' he explains.

Grape maturity is pushed a little further at Bollinger through careful choice of harvest date, a blessing the house attributes to vineyard ownership. The balance of fruit is sourced from winegrowers who have worked

The Champagne Guide

with the house for many generations (every one of 120 parcels is vinified separately at Bollinger; there is no purchase of 'vins sur lattes'). This accounts for the consistency, depth and complexity in Bollinger's wines.

NEW PRESS HOUSE
To reduce pre-ferment oxidation, Kauffmann's first job was to construct a new press centre in neighbouring Mareuil-sur-Aÿ, within line of sight of the maison in Aÿ, completed in time for the 2003 vintage. All the grapes of the house are transported by truck or tractor to Mareuil, where large, eight-tonne pneumatic presses are worked 24/7 to press 200 tonnes every day.

BARREL FERMENTATION
Bollinger uses only the cuvée (the first and best pressing) and ferments under temperature control in both stainless steel tanks and oak barrels. Use of barrels for fermentation and ageing is a key element in reinforcing Bollinger's house style, and Kauffmann has gone to great lengths to retain freshness and fruit purity through diligent barrel cleaning and cellar hygiene.

The magnitude of this task becomes apparent after seeing 3200 champagne barrels of 225-litre capacity stacked long and high, row after row, plus 208 barrels of 400-litre capacity, made by Bollinger in 1903. To increase consistency, old barrels of at least three years of age are purchased annually from Bollinger-owned Burgundy négociant Chanson and maintained until they are 20–30 years old, by what Bollinger claims to be the last in-house cooper in Champagne. Bollinger's vintage wines are 100% barrel fermented, as are all of its reserve wines, and any other parcels with sufficient acidity to handle 6–7 months in barrel.

I was privileged to participate in an enlightening tasting in 2010 that exemplified the point of all this. Comprising four vins clairs (fermented still base wines) from the 2009 vintage, chardonnay from Cramant and pinot noir from Aÿ, we compared the same parcels fermented in stainless steel and oak. The difference was profound, the barrel-fermented samples in no way woody (thanks to the age of Bollinger's barrels) but better integrated, more textured, more complex and better balanced. Bollinger considers barrels an insurance policy for the wine, providing controlled oxidation, and drawing out the longevity of Grande Année to 20 years and beyond.

FAMILY OWNERSHIP
With an annual production of a little more than 2.5 million bottles, Bollinger is the largest independent champagne house after Louis Roederer, owned and

The cathedral proportions of Bollinger's cuvées are derived from Champagne's pinot noir epicentre, Aÿ.

run completely by members of the Bollinger family. This provides the freedom to uphold practices, such as longer ageing under cork, that might be considered infeasible under a large owner.

LONGER AGEING
Bollinger keeps its cuvées on lees for long periods: a minimum of three years for non-vintages (until recently two and a half years), and eight years or longer for Grande Année (previously six). Kauffmann considers this crucial for producing small bubbles and very fine, velvety textures.

More than 12 million bottles are held in storage in Bollinger's six kilometres of cellars over four levels under Aÿ, including some 600,000 magnums of grand crus and premier crus fermented in barrels, bottled with natural corks and kept for between five and 15 years, or longer. There is a desire to increase production, but only at the very slow rate of 5000 bottles per year, so as to uphold quality. 'If I want to sell one more bottle in five years' time, I need to put five more bottles in the cellar now!' Kauffmann explains.

Infused with the resilience of barrel maturation, Bollinger's white cuvées are rock-solid, and I rarely encounter bottle variation whenever and wherever in the world I taste them. They also possess propensity for great longevity (but its rosés are best drunk as youthful as possible). While Kauffmann prefers Special Cuvée within two years of disgorgement, the Queen of England cellars hers for 10 years, and reportedly did not pop the 2001 disgorgement until 2010!

AGEING UNDER CORK

Bollinger upholds that ageing its reserve wines in magnum on natural cork rather than crown seal affords more complexity, a practice followed by a small number of growers and small houses, but no other sizeable house. Six grams of sugar is added for a 'prise de mousse' (carbonic fermentation) to produce a light sparkle to retain fresh flavour and aroma in these reserve magnums, dubbed 'aromatic bombs' by the house.

It's not hard to see why very few houses age reserve wines under cork — it necessitates riddling and disgorgement by hand, not to mention wastage to cork taint. Indeed, 80,000 reserve magnums are opened by hand every year for the Special Cuvée alone. It's a tedious and expensive process to check every bottle for cork taint by nose. Workers are instructed not to wear perfume on disgorgement days, and not to front up at all if they have a cold. Kauffmann reports a rejection rate to cork taint of just half of 1%, but admits that even this is too much. He acknowledges the benefits of DIAM corks in eliminating cork taint, but prefers contact with natural, unglued cork and considers DIAM aesthetically inferior.

It's not only Special Cuvée that's produced using a labour-intensive process at Bollinger. Vintage wines are hand disgorged, with every bottle tasted at disgorgement, and non-vintage rosé is hand riddled.

Asked about the practice of ageing under cork, Christian Pol Roger allegedly replied: 'It's a great idea, but we are not as crazy as you are at Bollinger!'

MALOLACTIC FERMENTATION

In the past, malolactic fermentation occurred haphazardly, only in those barrels and tanks that happened to progress naturally. In pursuit of greater consistency, malolactic bacteria are now introduced to ensure systematic completion of malolactic fermentation.

ONE BLEND

All 2 million bottles of Bollinger's Special Cuvée are triaged at once in a single blend in February, to maintain the consistency of each blend. To further promote freshness, Bollinger disgorges three times a year, with each disgorgement from the same original blend, yet subtly different due to a different length of time on lees.

Annoyingly, disgorgement dates are not stamped on non-vintage bottles (they are on the vintage wines), and the labelling code has changed so it's difficult to decipher precisely. The year of labelling remains easy, thankfully — the first two digits of the code.

Previously, disgorgement was three months prior to labelling, but this has been extended to six months to allow the wines to settle sufficiently after disgorgement.

MODERN FACILITIES

To further reduce post-ferment oxidation, in 2012 Bollinger installed one of Champagne's most modern disgorgement lines. A computerised system checks for defects in the seal of cork-sealed bottles, and rejects 3–4%. (If only it could detect cork taint, too!) When I visited, a cart was stacked 10 high with rejects destined to be used as liquor.

Bottling facilities were updated in 2005, 2008 and again recently, this time in preparation for a new bottle.

NEW BOTTLE

In 2012, Bollinger launched its gloriously refined '1846' bottle with a wider base, narrower neck and elegant curves. It is based on an original champagne bottle found in the Bollinger cellars dated 1846, and Kauffmann suggests that the benefits are more than just aesthetic.

'The neck of a standard champagne bottle is too big,' he claims. With a neck three millimetres narrower, the new bottle has a neck cross-sectional area 20% smaller than the last, which he suggests will slow the oxygen exchange, better for ageing.

Kauffmann also proposes that this neck takes up 40–50% less oxygen during disgorgement. The house PR material proposes that the ageing of the new bottle is more like a magnum, by comparing ratios of neck diameter to base diameter. The correct comparison is the ratios of neck cross-section to bottle volume, which places the 1846 decidedly closer to a standard bottle than a magnum — but that narrower neck can only be a good thing, and it does look spectacular.

Mathieu Kauffmann announced his surprise resignation from Bollinger in March 2013. He had been Bollinger's tenth Chef de Cave — the third in more than 70 years, and its first to resign rather than retire. His exacting attention to the finer details of Bollinger over the past decade lifted its wines to the cleanest, most precise, least aldehydic the house has ever made.

For a champagne of breadth and depth, and one that is readily available and affordable, Bollinger is in a world of its own.

Bollinger Special Cuvée Brut NV • $$

96 points • Disgorged late 2012; 8g/L dosage • Tasted in Aÿ

The complexity and richness of Special Cuvée is unrivalled among the entry-level non-vintage blends of every champagne house, short of ascending to the mesosphere of Krug. Its grand recipe explains why. The current release is a blend of some 200 parcels of 60% pinot noir, 25% chardonnay and 15% pinot meunier from each of the 2008 and 2007 vintages in equal measure, with between five and eight vintages of older reserve wines (5–10%) vinified in oak barrels and aged in magnum under cork for between five and 15 years. Kauffmann highlights the small percentage of older reserves as crucial for maintaining a consistent style. In all, this equates to a mind-boggling 400 wines and a massive 55% of reserve wine — astonishing numbers unrivalled by other champagne producers. Further intensity is derived from 30–40% of the blend in oak barrels, and a very high proportion of grand cru and premier cru fruit sources (more than 85%). Post-blending, the wine matures for a minimum of three years on lees in the cellar before it is disgorged and a light dosage of 8g/L is added. This cuvée represents 90% of the production of the house — more than 2 million bottles annually.

This is the finest Bollinger Special Cuvée I have tasted. The pristine high notes of the great 2008 vintage are a wonderful counterpoint to the resonant depth and triumphant complexity that set Special Cuvée apart. It is at once rich and full, with fleshy, cooked yellow summer fruits, figs and cherries. The depth of its reserve parcels reverberates with Bollinger's signature notes of ginger, Christmas cake, almonds, nougat and honey. The finish lifts in a masterful crescendo of fine, fresh 2008 acidity, more achingly pristine and more chalky mineral than ever, with a persistence of aftertaste nothing short of a revelation. Look for the new 1846 bottle with a bottling code beginning 'L12'.

Bollinger Rosé Brut NV • $$

96 points • 2008 and 2007 vintage base; disgorged October 2012; 7.5g/L dosage • Tasted in Aÿ and London

95 points • 2007 and 2006 vintage base; disgorged October 2012; 8g/L dosage • Tasted in Aÿ

62% pinot noir, 24% chardonnay, 14% pinot meunier

Bollinger Rosé NV has doubled in volume since its much-celebrated addition to the Bollinger family in 2008, though it still represents just 200,000 bottles, merely one-tenth of Special Cuvée. Red wine from the grand cru villages of Verzenay and Aÿ is given long pre-ferment maceration and matured in barrel for 12 months before it is added to Special Cuvée. The house prides itself on its red wine, and such is its strength, concentration, depth of colour and robust tannin structure that a tiny 5% is all that is required.

The magnificent 2008 base vintage is the first Bollinger Rosé to land in its ultra-sophisticated 1846 bottle, adorned with a breathtakingly stylish new label and neck label, making this new blend's arrival impossible to miss. Working its magic again, 2008 brings electric acidity, charging it with great freshness of structure and grand chalk mineral presence. In spite of higher acidity, Kauffmann has tactically wound back the dosage just a touch, in the hope of confirming a style of greater elegance. It meets the brief with effortless grace, a pale salmon hue with a tint of pink, singing with delightful purity and freshness of rose petals, strawberry hull and white cherries over a backdrop of classic Bollinger complexity of nougat and mixed spice. Testimony to the power of just 5% in transforming a blend.

BOLLINGER LA GRANDE ANNÉE BRUT 2004 • $$$$

96 points • DISGORGED JULY 2012 • TASTED IN AŸ

67% pinot noir, 33% chardonnay; majority from Bollinger vineyards; fermented and matured entirely in old barrels; a blend of almost 300 different wines; aged under natural cork; 8g/L dosage

If the 2002 La Grande Année was as sophisticated and suave as Pierce Brosnan, 2004 is Daniel Craig, more impetuous, more chiselled and more built. Ladies, look out. This is an LGA of a very different personality, driven more by structure and texture than acid, yet with the same core of immense energy and great stamina. It's taut and sinewy, layered with all the complexity of barrel fermentation: nougat, almond, brioche, vanilla, even a touch of fresh coconut. The finish lingers very long, with a soft minerality enclosed in its textural exterior. This is a less powerful vintage for LGA, a wine of poise and balance that will peak a little earlier than the 2002. Yet it remains irrefutably Grande.

BOLLINGER LA GRANDE ANNÉE BRUT 2002 • $$$$

97 points • DISGORGED FEBRUARY 2011 • TASTED IN ADELAIDE AND MELBOURNE

60% pinot noir, 40% chardonnay; majority from Bollinger vineyards; fermented and matured entirely in old barrels; a blend of almost 300 different wines; aged under natural cork for 8 years; 8g/L dosage

The 2002 is an exhilarating LGA that has barely moved since its release two years ago. Calling on a higher proportion of chardonnay to offset the strength of pinot noir in 2002, this is a vintage that brings driving energy, structure and linearity to inimitable Bollinger power. A razor edge of preserved lemon rides over a mountain of plums, fruit mince spice and orange rind. After more than a decade, it still sings with marvellous red berries and stone fruits, lingering with a deep undercurrent of chalk minerality. It will easily improve for another decade yet, and perhaps two.

BOLLINGER LA GRANDE ANNÉE ROSÉ 2004 • $$$$$

96 points • DISGORGED FEBRUARY 2012 • TASTED IN AŸ

68% pinot noir, 32% chardonnay; 6% red wine from the tiny Bollinger vineyard 'La Côte aux Enfants' in Aÿ; aged under natural cork at least 6 years; 7–9g/L dosage

LGA Rosé is La Grande Année with a tiny inclusion of red wine from the same vintage, staining it a pretty pale salmon and tuning its bouquet toward the red spectrum of rose petal perfume, strawberry hull and white cherries, with a refined background of mixed spice. The palate shows impressive focus and linearity, within the inimitable depth that defines Bollinger. With the same immense texture of the white, a grand finish of persistent red fruits and chalk minerality lingers long and steady. Another devastating LGA Rosé.

The Champagne Guide

CAMILLE SAVÈS

(Cah-mill Sah-ves)

6/10

4 RUE DE CONDÉ BP 22 51150 BOUZY
www.champagne-saves.com

$\mathcal{E}$ugène Savès began estate-bottling champagne in Bouzy in 1910. Today, fourth-generation grower Hervé Savès riddles bottles for an hour every morning before carefully tending 10 hectares of family vineyards on the famed Montagne de Reims terroirs of Bouzy, Ambonnay, Tours-sur-Marne and Tauxières-Mutry. Mature pinot noir and chardonnay vines are managed naturally with respect for the soil and crop-thinned to emphasise site character. Wines are fermented in small enamel-lined stainless steel tanks and matured in stainless steel and older oak. Malolactic fermentation is blocked to conserve freshness and acidity, and all wines spend at least four years on lees. An annual production of about 85,000 bottles includes a still pinot noir from old Bouzy vines. Savès champagnes are confident, intense, pinot-led styles, impeccably crafted, honed by malic acidity, and excellent value for money.

CAMILLE SAVÈS CARTE BLANCHE BRUT NV • $

94 points • DISGORGED MAY 2012 • TASTED IN BRISBANE

60% 2008, 40% 2007; 75% pinot noir, 25% chardonnay; Bouzy, Ambonnay, Tauxières-Mutry and Tours-sur-Marne; 4 years on lees; no malolactic fermentation; 8g/L dosage

Hervé Savès calls Bouzy 'the Chambertin of Champagne', and to temper its strength and dominance he adds a touch of chardonnay to this blend. I loved the 2006 base last year, and I love the 2008 even more; a sensational season that charges this intense, pinot-focused blend with scintillating energy and electric acidity. A gorgeous bouquet erupts with the fragrant beauty of freshly picked rose petals and the precision of white cherries and strawberry hull. The palate is intense and lively, with tightly honed malic acidity immaculately counterbalancing the impact of pinot noir from some of Champagne's most powerful villages. It finishes long and even, with subtle pinot noir spice and impeccably restrained dosage. One of best bargains of the year.

CANARD-DUCHÊNE

(Cah-nah Dew-shen)

1 RUE EDMOND-CANARD 51500 LUDES
www.canard-duchene.fr

MAISON FONDÉE EN 1868
FRANCE

From its home in the village of Ludes on the northern slopes of the Montagne de Reims, Canard-Duchêne draws pinot noir and chardonnay from a significant spread of growers, spanning 60 communes in Ludes, the Marne Valley, Côte des Blancs, Sézanne, and a significant proportion from the Aube. Purchased in 2003 by entrepreneur Alain Thiénot (see page 58), the house upholds a sustainable focus, including a certified organic champagne. Canard-Duchêne has traditionally been an inexpensive champagne, and all five cuvées that I tasted this year are relatively affordable. These are largely simple, fruity champagnes, and its prestige cuvées are a significant step up in quality, for a small price premium.

CANARD-DUCHÊNE CUVÉE LÉONIE BRUT NV • $$

87 points • TASTED IN BRISBANE

Pinot noir takes the lead here, with its candied red berry and musk fragrance, and its rounded, fruity palate of musk sticks and red apples. It's a primary and simple champagne with a clean, short finish and balanced dosage.

Canard-Duchêne Brut Rosé NV • $$

88 points • Tasted in Brisbane

A blend of pinot noir and chardonnay, with a pale to medium salmon hue and a pretty bouquet that captures the primary strawberry, raspberry and rose petal characters of pinot noir. The palate changes gears, with both bottles I tasted grinding into a flat landscape, lacking fruit expression, vibrancy and life, with fleeting red berry notes, but ending up hollow, short and dry on the finish. The acidity and dosage find a pleasant balance in a restrained and clean style.

Canard-Duchêne Charles VII Grande Cuvée des Lys Blanc de Blancs Brut NV • $$

94 points • Tasted in Brisbane

This is a different world to Canard's entry cuvées, a well-gauged and even style that accurately highlights beautifully mineral chalk structure. It unites the delicate restraint and taut acidity of chardonnay with slowly emerging toasty, buttery nuances of maturity, topped off with low dosage and considerable persistence.

Canard-Duchêne Charles VII Grande Cuvée des Lys Blanc de Noirs Brut NV • $$

92 points • Tasted in Brisbane

A fruit-focused style of well-gauged balance and lingering persistence. The bouquet is engaging, laced with mixed spice and dark berry fruits, introducing a palate that leads out with blackcurrant notes, culminating in a lingering finish of focused depth of dark berry fruits and an undercurrent of soft mineral texture.

CATTIER

(Ca-tiay)

6 RUE DOM PÉRIGNON 51500 CHIGNY-LES-ROSES
www.cattier.com

CHAMPAGNE

FRANCE

Every summer, roses burst into colour along the streets and premier cru vineyards of the romantic village of Chigny-les-Roses, on the northern slopes of the Montagne de Reims. The family-owned house of Cattier is the most famous in the village, a small négociant house with an annual production of a million bottles, matured in some of the region's deepest cellars. Cattier tends 31 hectares of mainly premier cru vineyards, mostly in Chigny-les-Roses and nearby Ludes, Rilly-la-Montagne and Taissy, with an environmentally sustainable philosophy, supplemented with grapes from across Champagne. Its entry non-vintage cuvée is particularly good value.

CATTIER BRUT PREMIER CRU NV • $

91 points • TASTED IN BRISBANE

Three-vintage blend; 50% pinot meunier, 30% pinot noir, 20% chardonnay; 10g/L dosage

Up from 40% last year, a full 50% pinot meunier lends a depth of colour to its medium straw hue, and a strong red berry theme to its bouquet. A clean, primary, zesty grapefruit and pear focus is retained on the palate, with lively acidity and candied dosage finding a comfortable balance. A reliable bargain.

CATTIER BRUT ABSOLU NV • $

89 points • TASTED IN BRISBANE

45% pinot noir, 30% chardonnay, 25% pinot meunier; zero dosage

Don't be seduced by appearances. Its elegantly streamlined missile-head-shaped bottle and expressive bouquet of pinot noir's red cherries, strawberries and musk are enticing. Then it detonates in an explosion of assertive structure followed by the fallout of a callow finish, screaming out for the finishing touch of dosage to enliven its fruit and calm its structure. A strong case for the value of even a touch of dosage to polish a clean, crisp and lively style.

CHAÎNE D'ÉTOILES

(Shen de-twahl)

6/10

J.P. MARNIQUET, 8-10 RUE DES CRAYÈRES 51480 VENTEUIL
www.champagne-marniquet.com

CHAMPAGNE
CHAÎNE D'ÉTOILES
BRUT RESERVE

*C*haine d'Etoiles is the buyer's brand champagne of Australian agency Echelon Wine Partners, created by J.P. Marniquet in the village of Venteuil, in the heart of the pinot meunier country of the Vallée de la Marne. Here, third-generation winemaker Jean-Pierre Marniquet tends seven hectares of vines biodynamically. In response to the roundness of his pinot meunier-focused blends, purity and finesse are preserved by blocking malolactic fermentation and using low dosages of 6g/L across each of Marniquet's cuvées. Echelon has purposely opted for a slightly lower dosage of 5g/L and it works refreshingly well.

CHAÎNE D'ÉTOILES BRUT RESERVE NV • $

92 POINTS • TASTED IN BRISBANE

Similar blend to J.P. Marniquet's Brut Tradition; 50% pinot meunier, 35% chardonnay, 15% pinot noir; vinified in stainless steel tanks; 3 years on lees

Chaîne d'Étoiles is an enticingly affordable way to discover the joys of pinot meunier-led aperitif champagne. Its meunier presence is declared in the palest hint of blush in its hue and its air of musk sticks and candied red fruits. A fresh fruit palate opens with white cherries and strawberry hull, quickly pulling into a taut finish, accented by tense malic acidity, finishing elegant, refreshing and persistent. The right banks of the Vallée de la Marne leave their signature in fine, mineral chalk texture.

CHARLES HEIDSIECK

(Shahl E-dseek)

7/10

12 ALLÉE VIGNOBLE 51000 REIMS
www.charlesheidsieck.com

CHAMPAGNE
CHARLES
HEIDSIECK

Maison fondée à Reims en 1851

There are three champagne houses named Heidsieck, all from families once related, and Charles is the smallest and the best of them. With an annual production declared to be significantly less than 1 million bottles, Charles Heidsieck is made alongside the larger Piper-Heidsieck in an impressive cuverie at Bezannes on the southern outskirts of Reims, using the same production methods, from essentially the same pool of vineyards and reserve wines. The two houses admirably uphold distinctly unique styles, thanks to their insightful and talented Chef de Cave, Régis Camus, who celebrated his 20th anniversary with the house the day after my most recent visit. With the relaunch of Charles Heidsieck last year, Thierry Roset was appointed Chef de Cave under Camus. His 25 years' experience with the house ensures Charles Heidsieck remains in capable hands.

THE HOUSE STYLES OF CHARLES AND PIPER-HEIDSIECK were once distinguished by their vinification, with Charles always passing through malolactic fermentation. Talented and much-celebrated Chef de Cave, the late Daniel Thibault, transformed and elevated Piper-Heidsieck before his untimely death in 2002, taking it from a non-malolactic to a full malolactic style.

Régis Camus, Daniel's friend and offsider since 1994, was nervous to fill such big shoes, but determined to maintain Thibault's legacy in Charles and to take it further in revitalising Piper. Since the mid-2000s, the houses have found their own separate lives in the selection of crus, styles and ages.

Over several recent tastings, Camus has presented dozens of vins clairs, reserve wines, just-bottled future blends, current release cuvées and old wines from the cellar to illustrate the distinctive styles of the two houses, offering an insight into the past, present and future of Charles Heidsieck and Piper-Heidsieck.

'It is all about the magic of the blend!' Camus announced as he poured the still blends of Piper-Heidsieck Cuvée Brut NV and Charles Heidsieck Brut Réserve NV from the 2010 base vintage.

'It is very important for me that the nuances of the wines speak so as to express the styles of the two different houses.'

Camus introduced a floral register, a fruity register and a toasty register in each of the wines. 'I assign a flower from a different season to each wine. I aim to evoke the first days of spring in Piper, with springtime flowers, sun, vegetal nuances, chlorophyll, fog and smoke. Charles is more about late summer and early fall, with its aromatic flowers, dried flowers and leaves.'

The fruity register follows the floral register. 'Piper is all about apples, pears and citrus, like biting into a crunchy granny smith apple, with a nervousness, minerality and tension. Charles is more about generosity and fleshy expression of late summer fruits, like biting into a peach and having the juice run down your face. It evokes dates, cream and a toasty register of warm brioche just out of the oven, or a crusty Parisian baguette.' The vivacious, dynamic Piper style, with its lighter colour, is designed for warmer weather, to be poured at 6–8°C; the more contemplative, mature, darker Charles for cooler weather, at 8–10°C.

For Camus, the true measure of a house is the quality of its brut NV. In his frank and unpretentious manner he shares how much he had enjoyed Taittinger NV with friends recently. 'The NV wines are the real business for me,' he says. 'After that it's all about having fun! The vintage wines are the vacation photos of the season, signed by Piper or by Charles!'

Non-vintage wines are blends of all three champagne varieties. He uses pinot noir as the core of the blend, the 'vertebra' or 'DNA molecule'; chardonnay for its dynamic liveliness ('It's me on Saturday night!'); and meunier for its fruitiness and freshness, and because 'we particularly like its crunchiness'.

Reserve wines represent about half of the harvest, with Charles Brut Réserve receiving 40% reserve wine, and Piper as little as 6% and as much as 18%. 'Sometimes you meet people in life that you just want to help and see grow to their full potential,' Camus alludes. 'I want to see just how far certain wines will go.' Most of his reserves are chardonnay and pinot noir, but he is proud to show off a tank of 2004 pinot meunier from Verneuil of stunning freshness and vivacity. 'This breaks the absurd impression that pinot meunier can't age!' Reserve wines are stored in 300–500hL stainless steel tanks to guard their freshness, 'so we can use them whenever they're needed, frozen in time like an ice man!'.

Fermentation and maturation are performed exclusively in stainless steel. 'The only wood here is the boardwalk above the tanks!' he quips. The wines are finished with a full dosage of 11g/L to balance the vivacity of Piper, and 12g/L for Charles to 'glorify the wine'. These are generous levels of dosage for modern Champagne, but they integrate neatly into the wines.

Charles Heidsieck Brut Réserve NV replaced Thibault's 'mis en cave' concept, a non-vintage wine clearly labelled with the year in which it was first bottled (an invaluable guide for the astute consumer, since 60% of the blend was from the preceding vintage). The concept was ingenious and the wine was impressive — the best non-vintage style to emerge from the Heidsieck cellars. Camus successfully fought to maintain the concept, in spite of marketing forces that boringly renamed it 'Brut Réserve' and removed the bottling date.

In addition to smart new front labels, back labels of this cuvée have recently been upgraded to some of the most informative among Champagne houses, detailing bottling and disgorgement dates, base vintage, proportion of reserve wines and number of crus in the blend. Let's hope Charles Heidsieck's other cuvées follow.

The global financial crisis hit Piper and Charles Heidsieck hard, throwing the company into some €240 million of debt, and laying off of a quarter of its staff.

Owner Rémy Cointreau put the brand on the market in late 2010, and by March 2011, the sale had been secured by French fashion-led luxury company Société Européenne de Participations Industrielles (EPI). President Christopher Descours named Régis Camus as one of the key reasons the company committed to the purchase. The €412.2 million transaction (including an impressive 800 hectares of vineyards, an inventory of 40 million bottles and California sparkling brand Piper Sonoma) was completed in July 2011. It seems the company is in good hands, under former Veuve Clicquot Managing Director Cécile Bonnefond.

The vineyards of Sacy overlook Bezannes.

CHARLES HEIDSIECK BRUT RÉSERVE NV • $$

94 points • DISGORGED 2012 • TASTED IN BEZANNES

Informative back label: 60% 2007; 40% reserve wines; 60 crus; 3 years in the cellars; bottled 2008; 11g/L dosage

A medium yellow colour and dried flower and autumn leaf notes reflect the maturity of a high proportion of reserve wines and long ageing on lees. A beautifully alluring champagne of comfortable, soft, rounded generosity of honey, white peach and anise, freshened with well-balanced acidity. Lingering chalk minerality provides structure to gentle, caressing persistence.

CHARLES HEIDSIECK ROSÉ RÉSERVE NV • $$$

92 points • TASTED IN BEZANNES

2009 base vintage; one-third of each of the champagne varieties; 20% reserve wines; 10% pinot noir vinified as red wine; 11g/L dosage

The back label of this cuvée used to declare the disgorgement date. No longer, which is a shame, because the rounded autumn-leaf mood of this style is best captured young, when it retains some freshness. Even here, tasted in the cuverie, it's already quite secondary and soft, with hints of wood spice, baked apples and roast chestnuts. There's a dryness to the mouthfeel, which honeyed dosage rounds out at the end. Lost is the lively edge that flattered blends of a few years ago.

CHARLES HEIDSIECK MILLESIME BRUT 2000 • $$$

95 points • TASTED IN BEZANNES

11g/L dosage

This accurate and enticing edition of the generous and rounded 2000 vintage was impressive on release a couple of years ago, and has since evolved to an even more comfortable demeanour. Juicy golden peaches have become baked peaches, dried fruits and figs, with a rising background of butterscotch, patisserie, woodsmoke, toast and even truffles. Its long, spice-accented finish is underlined with soft minerality. A calm and contemplative champagne for long conversations on cool nights.

CHARLES HEIDSIECK BLANC DES MILLÉNAIRES 1995 • $$$$

97 points • DISGORGED 2012 • TASTED IN BEZANNES

The A-list of the Côte des Blancs: Cramant, Avize, Oger, Le Mesnil-sur-Oger and Vertus; 100% chardonnay; minimum 10 years in cellar; 11g/L dosage

Blanc des Millénaires was the oldest currently available champagne in the last edition of this Guide, and — remarkably — it's still available. More incredibly, it's transcended to another plane of silken magnificence at a full 18 years of glorious age. The greatest soils of the Côte des Blancs rumble in precise, finely chalky mineral tones, energising a dizzyingly primary energy of lemon and grapefruit. Its voice has deepened as it's grown through adolescence, textured with nougat and spice, wisps of smoke and nuances of hearth. The finish is an epic revelation, undeviating and undiminished for minutes. No one would have ever expected 1995 to blossom at this age, and such is its monumental poise and seamless completeness, who knows what it might have in store in the decades to come? Sit back and enjoy the spectacle with the one you love, in the largest glasses you can procure.

CHARLES HEIDSIECK BLANC DES MILLÉNAIRES BRUT 1983

96 points • DISGORGED EARLY 2000S • TASTED IN BEZANNES

Charles' sheer stamina is proclaimed at a splendid 30 years of age, even a decade post-disgorgement. The grand slopes of the Côte des Blancs assert their position as the epicentre of the longest-ageing sparkling chardonnay on the planet, projecting a flash of primary lemon zest and white peach as pure and stark as high-noon daylight. Three decades in the bowels of the earth have generated toasty, buttery layers of grilled pineapple and honey. The fine chalky mineral fingerprint of Côte des Blancs grand crus is eternal, energising an astonishingly fresh finish of profound persistence.

Charles Heidsieck aims to evoke the characters of the seasons of Champagne, like these of Ville-Dommange in winter.

CHARTOGNE-TAILLET

(Shah-tone Tie-yair)

6/10

www.chartogne-taillet.com
chartogne-taillet.typepad.fr

CHAMPAGNE
CHARTOGNE-TAILLET

Vigneron à *Merfy* depuis 1683

'*I didn't make this wine, the plants gave it to me,' the young Alexandre Chartogne proclaimed as he hand disgorged a bottle of single-vineyard pinot meunier from 50-year-old vines. Fanatical about drawing every detail of expression from his family vines, he's conducted in-depth studies of root growth and microbiological life, experiments with planting at different densities, he cultures yeasts from the vineyards, vinifies in anything that produces the best result (including concrete eggs and clay pots), and even pulled a vineyard out a few years ago because it didn't produce a wine of 'vibration' — his translation of 'terroir.' I like that.*

THE CHARTOGNE FAMILY HAS BEEN GROWING WINE ON its 11-hectare domain spanning the villages of Merfy and Chenay, just to the north of Reims, since the 16th century. Today, young Alexandre Chartogne, with his parents Elisabeth and Philippe, are the only grower producers in their village.

Once a famed winegrowing district, this area was ravaged during both world wars and has never been replanted to its former glory. The bombings claimed all of the family's vines, their home, cuverie behind, and all but a small section of the original cellar below.

Replanted and rebuilt, their wines today showcase the area's style: less fruity, more rounded, more complex than the wines of the southern Montagne de Reims.

The chalk in Merfy is much deeper than in, for instance, Cramant and Avize, where Alexandre has also worked recent vintages with fellow terroirist and mentor Anselme Selosse. The soil is far more variable here, too, with pockets of limestone, clay and sand, producing some parcels of inferior fruit, and others of grand cru heights. It takes experience, diligence and talent to draw distinguished wines from such terroirs. Chartogne-Taillet is blessed with all three.

'My most important goal is to present the village,' declares Alexandre, whose range includes five single-vineyard wines. In an era in which the holdings of many Champagne growers are sprawling into other villages, Chartogne-Taillet champions a more traditional philosophy, all the more noble in a village in which no other grower makes champagne. The fruit of two hectares of Chartogne-Taillet vineyards in the Vallée de la Marne is sold every year.

'How could I say that I produce good wine in the Marne Valley when I live in Merfy?' Alexandre questions. 'Making our own wine is not about making money,' he reveals.

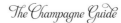

Since he began working his family's estate in 2006, Alexandre has adopted a low-intervention, hands-on, organic approach to encourage soil health, ploughing soils by horse to reduce compaction. He has called on the assistance of famed Burgundian soil expert Claude Bourguignon, and their analyses have shown that when herbicides are not used and the soil is aerated and not compacted, microorganisms are active at all levels, encouraging deep roots and expressive, terroir wines.

Alexandre pulls out vineyards with shallow roots and replants with ungrafted vines. Yields are kept in check by green harvesting (crop thinning) to maintain an average of just 60hL/hectare — two-thirds of the regional average — and as little as 20hL/hectare in his oldest vines. This produces 80,000–100,000 bottles annually, a conservative yield from 11 hectares.

'It is the vineyards that explain the harmony of the wines,' Alexandre emphasises. He sources wild yeast from each plot, which he upholds as crucial for maintaining the purity of his cuvées. So much so that when he was recently offered two hectares to rent in nearby St Thierry, he resolved to buy another cuverie on the other side of the road, just to keep the fruit separate and avoid cross-contamination of wild yeasts.

Since 2008, fermentation has taken place mostly in concrete eggs and old barrels (aged 4–9 years), and occasionally in stainless steel. He considers the reductive character of stainless steel and the woody notes of oak to be a distraction from terroir, favouring concrete eggs for wines requiring more air and lees contact, without the influence of wood. Low sulphur and low dosage are used in every cuvée.

Alexandre's interactive website is one of the best in Champagne, detailing the philosophy and vinification of each cuvée, vineyard maps and soil strata. Back labels are also refreshingly informative, stating base

Alexandre Chartogne ferments in concrete eggs, stainless steel vats and old oak barrels to enhance terroir expression.

vintage, blend, vinification and disgorgement date. A clean, sophisticated new front label brings a Burgundian feel to the brand, in tune with its terroir focus.

These are champagnes of precision, harmony and grace that represent exceptional value for money. It's no surprise that the full production sells out every year.

CHARTOGNE-TAILLET CUVÉE SAINTE-ANNE BRUT NV • $$

93 points • TASTED IN MERFY

2009 base vintage; 50% chardonnay, 50% pinot noir; 100% Merfy; average vine age 25 years; vinified in stainless steel tanks; 4.2g/L dosage

Chartogne-Taillet's entry wine is always good value, and the first disgorgement of the 2009 base vintage is as clean, fresh and harmonious as I've seen it. A blend from across estate Merfy vineyards, with a little more pinot noir in the blend than it has seen in recent years, yet retaining impressive restraint of fresh lemon blossom perfume and very fine pear, apple, lemon and anise flavours. Beautifully integrated, it's at once zesty and soft, with imperceptible dosage and gentle persistence. Definitive Merfy.

CHARTOGNE-TAILLET CUVÉE LE ROSÉ BRUT NV • $$

94 points • DISGORGED JANUARY 2012 • TASTED IN BRISBANE

2008 base vintage; 60% chardonnay, 40% pinot noir; vinified in stainless steel tanks;
red wine from Merfy vineyard Les Orizeaux; 5.5g/L dosage

The understated definition of Merfy fruit is well suited to graceful rosé, and Le Rosé is
consistently one of Champagne's finest at a very enticing price. A wafting and elegant bouquet
sings with rosehip, strawberry hull, red cherries and pomegranate, while the palate strikes a
wonderful contrast between the red fruit generosity and lively acid core of 2008. Light-footed
and delicate from start to finish, this is a masterfully crafted rosé of layered intrigue, with a
crunchy white cherry bite accented by refined, skinsy texture, providing depth and dimension
without interrupting its fragrant flow.

CHARTOGNE-TAILLET BRUT 2006 • $$

89 points • TASTED IN MERFY

60% pinot noir, 40% chardonnay; Les Courres vineyard in the middle of Merfy, rich in clay;
vinified in stainless steel tanks and aged on its lees until March of the following year; 4g/L dosage

This wine has a black label because Alexandre explains that his 'intervention in 2006 was
higher than it is now'. While he describes 2006 as a good year, the wine suggests a weaker
vintage for Chartogne-Taillet. It's toasty and characterised by dried pear and apple fruit, with
notes of bitter almond and a dry finish, reflecting some reduction, which Alexandre attributes
to stainless steel fermentation. It finishes clean, with low dosage and a drying finish.

CHARTOGNE-TAILLET CHEMIN DE REIMS EXTRA BRUT • $$

94 points • TASTED IN MERFY

100% 2008 chardonnay, though only labelled as such on the back label; single vineyard planted 1981; vinified
and aged in an egg fermenter for the first time; 1.4g/L dosage; fewer than 2000 bottles

Alexandre explains that the Chemin de Reims vineyard just below the village of Merfy has historically not
produced great wines, but was already planted by the monks in the 8th century. He's revived the tradition
capably in this well-crafted champagne, contrasting the wonderfully fresh lemon blossom perfume and taut
acid line of chardonnay with a savoury undertone of charcuterie, notes of flinty reduction and the very creamy
mouthfeel derived from enhanced lees texture of egg-fermenter maturation. A wine of fruit character, texture,
interest and balance that unravels beautifully to reveal nuances of spice and grapefruit. The real highlight is its
spine, showcasing the splendid, lingering acidity of 2008, promising great longevity.

CHARTOGNE-TAILLET LES ORIZEAUX EXTRA BRUT 2008 • $$

95 points • TASTED IN MERFY

100% pinot noir; single vineyard on sand over limestone; average vine age 55 years; vinified in barrels aged 2-7 years; 1.4g/L dosage; 2400 bottles

The standout of Chartogne-Taillet's single vineyards this year, tactically utilising the fine chalk mineral texture of its limestone subsoils, beautifully balanced low dosage and classic 2008 acidity to create an electric finish to a deep and generous style. A full yellow hue pre-empts a creamy and immensely textured wine of gingernut biscuit, plum cake and mixed spice generosity, with oak perfectly tucked into its folds, retaining impressive freshness on a long, tangy strawberry hull finish.

CHARTOGNE-TAILLET LES ALLIÉES EXTRA BRUT 2007 • $$

91 points • TASTED IN MERFY

100% pinot meunier; single vineyard, planted 1969 on sand; two new barrels; 1.4g/L dosage; 1792 bottles

Using 100% new oak is usually too much for champagne, though here it is held remarkably well, interrupted only by some fine wood tannin that makes the texture more rustic on the finish. The richness of pinot meunier stands up to wood work, with its plum, red apple and butterscotch flavours melding neatly with the toast, coffee and mixed spice of oak on a full and creamy palate.

CHARTOGNE-TAILLET HEURTEBISE EXTRA BRUT 2008 • $$

91 points • TASTED IN MERFY

100% 2008 chardonnay; 1.07 hectare single vineyard; sand and clay over rich limestone; average vine age 35 years; vinified in stainless steel tanks; 3.4g/L dosage

It is indicative of the scale of Chartogne-Taillet that one of its largest parcels is barely a single hectare. With accessible chalk, this site expresses itself in pronounced mineral mouthfeel, which tussles with the reductive character of stainless steel fermentation to produce a very textural wine, creamy and savoury. Its reduction adds a subtle gherkin-like note to its lemon and lime zest fruit, finishing with good length, refreshing acidity and invisible dosage.

CHARTOGNE-TAILLET 1996

94 points • TASTED IN MERFY

8.5g/L dosage

Chartogne-Taillet's great vintages age confidently for a decade beyond release, and the 1996 retains impressive persistence and balance, only just beginning to dry out on the finish. Rich, powerful and full-bodied, with succulent yellow mirabelle plums and honey becoming toast, butter and cinnamon.

Claude Carré et Fils

(Clawd Cah-ray e Feess)

5/10

42 RUE VAUDEMANGE 51380 TRÉPAIL

*N*ext door to Ambonnay, the premier cru village of Trépail is one of Champagne's highest villages, and unique in the Montagne de Reims as better suited to chardonnay than pinot noir. Growers here for four generations, the Carré family produce 140,000 bottles of appealingly juicy, fruit-focused champagnes exclusively from their 13 hectares in the village. Their blanc de blancs cuvées are the highlights, led by the vintage Cuvée Passion. With very little spread in price across the range, it's well worth trading up. All are now reliably sealed under DIAM.

CLAUDE CARRÉ ET FILS BLANC DE BLANCS BRUT NV • $$

92 points • TASTED IN BRISBANE

A succulent, fruity blanc de blancs that unashamedly proclaims the style of Trépail chardonnay in ripe nectarine and dried-peach fruit, pulled into control on the finish by grippy, crunchy grapefruit zest. It's generous and well composed, with appealing fruit focus, perfect for big parties, certain to keep any crowd well entertained.

CLAUDE CARRÉ ET FILS CUVÉE PASSION BRUT MILLÉSIME 2002 • $$

94 points • TASTED IN BRISBANE

100% chardonnay

A generous and enticing blanc de blancs at its prime, a celebration of 11 years of maturity in tantalising temptations of roast cashew nuts, crème brûlée, burnt butter and the crunchy outside shell of toasted marshmallows. It's creamy and silky, yet retains a refreshingly bright pale-straw hue, and just the right level of vibrant 2002 fruit energy in preserved lemon, dried pear and white summer fruits to keep things lively.

The Champagne Guide

DE SOUSA & FILS

(De Soo-za e Feess)

9/10

12 PLACE LÉON BOURGEOIS 51190 AVIZE
www.champagnedesousa.com

CHAMPAGNE

Sousa

à Avize

Un Champagne de Précision

If you could write the perfect recipe for the greatest champagnes it might read something like this: A tiny grower based in Avize in the exact centre of the grand crus of the Côte des Blancs, sourcing chardonnay from estate vineyards on the finest slopes of the grand crus of Avize, Oger, Cramant and Le Mesnil-sur-Oger, and pinot noir and pinot meunier from the grand crus of Aÿ and Ambonnay. Vines would be very old and painstakingly tended biodynamically by an experienced artisan, fanatical about drawing every detail of character and minerality from every site. Crop levels and dosage would be low, oak would be used generously when the fruit called for it and sparingly when it did not, blending would be performed from a deep pool of reserve wines, cuvées would mature long on their lees in cold cellars, and disgorgement dates and dosages would be printed on every bottle. Welcome to the wonderful world of De Sousa.

ON PAPER, THIS MIGHT BE THE FINEST RECIPE IN ALL of Champagne. But do the wines live up to it?

I first met third-generation head of the house Erick de Sousa over his gigantic French oak table in his tasting room in the heart of Avize. 'My job is to maximise the minerality in the vines,' he commenced, and everything from this point served to demonstrate his vision — every cuvée opened, every vineyard technique expounded, every cellar procedure demonstrated.

Over almost 30 years, Erick has refined the best of traditional thinking and progressive new methods to revitalise, transform and grow the estate to become one of the finest on the Côte des Blancs. Production has increased to 100,000 bottles annually and

vineyard holdings have grown to 42 plots spanning 11 hectares, including 2.5 hectares of coveted old vines in Avize, Cramant and Oger. With the exception of his entry Brut Tradition, every vineyard source is grand cru, with 70% of vines over 40 years of age and a significant percentage 50–60 years old. Some planted by his grandfather are more than 70 years old. 'I must give my wine the minerality that can only come from old vines,' he emphasises.

The roots of these old vines plunge deep into the soil, even as far as 35–40 metres into the chalk, he suggests. Here they extract the salts and trace elements that are fundamental to the structure of these wines. 'Minerality comes from the chalk,' he says.

Old vines have a natural moderating effect on yields, which generally average just 60hL per hectare from 8000 vines, 25–30% less than the average of the appellation. Such yields provide greater concentration and permit him to harvest only when the grapes have attained full ripeness. 'I want to maintain the maturity in the sugar level at harvest, but not too high, so as to keep a balance of acidity and minerality,' he explains. 'High maturity at harvest provides opulence, while minerality maintains freshness.'

In his own words, Erick De Sousa 'lives in the rhythm of the vines' and regards his work in the vineyards as the key to the quality of the grapes. Respect for the vine and the earth is paramount, and he has spent a decade converting the domaine to biodynamic viticulture, with full certification granted in 2010. Biodynamics for him is about equipping his old vines to capture minerality, 'to encourage the vine to draw deeply the trace elements specific to each terroir and provide different characteristics to each cuvée'. The soil is ploughed for ventilation and to restore microbial life, with a horse in some vineyards.

To increase production, de Sousa purchased new cellars on the opposite side of the village square in 2004 for his négociant label, Zoémie de Sousa. With walls at least half a metre thick, the stable temperature is ideal for ageing wines. When he showed me through, I was surprised by the small scale of production. His enamelled tanks are tiny, he owns one foudre for ageing red wine, a small wooden vat for red wine fermentation, and little 225-litre barrels made from oak harvested in Avize and from a cooper friend in Burgundy.

Fruit from vines older than 50 years is fermented in small oak barrels, with regular bâtonnage to enhance depth and breadth. He has used about 15% new barrels for his top cuvées, but increased the proportion slightly in 2004. Chaptalisation is performed when necessary, the first fermentation is initiated with natural yeasts, and all wines pass through malolactic fermentation. Sulphur dioxide is used sparingly.

Narrow and atmospheric, the 200-year-old cellars under the house run 800 metres directly under the square in the middle of the village. A stable temperature of 10°C is ideal for long ageing. Here, the old method of poignettage is practised, in which autolytic flavours are enhanced by shaking the bottles by hand to stir up the lees. Bottles are also riddled by hand. All now display the bottling date on back labels, allowing the base vintage of NV cuvées to be determined, since bottling always occurs in the year following harvest.

De Sousa's profound prestige Cuvée des Caudalies' claim to uniqueness is not so much that it is a prestige cuvée of non-vintage blend, but just how this blend is assembled. Sourced from chardonnay vines exceeding 50 years of age in Avize, Oger, Le Mesnil-sur-Oger and Cramant, and vinified in small barrels with no chaptalisation, it is blended as a solera of reserve wines that currently spans the 11 harvests from 1995 to 2005. Cuvée des Caudalies is also released as an ultra-complex vintage wine and a mesmerising rosé.

De Sousa has risen to a rightful place among Champagne's greatest producers under Erick's visionary guidance over the past quarter century, now ably assisted by his three children, Charlotte, Julie and Valentin, all of whom have completed degrees at the local wine school. Theirs are masterfully grown and crafted wines, every one of which is brilliantly mineral, profoundly exact and beautifully fresh. At the end of a long tasting and vigorous conversation over a massive oak table, I told Erick as much.

'It's all about mature vines with roots that go deep into the soil,' he replied with unassuming humility.

And it must also have a little to do with what is indeed the finest recipe in Champagne.

ZOÉMIE DE SOUSA BRUT PRÉCIEUSE NV • $$

91 points • DISGORGED JANUARY 2012 • TASTED IN AVIZE

2009 base vintage; from purchased fruit and younger estate vines in Avize, Oger, Le Mesnil-sur-Oger, Cramant and Chouilly; vinified in 400-litre barrels; aged 2 years on lees; 7g/L dosage; 20,000–25,000 bottles

Zoémie is De Sousa's négociant brand, and doesn't carry the finesse or persistence of the estate wines. Précieuse is a softly mineral wine with good fruit expression of golden delicious apple, ripe lemon and white peach, with bready development and notes of brioche and honey.

Zoémie De Sousa Brut Merville NV • $$

92 points • Disgorged February 2012 • Tasted in Avize

2009 base vintage; 50% chardonnay, 40% pinot noir, 10% pinot meunier; similar blend to Brut Tradition, but from younger vines of 20–25 years of age, with shorter lees ageing of almost 2 years; 7g/L dosage

A well-made, clean, fresh, fruity style that meets its brief of uncomplicated, easy drinking for apéritifs and weddings. Its simple fruit focus accents golden delicious apples, supported with subtle biscuit notes, well-balanced dosage, linear acid persistence and subtle mineral texture.

De Sousa Brut Tradition NV • $$

94 points • 2008 base vintage with 20–30% 2007 reserve, disgorged October 2012 • Tasted in Avize

93 points • 2007 base with 20–30% 2006 reserve; disgorged 16 December 2011 • Tasted in Brisbane

50% chardonnay, 40% pinot noir, 10% pinot meunier; vinified in tanks; aged 3 years on lees; 7g/L dosage

The mineral presence of De Sousa's wines speaks loud and clear, right from his entry non-vintage blend, and it looks finer in the great 2008 vintage than I've ever seen it. Beautifully pure and pristine, with a confident chardonnay lead, an air of lemon blossom, white pepper and fennel, and a crisp, fresh palate of lemon zest and granny smith apple. A delightfully refreshing and persistent apéritif style that carries soft, chalky mineral expression.

De Sousa Grand Cru Réserve Blanc de Blancs Brut NV • $$

95 points • Disgorged February 2012 • Tasted in Avize, Adelaide and Brisbane

2008 base vintage with 30% 2007 aged in barrels; 35–45-year-old vines in Avize, Oger, Cramant and Le Mesnil-sur-Oger; aged 3 years on lees; 7g/L dosage

A breathtakingly refined De Sousa, the very definition of chardonnay from the heart of its finest terroirs, bursting with the delicacy of lemon blossom, lemon zest and anise aromas. The palate is pristine, seamless and delightfully pure, with white-peach fruit becoming crunchy pears and almonds on the finish. Its minerality is a revelation, frothing with salty sea-surf chalk of impeccable definition. Intricately integrated, almost silky in its polish, yet at every instant poised and pristine; it will age long, charged with the sustaining vibrancy of the magnificent 2008 vintage.

De Sousa Rosé Brut NV • $$

93 points • Disgorged April 2013 • Tasted in Avize

2011 base vintage; 90% chardonnay, 10% pinot noir red wine from Aÿ, aged 1 year in oak for concentration; 7g/L dosage

Freshness and fruitiness are the aspirations of this young blend, yet in the midst of its pretty red cherry, rosehip, blackcurrant and anise preciousness, the salty chalk minerality of Avize makes its statement. Barrel ageing of red wine contributes to its savoury complexity, reinforcing notes of tamarillo and pepper. Finely poised tannins build impressive back palate textural structure, making for a particularly versatile food-matching style.

De Sousa Cuvée 3A Extra Brut NV • $$

96 points • Disgorged October 2012 • Tasted in Avize

2008 base vintage; a blend of the 3 'A' grand crus of Avize chardonnay (50%) and Aÿ and Ambonnay pinot noir (50%); blended prior to fermentation to increase harmony; 50% vinified in old oak barrels; 3g/L dosage; 8000 bottles

The trend in Champagne is towards keeping parcels separate to increase definition, but De Sousa has boldly co-fermented to create a profoundly seamless union between chardonnay and pinot noir from three of Champagne's most distinctive villages. Chardonnay's pristine white peach, grapefruit, apple and pear is gently interwoven with pinot's rich red cherry, cherry kernel, anise and fig, never compromising the character of each village. Oak is sensitively played, giving deep voice to a tremendous undercurrent of salty chalk minerality. It's so popular it's sold out for four months of the year. Little wonder.

De Sousa Cuvée des Caudalies Blanc de Blancs Grand Cru NV • $$$

96 points • Disgorged 16 December 2011 • Tasted in Avize and Brisbane

2006 base vintage with 50% from a solera of every vintage from 1995 to 2005; 100% Avize chardonnay from vines aged over 50 years; fermented entirely in small oak barrels; 5–6g/L dosage

From 12 vintages, all oak fermented, it might appear that this recipe could play havoc with purity and focus. To the contrary, and to the credit of the genius of Erick de Sousa and the all-conquering presence of Avize chalk, this is a wine of remarkable purity. Its minerality is an epiphany, mouth-filling and all-encompassing; one of the most profoundly deep-set, salty chalk signatures in all of Champagne. A magnificent celebration of controlled power, with pristine white fruits, lemon, grapefruit zest and fennel, and the depth, breadth and height of stone fruits of all kinds. Eighteen years of maturity brings a walk through an autumnal landscape, a layered, spicy complexity of golden leaves, nutmeg, cloves, anise, figs, cherry kernel and roast chestnuts, bringing a depth and generosity to the finish unusual for blanc de blancs. In the midst of such complexity, it maintains utter control and poise.

The Champagne Guide

De Sousa Cuvée des Caudalies Brut Rosé NV • $$$$

98 points • Disgorged 17 November 2011 • Tasted in Avize, London and Brisbane

2006 base vintage with 50% solera of every vintage from 1995 to 2005, same chardonnay base as
the Caudalies; 10% Aÿ pinot noir red wine vinified and matured in oak for 1 year; 48 months on lees

Such is the powerful colour, pure fruit and delicate structure of De Sousa's red wine that a
10% dose transforms a pristine blanc de blancs into one of Champagne's most spectacular rosés.
Drinking Cuvée des Caudalies Rosé is nothing less than a deeply moving emotional experience,
such is the relentless beauty of haunting red cherry fruits and pomegranates that hover in
suspension long through the finish. A maelstrom of complexity erupts from the bouquet in
freshly picked red fruits of all kinds, florist shop, baked figs, cherry kernel, anise, licorice and
plum pudding. The palate is a riveting spectacle of understated power and immense complexity,
in a refined frame of tightly defined Avize focus and monumental mineral presence. A frothing
wave of sea-salt minerality lifts the wine in a towering spray, like a big ocean swell crashing
against rocks. The layered spice of a deep solera and barrel work are intricately entwined and
perfectly integrated, concluding with immense depth and pencil lead definition.

De Sousa Cuvée des Caudalies Grand Cru Millésime Brut 2006 • $$$$

95 points • Tasted in Avize

Avize, Oger, Le Mesnil-sur-Oger and Cramant chardonnay with Aÿ and Ambonnay pinot noir;
100% barrel fermented; 2000 bottles

The contrasting shades of this wine make for a captivating journey, beginning generous and
deep with the savoury spice complexity of barrel fermentation, built out with subtle notes of
smoked bacon and roast nuts. A core of fresh lemon and white peach fruit, becoming tangy
preserved lemon, finishes tense and structured, with the stamina to age long. Signature
De Sousa minerality leaves its stamp in full, fine, mouth-filling, salty chalk.

De Sousa Cuvée des Caudalies Le Mesnil Extra Brut 2005 • $$$$

94 points • Disgorged November 2011 • Tasted in Avize

100% Le Mesnil-sur-Oger chardonnay; held in the cellar another year for release after the
2006 Cuvée des Caudalies; aged 72 months on lees; 1500 bottles, with an allocation of just
300 to be released each year

This wine proclaims its texture and structure before its fruit, a blessing in the smooth
and warm year of 2005, which was better weathered by the soil of Le Mesnil-sur-Oger than
elsewhere. Accessible pure chalk builds majestic structure of pronounced salty chalk mineral
texture, accentuated by the drying, nutty influence of barrels and the characteristically dry
finish of 2005. The result is a wine of solid structure, with a note of bitter hazelnut on the
finish, admirably upholding characters of lemon, white peach, fennel, marzipan and vanilla.

DELAMOTTE

(Deh-la-mot)

6/10

5-7 RUE DE LA BRÈCHE D'OGER 51190 LE MESNIL-SUR-OGER

www.salondelamotte.com

CHAMPAGNE

DELAMOTTE

Le Mesnil sur Oger depuis 1760

For all intents and purposes, Delamotte is effectively the second label of Salon (page 315), though the house prefers to refer to the two as 'sister houses'. It celebrated its 250th birthday recently and has been Salon's neighbour for more than a century, but the two joined forces in 1988 and were purchased by Laurent-Perrier the following year. Laurent-Perrier handles the winemaking for both brands.

DELAMOTTE PRODUCES 700,000 BOTTLES ANNUALLY from 35 hectares of its own vineyards, largely in Le Mesnil-sur-Oger, and a similar volume of purchased fruit. Chardonnay is sourced principally from the grand crus of Le Mesnil-sur-Oger, Oger, Avize and Cramant, and pinot noir for its Brut NV and Rosé from the southern Montagne de Reims, primarily Bouzy, Ambonnay and Tours-sur-Marne.

Delamotte also receives all the leftovers from Salon, and in years when Salon doesn't declare (two in five, to date), this means the entire Salon harvest is dedicated to Delamotte's Blanc de Blancs vintage and non-vintage and Brut NV. All the fruit of the Jardin de Salon itself currently goes to Delamotte, and will for at least the next few years, since the vines are only 12 years of age. For other parcels, the ultimate destiny of each tank (there are no barrels here) is quickly determined post-fermentation, since Delamotte undergoes malolactic fermentation while Salon does not.

Delamotte has been riding a steep growth curve for the past 15 years, almost quadrupling its output from 250,000 bottles, with a target of 1 million in the next five to six years, spurred by strong demand across Asia. The vision of Salon Delamotte President Didier Depond is to make Delamotte the reference house for blanc de blancs.

Since Salon is blanc de blancs, it is no surprise that Delamotte's blanc de blancs (both its vintage and non-vintage) are its soaring highlights, and today represent close to 50% of Delamotte's production.

Delamotte Brut NV • $$

85 points • Tasted in Le Mesnil-sur-Oger

2008 base vintage; 50% chardonnay, 30% pinot noir, 20% pinot meunier

On the reputation of 2008, this blend should sing with even greater clarity than those preceding it. Instead, the bottle poured for me by the house was an awkward accord of candied fruits and freshly tilled earth. Far from the clean precision of last year's blend, an earthy grubbiness dulls its focus and vibrancy.

Delamotte Blanc de Blancs NV • $$

93 points • Tasted in Le Mesnil-sur-Oger

2005 base vintage

After the magnificent 2004 base vintage last year, it was inevitable that the riper 2005 vintage could never hit the same high notes, yet Delamotte has pulled a more than respectable result from a less than outstanding season. A refreshing, clean and lively bouquet of lemon blossom and apple is a credit to a non-vintage aged so long on its lees. A taut, honed palate is accented with subtle notes of gunflint reduction. Well-defined mineral purity lingers long on the finish, contrasting with the ripe stone fruits of 2005 and slowly rising notes of bottle-developed toast.

Delamotte Rosé NV • $$$

92 points • Disgorged April 2012 • Tasted in Le Mesnil-sur-Oger

2005 base vintage; 80% pinot noir from Tours-sur-Marne, Bouzy, Ambonnay and Louvois, co-fermented with 20% Le Mesnil-sur-Oger chardonnay; similar saignée process as Laurent-Perrier; aged at least 36 months in the cellar, but for this bottle more than double this time; 7g/L dosage

Last year I raised the alarm on horribly stale bottles still lingering on shelves. This is a more recent disgorgement, though the consumer is none the wiser, since the house refuses to print disgorgement dates on bottles. If you can be sure the stock is fresh, you'll be rewarded with an extroverted rosé of medium salmon hue and expressive strawberry and caramel aromas. The palate is spicy and flavoursome, true to the generosity of its pinot noir sources and the rounded, plush shape of the 2005 vintage, finishing soft, with subtle minerality.

Delamotte Blanc de Blancs 2002 • $$$

95 points • Disgorged April 2012 • Tasted in Le Mesnil-sur-Oger

Le Mesnil-sur-Oger, Oger and Avize, with 5–10% purchased fruit from Cramant, which Didier Depond adores as 'the cream to link the villages of the south'

Salon Delamotte President Didier Depond waxes lyrical about the 2002 Salon, due to land some time in 2014. Delamotte's take on this vintage is a much more immediate style, right at the peak of its life. Toasty development of brioche, roast nuts and honey meshes beautifully with an undercurrent of grapefruit, lemon and succulent yellow plum and white peach. A wine of buttery smoothness and gentle generosity, upholding the lively acidity of 2002 and the inimitable chalk minerality that defines the grand crus of the Côte des Blancs.

DEUTZ

(Derts)

8/10

6 RUE JEANSON 51160 AŸ

www.champagne-deutz.com

FONDÉ   EN 1838

Champagne

DEUTZ

AY- FRANCE

Deutz is growing like a mad thing, tripling sales and production from 600,000 bottles in the late 1990s to more than 2 million every year from 2004 to 2008, dipping only slightly in response to the global economy and returning to 2 million in 2012. For such a breathtaking pace of expansion, the standards it has maintained are not only admirable, they're downright remarkable. A couple of rough vintages aside, there isn't one wine out of place in this line of crisp, pure champagnes, impeccably crafted in a style of elegant finesse.

DEUTZ IS STILL SETTING A CRACKING PACE. THE MAIN press house in Aÿ was razed in 2010 and two new layers of cellars dug underneath. A completely new press house was completed just in time for vintage 2011, with new four- and eight-tonne presses, a new bottling line and increased capacity for reserve wines. These extensions increased cellar capacity from 8 million to 11.5 million bottles, and Deutz is now bottling its annual production target of 2.5 million bottles.

Owned by Louis Roederer, the house lays claims to just 42 of the total 200 hectares from which it sources fruit. Most of the supply increase in recent years has come from purchased fruit. 'We are looking for vineyards to buy, but the availability of good vineyards is not high,' president Fabrice Rosset explains. To reward quality, growers are paid not only based on the standard of their terroir, but the quality of grapes delivered.

Can the house continue to maintain quality while following such a steep trajectory of growth? 'It is crucial that we maintain the same quality of supplies,' Chef de Cave Michel Davesne emphasises. The intention is to maintain the same suppliers, continuing to source from within 35 kilometres of Aÿ and using only the first pressings. He is confident that the investments in the new winery and cellars will only aid the pursuit of quality. 'There has been no compromise in growing to 2 million, and there won't be in growing to 2.5 million.'

Assuming the house can maintain reliable supply channels, Deutz will be well equipped to continue to achieve its target. Recently modernised disgorgement and warehousing facilities are already in operation, and 8 million bottles wait in anticipation in three kilometres of cellars extending into the hill, up to 65 metres deep beneath the vineyard behind Aÿ.

With sustainable agriculture a priority, Deutz is trialling organics. Chemical pesticides have been abandoned, and grasses cultivated in the mid-rows of some plots to avoid the use of herbicides and reduce yields.

Pruning techniques and green harvests have also been adopted to reduce yields to slightly below the average.

Even in its young vins clairs, the clean, crisp, fresh, pristine focus of the house is abundantly clear. Deutz preserves the purity of its fruit through fermentation in stainless steel tanks (no barrels), temperature controlled to 16–17°C. Malolactic fermentation is encouraged systematically. Non-vintage wines are aged for two and a half years on lees, and are rested in the cellar for a further six months post-disgorgement.

Its consistently refreshing, pure lemon sunshine freshness is presented in classic, smartly labelled bottles.

DEUTZ BRUT CLASSIC NV • $$

93 points • DISGORGED JULY 2012 • TASTED IN AŸ AND BRISBANE

2009 base vintage with 25% reserves from 2008 and 2007; one-third of each of chardonnay, pinot noir and pinot meunier; a blend from villages across the Marne, with a focus on Aÿ and Mareuil-sur-Aÿ; 9g/L dosage; around 1.6 million bottles annually

Brut Classic is the barometer of Deutz, representing 80% of the volume of the house, so if any cracks develop in the wake of increasing production, they will surely appear here. To the contrary, this refreshing apéritif style is as clean and lively as ever, a honed and taut champagne of focused lemon zest, pure lemon juice and red apples, finishing with well-expressed chalk minerality. A hint of wild honey dosage sits neatly behind tense, fine acidity. Subtle notes of flinty reduction are not out of place in this style, and quickly evaporate in the glass.

DEUTZ BRUT ROSÉ NV • $$

94 points • TASTED IN AŸ AND BRISBANE

2009 base vintage; 90% chardonnay; 10% pinot noir red wine blended from old vines in Aÿ and Mareuil-sur-Aÿ

The pure, fresh style of Deutz is perfectly suited to elegant and restrained rosé, and the house is unusual in producing the style at three different levels. The prowess of the house in crafting pristine rosé is displayed right from the entry NV rendition. A subtle and pretty perfume of rose petal, red cherry and strawberry hull carries evenly through the palate. The finish is refreshing, enlivened with vibrant acidity and textural mineral mouthfeel, with dosage impeccably measured for the restraint of the style.

DEUTZ BLANC DE BLANCS 2007 • $$$

95 points • TASTED IN AŸ AND BRISBANE

45% Avize; 40% Le Mesnil-sur-Oger; 8% Villers-Marmery; 7% Cramant, Oger and Chouilly

Embedded into two of the Côte des Blancs' most confident grand crus, this is a delightful blanc de blancs and an impressive expression of 2007. Delicacy meets power, juxtaposing the freshness of white lilies, the flavour of lemon zest and the structure of racy acidity with the grand cru depth and intensity of white peach and yellow mirabelle plum. Six years in the cellar have built notes of brioche, nougat, vanilla pod, nutmeg and cinnamon, framed in focused, mouth-filling chalk texture that crashes like a wave with sea-salt minerality.

Deutz Brut Millésime 2006 • $$$

94 points • Tasted in Aÿ

60% pinot noir from Aÿ, Mareuil-sur-Aÿ, Bouzy, Ambonnay and Verzenay;
30% chardonnay from Avize and Le Mesnil-sur-Oger; 10% pinot meunier from the
Vallée de la Marne; 10g/L dosage

This vintage has been current for a couple of years, and its slow evolution is testimony to
its endurance, still upholding primary lemon zest flavours and lively acidity. The passage
of time has built excellent mature notes of long-lingering toast, roasted walnuts and
preserved lemon, sitting comfortably alongside a subtle wisp of gunpowder reduction.
Its finesse and soft, mineral definition are impressive, particularly for a cuvée confidently
led by pinot noir from some of its boldest villages, building great persistence and considerable
depth to the mid-palate.

Deutz Brut Rosé Millésime 2008 • $$$

96 points • Tasted in Aÿ

There is a buzz in the air in Champagne as some of the first great 2008 vintage wines begin
to hit the streets, and I have an ever-rising feeling that this may prove to be Champagne's
finest season of the past 20 years, after 1996. Deutz Rosé adds further weight to this claim,
a magnificently graceful, ultra-sensual, medium salmon-tinted celebration of the remarkable
freshness and wondrous acidity delivered by this vintage. Capturing a knife-edge balance of
breathtaking elegance and alluring fruit presence in vintage rosé is one of Champagne's finest
arts, and Deutz has nailed it in this cuvée. Gorgeous red cherry, cherry kernel and strawberry
fruit purity finds pristine focus on a finish of fine acidity and wonderful texture, frothing and
churning with sea-salt minerality.

Deutz Amour de Deutz Blanc de Blancs Brut
Millésime 2005 • $$$$

89 points • Tasted in Aÿ

Avize, Le Mesnil-sur-Oger and a little Villers-Marmery; 9g/L dosage

A lesser vintage of Amour de Deutz, plagued by the drying ripeness that characterises this
season. It leads out with generous pear fruit, dried apple and hints of lemon zest, closing
dry and textural with roast chestnut development and a chewy, almond skin finish.

The Champagne Guide

Deutz Amour de Deutz Blanc de Blancs Brut Millésime 2003 • $$$$

92 points • Tasted in Brisbane

There is a concerning trend to release prestige cuvées in Champagne's lesser seasons; and two such vintages of Amour de Deutz on the loose at once is alarming. To its credit, this bottle has held its fruit admirably for a late-release 2003, in layers of ripe pears, mirabelle, golden delicious apples and wild honey. It's a rich, voluptuous champagne of creamy, custardy sweetness, even hinting at caramel. A little unsteady on the finish, its fruit fades in the wake of the firm phenolic structure that characterises 2003. Still, quite impressive for this tough season.

Deutz Cuvée William Deutz Brut Millésime 2000 • $$$$

96 points • Tasted in Aÿ

The year 2000 in Champagne was all about golden sunlight, fleshy succulence and layers of intensity. William Deutz bottles the essence of the season in this deep-hued and explosively concentrated champagne. Gorgeous fruit intensity of mirabelle plums, baked peaches and honey is accented by brioche and lingering spice. In spite of its proportions, it is pulled obediently into line by fresh, crisp acidity and long-lingering chalky, salty minerality. A vintage to drink right away with rich main-course fish or roast chicken dishes. The first bottle opened was slightly cork tainted; the second was magnificent.

Deutz Cuvée William Deutz Brut Millésime 1999 • $$$$

96 points • Tasted in Brisbane

55% pinot noir, 35% chardonnay, 10% pinot meunier

Some years have passed since its release, and nothing has interrupted the magnificent upwelling of chalk minerality that elevates this champagne. Presence, poise and balance are as impeccable as ever, a wonderful culmination of primary white fruits, accented with the complexity of dried pear, vanilla, roast nuts, even toasted marshmallows. A marvellous William Deutz with the presence to partner main-course fare.

Deutz Cuvée William Deutz Rosé Millésime 2002 • $$$$

97 points • Tasted in Aÿ and Brisbane

65% pinot noir, 35% chardonnay; 8000–9000 bottles

The king of Deutz's rosé trilogy is crafted around a fine structure and deep-set chalk minerality that elevate it to another spiritual level. The electric energy of 2002 contrasts the grand proportions of intensity built over a decade in the cellar. Delicate and elegant, with an exquisite air of rose petals, black cherries, raspberries and wild strawberries, rich with plum cake, baked apples, cherry kernel, anise, vanilla, honey, even toffee and Christmas cake spice, yet never heavy or clumsy. A triumph of pinot noir from a sensational vintage, exemplifying profound generosity and inexplicable complexity, while grasping impeccable freshness, detail and purity. One of the most triumphant wines to emerge from this great house in the modern era.

DEVAUX

(Deh-voh)

6/10

DOMAINE DE VILLENEUVE, 10110 BAR-SUR-SEINE
www.champagne-devaux.fr

CHAMPAGNE

*C*hampagne Devaux is the label of the large Union Auboise cooperative based in Bar-sur-Seine in the heart of the Champagne outpost of Côte des Bar. Owned by more than 800 growers, with some 1400 hectares under vine, the cooperative is the largest grower in the region and sells a substantial quantity of juice to other houses. Its headquarters are located in the country, on the banks of the Seine, where the soil is too moist for subterranean storage, so air-conditioned, industrial warehousing is employed. This hardly reads like an endorsement, but the cooperative is innovative and progressive, and its value-for-money champagnes are well made, showcasing the fruit power and definition of the Côte des Bar.

THE UNION AUBOISE DEDICATES JUST 100 HECTARES TO the production of Devaux, and even this is more than 1.5 times the requirement for producing 650,000 bottles annually. Chef de Cave Michel Parisot visits every vineyard prior to harvest to decide which will be rejected.

Twenty-one years at Devaux have blessed Parisot with a keen insight into the diversity of terroirs across the many valleys of the large region of the Aube. He compares some with the soils of Chablis, and others with those of Burgundy — no surprise, with many of his vineyards closer to both than the Côte des Blancs.

'We are not about comparing the Côte des Bar with the Côte des Blancs,' he emphasises. 'We have vineyards in both, and we focus on the diversity of Champagne in its villages, landscapes and finished products.'

Pinot noir rules in the Côte des Bar, and leads most of Parisot's cuvées, but chardonnay is increasing in the region, showing particular promise in Urville, and finding representation in the wines accordingly. Since 1987, Devaux has honed its attention more resolutely toward the Aube, focusing on pinot noir and chardonnay, removing pinot meunier from its cuvées.

Parisot works closely with his growers, though a count of more than 800 growers requires a team of six full-time liaison officers to help them better manage their vineyards. 'We decided some years ago that we want to have a large representation of organic vines, and we tell our growers that this is how they should manage their vineyards,' Parisot reports. Devaux performs extensive experimental work, investigating different techniques in its vineyards.

Growers are paid a premium for fruit destined for the premium D de Devaux range, which currently represents 30% of the brand. There is an aspiration to increase this to 50%, and to slowly grow production by 5% every year, a conservative target given the vineyard resources at Devaux's disposal.

The house is equally progressive in vinification, creating a vast array of different parcels from every vintage. Parisot compares his philosophy to that of a perfumer, creating different flavours to assemble a blend of great complexity. 'The first work is in the vineyard; the second is to create many different possibilities for fermentation and vinification, so as to produce a large palette of flavours,' he says.

This defines an interesting and unusual house style that encompasses a bit of everything — tank fermentation, barrel fermentation, large barrels and small, bâtonnage, full malolactic, no malolactic. With 500 tanks and barrels of all sizes at his disposal, the permutations for Parisot's experimentation are vast, and in the rare and privileged position of selling an enormous 95% of every harvest to other houses, he is afforded the luxury to keep only those ferments that suit his blends.

Malolactic fermentation is completed for the Devaux range, and carried out or blocked for D de Devaux, according to the parcel and the year. Parisot likes the complexity of blending with the two so much that he will sometimes split parcels and allow part to go through malolactic fermentation.

The D de Devaux wines are fermented in oak barrels, and large stocks of reserve wines are kept in large oak tuns of 3000–7000-litre capacity for up to three years. This affords the opportunity for slow, natural oxidation. 'I don't like oxidative wines, I like well-developed wines,' Parisot emphasises. 'For me a good champagne should have just the beginning of oxidation flavours, but always maintain its freshness.'

A small percentage of reserves are fermented in small barrels and matured on lees with weekly bâtonnage for four months. After extensive trials fermenting in 300-litre barrels and 600-litre demi-muids over the past decade, Parisot has settled on 300-litre barrels. 'We thought we would obtain a finer and more elegant wine from the demi-muids, but it was not true! They never ranked first in our tastings,' he explains.

Parisot's latest pursuit has been in pioneering the use of local oak from the Côte des Bar, motivated by an imperative to improve the company's carbon footprint. He is working with the University of France to compare oak from the Côte des Bar, Montagne de Reims and Argonne, but admits that just two years into the trial, he is yet to identify any differences in flavour. 'We would like to determine whether a certain forest suits a particular parcel of pinot noir or chardonnay, but it will take us many years, and maybe we will find that the place of origin doesn't matter!' he admits.

A focus on raising quality since 1987 has seen a trend towards increasing use of reserve wines, an impressive increase in bottle age of non-vintage cuvées from two years to between three and five, and a progressive decrease in dosage to under 10g/L. Each of three or four different disgorgements for each cuvée receive a different dosage, generally 7–9g/L.

A number of cuvées are sealed under DIAM closures and Parisot is delighted. 'We have only had two complaints in four years regarding the look of these closures,' he says. Unfortunately, the D de Devaux range is still consigned to natural cork, but Parisot believes he's close to convincing the company's president to move the entire range across to DIAM.

Parisot's innovative and progressive spirit continues to drive progress at Devaux. 'It is always possible to improve,' he maintains. 'We don't know the figures yet, but this year won't be a good year for champagne sales. We can't sit on our reputation. We must always look for ways to improve.'

DEVAUX GRANDE RÉSERVE BRUT NV • $$

92 points • DISGORGED MID-2012 • TASTED IN BAR-SUR-SEINE AND BRISBANE

2007 base with 20–25% reserves from 2006, 2005, 2004 and 2002; a small portion of reserves aged in large oak tuns; 70% pinot noir, 30% chardonnay; full malolactic fermentation; aged at least 3 years; 9g/L dosage; DIAM closure

An impeccably assembled blend, showcasing the enticing generosity and definition of the Côte des Bar at an affordable price. The richness of pinot noir's rounded peach personality, complexity of honey and lingering mixed spice are enlivened with a vibrant acid backbone and soft minerality, bringing balance and focus to the finish. Bottles tasted in Australia showed a little more brioche development.

Devaux Blanc de Noirs NV • $$

91 points • Tasted in Bar-sur-Seine

2009 base with 20% reserve wines; 100% Côte des Bar pinot noir; full malolactic fermentation; aged at least 3 years; 9g/L dosage; DIAM closure

Close your eyes and you could be drinking rosé, such is the precision of strawberry hull and red cherry fruit paraded here. The 2009 vintage emphasises the generous fruit expression of pinot noir, and Michel Parisot says he's never seen such clean, disease-free fruit in the Côtes des Bar, albeit lower in acidity than 2008. A soft, early-drinking style with succulent fruit sweetness, yet finishing fresh and focused.

Devaux Cuvée Rosée Brut NV • $$

92 points • Tasted in Bar-sur-Seine

20% reserve wines, partially aged in barrel; 80% pinot noir and 20% chardonnay; 12–14% red wine; full malolactic fermentation; aged at least 3 years; 9g/L dosage; DIAM closure

The aim here is for an easy-drinking, fruity rosé, with a medium crimson hue infused by the addition of both red wine and maceration skin-contact rosé from Les Riceys. The result meets the brief in an appealing, attractively fruit-focused and well-balanced style of strawberry and raspberry fruit, notes of nutmeg spice and a soft, fleshy finish.

D de Devaux La Cuvée Brut NV • $$

92 points • Tasted in Bar-sur-Seine and Adelaide

2006 base with 40% reserve wine from a perpetual solera; 60% pinot noir, 40% chardonnay; 80–85% malolactic fermentation; aged at least 5 years; 8g/L dosage

Michel Parisot has maintained a reserve solera in large oak tuns since 2002, and a sample including every vintage to 2011 showcased the complexity of maturity that can be built in a solera, while upholding wonderful purity, freshness and finesse. The 2006 base was blended with an earlier version of the same solera and retains an impressive focus of lemon and grapefruit, apple, pear and mixed spice. Notes of anise and licorice are classic Les Riceys pinot noir, and a hint of menthol is true to the Côte des Bar. Layered complexity harmonises seamlessly with a taut and well-focused finish. Bottles tasted in Australia demonstrated more gingernut and honey-biscuit development.

D DE DEVAUX ULTRA EXTRA BRUT NV • $$

91 points • TASTED IN BAR-SUR-SEINE

Identical to D de Devaux La Cuvée Brut, with 2g/L dosage

Devaux purposely avoids a zero-dosage cuvée, favouring a dosage of 2g/L to provide better balance and persistence to the finish. The result is more taut, metallic and coiled than the equivalent La Cuvée, accenting lemon zest on a firmer and more aggressive finish. A searing champagne for the brave, while the rest of us can save a few pennies and bask in the comfortable territory of La Cuvée.

D DE DEVAUX LE ROSÉ NV • $$$

94 points • TASTED IN BAR-SUR-SEINE

100% 2007, though not labelled as a vintage; 40% pinot noir, 50% chardonnay, 10% pinot noir red wine; 80–85% malolactic fermentation; aged at least 5 years in the cellar; 8g/L dosage

Purposely the fresher and more elegant aperitif style alongside Devaux's more colourful and fruity Rosée, this is a delightfully subtle rosé and a triumph of Devaux. It sings of Les Riceys, the Aube's most celebrated terroir, in nuances of anise and velvet texture. A restrained, lively strawberry and morello cherry fruit tang is accented by nuances of spice and cherry kernel. It finishes with wonderfully fine texture and lingering cherry character.

D DE DEVAUX CUVÉE MILLÉSIME 2002 • $$$$

94 point • TASTED IN BAR-SUR-SEINE

50% Côte des Bar pinot noir, 50% Côte des Blancs chardonnay; no oak vinification, to emphasise freshness and elegance; 50–70% malolactic fermentation; aged at least 5 years; 9g/L dosage

Whatever it was that wrote off all three bottles of this cuvée that I tasted last year with a dank, mushroomy character certainly did not plague this bottle. Parisot's vintage philosophy is to emphasise the vintage, without the oak influence used to build complexity in his non-vintage cuvées. The beautiful and rich 2002 season is captured in a wonderfully balanced champagne of appealing approachability and delightful complexity. A core of attractively poised white peach fruit is developing depth of toast and honey and notes of mixed spice. Les Riceys pinot noir articulates its presence in hints of anise, lingering on a soft, creamy finish.

Dom Pérignon
(Dom Pe-ri-ngon)

9/10

20 Avenue de Champagne 51200 Épernay
www.domperignon.com
www.creatingdomperignon.com

Dom Pérignon

Dom Pérignon is the prestige cuvée of Moët & Chandon, but so distinct are the production, style and sheer class of the wines that the two brands are best considered completely autonomous. The two are made in the same premises in Épernay, and some facilities are shared, but the winemaking teams are quite separate. Of Moët's colossal resource of 1500 hectares of estate vineyards, some are designated as Moët, others Dom Pérignon, and the rest are vinified by Dom Pérignon and allocated at the time of blending. 'The Dom' is a wine of tension, power and long-ageing endurance, the king of the most readily available and perpetually discounted prestige cuvées.

DOM PÉRIGNON IS THE VISION OF THE TALENTED AND insightful Richard Geoffroy, dedicated exclusively to this cuvée since 1990. The man who deserves much of the credit for the rise of one of Champagne's most famous and most celebrated brands of the modern age carries his responsibility with unassuming humility, praising the positive energy of his team and the extensive resources at his disposal. 'I must be the most privileged winemaker in the world!' he grins.

Geoffroy works painstakingly to draw out the best wines he can in each season, while juggling the politics of big business and a frenetic travel schedule to introduce his wines to the world. While deeply embedded in the history and tradition of Champagne, he steers this sizeable house with a courageous sense of daring. Although the course he has set is at times unexpected (more on this later), there is no doubt he is one of the great minds of modern Champagne.

Alongside Louis Roederer Cristal, Dom Pérignon was the very first of champagne's prestige cuvées, introduced in the mid-1930s with the 1921 vintage. There are only two wines: a vintage and a vintage rosé, traditionally produced less than one year in two, released after a minimum of seven years' bottle ageing on lees, and again selectively in later life as Dom Pérignon Oenothèques. There are no non-vintage wines. Every vintage is harvested and vinified, and the decision is made at the blending table as to whether the wine will be made and released, or the entire vintage sold off.

Dom Pérignon's production remains a closely guarded secret and rumours abound in Champagne, with some putting annual sales at 3.5 million bottles, and others suggesting as many as 8 million each vintage. The company maintains it is very much less than this, although how much less they will not say, divulging only that it's more than Krug's 600,000 bottles. There is a desire to increase production, but opportunities to increase estate holdings are extremely limited. 'I would love to have more grand cru vineyards!' Geoffroy exclaims. 'We're already making as much as we can.'

VAST VINEYARD RESOURCES

Dom Pérignon is based on a core of five grand cru villages of pinot noir and four of chardonnay, in which the company is privileged to own 'huge' resources. Estate vineyards in 14 of Champagne's 17 grand crus are called upon, and fruit is sometimes purchased from the other three, but over the past decade more than 98% has come from estate sources, including the oldest vines of the premier cru of Hautvillers, the historical and spiritual home of Dom Pérignon.

The key to Dom Pérignon's sourcing is the vast diversity of vineyards at its disposal. Historically, particular sites have been dedicated to each Moët Hennessy house, and Dom Pérignon has had first choice. 'There are core grand crus for Dom Pérignon and we have a privilege to access the fruit sources of the other houses as we desire,' Geoffroy divulges. His offsider, Vincent Chaperon, adds, 'We have the great ability to change the plots from one year to another, because even a grand cru vineyard can give shit if it's hit by hail or botrytis!'

Blending is fundamental to Dom Pérignon, and Geoffroy upholds that this is more important than ever in vintage champagne. 'If there is one house able to make vineyard-specific wine styles, surely it is Dom Pérignon — we own more vineyards than anyone else in every grand cru,' he points out. 'If anyone is capable of making Le Mesnil, it is Dom Pérignon! But I want to use Le Mesnil in the blend.'

The Dom Pérignon house style is about a tension between chardonnay and pinot noir, in a blend of roughly 50/50, though it can drift to 60/40 in either direction, according to the season. Chardonnay is the limiting ingredient in production, and in the current time of short supply, Geoffroy is pleased to have the security of a majority of estate vineyards and a single contract with a 'top cooperative'.

The precise moment of harvest is given the utmost attention, and the grapes are tasted twice every day. The window of picking is short — 'in 2008 it was vegetal on Monday and too ripe on Tuesday!' Geoffroy uses pH over acid, flavour and sugar as the most important indicator of properly ripe fruit. Waiting for sugar ripeness doesn't work in the wildly fluctuating vintages of current times. 'Ten degrees of sugar ripeness in 2003

was not like 10 degrees in 2004!' he points out.

Work is underway to redefine the vineyard plots using observation tools including aerial surveying, and to separately vinify each plot to further hone the detail of each parcel. Trials have also been conducted into an acceptable distance for fruit to be trucked between vineyard and press house, finding that a distance exceeding 15–20 kilometres can be problematic. Dom Pérignon is not afraid of some oxidation prior to fermentation in order to reduce phenolics in the juice, but this needs to be carefully controlled, according to the maturity of the grapes and their phenolic content.

REDUCTIVE WINEMAKING

'We are very dedicated to the fruit and the vineyards, but fermentation is just as important as the fruit,' Geoffroy declares. Wines are fermented exclusively in stainless steel tanks, using a cultured house yeast strain, with sulphite added at the press to kill off indigenous wild yeasts. The wine is judiciously protected from oxidation post-fermentation. 'Our vision is to age our wine in a reductive way, as too much oxidation kills champagne's complexity, making it fat and heavy,' he says.

Malolactic fermentation is run to completion using a culture co-inoculated with the primary fermentation, upheld as a key to achieving freshness as the wines build complexity and texture through long ageing. If vintages continue to warm, malolactic may be blocked in some parcels to maintain balance.

There is no rule for the dosage level in Dom Pérignon, which is determined through trials of different reserve wines and varying levels of sugar and sulphur dioxide six months prior to release. The dosage sweetness has diminished from 10g/L in 1996 to less than 7g/L in current cuvées. 'Perhaps the maturity of the grapes is higher, or perhaps we're doing different things in the making?' Chaperon postulates.

The decision to release a wine is made at the point of blending. 'Even in the lousiest years we go to the final blend with no preconceived ideas,' Geoffroy says. 'Since Dom Pérignon has been Dom Pérignon we have always harvested a vintage every year.'

First released in 1959, Dom Pérignon Rosé represents just a few percent of the blanc volume, and typically sells for close to twice the price. Only made in vintages in which phenolics are in balance, there is an attempt to make rosé in every vintage, but it is typically released every second year. It displays a riper fruit profile than the blanc since the pinot noir for the red wine for blending is picked riper, with more aromatics and more jammy character. 'The challenge is to balance this to maintain delicacy in the wine,' Chaperon explains. 'It's a highly bodied wine that needs to maintain an equilibrium between authority and seduction.'

The key to Dom Pérignon lies in blending to achieve 'a state of completeness', a perfect balance of white and black grapes. 'Harmony is so intense,' is Geoffroy's line. 'It's like playing tennis. If you're not experienced you try to make it up with power, but if you have the right swing, it's effortless. You can forget about power and deliver intensity. When you hit it right, you hear it because the sound of the ball is different. You hear the pop! That's my quest. Dom Pérignon is about the pop.'

THE NEW DOM PÉRIGNON

Prior to 1990, Dom Pérignon released 29 vintages in 70 years — one release every two and a half years. Since Geoffroy commenced in 1990, the frequency has almost doubled, to 11 vintages in 15 seasons. This has recently increased further still. Since 1997, so far only 2001 has not been released. This is the first time in its almost century-long history that Dom Pérignon has released six out of seven vintages.

Conspiracy theories abound, but Geoffroy thanks an improvement in Champagne vintages for this trend. 'I have often been asked about global warming, and I am embarrassed to say that so far it has been for the better in Champagne!' he exclaims. 'Good crop sizes, more consistent yields, good consistency of quality, good levels of ripeness, lower acids and more rounded wines, which I'm very excited about.'

Much controversy surrounds the 2012 release of the 2003 vintage, a challenging and atypical season, recording the hottest summer to ever hit Champagne. Geoffroy says that '1996 had the highest acidity we've ever recorded and 2003 had the lowest', and then makes an unexpected announcement: 'I take it as it is. It's not about the style of Dom Pérignon, it's about the vintage. I am sick of the word "style". There is no style. Dom Pérignon is pushing the idea of vintage more than anything else.'

There's something noble and inherently authentic in this statement, something perhaps more Burgundian than it is Champenois — a wholesome celebration of the voice of the elements over the force of the hand of man. Yet in a climate as tumultuous and increasingly erratic as Champagne's, there is something deeply disturbing in this statement, too. It changes the game for Dom Pérignon.

The Dom Pérignon that we know and love has never been all about the vintage. Chaperon explained to me two years ago that 'Dom Pérignon is about creating a balance between the style of the vintage and the style of the house, and we are able to drive the vintage in the direction of our style by selecting the finest sites in each season. Whether we release a vintage is more a question of style than of quality.'

'Style' hasn't always been a dirty word for Dom Pérignon. Until recently, if the style of the vintage hasn't met the style of Dom Pérignon, it has never been released. And there will always be Champagne vintages unworthy of standing alone. But is seems something changed in 2003. Geoffroy admits that '2003 is border territory for Champagne, as border as it can be. We took the risk, a technical risk. Frankly, we never lacked confidence, but we had to push harder.'

Is 2003 a one-off? Geoffroy alludes to a fundamental shift in the philosophy of the house. 'Some future vintages will be more than you might expect from Dom Pérignon,' he warns. 'In the past, Dom Pérignon has been very gentle and very accessible. But the decade of the 2000s is more about pushing the style.'

Are we entering an era in which the consumer must exercise greater discretion in selecting vintages of Dom Pérignon? Time will tell.

OENOTHÈQUE

Geoffroy speaks of three ages of peak maturity in Dom Pérignon's life, the first after 7–8 years (the standard release), a second at 12–20 years and a third at 35–40 years. Dom Pérignon makes these mature vintages available through an extremely limited library of 'Oenothèque' releases, representing just 1–2% of only the most age-worthy vintages, and typically at double the price of the first release. Oenothèques are a testament to the remarkable battery pack of energy and vitality contained within the lees in a bottle of champagne, capable of sustaining a bottle for a lifetime.

Oenothèque is based on the same wine as the standard release, sealed from the outset with a cork and aged on lees for an extended time in the cellar. Bottles are orientated upside down so the lees settle inside the cork and act as a barrier to oxygen ingress. Surprisingly, trials have found crown caps to be less reliable than corks beyond 10 years, perhaps due to phenolics and antioxidants leaching from the cork. 'After 10 years a cork is so superior to crown cap,' Geoffroy believes. 'There is a wonderful chemistry, which would be very difficult to reproduce with a different closure.'

The cork seal necessitates manual disgorgement of Oenothèque releases, and each bottle is checked for cork taint as it is disgorged. 'On tirage you have an added effect from the first and second cork,' he explains. 'You may not detect any problem from the first cork, but

The Champagne Guide

after you insert the second cork it may become noticeable.' Further, as in any wine style, long-ageing under natural corks creates bottle variation, and no two Oenothèques are alike, adding an element of risk to a significant outlay.

Dom Pérignon's best buy is always its standard blanc, and frequently discounted.

DREADED CORKS

The level of cork taint I've encountered in Dom Pérignon in recent years is alarming. One of two bottles of the Rosé 1998 that I opened last year went straight down the sink, as did one of two bottles of the Oenothèque 1996 this year. Of six bottles Geoffroy opened for me in Épernay recently, one was tainted, and the Oenothèque 1990 was sufficiently corky to disqualify it from assessment.

'The truth is, I have really started to like the wood character from cork,' Geoffroy responded, to my bewilderment. He considers that the house suffers around 2% cork taint. If this is true, the odds of three corked bottles in 10 (plus one corky) is extremely unlucky, if not nigh-on impossible.

Others have confirmed similarly disturbing findings, and I know of at least one cancellation of a significant wholesale order after abnormal cork-taint rates were detected. This is an embarrassment in any wine, and especially one of this reputation and price.

The house has been trialling alternatives to cork for five years, but will see the trials out for 10 years before drawing conclusions.

As always, be sure to have any suspect bottle replaced.

The abbey of Hautvillers, where Dom Pérignon lived and worked, remains the spiritual home of the house.

DOM PÉRIGNON 2004 • $$$$$

98 points • DISGORGED MAY 2012

52% pinot noir, 48% chardonnay

At the time of writing, a stunning Dom Pérignon is about to be unleashed to wow the world. After the powerful 2002 and the abrasive 2003, 2004 is a backward and honed Dom Pérignon of understated intensity, charged with dramatic tension of high-voltage electricity. At almost a decade of age, it seems to transcend the very passage of time itself, projecting an aura of impossibly youthful grapefruit and immaculately defined lemongrass, with a lightning bolt of pure lemon shattering its brittle core of pristine mineral chalk. A champagne of supreme purity and tightly coiled focus, unravelling to reveal fresh pear and anise. The first bottle opened was faintly cork tainted; the second confirmed one of the truly great and long-lived Doms of the modern era.

DOM PÉRIGNON 2003 • $$$$$

91 points • TASTED IN ÉPERNAY, PERTH, ADELAIDE, MELBOURNE AND BRISBANE

60% pinot noir, 40% chardonnay

The 2003 is a rich and generous Dom, a champagne of flamboyant fruit character of preserved lemon, fleshy peach, ripe fig, exotic apricot and even tropical fruits on first release, quickly evolving to become bruised red apple, roast cashew nuts, honey and mixed spice. It wears the battle scars of its challenging season, parading the exuberance of pinot noir that survived the hottest summer to ever hit Champagne. Heavy mid-spring frost and snow devastated 70% of Dom Pérignon's chardonnay crop, forcing a change in the villages and a focus on pinot noir in the blend. In an attempt to rescue the vintage from oxidation in the bottle, the juice was allowed to oxidise for two to three hours as it came off the press. Under such unprecedented conditions, it is surprising that Dom Pérignon 2003 was released at all, perplexing that it followed 2002 (even Moët cleverly released its 2003 vintage first), and bewildering that its volume represents full production levels. Richard Geoffroy sums up the 2003 as 'a vintage that was out of the box... a case of phenolic ripeness and bitterness, which makes up for its low acidity; a different balance, more chewy and less creamy'. I have had many opportunities to reassess Dom Pérignon 2003 across its full release cycle, and it is this hard phenolic bitterness that troubles me most about this vintage, leaving the finish astringent, coarse, dry and short. Geoffroy is adamant that it will live very, very long. Really? Of 20 bottles that I opened for masterclasses across Australia, 10 were rejected, some to cork taint, but most to premature development. It appears this vintage does not possess Dom Pérignon's usual resilience to oxidation through slight variations in the cork or the handling of the bottle. The 2003 is an awkward and challenging vintage, completely unworthy of Dom Pérignon. The question of why it was ever released remains elusive.

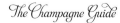

DOM PÉRIGNON ROSÉ 2002 • $$$$$

96 points • TASTED IN BRISBANE

There is classically a luxurious decadence to Dom Pérignon rosé, exuding a warm amplitude built around ripe pinot noir red wine. The 2002 delivers a cunning twist to this recipe, an enchantingly refreshing take on savoury, charged with the confidence of high-strung acidity. Breathtakingly youthful at 11 years of age, its hue is a striking pale salmon with a vibrant pink tint. A pristine bouquet sizzles with freshly cracked pomegranate, ripe strawberries and a wisp of pipesmoke. The palate opens with a hint of gunpowder, a fingerprint of Dom Pérignon's reductive style, then inviting flavours of cherry kernel and roast pecan nuts. It takes some time for its cherry fruit to unravel, and it does so tentatively and gracefully. An impeccably crafted 2002 with magnificent chalk mineral texture that bores deep into a very long finish.

DOM PÉRIGNON ROSÉ 2000 • $$$$$

97 points • DISGORGED EARLY 2011 • TASTED IN ÉPERNAY

Attaining refinement and complexity, precision and intensity, energy and drive in a long-aged rosé is perhaps the most precarious equilibrium to achieve in Champagne, and the warm generosity of 2000 made the chase all the more challenging. Dom Pérignon Rosé 2000 is testimony to the genius of Richard Geoffroy, not only meeting such a lofty ideal with exquisite precision, but doing so two years after the release of the white (most houses release their rosé earlier), at a height that transcends even its predecessor from the superior 1998 vintage. After 13 years, 2000 has grown in that slow, assured manner that is Dom Pérignon, sustaining a beautifully vibrant, medium crimson hue, presenting the ultimate tension between lively elegance and layered complexity of pink pepper, tangelo zest, tamarillo and subtle spice. Understated concentration gives voice to deep strata of soft chalk mineral texture. Geoffroy discloses that he's far happier with the rosé than the white. Mais oui!

DOM PÉRIGNON OENOTHÈQUE 1996 • $$$$$

100 points • DISGORGED 2008 • TASTED IN ÉPERNAY AND ADELAIDE

50% pinot noir, 50% chardonnay; first release 10g/L dosage, Oenothèque 6g/L

Dom Pérignon Oenothèque 1996 is not only one of the greatest Dom Pérignons of all, ranking among the top few champagnes on the shelves this year, but it's on the rise. Scoring it 99 points on its release in 2011, I wrote, 'Most profound of all, it'll get even better'. This year, impossibly, fresher still, a perfect 100. Oenothèque 1996 is almost completely devoid of time evolution. Never have I tasted a champagne of this age of such sheer energy, drive and acid tension. Alongside 2004, 2003 and 1990, this was the palest wine on the table, achingly youthful in its lemon blossom breath. In the ultimate contradiction, there is an airy lightness to its finesse, drawn out with a high-strung poise that belies the dehydrated concentration and low ripeness that marked this bizarre and inimitable vintage. Its mineral texture is an epiphany, dancing with fairy lightness on a stage of solid chalk. Dom Pérignon absolutely, finally and resoundingly silences the question on the lips of critics and connoisseurs for the past 17 years: Will the perfect 10/10 season of 1996 (10g/L acidity and 10 degrees of potential alcohol) ever find balance between its intoxicating concentration and its searing acidity? It will and, my goodness, it has. Richard Geoffroy believes it will live forever. This time, I'm a believer. One bottle opened in Adelaide showed corky character and a contracted finish.

DOSNON & LEPAGE

(Do-noh e Ler-pahg)

6/10

4 BIS RUE DU BAS DE LINGEY 10340 AVIREY-LINGEY
www.champagne-dosnon.com

The small cellar run by the young Davy Dosnon and Simon-Charles Lepage in Avirey-Lingey in the south-western reaches of the Côte des Bar is on the rise. A small production of just 50,000 bottles annually reflects an ever-more comfortable disposition of integration of low dosage and old oak. There is refinement, skill and craftsmanship on display in every bottle, and the best represent great value for money.

LESS THAN 50 KILOMETRES NORTH-EAST OF CHABLIS, a little over a half-hour drive, Avirey-Lingey perhaps has more in common with the northern end of Burgundy than it does with other parts of Champagne, a comparison well familiar to the Gevrey-Chambertin-trained Simon-Charles. The local clay-limestone soils make for particularly rich fruit, and pinot noir takes a confident lead, though this estate also takes pride in showcasing the rising credentials of Côte des Bar chardonnay in flying solo.

Complexity and fullness are the goals here. Fruit is sourced from two hectares of 25-year-old estate pinot noir vines (and a little chardonnay) and seven hectares of growers, farmed using sustainable viticulture. Harmony is the buzz word for Dosnon & Lepage and vines are essentially worked organically, while maintaining the flexibility to apply treatments in adverse seasons. Grasses are grown in the mid-rows, soils are tilled for aeration, no chemical treatments are employed, and yields are controlled.

Minimal intervention is the philosophy in the winery, too, and fermentation and ageing take place exclusively in oak (minimum barrel age five years).

Indigenous yeasts are increasingly employed for primary fermentation, to build character and complexity. An intuitive philosophy sees malolactic fermentation allowed or blocked and bâtonnage performed or not, according to the character of the wine. A high 40% of reserve wine is used, and bottle maturation is never less than two years.

Ultra-modern labels appropriately set off the progressive approach of this boutique négociant.

The Champagne Guide

Dosnon & Lepage Recolte Blanc de Noire NV • $$

93 points • Tasted in Brisbane

100% Côte des Bar pinot noir; vinified and aged in barrel; 9g/L dosage

This well-crafted blanc de noirs could confidently stand in for rosé at the table, though its medium straw hue is refreshingly pale for barrel-fermented Côte des Bar pinot noir, accurately reflecting its lively freshness. Well-defined red cherry and strawberry fruit is set against a rich yellow mirabelle plum, ginger and mixed spice background, structured with a primary backbone of lemon juice acidity. Finely structured tannins and hints of wood spice add texture to a well-balanced mouthfeel, finishing crisp, clean and long, with refreshingly low dosage that appears less than the stated 9g/L.

Dosnon & Lepage Recolte Blanche Blanc de Blancs NV • $$

92 points • Tasted in Brisbane

100% Côte des Bar chardonnay; vinified and aged in barrel

Côte des Bar chardonnay is richer than that of the Côte des Blancs, and the current blend is more generous than usual for Dosnon & Lepage, with honey and roast nuts packed around a core of intense white peach and yellow mirabelle plums. The mixed-spice complexity of barrel fermentation leads out, pulling decisively into a taut tail of primary lemon and grapefruit zest, and soft, underlying mineral structure. Finely textured mouthfeel and low dosage allow space for generous fruit and taut acidity to command the finish.

The Côte des Bar has enjoyed a rising reputation as its vines reach maturity, with villages like Les Riceys now widely celebrated.

DRAPPIER

(Drah-piay)

RUE DES VIGNES 10200 URVILLE
www.champagne-drappier.com

CHAMPAGNE

DRAPPIER

DOMAINE À URVILLE DEPUIS 1808
CAVES À REIMS - FRANCE

This medium-sized, family-owned house makes lively, fruity wines from 53 hectares of estate vineyards in and around Urville in the Côte des Bar, planted to 70% pinot noir. Fruit is also sourced from a further 40 hectares, notably chardonnay from Cramant and Chouilly, and pinot noir from Bouzy and Ambonnay. Georges Drappier was the first to plant pinot noir extensively here in the early 1900s, and today Michel Drappier is the seventh generation to grow grapes, using minimal intervention and organic practices, though organic certification is not sought. Fermentation takes place partly in large oak casks, and liqueurs d'expédition are aged in oak casks and large foudres for more than a decade. Use of the lowest levels of sulphur dioxide is a mixed blessing, as this can make for darker colours and premature biscuity flavours. These are not champagnes to hang on to, but a production scale of 1.5 million bottles annually makes for enticing value for money across its finer offerings.

DRAPPIER SIGNATURE BLANC DE BLANCS BRUT NV • $

91 points • TASTED IN BRISBANE

Cramant, Bouzy and Urville chardonnay; a touch of pinot blanc for complexity and roundness

Lovely richness of yellow summer fruits and dried pear neatly contrasts with crunchy lemon zest and clean acid. There are notes of complexity of roast nuts and cinnamon, finishing with a touch of stale biscuit. Pretty good value.

DRAPPIER GRANDE SENDRÉE BRUT VINTAGE 2005 • $$

89 points • TASTED IN BRISBANE

100% pinot noir, partly matured in large casks

A succulent, soft style, leading out with ripe pear and luscious white peach, accented with honey. It flows into a dry finish of apple skin grippiness, structured by firm phenolics and acidity. Buy the cheaper Signature instead.

DUVAL-LEROY

(Dew-val-Lair-wah)

6/10

69 AVE DE BAMMENTAL BP 37 51130 VERTUS
www.duval-leroy.com

CHAMPAGNE
DEPUIS 1859
DUVAL-
LEROY

he scale of Duval-Leroy's modern winery is a physical statement of the rapid progress at this family-owned company. Recently celebrating its 150th birthday, it now ranks in the top 15 Champagne houses, thanks to its dynamic, visionary leader, Carol Duval-Leroy, who has grown the estate during the past 20 years. Chardonnay takes the lead in these graceful and elegant wines, reflecting the bright fruit purity of the village of Vertus.

THE IMPOSING DUVAL-LEROY BUILDING LOOKS MORE at home in Silicon Valley than a small village in Champagne. The entire façade is covered by 250 square metres of solar panels, sufficient for the electrical needs of the barrel room, tasting room and reception area. It makes a bold, immediate statement that Duval-Leroy has sunk a serious investment into its modernisation and growth. And that's just the beginning.

Step inside the largest facility in Vertus and you're greeted by lines of gleaming new tanks, all temperature controlled to between 16°C and 20°C to preserve delicacy during fermentation. Five gentle eight-tonne pneumatic presses are cleverly positioned above 30 settling tanks, gently delivering the must by gravity.

Dug deep underground, this facility operates on multiple levels. Operations were modernised in 2009 when the facility was extended to integrate the entire production under one roof to improve efficiency and quality. At the same time, a new barrel room was added for fermentation of grand cru parcels.

Estate holdings comprise 60% chardonnay. The house controls 200 hectares in the Côte des Blancs (including an impressive 150 hectares in Vertus, and holdings in every grand cru), Montagne de Reims and Côte de Sézanne, providing a generous one-third of all fruit required to produce 5–5.5 million bottles annually. It is serviced by five press centres, and 18 million bottles stored 30 kilometres away in Châlons-en-Champagne.

Duval-Leroy manages a sustainability regime that's more than just a solar panel façade. A 10-page document on its website details a diverse list of initiatives. Herbicide use has more than halved in the past decade, and all estate vineyards are cultivated organically or biodynamically — quite a feat for a house of this size. Fruit purchased from a number of organically certified growers finds its way into two organic champagnes.

It is apparently possible to ascertain the disgorgement date from the bottling code, but the house keeps this and the tech sheets for each cuvée a closely guarded secret, for reasons I fail to understand.

Duval-Leroy Brut NV • $$

91 points • Disgorged October 2012 • Tasted in Vertus •

2008 base vintage; 70% pinot noir, 20% pinot meunier, 10% chardonnay from 20 villages; aged a minimum of 30 months; 8g/L dosage

Duval-Leroy's two entry cuvées together total more than 4 million bottles annually, making up 80% of the production of the house. A very strong pinot noir lead in this cuvée creates a sumptuous style of white nectarines and red berries. A fresh, lively, clean and fruit-focused style, with dosage contributing a touch of sweetness.

Duval-Leroy Fleur de Champagne Premier Cru NV • $$

92 points • Disgorged November 2012 • Tasted in Vertus •

2008 base vintage with 10% reserve wines; 75% chardonnay, 25% pinot noir; 100% estate vines on 15 premier and grand crus in the Côte des Blancs and Montagne de Reims; 8g/L dosage

Duval-Leroy's signature NV is confidently led by estate-grown chardonnay, giving it a decisive edge over the pinot-dominated Brut NV. It's clean, fresh and balanced, with focused lemon and lemon blossom expressing the purity of chardonnay, underlined by chalk mineral texture.

Duval-Leroy Rosé Prestige Brut NV • $$

89 points • Tasted in Vertus

66% pinot noir saignée, 34% chardonnay from grand cru and premier cru villages; aged 24 months on lees; 9g/L dosage

With a particularly pale, pretty salmon hue, this is a saignée rosé with aromas of cherry, strawberry and cherry kernel. A savoury, textural and mineral-accented palate adds notes of pink pepper and anise, though ultimately lacks fruit freshness and vivacity.

Duval-Leroy Blanc de Blancs Brut Nature 2002 • $$$

95 points • Tasted in Vertus

Chardonnay from Avize, Cramant, Chouilly, Oger, Le-Mesnil-sur-Oger and Vertus; 2.5g/L dosage

The great grand crus of the Côte des Blancs deliver their strength and generosity, intricately offset by the crisp freshness of Vertus. The result is a triumph of deep, chalky mineral presence and tremendous persistence, capturing the tension of 2002 and contrasting the bountiful richness of this great season with tightly clenched acid structure. Enticing yellow summer fruits and citrus of all kinds are set against a slowly rising backdrop of mature toast, butter and mixed spice character. It's intelligently topped off with the lightest touch of dosage.

DUVAL-LEROY BLANC DE BLANCS BRUT 2004 • $$$

93 points • DISGORGED AUGUST 2012 • TASTED IN VERTUS

100% chardonnay from Vertus, Le Mesnil-sur-Oger, Oger, Avize, Cramant and Chouilly; 6g/L dosage

A generous 2004 that has evolved from its determined linearity and energetic drive at release two years ago to find itself in a comfortable and generous place of butterscotch, succulent white peach, fig, yellow mirabelle plum, ginger and mixed spice. It upholds its underlying chalk mineral texture and overlays this with a creamy suppleness and ripe fruit sweetness that equip it for main-course action.

DUVAL-LEROY LADY ROSÉ SEC NV • $$$

88 points • TASTED IN VERTUS

80% pinot noir, 20% chardonnay; 24g/L dosage

In its gaudy Barbie-pink sleeve, this is an unashamedly sweet rosé with a dry, savoury palate masked by heavy, honeyed dosage. Ripe strawberry and raspberry flavours are accented with notes of ginger, finishing rounded and buttery with phenolic texture, but this ultimately lacks the vibrancy and acidity to support the level of dosage.

DUVAL-LEROY CLOS DES BOUVERIES 2005 • $$$$

92 points • TASTED IN VERTUS

100% chardonnay; single vineyard in the heart of Vertus; half fermented and aged in barrel; full malolactic fermentation; 4g/L dosage

The concept of releasing a single-variety, single-vineyard wine in every single vintage in a climate as fickle as that of Champagne's is more than a little disconcerting, though it's a testimony to the site that this wine has stood up to the challenging 2005 vintage confidently. It's released altogether too young for a wine with significant oak treatment, and two years after release that wall of oak has hardly subsided. Fruit has evolved from its primary lemon and grapefruit freshness, into a realm of preserved lemon and generous star fruits and golden delicious apples, lingering with impressive fruit presence. Oak distracts on the finish, leaving it dry and astringent. This is clearly a special patch of Vertus, and it deserves to be captured with long lees ageing minus the distraction of heavy-handed oak.

DUVAL-LEROY FEMME DE CHAMPAGNE 2004 • $$$$

95 points • TASTED IN VERTUS

87% chardonnay from Avize, Chouilly and Le Mesnil-sur-Oger; 13% pinot noir from Ambonnay;
13% vinified and matured in old oak barrels; 5g/L dosage

Strangely, this vintage was only made in half bottles and released earlier than usual, though
the house couldn't tell me why. In the context of the lofty heights that Femme has attained in
recent vintages, this is a slightly lesser release, with a generous fruit ripeness uncharacteristic
of 2004, lending something of a richness to its core. To its credit, its fruit focus and
lingering persistence are wonderful, led by the lemon and succulent yellow summer fruits of
chardonnay, with a touch of red cherry and strawberry disclosing a subtle touch of pinot noir.
Well-gauged barrel influence adds vanilla, butter and brioche notes, underlined by the classic
salty mineral texture that characterises Femme.

DUVAL-LEROY FEMME DE CHAMPAGNE 2000 • $$$$

96 points • DISGORGED MID-2012 • TASTED IN VERTUS (TWICE)

95% chardonnay from Avize, Chouilly, Oger and Le Mesnil-sur-Oger; 5% Bouzy pinot noir;
25% vinified and matured in oak barrels; 6g/L dosage

The rounded, succulent summer yellow fruits and figs that are representative of the warm
2000 vintage are evolving more slowly than anyone expected, still flaunting their beautiful
curves two years after release, and introducing new layers of mature complexity in gingernut
biscuits, mixed spice, honey, and even the subtle note of green olive that typifies many mature
Côte des Blancs chardonnays. The deep-set mineral presence of grand cru chardonnay stands
undeviated by the passage of time, with wonderful salty, sea-foam mineral texture churning,
frothing and gliding very long on the finish.

Duval-Leroy's barrel hall (left) ferments grand cru parcels, but the house focus remains on its premier cru village of Vertus (right).

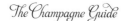
The Champagne Guide

EGLY-OURIET

(Eglee-Ou-ree-yair)

9/10

15 RUE TRÉPAIL 51150 AMBONNAY

CHAMPAGNE
Elaboré par SAS EGLY-OURIET à Ambonnay France

EGLY-OURIET

Propriétaire - Récoltant

BRUT TRADITION GRAND CRU

Issu des Grands Terroirs d'Ambonnay, Bouzy
et Verzenay Classés Grand Cru.

BRUT

ALC. 12.5% BY VOL.   750 ML

Egly-Ouriet is privileged to enjoy a cult status shared by no other grower on the Montagne de Reims. This tiny, exactingly pristine operation in Ambonnay deserves its acclaim, capturing the profound complexity, intensity and grandeur of the Montagne de Reims' finest terroirs, without for a moment sacrificing the precision that underlines the most revered champagnes. These are ravishingly vinous sparkling wines, consistently among the most exactingly balanced of Champagne's power set, handcrafted by an artisan who painstakingly tends his vines naturally to low yields and full maturity.

EGLY-OURIET OWNS 8.5 HECTARES OF GRAND CRU vineyards planted to 70% pinot noir and 30% chardonnay, primarily in Ambonnay, 1.5 hectares in Verzenay, a few rows in Bouzy, and a plot of very old pinot meunier vines in Vrigny that produce a single-vineyard premier cru. Fourth-generation head of the estate, Francis Egly, has bottled the entire harvest since he took over in 1982 — 100,000 bottles, a small annual production for a 12-hectare estate. Previously, his father, Michel, bottled a small proportion since the 1970s, and his grandfather, Charles, bottled tiny quantities for family and friends since the 1950s.

An eco-friendly approach has seen a radical reduction in the use of fertilisers and chemical pesticides. The soil is manured, ploughed for aeration and, most radically of all for Champagne, green harvests reduce crop levels by up to 50%. From vines averaging more than 45 years of age, dramatically lower yields than Champagne's average allow Egly to harvest at full maturity, typically at 12 or 13 degrees of potential alcohol, extremely ripe for Champagne. His goal is to harvest grapes as ripe as possible, and cites the best vintages as those of high maturity, naming undermaturity as Champagne's biggest problem.

Grapes are pressed slowly and fermented in barriques and enamelled tanks (not stainless steel) using only natural yeasts. Egly maintains some 200 barrels, sufficient for about half his production, not only for structure and longevity, but to facilitate vinification of different parcels separately to draw out more character of the terroir. Used barrels are purchased from his friend Dominique Laurent in Nuits-Saint-Georges.

Egly works intuitively in the cellar to preserve the detail of his grapes and their terroirs. Malolactic fermentation is allowed or barred depending on the vintage. Very low dosages are used — typically just

1–3g/L. Long ageing on lees in barrel for 8–10 months and in bottle for at least 3–4 years furnishes considerable longevity after release.

A 2006 cellar expansion brought all winemaking operations together in the same building, with pressing, vinification and storage on successive levels, temperature controlled at every stage. In 2008, Egly acquired two new presses, which he says have improved quality.

Egly-Ouriet's back labels are among Champagne's most informative, declaring disgorgement dates, terroirs and number of months on lees. Wines are bottled in July following harvest, so it's easy to determine the base vintage. Francis Egly does not maintain a website, but important details are proclaimed on every bottle alongside the philosophy of the house: 'This champagne is the expression of a "family" style that comes first and foremost from perfectly tended vineyards. The quality of grapes, the precision of blending and long "élevage" in the cellar allows us to offer you non-filtered champagnes in the purest champagne style.'

A breath of fresh air in a region saturated with marketing froth.

EGLY-OURIET LES VIGNES DE VRIGNY PREMIER CRU BRUT NV • $$$

95 points • DISGORGED JULY 2012 • TASTED IN BRISBANE

2008 base vintage; aged 36 months on lees

Egly-Ouriet crafts one of Champagne's most flattering single-vineyard pinot meuniers, faithfully translating every detail of the succulent depth of this grape's enticing juicy yellow peach, rich baked apple, wild honey and nutmeg character. Its full yellow hue reflects the long-aged style of the house. The energy of the 2008 vintage infuses this release with a cut of impeccable acidity and a pink grapefruit tang not usually seen in this cuvée. A skilfully crafted pinot meunier of refined, expressive chalk minerality, seamlessly dovetailing expansive generosity with tightly focused definition, finishing impeccably dry, gloriously persistent and exactingly honed.

EGLY-OURIET BRUT TRADITION GRAND CRU NV • $$$

95 points • DISGORGED APRIL 2011 • TASTED IN ADELAIDE AND BRISBANE

2006 base vintage; 70% pinot noir, 30% chardonnay; part vinified in barrel; aged 45 months on lees

A vinous wine of calm authority, carrying the full grandeur and complexity of carefully tended, low-yielding, old-vine pinot noir on some of Champagne's most revered grand crus, yet simultaneously fresh, pure and mineral-infused. Warm generosity ripples with baked peach, wild strawberries and cherries, with almost four years on lees fostering burnished notes of gingernut biscuits, brioche and vanilla, pulling into a scintillating finish of crunchy lemon zest and zippy acidity, layered with all the texture of barrel fermentation and mineral definition. A paradox of luxurious generosity and crystalline purity.

EGLY-OURIET GRAND CRU BRUT ROSÉ NV • $$$

95 points • TASTED IN REIMS

Similar composition to Brut Tradition, with 8% red wine from Ambonnay

Egly-Ouriet's rosé unravels with a universe of complexity of red cherry skins, secondary fruit development, hints of smoke and a whiff of gunpowder. True to the Egly style it carries its detail with impeccable control, built around well-textured structure and mineral chalk, finishing savoury, very long and with focused control.

EMMANUEL BROCHET

(Eman-yoo-el Bro-sheh)

8/10

7 IMPASSE BROCHET 51500 VILLERS-AUX-NOEUDS

Champagne

EMMANUEL
BROCHET

In the turning wheel of Champagne succession it is virtually unheard of for a young grower producer to be the first in his family to tend vines. All the more daring in the little-known premier cru village of Villers-aux-Noeuds, in which no one has made champagne for generations. Emmanuel Brochet defines a bold new frontier for Champagne, bringing an old terroir to life with an intuition derived not from local knowledge, family history or personal experience, but from the sheer courage to respond to each plot, each season and each ferment individually. Most remarkable of all is the beautiful fruit character and pronounced terroir expression that he has drawn from this place in a very short time. I know of no one in Champagne today who has achieved so much from so little so quickly as Emmanuel Brochet.

IN THE PLAINS BETWEEN THE SLOPES OF THE MONTAGNE de Reims and the sprawling southern suburbs of Reims, Villers-aux-Noeuds was once the proud custodian of 250 hectares of vines. The quaint little village is now home to just 27 hectares, spanning a wide diversity of soils.

Emmanuel Brochet's family has owned vines here for generations, hiring them to others to tend until Emmanuel commenced in 1997. His mother's 2.5 hectare single vineyard 'Le Mont Benoit' is one of the better sites in the village, with a thin layer of 40 centimetres topsoil directly over chalk, and just 25 centimetres at the top of the slope. Planted to 37% pinot meunier, 30% chardonnay and 23% pinot noir dating from 1962, half the block was replanted in 1986

after devastating frosts. Emmanuel manages the site for his mother, paying her a rent of 0.6 hectares of fruit, leaving 1.9 hectares for his modest production of 10,000 bottles.

Without the constraints and expectations of family and village history, Emmanuel Brochet is blessed with the freedom to forge a brave path with a spontaneity rarely possible in this staid region. 'I do things because I want to, not because I have to,' he tells me just moments after we first meet, affording him full licence to pursue his elegantly simple philosophy: 'If there is good balance in the soils and in the vine, then there is good balance in the wine.

'Every year is different, and we work it according to the season, not because we did it that way last year,' he says, admitting that he's never written down anything he's done each vintage. 'I practise biodynamics, but this is not the most important thing, no more important than the soil, the vines or my state of mind.'

Brochet abandoned use of chemicals in 2005 and commenced biodynamic certification in 2008, though he has no intention of mentioning biodynamics on his labels once certification is granted. 'It is important that my wines have no residues of pesticides, but many other elements are equally important,' he explains. 'If I put biodynamic certification on my labels then I should also include my press, the house, the grapes, the soil, the place and my state of mind!'

An annual production of 10,000 bottles is little more than half of what 1.9 hectares would normally produce in Champagne, and Brochet has found that biodynamics has reduced his yields. 'Perhaps it's not that we produce too little yield, but that conventional viticulture produces too much?' he pointedly suggests. The equilibrium he has achieved in his vines produces a balance of sugar and acidity sufficient that he has no need to chaptalise, unusual in Champagne, and virtually unheard of in a lesser premier cru village.

With no winery to inherit, Brochet sold his grapes until 2002 to finance the purchase of all of his equipment. He found a traditional 1960s two-tonne Coquard press in 2006, half the size of a traditional champagne press, and restored it 'like an old car'. Grapes are pressed on the day they are harvested and settled overnight before fermentation entirely in barrels, in which the wine remains until a month before the following harvest.

'My winemaking is very simple,' he explains, 'an oxidative vinification and ageing on lees, which consume the oxygen, creating a balance between oxidation and reduction.' Adamant that champagne should not have a woody taste, he purchases old barrels as well as new, and keeps wines in barrel on their lees to reduce the pick-up of oak flavours. Brochet likens winemaking in barrels with biodynamics: 'It's easier than in tanks, and the wines are more natural.' There is no bâtonnage, no filtration and no cold stabilisation.

In his short history, Brochet's experimentation has already refined his style. 'I tried putting my reserve wines in barrel, but without lees they became tired and woody, so for the past three years I've kept reserve wines in tank.' Generally he blocks malolactic fermentation in his vintage wines, but in 2012 he allowed it to proceed. 'With our warming weather, some people are saying that we should stop malo so as to retain acidity, but if you don't have a lot of acidity it's very hard to stop malo,' he explains. 'I would have to use a lot of preservative, and I don't want to do that.'

Brochet uses an extra brut dosage of around 4g/L in his cuvées, and trialled a zero-dosage wine from the same blend as his Le Mont Benoit NV last year, but found the acidity too pronounced at low temperatures. 'A little sugar is a technical support if you drink champagne too cold!' he says. The blend of this cuvée changes each year. 'The soil is more important than the varieties,' he upholds. 'The cépage is not important, and we can achieve great consistency each year even with different proportions of each variety. The wines taste of the vineyard and the soil, and that's the important thing.'

He maintains the flexibility to release wines 'when they are good to drink, not because I need the money', a rare opportunity in any young business. He has also broken with Champagne tradition in releasing non-vintage blends non-sequentially, releasing the 2009 base vintage after 2007 because 2008 was too young. Back labels are informative, specifying vintages, varieties and vinification details.

Brochet's wines showcase the unique mineral expression of his vineyard in a savoury chalk mouthfeel, a little coarser-grained in texture than that of the Côte des Blancs. I ask him if this is unique to the village, or particular to the accessible chalk in his vineyard, and he says he has no idea. 'There is just one producer who makes wine in this village and it is me!' he exclaims. 'Everyone else sells their grapes to the cooperatives and négociants. Old wine growers always said they could make very good wines in this village. Two generations ago they kept the grapes separate and made very good wines.'

To Brochet, state of mind is an important ingredient of terroir. 'There is no stress here during harvest,' he says, having employed his two best friends to assist. 'It's very important to enjoy your work and I like working in the vineyard on the tractor. When I was young I played with toys and now I like to have fun playing with bigger toys in the vineyard and the winery!' A refreshing mindset for one who has achieved so much so quickly.

EMMANUEL BROCHET LE MONT BENOIT EXTRA BRUT NV • $$

94 points • DISGORGED SEPTEMBER 2012 • TASTED IN VILLERS-AUX-NOEUDS

80% 2009 and 20% 2008; 40% pinot meunier, 35% chardonnay, 25% pinot noir; vinified for
11 months in barrels; full malolactic fermentation; 4g/L dosage

Emmanuel Brochet's complete lack of pretence makes a valiant statement in Champagne. To
him, 2009 was a 'high-tension year', so the picture on the label is a photograph he took of
the high-tension power lines that run near his vineyard. 'Some say it's provocative to put this
on an organic wine, but it's not, it's just an aesthetic label!' he defends. Blended from parcels
across the vineyard, he keeps part of the blend each year as the reserve wine, to maintain
consistency in the blend. True to 2009, this is a rich wine with impressive concentration
and expression of fig, dried pear and custard apple. Savoury texture builds great mouthfeel,
emphasising the delightfully pronounced salty mineral character of the site. For such
dimensions, it retains control and balance, finishing with excellent poise and persistence.

EMMANUEL BROCHET EXTRA BRUT PREMIER CRU MILLESIME 2006 • $$$

96 points • DISGORGED SEPTEMBER 2012 • TASTED IN VILLERS-AUX-NOEUDS

40% chardonnay, 30% pinot meunier, 30% pinot noir; vinified for 11 months in barrel;
no malolactic fermentation; 4g/L dosage

Brochet sets aside his parcels of old-vine chardonnay and pinot meunier for his vintage wines,
blended here with younger pinot noir. He admired the elegance of chardonnay in 2006,
so increased its representation accordingly. The result is a distinctive and impressive fruit
personality that resembles generous apple and pear character, laced with mixed spice and notes
of custard apple. Woodwork melds seamlessly, building texture but not flavour, creating a soft,
creamy mouthfeel, impeccable balance and profound length. Its display of chalk minerality is
pronounced, frothing with sea-surf salt, the signature of Villers-aux-Noeuds and of Brochet.

With no winery to inherit, Emmanuel Brochet restored old equipment to make the first champagne in his village in generations.

ERIC RODEZ

(E-ri Roh-day)

7/10

RUE DE ISSE 51150 AMBONNAY
www.champagne-rodez.fr

ERIC RODEZ
CHAMPAGNE

*O*rganic viticulture has become something of a catch cry in the modern wine world, but never have I seen a more profound statement of its impact than in Eric Rodez's magnificently positioned vineyard of 6.5 hectares on the glorious mid-slopes of Ambonnay. Standing on the edge of his rows of vines, he showed me tiny, sparse bunches. In the very next row, not more than a metre away, his neighbour's vines were loaded with full-sized bunches. The fanatical approach of this eighth-generation winegrower permeates every detail of his work, which embraces vinification in barriques, light dosages and a colossal resource of reserve wines spanning 20 years. The aspiration for Rodez is to let the salty minerality and generous expression of his vines sing through every cuvée. And sing they do.

WHEN I FIRST MET ERIC RODEZ, WHO MOONLIGHTS AS mayor of Ambonnay, he immediately admitted that 'Mon anglais est limité' ('my English is limited') and, my French being far worse, he proposed, 'Nous pourrons parler la langue des bulles!' — 'we can speak in the language of the bubbles!' As I soon discovered, where his bubbles are concerned, a particularly fine language it is.

Rodez makes eight wines, which he thinks of as eight 'melodies'. He likens them to a concert, where every tune evokes a different emotion. 'There is not enough emotion in champagne today!' he exclaims. 'I will not be the Coca-Cola of champagne – I will make emotional wine!' He thinks of his 35 parcels as 35 notes of music, each expressing five emotions, in their grape variety, vintage, vineyard location, method of fermentation, and malolactic fermentation ('forte') or not ('allegro').

The Rodez family has grown grapes in Ambonnay since 1757, and have made their own champagnes since the time of Eric's grandparents, but things changed when Eric began in 1984. 'That was not a good vintage,' he recalled, and it prompted him to do things differently in the vineyard, initiating a methodology that he prefers to call 'integrated' rather than 'ecological.'

He borrows practices of organics and biodynamics, without seeking certification under either. Use of chemicals is limited, grasses are cultivated in the mid-rows and yields are restricted to a tiny 30–40% of the permitted levels. He is working hard to reduce the use of copper sulphate as a fungicide in the vineyards, aiming for just six kilograms per hectare in 2014, and ultimately four kilograms per hectare.

'To my colleagues, I am a little crazy!' he exclaims. 'But I am very happy.'

'When you want to see the soil in the glass, you need to get the vine roots to go into the chalk,' he says. In his vineyards, the chalk is just 40 centimetres below the surface, but this is still deeper than in many parts of the Côte des Blancs, and it took 10 years from when he commenced biodynamics in 1989 before the roots tapped deep into the minerality of the chalk.

His philosophy now translates accurately into his wines, expressed as profoundly salty minerality in his champagnes. He showed me a stunning barrel sample of 2010 pinot noir that displayed none of the botrytis problems that dogged this wet vintage. 'Thanks to low vegetation in the canopy, we had good ventilation and no botrytis in the vineyard,' he explains.

Expression of terroir is everything to Eric Rodez, and he cheerfully admits that he doesn't aspire to make consistent wine for the consumer each year. 'Every year is different and I will adapt my processes in the vineyards and in the cellar to suit. It is very important to me to make a wine of terroir, where you can taste the emotion.'

Exclusively in the heart of Ambonnay's mid-slope, his vineyards are planted to 60% pinot noir and 40% chardonnay, with an average vine age exceeding 30 years. As we left his vineyard and passed Krug's Clos d'Ambonnay on the lower slopes, he commented, 'There is more complexity in the mid-slopes and more minerality lower on the slopes.' I asked which was better and he paused for a long time, smiled knowingly and responded, 'Both are very important for blending!'

There are few small growers who understand blending more intricately than Rodez. His annual production of 40,000 bottles comprises eight cuvées, including six non-vintage blends, benefiting from a deep stock of reserve wines, currently extending as far back as 20 years.

His 35 plots of two varieties are vinified separately to produce 60 different wines, 80% of which are fermented and matured in small Burgundian barrels, mostly aged between three and 20 years. Three vintages in Burgundy and one at Krug taught him to how to use barrels 'for sensuality, not oak flavour,' maintaining that new barrels are not good for the equilibrium and personality of champagne. He is currently increasing old barrel vinification, finding that it offers greater persistence and complexity.

His reserve stocks presently comprise barrels of every vintage since 2000 except the dreaded 2001 and 2003. He showed me a 2006 chardonnay with power and length resembling a great white Burgundy. 'It's too big for champagne,' he said, 'but five or seven percent is very important for the blend.'

Rodez tactically utilises the generosity of Ambonnay and the complexity of barrel fermentation, then enlivens his cuvées with selective use of malolactic fermentation, according to the parcel and the season, and low dosage. Grape juice rather than sugar is used to sweeten liqueurs, and all his wines currently contain no more than 6g/L dosage, allowing the character and minerality of these distinguished vineyards to sing with clarity and harmony.

For all they represent, the wines of Eric Rodez are largely undiscovered, and offer incredible value for money.

Eric Rodez Cuvée des Crayères NV • $$

92 points • Tasted in Ambonnay

46% 2008, 27% 2007, 9% 2006, 8% 2005, 7% 2004, 3% 2002; 55% pinot noir, 45% chardonnay; average vine age 30 years; 30% vinified in barrels; 75% malolactic fermentation; aged 3 years on lees; 6g/L dosage

Eric Rodez captures the personality of Ambonnay from his very first cuvée, enticingly generous in its layered complexity of white peach, baked apple and honey, with oak contributing notes of spice. It's supple, persistent and expressive of the sea-spray salt minerality of the village.

Eric Rodez Cuvée Blanc de Blancs NV • $$

89 points • Tasted in Ambonnay

41% 2007, 20% 2006, 17% 2005, 15% 2004, 3% 2003, 4% 2002; average vine age 32 years;
70% vinified in barrels; 30% malolactic fermentation; 5g/L dosage

This blend doesn't sing with quite the freshness that it paraded last year, with the subtle, savoury, meaty complexity of reduction now a slight disruption. The highlight remains its rounded, rich layers of white peach and lemon, showcasing the breadth and generosity of the village. Pinot noir may be the star of Ambonnay, but chardonnay can certainly perform here, too, expressing the soft, lingering minerality of the village on a long and well-balanced finish.

Eric Rodez Cuvée Blanc de Noirs NV • $$

95 points • Tasted in Ambonnay

45% 2007, 30% 2006, 13% 2005, 8% 2004, 2% 2002, 2% 2000; average vine age 32 years;
75% vinified in barrels; 35% malolactic fermentation; 5g/L dosage

Eric Rodez has again crafted a definitive blanc de noirs, and one of the finest at its price anywhere in Champagne. The enticing purity of Ambonnay pinot noir on show is something to behold, encapsulating the personality of the village in voluptuous black cherries, cherry kernel, red apples and mixed spice. Malic acidity is cleverly utilised to pull the tail into taut, refined definition, emphasising the pronounced salty chalk minerality of the Rodez vineyards.

Eric Rodez Cuvée Zéro Dosage NV • $$

95 points • Tasted in Ambonnay (twice)

65% 2005, 20% 2004, 12% 2002 and 3% 2000; 100% chardonnay; average vine age 32 years;
80% vinified in barrels; 25% malolactic fermentation; zero dosage

Rodez admits that it's very difficult to create a good equilibrium in zero-dosage champagne every year. Testimony to his intuitive flexibility, last year this cuvée was 70% pinot noir, and here it is a pure blanc de blancs. What remains unchanged is that this is one of Champagne's richer zero-dosage offerings, and one of the most delicately balanced. While others create bone-dry champagne from taut, young fruit vinified in stainless steel and softened with malolactic, Rodez turns the entire concept on its head and ingeniously blends a tremendous depth of old wines vinified and aged in barrel from his wonderfully opulent Ambonnay fruit and kisses it with the lightest touch of malolactic. Already a magnificent nine years average age on release, the purity he achieves is game-changing, tactically utilising the lemon, yellow mirabelle plum and white peach richness of Ambonnay chardonnay and the toasty, brioche, vanilla and ground almond notes of reserve wines to create internal harmony without any need for dosage. It finishes dry and structured, with profound persistence and the inimitable signature of Ambonnay salty minerality.

The Champagne Guide

Eric Rodez Cuvée Rosé NV • $$

95 points • Tasted in Ambonnay

45% 2007, 25% 2006, 15% 2005, 12% 2004, 2% 2002; 45% pinot noir maceration; 30% white wine of pinot noir and 25% chardonnay; average vine age 32 years; 75% vinified in barrels; 40% malolactic fermentation; 5g/L dosage

'I will not assemble a red wine and a white wine,' declares Rodez. 'For harmony, I will assemble pink wine of pinot noir macerated on its skins with white wine,' thus merging the maceration and blending techniques of rosé production. His pinot noir suits rosé very well, making, as he puts it, the red berries more explosive. There's real focus here, and excellent concentration of red cherries, strawberries and mixed spice, breathtakingly fresh and primary for a rosé already an average age of seven years on release. Its salty mineral expression is outstanding, all the more incredible for its tremendous fruit presence. An expertly crafted rosé that captures an elusive balance of character, presence and finesse.

Eric Rodez Cuvée Millésime 2004 • $$

96 points • Disgorged September 2012 • Tasted in Ambonnay and Brisbane

55% pinot noir, 45% chardonnay; average vine age 34 years; 85% vinified in barrels; 15% malolactic fermentation; 5g/L dosage

Unusually, 2004 was not a large vintage for Rodez, even smaller than 2002. The precision that he has extracted from this vintage is magnificent, and this is the season that he goes back to as confirmation of his biodynamic techniques. And so it is: the minerality is an epiphany, its shards of pure chalk boring deep into the core of the wine, then frothing up like an ocean swell in a blowhole. There's freshness here, even delicacy for Ambonnay, with an air of lemon and strawberries, harmonising with great intensity and body of plum, cherry liqueur, even plum pudding and espresso, slowly beginning to build nuances of toast and brioche. Skilfully handled barrel work enhances texture, minerality and toastiness without beginning to interrupt freshness, purity and thundering persistence.

Eric Rodez Cuvée des Grands Vintages NV • $$$

95 points • Tasted in Ambonnay

30% 2004, 21% 2002, 18% 2000, 13% 1999, 9% 1998, 6% 1996 and 2% 1995, all aged separately in barrel or tank; 70% pinot noir, 30% chardonnay; average vine age 33 years; fully vinified in barrels; no malolactic fermentation; 4g/L dosage

The philosophy here is an assemblage of the fruits of the first pressings of the best parcels across many years. The roll-call of vintages is mind-blowing, not only in that it averages 12 years of age on release, but that it plunders the greatest seasons of two decades, a line-up that must be unparalleled in all of Champagne, except perhaps in Krug itself, at three times the price. Its deep, layered complexity matches the recipe: generous stone fruits, figs, honey, toast, roast nuts and mixed spice of all kinds. For all of its vast intensity and full-bodied proportions, it maintains absolute control and balance, making way for fine-grained, pronounced, salty minerality to draw the finish out long and fine. The harmony on show in this melody is a masterpiece of Rodez's talent as a composer.

ERNEST RAPENEAU

(Er-nes Rah-pen-noh)

17 RUE DES CRÉNEAUX 51100 REIMS

www.champagne-ernest-rapeneau.com

Champagne
ERNEST RAPENEAU

*E*rnest Rapeneau is produced by the house of G.H. Martel in Reims, from a pool of some 170 hectares of vineyards across 52 villages. The house acquired a majority shareholding in G.H. Martel in 1979, and by the early 1980s was producing more than 2 million bottles annually. Today, its inexpensive champagnes express clean fruit quality, yet have a hurried, unpolished feel of youthful, edgy acidity and robust phenolic structure. All are sealed with DIAM closures.

ERNEST RAPENEAU BRUT SÉLECTION NV • $

88 points • DISGORGED SEPTEMBER 2012 • TASTED IN BRISBANE

50% pinot noir, 45% chardonnay, 5% pinot meunier; DIAM closure

A fruity and young champagne of medium straw hue, with bold, tangy lemon meeting pineapple flavours. It's fresh, vivacious and clean, with taut acidity offset by plenty of dosage, leaving the finish a touch sweet.

ERNEST RAPENEAU GRAND RESERVE PREMIER CRU BRUT NV • $

89 points • DISGORGED SEPTEMBER 2012 • TASTED IN BRISBANE

50% chardonnay, 50% pinot noir; DIAM closure

A strong representation of chardonnay gives this pale, young and primary champagne a tangy, somewhat aggressive acid cut. Fresh, clean lemon and apple fruit has a one-dimensional feel to a short finish. Dosage is well balanced for its firm, youthful acidity.

FLEURY PÈRE & FILS

(Floo-ree Pear e Feess)

6/10

43 GRANDE RUE 10250 COURTERON
www.champagne-fleury.fr

CHAMPAGNE

FLEURY

*J*ean-Pierre Fleury pioneered biodynamic viticulture in Champagne, tending his vines organically since 1970 and biodynamically since 1989. His family have been growers in the village of Couteron in the south of the Côte des Bar since 1895, and his grandfather was selling his own champagnes as early as the 1930s. Since 2004, the estate has been under the keen eye of Jean-Pierre's son, Jean-Sébastien, a trail-blazer who brings a sense of flair and daring no less courageous than his father, constantly trialling new and at times brave techniques in the vineyard and winery. His wines encapsulate the character and expression of Côte des Bar fruit with carefully balanced oak, limited dosage and malolactic fermentation tweaked to draw out the personality of each cuvée. These value-for-money champagnes rightfully rank among the most respected in the Aube.

PIONEERING BIODYNAMICS

JEAN-PIERRE FLEURY WAS REGARDED BY SOME AS A 'crazy hippie' when he started composting and tilling in 1970. 'When my father first talked about biodynamics, it was like something from a different planet!' Jean-Sébastien recalls.

Jean-Pierre's first trial in 1976 was a catastrophe, producing no grapes at all, due to excessive silicon sprays supposed to control mildew. It was not until 1989 that he trialled biodynamics again, and the whole estate was converted in 1992. Within three years, two other growers in the village followed. Fleury now sources from 15 hectares of its own vines and eight hectares from these two neighbours, all biodynamically certified. Characteristic of the area, the estate is planted to a vast majority of pinot noir and a little chardonnay, pinot blanc, pinot meunier and pinot gris.

'Our philosophy is to have healthy grapes,' says Jean-Sébastien. With 22 years of hindsight, they have found biodynamics delivers more consistent crops. 'In seasons when others have low yields, we have higher volumes, and when they have high volumes, ours are medium.' Aiming for lower yields is not Fleury's philosophy. 'We try to take what the vines can bring,' Jean-Sébastien explains, adding that every vineyard brings something different each year, and he needs to be very careful to manage each parcel individually to maintain balance. In 22 years of biodynamics, Fleury was able to reach the yield set for the appellation in every year but three (2003, 2007 and 2012).

A biodynamic approach in Champagne's wild climate can be a nail-biting affair, and it's not getting any easier. The year 2012 was 'a good year for us to learn some new things, and we hope we won't have another year like it!' Jean-Sébastien bemoans. Winter brought frosts of minus 15°C for two weeks straight, followed by two spring frosts, rain disrupting flowering, outbreaks of mildew, followed by two singeing summer days of 38 and 41 degrees. 'The worst conditions for a good harvest,' he says.

Fleury continues to learn more from its biodynamic approach. Recent comparisons between organic, biodynamic and traditional viticulture in the Côte des Bar have found Fleury to achieve 1g more acidity at harvest in regular years, and 2.5g more in hot years. 'Acidity is very important to us,' Jean-Sébastien emphasises. 'Before we embarked in biodynamics our malolactic fermentation was inconsistent, but high acidities now make it more consistent.' Fleury employs malolactic fermentation strategically, according to the acidity of each parcel.

Fleury has discovered that the roots of its vines have plunged deeper into the chalk following biodynamic conversion. With topsoil depths of between 40 centimetres and 1.5 metres, such deep roots are important for tapping into the mineral expression of each site. Prior to full conversion, comparisons were made between biodynamic and traditional viticulture and Jean-Sébastien recalls many tasters enquiring as to the percentage of chardonnay in blanc de noirs, such was the mineral expression of biodynamic parcels.

Fleury's inquisitive approach remains strong. 'We are always experimenting!' Jean-Sébastien announces, with wide eyes. Fleury is part of a group of biodynamic producers trialling alternatives to spraying copper sulphate as a fungicide, including essential oils and lower doses of new copper sprays. Others are trialling preparations based on local plant concoctions, harvesting on certain days of the biodynamic calendar, even playing different music to the vines.

Fleury's own trials are somewhat less far-fetched, employing a horse to cultivate the soil to determine whether or not there is a reduction in soil compaction, replanting using a massal selection of a variety of clones from biodynamic producers, and testing different grafting techniques.

BIODYNAMIC WINEMAKING

In the winery, Fleury has sought ways to introduce the principles of biodynamics in vinification. Its small, gravity-fed winery is intelligently constructed to follow the slope of the hill, with the press house at the top, cuverie directly underneath, and barrels suspended on high frames on the lowest level. Jean-Sébastien's aim is to use no pumps, but admits that this is complicated. Two vertical presses were installed in 1990 and an automatic Coquard press in 2004. 'The pressing makes 50% of the quality,' claims Jean-Sébastien, who loves the delicacy of the new press for reducing colour pick-up and oxidation.

Reducing oxidation is a key priority for Fleury, which hasn't added sulphur as a preservative since 2008. 'In 2011 we made a half press with sulphur and half without and found that adding sulphur removed purity and expression of flavour,' Jean-Sébastien explains. 'We only adjust sulphur levels at disgorgement, because this is crucial for the wine to travel. I hope, touch wood, that we will not have a bad experience!' His no sulphur Sonate No 9 cuvée shows pristine freshness at the winery, and time will tell how it travels, though he reports no problems in the first two and a half years in the market.

Fleury vinifies all parcels separately and, since 1997, 10% of production has been fermented and aged in oak barrels, mostly destined for vintage and reserve wines. To downplay oak flavour, barrels are purchased after three or four uses and maintained for 10–15 years. Reserve wines are stored in an impressive line of large 6000-litre foudres. Jean-Sébastien is keen to trial different fermentation vessels, and hopes to buy eggs and concrete tanks this year to assess their effect.

Jean-Pierre Fleury plans to retire this year, leaving the estate in the capable hands of Jean-Sébastien, his artistic sister and viticulture-trained brother. Their imperative is to uphold the style of Fleury's existing cuvées, while actively pursuing the introduction of new labels, including a 100% oak-fermented pinot blanc, a low-sulphur, zero-dosage pinot noir and a distinctive extra brut pinot noir. The estate has doubled production to a total of 200,000 bottles in recent years, and is working to increase its export markets.

While disgorgement dates are printed on every bottle, they're not always easy to read. Labelling dates are printed much more clearly. Labelling generally occurs 1–6 months after disgorgement.

'Biodynamics explains how we can make our wines unique, but ultimately it's about the wine,' Jean Sébastien emphasises. 'We'd like to be considered not only because our wines are organic or biodynamic, but because we have good grapes and make good wines.'

The champagnes of Fleury certainly live up to this aspiration and are worth discovering for their noble philosophy, and, more importantly, for the character they bring at an affordable price.

The Champagne Guide

FLEURY PÈRE & FILS BLANC DE NOIRS BRUT NV • $$

93 points • 2009 BASE VINTAGE WITH 2008 RESERVE; DISGORGED NOVEMBER 2012;
8G/L DOSAGE • TASTED IN COURTERON

94 points • 2008 BASE VINTAGE WITH 2007 RESERVE; DISGORGED OCTOBER 2011;
8.75G/L DOSAGE • TASTED IN BRISBANE

100% pinot noir; vines aged 15–20 years; enamelled tank fermentation; part of the blend kept as
next year's reserve and aged in 60hL foudres; full malolactic fermentation

A beautifully generous, well-poised blanc de noirs. The 2009 base vintage brims with a richness
of Christmas cake, baked apples and cinnamon spice, while the magnificent and bracing 2008
base vintage reverberates with powerful aromas of blueberries, strawberries and red cherries.
The palate glides effortlessly through fields of crunchy strawberries and orchards of tangy red
cherries, underlined by soft, Aube chalk minerality on a long, even and refreshing finish.

FLEURY PÈRE & FILS FLEUR DE L'EUROPE BRUT NV • $$

94 points • TASTED IN COURTERON • DISGORGED NOVEMBER 2012

2005, 2004 and 2003 vintages; 85% pinot noir, 15% chardonnay; less than 6g/L dosage

Fleur de L'Europe is purposely a more mature style, to contrast with Fleury's Blanc de
Noirs. Its age conspires with the generous fleshiness of Aube pinot noir to build a gloriously
succulent and pure style of strawberry, white peach, fig and red apple fruit, accented with
brioche and nougat. Fine, chalky, almost slatey mineral texture finds a seamless harmony
with a very pure acid line. A showcase for the greatness of Aube pinot noir, and good value.

FLEURY PÈRE & FILS NOTES BLANCHES BRUT NATURE NV

91 points • TASTED IN COURTERON • DISGORGED NOVEMBER 2012

100% 2009, though released too young to be labelled as a vintage; 100% pinot blanc;
100% oak fermented; zero dosage

The first release of Fleury's 'White Notes' is a unique and compelling expression of sparkling
pinot blanc to drink young and fresh. Texturally, pinot blanc behaves quite differently to
chardonnay, making this a blanc de blancs of taut structure and fine-grained phenolic grip.
Its aroma profile is distinctive, too, very spicy and exotic with fig, star fruit and fresh nutmeg
characters. The palate is honeyed, ripe and generous, toned with fine acidity and salty
minerality on a long, refreshing and dry finish.

FLEURY PÈRE & FILS SONATE NO 9 EXTRA BRUT NV

92 points • TASTED IN COURTERON • DISGORGED NOVEMBER 2012

100% pinot noir; no oak; full malolactic fermentation; no added sulphur, though analysis shows 5mg/L of residual sulphur produced naturally during fermentation; no added dosage, but analysis reveals 4g/L residual sugar from fermentation ('It's like it's self-dosaged!' Jean-Sébastien quips)

A lively and fresh pinot noir that shows no deterioration from low sulphur at the winery two months after disgorgement. Its bouquet hits pure high notes of lemon blossom, red apple, star fruit, crunchy pear and almond. Tense, focused acidity drives the palate through layers of spice and even a hint of wood spice, though there is no oak here. Fine, mineral texture defines a refreshing finish. A champagne to enjoy right away.

FLEURY PÈRE & FILS ROSÉ DE SAIGNÉE BRUT NV • $$

93 points • TASTED IN COURTERON • DISGORGED NOVEMBER 2012

2009 base vintage; 100% pinot noir; macerated for 24 hours; average vine age 20 years; enamelled tank and a small percentage of oak fermentation; no malolactic fermentation; 8g/L dosage

Rosé de Saignée is the pinnacle of Fleury, and its stunning new label designed by the family makes it almost as spectacular in its clear bottle as it is out. Different lengths of maceration make for a different colour every year, and the 2009 is a particularly full crimson hue, landing at the deeper end of the champagne rosé pool. It's swimming with fresh rosewater, crunchy strawberries, juicy raspberries and cherries. A touch of reductive complexity lends a hint of gunpowder. Finely managed tannins and lively acidity complement its fruit concentration and build a long, textural finish.

FLEURY PÈRE & FILS ROSÉ DE SAIGNÉE BRUT NV • $$

95 points • DISGORGED DECEMBER 2010 • TASTED IN BRISBANE

2008 base vintage; as for the 2009, except no oak; 6.9g/L dosage

Confident presence and calm sophistication is a difficult tightrope act in champagne rosé, and the balance is all the more challenging to achieve in saignée styles. Fleury has pulled off a particularly tense and exciting rosé, charged with the energy of the 2008 vintage. Its medium salmon hue is at the lighter end of the Fleury spectrum, but there's nothing lightweight about its well-defined pomegranate, raspberry and pink pepper fruit. It's spicy and taut and at the same time soft, drawing a masterful tension between finely honed phenolic grip and refreshing malic acidity. Leading out generous and succulent, it finishes under strict control.

The Champagne Guide

FLEURY PÈRE & FILS CÉPAGES BLANCS EXTRA BRUT 2005 • $$

90 points • TASTED IN COURTERON • DISGORGED NOVEMBER 2012

100% chardonnay; 12% vinified in barrel; 5g/L dosage

The warm 2005 vintage has yielded a generous and rich Fleury of baked peach, exotic spice and butter, already developing into notes of bees wax and nougat. A hint of flinty reduction adds complexity. It pulls into a drying finish of firm, grippy texture, lacking a little in fruit vibrancy on the close.

FLEURY PÈRE & FILS CÉPAGES BLANCS BRUT 2004 • $$

93 points • DISGORGED JULY 2010 • TASTED IN BRISBANE

100% chardonnay; 20 year old vines; enamelled tank fermentation; no malolactic fermentation; 6.65g/L dosage

A similar disgorgement to that which I tasted two years ago, and it's held its composure confidently. Just 50 kilometres from Chablis, this is a showcase for the rounded generosity of Courteron chardonnay in wonderfully expressive characters of dried pear, fig, wild honey, ginger cake, even grilled pineapple and hot wax. There's an intensity to this vintage, yet it does not waver for a moment, carried by primary acidity, and finishing dry and even.

FLEURY PÈRE & FILS BOLERO EXTRA BRUT 2004

90 points • TASTED IN COURTERON • DISGORGED NOVEMBER 2012

100% pinot noir; 30% oak fermented; aged on lees under cork; 4g/L dosage

I was the first person to taste this new release, and with no clues as to what it was, I did not guess pinot noir. It certainly meets the brief of showcasing a different style of this grape. It projects a complexity and an exotic flamboyancy not often seen in champagne, reminding me of lime cordial, quince and passionfruit. It's rich, fruity and generous, yet not sweet, held confidently in line by its firm texture and expressive acidity, finishing long and even. A champagne of idiosyncratic personality as distinctive as its modern label.

FLEURY PÈRE & FILS CUVÉE ROBERT FLEURY EXTRA BRUT 2004 • $$

93 points • TASTED IN COURTERON • DISGORGED NOVEMBER 2012

40% pinot noir, 35% chardonnay, 25% pinot blanc; 100% vinified in oak; full malolactic fermentation; aged on lees under cork

Fleury's tribute to Jean-Pierre's father is an enticing champagne of solid structure, present oak and full body, ready for main-course action. There's power here of secondary yellow fruits, ginger, nutmeg, butter, even notes of smoke. Oak contributes notes of vanilla and wood spice without overpowering. The palate epitomises the savoury, grippy texture that defines the house style, with suggestions of bruised apple development, yet finishing clean and tight, with low dosage.

....

FLEURY PÈRE & FILS CUVÉE ROBERT FLEURY BRUT 2000 • $$

93 points • TASTED IN BRISBANE • DISGORGED MAY 2011

Equal thirds pinot blanc, pinot noir and chardonnay; 100% vinified in oak; full malolactic fermentation; aged on lees under cork; 6.5g/L dosage

Loaded with tons of character and complexity, in the slightly rustic manner of pinot blanc, yet evenly controlled by equal doses of pinot noir and chardonnay, this is one of the friendliest champagnes from left-field. Aromatically, it has as many allusions to Alsacian pinot blanc or even mature riesling as it does to champagne, in characters of honey, toast, kerosene, dried pear and crème brûlée. The palate is fleshy and ripe, with a skinsy texture, yet beautifully controlled by finely poised acidity, every bit as lively as the day it was released two years ago.

Famous for its saignée rosé, Fleury demonstrates that there's more to Côte des Bar rosé than Les Riceys (left).

G.H. MUMM

(G.H. Moom)

29 RUE DU CHAMPS DE MARS 51199 REIMS
www.mumm.com

An annual production of 8 million bottles ranks Mumm number four by volume in Champagne after Moët, Clicquot and Feuillatte. Despite a turbulent history of acquisitions over the past century, Mumm has admirably retained its almost 218 hectares of vines, the majority planted to pinot noir, meeting 25% of its needs. The house has come a long way since my first visit during the snowfalls of Christmas 2001, recovering from its dark days of the 1980s and 1990s, due in part to the somewhat controversial appointment of the 31-year-old Dominique Demarville as Chef de Cave in 1998 and his 35-year-old successor, Didier Mariotti, in 2006. Mumm now enjoys a higher percentage of chardonnay in its 'Cordon Rouge' house blend, as well as more reserve wine, longer maturation times and lower dosages, all of which have helped to lift the style. And there is more at hand.

IN 1995, MUMM LAUNCHED A 12-YEAR PLAN TO resurrect Cordon Rouge, encompassing harvesting, pressing and vinification, with a focus on building reserve wines since the late 1990s, but it was not until Pernod Ricard purchased the company in 2005 that sufficient funds were injected to fully realise this vision. 'The quality of Cordon Rouge was so bad 10–15 years ago, because of insufficient reserve wines, short ageing in the cellar and inconsistent blends for each vintage,' Mariotti admits.

A gleaming new winery was constructed in Reims in 2008 and extended in 2010 to house row after row of sparkling new stainless steel tanks, new disgorgement and bottling lines, and space for greater stocks of reserve wines. 'With a new winery and smaller vats we are able to hone in on the terroir more accurately by producing smaller parcels for the blends,'

Mariotti explains. New press centres were constructed in Mailly-Champagne and Verzy in 2010 to address concerns with fruit waiting for up to 10 hours to be pressed. Grapes can now be moved just a few kilometres between press houses to avoid these delays.

Cordon Rouge is moving from 20% to an impressive 30% reserve wines, spanning four vintages, which Mariotti upholds as crucial for maintaining the consistency of the blend. It spends a minimum of two and a half years on lees in the cellar, and Mariotti has worked to lower the dosage from 10g/L to 8g/L. 'I am very proud of this dosage, one of the lowest of any of the houses,' he claims.

The magnitude of his new winery is sufficient that all 8 million bottles of Cordon Rouge are now the same blend each year, a remarkable feat of logistical engineering. An identical blend is made once a week for 15–20 weeks. An extra 30% is produced, and kept in tank as the reserve for the following year.

Didier Mariotti is enthusiastic about raising the quality of Mumm, bringing an acute attention to detail to every part of the process from the vineyard to the market. He spends 70% of his time during harvest visiting growers, building relationships, seeing the quality of the fruit and gaining an insight into the vintage. At the other end of the process, he tastes every wine from each warehouse in most export markets every six months, and checks the disgorgement date of cuvées in every restaurant he visits. 'It is important to be sure that the quality is maintained at every step,' he emphasises. 'You can work hard on the blend, ageing and disgorgement and if you don't focus on the supply chain you can destroy everything.' Mumm prints disgorgement dates only on its Brut Selection for the French market, but Mariotti believes it is always best to disclose the disgorgement date, and is working on introducing a bottle code in the same manner as Krug.

In a region where change comes slowly, Mariotti is eager to embrace innovation, even appointing a new winemaker dedicated to this purpose last year, with a focus on testing stoppers, lightstruck damage, matching champagne glasses to particular cuvées, as well as driving all manner of experiments in the winery.

'If you are not trialling, you are not moving,' declares Mariotti. 'Global warming, the markets and other things are changing, so we need to be asking questions about winemaking all the time.' This philo-sophy has inspired small trials of bâtonnage, malolactic fermentation, barrel ageing of liqueurs, even barrels of different coopers and varying levels of toast. All Mumm cuvées currently undergo full malolactic fermentation, though parcels with no malolactic are trialled each vintage. 'We need to be prepared for global warming,' Mariotti reveals, 'but so far our only response has been to harvest earlier.'

Mariotti has a vision to bring more structure and complexity to the non-vintage cuvées, by increasing ageing on lees, facilitated by having 25 million bottles maturing in its cellars at any time, and through greater proportions of reserve wines. 'With five years of wines in reserve I am able to think about which reserves I use for each blend,' he explains. Barrel ageing with bâtonnage may be the third step in future, though Mariotti admits that 'in some of our experimentation with barrels, the results have been very, very bad! But it's good for the kids to play!'

Mumm has bottled half bottles of Cordon Rouge under DIAM closures for two years and is hoping to do the same for full bottles for export markets. Mariotti is convinced of DIAM's superiority. 'If we can guarantee no more cork problems, I don't know why we are waiting!' he exclaims. (This can't come too soon, as I've seen some cork effect in this cuvée.)

'It takes a long time to turn things around in Champagne!' he adds. This is especially true in a house the size of Mumm. Its non-vintage cuvées are on a slow ascent, with hope for further gains in years to come.

Mumm's distinctive windmill overlooks its vineyards in Verzenay, historic birthplace of the house and important source of grand cru pinot.

The Champagne Guide

G.H. Mumm Cordon Rouge Brut NV • $$

90 points • Disgorged March 2012 • Tasted in Brisbane

2009 base vintage; 45% pinot noir, 30% chardonnay, 25% pinot meunier from 77 crus
and more than 2000 parcels; 8 million bottles; aged 30 months on lees; 8g/L dosage

A primary, up-front and fruity apéritif champagne of lemon zest and red apple fruit,
demonstrably fresher today than it was some years ago. It's clean and crisp, simple and
one-dimensional, with plenty of fruit on the front and not much on the finish. The first
bottle I opened showed a grubby, earthy cork character that suppressed aromatics and
contracted the finish; the second was pristine.

G.H. Mumm Brut Selection Grand Cru NV • $$

88 points • Disgorged April 2011 • Tasted in Reims

2005 base vintage with reserves from 2004, 2002, 1999 and 1998; pinot noir from Aÿ, Bouzy
and Verzenay; chardonnay from Avize and Cramant; aged 5 years in the cellar; 6g/L dosage

The new child in the Mumm family arrives with impressive credentials, though suffers from
the drying, contracted, savoury finish of the 2005 vintage. It's quite nutty, cheesy and earthy
on the front, and recovers somewhat on the finish, with impressive mature notes of roast nuts
and butter, highlighted by well-balanced dosage.

G.H. Mumm de Cramant Blanc de Blancs NV • $$$$

89 points • Disgorged January 2012 • Tasted in Brisbane

100% 2006 Cramant chardonnay; 36 months on lees; 4.5 atmospheres of pressure; 6g/L dosage;
100,000 bottles

In philosophy and pedigree, de Cramant is an altogether different tier in the world of
Mumm, and its only cuvée that I buy. As a relatively young release, the acidity of Cramant
is too aggressive for a full bead, so it is bottled at 4.5 atmospheres of pressure rather than the
usual 6. It's always been one variety (chardonnay), one village (Cramant) and one vintage,
though frustratingly never labelled as such. This is particularly troubling, as the current
release 2006 vintage is the least that I have seen this cuvée in the past decade, and there's
nothing on the bottle to distinguish it from its far superior predecessors. All four bottles
I opened lacked life and verve; the bouquet muted and toasty, the palate firm and phenolic,
with a bitter grapefruit-zest finish. It attempts to redeem itself with clean, crisp, youthful,
zesty lemon and apple fruit, which quickly vanishes on a short, contracted finish.

G.H. Mumm Cordon Rouge Brut Millésimé 2004 • $$

91 points • Disgorged March 2011 • Tasted in Brisbane

70% pinot noir, 30% chardonnay; 6g/L dosage

This vintage looked fairly simple and one-dimensional on release, and two years have blessed it with a touch of nougat and honey complexity. It holds its vibrancy at nine years of age, retaining primary, rounded white peach, lemon zest and apple fruit, finishing a little sugary, and shy of character and persistence. It's clean, balanced and friendly.

G.H. Mumm Cuvée R. Lalou Brut 1999 • $$$$$

91 points • Disgorged March 2010 • Tasted in Brisbane

50% pinot noir from Verzy, Verzenay, Aÿ, Mailly, Bouzy and Ambonnay; 50% chardonnay from Cramant and Avize; 6g/L dosage

Lalou was the prestige wine of the house between 1969 and 1985, but the bottle mould and recipe were lost somewhere in the wild ride of ownership changes. In 1998, Demarville revived the cuvée, this time a blend of 12 parcels in estate grand cru vineyards. Only at the point of blending is the decision made as to which parcels will win the golden ticket (it may be as few as two, if the vintage is deemed worthy at all). The only absolute is an equal blend of chardonnay and pinot noir. A liqueur of Cramant and Bouzy is aged in barrel to build sufficiently to meet the power of the wine.

The 1999 Lalou is unashamedly built as a strong wine and has evolved considerably from the lemon zest and citrus blossom personality of the first release of the same disgorgement two years ago. The nougat and vanilla of long lees ageing have developed into biscuit, toffee, honey and praline, overlaying soft, succulent peach fruit. Its ripe fruit presence and soft acidity conspire to generate an impression of sweetness that belies its low dosage.

On the Montagne de Reims foothills, Rilly-la-Montagne is one of Champagne's oldest wine villages.

GASTON CHIQUET

(Gas-toh Shi-khe)

7/10

912 AVE DU GÉNÉRAL LECLERC 51530 DIZY

www.gastonchiquet.com

CHAMPAGNE

Gaston Chiquet

PROPRIÉTAIRE - RÉCOLTANT

'The point is to make "vin de terroir",' emphasises the young eighth-generation Dizy grower Nicolas Chiquet. 'We are lucky to have some very nice vineyard locations, so our goal is to preserve the character of the fruit.' His assessment of the family's 23 hectares is politely modest. These are well-established vineyards on the privileged mid-slopes of Dizy, Hautvillers, Aÿ (including an impressive five hectares of chardonnay), Mareuil-sur-Aÿ, as well as in the Valley of the Ardre, close to Reims. With careful attention to sustainable viticulture, meticulous fruit handling and sensitive vinification, Nicolas and his brother Antoine's 'vin de terroir' ambition is brought to life in champagnes of fruit purity and fine, chalky minerality that represent impressive value for money.

THE CHIQUETS HAVE TENDED VINES SINCE 1746 AND were among Champagne's first growers to make their own wines in 1919. The property in Dizy was purchased by the brothers' grandfather Gaston in 1935, with a deep and extensive cellar, more than sufficient for the current production of 220,000 bottles annually.

In villages famed for pinot noir, Gaston Chiquet is unusual in its 40% holdings of each of pinot meunier and chardonnay. 'We speak well of the quality of meunier, even though it does not have the finesse to age like chardonnay or pinot noir. It provides roundness in the mouth for our non-vintage wines,' Nicolas Chiquet explains.

'Terroir is the most important thing and we have to be very humble in our approach,' adds Chiquet, who distinguishes his role as a Chef de Cave from that of a winemaker. 'We want to work more on our vineyards than our wine, making "vin de terroir" rather than adding oxygen through vinification in oak.' He compares this process with cooking.

'When you have good produce you have very little to do and it is perfect! This is why we have very natural winemaking processes. We do not want to change our fruit. We are very careful to adapt our vinification to keep the freshness in the juice, as we have a lot of power in our fruit.'

Vinification begins with one of the most sophisticated presses in Champagne, extracting the purest juice, though the old press is still used sometimes. 'The new press has had little influence, but how it's controlled is the key,' Chiquet says. Each of 35 different parcels is vinified separately in small stainless steel tanks, not oak barrels. To further protect from oxidation, wines are not aged long in tank, with bottle ageing preferred. Malolactic fermentation is carried out on all parcels and low dosages of typically 8g/L are used.

True to the ambition to preserve fruit character and reduce oxidation, DIAM closures have been used on every cuvée since 2009. 'The crown caps we use in the cellars are the best closures, but we can't sell our wines with them,' he says. 'DIAMs are very reliable, with a consistent level of oxygen ingress and no cork taint.' Pleasingly, every bottle is labelled with its disgorgement date. 'This is very important to us. We have educated our customers and they know not to open a bottle soon after it has been disgorged.'

Along with their cousins just around the corner at Jacquesson, the Chiquets make the finest champagnes of Dizy. True 'vin de terroir'.

GASTON CHIQUET INSOLENT BRUT NV • $

88 points • Disgorged July 2012 • Tasted in Dizy

2010 base vintage; sourced largely from Dizy and Hautvillers; average vine age 25 years; blend of first- and second-press juice; tank fermented; full malolactic fermentation; aged 2 years on lees; 8.8g/L dosage; DIAM closure

Intentionally a soft, light, pinot meunier-led champagne for summer parties, blended from any estate fruit of insufficient character or ageability for the house's other cuvées. It's by definition the least of the range, a fresh, sweet and simple style of rounded stone fruits and citrus, with an earthy undercurrent, crisp acidity and some phenolic texture from second-press juice.

GASTON CHIQUET BRUT TRADITION PREMIER CRU NV • $$

94 points • Disgorged June 2012 • Tasted in Dizy

2008 base vintage with 20% 2007 and 2006 reserves; 45% pinot meunier, 35% chardonnay, 20% pinot noir; 95% first juice; 8g/L dosage; DIAM closure

All hail the great 2008 vintage! Never have I seen Brut Tradition shine with such vivid clarity of red fruit perfume, lively lemon juice and expressive fruit persistence. Subtle mixed spice is underlined by fresh, taut acid persistence that lingers long on a refined finish. A consummately complete apéritif style, and great value.

GASTON CHIQUET BLANC DE BLANCS D'AŸ NV • $$

95 points • Disgorged June 2011 • Tasted in Dizy

100% 2008; 8g/L dosage; DIAM closure

In 1935, Gaston Chiquet was among the first to plant chardonnay in Aÿ, and today claims the only blanc de blancs in the village, a blend made by Nicolas' father and grandfather since 1950. It's always a vintage wine, yet released too young to be labelled as such. Chiquet is disappointed the 2008 vintage is so distinctive in its acidity because 'the point is to show the character of chardonnay in Aÿ, highlighting the terroir rather than the year'. Pedantics aside, this is a remarkable blanc de blancs, harmonising the elegance of the season with the rumbling power of the village. Refined lemon blossom perfume juxtaposes an understated yet rich core of fleshy white peach and apple. The chalk of the village speaks loud and clear above the voice of fruit and season, with well-defined fine chalk mineral texture. The length is outstanding: fresh, mineral and enlivened with classic 2008 acidity. An NV to age.

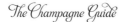

GASTON CHIQUET CUVÉE DE RÉSERVE PREMIER CRU BRUT NV • $$

94 points • DISGORGED SEPTEMBER 2012 • TASTED IN DIZY

Brut Tradition base vintage 2005; 45% pinot meunier, 35% chardonnay, 20% pinot noir; average vine age 27 years; aged on lees at least 5 years; 8g/L dosage; DIAM closure

Nicolas Chiquet doesn't leave it to chance for his customers to discover that the finest vintages of Brut Tradition age magnificently. With three years longer on lees, it's a soft and enticingly drinkable champagne of balance, generosity and poise. Impressive complexity of brioche, vanilla and custard has developed, while retaining the white peach generosity and creamy intensity of 2005. Fine chalk mineral texture remains unperturbed.

GASTON CHIQUET ROSÉ BRUT PREMIER CRU NV • $$

94 points • DISGORGED AUGUST 2012 • TASTED IN DIZY

2009 white wine base vintage; 12% red wine from 2008; 40% pinot meunier, 30% pinot noir, 30% chardonnay; 8.8g/L dosage; DIAM closure

Nicolas Chiquet's honesty is refreshing, openly declaring that it's tricky to make good red wine from pinot noir in Aÿ, often necessitating as much as 18% in his rosé, limiting volume to just 10% of the production of the house. Impressive colour in 2008 allowed a smaller red wine addition, giving life to a wonderful apéritif-style rosé. A bright, pale salmon pink hue anticipates an elegant bouquet of rose petals, strawberry hull and pink pepper. Its elegantly calm palate of soft, chalky minerality and fine-grained tannin texture carries well-defined focus of black cherry fruits and kirsch.

GASTON CHIQUET CUVÉE OR BRUT MILLÉSIMÉ 2004 • $$

95 points • DISGORGED SEPTEMBER 2012 • TASTED IN DIZY

60% pinot noir, 40% chardonnay; 8g/L dosage; DIAM closure

Parcels for vintage wines are chosen on their power and ability to age for 10 years without sensitivity to oxygen. This vintage will age for considerably longer, too, if its freshness and vitality at nine years of age are any indication. It retains a primary lemon core, layered with the presence of yellow summer fruits, white cherries, and all the complexity of brioche, almonds, ginger and mixed spice. A great vintage for Gaston Chiquet — majestic, complete and intricately assembled, with a lingering fruit line, supported by soft minerality.

GASTON CHIQUET SPECIAL CLUB BRUT MILLÉSIMÉ 2005 • $$

92 points • DISGORGED JUNE 2012 • TASTED IN DIZY

70% chardonnay, 30% pinot noir; 8g/L dosage; DIAM closure

A well-made champagne, yet true to a lesser season. The 2005 vintage exudes its rich, honeyed, spicy personality, balanced here with fine texture and more freshness on the finish than many in this warm vintage. Brioche, toast and mixed spice have grown in the cellar. Drink up soon.

GATINOIS

(Ga-tin-wah)

8/10

7 RUE MARCEL MAILLY 51160 AŸ
www.champagne-gatinois.com

CHAMPAGNE

GATINOIS

AŸ GRAND CRU

In the elegant reception room of Gatinois in the back streets of Aÿ, alongside a magnificent wine press still standing where it was constructed five generations ago, the Gatinois family tree is proudly displayed, tracing the family history in the village back to 1696. Young Louis Cheval-Gatinois is the 12th successive generation to farm seven hectares of his family's vineyards, enviably positioned on the majestic slopes of Aÿ. His family has made champagne here for so long they can't put an exact date on it, suggesting the mid-1800s, which must place Gatinois among the oldest grower producers in all of Champagne. Gatinois' generously coloured champagnes are among the finest in this revered village, resonating with the history of the house and the thundering power of its grand cru slopes, at every moment retaining exceptional definition and freshness.

IN THE CONVOLUTED HISTORY OF CHAMPAGNE succession and inheritance, the vineyards of the ancient village of Aÿ have been divided into ever-smaller plots, creating what Louis Cheval-Gatinois describes as 'a mosaic on the hillside.'

Gatinois has been privileged to retain seven hectares that have scarcely changed since the inception of the house, divided into 27 parcels of exclusively south-facing old vines (young vine fruit is sold). A wide spread of sites across the full breadth of the village creates complexity. 'Some respond better in particular seasons, so we can pick what we want in each vintage,' Cheval-Gatinois explains.

Pinot noir comprises some 90% of plantings, with a little less than one hectare of chardonnay to bring freshness and endurance to pinot's fleshy structure and aromatic intensity. Fruit is green harvested if appropriate to give low harvests of 65hL/hectare, yielding an annual production of just 50,000 bottles. Low yields enable Gatinois to pick at a high level of maturity, bringing colour and intensity to its champagnes.

The house maintains that careful picking is crucial for quality, so employs its own team of pickers. Every bad grape is sorted from each basket that is brought to the press. 'The quality of the grapes is the thing that makes our champagnes,' Cheval-Gatinois declares.

'The secret to the colour and style of our champagnes is what we put in our press. My father taught me to be proud of what is in the press before we close it, to be able to pick any grape and have the very best quality.'

Vinification at Gatinois is meticulously hands-on, shared between just three workers in the vineyards and cellars. The house still maintains its manual press. 'People are surprised to see me working with a traditional press, but this is important to ensure that we do not lose any quality,' he explains. 'We have a very humble vinification as we do not want to have too much impact on the taste.' Vinification takes place entirely in stainless steel tanks, to preserve the purity of the grape aromas. The only barrels in the house are for red wines, and these are very old, so as to produce gentle oxidation without imparting wood characters.

All cuvées undergo full malolactic fermentation and receive low dosages of around 6g/L. Zero-dosage champagne is not on the agenda here, because 'dosage is important to produce smoothness and openness in the mouth without feeling the sweetness.' Blending is conducted slowly and carefully in May following the harvest, achieving very clear base wines by allowing plenty of time for natural settling prior to bottling. Bottles are matured in Gatinois' cellars under Aÿ, and all 50,000 are painstakingly hand disgorged on site every year. 'If it weren't for the history of the estate I wouldn't hand disgorge, but I watched my father and my grandfather do it, so I do the same!'

Since taking responsibility three years ago, Louis has no desire to change the style. 'With such rich history behind me, I have a great opportunity to continue the philosophy of the house.' Skilfully capturing the exact character and great concentration of Aÿ, this tiny estate remains in capable and hard-working hands. Eleven generations would certainly be proud.

GATINOIS GRAND CRU BRUT TRADITION NV • $$

94 points • 2009 BASE VINTAGE; 80% PINOT NOIR, 20% CHARDONNAY • TASTED IN AŸ
95 points • 2008 BASE VINTAGE; DISGORGED OCTOBER 2011; 90% PINOT NOIR,
10% CHARDONNAY • TASTED IN BRISBANE

30-35% reserve wines; full malolactic fermentation; aged 2 years on lees; 6.5g/L dosage

A deep colour for a young wine, expressing the magnificent depth of character and concentration of Aÿ pinot noir. A grand parade of cherries, strawberries, orange rind and all the fanfare of layers of spice reflect the primary complexity of Gatinois' 27 sites across the village. Structure and definition rise to meet the fruit spectacle, with vibrant acid definition and soft, chalky mineral texture interlocking seamlessly and carrying forth into a wonderfully enticing finish. The vivacious 2008 base vintage is even brighter than the 2009, with an air of intricately honed harmony of fresh rose petal.

GATINOIS GRAND CRU BRUT RÉSERVE NV • $$

95 points • TASTED IN AŸ

2008 base vintage; 80% pinot noir, 20% chardonnay; aged 3 years on lees; 6.5g/L dosage

Made in the same manner and from similar parcels as Brut Tradition, and aged on lees for another year, this is purposely a more generous style, but the real distinction here is the radiant splendour of the 2008 vintage. A triumphant wine that trumpets the magnificence of Aÿ pinot noir in all its cherry, cherry kernel, anise and plum glory, framed impeccably in tense acidity, vivacious freshness and chalk mineral depth. Its authority lends a hint of salmon to its hue, and tremendous vigour to the palate, yet its purity is unerring and breathtakingly lively, finishing dry, tense and focused.

GATINOIS GRAND CRU BRUT ROSÉ NV • $$

95 points • TASTED IN AŸ

2009 base vintage; 95% pinot noir, 5% chardonnay; 7% very concentrated red wine from two parcels of Aÿ pinot noir of vines older than 60 years, yielding just 60% of Gatinois' normal yield; macerated for 10 days; 6g/L dosage

Such is the intensity of Gatinois' red wine that even a tiny addition creates an impressive medium salmon hue. This refined rosé epitomises the personality of great Aÿ pinot noir in all of its succulent, fleshy generosity, yet presents an impeccably tense and crisp structure. Pretty cherry and strawberry fruit purity meets gorgeous rose petal perfume on the bouquet, while the palate counters beautifully balanced fruit presence with tremendous, super-fine tannin texture and invisible dosage, at every moment lively and refreshing.

GATINOIS GRAND CRU BRUT MILLÉSIMÉ 2006 • $$

95 points • TASTED IN AŸ AND WELLINGTON

85% pinot noir, 15% chardonnay; aged on lees a little under 5 years; 6g/L dosage; 5000 bottles

Gatinois' vintage aspiration is to produce champagnes particular to Aÿ and to the season, blending parcels from the middle of the slope that best encapsulate this balance for the vintage; 2006 was a season of generosity, without sacrificing focus. It's a fleshy, succulent wine with a plethora of concentrated flavours and aromas of yellow mirabelle plums, white peach, honey, nougat, gingernut biscuits and mixed spice, enlivened by Gatinois' signature structure of refreshing, lively acidity well-controlled, mouth-filling chalk texture, finished with a creamy bead and perfectly matched dosage.

GATINOIS COTEAUX CHAMPENOIS GRAND CRU AŸ ROUGE 2004 • $$

92 points • TASTED IN AŸ

Gatinois' well-balanced and rare still red wine takes impeccable weather and half a day for the team in the press house to produce between just 1000 and 2000 bottles. Pretty aromas of cherries are beginning to become forest floor, game and truffles. Excellent persistence of pepper, anise and blackberry flavours are underlined by very soft, fine, silky tannins and well-defined acidity, without becoming too tense.

GEOFFROY

(Zhof-wah)

7/10

4 RUE JEANSON 51160 AŸ
www.champagne-geoffroy.com

CHAMPAGNE
GEOFFROY

The finest grower in Cumières is no longer in Cumières. With winemaking facilities and cellars shared between his grandmother's house, his father's house and a neighbour, when the opportunity came to consolidate in 2008, young fifth-generation vigneron Jean-Baptiste Geoffroy moved the whole operation 20 minutes (by tractor) down the road to Aÿ. Importantly, the vineyards remained, all 11 glorious hectares in Cumières, and one in each of the nearby villages of Damery, Hautvillers and Fleury-la-Rivière. This is what matters most for Geoffroy. 'I am a winegrower,' he says. 'I need to be in the vineyard, this is my passion.' There is a well-considered sensibility about Geoffroy, and every detail of his work in the vineyard and winery follows a stringent regime, while maintaining practical common sense. He is now better placed than ever to capture the fruit purity, poise and deep mineral fingerprint of some of the finer premier crus of the Vallée de la Marne.

WHEN I FIRST MET JEAN-BAPTISTE IN HIS PROUD AND spacious facility in Aÿ, my schedule didn't permit opportunity to visit his vineyards, so he took me to the rooftop, which enjoys a direct view of the slopes of Cumières.

'Nothing has changed in the vineyards,' he assured me. 'I want to create a champagne of terroir, to achieve the best expression of the soil in the grapes.' To this end, his highest goal in the winery is to maintain freshness in every cuvée. This proved to be a challenge, working from three sites in Cumières, necessitating regular pumping and moving of bottles.

Now he can guarantee that his grapes are on the press less than an hour after they are harvested, in a facility ingeniously designed to do away with pumping

altogether. Taking advantage of the hill behind, the harvest is delivered to the press on the third level of the building, and the juice flows by gravity to settling tanks immediately below the press on the second level, then to fermentation on the first level and finally to two levels of deep maturation cellars below.

In 2012 he purchased a further 500 square metres of storage space in the village, not to increase production, but to relocate bottles to provide space to move his barrels deeper into the cellar, where the temperature is more stable.

Every step of production is geared towards maintaining freshness and vineyard character, which Geoffroy achieves with admirable consistency, even with low use of sulphur dioxide as a preservative.

A traditional press is employed, which he admits is difficult to operate by hand, but worth every effort for quality. Each of 45 different parcels is pressed and vinified separately, and the tailles of each pressing separated and vinified independently.

Fermentation is conducted variously in the best vessels to facilitate controlled oxidation, generally small tanks for non-vintage wines, and small barrels and large foudres for vintage wines and the best pinot noir parcels. Previously using only older barrels, Geoffroy has recently introduced a turnover of younger barrels, though the oak flavours and tannins that this has introduced in at least one of his cuvées do not flatter the elegance of his fruit.

Ferments rely on wild yeast, but are inoculated if they don't start naturally. To further preserve freshness, malolactic fermentation is avoided (but will occasionally start spontaneously). Only concentrated grape juice is used for dosage, because he says he couldn't find a good balance using sugar. 'This emphasises the taste of the grapes and the character of the soil,' he says.

Geoffroy generally uses extra brut dosages of less than 5g/L, though a couple of cuvées are currently at double this level, and probably don't need to be. As he puts it, 'A champagne must always be very fine, elegant and fresh. If you have good ripeness and good practice in the winery you don't need dosage'.

Ripeness is achieved through painstaking attention to every detail in the vineyard. Geoffroy's annual production of 130,000 bottles is sourced exclusively from his own vines, apart from 5% permitted under récoltant-manipulant registration. Pinots rule in this part of the world, and his holdings comprise 40% each of pinot noir and pinot meunier and 20% chardonnay.

EARTH-FRIENDLY APPROACH
His eco-friendly approach is close to organic, but falls purposely short of the constraints of certification. 'I like to say I am bio-logical, without being bio-dynamic,' he says. To best express the soil in the grapes, vineyards are ploughed to discourage surface roots and drive the vines deeper into the subsoils.

To the same end, a number of species of natural grasses are cultivated in the mid-rows to provide competition at the surface. He is currently introducing a horse to plough one vineyard in an attempt to reduce tractor compaction. Organic fertilisers encourage soil health, and herbicides are avoided. Sulphur and copper sulphate sprays are used where possible, but here he sometimes deviates from a strict organic regime, calling on other chemicals as required.

Geoffroy knows each of his 45 plots intimately, and treats each separately, regarding them variously as grand cru, premier cru or unclassified. The blanket classification of Cumières as premier cru makes no sense to him. 'On the poor soil and sand at the top of the hill near the forest, it is inferior to Damery, which is unclassified,' he clarifies. 'The early-ripening middle slope of the south-facing amphitheatre of Cumières north of the city is of grand cru quality, and to the west it is premier cru.'

He points out each on a satellite photograph, and his designations corresponded precisely with the green patches that betray the most vigorous vines. There is a natural regulation of vigour in Geoffroy's vines, with old vines and mid-row grasses limiting yields, ensuring earlier ripeness.

COTEAUX CHAMPENOIS RED WINES
This approach allows him to produce one of the most celebrated Coteaux Champenois still red wines, a passion he inherited from his father and grandfather. 'I make a red wine from the best grapes of my terroir, from the oldest vines and the lowest yields,' he says.

After experimenting extensively with red wine production in Beaujolais and Burgundy, Geoffroy produces his red wine only in warmer vintages from Cumières pinot noir (pinot meunier for the first time in 2008), and releases it as both a non-vintage and a vintage cuvée. The wines undergo malolactic fermentation and mature in 600-litre demi-muids for a minimum of 12 months. These are long-ageing wines, with the potential to live for decades, and are only released when he deems them ready. Production is small and sporadic. 'It's good to make Coteaux Champenois when you don't need to!' he says. 'You can't make it to demand or in every vintage.'

In 2012, Geoffroy simplified the name of the estate from 'René Geoffroy' to 'Geoffroy' and introduced a new label, depicting the gate of the house in Aÿ to represent his new identity. 'It is not my philosophy to put my first name on the label as I hope to one day pass the estate on to my children. There is no point changing the name with every generation,' he says.

Vintages, varieties, dosage and date of disgorgement are now displayed on the back of every label, a laudable commitment for a small grower who disgorges every 2–3 months and tweaks the dosage for each disgorgement.

With undeviating attention to well-situated vineyards, an enviable production facility larger than his needs — and no intention to grow production — Cumières' finest grower is as fine as ever.

The Champagne Guide

GEOFFROY EXPRESSION BRUT PREMIER CRU NV • $$

98 points • DISGORGED OCTOBER 2012 • TASTED IN AŸ

2009 base vintage and 2008 reserve; 50% pinot meunier, 40% pinot noir, 10% chardonnay;
6g/L dosage

The 2008 was the first vintage that Jean-Baptiste made himself, and this is the finest I've
seen his entry cuvée. It's a beautifully balanced, clean style of crystal-clear fruit expression
of zesty citrus freshness and the pinot meunier lead of gentle red cherry and strawberry
character. A lively aperitif style, with fine acidity and soft, chalky minerality building a long,
fresh, crisp finish.

GEOFFROY PURETE BRUT ZERO NV • $$

92 points • DISGORGED JANUARY 2012 • TASTED IN AŸ

2007 base vintage and 2006 reserve; same base as Expression; 2 years older; 50% pinot meunier,
40% pinot noir, 10% chardonnay; zero dosage

The same base that I tasted with Jean-Baptiste two years ago is still current, and from a
younger disgorgement it holds its poise confidently. Its fine citrus fruits have evolved to a
fleshier demeanour of succulent white peach, red plums, nutmeg and five-spice, becoming
subtly toasty with brioche suggestions, accurately proclaiming its pinot meunier lead. This
works well in this zero-dosage style, giving a stronger voice to chalky minerality, and finishing
with pronounced, firm acidity.

GEOFFROY EMPREINTE BRUT PREMIER CRU 2007 • $$

94 points • DISGORGED NOVEMBER 2012 • TASTED IN AŸ

76% pinot noir, 10% pinot meunier, 14% chardonnay; fully fermented in oak barrels; 10g/L dosage

Cumières' pinot noir is beautifully portrayed here, structured with the tension of a higher-
acid season. Its personality is captured in gorgeous rose petals, succulent strawberries, ripe
raspberries and mixed spice, with subtle notes of brioche beginning to rise. A vintage of line,
length and precision, with soft, mineral texture. High dosage is well matched to the vibrancy
of its acidity, and Geoffroy plans to decrease dosage with successive disgorgements.

GEOFFROY ROSÉ DE SAIGNÉE BRUT NV • $$

90 points • DISGORGED SEPTEMBER 2012 • TASTED IN AŸ

100% 2010, but released too young to be labelled as such; saignée of 100% skin-contact pinot noir; 10g/L dosage

Geoffroy's saignée has produced a full crimson hue in 2010. A very pretty bouquet sings with the primary vibrancy of violet perfume, red apple, pomegranate, red cherries and strawberries. The palate has a raspberry generosity and an assortment of rich red berry fruits of all kinds, finishing with candied dosage notes and soft minerality. Without sufficient time to build persistence or complexity, its up-front fruit freshness doesn't carry through to the finish.

GEOFFROY BRUT PREMIER CRU VOLUPTÉ 2006 • $$$

91 points • DISGORGED SEPTEMBER 2012 • TASTED IN AŸ

80% chardonnay, 20% pinot noir; 94% fermented in large- and small-format oak; aged 5 years on lees; 5g/L dosage

I first tasted a younger version of this vintage with Jean-Baptiste two years ago, and after three years on lees and just 2g/L dosage it was a magnificent lemon-zest-accented expression of Cumières chardonnay. It has softened and rounded considerably with a further two years on lees, and I'm not sure that a higher dosage is necessary. Creamy, concentrated and fleshy, its theme is now juicy yellow summer fruits with baked apple, wild honey, ginger, almond and mixed spice. Its smooth silkiness is classic mature Cumières.

GEOFFROY BLANC DE ROSÉ EXTRA BRUT NV • $$$$

91 points • DISGORGED JUNE 2012 • TASTED IN AŸ

100% 2010, though too young to be labelled as such; 50% chardonnay and 50% pinot noir macerated in a saignée method; 2g/L dosage; 4000 bottles

This is purposely a very different rosé, a fresh citrus fruits and mineral-accented style, designed as an aperitif or partner for Japanese cuisine. A full crimson pink hue announces a very young, primary and fresh thing of perky pink pepper, rhubarb, nashi pear, pomegranate and pink grapefruit. It's all up-front and fruity, with a short finish underlined by crisp acidity and a creamy bead. For such simplicity, its considerable price has always puzzled me, perhaps reflecting scarcity more than style. It will benefit from time to build persistence and complexity, and Jean-Baptiste has doubled production this year, with the intention of holding 1000 bottles back as a late-disgorged release.

GEOFFROY EXTRA BRUT MILLÉSIME 2004 • $$$$

87 points • DISGORGED OCTOBER 2012 • TASTED IN AŸ

Geoffroy's vintage wine is a blend of the best barrels, hence a different blend every year —
here 71% chardonnay and 29% pinot noir; totally vinified in barrels; no chaptalisation, no added
yeast, no malolactic fermentation, no fining or filtering; aged 7 years on lees; 2g/L dosage

Sadly dominated by coarse oak, imposing its wood spice flavours and firm wood tannins,
which trod on otherwise pristine and honed grapefruit and lemon fruit character. This is not
a concern I've had with any other vintage of this cuvée. Don't drink it from a small flute, too
cold, or too soon. It demands a very long time to come into balance, and has the acid drive
and fruit energy that perhaps one day it will?

GEOFFROY EXTRA BRUT MILLÉSIME 2002 • $$$$

95 points • DISGORGED SEPTEMBER 2011 • TASTED IN ADELAIDE

A grand vintage for Geoffroy, tapping deep into chalk minerality and great fruit expression of lemon zest,
yellow summer fruits and dried pear, evolving to wonderful complexity of nougat, almond and vanilla. Its
mineral mouthfeel is exceptional, and it lingers with consummate precision and great persistence. The first
bottle opened lacked freshness, drying out and becoming bitter on the finish, presumably oxidised.

RENÉ GEOFFROY CUVÉE AUTREFOIS 1996

97 points • TASTED IN AŸ

Geoffroy's first vintage; full barrel fermentation and no malolactic fermentation, in the same philosophy as
Volupté and Empreinte today

The magical ability of malic acidity to sustain Geoffroy's cuvées for a long and magnificent future is exemplified
in his first vintage. This glorious high-acid and high-ripeness season has evolved to a beautifully silky and fine
demeanour of impeccable integration, with malic acidity providing delightful focus to softly mineral texture.
Layers of complexity of glacé fig, dried apple, preserved lemon and bees wax make for quite an enchanting
experience now, or any time in the coming decade.

GEOFFROY COTEAUX CHAMPENOIS CUMIÈRES ROUGE MILLÉSIME 2008 • $$

93 points • TASTED IN AŸ

Geoffroy makes one of the great red wines of Champagne, with excellent medium-red hue
using 100% pinot meunier for the first time, communicating all the personality of this grape in
violet perfume, pure red cherries, cherry kernel and even touches of white pepper. The lively
acidity of 2008 infuses a bright vibrancy, propelling silky minerality and beautifully managed,
super-fine tannins. It will age exceedingly long.

GEORGES LAVAL

(Zhor-zheh Lah-vahl)

7/10

16 RUELLE DU CARREFOUR F-51480 CUMIÈRES
www.georgeslaval.com

'*I have a Burgundy vision of champagne,' declares Vincent Laval. 'I want to taste grapes in the glass. First I make wine, then I make champagne.' His business card simply says 'Vigneron', and here, as in Burgundy, it's all about the vineyards. The tiny 2.5-hectare estate on the slopes of Cumières was one of the first seven in Champagne to be tended organically in 1971, and is now fully certified. The pure expression of its fruit is maintained by religious avoidance of chaptalisation (radical for Champagne), and grapes are harvested at full maturity with a high 11-degrees potential alcohol. 'Even if the potential is not high, we don't add sugar to increase the alcohol,' he says. 'We don't make wine to get drunk, but to enjoy as a drink.'*

THERE IS NO SIGN ABOVE THE DOOR TO LAVAL'S TINY premises on Ruelle du Carrefour in Cumières, a reflection of the minute scale of this grower, with a total production of less than 10,000 bottles annually.

This allows Vincent and his father Georges, who still helps out, to do everything by hand. A horse ploughs almost half the vineyard, with hopes to encompass the full estate. By reducing soil compaction, and by using natural composts and avoiding pesticides and herbicides for more than 30 years, they have established vineyards with very deep root systems, drawing on the salty minerality of the Cumières chalk.

A dramatic display on their cellar wall (see photo opposite) bears stark testimony to this — two vines, one on the right with deep, strong roots plunging vertically downward, the other with just a thin web of surface roots. The first was planted by Vincent's grandfather, Albert Laval, in an organic vineyard, and the second at a similar time on the same soils in a neighbour's vineyard, managed using traditional viticulture. When the family purchased the neighbour's vineyard, they ripped it up and replanted it. 'We are lucky to be on chalk, and we must taste the chalk in our wines,' Laval declares.

The Champagne Guide

His philosophy is to consider his wines in the same spirit as white Burgundy, and the same hands-on, low-intervention approach follows through every stage of production. No chaptalisation, natural fermentation and no fining or filtering mean the only addition is sulphur as a preservative, and this only in very small amounts at the press. 'After the wine is finished, it is rich and can defend itself against oxidation, so it doesn't need more sulphur at bottling,' he says.

There is no dosage in any cuvée, except the entry Premier Cru Brut, with a tiny 4g/L. Every wine is fermented slowly in barrels varying in age from three to 15 years, which he buys from Chassagne Montrachet in Burgundy. Malolactic fermentation occurs naturally and wines remain on lees in barrel, tasted regularly until he deems them ready to be bottled. Even riddling is performed, 'handly', as Laval puts it.

Half the estate vines are now aged over 30 years, and some date from 1966, 1946 and 1931, planted to 40% chardonnay, 40% pinot noir and 20% pinot meunier. These are very old vines for a region that typically replants every 30–35 years, and yield a miniscule 23–30 hL/hectare — just one-quarter to one-third of Champagne's average. 'If a plot produces good fruit even with low yields, it is fine for me,' he says. 'Champagnes of low yield are completely different to those of high yield. Small yields give more character, more concentration and more expression of the soil.'

The tiny scale of the vineyard means that Laval needs to purchase from friends, keeping organic fruit and selling the rest. He currently cannot meet demand, selling out every year. He expects to have sufficient fruit to grow production by 8000 bottles, and is expanding his cramped premises to accommodate. The house next door was acquired in 2009, and the renovation was in full swing when I visited this year, with jackhammer vibrations reverberating through the cellar, and a crane working on the roof. The extension will also provide space to age his wines longer before release, doubling the area of the cellar. 'Not difficult, because it's so small!' he grins.

Laval's Brut Non-vintage is blended from three vintages of reserve wines kept in barrel on their lees. Before the new vintage is fermented, parcels from the same vines are added to the reserves in barrel for fermentation, in something of a modified solera system. This unusual practice increases the complexity of the wine, while long barrel ageing on lees instils deep texture and wood spice notes. Laval favours younger vine fruit for reserves, thanks to its higher acidity and greater ageing capacity.

These are champagnes that age long, and even his non-vintage benefits from some years in the cellar. Laval proposes considering these wines in the manner of white Burgundy, an accurate comparison for his generous champagne style. Managing them in the cellar is greatly simplified, thanks to impressively informative back labels, declaring vintages, blends, disgorgement dates and dosage levels.

Sensibly, Laval's non-vintage philosophy is to make the best wine he can every year, rather than attempting to maintain a consistent style. For a producer as small as this, with a blending palette constrained to but one village, vintage fluctuations are invariably dramatic. His vintage philosophy is daring, perhaps too daring, in producing single-vineyard vintage cuvées of just one variety, a style that does not bode well in weaker seasons like 2005, 2006 and 2007. But in great vintages, his wines shine.

With well-situated vineyards and painstaking attention to every detail, this is an estate whose pedigree exceeds its minute size. 'I don't produce champagne to make money, but to make taste,' Laval sums up. 'It is my life.'

In Laval's vineyards, organic viticulture encourages deep roots (right) to draw mineral character from the chalk of Cumières.

GEORGES LAVAL CUMIÈRES PREMIER CRU BRUT NV • $$

96 points • DISGORGED FEBRUARY 2012 • TASTED IN CUMIÈRES

95% 2008, 5% 2006; 50% chardonnay, 25% pinot noir, 25% pinot meunier; pinot noir fermented and aged 2 years in oak barrels; full malolactic fermentation; 5g/L dosage; 7000 bottles

The magnificent generosity of fully mature Cumières is something to behold in the bright and energetic 2008 season, drawing out the inimitable sea-salt mineral personality of the village with breathtaking clarity. Rich layers of brioche, honey, pear and nutmeg open into a wonderland abounding in red cherry and white peach fruit. It pulls into a beautifully controlled and focused finish of remarkable persistence and medium-term longevity, a rousing celebration of the dazzling minerality of Cumières.

GEORGES LAVAL CUMIÈRES PREMIER CRU BRUT NATURE NV • $$

92 points • 90% 2010, 10% 2009; DISGORGED OCTOBER 2012; 50% CHARDONNAY, 30% PINOT NOIR, 20% PINOT MEUNIER; ZERO DOSAGE; 7475 BOTTLES • TASTED IN CUMIÈRES

94 points • 70% 2007, 30% 2006; DISGORGED JANUARY 2013; ZERO DOSAGE • TASTED IN CUMIÈRES

On the eve of its release, the 2010 base is a delightfully fresh champagne of lingering lemon-zest purity, reflecting beautifully ripe fruit in its succulent peach, honey and nutmeg generosity, accented with wood spice barrel character. The palate is tightly wound and well focused, with tense acid line, strong barrel ferment texture and zero dosage conspiring to create a well-structured wine of mouth-filling presence and assertive texture. All it needs is time, and plenty of it — come back in five years. The 2007 base is currently drinking magnificently, still exactingly fresh and just beginning to build toasty complexity, with many years before it yet.

GEORGES LAVAL CUMIÈRES PREMIER CRU ROSÉ BRUT NATURE NV • $$$

94 points • DISGORGED OCTOBER 2012 • TASTED IN CUMIÈRES

50% 2009 pinot meunier of old vines, macerated 1.5 days, co-fermented with 50% 2010 pinot noir of old vines, some dating from 1947; fermented and matured in old barrels (1998) for 10 months; pressed by foot; zero dosage; just 1500 bottles

Laval only produces rosé in seasons that yield sufficient fruit character and structure, and this is a rosé that proclaims both with considerable amplitude. Its bright, vibrant crimson hue announces a bouquet of great intensity and focus, layered with pink pepper, cherries, strawberries, brambles, wood spice, even a hint of fresh ham. Fruit tannins meet the textural structure of oak maturation, building a creamy palate of immense, mouth-filling texture. In the midst of this maelstrom, it retains a sense of restraint and focus. This is a rosé to contemplate long. Drink it at white wine temperature from large glasses, and let it loose on dishes of complexity and weight — it will handle game birds and chicken effortlessly.

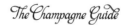

GODMÉ PÈRE ET FILS

(Gurd-may Pear e Feess)

7/10

10 RUE DE VERZY 51350 VERZENAY
www.champagne-godme.fr

CHAMPAGNE GODMÉ
Père et Fils

*P*inot noir rules the northern slopes of the Montagne de Reims, and it's unusual for chardonnay to account for more than half a growers' plantings. The Godmé family has tended its vines in the village of Verzenay on the northern slopes of the Montagne de Reims for five generations, bottling estate champagnes since as early as 1930. Today, 100,000 bottles are produced each year from 11 hectares, widely spread across 84 parcels spanning five villages. An impressive four hectares of chardonnay in Villers-Marmery is responsible for blanc de blancs cuvées that outshine even Godmé's blanc de noirs.

VITICULTURE IS THE FIRM FOCUS FOR HUGUES Godmé, the fifth generation to tend his family's vines in Verzenay. He maintains a largely organic approach, without seeking full certification.

Insecticides and herbicides are avoided, organic treatments and composted manure are embraced, and mid-rows are ploughed and planted to cover crops, encouraging deeper roots. The result has been later ripening, producing wines that retain greater acidity at the same level of ripeness.

Fermentation takes place in enamelled steel tanks, and about 40% of production is aged in oak barrels, with the intention of increasing in future.

As the climate continues to warm in Champagne, malolactic fermentation is blocked in an increasing number of parcels, including all reserve wines.

Concentrated grape must is used for dosage, retaining purity and clarity, the finishing touch to carefully balance cuvées that sensitively reflect the fine salt mineral texture of Verzenay.

Godmé Père & Fils Blanc de Blancs NV • $$

94 points • Disgorged May 2012 • Tasted in Brisbane

2009 base vintage; 100% Villers-Marmery chardonnay; 7g/L dosage

A beautifully crafted apéritif-style blanc de blancs of crystalline grace and primary purity, capturing both the white-fruit precision of chardonnay and the understated intensity of Villers-Marmery. It's crunchy and focused, emphasising pear, apple and tangy lemon zest fruit with subtle nougat complexity, underlined by impressively expressive, finely chalky mineral texture.

Godmé Père & Fils Blanc de Noirs Brut NV • $$

92 points • Disgorged April 2012 • Tasted in Brisbane

2009 base vintage; 100% Verzenay pinot noir; 9g/L dosage

The power of Verzenay pinot noir is paraded in a tint of gold in a full straw hue and a flamboyant bouquet that leaps of out of the glass with generous white nectarine, white cherry, honey and quince aromas, evolving to blueberry proportions in time. The palate is a generous concoction of all of the same, bringing orange zest, dried apricots and vanilla to the party. The finish is well-toned with crunchy grapefruit zest and just the right level of phenolic texture to keep lively fruit in check. Refreshingly, primary acidity has the final say on a long, spice-accented, blue-fruited ending.

Godmé Père & Fils Les Allouettes Saint Bets Chardonnay Brut Millesime 2004 • $$$

95 points • Disgorged February 2012 • Tasted in Brisbane

100% Villers-Marmery chardonnay; fully vinified in oak barrels; 5g/L dosage

A blanc de blancs of impressively controlled confidence, generous but not intense, full but not powerful. Precise white summer fruits meet crunchy white citrus, softened and caressed by barrel fermentation to build impressive presence of custard apple, lemon curds, nutmeg spice, even subtle, savoury charcuterie notes. It admirably upholds the honed, lemon zest crunch of 2004, perfectly balancing its creamy mouthfeel with crisp, tense acidity. A long finish froths with Villers-Marmery's salty mineral depth.

North-east facing vineyard slopes form an amphitheatre behind the premier cru village of Chamery on the Petite Montagne.

GOSSET

(Goh-say)

7/10

3 RUE DE MALAKOFF ÉPERNAY 51200

www.champagne-gosset.com

GOSSET
CHAMPAGNE

Established in 1584, centuries before the bubble was ever put into champagne, Gosset rightfully claims to be the oldest wine house in the region. Far from a staid, traditional establishment, Gosset is on the move, having relocated its production to the impressive Épernay cuverie and cellars of Château Malakoff, purchased from Laurent Perrier just in time for vintage 2009. In the midst of change, the house maintains an unwavering consistency, thanks largely to one man, Jean-Pierre Mareigner, its talented Chef de Cave of 30 years. Under his direction, the house style of no malolactic fermentation, clean-cut structure and enduring longevity remains as fine as ever, with the exception of its Brut Excellence NV entry wine, which seems a strange misfit, in both philosophy and quality.

A FRENZY OF ACTIVITY HAS TRANSFORMED CHÂTEAU Malakoff into the new home of Gosset over the past four years, with the finishing touch of an elegant new reception room added in 2012.

Previously, the house operated from five different locations, and it's now basking in the opportunity to grow into a huge cuverie with a capacity of 2.6 million litres, far exceeding the requirement for an annual production of 1.1 million bottles.

The substantial premises, constructed in 1860 on two hectares of parkland next door to Pol Roger, came fully equipped with vinification facilities and disgorgement and labelling lines. Its 1.5 kilometres of deep cellars have a capacity for 2.5 million bottles, and house part of the house's stock of more than 4 million. The rest remain in Gosset's historic headquarters in Aÿ, where riddling and disgorgement are still conducted.

Gosset's roots in Mareigner's birth town of Aÿ remain strong in spite of the move and the company's tiny vineyard holdings. With just one hectare to its name, 99% of fruit is purchased from 200 growers in 60 different villages, exclusively premier and grand cru in the Marne department.

The consistency of supply is a credit to Mareigner's long-term relationships with growers, some of whom have supplied Gosset for three generations. As evidence of its faith in these relationships, Gosset does not operate press houses in the villages, instead entrusting its growers to crush on its behalf.

Every village and grower is kept separate during vinification, which is performed in stainless steel tanks, temperature regulated to maintain ferments below 180°C. 'Our goal is to keep what nature has given us,' explains Mareigner. 'No centrifuge, no filtering until immediately before bottling, and no malolactic fermentation.'

The impressive freshness and remarkable ageing potential of malic acidity calls for long cellaring prior to release, and the great vintages of Gosset will live exceedingly long. Like Pol Roger next door, Gosset's deep cellars maintain a temperature below 11°C, drawing out the second ferment over six months to produce a very fine bead. A low dosage of 8g/L or less is used across the Grande range, and no more than 5g/L across the prestige Celebris trio, which accounts for a tiny 2% of the production of the house.

The beautifully poised Grande Réserve is on the rise, now representing more than 40% of production, pushing Brut Excellence down to just 30% (a tiny representation for an entry wine in the grand scale of champagne-house production). This is just as well, because Brut Excellence is something of an ironic aberration to the excellence of the house, made using partial malolactic fermentation and a full dosage of 11g/L. The bottle and label are appropriately quite a disparity to the rest of the range.

Let's hope the blessings of a new facility present opportunities for the Brut Excellence to mature into a true Gosset.

GOSSET BRUT EXCELLENCE NV • $$

87 points • 2010 BASE VINTAGE; DISGORGED OCTOBER 2012 • TASTED IN
ÉPERNAY
89 points • 2008 BASE VINTAGE; DISGORGED EARLY 2011 • TASTED IN BRISBANE

45% pinot noir, 36% chardonnay, 19% pinot meunier from 28 villages; 11g/L dosage

A blatantly more commercial style that Mareigner refers to as 'the Gosset range', with rounded baked apple fruit, grapefruit zest and a bruised apple texture. Dosage pokes out in notes of boiled sweets, finishing short and simple. The 2008 base vintage is clean and fresh, while the 2010 base carries subtle mushroom notes.

GOSSET GRANDE RÉSERVE BRUT NV • $$

94 points • 2008 BASE VINTAGE WITH 30–35% RESERVES FROM 2007 AND 2006;
DISGORGED JULY 2012 • TASTED IN ÉPERNAY
94 points • 2007 BASE VINTAGE WITH RESERVES FROM 2006 AND 2005
• TASTED IN ADELAIDE AND BRISBANE

43% chardonnay, 42% pinot noir, 15% pinot meunier; no malolactic fermentation; 8g/L dosage

Grand Réserve is perpetually among the most reliable NVs on the shelves, and the latest two blends are as fresh and lively as ever. The wonderfully refreshing malic acidity of the 2008 base vintage charges the palate with bolts of lively lemon and grapefruit zest of immaculate poise. The lesser 2007 vintage has landed equally refined, boosted with a higher proportion of reserves from 2006 and 2005. Both blends celebrate Gosset's signature, gently rolling, chalky minerality, a graceful undercurrent to a concentrated fruit palate of succulent yellow mirabelle plums, red apple and ginger. Lingering persistence and seamless integration make them ready to enjoy right away.

Gosset Grand Blanc de Blancs Brut NV • $$$

94 points • 2008 base vintage with reserves from 2007 and 2006 • Tasted in Épernay

94 points • 2007 base vintage with reserves from 2006 and 2005; disgorged late 2011 • Tasted in Brisbane

A blend of 15 villages, predominantly in the Côte des Blancs, with some Trépail and Villers-Marmery; no malolactic fermentation; 8g/L dosage

Gosset's refined mineral style and thrilling malic acid vitality suit blanc de blancs precisely, and the new member of the Gosset family hasn't deviated since its first release two years ago. The latest two blends are exactingly crafted apéritif styles of refreshing liveliness, linear drive, crystalline citrus purity and considerable persistence. The 2008 base vintage is flinty and structured, with hints of gunpowder reduction providing elements of focused complexity behind grapefruit, lemon and crunchy red apples, supported by pronounced minerality. High-tensile acidity keeps the 2007 base honed and backward. Both will live long.

Gosset Grand Rosé Brut NV • $$$

94 points • Disgorged late 2011 • Tasted in Épernay
95 points • Tasted in Brisbane

2008 base vintage with 2007 and 2006 reserves; 58% chardonnay, 35% pinot noir; 8% red wine from Bouzy, Ambonnay and Cumières; no malolactic fermentation

With its confident chardonnay-lead, low representation of red wine and signature cut of malic acidity, this wine meets its brief of elegant lightness more confidently in the energetic 2008 vintage than any other season I can recall. A brilliantly mineral palate of deep-set chalk texture is enlivened by delicately understated pink pepper, strawberry hull and white cherry fruits. Haunting persistence of nutmeg, struck flint and red liquorice fills out a very finely textured palate of silky, soft tannins and invigorating 2008 acidity. Its vibrant, pale salmon hue in Champagne has developed slightly to an orange tint with deeper brioche complexity abroad.

Gosset Grand Millésime Brut 2004 • $$$

96 points • Disgorged late 2011 • Tasted in Épernay and Brisbane

55% chardonnay, 45% pinot noir; no malolactic fermentation; 8g/L dosage

Gosset's splendid mandate of beautifully ripe fruit in tension with the electric zap of malic acidity is exemplified in 2004, a wine of inherent internal harmony, grace, poise and superb balance. A warm richness of white peach, fig, honey, brioche and nutmeg contrasts with refined lemon freshness, at every moment unswervingly pure and lively. Tense acidity accentuates its immense mineral presence, carrying the finish with profound length and seamless line.

GOSSET CUVÉE CELEBRIS BLANC DE BLANCS EXTRA BRUT NV • $$$$

97 points • DISGORGED LATE 2007 • TASTED IN MELBOURNE

55% 1999, 45% reserve wines from 1998, 1996 and 1995; no malolactic fermentation; 2.5g/L dosage

A grand statement of the longevity of Gosset, this wine has barely moved since its release two years earlier. All the more remarkable that a bottle disgorged more than five years ago could be even more superlative today. The sustaining power of malic acidity is immense indeed. The Celebris label reveals nothing of its vintage composition, which is a shame, because it reads like a roll call of the heroes of the 1990s, infusing the palate with the lacy web of chalk mineral texture that embodies grand cru chardonnay. At an average age of more than 15 years, its presence is monumental and its complexity mind-blowing, a lively throng of dried fruits, succulent stone fruits, preserved lemon, anise and nutmeg, pulled into line dutifully by a wonderfully taut finish of malic acidity and immaculately honed, silky structure.

GOSSET CUVÉE CELEBRIS EXTRA BRUT VINTAGE 2002 • $$$$

96 points • TASTED IN BRISBANE

52% chardonnay, 48% pinot noir; no malolactic fermentation; 5g/L dosage

The ultimate 21st present for 2002 babies, Celebris shows all the signs of living for a lifetime. It takes the energy of 2002 and the depth of a decade on lees and zaps it with a charge of malic acidity that jolts everything into a state of frenzy, slaying innocent, youthful white peaches, white cherries and golden delicious apples with an ice shard of acidity that screams out for years to soften. Notes of preserved lemon, brioche and a hint of crème brûlée build a delightful interplay between intensity and complexity, defining one of the great vintages for Celebris — though it will take at least a decade to confirm this.

GOSSET CUVÉE CELEBRIS EXTRA BRUT VINTAGE 1998 • $$$$

97 points • DISGORGED MAY 2012 • TASTED IN ÉPERNAY

64% grand cru Côte des Blancs chardonnay, 36% grand cru Montagne de Reims pinot noir; no malolactic fermentation; 3g/L dosage

Gosset's profound longevity is epitomised in the fourth vintage of its flagship, a champagne which I adored on its release as a grand expression of an outstanding season. Two years later, after a remarkable 13 years on lees, to my astonishment, it has ascended to a yet higher plane. It's voluptuously complex and simultaneously breathtakingly fresh, epitomising the seamless evolution from yellow summer fruits and pristine citrus to the richness of fig, dried pear, brioche and roast almonds. Charged with the high-voltage energy of malic acidity, it's unbelievably lively at 15 years of age, and will continue to blossom for many years yet. Its years have only heightened its textural expression, amplifying the pronounced chalk mineral personality of Champagne's finest grand crus.

The Champagne Guide

GOSSET CUVÉE CELEBRIS ROSÉ EXTRA BRUT 2007 • $$$$

96 points • TASTED IN BRISBANE

59% chardonnay, 33.5% pinot noir, 7.5% pinot noir red wine from Ambonnay and Bouzy; no malolactic fermentation; 5g/L dosage

The most subtle rosés are the most enchanting, and Gosset has conjured the epitome of elegance. A very pale and luminous salmon hue, brushed by the lightest touch of white cherries, strawberries and rose petals, its rosé aspirations are declared less in colour and fruit and more in structure, a delightfully refined tannin profile so fine it's impossible to tell when tannins finish and chalk mineral texture begins. Malic acidity sits surprisingly comfortably in the midst of this, drawing a tight finish out very long. It is desperately youthful and can be enjoyed immediately for its refreshing verve and tension, or confidently matured to build vast layers of complexity.

GOSSET CUVÉE CELEBRIS ROSÉ EXTRA BRUT 2003 • $$$$

94 points • TASTED IN ÉPERNAY

68% chardonnay, 25% pinot noir, 7% pinot noir red wine from Ambonnay and Bouzy; no malolactic fermentation; 5g/L dosage

'I wanted to have some fun with our very special, hot year!' says Jean-Pierre Mareigner. He has used a high proportion of chardonnay to balance the strength of the season, but its scarcity resulted in a very small production. The refreshing liveliness of malic acidity has sustained this vintage remarkably well, holding freshness and dynamism amidst the richness of plum, black cherry and exotic spice. The firm phenolic texture of the season makes for a full and robust finish. Notes of vanilla and creamy custard underline the richness of the year, yet it retains admirable acid tension, persistent length and seamless balance. A decade on from this challenging vintage, this is one of its most confident expressions. 'I like a challenge!' Mareigner smiles.

Gosset retains its historic headquarters in Aÿ (left) while recently opening a new reception room to its Épernay facility (right).

H. BILLIOT FILS

(H. Beey-yoh Feess)

5/10

1 PLACE DE LA FONTAINE 51190 AMBONNAY
www.champagnebilliot.fr

enri Billiot showcases the ripe intensity of one of Champagne's finest pinot noir villages. With fastidious attention to detail, he strives to capture the expression of his five hectares of old, low-yielding pinot noir (75%) and chardonnay vines exclusively in grand cru Ambonnay. All but one of his 18 parcels are enviably positioned on the mid-slopes of the village. Everything is done by hand in the cellar, an achievable feat for an annual production of just 45,000 bottles. To preserve freshness, fermentation takes place in enamelled steel tanks, malolactic fermentation is avoided and virtually no dosage is used. His wines carry a rounded ripeness and powerful fruit sweetness that will appeal to some. I have found an inconsistency in Billiot's wines in recent years, which may be related to what commentator Peter Liem suggests is problematic corks producing volatility. It appears to have since been resolved. It's great to see disgorgement dates now declared on back labels.

H. BILLIOT FILS CUVÉE TRADITION BRUT NV • $$

92 POINTS • DISGORGED OCTOBER 2011 • TASTED IN BRISBANE

75% pinot noir, 25% chardonnay; no malolactic fermentation

Billiot captures the stature of Ambonnay pinot noir in a full straw hue with a hint of pink and an intense bouquet that leads forth with lifted, lively cherry blossom and strawberry. The palate is textural, firm and dry, with malic acidity providing tense drive. It has a feeling of authenticity, albeit in a slightly unpolished demeanour, with a gently robust phenolic firmness that tussles with its raw acidity. This tension is well controlled, and not out of place for fruit of such magnitude.

HENRI GIRAUD

(On-ree Zhi-row)

6/10

71 BOULEVARD CHARLES DE GAULLE 51160 AŸ

www.champagne-giraud.com

1625

CHAMPAGNE
HENRI GIRAUD

The Giraud-Hémart family has diligently tended vines on the south-facing slopes of Aÿ since 1625, making this the oldest champagne house still owned by its founding family. It was not until current head of house, 12th generation Claude Giraud, that champagnes were made under the family name. An annual production of about 250,000 bottles is sourced from the family's 10 hectares, spread across 35 small plots, supplemented with fruit purchased largely from family and friends, all of which is pressed by Giraud. Planted to 70% pinot noir and 30% chardonnay, the magnificence of Aÿ is captured, thanks to vines of a minimum of 30 years of age, planted on thin topsoils and deep chalk, tended according to organic principles and harvested at full ripeness. Musts are cold settled at 10°C prior to fermentation, to enhance clarity and aroma, and all cuvées go through full malolactic fermentation. About one-third are vinified in 228 litre barrels from the Argonne forest southeast of Aÿ, an oak industry which Claude has been instrumental in reviving since 1989. He says his generous and silky Fût de Chêne and Code Noir cuvées are fresher and more lively as a result. These are worthy highlights of Giraud's characterful champagnes.

HENRI GIRAUD ESPRIT DE GIRAUD BRUT NV • $$

94 points • TASTED IN BRISBANE

70% pinot noir, 30% chardonnay; fermented in stainless steel and aged in tank on lees for 1 year

This invitingly rich, fruitful expression of Aÿ is a cracking entry point for Giraud, epitomising the strawberry and red cherry fruits of pinot noir, the crunch of fresh pear and apple, the sumptuous juiciness of white peach and the lemon zest of chardonnay. Its breadth is pulled into tight focus on the finish by a cut of citrus zest and lively acid. A characterful expression of the glories of Aÿ, trailing off with nuances of ginger, fruit mince spice and honey.

HENRI GIRAUD ESPRIT BLANC DE BLANCS NV • $$

93 points TASTED IN BRISBANE

Montagne de Reims chardonnay; fermented in stainless steel tanks and 10% in oak barrels

The slopes of the Montagne de Reims are home to chardonnay of affable character, and this soft blanc de blancs offers an enticing counterpoint to the tension of the Côte des Blancs. It's a toasty, roasty, creamy style of impressive proportions, dripping with succulent poached pear, golden delicious apple and tangy grapefruit, spiced with the roast almond notes of oak barrel fermentation. Buttery generosity carries long through a well-textured palate and balanced finish.

HENRI GIRAUD CUVÉE HOMMAGE BRUT NV • $$

92 points • TASTED IN BRISBANE

70% pinot noir and 30% chardonnay from Aÿ; vinified in stainless steel vats, matured for 6 months in small barrels

Giraud packs the full impact of Aÿ into this voluptuous champagne of powerful wild honey, fleshy berry fruits, wood spice and mixed spice. It finishes generous and creamy, with an unashamedly honeyed sweetness. Such generosity calls for nothing like this level of sugar, but it will appeal to those seeking a sweeter style.

Pruning in the magnificent grand cru of Aÿ during the winter snowfalls of 2013.

The Champagne Guide

HENRI GIRAUD ESPRIT ROSÉ NV • $$$

93 points • TASTED IN BRISBANE

70% pinot noir, 22% chardonnay; vinified in stainless steel tanks; 8% oak-matured pinot noir red wine from Aÿ

Giraud sensitively sustains a delicate sense of poise and energetic liveliness, offsetting the thumpingly powerful rosehip, raspberry jube, ripe strawberry, pomegranate, red cherry and pink pepper intensity of Montagne de Reims pinot noir. Oak adds a subtle savoury edge, giving its bold red fruits the impression of tomato, with very fine tannin texture providing depth and dimension, without interrupting its even flow, lingering long, linear, ripe and fruity, yet never sweet. The disgorgement date is not declared, but the fresh cork of this bottle betrays its glorious youth. A rosé to drink young and lively.

HENRI GIRAUD CODE NOIR BRUT NV • $$$$

94 points • TASTED IN BRISBANE

100% pinot noir vinified and aged in Argonne oak

In its sleek, modern, streamlined bottle, this deep golden yellow-tinted blanc de noirs is a celebration of the bountiful grandeur of Aÿ. Its grand dimensions embrace the far-flung realms of loquat and orange peach, against an elegant backdrop of gingernut biscuit and complex, toasty spice. Familiar tones of rich red berries pull into a well-honed close of zesty citrus fruits. Gentle, chalky minerality glides effortlessly under this captivating spectacle.

HENRI GIRAUD CUVÉE FÛT DE CHÊNE BRUT MILLÉSIME 2000 • $$$$$

95 points • TASTED IN BRISBANE

70% pinot noir and 30% chardonnay from Aÿ; vinified and aged for 12 months in small new barrels of Argonne oak

The voluptuous curves of pinot noir are amplified three-fold, in the stature of Aÿ, the luscious warmth of 2000 and the voluminous character of small-barrel fermentation, flinging Fût de Chêne to the outer realms of champagne concentration. Its richness of ginger, brioche, roast nuts, figs and yellow mirabelle plums glide like butter with silky, slippery generosity, calling for main-course fare of entire turkey proportions. In the midst of this maelstrom, it retains comfortable control and direction, gliding with impressive length and confident poise. Classic Aÿ, signature 2000 and definitive Giraud.

HENRI GOUTORBE

(On-ree Goo-tawb)

6/10

9 BIS RUE JEANSON 51160 AŸ
www.champagne-henri-goutorbe.com

*T*he Goutorbe family ran a viticultural nursery before becoming winegrowers in their home town of Aÿ. The label was established in the late 1940s and has since grown to encompass an impressive 25 hectares, including six in Aÿ, as well as good sites in nearby Mareuil-sur-Aÿ, Mutigny, Bisseuil, Avenay-Val-d'Or and Hautvillers, providing for an annual production of 200,000 bottles. Pinot noir takes the lead, representing more than two-thirds of plantings, with chardonnay comprising the majority of the remainder. Every cuvée is sourced exclusively from the estate, is fermented in stainless steel tanks, undergoes full malolactic fermentation and is aged at least three years on lees in Goutorbe's deep, cold cellar. Dosages are based on concentrated wine must rather than sugar. The result is a style that captures the rich expression of these privileged terroirs, while maintaining impressive control.

HENRI GOUTORBE CUVÉE MILLÉSIME BRUT GRAND CRU 2004 • \$\$

93 points • DISGORGED APRIL 2012 • TASTED IN BRISBANE

75% pinot noir, 25% chardonnay from Aÿ; 8g/L dosage

An enticingly powerful champagne that makes more impact on the palate than the purse, just the thing for anyone who finds champagne's more bracing styles a challenge. The authority of Aÿ pinot noir builds a formidable yet inviting presence of fleshy white peach, grilled pineapple, even a suggestion of cumquat marmalade. It's like biting into a succulent white peach, spiked with honey, fig and nutmeg, finishing rounded and cuddly, yet upholding flawless balance and self-assurance. Don't be afraid to serve it a little cooler than you might any other grand cru pinot noir.

HENRIOT

(On-ree-oh)

6/10

81 RUE COQUEBERT 51100 REIMS
www.champagne-henriot.com

CHAMPAGNE
HENRIOT
FONDÉ EN 1808

The independent and family-owned house of Henriot has been run continuously by the founding family for more than two centuries. This has afforded the privilege of building a long-ageing house style that might otherwise be infeasible for a house producing 1–1.2 million bottles annually. This is achieved through a strong reliance on chardonnay and virtually no pinot meunier. Long ageing on lees is reflected in a whopping 5–6 years of stock held continuously in the company's extensive cellars under Reims, as well as reserve wines back to 1990.

THIRTY-FIVE HECTARES OF ESTATE VINEYARDS ARE located mainly in the great Côtes des Blancs villages, with smaller holdings in Avenay-Val-d'Or, Verzy and Verzenay. Vines, averaging an impressive 25–30 years of age, are tended respectfully, with grasses cultivated in mid-rows, and herbicides and fertilisers avoided.

The family sources from a further 120 hectares of vineyards under long-term contracts. Every parcel is kept separate and fermented in small stainless steel vats, which can lead some cuvées to tend towards a reductive savouriness, not unusual for chardonnay-led blends. Full malolactic fermentation provides soft structures, while dosages between 8 and 11g/L can appear somewhat heavy-handed.

Henriot's long-aged Cuvée des Enchanteleurs is a powerfully characterful flagship.

HENRIOT BRUT SOUVERAIN NV • $$

92 points • DISGORGED NOVEMBER 2012 • TASTED IN BRISBANE

2008 base vintage; 50% pinot noir, 50% chardonnay; 20% reserve wines; 8–10g/L dosage

The great 2008 season has elevated Souverain to new heights of clarity and purity of lemon zest and apple crunch, with the toasty brioche complexity of maturity, and a subtle hint of struck-flint reduction. Honeyed dosage is a little more than it needs to be, but nonetheless an impressively fruity and persistent style.

Henriot Blanc de Blancs NV • $$

91 points • Disgorged June 2012 • Tasted in Brisbane

2006 vintage base; 30% reserve wines; 8–10g/L dosage; DIAM closure

After a run of stale 2005 base bottles last year, the 2006 is on form, with a vibrant pale straw hue and generous and focused apple and pear characters. A whiff of flinty reduction adds to its complexity as it becomes toasty and nutty, thanks to an impressive seven years of maturity. The dosage is higher than it needs to be for this age, leaving the finish sweet and rounded.

Henriot Brut Rosé NV • $$$

92 points • Disgorged August 2012 • Tasted in Brisbane

2008 base vintage; 60% pinot noir, 40% chardonnay; 25% reserve wines; 8–10g/L dosage

A captivating accord between elegant strawberry and raspberry fruit, pink pepper and rose petal fragrance, and the roast chestnut complexity of five years of bottle age. Reductive charcuterie notes quickly evaporate to reveal a gentle style of pale salmon hue and soft, mineral tannins offering refined structure. The energetic acidity of 2008 handles its dosage effortlessly.

Henriot Cuvée des Enchanteleurs 1998 • $$$$$

96 points • Disgorged January 2011 • Tasted in Brisbane

50% pinot noir, 50% chardonnay; from Mailly-Champagne, Verzy, Verzenay, Le Mesnil-sur-Oger, Avize and Chouilly; aged 12 years on lees; 8–10g/L dosage

Throbbing with dried nectarines, grilled pineapple, even marmalade and dark fruit cake, this is a rich and powerful Enchanteleurs, wanting for nothing in character and completeness. It's an engaging juxtaposition between fruit presence and the burnt butter and roast cashew nut development of 15 years of maturity. A vintage of considerable amplitude and breadth that upholds strict control, pulling into a refined finish of beautifully fine, chalk minerality, lively acid structure and immense persistence.

The Champagne Guide

J. DUMANGIN FILS

(J. Dew-mohn-zhan Feess)

6/10

3 RUE DE RILLY 51500 CHIGNY-LES-ROSES
www.champagne-dumangin.com

CHAMPAGNE

J. DUMANGIN Fils

ÉLABORATEURS DE CHAMPAGNE DEPUIS 5 GÉNÉRATIONS

'*The secret to making great wine is attention to the fine details at every stage,' is the mantra of Gilles Dumangin. The fifth-generation chef de cave must be the hardest worker in Chigny-les-Roses. When I visited late one Sunday afternoon in July, he'd been at the bottling machine since 4am, as he had been every morning for the past two weeks. The week before, his air-conditioner had died, then his brine chiller, then his labelling machine. He fixed all three himself. A self-confessed control freak, Gilles works 20–22 hours every day during harvest. And he loves it.*

SUCH FANATICISM DEFINES EVERY STAGE OF PRODUCTION at J. Dumangin Fils. 'My wife spent one harvest with me and declared, "You are in love with your presses! You do not leave them for a moment!"' Gilles recounted. And he doesn't disagree. 'The week and a half of harvest is a lovely time. I listen to my presses the whole time. I know them so well that if anything sounds different, I know something is wrong. If you can't press well, you can't make good champagne.'

I have not seen more focused attention to detail anywhere in Champagne. These are hand-made champagnes, and a production of just 150,000 bottles permits every step in the process to be performed manually by Gilles and his father Jacky, including riddling (by transfer between pallets). Every parcel is kept separate, thanks to tiny tanks, some not much larger than a bar fridge. 'A house this size would normally have 20 tanks,' Gilles points out. 'I have 80.'

Based in the romantic little village of Chigny-les-Roses, on the northern slopes of the Montagne de Reims, in the old school building that Gilles' grandfather converted, the estate sources from 15 hectares in this and the surrounding villages. Gilles owns a little more than three hectares of his own vines; he purchases from his parents' vineyards of a similar size and a further nine hectares from growers with long-term contracts.

Irrespective of ownership, Gilles' principles for the management of the vines are consistent across all of his sources, and he interacts with each of the vineyards in the same way, monitoring the vines during the year, going into the vines to determine the optimal time for harvest and supporting his own managers throughout the year in the same manner as he supports his growers. He is therefore technically a négociant-manipulant, but very much with the approach of a dedicated récoltant-manipulant. 'Would I produce better wines if I grew all the grapes myself?' he asks. 'No. I'd do everything the same way.'

This is pinot country, and both pinots feature heavily in the Dumangin style. Chardonnay finds its place, too, and the local quality is impressive, as his expressive single-vineyard, single-vintage blanc de blancs attests. Pinot meunier is more important here than it is in most champagne houses. 'This is the grape that makes champagne what it is, providing its fruit and its easy-drinking style,' says Gilles, whose entry Grande Réserve NV contains an impressive 50% of the variety.

Gilles is obsessive about preserving fruit in optimal condition. In 2008 he terminated some contracts with growers of inferior vineyards, and signed up other vineyards to bring all of his sources to within seven kilometres of his beloved old Coquard PAM presses. 'They're so gentle,' he says, 'that the pips stay on the skins and the seeds remain inside!'

Gilles pioneered 18 kilogram picking crates rather than the usual 50 kilogram crates, so as not to crush the fruit at the bottom of the crate. When fruit arrives it never spends more than five minutes in the sun before he brings it into his air-conditioned press room. He personally presses every grape. 'I don't believe you can make very good wine if you do not press your own grapes,' he explains.

The J. Dumangin Fils non-vintage cuvées rely on deep stocks of reserve wines, with the Grande Réserve and Extra Brut cuvées each boasting a whopping 60%. In every vintage 40% is kept as reserves. All cuvées have traditionally undergone full malolactic fermentation, but such was the acid and sugar balance of his 2012 fruit that he blocked malolactic fermentation in some parcels for the first time. This was also his first year of trialling barrel fermentation.

Every shipment of non-vintage wine that leaves the cellar is disgorged to order, with the dosage tweaked from its usual 10g/L sugar to suit. 'From my tests, the wines stay fresher if they're disgorged just prior to shipment,' Gilles says. It's different for the vintage wines, which he finds hold their freshness best if disgorged 3–4 years after bottling. To further refine quality, dosages have been progressively lowered across the range over the past few years, and Dumangin now seals every bottle with DIAM cork. 'In my trials, the wines keep fresher under DIAM.'

For champagnes disgorged to order, back labels are impressively informative, disclosing disgorgement date, blend and dosage information. Each disgorgement for every market now receives a unique QR code to provide great depth of information, including disgorgement date, blend, vineyards, food matches, reviews and importer's address.

Gilles' painstaking attention to detail shines in every bottle. I have been following his champagnes for seven years and his non-vintage wines are currently as dashing as ever. These rank high among the best-value small-producer champagnes.

J. Dumangin Fils Brut 17 NV • $

93 points • Disgorged October 2012 • Tasted in Chigny-les-Roses

2009 base vintage; 34% pinot meunier, 33% chardonnay, 33% pinot noir; 8.8g/L dosage; DIAM closure

After changing contracts to improve fruit sources, the 2009 base is as refreshing and pure as I have ever seen Brut 17. A beautifully refined apéritif champagne that captures the red-fruits freshness and crunchy red apples of pinot meunier and pinot noir, with a gentle, lingering refinement, a subtle rose petal air and soft, chalky minerality. A cracking entry champagne.

J. Dumangin Fils Grande Réserve Brut NV • $

93 points • Disgorged November 2012 • Tasted in Chigny-les-Roses from magnum

2009 base vintage; 50% pinot meunier, 25% chardonnay, 25% pinot noir; 2–3% oak aged; 8.8g/L dosage; DIAM closure

Unlike most champagnes meaninglessly labelled 'Réserve', Dumangin's Grande Réserve is just that, boasting a whopping 60% reserve wine. Pinot meunier leads confidently here, projecting its fragrant bouquet of red apple and pink grapefruit and its creamy strawberry palate. A beautifully clean, precise and elegant expression of the northern Montagne de Reims, finishing fine and textural, with soft mineral presence, vibrant acidity and well-integrated dosage. As grand as I've ever seen it, and sensational value.

J. Dumangin Fils Brut Premier Cru Rosé NV • $

93 points • Disgorged October 2012 • Tasted in Chigny-les-Roses

2009 base vintage; 47% chardonnay, 37% pinot noir, 16% pinot meunier; 8.8g/L dosage; DIAM closure

Dumangin's Rosé now represents 50% of the production of the house. This is one of Champagne's most finely crafted and elegant rosés at a refreshingly affordable price. Its pretty, bright pink/salmon hue introduces a lively and fruit-fresh style of just-picked strawberries and pink pepper. It finishes crisp and tangy, with well-managed tannins offering gentle textural support.

J. Dumangin Fils Vintage Brut 2000 • $$

94 points • Disgorged June 2012 • Tasted in Chigny-les-Roses from magnum

54% chardonnay, 46% pinot noir; 4.4g/L dosage; DIAM closure

Gilles' meticulous attention to pressing guarantees pale juice and wines of vibrant, bright hues, even after long ageing. His 2000 is ageing slowly and confidently, with the generous character of the vintage preserved in fantastic fruit clarity of golden delicious apple and yellow mirabelle plums, gradually becoming honey, ginger and vanilla. The acidity remains lively on the finish, accenting well-honed texture and impeccably integrated dosage.

J. Dumangin Fils Vintage Brut 2003 • $$

92 points • Disgorged October 2012 • Tasted in Chigny-les-Roses

54% chardonnay, 46% pinot noir; 4.4g/L dosage; DIAM closure

Dumangin's 2003 is holding its lemony acidity with surprisingly lively poise, making this one of the freshest 2003s I've tasted at 10 years of age. With a lower dosage than my tastings in 2010 and 2011, it's looking even more refined and less honeyed now. Its yellow mirabelle plum and white peach fruit still has life, with the complexity of gingernut biscuits. It finishes with full texture, true to the vintage, yet lively and in no way dried out.

J. DUMANGIN FILS PREMIUM BLANC DE BLANCS SINGLE VINEYARD DESSUS LE MONT NV • $$

91 points • DISGORGED NOVEMBER 2012 • TASTED IN CHIGNY-LES-ROSES

100% 2006 Chigny-les-Roses chardonnay; 8.8g/L dosage; DIAM closure

A soft and approachable blanc de blancs and an attractive expression of Chigny-les-Roses. It's clean and fruit-focused, with lemon pith character, notes of honey and a softly textural finish. Acid zest is a little lacking (apparently due to this clone of chardonnay), and there's a touch of heaviness in the back palate, derived from clay in this vineyard.

J. DUMANGIN FILS TRIO DES ANCETTRES • $$$$

Trio of single-vineyard, single-variety champagnes sold as a three pack in a magnificent oak ice bucket; 2000 vintage, though not declared on the labels; wood aged for 1 year; 10 years on lees in bottle; disgorged April 2012; zero dosage; DIAM closure; tasted in Chigny-les-Roses

Achille Blanc de Pinot Meunier (90 points) from a single vineyard in Chigny-les-Roses is a savoury, honed style, with the yellow summer fruits of meunier becoming savoury and a touch mushroomy, finishing with good acid freshness and some textural wood spice from oak ageing. Hippolyte Blanc de Pinot Noir (93 points) from a single vineyard in Rilly-la-Montagne has shed some of the oak character that dominated in its earlier life, opening up to expressive musk, red berry and strawberry shortcake aromas. The palate carries soft expression of red cherry and strawberry fruit, with layers of brioche and nougat, concluding with lively acidity and textural wood spice. Chardonnay stands alone confidently, and Firmin Blanc de Chardonnay (94 points) from Taissy just south of Reims sings with expressive, intense and persistent golden delicious apple and preserved lemon fruits, becoming nutty and buttery, enlivened with crunchy lemon zest acidity.

J. DUMANGIN FILS VINOTHÈQUE BRUT 1996 • $$$$

95 points • DISGORGED JUNE 2012 • TASTED IN CHIGNY-LES-ROSES

54% chardonnay, 46% pinot noir; 11g/L dosage; DIAM closure

Such was the acidity of Dumangin's 1996 ('It's off the chart!') that Gilles never released it, keeping all 9000 bottles in the cellar in the hope that it might some day soften. It's now reached a delightful point in its maturity, and still has decades of life in it. Its vibrant medium straw hue is remarkably bright for its age, as is its exceptionally primary fruit expression, still firmly in the lemon, grapefruit and white peach spectrum, with slowly building notes of ginger cake and nutmeg. The length is a revelation, and the acid line is pristine.

J. LASSALLE

(J. Lah-sahl)

7/10

21 RUE CHÂTAIGNIER 51500 CHIGNY-LES-ROSES
www.champagne-jlassalle.com

CHAMPAGNE
J. LASSALLE
PROPRIÉTAIRE DE VIGNOBLE

It takes great sensitivity to create wines that communicate the subtleties not only of the place that has given them birth, but the very personalities of those who have brought them to life. When I first tasted the enchanting champagnes of J. Lassalle, I knew nothing of the estate or the family behind them and was immediately captivated by their dainty restraint and feminine beauty, arousing my curiosity to discover how such delicate sophistication could be achieved. It all made sense when I met the three generations of delightful women who, for more than 30 years, have nurtured this immaculate estate in the charming village of Chigny-les-Roses.

EVER SINCE JULES LASSALLE PASSED AWAY IN 1982, HIS wife, Olga, daughter Chantal and grand-daughter Angéline Templier have worked closely together to double the size of their family estate to 11.2 hectares and an annual production of 100,000 bottles. Templier oversees winemaking, ably assisted by her mother. Olga, now 92, still helps with management and administration. 'We don't need any men to help!' Templier grins.

The meticulous attention to detail of these women shines in every stage of production. The winery at their home in the village is pristine, bathed in white light, one of the cleanest little facilities I've visited anywhere. 'We do everything as my grandfather did, but because we are girls we have a feminine touch, and you can feel it in the wines,' says Templier.

These are not wines to be taken lightly. The Lassalles have been making champagnes exclusively from their premier cru vineyards since 1942. Their aspiration is to express the terroir of the northern slopes of the Montagne de Reims, so all vineyards are tightly located within 10 kilometres of the house. Pinot noir is king here, and comprises 60% of plantings. Chardonnay (25%) takes a confident, if surprising, lead in Lassalle's most sublime cuvée, and pinot meunier makes up the remaining 15% of the estate. The family is privileged to own a significant proportion of old parcels, with some vines up to 50 years of age. 'They make great wines, so we don't replant them!' Templier exclaims. Any fruit of insufficient quality is sold to large houses.

Blends comprise all three champagne varieties in proportions varied according to the season, bolstered by a generous stock of five years of reserve wines. Preserving freshness at every stage is a high priority. Grapes are pressed on the first floor and the juice is piped directly to settling tanks below to avoid oxidation. Every cuvée undergoes full malolactic fermentation. The philosophy in the winery is to maintain the tradition of Templier's grandfather, while growing progressively. Much of the historical equipment of the estate is still in use, including enamelled tanks and the traditional press installed in 1965, and all cuvées are still riddled by hand.

Long ageing is inherent to the house style, and when rosé demand outstripped supply two years ago, the cuvée was put on allocation rather than releasing it earlier. 'The only thing we have to sell the house is our quality, and it is very important for us to respect this, so we told our clients to wait,' Templier explains.

Non-vintage cuvées are aged a minimum of four years and vintage cuvées between six and 10 years,

necessitating a large cellar stock of 400,000–450,000 bottles. The estate also holds back unusually large reserves, and currently holds as much reserve as new wine in storage. 'We're always full and running out of room!' says Templier.

To facilitate the growth of the estate, the building next door was purchased in 2007 and the winery expanded to a capacity of almost 100,000 litres. A new press was purchased, new cellars were dug under the building, and temperature-controlled stainless steel tanks installed to allow separate vinification of the estate's many small parcels.

It seems the attention to detail of the ladies of Lassalle has a new lease on life. Don't miss these impeccably crafted cuvées of generous fruit presence, purity and intricately judged balance.

J. LASSALLE BRUT PRÉFÉRENCE PREMIER CRU NV • $

92 points • TASTED IN CHIGNY-LES-ROSES AND BRISBANE

70% 2008 and 30% 2007; 60% pinot meunier, 20% chardonnay, 20% pinot noir; 8–10g/L dosage

Templier likes emphasising the aromas of pinot meunier, structured with chardonnay and pinot noir. There is a delicacy and purity to this lively, fruit-focused style, with a fragrant rose petal bouquet, blending red and white fruits of strawberry hull, white cherries and lemon blossom with the layered complexity of long lees ageing, in notes of ginger, cherry kernel, almond, mixed spice and honey. A finely mineral mouthfeel lends a softly textural structure. The lemon fresh purity of the 2008 season shines through in a clean acid line, balancing its dosage, which contributes a creamy roundness to the finish.

J. LASSALLE BLANC DE BLANCS BRUT MILLÉSIME 2005 • $$

93 points • TASTED IN CHIGNY-LES-ROSES

Single parcel of 25-year-old vines in Villers-Allerand; always less than 10,000 bottles

The aspiration of this cuvée is to express the rounded character of Villers-Allerand chardonnay. In the hands of lesser beings, it might seem an impossible task to draw a balanced wine from the generous 2005 vintage, but the exacting touch of the Lassalles has created a well-honed wine of focused fruit complexity. Appealing generosity of pure fig and white peach fruit is layered with spice, roasted nuts, butter and a touch of honey, culminating in caressing fruit texture and admirable persistence.

The Champagne Guide

J. Lassalle Premier Cru Brut Rosé NV • $$

94 points • Tasted in Chigny-les-Roses

70% pinot noir, 15% chardonnay, 15% pinot meunier; 6% pinot noir red wine

A tiny dose of red wine creates a gorgeous pale salmon hue, enlivening a dainty and fresh rosé with a fairy touch of rose petal perfume that wafts from the start of the bouquet to the lingering finish of the palate. Lively strawberry hull and elegant red cherry fruits are invigorated by bright acidity and gentle minerality, meshing seamlessly with soft dosage.

J. Lassalle Cuvée Angéline Premier Cru Brut 2007 • $$

95 points • Tasted in Chigny-les-Roses

60% pinot noir, 40% chardonnay; never more than 6000 bottles

Such is the exacting precision of the Lassalles that even a pinot-noir led blend can sing with soprano high notes of fresh lemon blossom and pristine lemon zest. There is a determined focus to the palate, with a crisp citrus lead, opening out slowly into great depth, flesh and structure of pinot noir fruit expression. Acidity and dosage are perfectly integrated on a finish of outstanding persistence, allowing soft, finely chalky minerality the final say.

J. Lassalle Special Club Brut 2004 • $$$

96 points • Tasted in Chigny-les-Roses and Brisbane

60% chardonnay, 40% pinot noir

Templier does not like to think of Special Club as her top cuvée, as she gives every wine the same attention, but one cuvée has to rule them all, and for as long as I have known Lassalle, Special Club has been that cuvée. The philosophy here is of greater freshness and delicacy, hence a stronger representation of chardonnay, though the wine does its best to deny it. After a cork-affected sample in Champagne, a replacement in Brisbane was utterly sensational. At almost nine years of age, it's a beautifully bright and radiant pale straw hue. I was surprised to see such pronounced anise character in the 2002, and here it is again, in a bouquet that's more black than white, reverberating with a depth of blackberries, plum liqueur, licorice, white peach and lemon. The palate follows, with an enthralling presence that transcends its pale hue and elegant stance, with darker shades of black cherries, cherry kernel, licorice, even plum liqueur and dark chocolate. In signature Lassalle delicacy, it is in no way heavy or broad, retaining a delightfully lively stance from start to finish, with elegantly entwined acidity, beautifully refined chalk minerality, impeccably integrated dosage and tremendous persistence. It's deep, shadowy, enchanting, and downright delicious.

J.L. VERGNON

(J.L. Vair-ngoh)

(6/10)

1 GRANDE RUE 51190 LE MESNIL-SUR-OGER
www.champagne-jl-vergnon.com

'*Daring' is the only word to describe Christophe Constant, the talented chef de cave of the little estate of J.L. Vergnon in Le Mesnil-sur-Oger. In a village renowned for chardonnay of greater longevity than any other in Champagne, no other grower-producer dares avoid malolactic fermentation. And he goes further. Dosages are very low, never more than 7g/L, and often just 3g/L. His top cuvée, appropriately named 'Confidence', is vinified entirely in oak, a whopping 50% of which is brand new. With such an ambitious recipe, the proof of his skill is a well-crafted range of long-lived blanc de blancs that capture the vibrant, clean expression of the finest grand crus of the Côte des Blancs.*

AND HEREIN LIES THE SECRET OF J.L. VERGNON. With nothing but estate chardonnay harvested ripe from just five hectares of vines averaging more than 30 years of age, enviably situated in Le Mesnil-sur-Oger, Oger and Avize, he has no need of malolactic fermentation, chaptalisation, dosage, or any other trick to soften or mask such riveting fruit.

The aim at harvest is to achieve maximum maturity so as to produce balanced wines of vinosity and finesse. To this end, cover crops are used to naturally regulate yields, and there is a focus on sustainable viticulture, avoiding pesticides where possible.

With supply limiting current production to 50,000 bottles, J.L. Vergnon surrendered its grower producer status in late 2012 to function as a négociant and purchase fruit from the 2013 harvest, with the plan to increase the volume of its Conversation cuvée.

'I buy grapes in the vineyard, like they do in Burgundy, though this is not done much in Champagne,' Constant explains. 'I don't want to buy must, only grapes, so we can press everything ourselves, with one exception. We have found an old vineyard in Le Mesnil managed by someone who works like me and makes wine without malolactic fermentation, and we would like to one day buy vins clairs from him.'

Constant vinifies in stainless steel tanks or oak, according to the cuvée, with all reserve wines fermented in oak since 2010. Disgorgement is by hand and disgorgement dates are printed on every back label. Blending of different plots creates distinct personalities in four cuvées, whose evocative names neatly sum up the character of the house in both French and English: 'Conversation', 'Éloquence', 'Résonance' and, most of all, 'Confidence'.

J.L. Vergnon Conversation Blanc de Blancs Brut NV • $

94 points • 2008 base vintage; disgorged July 2012; 7g/L dosage
• Tasted in Le Mesnil-sur-Oger and Brisbane

92 points • 2009 base vintage; disgorged September 2012; 6g/L dosage
• Tasted in Le Mesnil-sur-Oger

Le Mesnil-sur-Oger, Oger and Avize; 20–25% reserve wines; vinified in stainless steel tanks; no malolactic fermentation; aged more than 3 years on lees

The 2008 base vintage makes for an engaging Conversation and a consummate apéritif. The generosity of pristine grand cru chardonnay defines wonderful purity and depth of primary lemon and red apple fruit, nuanced with the complexity of brioche and almond. It lingers long and clean amidst scintillating chalky minerality. The 2009 vintage was riper, less acidic and less focused than the magnificent 2008 season, articulated in a Conversation of more generous golden delicious apple fruit, balanced with slightly lower dosage.

J.L. Vergnon Éloquence Blanc de Blancs Extra Brut NV • $$

94 points • 2008 base vintage; disgorged November 2012 • Tasted in Le Mesnil-sur-Oger

93 points • 2009 base vintage; disgorged September 2011 • Tasted in Le Mesnil-sur-Oger

Le Mesnil-sur-Oger, Oger and Avize; the same wine as Conversation, with a lower dosage of 3g/L

Testimony to Constant's flair, with lower dosage, Conversation lowers its tone to become more refined and shy on the bouquet and more focused and crystalline on the palate, giving greater voice to salty mineral chalk expression. Acidity is taut and refreshing, energising impressive power of grapefruit and lemon in the 2008 base, more apple-accented in the richer 2009 season. Seamless and precise, it's eloquence, indeed.

J.L. Vergnon Résonance Extra Brut 2006 • $$

92 points • Tasted in Le Mesnil-sur-Oger

Le Mesnil-sur-Oger and Oger, vinified in stainless steel tanks; aged more than 5 years on lees; 3g/L

The rich, ripe and expressive 2006 vintage has been strategically toned with half the usual dosage of this cuvée. It resonates with powerful fruit concentration of apple, pear, white peach and lemon, beginning to develop brioche overtones in the cellar. A vintage of calm fruit persistence, albeit without the acid definition or mineral expression of cooler seasons, finishing with a touch of very fine, drying phenolic texture.

J.L. Vergnon Blanc de Blancs Confidence Brut Nature Millésime 2008 • $$$

95 points • Disgorged December 2012 • Tasted in Le Mesnil-sur-Oger

Le Mesnil-sur-Oger with a little Oger; fully vinified in 50% new oak

I was privileged to share Constant's first post-disgorgement tasting of the sublime 2008 vintage. It's a masterfully executed creation that holds a forest of oak more eloquently than the 2007 and 2006 before it, testimony to both the heights of the season and to his growing experience in integrating fruit and wood. Vibrant and taut lemon and lime fruit sits comfortably in the presence of beautiful lemon blossom purity and confident structure of high-strung malic acidity. Its mineral expression is profound, boring to the core of Le Mesnil, stirred and propelled by oak, though never clashing. Expect this vintage to unravel in the months and years to come, and to blossom into an extended future of determined confidence.

J.L. Vergnon Blanc de Blancs Confidence Brut Nature Millésime 2007 • $$$

91 points • Disgorged March 2012 • Tasted in Le Mesnil-sur-Oger

As above

A clean and well-formed representation of a difficult and early season with a wet, cold August producing high acidity and some botrytis. This leads to a feeling of clumsiness, lacking focus and definition, never quite deciding whether it's a rounded apple and pear style, spicy and bready or citrus zesty. Barrel work adds toasty vanilla notes to the mayhem, contrasting with nail-biting lemon/lime malic acidity. It bursts from its confusion with a creamy bead and surprising persistence. It's hard to say whether it's already achieved its finest, or simply demands a long time to pull itself together.

Le Mesnil-sur-Oger, the most confident grand cru of the Côte des Blancs and home to the daring house of J.L. Vergnon.

The Champagne Guide

JACQUART

(Zhah-khah)

34 Boulevard Lundy 51100 Reims
www.champagne-jacquart.com

*J*acquart is the brand of the Alliance Champagne Group, a cooperative representing one of Champagne's largest sources of grapes. The group is owned by 1800 growers, holding over 2600 hectares, spanning more than 60 crus across the Côte des Blancs, Vallée de la Marne and Côte des Bar. Jacquart has grown dramatically since it was founded just over 50 years ago, now sourcing from 350 hectares of this vineyard pool to create its pleasant chardonnay-led blends of prominent dosage. It's worth spending a little more to trade up to its top cuvée this year.

JACQUART BRUT MOSAÏQUE NV • $$

90 points • DISGORGED LATE 2011 • TASTED IN BRISBANE

2006 base vintage with 20% reserves; 40% chardonnay, 35% pinot noir, 25% pinot meunier; 60 different villages; aged more than 3 years on lees; 10g/L dosage

A clean and accurate blend, with chardonnay clearly in the lead, speaking in articulate notes of lemon meringue and white peach, with the complexity of pinots' red apple, and mature cellar notes of toasted coconut and vanilla marshmallow. The dosage of 10g/L could be lighter, leaving a sweet, candied suggestion to the finish.

JACQUART BRUT DE NOMINÉE NV • $$$

94 points • DISGORGED LATE 2011 • TASTED IN BRISBANE

2004 base vintage; aged 6 years in the cellar; 60% chardonnay from Chouilly, Oger, Le Mesnil-sur-Oger, Avize and Vertus; 40% pinot noir from Mailly-Champagne, Verzy and Louvois; 8g/L dosage

Jacquart's flagship is a non-vintage blend with a label that declares nothing of its vintage composition, a shame, as it's older than the current vintage wines of many houses. The wine rejoices in a decade of maturity in its creamy, silky, rounded texture, succulent yellow summer fruits, wild honey and butter on toast. It finishes refreshingly taut and structured, with a grapefruit-pith texture and preserved lemon notes, underlined by Côte des Blancs acidity that proclaims its chardonnay lead. It concludes with impressive persistence, line and definition.

JACQUES PICARD

(Zhak Pee-khah)

7/10

12 RUE DU LUXEMBOURG 51420 BERRU
www.champagnepicard.com

CHAMPAGNE
JACQUES PICARD

PROPRIÉTAIRE-RÉCOLTANT

From its home on the slopes of Mount Berru, seven kilometres north-east of Reims, the Picard family crafts champagnes with an insightful touch. Well-considered, strategic use of generous proportions of chardonnay, abundant reserve wines and selective employment of oak fermentation and maturation conspire to build fleshy, layered complexity, sensitively tweaked with low dosage and selective blocking of malolactic fermentation to preserve vivacity. With no other estate bottling champagnes in Berru, it is difficult to distinguish the skill of the maker from the potential of the place. Wherever the credit is directed, there is no denying that this beautifully complete set of champagnes transcends lesser terroirs.

THE VINEYARDS OF BERRU WERE COMPLETELY DES-troyed in the First World War and replanted by Roger Picard, then mayor of the village, after the Second World War.

Jacques Picard made his first sparkling wines in the early 1960s and his daughters Sylvie and Corinne and their husbands took over in the 1990s. Today, the estate is privileged to own 17 hectares in Berru, Montbré and a small parcel in Avenay-Val-d'Or.

Berru chardonnay is the focus of the estate, compri-sing 70% of holdings, supported by 20% pinot meunier and 10% pinot noir. Berru is geologically similar to the Montagne de Reims in its limestone and clay soils, producing chardonnay of body and roundness.

The Picards believe in 'lutte naturelle' (natural control) and practise 'culture raisonnée' (reasoned culture), some time ago convincing the entire com-munity of the village to use sexual confusion through the use of hormones as a method of insect control to reduce use of pesticides. Sustainable viticulture is the focus, and grasses have been planted in mid-rows to reduce erosion.

Picard's wines are aged at least three years in cellars dug into chalk under the house.

JACQUES PICARD BRUT NV • $$

98 points • DISGORGED SEPTEMBER 2011 • TASTED IN BRISBANE

Base vintage 2008 with 40% reserves from 2007, 2006, 2005 and 2004; 60% chardonnay, 35% pinot noir, 5% pinot meunier; vinified in stainless steel tanks; full malolactic fermentation; aged 3 years in bottle; 8g/L dosage

Picard successfully tones the fleshiness of Berru chardonnay with low dosage, building complexity with large proportions of reserve wines and long ageing on lees. A strong chardonnay lead retains the precision and focus of lily blossom and lemon juice in the midst of rounded generosity of pear and fleshy white peach fruit. The effect is impressive, and masterfully handled, finishing long and even.

JACQUES PICARD BRUT ROSÉ NV • $$

92 points • DISGORGED SEPTEMBER 2011 • TASTED IN BRISBANE

2007 base vintage with 25% reserves from 2006, 2005 and 2004; 85% chardonnay, 15% still red wine of pinot noir; vinified in stainless steel tanks; 9g/L dosage

Effectively a blanc de blancs shot with red wine, infusing a freshness to the bouquet. A creamy palate captures the fleshy nature of the village, with subtle red cherry fruit, finishing with a tangy strawberry hull note and lively acid cut. Softly textured tannin presence integrates evenly on the finish. Well crafted.

JACQUES PICARD ART DE VIGNE BRUT MILLESIME 2002 • $$$

95 points • DISGORGED DECEMBER 2009 • TASTED IN BRISBANE

60% single-vineyard Berru chardonnay from 30-year-old vines; 20% single-vineyard Montbré pinot meunier from 22-year-old vines; 20% single-vineyard Avenay-Val-d'Or pinot noir from 50-year-old vines; fully fermented in barrels with bâtonnage (lees stirring) for 6 months; no malolactic fermentation; 6g/L dosage

Six months in oak and a decade in bottle are celebrated in a rich yellow-golden hue. The generous fleshiness of the village conspires with full barrel work to produce a generous complexity reminiscent of pinot-dominant cuvées. It's voluptuous and opulent, with baked white peach, stewed plums, nougat, brioche, honey, even crème brûlée and Christmas pudding, set off with a wonderful overlay of spices of all kinds. Resonating with lavish low notes of deep-set fruit generosity, malic acidity enlivens an even, clean, fresh finish.

JACQUES SELOSSE

(Zhak Sur-loss)

8/10

59 RUE DE CRAMANT 51190 AVIZE
www.selosse-lesavises.com

JACQUES SELOSSE

VINS DE CHAMPAGNE AVIZE

The expression of terroir has been one of the great advances of Champagne of the past three decades, and there is no grower who has been more influential in its progress than Anselme Selosse. 'We should take what nature has given us and not interfere' is a philosophy that he pursues more obsessively than any other, making him a visionary mentor who has inspired a generation of growers in Champagne. Since taking over from his father in 1980, his example has been a revolution in the region, radically pioneering lower yields farmed according to biodynamic principles and a handmade, Burgundian approach quite unlike any other in Champagne. His wines are as strong as the convictions behind them, and rank among the ripest and most expressive in all of Champagne. For some, his Burgundian approach pushes his wines beyond the realms of sound champagne and into the outer limits of oxidation. For others, the wines of Selosse rank high among the most prized sparkling wines of all, and each year his entire production of 57,000 bottles quickly vanishes into the cellars of collectors across the globe. These are rare champagnes, and priced accordingly.

THERE IS NO NAME IN CHAMPAGNE MORE TALKED about right now than Anselme Selosse, and no grower more controversial. He is one of the most profound thinkers in the modern wine world on the role of the soil as the interface between the terroir and the vine. 'The terroir expresses itself in the minerality, the flavour and the intensity of the wine,' he explains.

'The bedrock on which we plant our vines is rarely directly soluble, and it is only by the action of micro-organisms that it is able to be transformed to be absorbed by the roots and impart its mineral signature. The population of micro-organisms is specific to its location, and a short distance away, when the population changes, the terroir changes.'

For Selosse, terroir encompasses the entire eco-system, and anything that might disrupt the intricate balance of biodiversity is to be vigorously avoided. This is intuitive winegrowing of the highest order, a rigorous biodynamic regime, yet vigorously non-prescriptive, encouraging balance through such techniques as soil respiration by planting grasses in the mid-rows, abandonment of pesticides, and hard pruning to limit yields.

The result is fruit of full ripeness, capturing the detail and character of spectacular estate holdings totalling 7.5 hectares, located primarily in the grand crus of the Côte des Blancs, including four hectares of chardonnay in his home village of Avize, one hectare in each of Oger and Cramant and smaller plots in Le Mesnil-sur-Oger, and pinot noir in Aÿ, Ambonnay and Mareuil-sur-Aÿ.

A conspicuously Burgundian approach is pursued in the winery. 'A lot of people consider vintage to be finished when the grapes are picked, but for me it continues through the vinification and all the way to bottling,' he says.

In 2008 he purchased an old Avize château with 200-year-old cellars built on four levels. Each of 47 different plots is pressed separately in his press house at the level of the vines above the village, flowing by gravity into settling tanks below, then down to barrels on a third level. Every parcel is fermented using wild yeast in Burgundy barrels of all sizes, purchased from some of Burgundy's finest estates.

Maintaining solids in the fermentation juices is an important element of the Selosse style. 'Solids in the juice provide nutrients and antioxidant protection for the wine,' he explains, 'adding texture, nutty flavours and deep colour.' These characters build as the wines are held in barrel over one year, enhanced with weekly bâtonnage (lees stirring).

Malolactic fermentation is free to occur (or not) as each parcel evolves. Minimal sulphur dioxide is used, and only ever prior to fermentation. Selosse has been at the forefront of low dosage in Champagne, using less than 7g/L, and usually less than 3g/L. Each cuvée is aged long on lees prior to release — up to eight years in the case of 'Substance', made using a true solera going back to 1986.

These radical methods make the wines of Selosse unique in flavour and stature in all of Champagne. These are inherently textural, vinous wines that have as much in common with white Burgundy as they do with champagne. Not to be hurried, they benefit tremendously from a decant and plenty of time to open up in a large glass to allow volatility to blow off. They evolve dramatically and polarise even the most seasoned champagne drinkers. To the uninitiated, such big, oxidative, unashamedly broad styles with at times fino sherry-like development can come as something of a surprise. They are certainly as distinctive and original as the man who masterminded them.

There are signs that Selosse is working toward a less oxidative style, and has installed a new Coquard press, though it will be some years before the results come through in his cuvées. Anselme's young son Guillaume returned to the estate in June 2012 and is assuming increasing responsibility. Labels are impressively informative, detailing disgorgement dates, dosage, blends and often the base vintage.

A visit with Anselme Selosse brings no shortage of surprises. This year, I caught him on his return from travels in Spain, where he had been focusing on sherry production, 'because he is a bit obsessed with oxidation!' as one of his close grower friends put it. His luxury hotel, Les Avisés, goes from strength to strength, and his brilliant restaurant continues to serve up one of the most memorable and hospitable dining experiences in all of Champagne.

The Selosse revolution continues.

JACQUES SELOSSE V.O. GRAND CRU BLANC DE BLANCS EXTRA BRUT NV • $$$$

96 points • DISGORGED OCTOBER 2010 • TASTED IN MELBOURNE

2002 base vintage with reserves from 2001 and 2000; Avize, Cramant and Oger; vinified in oak barrels; aged 3.5–4 years on lees; zero dosage; 3600 bottles

Selosse's Version Originale is a full golden yellow hue, with such bombastic complexity that it resembles mature white Burgundy as much as it does champagne. Remarkable ripe intensity transcends Côte des Blancs chardonnay in its panoply of flavours of plum, dried fruit, baked peach, fig, honey, savoury spice and citrus zest. The pronounced structure of 2002 swoops in on the finish, with well-defined acidity drawing the finish out long and true. The mineral presence on show here is of dramatic proportions, with the deep-set, salty mineral texture of Avize penetrating deep into the back-palate. Of three bottles tasted, one showed subtle tiredness, and all three appreciated considerable time in a large glass to open up, blowing off volatile notes, showing some fino sherry-like oxidative character, evolving and changing vividly.

JACQUES SELOSSE LE MESNIL-SUR-OGER LES CARELLES EXTRA BRUT NV • $$$$$

94 points • DISGORGED JANUARY 2010 • TASTED IN AVIZE

Inaugural release, 100% 2003 (subsequent releases blended from a mini solera); single-vineyard Le Mesnil-sur-Oger; aged 5–6 years on lees; 0.5–1g/L dosage; 1800 bottles

This champagne has not moved one iota since I first tasted the same disgorgement two years ago, an extraordinary feat on two counts. First, that a wine should hold such freshness, hailing from the estate probably named more often than any other any time oxidation is raised in Champagne. But, more than this, that any wine exclusively from 2003 could sustain such vitality. In true Selosse form, it's a gold-tinted, full yellow hue, volunteering a universe of complexity in rich, creamy flavours of vanilla, burnt butter, toffee, dark fruit cake and cherry liqueur. Riding the outermost extremities of champagne intensity, this is the epitome of full-bodied, yet, crucially, the finish is honed and controlled, thanks to crunchy lemon zest and mouth-filling minerality.

A pruning cart and vineyard shed in Avize, where Anselme Selosse has inspired a new generation of attentive vineyard care.

The Champagne Guide

JACQUESSON

(Zhak-soh)

9/10

68 RUE DU COLONEL FABIEN 51530 DIZY
www.champagnejacquesson.com

champagne
JACQUESSON

No champagne house today is on a trajectory of ascent as steep as Jacquesson. While many houses are on the prowl for more fruit to increase production, Jacquesson is drastically slashing its yields and its contracts to radically improve quality in spite of lowering quantity. When others set out to make a consistent blend every year, Jacquesson throws uniformity to the wind to draw the best blend out of every vintage. Each time I look, this little house in the village of Dizy appears more like a fanatical grower producer. Purely on the refinement of its current cuvées, Jacquesson has leapt from ranking among Champagne's top 20 houses to a lofty position among its top 10.

THE CONCEPT OF NON-VINTAGE CHAMPAGNE HAS never sat quite right with me. Blending multiple vintages to deal with the ups and downs of the seasons makes sense. But creating a consistent style that tastes the same every year has never seemed quite right.

When a particularly blessed season arrives, why must it always be dumbed down for the sake of uniformity? Or must it?

'We were making a regular non-vintage at Jacquesson until we became progressively frustrated with it,' Jean-Hervé Chiquet told me as we tasted his oddly named Cuvée No 734 in the tasting room of the family estate in Dizy.

'We face such vintage variation at this extreme, with fantastic vintages followed by disasters, that our ancestors found that the only way to handle the seasons was to blend vintages to produce consistent wine. This is why 90% of Champagne's production does not carry a vintage. In spring 1998 we were working on our non-

vintage from 1997 base and we found a blend that was very nice, but not the same as the previous non-vintage and not able to be reproduced. At the time, we made an inferior wine to match the consistency of the house. We decided then that there should be a better rule. We thought, what happens if we don't try to imitate what we did last year, but start from a blank sheet of paper and make the best wine that we can every year?'

And so Cuvée 728 was born from 2000 vintage base. A different blend every year is reflected by a consecutively rolling number (1272 less than the vintage year) — a 'stupid number', according to Jean-Hervé. 'But two things don't change: the fruit sources and the taste of the two guys who do the blend!'

RADICAL CHANGE
Those two guys are brothers Jean-Hervé and Laurent Chiquet, whose family purchased the company in 1978 and transferred its headquarters to their own family's

historic estate. 'I spent 10 years campaigning to my father that we could do something differently,' Jean-Hervé says.

'Then in 1988 he allowed me and my brother to take over and we spent 12 years changing everything about the structures of the company and the vineyards. But in 2000 we realised that the changes were not reflected in the wines, so it was then that we changed the entire range. We took big risks in changing the style to introduce the 700 series. A risk of losing most of our customers and a risk of big investment with no return for some years. We had to be good friends with our bank manager!'

While 2002 marked the turning point, even a small champagne house is like an ocean liner and it takes a generation to turn around. 'Our last Late Disgorged 2002 will be sold between 2019 and 2021, from a regime we started talking about in 1978, so it takes 43 years for the change to fully take effect.' And the Jacquesson revolution is far from over yet.

The house has introduced a series of drastic changes to raise quality in recent vintages. At a time when many houses are seeking to extend their fruit sources, Jacquesson has radically initiated just the opposite. Yields were lowered in 2008 at the same time as fruit purchases were strategically slashed from 40 hectares to just eight, lowering annual production of 350,000 bottles by 23%, with estate vines now supplying almost 80% of needs. 'The quality of what we grow means we are less satisfied with the fruit we buy, so we dropped those vineyards that were not up to the standard of our rising expectations,' Jean-Hervé declares.

Further, the age of release of the 700 series has been progressively stepped up, from three years on lees for Cuvée 733 (2005 base) to four years for Cuvée 736 (2008), with the hope of stretching Cuvée 739 (2011) to 4.5 years. Meanwhile, allocations have been further lowered by holding back an average of 15,000 bottles from each release since Cuvée 733, to release as a Late Disgorged 700 series from 2014, with an additional 4–5 years of bottle age. These are radical measures for any wine region, unheard of for a champagne house, and reflect resoundingly in Cuvée 736.

FANATICAL GROWER

Jacquesson's cuvées are complex blends that age impressively and reflect the intricate attention to detail applied at every step of their creation. This begins in the vineyards. According to Jean-Hervé, there are five factors in wine: 'Terroir, viticulture, viticulture, viticulture and winemaking!' He describes Jacquesson as a grower more than a champagne house, and himself

Jean-Hervé Chiquet expounds rigorous principles to drastically slash yields in his vineyard in Dizy.

and his brother as 'frustrated growers'. It is this philosophy that underpins the recent transformation of the house.

Their goal in the vineyards is to grow less fruit, slightly riper, to draw out the mineral character of the terroir. Jacquesson directly controls 30 hectares of enviably located premier and grand cru vineyards, in Dizy, Aÿ, Hautvillers and Avize, with an additional eight hectares sourced from contract growers in the same villages, who Jean-Hervé describes as 'neighbours and friends'. The estate has experimented with organics, with 10 hectares now fully organic, and the remainder run under a minimal-sulphur regime. When I questioned why full organic certification was not the agenda, Jean-Hervé's sensible response was, 'We are here to make good wine as our primary priority.' And 2012 was a strong case in point, with his organic fruit lost to mildew. 'I have always been convinced that a 100% organic system is not reasonable in Champagne's climate,' he explains.

Jacquesson has recently encountered an unexpected menace to particularly ripe fruit. 'We try to harvest one of our single vineyards as late as possible, and in 2012 wild boar came in from the nearby woods and ate 1.2 tonnes — 800 bottles — in one night!'

Traditional methods are used throughout: little or no soil improvers, no herbicides or pesticides, minimal spray regimes, use of ploughing, cover crops between rows, and pruning to control vigour and limit yields to an average of around 60hL/hectare, just two-thirds of Champagne's average. 'The problem with Champagne is that every grower considers the maximum yield permitted by the appellation to be an economic minimum,' he admits. He describes cover cropping as particularly effective in controlling yields, but acknowledges that until recent environmental priorities became prominent, this was practised by significantly fewer than 1% of Champagne growers.

Jacquesson's attention in the vineyard allows its cuvées to capture the expression of the soil, exemplified in its trilogy of single-vineyard, single-varietal, single-vintage wines produced in minuscule volumes from three special little plots in Aÿ, Dizy and Avize. 'Terroir is the most unfair part of the wine business — you either have the right place or you don't!' Jean-Hervé says. 'It is very important to talk about terroir in champagne.' And talk terroir these cuvées do, articulating chalk mineral textures of disarming clarity.

HANDS-OFF WINEMAKING

Jacquesson's scrupulous practices in the vineyard are mirrored in its hands-off approach in the winery. All fruit used by the house is pressed in its own press houses. 'Pressing is very important in champagne because we have this stupid idea of making white wine from red grapes!' he exclaims. 'We must hand-pick and press close to the vineyard or we'll end up with jam.'

Gentle vertical presses are used, and the very first juice is removed 'because it has washed the outside of the grapes'. Each parcel is vinified separately in large oak foudres to allow the wine to breathe, after which it is left on lees and stirred for several months. This process produces creaminess and body, and has an antioxidant effect, reducing sulphur dioxide additions.

'Malolactic fermentation is the eternal debate in Champagne,' Jean-Hervé suggests. 'We favour malolactic fermentation as we don't want to use heavy sulphur dioxide additions or filtration.' There is also no fining, 'to maintain the aromatic potential of the fruit'.

All Jacquesson cuvées have been extra brut (less than 6g/L dosage) since 2000, although the current Cuvée 736 is the first to display this on its label. 'We never intended to make extra brut, but we just don't think our wines need more dosage,' says Jean-Hervé.

Dosages have become progressively lower, but this trend has never been a conscious decision. 'Some of our wines have no dosage, not because we wanted to make zero-dosage wine but because they were better wines this way,' he says.

Back labels are among the most informative of any champagne house, shamelessly declaring disgorgement date, dosage, base vintage, blend and even precise production quantities. There are no secrets here, just great champagnes, and better than ever. As Jean-Hervé puts it, 'At Jacquesson, we just want to grow great fruit and make great wines.'

JACQUESSON CUVÉE No 736 EXTRA BRUT NV • $$

96 points • DISGORGED JULY 2012 • TASTED IN DIZY

66% 2008, 34% 2007 and 2006; 53% chardonnay, 29% pinot noir, 18% pinot meunier; vinified in casks on lees with regular bâtonnage (lees stirring); 1.5g/L dosage; 273,000 bottles

The planets aligned in 2008, when the vintage of the decade coincided with Jacquesson's tearing up of every contract for fruit that wasn't up to scratch. It goes without saying that this is the finest 700 series release from Jacquesson yet, but it's more than that: its breathtaking elegance and electric brilliance position it firmly among Champagne's very finest entry NVs this year. The coiled expression of 2008 is encapsulated in concentrated focus of lemon blossom, lemon zest, granny smith apple and white peach. A beautifully linear and chiselled champagne of brilliant mineral presence and fresh lemon acidity, finishing very long, never hard, with structure seamlessly entwined with lingering citrus and stone fruits. Its sheer endurance will make for an exceedingly long life.

JACQUESSON CUVÉE NO 735 BRUT NV • $$

94 points • DISGORGED MAY 2012 • TASTED IN DIZY

72% 2007, 22% 2006, 6% 2005; 47% chardonnay, 33% pinot noir, 20% pinot meunier; vinified in casks on lees with regular bâtonnage (lees stirring); 3.5g/L dosage; 363,000 bottles

The Cuvée 700 series is Jacquesson's primary priority, representing more than 90% of the production of the house, supplemented only by single-vineyard wines in vintages when the blend doesn't need their fruit. The last disgorgement of 735 is a champagne of great depth and complexity, rippling with sumptuous fruit of gorgeous expression and allusions of dried peach, fresh pear, lemon, gingernut biscuits and mixed spice. An enticing and caressing style of creamy bead and softy underlying texture. Drink 735 while 736 comes back to earth.

JACQUESSON DIZY TERRES ROUGES ROSÉ RÉCOLTE EXTRA BRUT 2007 • $$$

95 points • DISGORGED MARCH 2012 • TASTED IN DIZY

Skin contact rosé of pinot noir; 28 hours maceration; 1.35 hectare single vineyard on the boundary of Dizy and Hautvillers, planted 1993; full malolactic fermentation; vinified in oak foudres; 3.5g/L dosage; 7320 bottles

Jacquesson's first skin-contact rosé of pinot noir, born of the frustration of lighter rosés made by the estate in the past, is a benchmark of red-blooded fizz. 'I want to be able to taste that this is a rosé, even in a black glass,' Jean-Hervé declares. 'I wanted to make something where you could really eat, drink and chew the pinot!' He's done just that, with one of champagne's deepest rosés, of unashamedly full crimson hue. If there is a spectrum that begins at champagne rosé and ends at full-bodied red Burgundy, this wine is further progressed than most champagnes, in intensity, structure and food-pairing versatility. It's layered with plums, cherries, even violets, blackberries and roast chestnuts, lingering with great freshness and purity, powered by an engine room of ultra-fine tannins of confident grip. He has no idea of how it will age, but imagines it might develop well — and with these tannins to propel it, I reckon he's right.

JACQUESSON MILLÉSIME 2000 • $$$$

96 points • DISGORGED 4TH QUARTER OF 2009 • TASTED IN ADELAIDE

50% pinot noir from Aÿ, Verzenay and Dizy; 50% chardonnay from Avize; vinified in cask; 2.5g/L dosage

A gloriously enticing 2000 with not one molecule out of place, as impeccably composed as the day it was released two years ago. Rich summer white fruits, ripe pear and yellow mirabelle plums quickly draw into a taut tail of lemon zest of profound energy, line and persistence. A wine of brilliant poise, inviting generosity and inherent grace, touched by the mature complexity of toast and roast nuts, rising on the finish to great texture of very fine, chalky, faintly salty minerality. Jacquesson ceased making this cuvée after 2002, since its 700 series replaced both a vintage and a non-vintage concept. Snap it up while you can.

The Champagne Guide

Jacquesson Dizy Corne Bautray Récolte Extra Brut 2004 • $$$$$

95 points • Disgorged October 2012 • Tasted in Brisbane

South-west facing single-vineyard Dizy on the boundary with Aÿ, planted 1960 on millstone-grit gravel over clayey marl and Campanian chalk; 100% chardonnay; vinified and aged in oak casks on lees; unfiltered; zero dosage; 5400 bottles

Such is the immense tidal wave of surging, heaving salt minerality of overwhelming texture that crashes through the palate of this dizzying chardonnay that it might fool the unsuspecting with the impression that it's phenolically heavy. It's not. This is the voice of the soil over the tones of the fruit and the expression of the barrels. It's powerful and pristine, with distinctive characters of cherry kernel, fennel, ginger, apple, lemon zest and Campari forming an intense background track to its mineral solo. It needs at least five years to calm down before daring to approach, and will likely live a lifetime.

Jacquesson Dizy Corne Bautray Récolte Brut 2002 • $$$$$

97 points • Disgorged February 2011 • Tasted in Dizy

As above, except vinified in a 40hL foudre; full malolactic fermentation; aged 8 years on lees; zero dosage; 5300 bottles

This is one of the most profound chardonnays of the Vallée de la Marne, yet from a site where no one believed good chardonnay could be grown, discovered only by the Chiquets when a 1995 vin clair stood out. The mineral impression of this wine is inexplicable, from a site with chalk no less than 2.5 metres under the surface, in a village unrecognised for chardonnay of structure. Its violent, deep, frothing, salty minerality fills the palate with immense texture, drawn out with incredible persistence by super-focused acidity. Such is its aromatic intensity that I could smell it the moment it was poured on the table before me. Wonderful layers of yellow summer fruits leap out of the glass amid nougat, brioche and almond aromas. Its mineral structure and lively acidity control this intensity on the palate, propagating a finish that does not stop.

Jacquesson Avize Champ Caïn Récolte Extra Brut 2004 • $$$$$

95 points • Disgorged October 2012 • Tasted in Brisbane

Due south-facing single-vineyard Avize; 1.3 hectares; planted 1962 on surface chalk; 100% chardonnay; vinified and matured in oak casks on lees; unfiltered; 1.5g/L dosage; 10,000 bottles

This blanc de blancs gives the impression of generosity, then quickly pulls into a chiselled and streamlined vector of crunchy pear and apple fruit, with a crisp grapefruit zest finish, accented with pristine aromas of pure apple blossom and a hint of nutmeg. Deep layers of fine, salty minerality are amplified by subtle barrel and fruit structure, and the textural influence of long lees ageing. An intricately structured champagne that will require at least five years to put flesh on its tense frame.

JACQUESSON AVIZE CHAMP CAÏN RÉCOLTE BRUT 2002 • $$$$$

96 points • DISGORGED FEBRUARY 2011 • TASTED IN DIZY

As for the Extra Brut 2004, except vinified in 75hL oak casks with lees stirring; full malolactic fermentation; aged 8 years on lees; 2g/L dosage; 6400 bottles

Nuances of exotic spice weave seamlessly amid white peach and fig, with notes of vanilla and nougat. A beautifully gauged hint of flinty reduction gives an air of sophistication to tight grapefruit and lemon aromas. Chalk minerality is soft, subtle and understated, in a graceful and elegant style of prolonged persistence and exacting poise. Signature Avize.

JACQUESSON AŸ VAUZELLE TERME RÉCOLTE EXTRA BRUT 2004 • $$$$$

96 points • DISGORGED OCTOBER 2012 • TASTED IN BRISBANE

Tiny plot of just 0.3 hectare, due south-facing on the mid-slope of Aÿ, not far from the Dizy border; planted by Jean-Hervé Chiquet in 1980 on calcerous soil 60–70 cm over chalk bedrock; 100% pinot noir; vinified and matured in oak casks on lees; unfiltered; 1.5g/L dosage; less than 1800 bottles

This tiny pocket is Jacquesson's finest terroir of all, giving birth to a champagne for long contemplation in large glasses, and preferably not for at least five years, if not ten. Six months post-disgorgement, it's coiled up tight. Understated aromas of apple, pear and nougat open into an impeccably poised palate, a celebration of the fine, textural structure of chalk and the mouthfeel of lees age in barrel. The finish is propelled by apple and pear fruit, defining by well-structured, quince-like texture, taut acidity and deep-set minerality. In time, pinot noir finally declares its presence, as introverted cherry and red berry fruits begin to unravel. Patience.

JACQUESSON AŸ VAUZELLE TERME RECOLTE BRUT 2002 • $$$$$

98 points • DISGORGED FEBRUARY 2011 • TASTED IN DIZY

As above, except vinified and aged in a 20hL oak cask with bâtonnage (lees stirring); full malolactic fermentation; aged 8 years on lees; 2g/L dosage; less than 2200 bottles

The greatest Jacquesson cuvée I have tasted, and an entrancing paradox: so light and fresh that it will lift you clean off the ground, yet reverberating with monumental depth of the most pristine red cherry and strawberry fruits. There's a breath of rose petal perfume, a glimpse of lemon blossom, darting notes of anise, slices of crunchy granny smith apple and flickers of spice. Its mineral depth is cavernous and immensely chalk-infused. With undeviating length and unwavering line, this is a champagne so complete it defies resistance. Few will ever experience what magnificence will unfold when it one day reaches its glorious maturity.

Janisson-Baradon

(Zhan-neesoh Bah-rah-doh)

5/10

2 RUE DES VIGNERONS 51200 ÉPERNAY
www.champagne-janisson.com

*F*ifth-generation head of his family estate, Cyril Janisson crafts champagne with a philosophy he learnt in Burgundy, even using horses in the vineyards and egg fermenters in the winery. It's unusual to find a Champagne grower within the town of Épernay itself, and eight of Janisson-Baradon's nine hectares of vines are located in the hills of Épernay, planted to 60% pinot noir, 30% chardonnay and 10% pinot meunier, the remainder shared between chardonnay in Chouilly and pinot meunier in Brimont. Largely from clay soils typically producing richer-bodied champagnes, the affordable wines of Janisson-Baradon are refreshingly youthful and lively.

'MY AIM IS TO DEFINE THE STYLE OF THE HOUSE,' explains young Cyril Janisson, 'as my father just focused on bottling.' Cyril commenced in 1997 and his brother Maxence took charge of the cellar in 2004. Together they produce 90,000 bottles each year under a regime of 'lutte raisonnée' (reasoned struggle), using no pesticides or herbicides since 1999.

Vinification is largely in tanks, with increasing use of egg fermenters and Burgundian barrels for fermentation and ageing of reserve wines. Vintage wines are never chaptalised. 'If I need sugar, I don't produce a vintage wine!' he declares. Malolactic fermentation has been blocked on vintage wines since 2005, and dosages progressively lowered from 11g/L to around 7g/L.

JANISSON-BARADON SÉLECTION BRUT NV • $

91 points • DISGORGED FEBRUARY 2012 • TASTED IN BRISBANE

2009 vintage with 30% 2008 reserve aged in oak barrels; 50% chardonnay, 50% pinot noir; 100% Épernay estate vineyards; aged 3 years on lees; 7g/L dosage

A restrained and lively champagne in a clean, crisp apéritif style. Crunchy lemon and grapefruit zest and granny smith apple fruit is balanced with subtle nutty notes. Well-integrated dosage accents a fresh and structured finish. A reliable and affordable entry champagne.

JÉRÔME PRÉVOST

(Zheh-rowm Preh-voh)

8/10

---

2 RUE DE LA PETITE MONTAGNE 51390 GUEUX

CHAMPAGNE

La Closerie

Les Béguines

*A*cross every style and region of the wine world, the very greatest makers share an intuitive approach that transcends any prescriptive grapegrowing or winemaking regime. Besides Anselme Selosse (of Jacques Selosse) himself, no one in Champagne personifies this more dramatically than Jérôme Prévost. When others follow regimes of traditional viticulture, organics or biodynamics, Prévost adopts a natural approach, keeping his senses attuned to the vines and responding gently. In a region that strives to mould every vintage into a house style, Prévost makes only a vintage wine and sees it as his role to support the vines to maximise the expression of the season, though sadly releases it too early to label it as a vintage. He harvests not on sugar or acidity, but on the sensation of the skins of the grapes in his mouth. He can't tell you if his wines go through malolactic fermentation ('I don't do analysis — the wines do what they want'). And he doesn't add dosage, not because this is his philosophy, but because the wine doesn't need it. 'Wine is not about philosophy,' he declares. This is winemaking by emotion, a world away from the formal, clinical approach of Champagne. With a big smile and a genuine, warm and unflustered approach, Prévost makes wines much like himself. Fleshy, vinous and brimming with exotic spice, these are some of the finest expressions of pure, single-vineyard, single-vintage pinot meunier in all of Champagne.

IN 1987, AT THE AGE OF 21, PRÉVOST INHERITED THE 2.2 hectare vineyard planted in the 1960s by his grandmother in Gueux on the Petite Montagne. There is only one vineyard and one variety and, until a recent foray into rosé, there was only one wine, too.

He made his first wine in 1998 with the help of his friend Anselme Selosse. It was a sign of the regard in which Anselme held the young Jérôme that he lent him space in his winery in Avize to make his first

four vintages. There is a clear synergy of philosophy between the two.

Prévost treasures the 55 million-year-old soils of his village and proudly showed me a sample, teeming with fossils of ancient sea life like some geology museum artefact — the secret, he says, to the minerality of his wine. Here, the chalk is deep, starting 25 metres below the surface, and he has spent 12 years working the soil to encourage deeper roots to build minerality in his wines.

'The soil used to be very hard, but now it is very easy to work. I plough the mid-rows and avoid herbicides. It's all about building up the micro-organism population in the soil, and that takes time,' he says.

He is emphatic that this is not biodynamics. 'Biodynamics is like a religion and I don't agree with that,' he explains. 'It's too much like a recipe, but every plot of land is different. You have to work with emotion and sensation and learn from nature, not from a book. You have to go out in the vines and feel the sun and the wind, with all of your senses attuned, to taste with your eyes and your ears.'

Grapes are harvested at a high level of maturity, achieved with tiny yields of 45hL/hectare, less than half of Champagne's average. His role is one of supporting his vines to draw out the expression of the year. 'I do not know which years are good years because for me every year is different,' he says. 'I have two girls, educated in the same way, but each is different and I love them both with the same love. My wines are the same. In the vineyard, every year is very different and this is what I enjoy about it.

'I do not understand the philosophy of making champagne taste the same every year. It is not my role to determine the style of the wine. The wine is the wine and it has its own way. In the winery, I do not want my stamp to show. I have to work very softly. To make a white wine I do nothing in the cellar — I work hard in the vineyard, press and put it in barrels,' he says.

Fermentation relies exclusively on natural yeasts from the vines. 'Different yeasts give different aromas, so you have to use natural yeast to make complex wines,' he explains. Since different yeasts have different tolerances of sulphur, he uses only very low levels of sulphur, so as not to inhibit weaker strains. Fermentation takes place entirely in barrels, both small and large, including a few Acacia barriques for the first time in 2012, and wines remain in barrel for 10 months, so as to breathe and not develop reductive characters. There is only one wine (the rosé is made from the same base

as the white), so the blend is made up of every barrel. Prévost prizes the complexity achieved by blending many small ferments of parcels from one vineyard. Every wine receives the same dosage of a minute 2g/L. 'I don't think about that, they all get the same!' he says.

It's a shame Prévost's wines are released so young, as it takes years for them to blossom. Bottles are not vintage dated, but the year of harvest is coded in the fine print of the front label, beginning 'LC'.

He was excited to make red wine for rosé from pinot meunier for the first time in 2007. A tiny volume of a single barrel is worked by hand, even using a bucket to 'pump' over twice a day. 'It's a marvellous thing!' he exclaims. 'Working directly with the grapes to make red wine is like a gift for me. In Champagne traditionally we never put the skin in the wine, but I don't understand this because all the good things about the grape are just under the skin!' Harvesting at full ripeness is the key, because maturity of the skin is more important to him than sugar and acid levels. This is achieved by sourcing red wine from an old part of the vineyard affected by a virus which produces very small and very few berries, reducing yields and intensifying the fruit. He always adds 10% to the white of the vintage to produce a rosé of slightly different colour each year.

Prévost makes just 13,000 bottles every year in the outhouses of his charming 1924 cottage in Gueux and a little cellar on his street. It's a small space, containing his barrels, one small blending tank, one forklift and a cellar in an old World War I armaments store. He has to move the labelling machine to get to his barrels. 'It is very small but enough for my two hands,' he says. Such is his tiny scale that he refers to his friend Pierre Larmandier's small estate of Larmandier-Bernier as 'a factory'.

The scarcity of Prévost's wines makes them hard to find, but the hunt is richly rewarded. Don't look for a bottle with his name on it. The name of the vineyard is prominent and his name is lost in the fine print.

This is just as he would have it.

Jérôme Prévost La Closerie les Béguines • $$$

92 points • Disgorged October 2012 • Tasted in Gueux

2010 base vintage ('LC10' on front label)

Don't be lured by enticing layers of gingernut biscuits, butterscotch, wild honey and nashi pear into thinking that Prévost's captivating meunier is a speed date. Give him time and wonderful raspberry fruits will emerge. This is an immensely textural wine with a dry finish and a savoury overlay of cashew nut oak that pleads for time in the cellar to properly integrate. It has the acid poise and persistence to go the distance.

JÉRÔME PRÉVOST LA CLOSERIE LES BÉGUINES • $$$

93 points • TASTED IN GUEUX

2009 base vintage ('LC09' on front label)

Another year in bottle and Prévost's 2009 still needs more time for its oak to integrate. A wonderfully inviting meunier of beautifully focused fresh pear, baked apples, wild honey, ginger and mixed spice. Poise, dimension and complexity abound, with balanced oak, texture akin to red apple skin and a very long, creamy finish.

JÉRÔME PRÉVOST LA CLOSERIE LES BÉGUINES • $$$

94 points • TASTED IN GUEUX

2007 base vintage ('LC07' on front label)

The 2007 exemplifies the longevity of Prévost's meunier, every bit as fine and fresh as it was two years ago, singing with lemons and brilliantly taut, refreshing acidity. It's simultaneously fleshy, vinous and wonderfully complete, with gingernut biscuit, spice and apple. The subtle toasty notes of savoury oak provide gentle support to a long-lingering finish, and it will only improve with more time in bottle.

JÉRÔME PRÉVOST LA CLOSERIE FAC-SIMILE ROSÉ NV • $$$$

95 points • TASTED IN GUEUX

2008 base vintage

Jérôme Prévost's 2008 white is his finest I have tasted, and from the same base, his rosé possesses the same core of layered spice and subtle red- and whitecurrants, overlaid with a revelation of gorgeous, pure, strawberry, red cherry and raspberry fruit of great finesse, subtlety, vinous depth and excellent definition. Wafting with delightful cherry blossom, lingering very long on the finish, charged with lively acidity, fine chalk minerality and subtle barrel texture. This disarmingly enduring rosé hasn't moved one iota since its release two years ago, promising great potential to age yet. Pinot meunier certainly makes for an enchanting rosé, particularly when it's handled as lovingly as this.

JOSEPH LORIOT-PAGEL

(Zhoh-sef Loh-ree-oh-Pah-zhel)

33–40 RUE DE LA RÉPUBLIQUE 51700 FESTIGNY
www.champagne-loriot-pagel.fr

CHAMPAGNE

Joseph Loriot-Pagel

The Loriot family has tended vines for more than a century and made its own wines for 80 years from Festigny in the Marne Valley. Almost nine hectares of estate vines span the surrounding villages and the Côte des Blancs grand crus of Cramant, Avize and Oger. Pinot meunier comprises more than two-thirds of the estate, the balance made up by chardonnay and pinot noir, farmed using integrated techniques that care for the soil and its people. Fermentation takes place in small stainless steel tanks, and reserve wines are matured in wooden barrels.

JOSEPH LORIOT-PAGEL CUVÉE DE RÉSERVE 2005 • $$

84 points • DISGORGED MAY 2012

Equal parts pinot meunier, pinot noir and chardonnay from the villages of Festigny, Cramant and Avize; 8g/L dosage

A ripe vintage of deep colour and powerful bouquet. It leads out with luscious white peach fruit but ends biscuity, dried out and dominated by a stale, bitter walnut character, leaving it coarse and contracted. A victim of a tough season.

JOSEPH LORIOT-PAGEL BLANC DE BLANCS 2006 • $$

88 points • DISGORGED MAY 2012

Cramant, Avize and Oger; 11g/L dosage

This vintage looked too sweet with a dosage of 10g/L two years ago. A more recent disgorgement would have benefited from a lower dosage, but has instead been subjected to a full 11g/L, which is unfortunate, because it's otherwise a clean and fruity expression of three great terroirs. A creamy palate of white peach, honey, nougat and spice finishes rounded and sweet.

KRUG

(Khroo-k)

5 RUE COQUEBERT 51100 REIMS
www.krug.com

KRUG

The call came at 4am one morning in March 2011. Olivier Krug braced himself for bad news. It was Maggie Henriquez, president of Krug. 'You have to read this book!' she exclaimed, to his bewilderment. An unlikely 4am conversation starter, but the book to which she referred would prove to be a revelation for the sixth-generation director of Krug. 'I've been talking about Krug for more than 20 years but four months ago, I really understood what it is about!' he exclaimed when he first showed me the book a few months later. Buried in the company archives for more than 160 years, the personal notebook of Olivier's great-great-great grandfather was written to document the philosophy of Krug just five years after he founded the house in 1843. In it he expounded the principles of creating a champagne of great richness and yet great elegance, of selecting only the finest elements from the greatest terroirs, rejecting mediocre fruit and — revolutionary at the time — making both a non-vintage and a vintage cuvée. To this day, a resolute commitment to these very ideals has secured Krug's position as the most luxurious, most exclusive and most decadent of all champagnes. And, most extraordinary of all, its champagnes are only getting better.

TO THOSE OF US GAZING IN FROM THE OUTSIDE IN wide-eyed wonder, Krug is to Champagne as Domaine de la Romanée-Conti is to Burgundy and Petrus is to Bordeaux. It possesses a grandeur, an other-worldliness, an amplitude that is as lofty as its meso-spheric price. Krug's grand hierarchy of prestige begins at a higher price than any other in Champagne, and its single-vineyard wines rank among the most expensive in the world. Krug is the king of champagnes. And it has something mystical, too.

I've always wondered if the magic of Krug is real. If one worked here for long enough, would the sparkle evaporate, the cellar turn into just a dank, dark hole,

the barrels become just dirty old kegs, the cracks in the walls reveal these old buildings for what they are, and the day-to-day reality expose the hyperbole of one of the most clever of all French marketing spiels?

I'm not the only one who has wondered. Julie Cavil, one of four in a talented young winemaking team headed by Eric Lebel, made a flippant passing comment when I first met her. 'When I joined here, I went behind the scenes because I suspected that not every-thing was done as it is said to be. But I found that it is,' she said. The sparkle in her eye and that glimmer of don't-pinch-me-in-case-I-wake-up wonder told me this was no marketing line. The magic, it seems, is real.

And it has to be, hasn't it? Some can fake wines of mediocre standards but no one, anywhere, ever, can fake wines at this level. The wines of Krug are among the most revered in the world.

PERFECTIONISM BEFORE TRADITIONALISM

From the outset, Krug has courageously pursued perfectionism ahead of traditionalism. 'Joseph was not a non-conformist, he was a very serious German guy, but he was ready to go beyond the rules to create something different,' Olivier reflects. 'He left the stability of the largest house in Champagne in 1842, with a vision to create a champagne that didn't exist.'

That same daring spirit flows in Olivier's blood, relentlessly pursuing the very finest grapes, regardless of variety, vineyard classification or village reputation, and fanatical vinification, regardless of cost.

Pinot meunier is prized, even in these wines of untiring longevity. Classification tastings are conducted blind, with no regard for a vineyard's cru. Krug purposely does not constrain itself to grand cru, nor even to premier cru, and its reach has extended as far even as the village of Les Riceys at the most southerly extreme of the Côte des Bar, on the border of Burgundy. A region not traditionally associated with longevity, its winegrowers were amazed when Krug invited them to taste their reserve wines at two, three, five and even 15 years of age. 'They were astounded that their wines could be kept all that time, and were extremely moved and very emotional,' Cavil recalls.

Krug owns just 21 hectares, 35% of the vineyards required to meet an annual production of some 600,000 bottles. The remainder is sourced from some 70–100 loyal growers, some of whom have supplied the house since its foundation. Olivier explains that they have recently formalised contracts based on individual plots, but with the flexibility to maintain quality in difficult vintages.

'One grower called us in 2010 and said, "I have a different plot for you because yours was done by rot",' he says. Few champagne houses can claim such loyalty.

OBSESSED WITH DETAIL

Krug's long-ageing style begins with fruit harvested with more acidity and less sugar, so pHs are usually lower than the rest of the region.

'In 2010 we started in Clos du Mesnil two days before the official regulated start of harvest,' Olivier explains. 'Everyone in the village said we were mad, but they were all watching for when we started because they know we are obsessed with detail!'

The secret at Krug lies in the detail. 'Joseph set some rules for an absolute detail for everything,' Olivier says. 'And we focus even more intently on the details today.' Grapes are selected plot by plot and pressed individually by their growers. 'Even if a grower chooses grapes from the same part of the village, we ask him to press as many parcels as he can.'

Olivier's late father, Henri Krug, told him, 'If you have a chance to vinify a wine on its own you will express more of its personality. The more individuality you get, the more precise you can be with your selection'. To this end, 36 stainless steel double vats of small capacity were installed in 2007, increasing the small-batch storage capacity of the winery. In keeping each plot separate, reserve wines are able to be kept fresher. 'Some plots have more potential to age than others, and if they were all vinified together, the blend would lose the freshness of the freshest parcels,' he explains.

Last year one of Krug's largest growers in Avize came to taste his six reserve wines back to 1998. 'He knows which plots are in each sample and we don't,' Oliver recounts. 'He went white when he tasted them. Out of 20 plots that he has supplied us over 13 years — more than 250 wines in all — five of those six reserves were from the same plot. None of us had any idea, because what we do is by taste, not by recipe. Such is our attention to detail in the tasting room.'

Krug's winemaking team admits to an obsession with numbers. Krug works with 200–250 very small parcels of fruit every vintage, all of which are tasted after vintage and again the following year. Any not up to Krug's exacting standards go somewhere else in the Louis Vuitton-Moët Hennessy group. At any time, more than 150 reserve wines are under consideration for Grande Cuvée, all of which are also tasted annually. Olivier and his uncle Rémi join the winemaking team for the tastings. The final blend comprises more than 100 parcels, spanning 8–10 vintages, reflecting a different recipe every year. 'Our job every year is to recreate the most generous character of champagne,' as is Olivier's aspiration. A particular 1995 reserve wine from Bouzy has been tasted every year for 16 years and is yet to be allocated to the blend. Reserves are kept fresh in 150 small tanks, deep in the cellar at a stable 11–12°C. At any given time there are 5 million bottles in the cellar, 10 times the annual production, a massive ratio that reflects this long-ageing style.

MAGNIFICENT LONGEVITY

Krug attributes its longevity to the primary fermentation of all of its wines in more than 4000 small, 205-litre oak barrels. When I arrived in July 2011, I was confronted by a sea of barrels in preparation for vintage in Krug's large courtyard, packed in so tight that there were but narrow accessways to each of the buildings. And Krug has more barrels on site at its Clos du Mesnil and Clos d'Ambonnay vineyards. It uses these not for oak flavour or aroma but to build richness, complexity, balance and a 'high fidelity' that is not possible in stainless steel.

This is achieved by using only old casks, of average age 20 years, currently dating back to 1964. They are decommissioned after about 50 years, when they become too difficult to repair. Seguin Moreau barrels were used exclusively in the past, but Taransaud have been introduced recently. 'It took six years of tasting trials to establish the best coopers for Krug,' Cavil tells me. Such is the attention to detail here. All barrels are purchased new and are seasoned for a few years by fermenting the second and third press before it is sold for distillation. A waste of a new barrel, but that's Krug!

Olivier is adamant that Krug is not special just because it is fermented in oak. 'When we started, every champagne was fermented in oak, and it still was 50 years ago!' he points out. When I asked to take his photo in front of the barrels, he politely proposed a different backdrop, eager to downplay the focus on oak.

To uphold freshness, Krug's wines spend just a few weeks in cask and are transferred to tanks following fermentation. Contact with oxygen during fermentation furnishes Krug with a resilience when it contacts oxygen as it ages, infusing its wines with rock-solid consistency. I have not seen the degradation of freshness in Krug bottles that plagues many other champagnes as they travel around the world. These are wines capable of ageing magnificently for decades.

When a bottle in Krug's museum cellar popped as its cage was replaced recently, the board and winemakers were immediately assembled to taste the wine blind. Vigorous debate ensued as to whether it was from the 1950s or the 1960s, but it was decided it was too fresh for the 1960s. It turned out to be 1915 — all the more remarkable because the Côte des Blancs was under occupation during the First World War and the wine was made exclusively from pinot noir, without the structural longevity of chardonnay.

Although Grande Cuvée is released when it is ready to drink, after a long ageing process, Olivier has been intrigued by the number of collectors who age it further. 'Visitors now talk about Grand Cuvées from the '40s, '50s, '60s and '70s,' he reports. 'Many of our customers now put it down for five years or more.' He has a dream to host dinners around the world for Krug lovers to bring their oldest Grand Cuvée.

It is now finally possible to ascertain the age of Krug's cuvées, thanks to an ingenious ID code printed above the barcode of every bottle, the first three digits of which indicate the trimester (first digit) and year (second and third digits) in which it was disgorged. Using this code, Krug.com will reveal the season and year in which the bottle was shipped, the number of years over which it has aged, the blend and the vintage story for vintage wines. For non-vintage blends, it will reveal the number of wines and each of the vintages.

RELENTLESS PURSUIT OF QUALITY

Krug's quest for quality in spite of the cost knows no limits. Krug Clos du Mesnil 1999 was to be released in 2010, but the final tasting pre-labelling was a disappointment. 'It did not have extravagant purity, it was shy and boring, you don't want to sit next to this wine!' Olivier explains.

So the decision was made to cancel its release, in spite of an offer from China to purchase the entire production of more than 10,000 bottles at full price. Olivier opened a bottle for me this year, 'to show that there is no compromise at Krug'. It was tense, introverted, deeply mineral and magnificent, though not as coherent as the 1998 or 2000. A secure 96 points. 'We will destroy the bottles and blend it away,' Olivier declared.

'The first thing you learn here is patience,' admits Cavill. 'There is a different time here. The clock in the courtyard is a symbol of the house. Time is very important in this place.'

Long ageing prior to release makes it impossible for Krug to follow trends, even if it wanted to. It takes 20 years to make a bottle of Grand Cuvée, since reserve wines are built up over 10 years, and seven or eight years of stock is perpetually ageing on lees.

Ownership of Krug rests with Louis Vuitton-Moët Hennessy, which has remained sufficiently hands-off to leave most of the decisions in the hands of the family. Since he joined the company in 1989, Olivier has built the Japanese market into the most important for Krug. 'Everyone in Champagne was laughing when we went to Japan,' he said. 'And that's the reason they are still not there today!' Hong Kong is strong, but he is uncertain of whether China will follow. The UK and France remain confident markets for Krug, but there is a lot of potential for development in the US.

While writing this book I received the sad news of the passing of Henri Krug. His place in the House of Krug and in Champagne will forever be treasured and held dear by many around the world. Such was the visionary daring of Henri Krug that when his father opposed the creation of a pink wine, he and his brother Rémi secretly produced a trial rosé. On pouring it blind for their father in 1976, he exclaimed, 'It is finished for us because someone in Champagne has copied Krug!' It was Henri who purchased Clos du Mesnil, and Henri who convinced his father to release it as the first single-vineyard wine of Krug.

For all he achieved, it was Henri Krug's unassuming humility and gracious welcome that I remember most of my first visit to Krug in the winter of 2001. He epitomised the ideals that have elevated the very pinnacle of Champagne to its inimitable place as the finest sparkling wine in the world today. It is for these reasons that this book is dedicated to Henri Krug.

KRUG GRANDE CUVÉE NV • $$$$

97 points • DISGORGED IN THE 3RD TRIMESTER OF 2011; BLENDED FROM 121 WINES FROM 12 VINTAGES FROM 1990 TO 2004 • TASTED IN REIMS AND BRISBANE

97 points • 2001 BASE VINTAGE, THREE YEARS OLDER THAN THE CURRENT RELEASE • TASTED IN REIMS, ADELAIDE AND BRISBANE

Krug leads off where most other champagne houses end, and this is every bit a prestige cuvée. Krug is adamant that it has no hierarchy in its cuvées, but price and style dictate that Grande Cuvée is always the starting point. Interestingly, the house pours in reverse order, tasting Grand Cuvée last. 'My father said, "Red carpet for every Krug!"' explains Olivier. 'There is no special treatment here, and every grape at Krug is given the same respect.'

Krug's winemaking team describes Grande Cuvée as its most exciting and most challenging wine to produce each year. It is a blend of the three champagne varieties, but there is no formula or recipe except to maintain the consistency of the style. Krug Grande Cuvée and Rosé are built on a high proportion (30–50%) and wide spectrum (6–10 vintages) of reserve wines. Reserves are kept in tank for five, 10 and even 20 years. After blending, Grande Cuvée spends at least a further six years on lees in bottle to build its characteristic golden amplitude. It accounts for 85% of the production of the house.

Grand Cuvée is more tense and fresh in its current late 2011 disgorgements than I have ever seen it. In spite of its profound maturity and inimitable complexity, it sings with a youthful definition that Krug has progressively refined in recent years. A zesty, crunchy amalgam of apple, pear and every form of citrus you can conjure opens into a maelstrom of molten wax, wisps of smouldering truffle, Christmas spice and kirsch. Decadently rich, extravagantly complex and thunderingly expansive, Grande Cuvée is a vinous champagne of multifaceted personality, yet ever-heightened tension and unerring focus, tapping into deep wells of scintillating, swirling minerality. Profound nuances of exotic spice flicker for minutes after you swallow. Every bit as enchanting as its legendary reputation promises, this is a champagne to drink slowly from large glasses, to witness an entire universe of captivating theatrics unfold as it warms.

Older disgorgements served at the house and around the world demonstrate the enduring consistency of this cuvée and its profound propensity to retain its vitality. Definitive and immovable, every one of six bottles of different ages that I have tasted in recent months has upheld a stability unmatched by any other house. Older disgorgements based on the 2001 vintage show more stone fruit generosity, green olive bite, bitter peach kernel character and gingernut biscuit warmth, yet still retain breathtaking tension and focus for old wines based on what Olivier describes as the worst vintage in Champagne in two decades.

The precision of recent releases is unprecedented, and just how many decades they might hold in the cellar is anyone's guess.

KRUG VINTAGE 2000 • $$$$$

98 points • DISGORGED SPRING 2010 • TASTED IN REIMS, ADELAIDE AND BRISBANE

43% chardonnay from Trépail, Villers-Marmery, Avize and Le Mesnil-sur-Oger; 42% pinot noir from Ambonnay, Bouzy and Aÿ; 15% pinot meunier from Sainte-Gemme and Villevanard

The potential for a Krug vintage wine is identified during the blending of Grande Cuvée, and only after the blend has been secured and all of the reserves earmarked. 'Our goal and challenge with Grand Cuvée is to make a consistent wine that erases all the character of the vintage,' Olivier explained. The most extreme and spectacular wines are kept aside as reserve wines, and those with the most pronounced character of the vintage become the vintage wine. Krug's vintage philosophy is to make a statement to reflect the story of the year, rather than a creative expression.

Krug dubs Vintage 2000 'gourmandise orageuse' — stormy indulgence — after its unusually climactically chaotic season. The end of 1999 brought the two biggest wind storms in France in the century, a violent tornado blacking out two-thirds of the country on the night before the turn of the millennium, and a July hailstorm of unprecedented violence. It was a year with little sun but above-average temperatures. Krug rates 2000 among its most intense vintage champagnes, one of its warmest declared vintage years, alongside 1947, 1959, 1976, 1982 and 1989.

There's a gentle and calm demeanour to Krug 2000 that belies its tumultuous season. In spite of its glowing generosity it's somehow transfixed in time, held in suspended animation and astonishingly unchanged from its release two years ago, yet somehow even more expressive than I have ever seen it. The sheer endurance of even a warm Krug vintage is a marvel indeed. This season has found a new lease on life in the capable hands of Krug, shot with indelible definition of crunchy lemon zest and tightly coiled acid line that draws its multifaceted complexity into tight control. It's aglow with yellow summer fruits and grapefruit, with the great intensity of Krug resonating in rumbling depth of figs, dried peaches, molten wax, exotic spice, vanilla, green olives and hints of smouldering hearth. Deep-set mineral expression and silky texture underscore a finish of sheer concentration and remarkable poise. Right at its prime, with a longer future before it than I ever expected.

....

KRUG VINTAGE 1998 • $$$$$

99 points • TASTED IN REIMS AND PERTH

A dramatic year made for a controversial Krug vintage. The hottest August since 1991 saw 40°C heat burning some vines and destroying 15% of the crop. Chardonnay held its freshness better than pinot, so this wine became the second in the history of the house to comprise predominantly chardonnay (the other was 1981). 'Krug is all about pinot noir, but this wine is much more about chardonnay,' Olivier explains. His father Henri declared, 'This is not Krug!' But to Olivier 'every vintage has to taste as different as possible from the previous one, otherwise there is no interest. We do not try to force the vintage into the house style.'

I adore the way that chardonnay holds this wine, utterly transcending its 15 years, vitalising an air of lemon blossom perfume, a shard of fresh acidity and an ageless primary citrus note that rings in clear peals like church bells. The palate darts with all the fruit velocity and agility of its release many years ago, building ever-deeper complexity in layers of brioche, nougat and honey, intricately interwoven with peach and fig generosity and subtle flickers of nutmeg and mixed spice. It swirls into a river of minerality that flows deep and swift across the palate, frothing with whitewash of mouth-filling, salty minerality that lingers and splashes long and strong.

The Champagne Guide

KRUG ROSÉ BRUT NV • $$$$$

98 points • DISGORGED FIRST TRIMESTER OF 2012 • TASTED IN REIMS AND BRISBANE

Like Grande Cuvée, Krug Rosé is a multi-vintage blend, but the association strictly ends here. This is a much smaller volume, assembled from the ground up. Pinot noirs from the best vines in Aÿ are treated to a short fermentation on skins and then blended with pinot noir, pinot meunier and chardonnay fermented in small oak casks as white wine, before ageing for a minimum of five years in bottle.

Rosé is a relative newcomer at Krug, first released in the 1980s. Its ethereal restraint and delicate air seems a paradox in the grand decadence of Krug, but such is the detailed intricacy of this medium salmon-tinted cuvée that it dances with light-footed grace on a stage of epic complexity. Absolute restraint and taut freshness of strawberry hull, white cherry, red apple and lemon zest slowly unravel to nuances of anise and mixed spice. An impeccable acid profile and pinpoint bead define a remarkable finish of mind-blowing seamlessness, impeccable line and unrelenting persistence. Most thrilling of all, its minerality is all-encompassing, mouth-embracing and emphatically chalk-infused.

KRUG CLOS DU MESNIL 2000 • $$$$$

100 points • TASTED IN REIMS

Clos du Mesnil is the most famous vineyard in all of Champagne, and one of the finest chardonnay sites outside the grand crus of Burgundy itself. An inscription in the vineyard states that vines were planted here and the wall built in 1698. The clos is divided into five or six plots across just 1.85 hectares in the heart of Le Mesnil-sur-Oger, the finest and most age-worthy of Champagne's chardonnay villages. On pure chalk, the east-facing slope achieves less ripeness than some of Le Mesnil's due south-facing slopes, making it all the more suited to Krug's long-ageing style.

'My father purchased the plot in 1971 to secure a supply of chardonnay at a time when many growers were starting to make their own wines,' Olivier explains. 'They did not expect this plot to produce amazing wines, but when they tasted all the still wines that year, they realised this little clos behind the big rusty gate in the middle of the village did not taste the same as the other wines from Le Mesnil. It was used in the blend at the time, but the same story repeated until the outstanding 1979 harvest, when my father suggested they should make a single wine. My grandfather said, "Never! You will ruin the philosophy of Krug! This is only one grape and one year and one little garden!" But my father made a test and they fell in love with the champagne.'

There is no fingerprint of place more pronounced than the mineral voice of the soil that resonates in the most distinctive champagnes. In all Champagne, I have not tasted a wine of such earth-shaking minerality as Clos du Mesnil 2000. It rumbles to the very core of the earth deep below this mesmerising site, then rises on the finish, like a shard of pure chalk erupting from the surface of the clos itself. Krug calls Clos du Mesnil 2000 'the miracle wine' after a hail storm destroyed half the vineyard, reducing the yield to 11,300 bottles. The surviving fruit escaped with remarkable endurance, still fresh and poised at 13 years of age, with a shining sabre of lemon and grapefruit acidity that slices through its core with razor precision, yet all the while impossibly creamy and gentle. Krug doesn't measure malolactic fermentation, but the breathtaking tension and eternal longevity of this cuvée is certainly charged with high-voltage malic acidity. A remarkable contradiction exists within its vector of pristine precision, unravelling a universe of complexity of anise, licorice, roast almonds, truffles, honey and molten wax.

Krug Clos du Mesnil is queen of blanc de blancs, and yet again the wine of the vintage.

KRUG CLOS D'AMBONNAY 1998 • $$$$$

100 points • TASTED IN REIMS

When Olivier joined Krug in 1989, his father suggested that perhaps the challenge of his generation would be to find another clos with terroir worthy of another Krug single vineyard. Just two years later, a clos surrounded by a protective wall since 1766 was found in Ambonnay, Krug's favourite village and largest source of pinot noir. The tiny site of just 0.68 hectares, just one-third the size of Clos du Mesnil, was purchased in 1994, and the first vintage was made in 1995. 'We called it ABC as a codename to keep it an absolute secret until it was released in 2007,' Olivier reveals. 'We even kept it a secret from Moët for some years!'

The third release of Clos d'Ambonnay, so scarce that the bottle Olivier opened for me was the first he'd tasted in some months. This is the most expensive current-release champagne, with a four-digit price tag in any currency, making for one of the rarest and most memorable tastings of all. On my first encounter, Clos d'Ambonnay reacted like no other I have tasted besides Clos du Mesnil of the same vintage. Such is its complexity and enthralling persistence that it morphed, unravelled and revealed itself for minutes after I swallowed. It reached out graciously, then paused, contemplated, interrogated, before resolving to divulge its secrets. Only after I said my farewells to Olivier and made my way back through the courtyard and out to the street did its haunting persistence declare its true pedigree as one of the finest champagnes I had tasted in more than 50 visits across the region. At a full 15 years of age, it is still shockingly fresh and lively, with an elegant purity that flies in the face of one of Champagne's most opulently voluminous creations. Its minerality is a revelation, deeply chalky, even spicy in texture. There is immense power here, with red fruits, plums, dried pear, blackberries, anise, truffles, licorice and exotic spice as if it were pinot noir uprooted directly from the grand crus of the Côte de Nuits itself. Clos d'Ambonnay is Champagne's very own La Romanée.

Krug's 36 new stainless steel double vats (shown left) provide capacity to keep small parcels separate, preserving the detail of magnificent sites such as Clos du Mesnil (right).

L. BÉNARD-PITOIS

(L. Bear-nah-Pee-twah)

6/10

23 RUE DUVAL 51160 MAREUIL-SUR-AŸ
www.champagne-benard-pitois.net

CHAMPAGNE

L. Bénard - Pitois

PROPRIÉTAIRE-RÉCOLTANT

Vignobles Premier Cru et Grand Cru

In Champagne's finest villages, the carving knife of succession is prone to shrinking the estate of each generation, but the Bénard-Pitois family has been blessed with something of the opposite. Laurent Bénard's paternal grandfather was privileged to holdings in Le Mesnil-sur-Oger and Oger, his mother in Avenay-val-d'Or and neighbouring Mutigny since 1850, and his wife in Bergères-lès-Vertus. The estate now draws from all five villages from its home in Mareuil-sur-Aÿ, one of the Vallée de la Marne's finest premier crus, and source of half its fruit. These are refreshingly affordable, terroir-driven wines, built around majestic pinot noir (two-thirds of the estate) from vines of average age exceeding 25 years.

BÉNARD'S GRANDFATHER MADE HIS OWN CHAMPAGNE in Mareuil-sur-Aÿ in small quantities from 1950. His father increased annual production to 20,000 bottles, and since 1991, Bénard has grown it to 70,000.

This is a conservative production for a 12-hectare estate, and the difference is sold to Bollinger and Duval Leroy. Pinot meunier has very little place in these cuvées 'because I don't like it', Bénard admits candidly. Most is sold to Duval-Leroy, who reportedly love it.

Bénard-Pitois upholds a natural approach in its vines, cultivating grasses in the mid-rows of every vineyard. Two hectares have been tended organically and ploughed with a horse since 2009, with certification approved in 2012. Organic fruit has already shown greater floral aromatics and complexity, as well as a lowering of yields by 20–30%, to less than 60hL/hectare — under two-thirds of Champagne's average.

Yields in 2012 were even lower, after outbreaks of mildew and oïdium. There is a hope to convert all estate vineyards to organics, though Bénard acknowledges that this will be quite a challenge across 40 far-flung plots. He will release his first organic champagne from Mareuil-sur-Aÿ in 2014 under the label 'LM Bénard'. As a grower, he is not permitted to market certified organic wines under the same brand as his traditional wines.

This organic philosophy carries over into vinification, with minimal use of sulphur as a preservative, and an attempt to make sulphur-free wine for the past two years. 'We prefer to use just enough sulphur at the beginning of vinification and a tiny addition at disgorgement,' he explains. All cuvées go through full malolactic fermentation, as it's very difficult to block with a low sulphur regime.

This creates something of a dilemma for Bénard, who is concerned by declining acidity in the wake of global warming. Warm summers are building good sugar concentrations and he has very little need to chaptalise, if at all. Reconstituted grape must rather than sugar is used for dosage. To balance lowering acid levels, Bénard has lowered dosage from 15g/L to 9g/L over two decades.

Each parcel is vinified separately in small enamelled tanks, or oak barrels for chardonnay and reserve wines. To minimise oak influence, barrels are purchased after two or three vintages in Burgundy. Growth of production over the past two decades has put pressure on space, and bottles are now aged in a rented cellar.

Disgorgement dates aren't printed on labels, but the date is on the cork. If you have a good eye, the bottling code on the glass is also the disgorgement date.

L. BÉNARD-PITOIS BRUT CARTE BLANCHE NV • $

94 points • DISGORGED NOVEMBER 2012 • TASTED IN MAREUIL-SUR-AŸ

2010 base vintage with 30% reserve wines; 75% pinot noir, 20% chardonnay, 5% pinot meunier; 9g/L dosage; 35,000 bottles

Bénard-Pitois' entry wine makes up half the production of the estate. It's an enticingly fruit-focused blend of young, fresh apple and nashi pear, fleshed out with pinot noir's gentle generosity. A clean, refreshing and well-made apéritif that balances fresh acidity with the soft roundness of premier cru pinot noir.

L. BÉNARD-PITOIS BRUT RÉSERVE NV • $

94 points • DISGORGED SEPTEMBER 2012 • TASTED IN MAREUIL-SUR-AŸ
AND BRISBANE

2009 base vintage with 2008 and 2007 reserves; 60% pinot noir, 40% chardonnay; 9g/L dosage; 20,000 bottles

There aren't many champagne producers that offer the chance to trade up from the entry NV for such a tiny outlay. With a larger representation of chardonnay and an extra year in the cellar, this is a big step up: a champagne of pristine freshness, fruit purity and soft minerality. Crunchy pear and apple fruit are the focus, delivering exacting definition, concentration and surprising persistence, with a subtle touch of honey, enlivened with fresh, vibrant acidity. A friendly, fruit-focused style, and one of the bargains of the year.

L. Bénard-Pitois Brut Nature NV • $

94 points • Tasted in Mareuil-sur-Aÿ

2007 base vintage; Brut Réserve kept 2 years longer on lees; 60% pinot noir, 40% chardonnay; zero dosage; 2g/L residual sweetness

A new label, released late 2012, showcasing the ability of Bénard-Pitois Brut Réserve to both age confidently and stand tall without added dosage. It retains impressive poise of lemon and purity of white peach, lively acidity and excellent mineral freshness, juxtaposed wonderfully with toasty, roast nut maturity. Finely crafted, beautifully balanced and quite a bargain.

L. Bénard-Pitois Demi-Sec Gourmandine NV • $$

90 points • Tasted in Mareuil-sur-Aÿ

2007 base vintage; 60% pinot noir, 40% chardonnay; Brut Réserve kept 2 years longer on lees; 38g/L dosage; just 2000 bottles

Heightened dosage makes the Brut Réserve honeyed and candied, exaggerating its fleshy stone fruits, yet retaining good acid definition and mineral structure.

L. Bénard-Pitois Brut Rosé NV • $$

95 points • Disgorged May 2012 • Tasted in Mareuil-sur-Aÿ

2009 base vintage; 50% pinot noir, 35% chardonnay, 15% pinot noir red wine; Brut Réserve blended with red wine from Mareuil-sur-Aÿ and Mutigny; 7g/L dosage

The pristine freshness, purity and chalk mineral expression of Brut Réserve is the perfect base for a beautifully elegant rosé. A splash of red wine transforms it into a gloriously medium salmon-tinted thing with a pretty air of pure red cherry and strawberry fruit and a delightfully understated palate. It's fine, mineral and precise, with a delicate finish nuanced with lingering cherry kernel and anise.

L. Bénard-Pitois Blanc de Blancs Millésime 2004 • $$

93 points • Disgorged December 2012 • Tasted in Mareuil-sur-Aÿ

50% Mareuil-sur-Aÿ, 25% Le Mesnil-sur-Oger, 25% Bergères-les-Vertus; half fermented in barrel; 8g/L dosage

A blanc de blancs of lively freshness, contrasting sour lemon and honeydew melon with slowly rising notes of almond and butter. Oak contributes spicy complexity and a savoury background, drawing out the finish long, linear and balanced, accenting fine minerality.

L. Bénard-Pitois Brut Rosé LB NV • $$

93 points • Disgorged September 2012 • Tasted in Mareuil-sur-Aÿ

2009 base vintage; 85% chardonnay, 15% pinot noir red wine; fermented in tank; 50% aged in older barrels for 1 year; 7g/L dosage; less than 2000 bottles

Bénard has achieved his aim of producing a different style of rosé, contrasting the vibrancy and mineral texture of chardonnay with the red berry fruits of pinot noir red wine and the spicy complexity of barrel ageing, holding with considerable persistence. Finely poised, grippy tannins make this a well-textured rosé that will age confidently.

L. Bénard-Pitois Brut Millésime 2005 • $$

90 points • Tasted in Mareuil-sur-Aÿ

60% pinot noir, 40% chardonnay; 20% barrel fermented, a smaller proportion than usual in response to the inherent power of 2005

Bénard's sincerity is refreshing, and he's the first to admit that he fought with fungus and harvested too late in the difficult 2005 season. The result is a generous and ripe vintage, leading out with honeydew melon and ripe white peach, quickly fading on the finish to close short and a little dried out. A spicy and fruit-sweet style, characteristic of this ripe season.

The Champagne Guide

LAHERTE FRÈRES

(La-airt Frair)

6/10

3 RUE DES JARDINS 51530 CHAVOT-COURCOURT
www.champagne-laherte.com
champagne-laherte.blogspot.com

CHAMPAGNE

DEPUIS 1889

Laherte Frères
à CHAVOT

'More than anything, my father and I are trying to respect the soil, expressing the style of the clay and limestone,' says the young Aurélien Laherte. This is the soil of the historic little village of Chavot-Courcourt, on the border of the Côte des Blancs and the Vallée de la Marne. 'The clay gives us chardonnay that is fruitier than the Côte des Blancs, and the limestone pinot meunier that is finer than the Vallée de la Marne,' he says. For a production of just 100,000 bottles, Laherte Frères boasts a very large portfolio of 11 cuvées that preserve the detail of its terroirs in wines of taut, linear persistence and at times assertive structure.

WITH A HISTORY OF GRAPE-GROWING IN THE VILLAGE spanning seven generations, the extended Laherte family accounts for almost one-third of Chavot's population of 350. The 10 hectares from which the estate sources across 75 parcels in 10 nearby villages have been passed down through the generations and all are still owned and tended by members of the immediate family. French law dictates registration of the domaine as a négociant-manipulant, but for all practical purposes it should be considered as a grower producer, with the exception of its entry Brut Ultradition NV, for which supply is supplemented with two hectares of purchased fruit.

A complex array of vineyard parcels span the Coteaux Sud d'Épernay (Chavot, Moussy, Épernay, Vaudancourt and Mancy, with chardonnay, pinot noir and pinor meunier), Côte des Blancs (Vertus and Voipreux, with chardonnay) and the Vallée de la Marne (Le Breuil and Boursault, with pinot meunier).

'We would like our wines to express that they are not from the Côte des Blancs or the Montagne de Reims, but to be expressive of our village,' Aurélien says. In tasting young vins clairs, the chalk minerality of Chavot is quite distinctive compared with his parcels from other villages. The oldest vines have been cultivated here by different generations of the family for more than 68 years.

An ecological approach is taken in the vineyards, with half the holdings managed biodynamically, and the remainder essentially organically, 'to facilitate the natural expression of the vine and increase its aromatic potential', Aurélien explains. He reports that he sees increased mineral character in biodynamic plots as vines push deeper into the chalk, encouraged by ploughing by horse in spring and autumn to break up the surface. Natural pesticides and herbicides are employed and yields are limited.

'When we started with biodynamics in 2005, we found the fruit was cleaner and more consistent during vinification,' he says. 'The wines were fruity, held good acidities and the bottles maintained their freshness for longer after they were opened.'

A vintage wine is made every year, even in the challenging 2010 season. 'If you work diligently, you don't need to be afraid of the quality of the vintage,' he suggests. 'In Champagne, many people just add more sugar or leave a wine on lees for longer if it's not right, but for us we simply make the wine.'

Villages, crus and varieties are separated, and assessed and matched to the age and style of one of 250 barrels as the musts leave one of two traditional presses. More than 80% of parcels are fermented and aged in oak, as has been the tradition here for more than 25 years. Barrels vary from four to 40 years of age, and include several large 100-year-old foudres from Alsace for reserve wines. Five small barrels are purchased each year from Domaine de la Romanée-Conti, where they have aged Le Montrachet, no less.

Some lees stirring is performed to build richness. Malolactic fermentation is blocked in most cuvées, but may be allowed to proceed in part for particular years and varieties. Laherte has trialled some barrels without sulphur, but is not yet certain that this is a good idea. 'Good acidity and low pH mean we don't need to use much sulphur, but without any we lose something of the soil and the precision of the fruit,' Aurélien explains.

A unique 'Le Clos' vineyard of just 0.3 hectares in Chavot has been planted to seven varieties to preserve the heritage of the estate.

'We found the lost varieties of our ancestors in our old plots, and we have embarked on a project to recreate champagne with the same taste as 250 years ago,' Aurélien explained as he showed me through the prized site at the top of the village. Chardonnay, pinot meunier, pinot noir, fromenteau, petit meslier, pinot blanc and arbane are harvested and pressed together, wild yeast fermented in barrel without malolactic fermentation, and blended with a reserve solera of every vintage since 2005 and bottled as 'Les 7'.

Attention to every detail is the key at Laherte, right down to the cork. Every wine has been sealed with DIAM for more than six years. 'I don't want to lose all our work to the cork!' Aurélien exclaims. 'Our goal is to preserve freshness, fruit and minerality in our wines and our tests indicate that DIAM is most effective, providing protection against changes in temperature and humidity as our wines travel around the world.'

Aurélien works alongside his father, uncle and grandparents to produce 11 cuvées each year, all but two of which are made in tiny volumes of just a few thousand bottles. Each boasts a refreshingly informative back label, detailing villages, assemblage, vinification, dosage and disgorgement date.

LAHERTE FRÈRES GRAND BRUT ULTRADITION NV • $

90 points • DISGORGED SEPTEMBER 2012 • TASTED IN CHAVOT AND BRISBANE

60% 2010 base; 40% 2009 reserves aged in barrel; 60% pinot meunier, 30% chardonnay, 10% pinot noir; blend of the Coteaux sud d'Épernay, Vallée de la Marne and Côte des Blancs; average vine age 28 years; 50% vinified in barrels; 60% malolactic fermentation; 7g/L dosage; DIAM closure; 50,000 bottles

Previously this was Brut Tradition, but with many growers now producing a brut tradition it has been cleverly renamed 'Ultradition'. 'Our work in the vines and the winery now is not traditional,' Aurélien explains. 'We are trying to do something different.' This is certainly a characterful expression of an entry cuvée, with plenty of barrel work contributing notes of charcuterie and buttery, savoury complexity. Its young pinot meunier contributes a medium straw-yellow hue and generous yellow summer fruits, preserved lemons and honey, while chardonnay lends zesty grapefruit and apple. A textural and structural champagne showing firm phenolic dryness on the finish, though not diminishing its fruit flow and persistence.

The Champagne Guide

LAHERTE FRÈRES BLANC DE BLANCS ULTRADITION NV • $

93 points • DISGORGED AUGUST 2012 • TASTED IN CHAVOT

50% 2010 base vintage; 50% 2009 reserves aged in barrel; Épernay and Côte des Blancs; vines over 30 years old; 5g/L dosage; 20,000 bottles

A bargain blanc de blancs that contrasts impressive fruit character of lemon and white peach with the fine, chalky, salty mineral texture that Chavot shares with the Côte des Blancs. The generosity of Chavot brings impressive balance and persistence to this youthful blend, with barrel-aged reserves building seamless depth without any sense of woodiness. All Laherte cuvées are good value, and this is one of the best this year.

LAHERTE FRÈRES BLANC DE BLANCS BRUT NATURE NV • $$

92 points • DISGORGED AUGUST 2012 • TASTED IN CHAVOT

As above for Blanc de Blancs Ultradition, with zero dosage

Predictably much like the Ultradition, with less generosity of fruit, making for quite a contrast between the taut, mineral structure of these villages, tense acidity and good expression of yellow summer fruits and preserved lemon, finishing with signature chalky, salty minerality.

LAHERTE FRÈRES BRUT ROSÉ TRADITION NV • $

90 points • TASTED IN CHAVOT

50% 2010 and 50% 2009; 15% red wine; 100% fermented and aged for 6 months in wooden barrels, foudres and vats; partial malolactic fermentation; average vine age 25 years; 8g/L dosage

Aurélien finds his blended rosé his most challenging wine to make, with the tannins of red wine clashing with the citrus of chardonnay, hence the blend is predominantly black grapes, including some from his wife's family in Bouzy. It's a clean, fresh and well-assembled style of full crimson hue. The bouquet expresses pretty strawberry and rose petal perfume, becoming gentle, elegant red fruits on the palate. A young, vibrant and simple rosé that finishes a little short.

LAHERTE FRÈRES LES VIGNES D'AUTREFOIS 2008 • $$

95 points • DISGORGED FEBRUARY 2012 • TASTED IN CHAVOT

100% pinot meunier from Chavot and Mancy vines planted between 1947 and 1953 in four vineyards in chalk soils; wild fermented in barrels at least 4 years of age; aged 6 months with regular lees stirring; no malolactic fermentation; 4g/L dosage

This is consistently the most delicious Laherte cuvée. The planets aligned and the great 2008 vintage shone on these biodynamically tamed old pinot meunier vines, deeply rooted in chalk soils, giving birth to one of the tightest and most age-worthy pinot meuniers of all. The vivacity and expression of the season is amplified by tense malic acidity and honed chalk mineral texture, impeccably offsetting meunier's generous, succulent yellow plum, raspberry and honey lusciousness. Flawlessly engineered and great value.

LAHERTE FRÈRES LES EMPREINTES NV • $$

94 points • DISGORGED MARCH 2012 • TASTED IN CHAVOT

100% 2008; 50% Chavot pinot noir, 50% Épernay chardonnay muscate (a particularly aromatic clone of chardonnay); fully vinified in barrels at least 2 years of age; 4g/L dosage

Laherte labels Les Empreintes as a non-vintage to avoid confusion with the vintage-dated d'Autrefois, which seems odd for an estate with nine non-vintage cuvées, and there's no overlap of varieties between these two. Laherte's second Les Empreintes is certainly a vintage to celebrate, singing with all the high notes of this exemplary season. It strikes a captivating contrast between the zesty crunch of lemon fruit and the generosity of succulent white peach, white cherries and honey. Layers of nutmeg and mixed spice fill out a creamy finish, underlined by finely structured, chalky minerality.

LAHERTE FRÈRES LES 7 NV • $$

92 points • DISGORGED JANUARY 2012 • TASTED IN CHAVOT AND ADELAIDE

Single-vineyard Chavot; previously labelled Les Clos; 18% chardonnay, 17% pinot blanc, 18% pinot meunier, 15% petit meslier, 10% fromenteau, 8% arbane, 14% pinot noir; planted 2003; 60% 2009; 40% perpetual reserve blend of 2005 through 2008; wild fermented in Burgundy barrels at least 10 years of age; matured in barrel for 6 months with regular lees stirring; no malolactic fermentation; 4g/L dosage (also made with zero dosage)

An opulent and multi-dimensional fruit character anticipated by its recipe, spanning the contrasting expressions of citrus and stone fruits of all kinds, star fruit, mixed spice, custard apple, even ripe table grapes. In the midst of this complex fruit salad, it retains a purity and focus to its crunchy lemon rind and fresh grapefruit palate. There is real textural dimension to this wine, encapsulating the grip and mouthfeel of its wide array of varieties. With full malic acidity to keep things lively, 4g/L dosage is my pick over the zero-dosage version.

The Champagne Guide

LAHERTE FRÈRES MILLESIME RECOLTE 2005 • $$

89 points • TASTED IN CHAVOT

85% chardonnay, 15% pinot meunier; average vine age 35 years; fully vinified and aged in 40% new barrels for 6 months with regular lees stirring; 3–6g/L dosage

From an era before Laherte was practising organics and when it still used new oak (thankfully, no longer), this is a wine that Aurélien admits is too oaky. Its expressive generosity of white stone fruits, preserved lemon and mixed spice is interrupted by the savoury grip of oak, which leaves the finish a little woody, firm and astringent.

LAHERTE FRÈRES LES BEAUDIERS ROSÉ DE SAIGNÉE NV • $$

90 points • DISGORGED JANUARY 2012 • TASTED IN CHAVOT

2008 vintage; 100% pinot meunier from old Chavot vines planted in 1953, 1958 and 1965; macerated for 12 hours; wild fermented and aged for 6 months in barrels of at least 6 years of age; no malolactic fermentation

A deep, vibrant, full crimson red hue anticipates a unique rosé style of intense pomegranate, cherry and red berry fruits and quite pronounced tannin grip. A touch of savoury reduction is apparently typical of the soils of this east-facing site at the bottom of the village.

LAHERTE FRÈRES LA TROISIEME VIE COTEAUX CHAMPENOIS • $$

92 points • TASTED IN CHAVOT

Blend of pinot meunier from 2009 and 2008; partial malolactic fermentation; 300 bottles

Such is the rarity of this tiny cuvée that I have only ever seen it in Laherte's little cellar in Chavot, where it sells for €45. Coteaux Champenois is about as acidic as red wine comes, and malic acidity can make for a particularly challenging style. Laherte has pulled this off with consummate skill, a focused style of tightly coiled black cherry fruit, rose bud, brambles, even smoky suggestions. Silky, fine tannins offer plenty of grip, and the acid line is unsurprisingly taut, promising profound longevity. Patience is the key. 'We did a Coteaux Champenois tasting last year and a 1959 and 1968 were wonderful, with balanced, soft acidity,' Aurélien recalls. 'They taught us not to be too concerned about the acidity when these wines are young.'

LALLIER

(Lah-liay)

---

4 PLACE DE LA LIBÉRATION 51160 AŸ
www.champagne-lallier.fr

The young house of Lallier was established in 1996, purchased by winemaker Francis Tribaut in 2004, and moved operations from its 18th century vaulted cellars in Aÿ to a new facility in Oger in 2011. The estate is privileged to eight hectares in Aÿ and four hectares in Cramant, Chouilly and Vertus, providing for one-quarter of its production of 450,000 bottles annually; the remainder is sourced from vineyards through the Montagne de Reims and Côtes des Blancs. Fermentation takes place in stainless steel tanks using only natural yeasts, and partial malolactic fermentation is used in each cuvée to maintain consistency of freshness. These are clean, well-balanced and fruit-focused champagnes, though entry cuvées somewhat lack character and presence.

LALLIER GRAND CRU GRANDE RÉSERVE BRUT NV • $$

89 points

65% pinot noir from Aÿ and Verzenay; 35% chardonnay from Avize and Cramant; 9g/L dosage

Impressive sourcing credentials that it sadly fails to live up to. A clean, fresh, lively and fruit-focused champagne with up-front, young, zesty grapefruit, apple and pear that drops away quickly to a thin finish. Some firm apple-skin texture contributes phenolic grip to the mouthfeel, giving an impression of heavy-handedness at the press. No indication of age is offered, but this seems a very young blend.

The Champagne Guide

LALLIER PREMIER CRU ROSÉ BRUT NV • $$$

90 points

80% pinot noir from Aÿ and Bouzy, 20% chardonnay from Avize and Mareuil-sur-Ay; 20% reserve wine; 10g/L dosage

Unusual for the typically characterful Aÿ and Bouzy pinot noir, there's not a lot of fruit definition or persistence to speak of, making for a neutral style with a gentle, creamy bead and a little phenolic, skinsy texture. It's clean, fruity and light with placid orange jube, tangelo and red apple flavours, rounded out with soft acidity and gently balanced dosage.

LALLIER GRAND CRU VINTAGE 2005 • $$$

86 points

55% Aÿ pinot noir; 45% Côte des Blancs chardonnay; 7g/L dosage

The powerfully ripe 2005 vintage bursts into the room with rich grilled pineapple, baked apple, grilled stone fruits and voluptuous tropical fruits, then immediately collapses on the floor in a dry, callow, stale mess. For what it's worth, acidity and dosage are well balanced.

LALLIER GRAND CRU BLANC DE BLANCS NV • $$$

91 points

70% Aÿ, 30% Cramant and Avize; 25% reserve wine; 8g/L dosage

The strongest of Lallier's cuvées this year, and a real step up in fruit definition and character. It's age is not disclosed, but this is clearly a young, racy thing, singing with lively, youthful acidity, fleshed out with some skinsy phenolic grip and bitter grapefruit notes. Lemon meringue flavour is offset with a taut, sour lemon cut.

LALLIER GRAND CRU ZERO DOSAGE NV • $$$$

91 points

70% pinot noir from Aÿ; 30% chardonnay from Avize and Cramant; 40% reserve wine; aged under cork; zero dosage

As clean and dry as a desert, this is a stark, lifeless yet strangely endearing landscape punctuated by softly skinsy phenolic texture. It's an edgy and honed zero-dosage of high-tensile bitter grapefruit and lemon zest flavours of considerable persistence, impressive concentration and streamlined, piercing clarity. This territory is strictly only for the most adventurous explorers.

LANSON

(Lohn-soh)

7/10

66 RUE DE COURLANCY 51100 REIMS
www.lanson.com

*T*here *is something about Lanson that has always struck me as quite extraordinary. For the ninth largest Champagne house, with a 4 million bottle annual production (the majority of which is Black Label Brut NV, frequently discounted to one of the lowest prices of any champagne on the shelves), this is a house that has maintained remarkable consistency. All the more astonishing considering that it was purchased by Moët in 1991 and cunningly on-sold less than six months later, with just two of its 208 hectares of magnificent vineyards. It should take 15 years for a house of this magnitude to recover from such a blow, but I have enjoyed Black Label as my house champagne many times over the past decade, and in recent tastings of vintage wines spanning 30 years, that ominous dip that everyone anticipated simply never came. How is this possible?*

ONE MAN. JEAN-PAUL GANDON COMMENCED HERE IN 1972, making his tenure of more than 40 years (and counting) extraordinary even in a region as historic as Champagne. More than this, he spent his first 15 years overseeing the sourcing of the grapes and must in the vineyards, a role which he retained when he was promoted to Chef de Cave in 1986.

His new owners astutely left him free reign to source, make and blend the wines as he saw best. He is a talented winemaker, certainly, but more than this, he is connected, and his relationships with the growers across the villages of Champagne have infused this house with a startling resilience in the midst of its tumultuous corporate ride of recent decades.

Lanson's distinctive house style of blocking malolactic fermentation makes for an excitingly high-strung, age-worthy champagne, true to Gandon's aspiration of 'maintaining freshness, power and fruit character'. The non-vintage receives complexity from a minimum of three years ageing on lees, power and structure from a 50% dose of pinot noir from the Montagne de Reims and Côte des Bar, minerality from chardonnay on the southern slopes of the Montagne de Reims, and a balancing touch of just 15% Vallée de la Marne pinot meunier. Lanson uses pinot meunier only in its entry non-vintage cuvées.

Thanks to Gandon, Lanson has been able to maintain grand cru fruit sources for all of its vintage

The Champagne Guide

wines, which are generally a 50/50 blend of pinot noir and chardonnay, aged a minimum of five years on lees prior to release, and usually considerably longer — remarkable for one of the lowest-priced vintage wines on the shelves.

Such maturation calls for a total cellar stock of 23 million bottles in Lanson's six kilometres of drives under Reims.

These are wines that age effortlessly, building slowly and purposefully in bottle, and I have recently been stunned by the stamina of late-disgorged 1983, 1988, 1990 and regular-disgorged 1996 and 1998.

Lanson is impressive in printing disgorgement dates on the back of every cuvée and its new website is refreshingly informative, with technical sheets detailing blends and villages for every cuvée.

To commemorate its 250th anniversary in 2010, Lanson launched a series of 'Extra Age' cuvées. The concept was unusual but inspired, a trilogy of three non-vintage cuvées, each from three mature vintages chosen to complement each other. These were not simply late-disgorged versions of its non-vintage cuvées, but purpose-assembled to age gracefully.

Lanson is the primary brand of the Lanson-BCC group, champagne's second largest after LVMH. In February 2013, it was announced that Hervé Dantan would join as Assistant Chef de Cave in anticipation of Jean-Paul Gandon's pending retirement.

Dantan comes with an impressive track record of 22 years as Chef de Cave at Mailly Grand Cru, following experience at Moët & Chandon and Piper-Heidsieck.

It seems Lanson's future will remain in good hands.

LANSON BLACK LABEL BRUT NV • $

93 points • DISGORGED FEBRUARY 2012 • TASTED IN REIMS AND BRISBANE

2008 base vintage; 50% pinot noir, 35% chardonnay, 15% pinot meunier; 50–60 villages; aged 3 years on lees; no malolactic fermentation; 9g/L dosage

As precise as ever, Lanson makes a profound statement of freshness and fruit expression right from its first cuvée, making Black Label one of the best of the readily available bargain champagnes. The great 2008 vintage base delivers more generosity than usual, lingering long, with depth of peach, wild honey, toast and ginger, freshened up with lemon and apple fruit and the classic malic acid signature of the house. One bottle opened in Australia was oxidised, dried out and lacking fruit definition, and another was corked.

LANSON ROSE LABEL BRUT ROSÉ NV • $

94 points • DISGORGED JULY 2012 • TASTED IN REIMS

2008 base vintage; 53% pinot noir, 32% chardonnay, 15% pinot meunier; 7% red wine; 50–60 villages; aged 3 years on lees; no malolactic fermentation; 7g/L dosage

There is a dazzling elegance and an understated delicacy to this gorgeous rosé that its blatant strawberry-mousse coloured livery completely belies. Don't be put off by this or its teeny price, because this is a beautifully crafted rosé of purity and subtlety. Jean-Paul Gandon seeks red wine of pretty aromatics and soft tannins and uses a judicious dose to create a medium salmon hue. Red cherry, red apple, strawberry hull and rose petal perfume all congregate and hang around for a surprisingly long finish, sustained by the delightful tang of malic acidity and softly mineral texture. One of the real bargains of rosé champagne.

LANSON BRUT VINTAGE GOLD LABEL 2004 • $$

93 points • TASTED IN REIMS

52% pinot noir, 48% chardonnay; no malolactic fermentation; 8–9g/L dosage

I love the energy of malic acidity in charging Lanson Vintage with tremendous potential to improve in the cellar. On the eve of its release, the youthful purity of 2004 is structured by a rigid scaffold of taut, drying malic acidity, giving a textural mouthfeel to juvenile grapefruit, apple and pear fruit. Its pretty fragrance of lemon zest proclaims its innocence, not yet having embarked on the journey towards complexity. A structured vintage, without the vibrancy, intensity or energy of 2002, but one which will undoubtedly blossom over the next two decades. Patience.

LANSON BRUT VINTAGE GOLD LABEL 2002 • $$

95 points • DISGORGED JUNE 2012 • TASTED IN REIMS AND BRISBANE

53% pinot noir from Aÿ, Louvois, Verzenay and Verzy; 47% chardonnay from Cramant and Le Mesnil-sur-Oger; no malolactic fermentation

A rare dry wind at the end of the season concentrated the grapes, infusing 2002 with a formidable tension between intensity and acid cut. Lanson captures this contrast with impeccable precision in its finest vintage since 1996. Considerable poise of delightfully fresh and pure lemon zest, lemon juice and white peach is charged with all the energy and cracking malic acidity of 2002, only slowly beginning to build complexity of brioche, roast nuts and honey. Seamless persistence, powerful drive and crystalline mineral texture unite with fine-tuned balance, guaranteeing an exceptional life and confirming one of the best bargain vintage champagnes on the shelves. I recently bought a case, sealed it up tight and buried it deep in my cellar. Come back in 10 years.

LANSON EXTRA AGE BLANC DE BLANCS BRUT NV • $$$

94 points • DISGORGED JUNE 2012 • TASTED IN REIMS

A blend of 2005 for suppleness, 2004 for finesse and 2003 for generosity; Avize, Cramant, Oiry, Oger and Le Mesnil-sur-Oger; no malolactic fermentation

A blanc de blancs of wonderfully seamless beauty and outstanding persistence and harmony. For a wine of this age, purity is proclaimed in a brilliant pale straw hue and a scintillating bouquet of white peach and lemon fruit. The palate is building subtle notes of toasty complexity, preserved lemon, wild honey and ginger, while maintaining the laser-like focus and freshness that define Lanson. Even with no malolactic fermentation, there's a buttery flavour and a welcoming creaminess to its bead.

LANSON EXTRA AGE BRUT NV • $$$

95 points • DISGORGED JUNE 2012 • TASTED IN REIMS

A blend of 2004, 2000 and especially 2002; 60% pinot noir, 40% chardonnay; Avize, Chouilly, Cramant, Oger, Le Mesnil-sur-Oger, Vertus, Cuis, Verzenay, Mareuil-sur-Aÿ and Bouzy; no malolactic fermentation

The leader of Lanson's senior citizens owes its superiority to a predominance of the majestic 2002 vintage, boring deep into the chalk bedrock of (particularly) Verzenay and Cuis to draw out intricate definition of mineral texture. A calm sense of completeness sets this blend apart, capturing the wonderful succulence of white summer fruits, the subtle, nuanced complexity of toast and mixed spice and the generosity of honey, all drawn together by the whip-crack of malic acidity, bringing harmony to a seamlessly persistent finish.

LANSON ROSÉ EXTRA AGE BRUT NV • $$$$

93 points • DISGORGED JUNE 2012 • TASTED IN REIMS

A blend of 2005, 2004 and 2002; 65% pinot noir, 35% chardonnay; Avize, Chouilly, Cramant, Oger, Le Mesnil-sur-Oger, Verzenay and Bouzy; no malolactic fermentation

A rosé of grand credentials, with a copper tint to its medium salmon hue revealing the onset of secondary complexity. It's a stroll through an autumnal environment, with crisp leaves falling on damp earth, a note of pipe smoke on the air and a suggestion of spices of unknown origins. It retains beautiful aromas of cherries and strawberries, though the palate is further progressed down the path towards savoury development. Its complexity lingers long on the finish, with subtle textural presence becoming dry on the close.

LANSON NOBLE CUVÉE BRUT ROSÉ NV • $$$$

95 points • DISGORGED SEPTEMBER 2012 • TASTED IN REIMS

2002, 2000 and a little 1998; 62% chardonnay from Oger, Le Mesnil-sur-Oger, Cramant and Chouilly; 38% pinot noir from Verzenay and Bouzy; no malolactic fermentation

In contrast to Lanson's Extra Age Rosé, its Noble Cuvée leads with chardonnay, bringing a sense of delicacy and harmony to a blend of considerable age. Freshness, deep-set complexity and fine definition are held in careful tension, as summer peaches, nectarines and subtle suggestions of strawberries and cherries evolve to enticing complexity of autumn leaves, anise, ginger and wild honey. It has upheld finesse and fullness in the midst of this transformation, without any hint of deterioration into dry savouriness on the finish — a daring tightrope stunt to pull off with rosé of such maturity.

LANSON NOBLE CUVÉE BLANC DE BLANCS 2000 • $$$$

95 points • DISGORGED SEPTEMBER 2012 • TASTED IN REIMS

Avize and Cramant; no malolactic fermentation; 10g/L dosage

The strength of the partnership of these neighbouring grand crus infuses a focus of lemon and grapefruit and a depth of succulent white peach, retained with impressive vibrancy for the generous 2000 vintage at 13 years of age. Powerful structure and taut malic acidity make this a particularly energetic release, with a very long life before it, just beginning to build complexity of toast and nougat, and on some days hints of smoky reduction, reminiscent of ginger and green olives. A blanc de blancs of impressive texture and mineral presence, proclaiming the signature of these great terroirs.

LANSON NOBLE CUVÉE BRUT MILLÉSIMÉ 2000 • $$$$

96 points • DISGORGED OCTOBER 2011 • TASTED IN REIMS

70.5% Avize and Oger chardonnay; 29.5% Verzenay, Bouzy and Aÿ pinot noir; no malolactic

One of the finest Lanson cuvées I have ever tasted, and undoubtedly the greatest of the modern era. Such was its searing acidity on our first encounter two years ago that I wrote, 'Don't chill it too much, for risk of being impaled by an ice shard of malic acidity!' It has since toned magically, with that acid-cut serving to tone the expressive fruit generosity of yellow summer fruits that define this sun-drenched season. Its mineral definition has erupted with the pure chalk of Avize and Oger, lingering with great determination and seamless poise, the epitome of persistence and of sheer longevity that transcends its vintage.

LANSON BRUT VINTAGE GOLD LABEL 1990 • $$$$

95 points • DISGORGED SEPTEMBER 2012 • TASTED IN REIMS

54% pinot noir; 46% chardonnay; Avize, Oger, Chouilly, Cramant, Aÿ, Verzenay and Bouzy; no malolactic fermentation

Lanson's Vintage Collection comprises 14 vintages back to 1976, all currently available from its cellars, preserved with the tremendous stamina of malic acidity. The 1990 evolves to tell a captivating story in hues of yellow and gold. It begins with green olives and pipe smoke, progressing from honey to wax before its fruit rises in complex notes of secondary white fruits and an ultimate crescendo of preserved lemon. At 23 years of age it upholds great focus, remarkable freshness and ultimate completeness.

LANSON BRUT VINTAGE GOLD LABEL 1979 • $$$$

96 points • DISGORGED 2011. TASTED IN REIMS FROM MAGNUM

52% pinot noir, 48% chardonnay; Oger, Chouilly, Verzenay and Mareuil-sur-Aÿ; no malolactic fermentation

Many privileged encounters with great old Lansons have led me to believe that it takes three decades for the most enduring vintages to achieve their full potential. The 1979 is one of the greatest I've met, and this magnum was still alive and energetic at 34 years of age, with plenty of years before it yet. Enchanting truffles, exotic spice, brioche, burnt butter, toast and even soy proclaim its age, sustaining profound remnants of baked peach, citrus zest, marmalade and quince. For 1979 babies, the answer is 'Yes!'

LARMANDIER-BERNIER

(Lah-mohn-diay-Bear-niay)

8/10

19 AVENUE DU GÉNÉRAL DE GAULLE 51130 VERTUS
www.larmandier.fr

CHAMPAGNE
LARMANDIER-BERNIER

'*To create a wine that deeply expresses its terroir' is Pierre Larmandier's aim, stated on the back of every one of the 140,000-odd bottles that leave his little cellar in Vertus each year. But to this fastidious grower, terroir in itself is not enough. 'Terroir is to wine what the score is to music,' he suggests. 'What's the point if the grape variety, the vine plant (the instrument) and the winegrower (the performer) are not up to standard?' Some growers are known for their focus on the vines, others for their attention in the winery, but few find a balance in every detail like Pierre Larmandier.*

LARMANDIER'S 12-HECTARE ESTATE IS BLESSED WITH impressive terroirs in the Côte des Blancs, spread across 50 plots in the premier cru village of Vertus, including substantial holdings on the mid-slopes close to Le Mesnil-sur-Oger, supplemented with an impressive four hectares in the grand crus of Cramant and Avize, 0.2 in Oger and 0.5 in Chouilly, belonging to his wife, Sophie.

Chardonnay is king here, and Larmandier tends just two hectares of pinot noir in Vertus for rosé and red wine. 'Chardonnay is very adaptable, and if you cultivate it carefully it will take its expression from the soil,' he explains, likening the diversity of his various plots with that of Puligny-Montrachet and Chablis.

'It would be a shame if we didn't bring our vineyards to your glass!' he says. And bring them he has, through one of the most sensible and diligent regimes anywhere in Champagne.

ORGANO-REALIST

Biodynamically certified since 2004, Larmandier describes himself as an 'organo-realist'. Every time I visit, he whisks me off in his four-wheel drive to one of his key plots in Vertus. One year, he'd heard rumours of an oïdium breakout around the village and wanted to get on to it right away.

As we approached one of his plots we passed other growers out treating for oïdium. 'That man,' he said, pointing out one, 'is the worst in the village for always treating'. We found a little oïdium in Larmandier's plot, 'but it is not so bad so we will not treat yet. We're not too concerned about a little disease in the vineyards. Some people say grass is a disease, too!'

Larmandier cultivates grasses in the mid-rows during winter and ploughs until close to harvest. He considers an absence of herbicides to be the key in the vineyard. 'Organic or not is less important than abandoning herbicides,' he suggests. 'Everyone says they control weeds by ploughing, but I see them spraying with herbicide!' With neighbouring vines in such close proximity, it's impossible to conduct a biodynamic regime without some influence from those who do not farm naturally. Larmandier is matter-of-fact: 'We try to do the best we can, but it is not ideal. We still manage to be different to the others, even though we are among them'.

Since beginning conversion to biodynamic viticulture in 2000, Larmandier has noted a drop in yields, regulated by grasses in the mid-rows. He currently produces just 60–70hL/hectare. 'In the village, you are considered a bad grower if you do not produce 100hL/hectare,' he says. 'People produce too much in the Côte des Blancs and the big houses just buy everything. They say I'm crazy to produce less than 100hL.'

He says 2012 was one of the toughest seasons he can recall in 25 years of managing his vines, yielding just two-thirds of his usual small harvest. Incessant rain made it difficult for him to get into the vineyards to cultivate the soil. 'We do our best with biodynamics, but when it's crazy, it's crazy!' he exclaims.

Larmandier likes old vines and tries to keep them as long as he can, and some are as old as 80 years. 'My ideal is to never replace them, which is all very well, but then you don't have any grapes!' he says. In order to create more competition and push the roots deeper, he is slowly replanting at 10,000 vines per hectare, more than the regional average of 7500. 'This is contrary to the way of thinking in Champagne, but if I want to improve concentration without increasing my harvest, I think this is the way,' he explains.

'You can only extract so much minerality per square foot before it is diluted, but with more vines you can extract more.' While others focus on grapes per square metre of leaves to produce more aromatic wines, for Larmandier the key is the more Burgundian focus on grapes per square metre of soil.

'The soil is the most important thing,' he emphasises. 'With deep roots in good soils, 80% of the work is done.' Here, on the lower slopes below the village of Vertus, the chalk lies 80 centimetres below the surface. He considers his average vine age of 35 years to be very important. 'The roots have a better depth and are better able to extract the minerality from the chalk. We are very lucky to have the place we do, and we work very hard in the vineyard to make the most of it,' he says.

Along with an expression of minerality, his priorities are the roundness and linearity achieved by harvesting grapes at optimal ripeness. 'It is important for us to work the soil to achieve a lower pH in the wine, allowing us to wait longer to harvest, to achieve ripeness without lacking freshness.'

He explains that even in the record heatwave of 2003 he was able to achieve freshness. 'Attention to the soil is increasingly important in these warmer vintages, so as to achieve phenolic maturity and not just sugar ripeness.' Larmandier harvests on the taste of the grapes rather than sugar levels.

NON-INTERVENTIONIST WINEMAKING

His sensitive and non-interventionist approach informs all he does. 'My philosophy used to be that terroir was everything and the hand of man was nothing, that our work in the vineyard was all that mattered,' Larmandier clarifies. 'But now we understand that the work we do and the choices we make in the winery are important, too.' Larmandier did not study oenology and says it's impossible to simplify winemaking to a recipe. 'If you work in the vineyards, your mind is not only on acid and alcohol numbers but on expression,' he says. 'Every year I have an oenology student come to work with me and they want to measure everything but I say, "First, you must taste!"'

To draw out the character of each site, wild yeast is used for primary and malolactic fermentations, with every ferment relying exclusively on its own natural yeasts. There is no filtration, 'because every time you filter or fine you lose a part of what you have worked hard to achieve in the vineyard'.

Very low levels of preservative (sulphur dioxide), and ever lower dosages of around 4g/L are used. 'After all the care lavished on our wines, we are not going to add anything which might go against them!' Larmandier exclaims. Low sulphurs dictate that every wine is free to proceed through malolactic fermentation, and reserve wines are kept in tank under temperature control to maintain freshness.

Larmandier doesn't like the 'austerity' of stainless steel fermentation, and has increased the proportion of oak vinification from 40% to 70%, for controlled oxidation and complexity. He appreciates the expression achieved in oak and is beginning to experiment with egg fermenters for rosé.

'With more concentration in our fruit, stainless steel is too closed and there's more risk of reduction,' he explains. He maintains a delicate balance to keep his wines fresh, admitting that he's afraid of oxidation. When I first visited in 2011, he was putting the finishing touches on a new building to provide space to work with more barrels. He still uses the first barrels he purchased in 1988, and has bought new barrels every year since 1999 'because a used barrel has a personality of the wine, but we only want to express the personality of our vineyards'.

He doesn't want new oak characters to interfere, so new barrels comprise just 3% of his larger non-vintage blends for their first two years. Even tastings of his young vins clairs from second-use barrels display very subtle oak influence. He has purchased large foudres of the more subtle Austrian oak since 2001 and three more arrived last year.

Extra space also provides opportunity to hold stock in bottle for longer, and his cellar now houses 500,000 bottles, sufficient for an average of 3.5 years

on lees across his cuvées, with the aim of increasing his non-vintages from two years to three.

Larmandier's non-vintage philosophy is to let every vintage express its character. 'We are not blessed with making our non-vintage wines taste the same every year,' he says. Bottling codes are easy to decode, with the last four digits denoting the month and year of disgorgement. The other digits in the code are the base year.

Larmandier-Bernier exemplifies the levels of purity and mineral focus that can be drawn out of primarily premier cru terroirs with sufficient care and attention. These exceedingly fine wines rightfully rank high among the finest of champagne's grower producers.

LARMANDIER-BERNIER LATITUDE BLANC DE BLANCS À VERTUS EXTRA BRUT NV • $$

94 points • TASTED IN VERTUS

2010 base vintage with 30% reserves; previously Brut Tradition; vinified and aged in casks, wooden vats and stainless tanks on lees for almost a year with bâtonnage; unfined and unfiltered; aged in bottle at least 2 years; 4g/L dosage

Larmandier has streamlined his Brut Tradition chardonnay pinot noir blend into a blanc de blancs to better articulate its sense of place, sourced exclusively from the same 'Latitude' of the generous terroir of southern Vertus. It encapsulates the gorgeous freshness of young Vertus chardonnay in its grapefruit, freshly picked apple and lemon blossom aromas, while boring deep into its chalk mineral structure, building great textural presence, amplified by the spicy, nutty complexity of barrel fermentation. It's quite a contrast to Larmandier's final blend of Brut Tradition, which has lacked a little in lift and definition in my most recent tastings.

LARMANDIER-BERNIER LONGITUDE BLANC DE BLANCS PREMIER CRU EXTRA BRUT NV • $$

95 points • TASTED IN VERTUS AND ADELAIDE

2010 base vintage with 40% reserves; previously labelled Blanc de Blancs Premier Cru; two-thirds Vertus, one-third Avize, Cramant and a little Oger; vinified and aged in casks, wooden vats and stainless tanks on lees for almost a year with bâtonnage; unfined and unfiltered; aged in bottle at least 2 years; 4g/L dosage

A new name, but the same captivating wine, blended from four of chardonnay's most beguiling villages, sharing roughly the same 'Longitude.' Purity of white peach and preserved lemon is impressive, with the complexity and depth of a lesser vintage base already building spicy notes of fig and toast. As always, it is the tremendous minerality of these terroirs that is most engaging, gliding long and seamless from start to finish. A complex and creamy blanc de blancs of great depth, upholding lively acid tension on a very long finish. It's more precise than the 2009 base, for which recent tastings have showcased the broader frame of the vintage, compared with the bright freshness of 2008, nonetheless upholding lemon zest focus and mineral definition.

LARMANDIER-BERNIER ROSÉ DE SAIGNÉE PREMIER CRU EXTRA BRUT NV • $$$

96 points • TASTED IN VERTUS

100% 2009 Vertus single-vineyard pinot noir; initially released too young to be labelled as a vintage, though this is now the end of its release; old vines harvested ripe at very low yields; cold macerated two–three days to achieve colour without tannin; fermented and aged for a year on lees in an enamel-lined steel vat; aged a further 2 years in bottle; full malolactic fermentation; 3g/L dosage

This wine is a paradox of the highest order, a salute to the genius of its maker and the depth of its old-vine sources. How a 100% Côte des Blancs rosé from an elegant east-facing Vertus site can land mid-way between a graceful champagne rosé and an expressive red cherry pinot noir is truly astounding. Larmandier set out to make 'a rosé, not a white champagne with colour', marrying the power of pinot noir with the elegance of the village and, goodness, has he done it! A profoundly vinous champagne of full crimson-red hue, with a breathtaking display of gorgeous rose petals, understated black cherries, raspberries and strawberries. Minerality of mouth-filling dimensions surges and froths, charged with acidity both tense and refined. An exceptional finish upholds benchmark rose petal freshness at every instant. It's as special as it is inimitable. Drink it young and fresh; two oxidised older bottles were browning in colour and flavour.

LARMANDIER-BERNIER TERRE DE VERTUS PREMIER CRU BLANC DE BLANCS NON-DOSÉ 2008 • $$$

96 points • TASTED IN VERTUS

Two vineyards on similar terroirs spanning 2.5 hectares of Vertus mid-slopes; vinified and aged in casks, wooden vats and stainless steel tanks on lees for almost a year with bâtonnage; unfined and unfiltered; aged in bottle for at least 4 years; zero dosage

Drawing life from the shallow chalk along the road to Le Mesnil-sur-Oger, this is a blanc de blancs that expresses more soil than sky, in a palate more about mouth-embracing, intensely textured minerality than fruit. Crystalline freshness of lemon blossom, pure grapefruit, white peach and even lime is set impeccably against a background of subtle complexity of fig and mixed spice from oak fermentation. Perfectly balanced without a drop of dosage, its vibrant acidity, ever-present chalk minerality and profound persistence confirm this magnificent vintage as one of Larmandier's greatest of the modern era, with a tremendous future before it.

LARMANDIER-BERNIER TERRE DE VERTUS PREMIER CRU BLANC DE BLANCS NON-DOSÉ 2007 • $$$

95 points • TASTED IN VERTUS

As for the Blanc de Blancs Non-Dosé 2008

The intense mineral texture and layers of mouth-filling chalk of the northern slopes of Vertus learn much from the neighbouring grand cru of Le Mesnil-sur-Oger, and Larmandier is astute in separating these from the more rounded character of southern Vertus (in his 'Latitude' cuvée). In spite of its season, Terre de Vertus is all about preserving this mineral fingerprint. In 2007, it does so within a spicy style of fig and apple fruit, with a taut backbone of vibrant lemon. Give it time.

The Champagne Guide

Larmandier-Bernier Vieille Vigne de Cramant Grand Cru Blanc de Blancs Extra Brut 2006 • $$$$

95 points • Tasted in Vertus

Two nearby vineyards in the heart of Cramant; vines aged between 49 and 76 years; vinified and aged on lees in casks and wooden vats with bâtonnage for almost a year; unfined and unfiltered; aged in bottle at least 5 years; 2g/L dosage

To Larmandier, Cramant is a different world that deserves to be showcased solo. Like the Terre de Vertus, he prints the vintage only on the back label, 'because the place is more important than the vintage'. He says that in this special part of Cramant, his carefully cultivated old vines are less sensitive to seasonal fluctuations, and he could make a vintage every year. There's inherent power here, indicative of the intensity of one of the Côte des Blancs' strongest villages, tamed with the classic finesse of Larmandier's sensitive touch. It celebrates the rich expression of the village in layers of creamy lemon butter, ginger cake, fleshy pear and exotic fig, yet retains immaculate freshness at every moment. The finish is very long and refined, embedded with deep layers of profound chalk mineral texture.

Larmandier-Bernier Les Chemins d'Avize Grand Cru Blanc de Blancs Extra Brut 2009

Tasted in Vertus

Single-vineyard Avize; vinified in casks and wooden vats and aged on lees with bâtonnage for almost a year; unfined and unfiltered; 2g/L dosage

Larmandier's single-vineyard trilogy is about to become a quartet, after Larmandier purchased a smaller press in 2009 to separate the juice of his two vineyards in Avize. Previously a component of 'Longitude', this site, almost on the flat of Avize, produces a more elegant style. Six months pre-release, it's a beach-fresh and youthful blanc de blancs, loaded with grapefruit and crunchy beurre bosc pear. It captures a picture-perfect snapshot of the soft, salty texture of Avize chalk, harmonious yet firm, with well-balanced oak providing structural definition and great sustaining power in the cellar. The small blend necessitated use of small barrels, and Larmandier suggests the oak is a bit strong. This sample was disgorged on the spot without dosage, hence is unscored, but worthy of at least 95 points, and perhaps more, with sufficient time to integrate. There's no doubt it will age long, and a small volume will be released in late 2013, with the remainder wisely held back for a later release.

Larmandier-Bernier Club de Viticulteurs Champenois Blanc de Blancs 1979

96 points • Disgorged mid-1980s • Tasted in Vertus

The old equivalent of Special Club; almost entirely Cramant, with a touch of Vertus; malolactic fermentation unknown; 7–8g/L dosage

The inimitable minerality of the soft chalk expression of Cramant is timeless, and 34 years on, this cuvée declares its origins with remarkable accuracy. Its colour has deepened to a medium yellow-gold, and its primary fruits have evolved to an enchantingly evocative place of white truffles, dried figs, Old Spice, coffee beans, green olives, wax, boot polish and wisps of hearth smoke. In time it opens magnificently to reveal tantalising glacé peach fruit. A grand testimony to the astonishing longevity of Larmandier-Bernier.

LARMANDIER-BERNIER VERTUS ROUGE COTEAUX CHAMPENOIS PREMIER CRU 2009

94 points • TASTED IN VERTUS

Old-vine Vertus pinot noir; macerated for 12 days and matured in casks for 18 months

Larmandier's still red wine is one of the great Coteaux Champenois, naturally more tense and mineral-focused in Vertus than the deeper style of the warmer slopes of the Montagne de Reims. Very small yields and full ripeness nonetheless build wonderful black depth of blackberries and black cherries, with an undercurrent of very fine tannins and the signature chalk mineral texture of Vertus, lingering with enthralling violet perfume.

LARMANDIER-BERNIER CRAMANT NATURE COTEAUX CHAMPENOIS BLANC GRAND CRU 2008

94 points • TASTED IN VERTUS

Fermented and matured as reserve wines in two barrels on lees for 18 months; aged in bottle 2 years; 11% alcohol

Larmandier reports that the still white Cramant Nature of his family was more famous than their sparkling wines at the beginning of the 20th century. Two reserve barrels of 2008 Cramant reminded them of the style, so they revived this unusual and compelling wine. It captures the concentration and the refreshing, lingering minerality of Cramant in a delightful culmination of ripe, succulent yellow mirabelle plums, grapefruit and butter, with champagne's characteristic acid tension and taut lemon juice finish.

The mightly slopes of Cramant, the Côte des Blancs' most powerful grand cru, increasingly showcased solo by growers such as Larmandier-Bernier.

The Champagne Guide
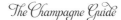

LAURENT-PERRIER

(Lohr-rohn-Peh-riay)

51150 TOURS-SUR-MARNE
www.laurent-perrier.com

aurent-Perrier is on a steep growth curve. Substantial expansion in recent years has seen the house climb to number five in Champagne by volume. A new cuverie, constructed in time for the 2009 harvest, added capacity for another 150 vins clairs and now handles production for the group, including de Castellane, Delamotte and Salon. With an annual production of 7 million bottles (almost two-thirds of which are L-P Brut), Laurent-Perrier is unusual in having found a reasonably comfortable equilibrium in that precarious balance between volume and finely tuned quality. These are champagnes with a flattering demeanour of precision, delicacy, elegance and tension, though some inconsistency has recently begun to creep into certain cuvées.

LAURENT-PERRIER'S SUCCESS IS LESS BY VIRTUE OF ITS domain vineyard holdings (which supply just 11% of its total needs of 150 hectares) than by the skill and vision of its people. The talented Alain Terrier was Laurent-Perrier's long-standing Chef de Cave from 1975 to 2005 and was succeeded by Michel Fauconnet, his offsider for more than 20 years.

But the secret to Laurent-Perrier's wines today delves even further into the history of a house that recently celebrated its 200th birthday.

The late Bernard de Nonancourt, founding president of the Laurent-Perrier Group, was a visionary who spent half of the last century transforming and expanding the company. His innovations changed the face of modern champagne. Under his leadership, the house boldly launched its non-vintage prestige cuvée, Grand Siècle, in 1957, a rosé well ahead of

its time in 1968 (considered a joke by the Champenois at the time, now the best-selling champagne rosé in the world) — and, perhaps most influential of all, inspired by brewers of beer, Laurent-Perrier was the first house in Champagne to use stainless steel tanks in the 1960s.

De Nonancourt's vision was one of freshness, finesse and elegance based on chardonnay, which to this day maintains the majority stake in every cuvée (representing double Champagne's average) except rosé. No pinot meunier is used, apart from a 15% touch in L-P Brut. This creates a house style of precision and tension, unique among houses of this scale.

To celebrate its bicentenary in 2012, Laurent-Perrier commissioned a major and spectacular addition and renovation to its cuverie. In the same location as Champagne's first winery to employ stainless steel tanks, The Grand Siècle winery is a striking and atmospheric display of stainless steel reserve tanks custom-built with graceful curves, no seams and narrow spouts to reduce oxidation.

Laurent-Perrier has a very real commitment to sustainability: vineyard manager Christelle Rinville refuses to fly in aeroplanes, encourages workers to use bicycles, plants grasses in the mid-rows and uses only non-invasive chemicals in all estate vineyards. The winery is almost self-sufficient in its use of water.

The tight, chardonnay-driven house style is softened through malolactic fermentation in all cuvées, and long

lees ageing of at least four years at 11°C in 10 kilometres of cellars under the house in Tours-sur-Marne.

Regrettably, consumers remain oblivious to Laurent-Perrier's long ageing as the house not only fails to disclose disgorgement dates and base vintages on labels but also refuses to provide this information when requested, for reasons I fail to understand. I was granted this detail on my tasting at the house, but declined for disgorgements later tasted in Australia, despite repeated requests.

These are long-ageing wines of a clean sophistication that transcend the scale of this operation.

LAURENT-PERRIER L-P BRUT NV • $$

91 points • TASTED IN TOURS-SUR-MARNE AND BRISBANE

2006 base vintage with up to 20% reserves from 2005 and 2004; 50% chardonnay, 35% pinot noir, 15% pinot meunier; aged 4 years on lees; 10g/L dosage

At 62% of Laurent-Perrier's production this cuvée alone accounts for something in the order of 5 million bottles annually, which makes its recipe of using a high proportion of chardonnay and long ageing all the more impressive. Dosage was lowered by one gram for the 2005 base and again this year. It's a happy party quaffer in a fresh, fruity and lively style, accenting lemon zest, white peach and red apples. Tangy acidity and well-integrated dosage create a comfortable balance, finishing short and simple. A grubby, earthy cork note detracted from the cleanliness and focus of a bottle opened for me by the house.

LAURENT-PERRIER L-P ULTRA BRUT NV • $$$

88 points • 2004 BASE VINTAGE WITH 2003 RESERVE • TASTED IN TOURS-SUR-MARNE
91 points • TASTED IN BRISBANE

55% chardonnay, 45% pinot noir; bunch selection of grapes with high sugar and low acidity from 15 villages; no added dosage; 1.2g/L residual sweetness from fermentation

Laurent-Perrier has a very long history with zero dosage, having first launched its 'Grand Vins Sans Sucre' in the 1800s, relaunched by Bernard de Nonancourt in 1981 from the 1976 vintage. Today, this cuvée is champagne's best-selling brut nature. It's custom-crafted from grapes of high sugar and low acidity from 15 villages in ripe vintages, making for a well-balanced and high-strung apéritif style. It leads out with clean nashi pear and grapefruit and a subtle flinty reductive note, with an understated white peach breadth to the back palate, finishing razor-tight with primary lemon juice acidity, fluffy minerality and softly textural mouthfeel. Four years of age add hints of biscuity complexity. The house is serving an older blend, the same that it showed me two years ago, and it's since deteriorated to a toasty and nutty style of textural grip and dry finish.

Laurent-Perrier Millesime 2004 • $$$

92 points • Disgorged mid-2012 • Tasted in Tours-sur-Marne
93 points • Tasted in Brisbane

50% Montagne de Reims pinot noir; 50% Côte des Blancs chardonnay; 10.4g/L dosage

I've long admired L-P vintage (1996 is still in my cellar) and the 2004 Champagne vintage was strong, but I'm disappointed that this new release doesn't quite live up to expectation. It's friendly, enticing and easy to drink, with a vibrancy to its lemony acidity, but lacks tension and intrigue. Its fruit simplicity seems humdrum, with generous red apple and stone fruits fleshing out a honeyed finish of top-heavy dosage, lacking acid stamina and mineral presence in a season that should not be short of either. The bottle I tasted at the house showed a subtle earthy note, as did its replacement, a character I didn't see three months later in Brisbane — perhaps a sign that it may appreciate another year to unwind?

Laurent-Perrier Millesime 2002 • $$$

95 points • Disgorged late 2011 • Tasted in Tours-sur-Marne
94 points • Tasted in Brisbane

50% chardonnay, 50% pinot noir; aged 9 years on lees; 8g/L dosage

A brilliant expression of vintage Laurent-Perrier, 2002 is evolving from the restrained purity of its release two years ago to develop subtle nuances of almond, brioche and toast. A delicate focus is retained in lemon and red apple fruits, hints of flinty reduction and intricate structure of mineral bath salts. A bottle tasted in Australia showed greater depth of toasty development approaching the end of its life, though retaining integrity and poise.

Laurent-Perrier Cuvée Rosé Brut NV • $$$

95 points • 2008 base vintage; 10.9g/L dosage • Tasted in Brisbane
94 points • 2006 base vintage; disgorged late 2012; 10g/L dosage
• Tasted in Tours-sur-Marne

100% pinot noir from 10 different crus, predominantly in the Montagne de Reims, including Ambonnay, Bouzy, Louvois and Tours-sur-Marne; hand sorted

Laurent-Perrier macerates its rosé for 12–72 hours, depending on fruit ripeness, until the colour is fixed and the aroma resembles freshly picked raspberries. So crucial is timing, legend has it that the first Chef de Cave, Edouard Leclerc, slept by the tank to stop it just in time! This wine has achieved that elusive ideal of volume and finesse; the world's best-selling rosé champagne epitomises the ultra-restraint of rosé's finest expressions. All the more remarkable for the challenging saignée method. The lively 2008 vintage has yielded one of the greats, walking the delicate tightrope between refined rose petal freshness and deep fruit definition. It's fragrant and playful, encased in red cherries, strawberry hull, pink pepper and pomegranate. A soft, creamy bead, beautifully fine, soft, mineral tannins and lingering aftertaste confirm quality can come even at this quantity. Strangely, the house is pouring a blend two years older than that on the market, lacking vibrancy and taking on subtle toasty, autumn-leaf savouriness.

LAURENT-PERRIER GRAND SIÈCLE NV • $$$$

97 points • TASTED IN TOURS-SUR-MARNE AND BRISBANE

60% 1999 and 40% 1997 and 1996 vintages; 55% chardonnay, 45% pinot noir; 8g/L dosage

De Nonancourt's vision was to produce a multi-vintage prestige cuvée able to maintain consistent quality. This is achieved by blending only grand cru fruit from the best crus in the finest years declared by Laurent-Perrier. The blend I tasted two years ago is still current, placing this among the oldest champagnes on the shelves this year. Sadly, the consumer is oblivious to this, as the bottle gives no clue to either its disgorgement date or its splendid maturity. Despite a huge internal debate, the house refuses to budge on this. This makes managing collections a challenge, which is a shame, as Grand Siècle ages magnificently, long beyond its release.

Even toward the end of its release, this wine is staggeringly youthful, somehow mustering even more pristine freshness than it revealed when it first landed. It sings with the zest of lemon and lemongrass, the crunch of pear, the spice of quince and the tang of granny smith apple. The bottle I tasted at the house declared its marvellous maturity in rising notes of toasted almonds, honeysuckle, dried pear, cedar, nutmeg and exotic spice, while the bottle in Australia resolutely upheld pristine, primary fruit focus, remarkable for its age. An undercurrent of minerality tosses and glides through the finish, meshing impeccably with beautifully refined acidity on a long-enduring finish. It will live for decades.

LAURENT-PERRIER ALEXANDRA GRANDE CUVÉE ROSÉ 2004 • $$$$$

94 points • TASTED IN TOURS-SUR-MARNE

Previously Grand Siècle Alexandra; 80% grand cru pinot noir, 20% grand cru chardonnay, macerated together; 7–8g/L dosage

The first vintage since 1998, as the quality of pinot noir was deemed insufficient in the intervening years. A beautifully elegant rosé of light to medium copper-salmon hue. It's in a calm place of complexity and balance; engagingly mature, in a savoury and restrained style. Secondary red fruits are becoming toasty and nutty, carried by a textural mouthfeel and a honed finish of poise and persistence.

LAURENT-PERRIER GRAND SIÈCLE ALEXANDRA BRUT ROSÉ 1998 • $$$$$

96 points • TASTED IN TOURS-SUR-MARNE

80% grand cru pinot noir from villages including Ambonnay, Bouzy, Louvois, Mailly, Verzenay and Tours-sur-Marne; 20% grand cru chardonnay from villages including Avize, Cramant, Chouilly and Le Mesnil-sur-Oger; macerated together

The bouquet is an enchanting wonderland filled with crunchy autumn leaves, the 'sous bois' of damp earth underfoot, a hint of game on the breeze and fields of spices of all kinds. Taste, and you step into the warmth of grandma's kitchen, with fresh gingernut biscuits just out of the oven, and a winter's breakfast of honey on toast in front of a smouldering hearth. For all its dreamy complexity and full maturity, it retains a refreshing finish, layered with mouth-filling texture, soft minerality and unwavering line and persistence. Drink it with foie gras, pheasant or wild boar... or simply pour large glasses for breakfast with grandma.

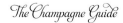
The Champagne Guide

LE BRUN-SERVENAY

(Ler Bru-Sair-veh-nay)

8/10

14 PLACE LÉON BOURGEOIS 51190 AVIZE
www.champagnelebrun.com

*W*hen Patrick Le Brun's parents were married in 1955, they brought together the house of Le Brun in Avize and the estate of Servenay in Mancy in the Coteaux Sud d'Épernay. His estate remains a seamless, if somewhat unusual, union of the two families, maintaining the Le Brun cellars directly next door to Erick de Sousa in Avize, and the Servenay press house and cuverie, six kilometres over the hill in Mancy, rebuilt last year. The Le Brun's almost six hectares of enviably positioned chardonnay in Cramant, Oger and (especially) Avize provide 80% of the estate's needs, supplemented by about 1.5 hectares of pinot noir and pinot meunier from Mancy and its surrounding villages. These are distinctive champagnes in their remarkable freshness, pristine purity and staggering longevity, particularly expressive of the chalk mineral signature of Avize, heightened through the blocking of malolactic fermentation across all cuvées.

IT WASN'T MANY GENERATIONS AGO THAT MALOLACTIC fermentation became commonplace in Champagne, before which every wine of the region was blessed with the sustaining endurance, if at times disarming austerity, of malic acidity.

Those houses and growers who have conscientiously retained malic acidity while upholding carefully balanced appeal are due high admiration.

Patrick Le Brun struggled to convince his father to block malolactic fermentation, maintaining that malic acidity is crucial for preserving the freshness and smoothness in his grape's aromas. It also charges

his cuvées with tremendous sustaining power. When he opened vintages spanning three decades recently, it became breathtakingly apparent that these champagnes mature at but half the pace that one might expect.

Built on majestic grand cru chardonnay and finished with low dosages of typically 7.5g/L, these could be challenging champagnes were it not for Le Brun's meticulous attention to picking at perfect ripeness, and his patience in long ageing in the cellar. Freshness is preserved through vinification in tank, with just a small amount of red wine in barrel for rosé.

'Our purpose is to translate in the glass the elegance and minerality of the terroir of our vineyards,' declares Le Brun, the fifth generation of the Servenay family, and the fourth on the Le Brun side to tend grapes in these sites. His vines are old by Champagne standards, some older than 80 years, with roots that plunge 10–12 metres into the chalk. 'We plough and plant grass in the mid-rows to encourage competition and force the roots deeper,' he explains. Yields of 60–80 hL/hectare (60–80% of Champagne's average), are important for achieving full ripeness.

The champagnes of Le Brun-Servenay live up to their brief with exacting clarity and represent outstanding value for money.

LE BRUN-SERVENAY BRUT SELECTION BLANC DE BLANCS NV • $$

94 points • TASTED IN AVIZE AND BRISBANE

50% 2009, 20% 2008, 20% 2007, 10% 2006; blanc de blancs from Avize, Oger and Cramant vines of average age 25 years; no malolactic fermentation; 7.5g/L dosage; DIAM closure

The pristine delights of Le Brun-Servenay are proclaimed for all to relish from its very first cuvée. A beautifully pale, fresh and pure expression of perfectly ripe chardonnay with aromas of granny smith apple and ripe pear and a taut, honed palate of lemon and grapefruit. Charged with electric malic acidity, this is an exceptionally affordable and accurate expression of the fine, chalky minerality of the Côte des Blancs, making for a refreshing apéritif of creamy bead and subtle dosage.

LE BRUN-SERVENAY BRUT RESERVE NV • $$

94 points • TASTED IN AVIZE

50% chardonnay from 2009, 2008, 2007 and 2006; 25% pinot noir from 2009; 25% pinot meunier from 2009; made in small stainless steel vats; no malolactic fermentation; 7.5g/L dosage

Mancy pinot noir and meunier bring pretty notes of red berries and red apples, which mesh seamlessly with the exactingly honed and pure lemon fruit expression of grand cru chardonnay. The result is a taut, refreshing and fruit-focused style with salty minerality that loiters long on the finish.

LE BRUN-SERVENAY CUVÉE ROSÉ BRUT NV • $$

94 points • TASTED IN AVIZE

2009 base vintage; same chardonnay base as Brut Selection; 10% red wine from pinot noir and a touch of pinot meunier, half aged in oak barrels; no malolactic fermentation; 7.5g/L dosage

Built on the fresh purity and electric structure of Brut Selection, the achingly pristine elegance of Le Brun-Servenay's rosé comes as no surprise. A touch of red wine creates a pretty, bright, pale salmon hue and a subtle rose petal and strawberry hull bouquet. The palate is ultra-refreshing and taut, with uplifting freshness of rose petal and strawberry hull. Its chalk minerality and tense malic acidity speak louder than its fruits, making for a quintessential apéritif rosé.

The Champagne Guide

LE BRUN-SERVENAY EXHILARANTE VIEILLES VIGNES MILLÉSIME 2004 • $$$

93 points • TASTED IN AVIZE

80% chardonnay; 10% pinot noir for structure; 10% pinot meunier for fruitiness; Avize, Oger and Cramant chardonnay; Le Brun's oldest vines of between 60 and more than 80 years of age on soil just 15 cm above the chalk; no malolactic fermentation; 8g/L dosage

Impressive fruit presence of pear, red apple and grapefruit pith proclaim perfectly ripe grapes. A consummately textural wine of great depth of chalk mineral expression. Some bruised apple notes and a hint of dried apple on the finish suggest that this bottle may not be at the prime of its freshness. Nonetheless, its hue is a pristine pale straw and its length impeccable.

LE BRUN-SERVENAY CUVÉE CHARDONNAY BRUT MILLÉSIME VIEILLES VIGNES 2003 • $$

94 points • TASTED IN AVIZE

Blanc de blancs from Avize, Oger and Cramant; old vines aged 45–80 years; no malolactic fermentation; 5g/L dosage

After frost destroyed 80% of Le Brun-Servenay's 2003 crop, a heatwave further decimated yields to a minute 20hL/hectare, merely 20% of Champagne's typical harvest. That they managed to resurrect anything from this calamitous season is remarkable in itself, and that it is still as fresh and primary as this a decade later is nothing short of astonishing. It's still quite pale in its medium straw hue, with predictably impressive concentration and surprising freshness of lemon, granny smith apple and grapefruit. Malic acidity is beautifully structured, accented with soft minerality, and the finish is long and exact. One of Champagne's very best from 2003.

LE BRUN-SERVENAY BRUT MILLÉSIME VIEILLES VIGNES 2004 • $$

95 points • TASTED IN AVIZE

Chardonnay from Avize, Oger and Cramant; a dosage trial with 5g/L, but Le Brun thinks he will increase this for its pending release

The large 2004 vintage yielded 100hL/hectare, a normal crop for Champagne, but very high for Le Brun-Servenay. This freak vintage surprised everyone with its devastating focus, tremendous concentration and astounding longevity. This wine epitomises the season, brilliantly taut and youthful in its elderflower perfume and crystalline lemon and apple fruit. Inimitable Côte des Blancs chalk mineral texture bores deep into its core. Consummate poise and enduring persistence assure an exceedingly long life. It will subsume higher dosage without flinching.

Le Brun-Servenay Brut Millésime Vieilles Vignes 1997

93 points • Disgorged 2008 • Tasted in Avize

From a vintage plagued by disease, this is an impressive result, still very youthful, ageing slowly and assuredly. It upholds exceptional fruit purity of granny smith apple, building layers of spice, cloves, honey, toast, even orange rind. With zero dosage, chalk mineral expression is amplified.

Le Brun-Servenay Brut Millésime Vieilles Vignes 1991

97 points • Disgorged late 2012 • Tasted in Avize

Any winemaker in the world would dream that their first vintage might age as beguilingly as this. With his father hospitalised two days before harvest, Patrick was thrust into the driver's seat. Almost a generation later, his first wine is still astonishingly backward and fresh, a delightfully pale medium straw hue, alive with the primary crunch of apple and lemon. Barely the slightest hints of maturity have emerged in wax, honey and toast. Its length is profound, line exact, and its chalk-filled minerality deep-set. Without an ounce of dosage, it will easily live for another 50 years.

Le Brun-Servenay Brut Millésime Vieilles Vignes 1990

95 points • Disgorged late 2012 • Tasted in Avize

Well into its glorious maturity, with a glowing medium straw-yellow hue and a panoply of fig, honey, toast, mixed spice, even orange rind and toffee. There's still vibrancy to its structure, just beginning to dry out a touch on the finish, with no dosage to support it. Incredibly, the only Le Brun-Servenay I've ever tasted that appears vaguely close to the end of its life.

Le Brun-Servenay Brut Millésime Vieilles Vignes 1988

98 points • Disgorged late 2012 • Tasted in Avize and Brisbane

If I did not know better, I would never believe this wine was a full quarter-century old. Everything points to youthful stamina, from wonderfully lively medium straw hue to impeccable purity of primary white peach, pear and apple, to beautifully integrated acidity and deep-set, chalky minerality. It's barely beginning to become creamy, buttery and faintly nutty, without a trace of the toasty, honeyed development that characterises champagne of such grand maturity. Patrick names 1988 the last typical harvest in Champagne, with every season since delivering greater richness and less minerality, perhaps a consequence of global warming. Whatever the reason, this 1988 still has a breathtaking future before it. Some say dosage is a prerequisite of longevity. This wine has none, and will effortlessly live another quarter-century, if not three.

The Champagne Guide

LE MESNIL

(Ler Meh-neel)

5/10

19-32 RUE CHARPENTIER LAURIAN 51190 LE MESNIL-SUR-OGER
www.champagnelemesnil.com

CHAMPAGNE
Le MESNIL
BLANC DE BLANCS
GRAND CRU

*L*e Mesnil competes only with Mailly Grand Cru as Champagne's greatest cooperative, and in value for money it has no rivals. This large establishment has 553 member growers who tend a good 305 hectares spanning some of the best sites in the most age-worthy grand cru of the Côte des Blancs. It presses grapes for many of the big names of Champagne, and bottles just 8% of production under its own label. Vinification is performed in stainless steel at a controlled temperature of 18°C to preserve the fresh expression of the village. Its finest cuvées proclaim the racy tension and commanding presence of Le Mesnil-sur-Oger, at enticing prices.

LE MESNIL BLANC DE BLANCS GRAND CRU BRUT NV • $$

93 points • DISGORGED MARCH 2011 • TASTED IN BRISBANE AND ADELAIDE

2007 base vintage with 10% 2006; full malolactic fermentation; 8.7g/L dosage; DIAM closure

The inimitable chalk mineral texture of Le Mesnil-sur-Oger forms an undercurrent to racy, taut grapefruit and lively lemon zest. A core of white peach and yellow mirabelle plum concentration lingers long and focused, with brioche and almond-like complexity and well-gauged dosage. One of the more affordable experiences of the elegance and power of Le Mesnil. One bottle was oxidised, stale and dried out, lacking fruit clarity and persistence, the victim of a mis-inserted DIAM closure.

LE MESNIL SUBLIME BLANC DE BLANCS BRUT 2005 • $$

87 points • DISGORGED JULY 2011 • TASTED IN BRISBANE

A blend of Côte des Blancs villages; 85% malolactic fermentation; 8g/L dosage

Generous lemon sherbet, white peach and pear fruit is sucked into a vortex of bruised apple texture, stale woodiness, drying grip and contracted sustain, characteristic of the warm and challenging 2005 vintage. Sublime it is not.

LE MESNIL SUBLIME ROSÉ BRUT NV • $$

93 points • DISGORGED JANUARY 2012 • TASTED IN BRISBANE

2009 base vintage with 42% reserve wines; 47% chardonnay, 37% pinot noir, 16% pinot noir red wine; 10g/L dosage; DIAM closure

Freshness and vitality meet wonderfully fruity expression in this young blend, with the acid drive and soft, chalky presence of Le Mesnil to dissolve 10g/L dosage and frame elegant rosehip, pomegranate, pink pepper, strawberry and red cherry fruits. The back label suggests 'this is perfect as an aperitif or in cocktails'. A sublime apéritif, certainly, but it would be a travesty to reduce this graceful and delicate rosé to cocktails.

LE MESNIL BLANC DE BLANCS 2004 • $$

95 points • TASTED IN BRISBANE

40-year-old vines; no malolactic fermentation; 8g/L dosage; DIAM closure

In its wide bottle of dramatic angles and its small front label with deep green highlights, this is a sophisticated package, and more than a little Salonesque. Pretensions to greatness aside, this is an impressive testament to the confidence and generosity of Le Mesnil charged with malic acidity, the personification of power with consummate control. The palate commands a wonderfully generous, expansive and creamy mouthfeel, filled with succulent white peach and fresh pear, becoming nougat, honey, nutmeg and butter. It pulls decisively into a strictly controlled finish of lemon zest freshness, grapefruit zest bite and silky chalk minerality. It's long, concentrated, delicious and great value for money.

The Champagne Guide

LENOBLE

(Ler-nob-ler)

6/10

35-37 RUE PAUL DOUCE 51480 DAMERY
www.champagne-lenoble.com

'The two important things for making great champagne are the quality of your grapes and the size of your stock,' declares Antoine Malassagne, who is richly blessed with both. With his sister Anne, he is the fourth generation to manage the family cellars and vineyards of the Graser-Malassagne family. The 18 hectares of the small house of Lenoble transcend its position in the centre of the village of Damery in the middle of the Vallée de la Marne, thanks to a majority of holdings in the core of the Côte des Blancs grand cru of Chouilly. The chardonnay from these vines defines Lenoble's finest cuvées, supplemented with chardonnay and pinot noir from estate vineyards in Bisseuil and Damery. The remainder of its needs, including all pinot meunier, is sourced from Damery growers. For an annual production of less than 400,000 bottles, Lenoble's cellar stock of 1.4 million is sizeable, furnishing long ageing of 3–4 years for non-vintage cuvées, and six or more for vintage wines. True to its name, a noble approach in the vines and the cellar produces well-composed and tantalisingly affordable cuvées that showcase the strength, structure and definition of Chouilly.

LENOBLE WAS ESTABLISHED IN 18TH CENTURY CELLARS IN Damery almost a century ago. The winery was rebuilt in 2008 and still maintains three wooden presses between 30 and 45 years of age. All parcels are vinified separately, with the best parcels from the finest seasons fermented in small Burgundy barrels.

'I like buying new barrels, as you know what you're getting,' Malassagne explains. Such is his attention to detail that the first year's fermentation is sold for distillation, to reduce new oak character — a costly and time-consuming process. A brand new 5000-litre foudre has been recently acquired for ageing reserves.

Lenoble adapts vinification to suit the harvest, with malolactic fermentation used selectively, according to the season and the parcel. 'It's difficult to find a balance between finesse and intensity,' Malassagne admits. Dosage is low, typically no more than 6g/L.

A natural approach in the vineyards has seen the elimination of herbicides and pesticides, ploughing to control weeds and aerate the soil and use of organic manure and cultivation of grasses in the mid-rows of some vineyards to moderate yields. For these initiatives, Lenoble was the second in Champagne after Bollinger to receive High Environmental Value certification.

LENOBLE CUVÉE INTENSE NV • $

94 points • DISGORGED LATE 2012 • TASTED IN DAMERY AND BRISBANE

2009 base vintage with 20% reserve wine; 15% vinified in barrel; 40% chardonnay from Chouilly; 30% pinot noir from Bisseuil and the Montagne de Reims; 30% pinot noir from Damery; aged 3 years on lees; full malolactic fermentation; 6g/L dosage

An impeccably crafted wine from noble fruit sources, offering sensational value for money. A delightful bouquet is filled with lifted lemon blossom, red berries of all kinds and stonefruit depth. The palate is honed and focused, structured around the taut lemon and grapefruit of chardonnay and understated generosity of white peach, pear and red berries of pinots. A bright finish is accented with tense energy and an undercurrent of salty Chouilly chalk minerality.

LENOBLE CUVÉE INTENSE BRUT NATURE DOSAGE ZÉRO NV • $

94 points • TASTED IN DAMERY

2008 vintage base; Cuvée Intense with 4 years on lees and no added dosage; 1g/L residual sweetness from fermentation

The 2008 base was responsible for one of the greatest expressions of Cuvée Intense last year, and with an extra year on lees and no dosage to speak of, the energy and vibrant acidity of 2008 sings as high-pitched as ever. This is a taut and electric take on the season, with high-tension acidity baring all, with no sugar to cover its edges. Fine, chalk minerality is given full voice amid clean lemon fruit and emerging complexity of brioche and almonds.

LENOBLE CUVÉE RICHE DEMI-SEC NV • $$

91 points • TASTED IN DAMERY

2008 base vintage; Cuvée Intense with 4 years on lees and 32g/L dosage

Lenoble Cuvée Intense provides a fascinating insight into the effect of dosage at three different levels. This is the sweetie of the trio, with its pure lemon and peach fruit transformed into candied lemon and glacé peach. It's clean and honeyed, with minerality still present, though less apparent at this level of sugar. The finish is long, without the purity, structure or precision of its lower-dosage counterparts.

LENOBLE GRAND CRU BLANC DE BLANCS CHOUILLY BRUT NV • $$

92 points • TASTED IN DAMERY

2007 base vintage, vinified in tank; 2006 and 2005 reserves, vinified in barrel; 100% chardonnay; two identical cuvées from the same plot, one vinified with full malolactic ferment, the other 50%; 4 years on lees; extra brut dosage of 5g/L

The full, rounded, buttery presence of Chouilly chardonnay is tightened and freshened with malic acidity, creating a blend that contrasts the fresh liveliness of lemon blossom with the generosity of mirabelle plums and white peach. The palate is honed and chiselled, with Chouilly's signature intensity and richness. It finishes with pronounced acid definition and a robust structure of slightly drying texture, accentuated by the oak of its reserves.

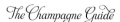

Lenoble L'Epurée Grand Cru Chouilly Blanc de Blancs NV • $$

93 points • Disgorged early 2012 • Tasted in Brisbane

2007 base vintage with 2006 reserves; 100% Chouilly chardonnay; 6% vinified in barrel; 50% malolactic fermentation; 3g/L dosage

The combination of Chouilly chardonnay, low dosage and 50% malic acidity makes for a bracing style, but one that has been well executed here. It's predictably tense and honed, with a dry, textural mouthfeel reminiscent of lemon pith, contrasting with the dynamism of malic acidity. Candied lemon peel and white peach are lifted by an attractive note of anise, with subtle barrel richness propelling it forth. The depth of Chouilly chalk mineral expression is impressive, powdery and fine. It concludes with commendable persistence and drying, textural finesse, holding its composition admirably.

Lenoble Grand Cru Blanc de Blancs Chouilly 2006 • $$

94 points • Disgorged mid-2012 • Tasted in Damery and Brisbane

100% Chouilly chardonnay; 13% vinified in barrels; 5g/L dosage

In an age in which champagne houses are increasing the frequency of their vintage releases, Lenoble is admirable in producing very few, and 2006 is its first since 2002, in spite of strong demand. 'I would prefer to frustrate myself and my clients than to sacrifice quality for quantity!' Malassagne explains. This release is testimony to his standards, a celebration of the contrasting dimensions of Chouilly, simultaneously bold in fruit presence, muscular in structural grip, prominent in chalk mineral texture and electric in its acid poise. It's a display of fresh lemon, lemon zest, white peach, nougat and nutmeg of considerable proportions, charged with great depth of salty chalk mineral intensity and drawn out long on a tense and lively finish. An impressive vintage blanc de blancs, and good value for money.

Lenoble Blanc de Noirs Brut 2006 • $$

87 points • Tasted in Damery

100% Bisseuil pinot noir; 30% vinified in barrel

Lenoble's least cuvée is predictably the one that is not led by the glorious Chouilly chardonnay of the house. Its cherry and plum fruits are disrupted by a firm oak backbone that lends overt woody flavours and a hard structure.

LENOBLE ROSÉ TERROIRS BRUT 2006 • $$

92 points • TASTED IN DAMERY

88% Chouilly chardonnay; 12% Bisseuil pinot noir vinified and aged in barrel as red wine

Lenoble's pinot noir and pinot meunier is too rich to stand alone as a rosé, so the house tactically calls upon the structure and fresh acid drive of its Chouilly chardonnay. With a full crimson hue, this is a structured rosé that collides the full texture of Chouilly chardonnay with the oak structure of red wine. There are notes of wood spice to its red berry and apple fruits, slowly becoming soft and secondary as they mature, yet retaining accurate line and good persistence.

LENOBLE CUVÉE GENTILHOMME GRAND CRU BLANC DE BLANCS MILLÉSIME 2006 • $$$

95 points • TASTED IN DAMERY

100% Chouilly chardonnay; part vinified in barrels

Lenoble's 'Gentleman' is an affable fellow of considerable depth and concentration. This is a champagne fully up to roast-chicken combat on the table, packed with fleshy white summer fruits, honey, nougat, roast nuts, even the full potency of fruit-mince spice. He holds impressive energy within his rich proportions, with biceps structured with the fibrous muscle of Chouilly, immaculately presented in a tailored tuxedo of tense, lively acidity. On the finish, his concentration does not break for minutes.

LENOBLE CUVÉE LES AVENTURES GRAND CRU BLANC DE BLANCS BRUT NV • $$$

94 points • TASTED IN DAMERY

60% 2006 and 40% 2002; 100% Chouilly Grand Cru; 40% vinified in barrel; aged on cork; 3g/L dosage

Blended only from seasons released as vintages in their own right, the philosophy of 'The Adventures of Lenoble' is to showcase what a small terroir in Chouilly can produce in top years. Quite a quest it is, engineered and structured with a scaffold of Chouilly tension, amplified by barrel fermentation. An action-packed future lies before it, propelled by coiled energy of textural structure as much as by tense acidity. Enticing complexity of toast, nuts, green olives and coffee beans already provide considerable entertainment to its classic Chouilly yellow fruits. This is a powerful and formidable experience for the adventurous, yet never heavy or broad, its rigid spine of structure bringing a honed balance to its long finish.

LOMBARD & CIE

(Lom-bar e See)

5/10

1 RUE DES CÔTELLES BP118 51024 ÉPERNAY
www.champagne-lombard.com

CHAMPAGNE

LOMBARD & C IE

MAISON FONDÉE EN 1925

EPERNAY

hierry Lombard is the third generation of his family to run the medium-sized Épernay house of Lombard & Cie. About 10% of an annual production of 1.5 million bottles is produced from 15 hectares of estate vines in the western Montagne de Reims and Épernay, planted to all three champagne varieties, the remainder sourced from growers. Fermentation is conducted parcel by parcel in temperature-controlled stainless steel tanks, producing a house style of freshness and vitality. It's a small price to trade up to the lively 2008 vintage.

LOMBARD & CIE BRUT ROSÉ PREMIER CRU NV • $$

90 points • TASTED IN BRISBANE

50% chardonnay, 40% pinot noir, 10% pinot noir red wine; Épernay fruit sources; aged 3 years on lees

A savoury rosé of medium crimson hue and characters of nuts, biscuits, dried herbs and tomato bush. Bright acidity and persistent pomegranate fruit lingers long on the palate, culminating in well-balanced dosage. A little shy on fruit definition and vibrancy.

LOMBARD & CIE BRUT GRAND CRU MILLESIME 2008 • $$

94 points • TASTED IN BRISBANE

The great 2008 vintage energises a wine of well-articulated structure with a deep, ultra-fine mouthfeel of chalky minerality. Bottle age is evolving captivating characters of generous white peach and fresh lemon into brioche, nougat and apple turnover. Honeyed dosage is balanced with lively 2008 acidity on a long and even finish. Value.

LOUIS ROEDERER

(Loo-ii Roh-dehr-air)

8/10

21 BOULEVARD LUNDY BP66 51053 REIMS
www.champagne-roederer.com

LOUIS ROEDERER
CHAMPAGNE

Louis Roederer is unlike any other champagne house of its magnitude. The largest independent, family-owned and managed champagne maker of all is privileged to 235 hectares of superbly located vineyards, supplying a grand 70% of its needs for an annual production of 3 million bottles. With 410 blocks and 500 tanks and casks at his disposal, Chef de Cave Jean-Baptiste Lécaillon describes his role as 'à la carte winemaking'. He hates the word 'blend'. 'We don't blend, we combine,' he says. 'I love art, and like a great painter we add colour rather than blending.'

THERE WAS ONCE A TIME WHEN LOUIS ROEDERER WAS purely a négociant house, but over the years it has strategically acquired vineyards to amass one of the largest proportions of estate vines among the big champagne houses. These are well situated across some 16 villages spanning the three districts of Montagne de Reims, Vallée de la Marne and Côte des Blancs. More than two-thirds are rated at grand cru level.

All of Louis Roederer's vintage wines are assembled exclusively from estate properties, and even its entry Brut Premier NV now boasts 55% estate fruit, with this percentage rising.

'I do not say that Roederer is a champagne house for the vintage wines,' says Lécaillon. 'We are three growers, one in Montagne de Reims, one in Vallée de la Marne and one in Côte des Blancs.'

Roederer is continuing to expand its estate and purchased another two hectares in June 2011, averag-ing an additional two hectares every year for the past decade, all on chalk soils. 'Chalk is the style of Roederer,' Lécaillon declares. 'It produces more focused wines, while clay produces more round and soft styles.'

The vast majority of estate vines are on chalk, with a particular focus on the chalk-rich Côte des Blancs, home to 80 hectares of Roederer vines. The company owns no vineyards beyond Cumières in the Vallée de la Marne because of the higher clay content here.

'We have wonderful terroirs and our goal is to express each of them,' Lécaillon says. For an operation of this scale, the attention to detail in the vineyards is unprecedented. Old vines are used to limit yields, as is green harvesting, in what Lécaillon dubs 'haute couture viticulture'.

A team of some 600 pickers sorts fruit in the vine-yard, and it is sorted again before it is pressed.

BIODYNAMICS ON A GRAND SCALE

Most remarkably, Roederer now tends more than 60 hectares of vineyards biodynamically, including more than half of those that contribute to Cristal. Biodynamics on such a scale is unheard of in Champagne, and Roederer's operation is the biggest in the region by an order of magnitude.

Plots have been set aside for experimentation in each of the three regions of Champagne, and fruit from biodynamic vines is compared with traditional viticulture from the same village. I was surprised at just how much more salty minerality and texture was evident in 2012 vins clairs from biodynamic sources.

'When the soil looks better, the vines look better, the fruit looks better and we get more ripeness, more acidity and more iodine salinity to the minerality,' explains Lécaillon. He attributes greater precision in biodynamic fruit to decreased vigour in the vines, and greater mineral expression to deeper roots. 'We cannot explain this with measurements, but this is the way with biodynamics — we can only see it by tasting.'

Roederer began experimenting with biodynamics in 2003, after a false start in 2000. Ten years on, it has been found that a different approach is necessary in each region. 'There are some years in which biodynamics is much better and some years in which it is not so effective,' Lécaillon explains. 'It performs well in vintages in which the vines struggle under particularly wet or dry conditions.' He suspects this may be a result of thicker skins providing greater resilience in biodynamic fruit. While he is convinced of the philosophy of biodynamics, certification is not the goal. 'We see it as just one means of achieving terroir expression,' he says. 'We are constantly learning.'

This learning curve was particularly steep in 2012, and Roederer reported losses of 30–50% in some plots, and greater under biodynamics than traditional viticulture. 'It involves so much risk,' Lécaillon explains. 'Biodynamics removes all the safety of chemicals, and if it's not done properly you can really get caught quickly.' He accepts the loss of 2012 and suggests that the experience was helpful for his team to really get on top of biodynamics.

À LA CARTE WINEMAKING

Roederer's focus on its vineyards has opened up opportunities for greater refinement in the winery. Regulated yields allow harvesting at full ripeness, rendering chaptalisation unnecessary, unless the season is particularly difficult — an impressive mandate, and to my knowledge unprecedented at this scale in Champagne. Wild yeast ferments have been introduced in recent years. Biodynamic plots are harvested early, fermented wild and used to seed other ferments.

Malolactic fermentation is generally avoided, except in some higher-acid parcels destined for the non-vintage Brut Premier, generally just 20–25% of the blend. 'The only way to avoid malo is to produce fruit in the vineyard that doesn't require it — ripe fruit with soft malic acid,' notes Lécaillon, who prefers to obtain the right acid balance in the vineyard than the winery.

'Malolactic fermentation was first conducted in Champagne in 1965,' he points out. 'It can be useful in a difficult year, but it must be a safety tool, not a systematic procedure, and this is especially true with global warming.' The house completely blocked malolactic fermentation on all estate and contract fruit in 2012, 2006, 2003, 2002 and 1999.

Basket presses run 24/7 throughout vintage, as it takes three hours for the first cuvée to be pressed. Unusually for Champagne, the solids are retained, producing a cloudy juice. 'We feel this expresses terroir better and gives greater protection against oxidation,' Lécaillon explains.

A new cuverie was built in 2007 to provide space for every block to be vinified separately in a custom-made tank or large oak vat, according to the power of the fruit tasted in the vineyard. About 20% of the vintage is fermented in oak, and aged on lees with bâtonnage for texture and roundness.

'We hate oxidation — it is a betrayal of terroir,' says Lécaillon. 'Lees contact and bâtonnage protect from oxidation.' This creates a reductive style, which can at times produce savoury overtones that distract from fruit purity in Roederer's vintage wines. Vins clairs fermented in oak show richer texture, without taking on oak flavour. Reserve wines are aged in 150 large old oak casks (aged 15–50 years), and liqueur d'expédition is kept in casks for as long as a decade. Four vintages of liqueur d'expédition are kept in vat at all times to allow the dosage for each blend to be tweaked. Dosages of typically 8–11g/L sometimes appear a little high for the natural ripeness of Roederer's fruit.

Non-vintage wines are aged on lees in bottle for three years, vintage wines for four years, and Cristal for five to six. This necessitates a large stock of 18 million bottles squirreled away in Roederer's cellars, with 3 million leaving every year.

Roederer's attention to detail in its vineyards and winery shine even in its non-vintage Brut Premier. For an annual production of more than 2 million bottles, this is a masterfully assembled cuvée. Lifted by the glorious 2008 vintage, Roederer's Brut Rosé is the best buy of the house this year.

LOUIS ROEDERER BRUT PREMIER NV • $$

94 points • TASTED IN MELBOURNE, ADELAIDE AND BRISBANE

2008 base vintage with 20% reserves from five harvests; 40% pinot noir, 40% chardonnay, 20% pinot meunier; 40 villages; 55% estate vineyards; base wines from estate vines fermented in oak casks with bâtonnage (lees stirring); reserves fermented in tanks and matured in large oak casks for up to 8 years; 20–25% malolactic fermentation; aged 3 years on lees; 10–11g/L dosage

I have long adored Brut Premier, a masterful presentation of impeccably ripe fruit of intricate balance and abundant appeal. The rounded richness of white peach, nectarine and grilled pineapple accelerates into a racy finish of tightly honed lemon zest and linear persistence. Dextrous handling of old oak builds gentle texture, with subtle nuances of nutmeg and mixed spice providing dimension. Chalk mineral texture shines on a long finish. Some bottles show hints of reductive struck flint complexity, which only add to the spectacle. A dependable bargain in the non-vintage champagne stakes.

LOUIS ROEDERER BLANC DE BLANCS 2006 • $$$

92 points • TASTED IN BRISBANE

15–20% aged in oak barrels with weekly bâtonnage; no malolactic fermentation; matured 5 years in bottle; 8–10g/L dosage

The child of a record hot July and cold, rainy August, building a lively lemon and energetic grapefruit demeanour. Reductive characters of fennel, struck match and charcuterie are prominent on the bouquet, conspiring with barrel work on the palate to create the impression of wet-wood funk. Dosage rounds out the finish a little more than it needs to, though doesn't distract from the well-defined flow of chalk mineral texture on a long finish.

LOUIS ROEDERER BRUT VINTAGE 2006 • $$$

93 points • TASTED IN BRISBANE

70% Verzy and Verzenay pinot noir; 30% grand cru Côte des Blancs chardonnay; 30% fermented and matured in oak casks with weekly bâtonnage; no malolactic fermentation; matured 4 years in bottle; 10.5–11g/L dosage; 100,000 bottles

Incisive definition of crunchy lemon zest and grapefruit is presented within a cradle of softly fleshy stone fruits, Christmas spice and red berries, showcasing the intensity and character of pinot noir from the northern slopes of the Montagne de Reims. Barrel work adds subtle savoury nuances amidst hints of reduction, without losing focus on its expressive fruit. A little dryness on the finish on release has filled out beautifully with a further six months in bottle, defining a long and well-poised palate of generous fruit presence, neatly offset by tense malic acidity, drawing the finish out long and taut, accented by an undercurrent of fine, chalky minerality. It will benefit from further time for its acidity to soften and integrate.

The Champagne Guide

Louis Roederer Brut Rosé 2008 • $$$

96 points • Disgorged mid-2012 • Tasted in Reims and Brisbane

66% Cumières pinot noir, saignée method, blended after cold maceration with 24% Le Mesnil-sur-Oger chardonnay; 20% matured in oak, weekly bâtonnage; 10% malolactic; aged 4 years in bottle; 9.5g/L dosage

The 2008 vintage snaps high-tensile acidity and chalk mineral texture from black-and-white into vivid high-definition 3D. Every element delicately placed, seamlessly connected and supporting the greater whole, like a masterpiece of cinematography in the hands of the most fastidious director. Prepare for a breathtaking flight over fields of red roses, orchards of tangy white cherries, endless plains of anise and perfect rows of strawberries. It pulls into a white-knuckle vertical ascent of intricately silky malic acidity and textured mineral chalk of lively poise and elegant focus. Lécaillon upholds that concentration is almost as important as acidity for longevity in champagne, and since 2007 a focus on lowering yields, decreasing phenolics and naturally sweet pinot noir have been the key to retaining freshness. He likens 2008 with 2002, though without its slight overripe concentration, and with a tension akin to 1996. Roederer's most riveting episode of the current season, certain to keep you on the edge of your seat.

Louis Roederer Brut Rosé 2007 • $$$

95 points • Disgorged mid-2011 • Tasted in Reims

As above; 10g/L dosage

A new winemaking facility in 2007 provided the tanks for more precise red winemaking and more intricate blending of rosé. This coincided with a pruning regime to decrease red wine yields from 50hL/hectare to a miniscule 30–35. The result upholds a wonderful tension between red berry and cherry fruits, slowly becoming secondary, and the fresh vivacity of malic acidity. Some savoury reductive notes on the bouquet quickly evaporate, revealing a palate dusted with pepper and built on fine minerality, excellent texture and wonderful line and length.

Louis Roederer Brut Rosé 2004

96 points • Disgorged in 2009 • Tasted in Reims

As above; 10g/L dosage

Roederer's classic medium salmon hue is still vibrant after almost a decade. The bouquet and palate continue the theme, upholding impeccable primary definition of pure red cherry, cherry kernel and red apple. Elegant notes of mixed spice and pepper accent a precise mineral tail of unwavering line and length.

Louis Roederer Brut Rosé 2000

95 points • Disgorged in 2006 • Tasted in Reims

As above; 10–11g/L dosage

After 13 years, half on lees and half off, 2000 has matured to an inviting place of dried pear, fig, butterscotch, tobacco, truffles and toasty complexity, behind a medium salmon-copper façade. Malic acidity invigorates its poise and streamlines its even fruit persistence, while a presence of soft, salty minerality hovers in the wings.

Louis Roederer Brut Rosé 1996

97 points • Disgorged in 2003 • Tasted in Reims

Few rosés are capable of sustaining their integrity post-disgorgement as effortlessly as Louis Roederer, and no vintage is charged with enduring stamina quite like 1996. A full decade since disgorgement, it has ventured to an intriguing and enchanting place of roast chestnuts, butterscotch, dried nectarine, fig, toasted coconut and all manner of spices. It celebrates the high-wire tension that defines 1996, contrasting energetic malic acidity and powerful fruit definition with unrelenting persistence.

Louis Roederer Brut Rosé 1988

94 points • Disgorged in 1995 • Tasted in Reims

10% malolactic fermentation

Celebrating its silver anniversary this year, 1988 is holding more than confidently for a rosé off its lees for 18 years. It's attained a tertiary place of truffles, roast fennel, dried fruits, butterscotch, exotic spices and a hint of sweet pipe smoke. Minerality remains transfixed, finely structured and textural. Just a hint of furniture wax is beginning to show, a sign that oxidation has finally begun to set in and it's time to drink up.

Louis Roederer Cristal 2006 • $$$$$

96 points • Disgorged June 2012 • Tasted in Reims

60% pinot noir, 40% chardonnay from a pool of 50 hectares of old vines on the most chalky sites; 20% matured in oak barrels with weekly bâtonnage; no malolactic fermentation; matured an average of 5 years on lees; 9g/L dosage; typically 150,000–300,000 bottles

The finest Cristal since 2002, a celebration of ripe fruit framed in tense malic acidity. Even in its extreme youth more than a year prior to release, it ripples with generous waves of pure white peach, fig, butterscotch, even candied fruits, grilled pineapple and fruit-mince spice. Roederer's stamp of malic acidity takes control of this revelry, pulling the finish into a refined focus of crunchy lemon zest freshness, shimmering with expressive, fine, mouth-filling chalk minerality. Another year will certainly help, but it screams out for at least a few years to build depth and complexity. The release of Cristal is timed according to sales of the previous vintage, typically making this the first of the big-gun prestige champagnes to be lobbed into the market. Such early release is to its loss, as Cristal is a champagne that blossoms with sufficient time for its reductive complexity to mellow, its fruit personality to assert itself, and its malic acidity to settle down, as recent tastings of mature vintages attest.

LOUIS ROEDERER CRISTAL 2005 • $$$$$

94 points • TASTED IN BRISBANE

As for the 2006, except: 55% pinot noir from Verzenay, Verzy, Beaumont, Vesle and Aÿ; 45% chardonnay from Avize, Cramant and Le Mesnil-sur-Oger; 8–10g/L dosage

The child of a challenging season, 2005 is the least Cristal of the modern era, though upholding an impressive standard for this warm vintage. It's predictably voluptuous, leading out with juicy white peach, yellow mirabelle plum and fig, contrasting refreshingly with the finesse of grapefruit and lemon zest, rescued by the saving stamina of taut malic acidity. It's spiced up with edgy reductive notes of fennel, white pepper and star anise, while upholding fruit focus and an undercurrent of chalk minerality. The finish was characterised by a dryness on release, which has since fleshed out neatly, with a honeyed dosage sweetness contrasting with the sour lemon tang of malic acidity.

LOUIS ROEDERER CRISTAL ROSÉ 2004 • $$$$$

97 points • TASTED IN REIMS

60% pinot noir from a single organic block in Aÿ; 40% Le Mesnil-sur-Oger chardonnay; 20% vinified in oak barrels with weekly bâtonnage; no malolactic fermentation; saignée method, cold macerated for 5–8 days; 8–10g/L dosage

The ultimate juxtaposition between breathtaking finesse and glorious concentration, showcasing the rumbling power and mouth-storming chalk minerality of Aÿ pinot noir. Consummate definition, exacting poise and undeterred persistence are reinforced by the tension of Le Mesnil-sur-Oger chardonnay, propelling the remarkable cherry definition, red berry concentration, violet perfume and long-lingering spice of pinot to mesospheric heights.

Louis Roederer's Reims premises, an illustrious testimony to Champagne's largest family owned and managed house.

MAILLY GRAND CRU

(My-ii Groh Khrew)

5/10

28 Rue de la Libération 51500 Mailly Champagne
www.champagne-mailly.com

CHAMPAGNE

MAILLY

GRAND CRU

*O*f Champagne's 137 cooperatives, only Le Mesnil rivals Mailly Grand Cru as the fairest of them all. Mailly's 80 growers supply fruit for more than 500,000 bottles each year, from some 480 parcels, exclusively on 70 hectares of glorious Mailly grand cru soil. North-facing slopes on chalk subsoils draw out the mineral freshness of pinot noir, which comprises 75% of plantings, with chardonnay making up the remainder. The cooperative works closely with its growers, maintaining many test parcels throughout the village and upholding an average vine age of 25 years. Individual vinification of many parcels provides a blending palette of more than 60 wines, including reserves spanning more than 10 vintages, stored in small tanks and oak tuns. The cooperative's glass building stands proudly in the village, above seven levels of cellars and a kilometre of chalk crayères, dug by hand by the founders of the cooperative every winter from 1929 to 1965. Mailly's non-vintage cuvées showcase the up-front fruit character of the area, while its finest prestige cuvées capture an elegant mineral precision that sets a benchmark for the village. Mailly's talented Chef de Cave since 1991, Hervé Dantan, accepted a position at Lanson in February 2013.

MAILLY GRAND CRU BRUT RÉSERVE NV • $$

90 points • Tasted in Brisbane

2008 base vintage; 75% pinot noir, 25% chardonnay; a blend of the 480 parcels of the cooperative with 10 years of reserves, 5–8% barrel aged; full malolactic fermentation; 9g/L dosage

A lively, fresh, up-front and fruity style exemplifies the flamboyant character of Mailly pinot noir. It carries a deep hue and an expressive array of ripe wild strawberry, red apple, pear, and raspberry candy fruits. Dosage is well integrated on a finish of drying phenolic grip.

Mailly Grand Cru Brut Rosé NV • $$$

93 points • Tasted in Brisbane

2008 base vintage; saignée style from 90% old-vine pinot noir, with 10% chardonnay for lightness, brightness and balance; full malolactic fermentation; 8g/L dosage

Mailly has nurtured a beautifully crafted saignée of refreshing elegance and youthful fruit expression, celebrating the accurate fruit intensity of grand cru pinot noir, while upholding an eminently refined style. A full salmon crimson hue announces the capacity of a saignée maceration to capture the concentration of the village, reinforced by aromas of strawberry hull, tangy red cherries, even a subtle hint of fresh tomato. The palate sings with the energy and refreshing acidity of 2008, balancing fresh, lively acidity and softly chalky mineral structure with well-integrated dosage.

Mailly Grand Cru Blanc de Noirs NV • $$$

89 points • Tasted in Brisbane

2008 base vintage; 100% pinot noir, selected from plots known for their finesse; full malolactic fermentation; 8g/L dosage

From slopes ruled by pinot noir, it seems ironic that the least of Mailly's cuvées based on the incredible 2008 vintage is its only blend without chardonnay. Perhaps the power of pinot has got the better of itself here? There's a tint of gold to its full straw hue, introducing an altogether golden palate of ripe peach, golden delicious apples and butter. It leads out rich and opulent and quickly runs out of steam, finishing with a drying phenolic structure that leaves it coarse and contracted.

Mailly Grand Cru Vintage 2006 • $$$

94 points • Tasted in Brisbane

75% pinot noir, 25% chardonnay; 6g/L dosage

The recipe says 25% chardonnay, but for all intents and purposes this wine should be treated as a blanc de noirs, making it spot-on for winter sipping or aligning with main-course seafood fare. It presents considerable depth of Mailly pinot noir character, built around black cherry, anise, figs, even licorice. Its fine texture neatly weaves mineral expression with well-judged phenolic structure, accurately guiding a powerful fruit finish with considerable persistence. A well-composed vintage that depicts the concentration of Mailly pinot noir and an accurate expression of its chalk structure.

MAILLY GRAND CRU L'INTEMPORELLE MILLÉSIME BRUT 2007 • $$$$

95 points • TASTED IN BRISBANE

60% pinot noir, 40% chardonnay; full malolactic fermentation; 8g/L dosage; 25,842 bottles

An impressively refined and honed Mailly that will benefit from considerably more age, making it a surprise that this prestige cuvée is released younger than the standard vintage wine of the house. Blended from a selection of fruit from the best plots of the village, there's an elegance here, reflected in a paler hue than Mailly's entry blends. A larger inclusion of chardonnay sings in lively aromas of white peach and pear against a backdrop of white cherries. The palate reflects its youth: taut, lively and primary, with tangy grapefruit and lemon zest holding out on a finish of profound line and length, underwritten by pronounced chalk mineral texture.

MAILLY GRAND CRU L'INTEMPORELLE ROSÉ BRUT 2007 • $$$$

95 points • TASTED IN BRISBANE

60% pinot noir, 40% chardonnay; pinot noir red wine from vines exceeding 40 years of age; 8g/L dosage; 5053 bottles

In its minuscule volumes, Mailly's prestige rosé is a glorious celebration of youth. An ultra-pale salmon hue heralds a subtle and precise bouquet of elegantly expressive rose petal, red apple and strawberry hull aromas. The freshness of the palate is true to its youth — taut, fine and light-footed, with primary white cherry and lemon zest accented with notes of anise. An undercurrent of fine, soft, yet well-defined Mailly chalk wells up from its core and carries its finish with lingering persistence. Very young for a prestige rosé, yet none the less for it.

MAILLY GRAND CRU LES ÉCHANSONS MILLESIME BRUT 2000 • $$$$

92 points • TASTED IN BRISBANE

75% pinot noir, 25% chardonnay; 6g/L dosage; 11,788 bottles

A powerful village, an intense vintage, a large majority of pinot noir and 13 years of bottle age make for a foreboding foursome, conspiring to create a champagne deep in colour and strong in its ripe fruit expression. A deep amalgam of raisins, tangelo, wild honey, cherry liqueur, dried fig, plum pudding and smouldering hearth makes for an explosively ripe entry, yet quickly collapses in a heap, finishing with subtle dry extract, showing signs of the beginnings of oxidation.

The Champagne Guide

MOËT & CHANDON

(Mo-wet e Shon-don)

20 AVENUE DE CHAMPAGNE 51200 ÉPERNAY
www.moet.com

MOËT & CHANDON
CHAMPAGNE

I thought I had Moët & Chandon figured out. We all know the wines, we've witnessed the PR machine in full grind, and I've visited command-central in Épernay a few times over more than a decade. The company that has 120 million bottles of fizz under its floorboards and sells a mind-boggling 28 million every year; the company that produces some 9% of all champagne; that could alone satiate Champagne's biggest export market of the UK, indefinitely; that buys grapes from 3000 growers and still supplies one-third of its needs from a whopping 1150 hectares of estate vineyards — that company — can't be that hard to pin down. But big developments are at hand. The giant of Champagne is on the move.

UNPRECEDENTED ANTICS

IN JUNE 2012, MOËT & CHANDON'S OWNER, LUXURY giant Louis Vuitton-Moët Hennessy, made a tactical and unprecedented play. An advertisement placed in local newspapers announced that company would pay 4% more for its grapes in the 2012 vintage.

An aggressive buyer in the champagne market for some years, this was the first public announcement of its intentions. At the same time, Moët & Chandon completed a major expansion of its production facilities in strategic anticipation of rising global demand for champagne, with record sales forecast for 2014.

On grand display to the stream of traffic on the main road from Épernay to the Côte des Blancs, Moët's new Mont Aigu winery in Oiry is like nothing I've ever seen. Magnificently showcased behind floor-to-ceiling glass on every side stand 137 sparkling new stainless steel fermentation tanks, with a capacity of 10 million

litres, with a further 5 million to be added this year. Dedicated exclusively to Moët Brut Impérial NV, this is likely the most sophisticated sparkling facility in the world, computer controlled to automatically direct juice from tankers to vats without a human hand touching a hose or tap. Every ferment is monitored every five seconds, with breathtaking precision. By 2017, this facility will add 21 million bottles to Moët's current production capacity of 60 million. It's a striking monument to Moët's growth, and the company is working overtime to secure supply to fill it, even door-knocking growers with enticing incentive offers.

There are loud grumblings in Champagne about this brazen wielding of power. As the largest purchaser in the region, when Moët sets a price, everyone follows. Some perceive the move as a strategic attempt to put pressure on grape supply and push smaller players out of the market. It's not as simple as this. Champagne has long paid its growers like no other appellation in France, and higher grape prices are ultimately to their benefit, shoring up the foundation of the region. Moët's commitment to purchasing fruit rather than vins clairs made by others producers can only be a good thing, both for the growers and for quality. And the rise of Moët to date has been for the greater good of Champagne in another way, too.

In conversations across the region, from the largest houses and cooperatives to the smallest growers, I am continually impressed by the high regard in which Moët & Chandon is held.

The Champenois salute Moët as an ambassador for their region, for its groundbreaking and ongoing work in breaking into emerging markets like China and India. There is genuine gratitude that this trailblazing paves the way for other champagne brands to follow.

And growing markets demand growing supplies. This is nothing new for Moët. Founded in 1743, the company claims to be the first house of champagne. It came into international prominence under Jean-Remy Moët, who inherited the house from its founder, his grandfather, Claude Moët, in 1789. It is said Jean-Remy was already dreaming about Asian markets before the end of that century.

Since this time, Moët has mushroomed like no other champagne house, and the real danger today is that its explosive growth topples the balance in Champagne. LVMH is already the giant of the region. Its brands of Moët & Chandon, Veuve Clicquot, Mercier, Ruinart, Dom Pérignon and Krug between them account for a whopping 20% of all champagne sales. The group is so far ahead in both value and volume that it more than exceeds its two nearest rivals, Lanson-BCC and Vranken-Pommery, put together.

The biggest question of all is how Moët can sustain quality in the wake of such unprecedented growth.

PERPETUAL EVOLUTION

'I believe bigger is better,' responded Chef de Cave Benoît Gouez when I recently put the question to him, deep in Moët's cellars in Épernay.

'I don't consider quality and quantity to be mutually exclusive in Champagne. A small grower in one village has nothing to compensate for difficult weather. Grower wines are very good, and I have friends among many of them, but by nature the quality of champagne is uneven. The more grapes you can access, the more you can be consistent.'

It's a principle that appears to have worked for Moët in recent years. At more than 20 million bottles every year, its Brut Impérial is the biggest blend in Champagne, and currently as fresh as I've seen it. 'This is a wine that is always evolving, because the climate, the technology, the market, the consumers and the world have changed,' Gouez explains.

Of course, quality does not automatically come with quantity, and his team has embraced innovation and worked hard to refine the style. 'We have worked on the preparation of our ferments to provide the right level of oxygenation so they don't get too stressed,' Gouez says. 'This reduces the reductive flavours, allowing room for the expression of the precision and cleanliness of the fruit.' This shows in most cuvées, though at least one vintage shows strong reductive character this year.

Lower dosage has also been a refreshing trend in recent years, though I still find the sweetness somewhat candied in his non-vintage cuvées. 'In the past, we were known for higher dosage, but today Brut Impérial is 9g/L, one of the lowest among the grande marques,' he points out. This comes in response to both riper fruit and a changing consumer palate, seeking elegance and purity. 'We will continue to evolve,' he says. 'It's perpetual, and we need to continually revisit our style and our values.'

The Moët ambition is a fruit-driven style of freshness, brightness and purity. 'We want our champagnes to taste of the grapes they're made of,' Gouez explains. To this end, winemaking is purposely reductive, vigorously minimising oxidation and religiously avoiding oak. 'The size and diversity of our vineyard sources is the key to consistency,' he says. Drawing from an unrivalled 1150 hectares of estate vines and twice this area of purchased fruit, Moët assembles some 800 different parcels every vintage, spanning 230 of Champagne's 319 villages.

Further complexity is built through fermentation using yeasts produced in its own lab. All Moët & Chandon cuvées are blends of the three champagne varieties, and all undergo malolactic fermentation. Prior to the commissioning of the Mont Aigu facility, all of its wines were stored in its 28 kilometres of cellars under Épernay, which took two centuries to carve.

These are sweet, rounded, commercial champagnes, but recent efforts have certainly refined the style in spite of the monumental scale of production.

'Whatever we do at Moët, we like to do it big and bold, to share Moët with the world!' Gouez rejoices. That they do.

Let's hope that when the wines of Moët & Chandon's current growth phase hit the ground in a few years' time, quality might increase at the same dramatic pace as production.

Moët & Chandon Brut Impérial NV • $$

88 points • Disgorged February 2012 • Tasted in Épernay, Brisbane and Dubai

2009 base vintage; 20-30% reserves, mostly from 2008 and a little from 2007; a big third of pinot noir (30-40%), a third of pinot meunier (30-40%) and a small third of chardonnay (20-30%); a blend of more than 100 different wines; matured 24 months on lees; 9g/L dosage

At more than 21 million bottles, and rising, this one wine accounts for some 7% of Champagne's production. To put this in perspective, the vines that supply this label alone would cover an area close to 4000 rugby fields! This is a blend of everything from everywhere, on an oceanic scale that makes a single blend impossible, dictating three or four quite different blends every year. The new vintage will be very young in the first blend, and balanced with up to 40% reserve wines, while the last blend might only call for 20% reserves. The aim is to use young and fruity reserves of two vintages to build consistency by contributing any elements missing from the latest harvest. There is thus no recipe, with a different dosage and different liqueur for every batch. 'I call this tailor-made winemaking,' says Gouez. 'We have to adapt and be flexible. How can a house of this size be flexible? For me, craftsmanship is not about being small but about having an ambition to focus on every detail.'

The mind-boggling scale of Brut Impérial makes its improvement in recent years all the more impressive, and this is the freshest and most fruit-focused I have seen it. The last blend of the 2009 base vintage retains a freshness and focus of grapefruit zest, lemon pulp and peach. There's a little earthiness and a dry grip on the finish, countered by dosage which leaves it a touch candied. It's better made than ever — quite an achievement at this volume.

Moët & Chandon Rosé Impérial NV • $$

88 points • Disgorged May 2011 • Tasted in Épernay and Brisbane

2009 base vintage (or 2010 — Gouez wasn't certain); 40-50% pinot noir (including 10-15% red wine); 30-40% pinot meunier (including 10-15% red wine); 10-20% chardonnay; 20-30% reserve wines; aged 21 months on lees; 9g/L dosage; around 3 million bottles annually

Moët has a very long history with champagne rosé, evidenced by a letter of order from Napoleon dated 1801. Today, rosé represents 17% of total sales, which must put its non-vintage rosé somewhere in the vicinity of 3 million bottles annually. It's intentionally in the same style as its Brut Impérial, though crafted from a unique blend. To create intensity of colour and lightness on the palate, Moët is unique in Champagne in employing a Beaujolais technique of heating and macerating pinot meunier at 70°C for a couple of hours to extract colour and flavour without tannins. Short macerations produce red wines of lighter colour, which explains a large dose of 20–25% red wine in the blend.

In spite of its full salmon-crimson hue, there's an elegance and a fruit freshness to this style, with well-defined primary strawberry, red cherry and pink pepper characters. Soft, drying tannin texture and a touch of phenolic grip and firmness are offset with a dosage that leaves a confectionery note to a short finish.

MOËT & CHANDON GRAND VINTAGE 2004 • $$$

87 points • DISGORGED JANUARY 2012 • TASTED IN ÉPERNAY AND BRISBANE

38% chardonnay, 33% pinot noir, 29% pinot meunier; 5g/L dosage; around 1.5 million bottles annually

Gouez has replaced 'Moët & Chandon Vintage' with 'Vintage by Moët & Chandon', with labels of bold vintage declaration, to focus more on the style of the season than the house. 'The idea is not to follow a recipe, but to listen to the wines and create a vintage with uniqueness and charisma,' he says. The blend and the selection of parcels changes to reflect the character of the season, looking for those that are most interesting and original. 'We start from scratch, I choose the grapes from anywhere I want, and I don't care if it's pinot meunier or if it isn't grand cru. The personality of the wine tasted blind is the key.' The maturation has also evolved, previously released after five years on lees and now after seven, allowing the dosage to be lowered to just 5g/L. Disgorgement date, dosage and blend are clearly displayed on the back label — impressive detail for a house of this magnitude.

Taut lemon zest fruit is backed by subtle complexity of honey and ginger cake, structured by crunchy acidity and a firm phenolic grip. A reductive onion/gherkin character leaves an astringent, dry awkwardness to the finish, which pulls up hard and abrupt.

MOËT & CHANDON GRAND VINTAGE ROSÉ 2004 • $$$

87 points • TASTED IN ÉPERNAY

45% pinot noir (including 22% red wine); 31% chardonnay; 24% pinot meunier; aged 7 years on lees; 5g/L dosage; around 300,000 bottles annually

Moët harvests red wine for its vintage rosé from its best estate pinot noir plots of low-yielding old vines, green harvested to reduce yields when necessary. Twice the necessary vineyard area is prepared, to permit choice of the grapes with the best phenolic maturity to provide structure. Red wine is macerated for 5–7 days to draw out ripe, soft character, without hard tannins.

There's a distinct earthiness to this spicy style of soft, rounded berry fruits, guava, pink pepper and creamy bead. It finishes with soft minerality and firm phenolic structure that contribute dryness.

MOËT & CHANDON GRAND VINTAGE ROSÉ 2002 • $$$

87 points • DISGORGED APRIL 2010 • TASTED IN BRISBANE

51% pinot meunier (including 27% red wine); 28% chardonnay; 21% pinot meunier; aged 7 years on lees; 5.5g/L dosage

Moët's intelligent and unprecedented decision to release its 2003 vintage before 2002 was driven by the youthful 2002 rather than the forward 2003, which does little to explain the rapid development of the 2002 and why it is still in the market three years after release. It already showed a distinct lack of freshness and vitality 18 months ago. It's now deteriorated to a full copper-crimson colour, with fully secondary characters of spice, nut and butter, devoid of primary fruit yet, admirably, not dried out on the finish and not oxidised, making for a creamy, nutty, smoothly textured close. It's well past its prime, yet desperately clinging to life.

The Champagne Guide

MOUTARD

(Moo-tahr)

RUE DES PONTS BP1 10110 BUXEUIL
www.champagne-moutard.fr

BRUT

*T*he Moutard-Diligent family have been vignerons in Buxeuil just outside Troyes in the Côte des Bar since 1642 and have made their own champagne since 1927. The domaine encompasses 21 hectares of vines, planted largely to pinot noir, with six other varieties, including the rare arbane and petit meslier. Estate holdings provide for 40% of an annual production of 750,000 bottles. Cold settling is used to settle the coarse lees prior to fermentation in small and large barrels, and malolactic fermentation is blocked. These are inexpensive champagnes of rustic character.

MOUTARD GRANDE CUVÉE BRUT NV • $

89 points • DISGORGED JUNE 2012 • TASTED IN BRISBANE

100% pinot noir; disgorgement date is printed discreetly on the back label

A blanc de noirs, though not labelled as such, and it needn't be, because this is a simple and neutral champagne. It's primary and fruit-focused, with sweet peaches, honey, apple and pear, finishing short, with dosage and acidity in even balance. The first bottle opened was corked.

MOUTARD CUVÉE DES 6 CÉPAGES BRUT 2006 • $$

90 points • DISGORGED JANUARY 2013 • TASTED IN BRISBANE

Arbane, petit meslier, pinot blanc, chardonnay, pinot noir and pinot meunier; fermented and vinified in barrels; 18,021 bottles; disgorgement date is printed discreetly on the back label

Spanning the full sweep of complexity of six varieties, this blend is layered with all manner of citrus, stone fruits and tropical fruits. Tasted a couple of months post-disgorgement, it's developing quickly, already a full yellow hue and packed with buttery, toasty, honeyed and roast almond maturity, though holding its balance in lemon pith and crunchy pear fruit. A hint of charcuterie leaves it a touch funky, with a firm undercurrent of phenolic texture. All four bottles tasted were sound, in contrast to the previous vintage, where all four were corked.

NAPOLÉON

(Nah-poh-lee-o)

5/10

30 RUE DU GENERAL LECLERC B.P.41 51130 VERTUS
www.champagne-napoleon.com

CHAMPAGNE
NAPOLÉON

Napoléon is a brand of the growers cooperative of Vertus, producing 100,000 bottles annually from the fruit of 100 growers, with vineyards largely in Vertus and neighbouring Le Mesnil-sur-Oger and Bergères-lès-Vertus. Covering the second-largest area of any village in Champagne, and the largest in the Marne, Vertus offers great diversity of sites and microclimates, and Napoléon vinifies its many parcels separately in small stainless steel tanks. The brand draws on equal proportions of pinot noir and chardonnay to produce long-ageing wines, with non-vintage cuvées typically matured for four years on lees, and vintage cuvées much longer, generally released around 13 years of age — extraordinarily old for a cooperative. Managing Director and Chef de Cave Jean-Philippe Moulin brings significant experience from his former positions as Chef de Cave of Ruinart and inaugural head of the CIVC Research & Development unit. Napoléon produces soft, fruity and creamy champagnes, also sold as Prieur in some markets. Its long-aged vintage wines represent good value.

NAPOLÉON BLANC DE BLANCS BRUT NV • $$

89 points • 2007 BASE VINTAGE WITH 2006 RESERVE • TASTED IN VERTUS
90 points • 2006 BASE VINTAGE WITH 2005 RESERVE • TASTED IN VERTUS

Predominantly Vertus; 7g/L dosage

A fruit-focused, soft and easy-drinking blanc de blancs of elegant lemon and white peach fruits, notes of almond, soft, creamy acidity and lively bead. A touch of reduction gives subtle savoury complexity in the 2007 base.

Napoléon Tradition Brut NV • $$

92 points • Disgorged October 2012 • Tasted in Vertus

2007 base vintage; 50% chardonnay; 50% pinot noir purchased from Verzenay, Hautvillers and Aÿ; 8g/L dosage

A fresh, fruity, creamy and well-balanced blend of ripe fruit, lingering acidity and soft mineral structure. Apple, pear and white peach fruit lingers with citrus zest notes, accented with subtle spice and almond complexity, reflecting almost five years maturing on yeast lees.

Napoléon Tradition Demi Sec NV • $$

85 points • Tasted in Vertus

Same blend as the Brut NV above, except 16–17g/L dosage

Clean and sugary, honeyed and toffeed, with candied fruits and notes of spice, finishing short and simple.

Napoléon Rosé Brut NV • $$

90 points • Tasted in Vertus

2007 base vintage; 50% chardonnay, 50% pinot noir; red wine from low-cropped old-vine Vertus pinot noir; 8g/L dosage

A generously fruity rosé of tangelo and strawberry fruits, with bottled-aged complexity of honey, ginger and biscuits. Clean and well made, with the creamy softness of long lees age.

Napoléon Brut Vintage 1998 • $$

95 points • Tasted in Vertus

50% chardonnay, 50% pinot noir; full malolactic fermentation; 5g/L dosage

Napoléon upholds a late-release philosophy for its vintage wines, making for impressive maturity at an affordable price. Its 1998 celebrates the stamina of the season, still impressively vibrant and well-composed at a full 15 years of age. Its hue has developed to a full straw-yellow, and roast nut, butter and honey complexity rises from a core of lemon zest and white peach.

Napoléon Brut Vintage 1996

95 points • Disgorged December 2012 • Tasted in Vertus

4g/L dosage

An impressively poised 1996 that presents delightful focus, charged by the honed acidity of this long-lived season. It's taken on an enticing array of anise, dried pear, green olives, tobacco and hints of smoke, finishing dry and taut, with brilliant persistence.

NICOLAS FEUILLATTE

(Ni-khoh-lah Fer-yat)

D40A PLUMECOQ 51530 CHOUILLY
www.feuillatte.com

CHAMPAGNE
Nicolas Feuillatte

*C*entre Vinicole — Champagne Nicolas Feuillatte' is Champagne's oldest and largest cooperative, and Nicolas Feuillatte is its key brand. The gargantuan operation comprises a collective of 82 cooperatives, with more than 5000 growers tending 2250 hectares of vines across more than 300 villages, comprising 7% of Champagne's surface. Production facilities span a full 12 hectares of high-tech buildings, with a capacity of 30 million litres — so large that they act as a second production and storage site for Moët & Chandon. At any time 65 million bottles of Nicolas Feuillatte are ageing here, with a capacity of 100 million, and more than 9 million are sold each year, making the brand Champagne's third largest. All cuvées are produced from premier and grand cru vineyards, in stainless steel tanks. The cooperative relies on a high proportion of pinot meunier (48%), and lesser amounts of pinot noir (27%) and chardonnay (25%). For its primary, fruity style, dosage levels are heavy-handed.

NICOLAS FEUILLATTE BRUT RÉSERVE PARTICULIÉRE NV • $$

89 points • TASTED IN BRISBANE

40% pinot noir, 40% pinot meunier, 20% chardonnay

Fresh white peach, spicy grapefruit and lemon zest lead out fruity and fresh, supported by a lively, taut acid line, finishing short and a little dried out, with notes of phenolic firmness jostling with full, honeyed sweetness. The cleanest I've seen this cuvée yet.

NICOLAS FEUILLATTE BRUT ROSÉ NV • $$

87 points • TASTED IN BRISBANE

60% pinot noir, 30% pinot meunier, 10% chardonnay

A medium copper-salmon hue suggests a little development, as do notes of bruised red apple and some dryness on the finish. To its credit, it retains some primary strawberry and raspberry fruit character, though lacks freshness and vitality, finishing with some textural phenolic grip.

NICOLAS FEUILLATTE GRAND CRU BLANC DE BLANCS 2004 • $$

88 points • TASTED IN BRISBANE
Aged in the cellars at least 8 years

A rich bouquet of honey and roast nut complexity. The palate is rounded, succulent and sweet, with heavy dosage pushing it well into the candied realm, which is unfortunate, because there's a reasonable fruit and acid profile behind it.

NICOLAS FEUILLATTE GRAND CRU BLANC DE NOIRS 2002 • $$

91 points • TASTED IN BRISBANE

An enticing red fruits and orange rind bouquet is replicated on a rich and fruity palate, accented by firm phenolic texture. The taut acid line of 2002 is balanced with honeyed dosage. A fine bead and admirable persistence confirm an impressive vintage for one of Feuillatte's better cuvées.

NICOLAS FEUILLATTE PALMES D'OR VINTAGE BRUT 1999 • $$$$

91 points • TASTED IN BRISBANE
50% chardonnay, 50% pinot noir; aged a minimum of 9 years

Nicolas Feuillatte's information sheet for Palmes d'Or 1999 reads, 'Palmes d'Or Brut vintage 1998 is sublime'. The 1999 doesn't attain the same heights as its predecessor — a generous, rich, creamy and sweet champagne of toasted pineapple, crème brûlée, toffee, honey, fig, baked peach and mixed spice conspiring to give an effect reminiscent of toasted marshmallows. It finishes long, with good acid line, plenty of character and more dosage than its ripe fruit calls for. It will appeal to those looking for an overt and sweet champagne style.

NICOLAS FEUILLATTE PALMES D'OR ROSÉ VINTAGE 2005 • $$$$

88 points • TASTED IN BRISBANE
Rosé de saignée of 100% pinot noir from Bouzy and Les Riceys; aged a minimum of 5 years on lees

The saignée process has produced a rosé of full crimson hue with an orange sunburst rim. This is a powerfully fruity and exotic champagne of bold red fruits, Campari, smoke and beeswax. For all its extroverted flamboyancy, it loses gusto on the finish, closing callow and firm.

PASCAL DOQUET

(Pas-khal Doh-khay)

7/10

44 CHEMIN DU MOULIN DE LA CENSÉ BIZET 51130 VERTUS
www.champagne-doquet.com

The annual release letter Pascal Doquet sends to his customers from his cellar on the outer edge of Vertus reads more like that of a tiny boutique in Burgundy than a champagne producer. In it he recounts the stories of recent vintages, the tribulations of a rigorous organic regime and the intricacies of each of 10 different cuvées, in their limited availability. Every detail of the philosophy and practice of this tiny estate translates into wines of effortless form and beguiling beauty, making this a mailing list that every lover of blanc de blancs should subscribe to.

THIRD-GENERATION WINEMAKER PASCAL DOQUET HAS been making champagne under his parents' label of Doquet Jeanmaire since 1982, and has led the estate since 1995. It was not until 2004 that he gained independent control and began marketing the brand under his own name, following acquisition of shares held by his sisters' family. This opened up the opportunity for Doquet to embark upon a daring organic regime to more accurately draw out the terroirs of each plot.

While he abandoned the use of herbicides as early as 2001, it was not until 2004 that he fully tuned in to sustainable viticulture, resolutely pursuing practices in harmony with nature and the planet, as he puts it. Full organic certification was granted in 2007. 'Respect of the soil is important,' he explains as he proudly shows photos of the health of his vines compared with neighbouring plots.

His is an intuitive approach, constantly experimenting and adapting his techniques and treatments to suit the plot and the season. All plots are ploughed, and spontaneous flora is maintained in the mid-rows for a rich and complex biodiversity.

Doquet prepares his own organic composts and applies hardwood bark, grape marc and shredded branches to encourage biological activity. He is exploring new alternatives to copper and sulphur sprays for protection against disease.

He admits that a meticulous organic approach is a constant challenge in Champagne's climate, and particularly tricky to manage in vineyards separated by 75 kilometres. His 8.66-hectare estate is solidly rooted in the Côte des Blancs, with 3.5 hectares in Vertus, Bergères-lès-Vertus and Le Mont Aimé just south of Bergères, and a magnificent 1.7 hectares in Le Mesnil-sur-Oger. A further 3.5 hectares are located in the communes of Bassuet and Bassu in the region of Perthois near Vitry-le-François to the east. Vines boast a maturity of up to 77 years, with a weighted average of 35 years, very high for Champagne. Chardonnay rules across the estate, with just 5% pinot noir, and no pinot meunier.

Doquet's goal is to harvest at full maturity to avoid chaptalisation. 'Chaptalisation should be the exception in Champagne,' is his radical suggestion. To this end, he green harvests to bring yields down to around 65hL/hectare, just two-thirds of the permitted appellation volume. This provides an annual production of 75,000 bottles, exclusively from estate vines.

Pascal Doquet makes wine by the philosophy of letting the vines and the wine tell him what to do, while forever experimenting and striving to improve. There are no strict rules and he varies his techniques in the cellar from year to year. Some wines go through malolactic fermentation, others do not. About one-third are fermented in oak and two-thirds in enamelled stainless steel, which he says is less prone to developing reductive characters. The natural yeasts of each vineyard are used for fermentation, and wines spend 4–5 months on lees in vats, and 11 months in barrels with moderate bâtonnage after malolactic fermentation. Dosage is low, always under 7g/L, and usually around 4.5g/L. Concentrated grape must is used instead of sugar because it tastes closer to the natural sweetness of the grapes.

A massive stock of 350,000–450,000 bottles is held in large cellars cut into chalk to permit long ageing periods of typically 4–5 years, crucial for blanc de blancs that hold their youthful vigour with pristine clarity. Vintages are released only when they're ready. DIAM closures have been used for exports since 2007. Doquet likes the closure, but admits that it's not so popular in France. Back labels are informative, declaring disgorgement date, dosage, base vintage and percentages of reserves.

The intuitive and sensitive approach of Pascal Doquet creates beautifully expressive and deeply terroir-driven wines. All but three non-vintage blends showcase individual villages, of which Le Mesnil-sur-Oger and Vertus are his jewels.

PASCAL DOQUET HORIZON BLANC DE BLANCS NV • $$

92 points • TASTED IN VERTUS

67% 2009, 33% 2008; Bassuet and Bassu in the region Perthois near Vitry-le-François; vineyards in conversion to organics; natural fermentation; no chaptalisation; 12% aged in oak; no fining or filtration; full malolactic fermentation; 6 months on lees in tank; 7g/L dosage; DIAM closure

Pascal Doquet's attention to detail elevates even lesser terroirs. Structure leads before fruit in his brand-new cuvée, resonating with the chalk and grey clay of Perthois, 50 kilometres east of his home in Vertus. This is a balanced and elegant champagne of pale straw hue and crisp definition of white peach, apple and grapefruit. A fine, creamy bead and tight finish define a precise style.

PASCAL DOQUET PREMIERS CRUS BLANC DE BLANCS EXTRA BRUT NV • $$

93 points • DISGORGED FEBRUARY 2012 • TASTED IN VERTUS

2005 base vintage with reserves from 2004 and 2002; Vertus, Villeneuve and Mont Aimé; 20–30% vinified in barrels; aged on lees for 3 months; full malolactic fermentation; 3.5g/L dosage; DIAM closure

An impressively assembled expression of the southern Côte des Blancs, capturing well-structured chalk minerality, amplified ingeniously by the texture of barrel fermentation. Fruit is well defined and enticingly exotic, with grapefruit, star fruit and golden delicious apple, even notes of coffee bean and cocoa. It finishes long and beautifully balanced with bright, crunchy acidity and creamy texture.

PASCAL DOQUET PREMIER CRU VERTUS 2004 • $$

95 points • Disgorged July 2011 • Tasted in Vertus

75% chardonnay, 25% pinot noir; one-third vinified in oak barrels; aged on lees in tank and barrel for 5 months; full malolactic fermentation; 4.5g/L dosage; DIAM closure

The finest mid-slope vineyards of Vertus are capable of rivalling any grand cru, and Pascal Doquet showcases their full potential in this intricately crafted cuvée. It's expressive and generous in juicy white peach, nectarine, fleshy pear, fig and mixed spice, even a hint of sultana, evidencing Doquet's focus on harvesting ripe fruit. At the same time, magnificently elegant and restrained, proclaiming the softly chalky minerality and well-integrated acidity of the village in an appealingly silky and supremely balanced finish.

PASCAL DOQUET PREMIER CRU LE MONT AIMÉ BLANC DE BLANCS 2005 • $$

89 points • Disgorged October 2011 • Tasted in Vertus

40% vinified in oak barrels, 60% in enamelled stainless steel tanks; aged on lees in tank and barrel for 6 months; 4.5g/L dosage; DIAM closure

Pascal Doquet has bottled the precise lemon zest, red apple and grapefruit of Mont Aimé at the southern end of the Côte des Blancs, accurately preserving the chalky minerality of its sandy and stony silica soils. It begins crunchy and finely structured, and quickly falters into a hard, dry, coarse finish, characteristic of this ripe vintage. Its acidity remains admirably bright throughout.

PASCAL DOQUET LE MESNIL-SUR-OGER BLANC DE BLANCS NV • $$$

94 points • Extra Brut disgorged February 2012 with 3.5g/L dosage
  • Tasted in Vertus
95 points • Brut disgorged October 2011 with 7g/L dosage • Tasted in Vertus

65% 2004, 35% 2003; 10% fermented in barrels; partial malolactic fermentation (none on 2003 parcels)

It says non-vintage, but after seven years on lees in bottle, this is as ravishing as any vintage wine, a glorious expression of all the concentration and theatrics of Le Mesnil-sur-Oger. Its textural, mineral style is a rousing celebration of the prominent chalk of the village, stirred by a touch of oak fermentation. Expression of apple and pear fruit is accurate, building complexity of brioche and almond. Pascal Doquet releases this cuvée as both a brut and an extra brut, and the brut has the edge at the moment, lifting its lemon freshness, toning its tense, dry finish and drawing it out with outstanding persistence and elegant freshness.

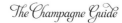

The Champagne Guide

Pascal Doquet Le Mesnil-sur-Oger Blanc de Blancs Brut NV • $$$

94 points • Disgorged November 2010 • Tasted in Brisbane

70% 2002, 30% 2001; 10% vinified in oak barrels; aged on lees in tank and barrel for 6 months and in bottle for 7 years; 7g/L dosage

With the high-strung definition of one of the finest seasons on the Côte des Blancs, and internal harmony infused by more than a decade in the cellar, this is a remarkable NV of ravishing precision. It's hardly moved since its release two years ago, holding youthful poise of white peach, grapefruit and fig, softening and slowly building complexity of spice and dried fruits. Remarkably, it hasn't yet ventured into the realm of honeyed toastiness, promising many years of life yet. Dazzling poise and energy are underlined by the inimitable chalk texture of Le Mesnil-sur-Oger.

Pascal Doquet Vielles Vignes Le Mesnil-sur-Oger Blanc de Blancs 2002 • $$$

96 points • Disgorged May 2012 • Tasted in Vertus

Vinified in tanks and 15% in oak barrels; aged 5 months in tanks and barrels on lees, and 9 years in bottle; no malolactic fermentation; 5.5g/L dosage

Doquet's oldest plots stand proud on three magnificent sites in one of Champagne's most thrilling villages. Vines date from 1929 and average 49 years of age, with roots plunging deep into solid Le Mesnil-sur-Oger chalk. This great terroir is translated with pinpoint exactness in an undercurrent of chalk minerality that is at once deep-set, while dancing through the finish graceful and light on its feet. Belying a decade of age and a touch of oak vinification, its hue is still impossibly bright and pale. Mesmerisingly youthful lemon blossom, lemon zest and freshly cut apples are preserved with breathtaking precision, only beginning to hint at preserved lemon, orange, vanilla and nutmeg. Such is its potential that it has not deviated one iota since its release two years ago, with decades of magnificent life stretching before it.

Pascal Doquet Le Mesnil-sur-Oger Blanc de Blancs Coeur de Terroir Brut 2002 • $$$

95 points • Disgorged May 2012 • Tasted in Vertus

30% vinified in oak; full malolactic fermentation; 4.5g/L dosage

Assembled in tiny volumes from four different Le Mesnil-sur-Oger sites to those that comprise Doquet's Vieilles Vignes — the thundering Chétillons, Champ d'Alouette, Finciart and Coullemets du Midi — this is a pristine expression of a splendid season, sustaining a brilliant pale to medium straw hue. Alluring poise is built on youthful character of fresh white peach, crunchy grapefruit zest and the rising complexity of preserved lemon, glacé fig, honey and layers of spice. The finish is long and creamy, defined by the inimitable voice of Le Mesnil-sur-Oger's salty chalk minerality.

PAUL BARA

(Pawl Bah-rah)

8/10

4 Rue Yvonnet 51150 Bouzy
www.champagnepaulbara.com

CHAMPAGNE

BOUZY

BRUT
GRAND CRU
100%

Paul Bara

*P*aul Bara knows Bouzy history so well he wrote the book on it. Celebrating its 180th anniversary this year, his family estate boasts 11 hectares of low-yielding grand cru vineyards on 33 parcels in the village. An annual production of 120,000 bottles embodies the characterful intensity of Bouzy pinot noir, comprising nine hectares of the estate, the remainder chardonnay. Impressive vine age averaging 35–40 years keeps yields in check and ripeness in balance. Exuberance is well toned, with freshness and vibrancy preserved by fermenting in small enamelled and stainless steel tanks, blocking malolactic fermentation and low dosages. Malic acidity is given long periods to soften, with NV cuvées relying on generous proportions of reserve wines and bottle ageing of almost three years; vintage wines at least five years. Long one of the village's great estates, the legacy lives on in the hands of Paul's daughter, Chantale. The NV cuvées are especially refined this year, charged with the splendid acid of 2008 base wines.

PAUL BARA BOUZY BRUT RÉSERVE NV • $$

95 points • Disgorged September 2012 • Tasted in Brisbane and Bouzy

50% 2008 and 50% reserve wines; 80% pinot noir, 20% chardonnay; 7g/L dosage

A remarkable release for Paul Bara, celebrating the full depth of Bouzy pinot noir in all of its wonderful splendour. A tint of salmon to its medium straw hue reflects great depth of perfectly ripe red fruits. An incredible display of fruit intensity, embracing the full spectrum of pinot noir character in black cherries, strawberries, plums, even mixed spice and plum pudding. The tremendous acid profile of the great 2008 vintage pulls everything into an impeccable finish of fine-spun malic acidity and wonderful chalk mineral texture. Thrillingly primary and enticingly moreish.

PAUL BARA GRAND ROSÉ DE BOUZY BRUT NV • $$

94 points • DISGORGED AUGUST 2012 • TASTED IN BRISBANE AND BOUZY

50% 2008 and 50% reserve wines; 80% pinot noir, 20% chardonnay; Brut Réserve with 12% pinot noir red wine; 7g/L dosage

A beautiful rosé that shines with the bright intensity of Bouzy pinot noir and the crystalline definition that characterises 2008. A small dose of 12% red wine is all it takes to generate a full crimson hue, which must make Paul Bara's red wine some of the deepest in all of Champagne. It infuses the palate with its red berry and red apple intensity and gorgeous rose petal fragrance, upholding the fresh vibrancy of 2008 in impeccable, tangy acidity, underlined by fine, chalky mineral texture.

PAUL BARA BRUT MILLESIME 2004 • $$

95 points • TASTED IN BOUZY

90% pinot noir, 10% chardonnay; 6-7g/L dosage

The bold and extroverted personality of Bouzy pinot noir is paraded in tremendous fruit intensity of red cherries, berry compote, and mixed spice, lifted by a waft of rose petal fragrance and the gleaming purity of lemon zest. The energy of the 2004 season charges lively malic acidity, toning its generosity and drawing out a finish underlined by fine, mineral texture.

PAUL BARA SPECIAL CLUB 2004 • $$$

96 points • TASTED IN BRISBANE AND BOUZY

70% pinot noir, 30% chardonnay; 6g/L dosage

Drawing vibrant energy, mineral-laden texture and impeccable control from vast, expansive fruit of old-vine Bouzy magnitude calls for quite some wizardry. Paul Bara uses a strong dose of chardonnay to counter pinot noir's exuberance, making for a refreshingly pale medium straw hue for a champagne almost a decade old. It's a powerful hit of gingernut biscuits, anise, fig, honey and red fruits of all kinds, even blackberries, blackcurrants and licorice, bathed in velvety warmth, underlined by the freshness of crunchy lemon zest and the dynamism of lively 2004 malic acidity. Achingly youthful and dynamic.

PAUL BARA SPECIAL CLUB ROSÉ 2006 • $$$

96 points • TASTED IN BOUZY

Special Club with 8% Bouzy rouge; 7g/L dosage; fewer than 2500 bottles

Taming Bouzy's extravagant fervour is an art of the highest order, and this wine is a case study in graceful strength. A monumental contrast of intensity and elegance, soaked in black cherries, pomegranate, pink pepper and pink grapefruit, pulled strictly into line by lively, taut malic acidity and well-defined chalk mineral grip. Restraint is achieved through a tiny addition of red wine, sufficient to build an impressive crimson hue. The result is enticingly generous and yet impeccably fine and fresh. A feisty enchantress.

PAUL BARA SPECIAL CLUB ROSÉ 2004 • $$$

93 points • TASTED IN BRISBANE

Special Club with 8% pinot noir red wine; 75% pinot noir, 25% chardonnay; average vine age 35 years; just 2000 bottles

A delightful rosé of sure-footed balance two years ago, but this bottle is slightly troubled. Its hue has developed to a sunburst rim and it's lost the fruit edge that flattered its earlier self. More toasty now, with a slightly contracted finish, the expansive presence of Bouzy pinot noir still asserts itself in secondary red berry fruits. Disgorgement date is uncertain, but a hard cork suggests that this could be the original 2009 disgorgement. Slightly corky; a bottle with a sound cork would likely present better.

PAUL BARA COMTESSE MARIE DE FRANCE 2000 • $$$$

95 points • TASTED IN BOUZY

100% pinot noir; 3700 bottles

With a history spanning a half-century, Paul Bara's original prestige cuvée reflects the golden glow of 2000 in deep layers of dried pear, baked apple and ripe stone fruit, evolving into brioche, vanilla, honey and spice of all kinds. Unashamedly blanc de noirs, this is purposely a richer style to Bara's Special Clubs. Well-integrated malic acidity keeps it on its toes, lending a lively grapefruit freshness and highlighting lingering chalk mineral structure.

The Champagne Guide

PAUL DÉTHUNE

(Pawl Deh-tune)

8/10

2 RUE DU MOULIN 51150 AMBONNAY
www.champagne-dethune.com

The Déthune family has tended its vines on the privileged slopes of Ambonnay since 1610. Today, the young Pierre Déthune and wife Sophie sensitively manage seven hectares of 70% pinot noir and 30% chardonnay entirely within the village. Seven cuvées draw complexity and diversity from 34 different parcels vinified separately, some in large oak foudres and small oak 'pièces' from the forests of Champagne. Their 50,000 bottles confidently express the luscious power and characterful poise of Ambonnay and quickly sell out every year.

THE DÉTHUNES EFFECTIVELY TEND THEIR VINES organically, having employed organic composts and avoiding insecticides and herbicides for 20 years, though purposely shunning organic certification over concerns surrounding copper sulphate fungicide.

'Pierre's grandfather was organic without knowing it, and 100 years later we still have copper in the vineyard from his treatments. This is not good for the vines,' Sophie explains. 'Champagne's difficult climate calls for liberal use of fungicides, particularly in wet vintages like 2012, but we do not want to use massive amounts of copper sulphate.' Pierre is instead trialling essential oils in the vineyards.

Pierre's father, Paul, introduced mechanisation in 1960. 'They had an easier job — and we are going backwards!' he exclaims, detailing the time and attention required to control grasses planted in the mid-rows

since 2001. 'We intend to leave the vineyards for the next generation, so it is important for us to preserve the environment.' Fifty-four square metres of solar panels on the roof of the 17th century buildings provide one-fifth of the winery's electricity, and rainwater services a similar proportion of water requirements.

The Déthunes are careful not to harvest too late, to hold freshness and check the exuberance of Ambonnay pinot noir. They buy two, three or four new 205-litre champagne oak barrels each year. 'We have 36 in all, and that's all we have room for!' says Sophie.

They aim to complete harvest of all 34 parcels within eight days. All are vinified separately, those destined for Brut NV in stainless steel, and reserves and other cuvées in wood. A dosage of 10g/L is used across all cuvées, suiting the strength and vitality of the house style.

Paul Déthune Brut NV • $$

93 points • Disgorged July 2012 • Tasted in Ambonnay

2009 base vintage with 25% reserves; 70% pinot noir, 30% chardonnay; vinified and aged in stainless steel tanks; 10g/L dosage; last three digits of bottle code are month and year of disgorgement

A true expression of grand cru Ambonnay pinot noir in its gorgeous roundness of plum and red cherry fruits of excellent persistence. Nutty notes and nuances of savoury spice provide complexity, lifted by a creamy bead and structured with balanced acidity and soft, gentle minerality.

Paul Déthune Brut Rosé NV • $$

94 points • Tasted in Ambonnay

2008 base vintage; 80% pinot noir, 20% chardonnay; Brut NV with 8–12% pinot noir red wine; 10g/L dosage; 4000 bottles; last three digits of bottle code are month and year of disgorgement

Déthune blends rosé from its Brut NV rather than macerating pinot noir, to retain higher acidity and freshness in its rich Ambonnay fruit. The 2008 base of Brut NV was a delightfully fresh and characterful champagne, and its rosé version captures the same mood. Its medium to full crimson hue anticipates devastating red flavours of strawberries and red cherries, lifted by rose petal perfume. An enticing undercurrent whispers with mixed spice, forest floor and a wisp of sweet pipe smoke, lingering with finely balanced tannin texture.

Paul Déthune Brut Blanc de Noirs NV • $$$

94 points • Tasted in Ambonnay

2008 base vintage; 100% pinot noir; made and aged entirely in old barrels; 10g/L dosage

Freshness rather than heaviness is Déthune's mantra for pinot noir, and 2008 furnished the lively acidity to nail this balance. It strikes a comfortable equilibrium between the generous yellow summer fruits and red berries of Ambonnay pinot noir, the spicy complexity of oak vinification, and the freshness of well-poised acidity. A mighty blanc de noirs of impressively rounded generosity and enduring persistence, perked up by a honed finish of well-defined minerality.

Paul Déthune Cuvée Prestige Brut NV • $$$

95 points • Tasted in Ambonnay

75% 2005, 25% reserve from a perpetual solera in oak vats going back 35 years; 50% pinot noir, 50% chardonnay; 10g/L dosage; 2500 bottles; last three digits of bottle code are month and year of disgorgement

More than 40 years ago, Pierre's father Paul commenced a solera to which every vintage since has contributed. The complexity that such depth of maturity contributes to a blend is mesmerising, evoking memories of dried fruits, gingerbread, butter, smoke, coffee and chocolate. One might expect a dissonance between such far-fetched exoticism and the precise, primary fruit depth of red berries and yellow plums of the 2005 vintage. The true skill of this cuvée comes first in harmonising the two seamlessly, and second in bringing poise to the ripe and too often rather clumsy 2005 vintage. This is an unusually textured wine of chewy structure, prolonged aftertaste and enchanting appeal.

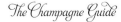
The Champagne Guide

Paul Louis Martin

(Pawl Loo-ii Mahr-tah)

3 Rue d'Ambonnay 51150 Bouzy
www.champagneplmartin.com

*P*aul Louis Martin is a 10 hectare family-owned estate established in Bouzy in 1864. It bottles young, simple and fruity expressions of the village exclusively from estate pinot noir and chardonnay, sealing them with a reliable DIAM closure. Vintage wines are rich and fleshy representations of a generous village, with plenty of firm phenolic grip.

Paul Louis Martin Brut Grand Cru NV • $

86 points • Tasted in Brisbane

60% pinot noir, 40% chardonnay; DIAM closure

A simple, young and fruity style of ripe stone fruits and citrus, with a honeyed dosage interplaying with acidity to give a sweet and sour effect. Subtle chalk minerality lends texture. It finishes short, with no apparent aged complexity.

Paul Louis Martin Grand Cru Cuvée Vincent Blanc de Blanc 2007 • $$

88 points • Tasted in Brisbane

DIAM closure

A softly generous, juicy roundness makes for a friendly blanc de blancs — an unusual cuvée for the pinot-oriented Bouzy. Summer white fruits of rich generosity meet grilled pineapple and subtle roast nut complexity, finishing with plenty of phenolic grip, medium length and integrated dosage.

PERRIER-JOUËT

(Per-riay Zhoo-ay)

5/10

23 AVENUE DE CHAMPAGNE 51201 ÉPERNAY
www.perrier-jouet.com

The past 15 years have been turbulent for Perrier-Jouët, changing hands three times before it was taken over by current owners, Pernod Ricard, in 2005. In the midst of this rollercoaster, the house has been fortunate to retain most of its vineyards, with a total of 65 hectares now providing for one-quarter of its annual production of 3 million bottles, ranking it as Champagne's tenth largest house. From its founding just over 200 years ago, the vision of the house has focused on the floral elegance of chardonnay, and today more than half of the estate's holdings lie in the Côte des Blancs, particularly in the grand crus of Cramant and Avize. Belle Epoque Blanc de Blancs, the finest creation of the house, is sourced exclusively from Cramant. Alongside similar houses, Perrier-Jouët's cuvées can appear creamy and rounded, tending to lack definition and fruit carry through the mid-palate, leaving rich, sweet dosage to dominate the finish.

SYMBOLIC OF ITS FOCUS ON CHARDONNAY'S FLORAL elegance, Perrier-Jouët's Belle Epoque flagships are presented in a distinctive, enamelled bottle of Art Nouveau Japanese anemones. The luscious branding of the house is likewise a tribute to the Art Nouveau era.

Its promotions took a new tack to celebrate its bicentenary in 2011. For a cool €10,000, a hundred wealthy individuals could purchase a 'Living Legacy' of two magnums of Perrier-Jouët's Belle Epoque 1998, one for now and one to remain in Perrier-Jouët's cellar for their heirs. Or for €50,000 they could secure a dozen Belle Epoque Blanc de Blancs with the dosage personally tweaked by Chef de Cave Hervé Deschamps to match one's personal taste.

It's all very grand, but leaves me wondering why the contents of Perrier-Jouët's bottles never quite seem to live up to the polish and glamour of their glossy exterior.

PERRIER-JOUËT GRAND BRUT NV • $$

91 points • <small>TASTED IN BRISBANE</small>

40% pinot meunier from Dizy, Damery, Venteuil, Vincelles and Vinay; 40% pinot noir from Mailly, Verzy, Aÿ, Rilly-la-Montagne and Verzennay; 20% chardonnay from Cramant, Avize, Le Mesnil-sur-Oger and Chouilly; 12–14% reserve wines; aged 3 years on lees; 10g/L dosage

Grand Brut is currently the freshest I've seen it, charged with young, lemon zest acidity, finishing crisp and softly mineral for an exuberant, pinot-led style. Its powerful red fruits burst from the glass with strawberries, raspberries and red cherries. The palate is loaded with candied red fruits, its ripeness and dosage conspiring to create a showily exuberant style, with dosage poking out a little on the end.

PERRIER-JOUËT BELLE EPOQUE 2004 • $$$$

93 points • <small>TASTED IN BRISBANE</small>

50% chardonnay from Cramant, Avize, Le Mesnil-sur-Oger and Oger; 45% pinot noir from Mailly, Aÿ and Mareuil-sur-Aÿ; 5% pinot meunier from Dizy and Venteuil; aged 6 years on lees; 9g/L dosage

To my surprise, this cuvée now looks even fresher than it did in Épernay two years ago, raising questions over the bottle that the house poured for me at that time. A core of white peach and lemon zest is bolstered with the complexity of brioche, toasted almonds and nougat. It sings with the fine chalk mineral signature of Côte des Blancs chardonnay, lingering long and true, drawn out by fine acid line. Rounded, honeyed sweetness distracts a little from the graceful refinement of 2004.

The Perrier-Jouët style derives from the magnificent chardonnay of Oger and other Côte des Blancs grand crus.

PHILIPPONNAT

(Fi-li-poh-nah)

13 RUE DU PONT BP2 51160 MAREUIL-SUR-AŸ
www.philipponnat.com

PHILIPPONNAT

CHAMPAGNE

If the finest vineyard sites are the most important asset of any Champagne house, Philipponnat is particularly privileged. Its 20 hectares of mostly pinot noir span Mareuil-sur-Aÿ, and its neighbours Aÿ, Mutigny and Avenay-Val-d'Or, but its most prized is the sun-drenched Clos des Goisses, one of the most powerful and distinctive sites in all of Champagne. The walled vineyard of 5.5 hectares lies on the east of Mareuil-sur-Aÿ at the very heart of Champagne, the juncture at which the Côte des Blancs, the Vallée de la Marne and the Montagne de Reims meet. With perfect south-facing aspect, a dramatic slope of 30–45 degrees towards the Marne, catching the sun in its full perpendicular strength, and shielded from the westerly winds, this is one of the warmest microclimates in Champagne, boasting temperatures to equal those of Burgundy. The subsoil is pure chalk, following the gradient of the hill under a thin layer of poor topsoil, so roots quickly strike chalk, pervading the wines with minerality. Mareuil-sur-Aÿ is a mere premier cru, and Clos des Goisses is perhaps the most striking case of all for a much more detailed classification of Champagne vineyards.

PHILIPPONNAT'S HOUSE STYLE IS PARTICULARLY intense, relying primarily on the power of Montagne de Reims pinot noir from south-facing estate vineyards. Additional supplies are sourced from a further 60 hectares of vineyards, particularly from the Côte des Blancs and Vallée de la Marne, and excess is purchased each vintage to permit lesser parcels to be declassified.

Yields are restricted and optimal physiological maturity is sought through slightly delayed harvests.

The opulence of Philipponnat's ripeness can be disarming, and the phenolic coarseness that this creates in many of its current vintage cuvées is disconcerting, and more pronounced than I have seen from this house before, though other commentators are somewhat more forgiving of this character than I.

Fruit of high sugar ripeness calls for winemaking processes that preserve freshness in every detail. This begins with vinification close to the vineyards in Mareuil-sur-Aÿ. When Philipponnat owners Lanson-BCC invited Charles Philipponnat to return and manage the family business in 1999, his first initiative was to construct a new winery in Mareuil-sur-Aÿ and discontinue processing in Reims.

Freshness is preserved through use of only the first pressings, cool fermentation in temperature-controlled stainless steel, blocking of malolactic fermentation in the most powerful parcels, use of a minimum of 30% chardonnay, and moderate dosage.

The strongest parcels of pinot noir and chardonnay (about 20% in all, representing 40–60% of vintage wines) are fermented in barrels, which vary between new and 5–6 years old, for complexity and oxidation. Walking into the barrel hall, the aroma of oak is intoxicating, like nowhere else in Champagne. Such is the strength of Philipponnat's bold fruit that oak flavour does not tend to dominate, though its structure can disrupt already heightened phenolic structures.

The barrel hall is climate controlled to block malolactic fermentation in every barrel. All reserve wines are matured for six months in small- and large-format oak. Reserve wines for Brut Royale are kept in a solera system of fractional blending, re-blended every year to incorporate mature wines without losing freshness. Non-vintage cuvées receive 20–30% reserve wines and are aged 3–4 years in bottle. Philipponnat

sells 600,000 bottles annually, all of which boast particularly informative back labels, declaring the date of disgorgement, the blend and dosage, and the house claims to be the first in Champagne to also indicate the base year of its blends.

The 14 Clos de Goisses parcels are vinified separately, half in tank and half in barrel, as has been tradition since 1935. The vineyard comprises about two-thirds pinot noir and one-third chardonnay, from vines aged 8–45 years, with an average of 30.

While 5.5 hectares has the capacity to produce 55,000 bottles, on average just 17,000 bottles are made annually — sometimes as few as 3000 or as many as 40,000 — with the remainder declassified into other Philipponnat cuvées. Clos des Goisses is produced every vintage, but not always released. It is testimony to the site that almost every year since 1956 has been released.

For its lofty credentials (and price to match), Clos des Goisses should consistently rank in the highest echelons of Champagne. But it never seems to rise to the heights of expectation.

PHILIPPONNAT ROYALE RÉSERVE BRUT NV • $

94 points • DISGORGED AUGUST 2012 • TASTED IN MAREUIL-SUR-AŸ

2008 base vintage with 28% reserves; 65% pinot noir, 30% chardonnay, 5% pinot meunier; 8g/L dosage

It seems preposterous that my favourite Philipponnat cuvée this year should be its bargain-priced entry wine, but such is the refreshing balance of 2008 acidity that it pulls the ripe style of the house into a wonderful place of fine-tuned balance that even its current prestige cuvées fail to emulate. The generosity of Mareuil-sur-Aÿ pinot noir leads out with fleshy peach, baked apple, honey and mixed spice, gliding into a refreshing finish of taut acidity and finely structured mineral expression. This is the best I've ever seen this cuvée.

PHILIPPONNAT NON DOSÉ ROYALE RÉSERVE NV • $$

86 points • DISGORGED OCTOBER 2012 • TASTED IN MAREUIL-SUR-AŸ

Brut Royale without dosage; 2007 base vintage with 28% reserves; 65% pinot noir, 30% chardonnay, 5% pinot meunier

This same base vintage with 8g/L dosage scored 92 points in my book last year, making the Non Dosé version a strong case for the importance of dosage and the inherent danger of making a zero-dosage champagne without designing it purposely from the ground up. Experience shows that this cuvée does not hold up well with age, and the current blend has developed quickly to a place of toasty brioche and nuts, its taut lemon juice acidity leaving the finish dry and callow.

PHILIPPONNAT BRUT RÉSERVE ROSÉE NV • $$

87 points • DISGORGED JULY 2012 • TASTED IN MAREUIL-SUR-AŸ

2007 base vintage with 24% reserves; 75% pinot noir, 20% chardonnay, 5% pinot meunier; 8% red wine; 9g/L dosage

A tiny dose of red wine is sufficient to produce a medium salmon-copper hue in this soft, creamy rosé. Secondary red fruits are already becoming savoury, finishing short and simple, with good acid definition and well-gauged dosage.

PHILIPPONNAT GRAND BLANC BRUT 2005 • $$

88 points • DISGORGED SEPTEMBER 2012 • TASTED IN MAREUIL-SUR-AŸ

Premier cru and grand cru chardonnay including some Clos des Goisses; half stainless steel, half barrel vinification; malolactic fermentation in tanks only; 5g/L dosage

The bouquet delivers lovely aromas of succulent yellow summer fruits, yellow mirabelle plums, pears and honey. The palate kicks off confident and fruity but falters on the finish, its ripe fruit lacking the stamina to pull through, finishing with firm phenolic texture, typical of 2005. Soft acidity and well-judged dosage hold their balance.

PHILIPPONNAT SUBLIME RÉSERVE SEC 2002 • $$

94 points • DISGORGED AUGUST 2010 • TASTED IN MAREUIL-SUR-AŸ

100% chardonnay; 30g/L dosage

This is a clever recipe. Philipponnat doesn't like to add a lot of sugar to create a sweet wine, instead choosing a strong base wine from a great vintage, with sufficient acidity to keep it fresh and structured. The ripe fruit style of the house lends itself particularly well to a sweet champagne, contributing lychees and nectarine to the toasty, honeyed characters of more than a decade of maturity. The palate shows a poise and balance rarely found in the often precarious realm of sweet champagne, its candied dosage pulled neatly into line by well-defined acidity and the fine, chalky minerality of 2002 chardonnay. Notes of cinnamon and cloves set off a very carefully constructed, proper sweet champagne.

PHILIPPONNAT RÉSERVE MILLÉSIMÉE 2003 • $$$

92 points • DISGORGED AUGUST 2010 • TASTED IN MAREUIL-SUR-AŸ

70% pinot noir, mostly from Aÿ and Mareuil-sur-Aÿ, 30% Côte des Blancs chardonnay; full malolactic fermentation; 5g/L dosage

Here's a surprise. Two years ago I reported that this was a balanced and well-made champagne, ageing confidently, in spite of the awkwardness of the season. It's now looking more impressive again, its fruit holding remarkably a decade after this challenging vintage. Characteristically generous 2003, it is custardy and creamy, layered with honey and dripping with ripe peach, plum, fig, pear, even fruit mince spice, and finishes with soft phenolic structure and lingering persistence. More reminiscent of a ripe white Burgundy from Meursault than a champagne, and none the less for it.

The Champagne Guide

PHILIPPONNAT CUVÉE 1522 2004 • $$$

90 points • DISGORGED SEPTEMBER 2012 • TASTED IN MAREUIL-SUR-AŸ

70% pinot noir, 30% chardonnay from grand cru vineyards; 40% oak fermented; malolactic fermentation in tanks only; 5g/L dosage

An excellent bouquet marries fresh lemon zest with the rich yellow stone fruits typical of Philipponnat. The palate is a different story, launching with crunchy nashi pear and peach, then swerving into a mid palate lacking in fruit body, and a dry, blocky, robust finish of coarse phenolic structure. For all that, its mineral presence holds confidently.

PHILIPPONNAT CUVÉE 1522 BRUT ROSÉ 2006 • $$$$

89 points • DISGORGED JULY 2012 • TASTED IN MAREUIL-SUR-AŸ

65% pinot noir, 35% chardonnay; 5% red wine; 5g/L dosage

Just a drop of red wine stains this rosé a pretty, pale salmon. A lovely bouquet sings of lifted rose petals, strawberry hull and red cherries. The palate is tight and elegant, with crisp acidity and refreshingly low dosage. The fruit lacks a little in definition and presence in the mouth, leaving the finish slightly blocky and coarse in phenolic presence.

PHILIPPONNAT CLOS DES GOISSES 2003 • $$$$$

92 points • DISGORGED AUGUST 2012 • TASTED IN MAREUIL-SUR-AŸ

65% pinot noir, 35% chardonnay; part barrel fermented; no malolactic fermentation; 4.5g/L dosage; just 7000 bottles

A powerful champagne of white Burgundian proportions, booming with intense, ripe, sweet white peach and fig, becoming spice, toffee, toast and wood smoke. Such is its thumping concentration and savoury complexity that it almost becomes meaty on the finish, rounding out soft and honeyed, with impressive persistence.

PHILIPPONNAT CLOS DES GOISSES 2002 • $$$$$

91 points • TASTED IN MELBOURNE

62% pinot noir, 38% chardonnay; 5.8g/L dosage

A voluptuous and monumentally ripe Clos des Goisses, riding the fine line between intense ripe peach and the woody core of a pineapple. This is an assertively structured Clos des Goisses that relies more on phenolic structure than acidity, toppling on the finish as phenolic grip interrupts and dries out its flow. Drink it soon, before it contracts any further.

PIERRE GIMONNET & FILS

(Pee-yair Zhi-moh-neh e Feess)

8/10

---

1 RUE DE LA RÉPUBLIQUE 51530 CUIS
www.champagne-gimonnet.com

CHAMPAGNE

Pierre Gimonnet
& Fils

'*The difference between a good wine and an exceptional wine is only a question of very, very small details, but we must focus on every detail all of the time,' declares Didier Gimonnet, who oversees his family's estate with his brother, Olivier. The champagnes of Pierre Gimonnet & Fils are intricately assembled by masterful hands exclusively from enviably positioned and painstakingly tended old vines. Every cuvée sings its aspiration of 'precision, purity and minerality', each speaking articulately of its place in the northern Côte des Blancs through expressive, chalky minerality, without one molecule of detail out of place. With high-strung tension, crystalline structure and rapier-sharp precision, these are blanc de blancs champagnes charged with an energy that will sustain them long indeed. They represent some of the best-value apéritif champagnes of all.*

'MY FATHER ALWAYS TOLD ME THE MOST IMPORTANT thing is to make wine, and after that to sell it at a reasonable price,' Gimonnet explains. From one of Champagne's most intelligent growers, wines of such purity and fine-spun, mineral-laden precision should sell for much higher prices. Little wonder Gimonnet has experienced high global demand in recent years, fully allocating its production capacity of 280,000 bottles. There is not a champagne in this collection unworthy of your table this year.

GRAND VINEYARDS

'Our champagnes have a personality because of the vineyards they come from,' Gimonnet says. 'In Champagne, as everywhere, the most important thing is the

origin of the grapes.' The family owns a substantial estate of 28 hectares, mostly proudly located in the heart of each of their village's terroirs, almost exclusively in the Côte des Blancs.

In a region afflicted with generally young vines, more than two-thirds of Gimonnet's are now over 40 years old, close to half are more than 50 and some are almost a century — incredible numbers for a region that typically replants every 35 years. Every bottle of Gimonnet comes exclusively from these vineyards; not a single grape is purchased from growers.

'When you have great terroir, it is a child's game to create a great blend,' he says. More than half of Gimonnet's vineyards are located in its premier cru home village of Cuis, which he is frank in admitting is not a great terroir. 'With less body and structure, Cuis does not have the character of a grand cru but it has higher acidity, giving us very fresh wines,' Gimonnet explains. 'Without doubt, the best of our domains are in Cramant. I compare Cramant with lace — it is precise and delicate, with an interesting, chalky minerality, and it has a concentration but is not heavy.'

One hectare in the more stony soils of Oger contributes concentrated, spicy, smoky power and graphite minerality, two recently acquired hectares in Vertus have less power but more exotic tropical fruit character, while substantial holdings in Chouilly add a fruity elegance. A little pinot noir is derived from just half a hectare, shared between Aÿ and Mareuil-sur-Aÿ.

'Fruitiness, elegance, power and minerality can therefore be determined according to the villages that we use in each blend,' Gimonnet clarifies.

UNCOMPROMISING MIXOLOGISTS

Of Gimonnet's considerable 12 hectares of grand cru holdings, three-quarters are located in the prized heart of the mid-slopes of their villages. Some in Champagne suggest that Gimonnet's blends do not do justice to the greatness of his terroirs.

In the hands of others, these holdings could yield thundering single-cru old-vine cuvées from the grand crus of Cramant, Chouilly and Oger, but to do so would deprive Gimonnet of the powerful blending material that so eloquently lifts the mood of Cuis in all but the very first of his nine blends. He singles out the strength of Oger as an exception, making it tricky to blend without dominating.

'I created a single Oger cuvée last year, as I am not clever enough to know how to blend all of it!' He defines the best terroirs as those that respect others in a blend. 'Champagne is a blend, and a grand terroir is one that can be blended without dominating,' says Gimonnet, who has been dubbed a 'mixologist'.

This blending is the key to the philosophy of the house. 'I am against monoterroir,' he says, 'but I am adept of very polished blends that combine the qualities of different terroirs to produce complexities. When I present the house I always say I'm not a winemaker, just an interpreter of the terroir'.

Gimonnet owns 12 grand cru vineyards, but does not produce a single wine that can be labelled grand cru, 'because they're better balanced when blended with premier cru parcels to confer freshness of acidity and balance between concentration, finesse and elegance,' he explains.

This is exemplified in his Special Club Cuvée 2005, one of the finest champagnes of the vintage.

The gleaming precision of Didier Gimonnet's winery is reflected in his pristine chardonnay-driven cuvées.

'The blend is the highest ideal here, more than the sum of the parts,' he explains.

His mantra is to produce the most balanced wines, not those that can be labelled to command the highest prices. A noble pursuit, rare in Champagne, and it begins in the vineyards.

METICULOUS ATTENTION TO PURITY

'The date of harvest is very, very important,' maintains Gimonnet. 'Just four days too early or too late and it will disrupt concentration, structure and elegance.'

Gimonnet prizes minerality and freshness above concentration, so does not harvest at the maximum maturity, but at the optimum level of ripeness to give a good balance of alcohol potential and high acidity. To achieve this, yields are moderated to around 11–12 tonnes/hectare (equating to about 75hL/hectare), compared with a potential of 18–20 tonnes.

The goal of every stage of vinification is to preserve purity, freshness and minerality with the utmost precision. Gimonnet's winery is a pristine declaration of this mandate, a bathroom-fresh environment of floor-to-ceiling tiles and gleaming stainless steel. 'It is like cooking,' he suggests. 'To create purity you must have the freshest ingredients.'

With 90% of vineyards within four kilometres of the house, all grapes are pressed within six hours of harvest. Gimonnet presses more lightly than most, so of the little he harvests he extracts even less juice, but juice of finer quality. As at Billecart-Salmon and Pol Roger, the juice is clarified at 10°C for 24 hours prior to fermentation, a crucial procedure for the refined elegance of the style. Selected yeast is then added to achieve a rapid start to fermentation.

'My goal is to have the juice in fermentation less than two days after picking, and this is very important for maintaining purity and freshness.' Fermentation and maturation take place only in temperature-controlled stainless steel tanks. 'Our grapes come from good terroirs and we want no other taste than that of the fruit in our wine.' The tendency of Cuis chardonnay to oxidise quickly in tank dictates that reserve wines are instead kept on fine lees in bottle under crown seal, allowing them to mature and develop body, while retaining purity and freshness, without evolving too rapidly. An unusual and painstaking process, it takes six people to open 10,000 bottles a day.

Malolactic fermentation is employed in all wines to soften the high acidity of Cuis. A light dosage of 8g/L of sugar is used, as little as 5g/L in the vintage cuvées, and there is no impression of sweetness. 'Dosage is very important to avoid angular wines without introducing the taste of sugar,' Gimonnet explains. He considers it crucial to oxidise the liquor before adding it to the bottle. 'It seems like nothing, but it makes a subtle difference to the taste.'

Timing of disgorgement is likewise given careful consideration, with every bottle freshly disgorged to order. Disgorgement dates are printed on bottles sent to countries that request them, including the US and Italy. 'The date of disgorgement is very important in champagne,' Gimonnet points out. 'A cuvée is very different six months after disgorgement than it is two years after disgorgement.' More than half of Gimonnet's non-vintage cuvées are sealed with reliable Mytik DIAM closures, as his trials have found these to preserve freshness more reliably than natural cork.

Enviable vineyards and meticulous practices stir strong demand, and Gimonnet has been working to increase production to keep up. Not as easy as it sounds, according to Gimonnet. 'We don't want to be wine merchants by buying grapes to increase production,' he emphasises. 'We don't want to make volume, we want to make the quality that we like and then offer it on allocation. We therefore need to buy vineyards with the potential of our style. But there are not many vineyards on the market, and when they are they are too expensive.' Over the past eight years, five hectares have been purchased in the Côte des Blancs to increase production by about 50,000 bottles.

Gimonnet's cuvées boast handsome new livery, with smaller, more distinctive and more refined labels, matching the mood of some of the Côte des Blancs' best buys this year.

The village of Cuis produces chardonnay of elegant freshness, bolstered by the depth of grand crus in Gimonnet's blends.

The Champagne Guide

Pierre Gimonnet & Fils Brut 1er Cru Cuis Blanc de Blancs NV • $

93 points • 80% 2010, 9.8% 2009, 4.2% 2008, 5% 2007, 1% 2002; 7.5g/L dosage; 143,000 bottles • Tasted in Cuis

92 points • 72% 2008, 13.3% 2007, 3.3% 2006, 7.5% 2005, 3.9% 2004; disgorged June 2010; 7g/L dosage; 200,000 bottles • Tasted in Brisbane

100% Cuis; 20% reserve wines; full malolactic fermentation; aged 2 years on lees

A merry celebration of the freshness of Cuis, the quintessential apéritif and one of the most pristine champagnes for its price. Impeccable phenolic maturity without high sugar levels in 2010, made for one of Cuis' great vintages. It sings with crystalline purity of lemon blossom, lemon juice and grapefruit, and an almond nut maturity providing a sense of dimension. Gentle chalk minerality and beautifully integrated dosage linger with outstanding persistence. The 2008 base still holds impressive freshness, with rising almond complexity, just beginning to fade.

Pierre Gimonnet & Fils Brut Selection Belles Années 1er Cru Blanc de Blancs NV • $

93 points • 21% 2009, 34% 2007, 45% 2006; 35.1% Cuis, 33.7% Chouilly, 15.5% Cramant, 12.7% Oger, 3% Vertus; 8g/L dosage; 12,400 bottles; DIAM closure • Tasted in Cuis

93 points • 85% 2007, 15% 2006; disgorged July 2010; 33.3% Chouilly, 30.3% Cuis, 20% Cramant, 16.4% Oger; full malolactic fermentation; aged 3 years in bottle; 8g/L dosage; 35,000 bottles • Tasted in Brisbane

A blend of 'Beautiful Years' of Gastronome in a style of greater power and complexity, led by a high proportion of grand crus. Purposely less fresh and more polished, accessible and food-friendly, it carries a 'petite mousse' of 4.5 atmospheres instead of the usual 5–6. A four-fifths majority of reserve wines balances the lesser 2009 season, making for a powerful Belles Années of ripe peach, preserved lemon, baked apple and mixed spice flavours. A touch of oxidative complexity gives maturity to a long, dry finish, upholding the salty mineral signature of the house. The 2007 base was a tighter-coiled blend on release two years ago, and still retains its zing of fresh lemon zest, while building almond nougat complexity.

Pierre Gimonnet & Fils Gastronome 1er Cru Blanc de Blancs Cuvée 2008 • $$

95 points • Tasted in Cuis

43% Chouilly for fruit and elegance, 29% Cuis for vivacity and freshness, 16% Oger for masculine structure and spicy minerality, 7.5% Cramant for plumpness, 4% Vertus for exotic fruit; full malolactic fermentation; 'petite mousse' of 4.5 atmospheres; 7g/L dosage; 33,066 bottles

Gastronome 2008 is like stepping outside and inhaling a breath of brisk winter morning air, such is its youthful freshness and breathtaking delicacy. It's delightfully coiled and focused, with airy high notes of lemon blossom, white peach and a hint of almond. A mouthful of shattering chalk minerality and unnerving texture articulates the voice of the northern Côtes des Blancs. Alongside 2002, 2008 is Gimonnet's standout vintage of the past decade, honing an elegantly refined champagne of the highest order, to partner only with the subtlest of flavours.

Pierre Gimonnet & Fils Rosé de Blancs 1er Cru NV • $$

94 points • Tasted in Cuis

12% Bouzy pinot noir and 88% Côte des Blancs chardonnay, from the same blend as the Gastronome cuvee: 33% Chouilly (mostly Mont Aigu) for fruit and elegance, 21.5% Cramant for plumpness, 8.8% Oger for masculine structure and spicy minerality, 15% Cuis for vivacity and freshness, 9.8% Vertus for exotic fruit; aged in bottle 18 months; 7g/L dosage; 9872 bottles; DIAM closure

Gimonnet has burst into the world of rosé with a cracking and cleverly named cuvée true to the fresh, crisp style of the house. It's blanc de blancs stained super pale salmon with a dash of pinot noir, purchased from a grower, because Gimonnet's vines aren't up to making red wine. It upholds its mantra of sustaining the mouthfeel, persistence and minerality of the Côte des Blancs with great accomplishment. Classic Gimonnet elegance is touched with the lightest reflections of red cherries and strawberry hull, lifted with pretty rose petal notes. Delightfully restrained, refreshingly tense and consummately mineral — the ultimate apéritif rosé.

Pierre Gimonnet & Fils Gastronome 1er Cru Blanc de Blancs 2006 • $$

93 points • Disgorged June 2010 • Tasted in Brisbane

45% Chouilly for fruity elegance, 19% Cramant for plumpness, 16% Oger for power, 20% Cuis for vivacity and freshness; full malolactic fermentation; 'petite mousse' of 4.5 atmospheres; 7g/L dosage; 37,000 bottles

An old disgorgement still sitting around on the shelves three years after disgorgement. It's lost the racy flamboyancy of its youth, having attained an appealing point in its evolution where flinty reduction perfectly harmonises with primary lemon and grapefruit citrus and slowly evolving toasty/nutty maturity. It's bang-on for drinking right now, underlined by soft, fine minerality that lingers evenly through a long finish.

Pierre Gimonnet & Fils Cuvée Fleuron Brut 1er Cru Blanc de Blancs 2006 • $$

94 points • Tasted in Cuis

39% Cramant, 36% Chouilly, 8% Oger, 17% Cuis; aged on lees in bottle at least 5 years; 6g/L dosage; 43,000 bottles

'Fleuron' means 'best of', created when there was only one non-vintage and one vintage wine in the house. Today it's Gimonnet's signature vintage cuvée, a blend of the best parcels from each village, boasting more than four-fifths grand cru Côte des Blancs, a preposterous proportion for a wine of this price. Gimonnet's goal here is to capture the taste of the domaine in a single blend. The 2006 season furnished a very complete style, permitting a higher proportion of Cramant. It encapsulates the wonderful persistence and elegant minerality of Gimonnet within an expressive and fruit-focused style. Star fruit, pear, apple and spice leap out of the glass and coast their way through a pure, Cramant-led, white-fruited palate that swoops into a taut finish, commanded by deep-set chalky minerality.

PIERRE GIMONNET & FILS FLEURON BRUT 1ER CRU BLANC DE BLANCS BRUT 2005 • $$

93 points • TASTED IN BRISBANE

45% Chouilly, 24% Cuis, 23% Cramant, 8% Oger; full malolactic fermentation; aged in bottle at least 4 years; 6g/L dosage; 55,000 bottles

Gimonnet was astute in employing a higher dose of structured Chouilly to temper the power of the rich, ripe 2005 vintage. It's a credit to the exacting attention of the domain and its magnificent fruit sources that this vintage can look every bit as fine two years after release as it did the day it landed. Its pale straw hue is testimony to its vibrancy, retaining intense lemon and grapefruit, with rising preserved lemon and almond complexity. It carries more evenly through the finish than most in this season, its soft, salty, chalky minerality remains prominent, and it's far from the end of its life yet.

PIERRE GIMONNET & FILS CUVÉE PARADOXE 1ER CRU 2007 • $$

91 points • TASTED IN CUIS

52% pinot noir (39% Aÿ, 13% Mareuil-sur-Aÿ); 48% chardonnay (14.7% Chouilly, 13% Mareuil-sur-Aÿ, 10.5% Cramant, 6.3% Cuis, 3.5% Oger); aged 4 years in bottle; 8g/L dosage; 6092 bottles

Gimonnet is very selective in the years in which it produces Paradoxe, with no release from 2005, 2009 or 2010. Didier admits that the long ripening cycle of 2007 lacked structure and complexity, so attempted to compensate with a higher proportion of chardonnay than usual, which he confesses was a mistake. The result is less complex, less structured and less acidic than usual. Instead, this is a fresh and immediate style of expressive red cherries and strawberries, with a refined tail of red apples, pears and mixed spice; ready to drink right away.

PIERRE GIMONNET & FILS SPECIAL CLUB BLANC DE BLANCS 2005 • $$

96 points • TASTED IN CUIS

57% Cramant (including 26% from 1911–1913 plantings), 30% Chouilly, 13% Cuis; blend of old vines, aged 40–90 years, from the core of each terroir; aged in bottle more than 5 years; 6g/L dosage; 25,400 bottles

It takes a tough season to truly define a great estate, and Gimonnet's Special Club is one of Champagne's finest expressions of the sunny and structured 2005 vintage — all the more noble at the top end of Special Club production volumes. Didier Gimonnet is justly proud of the balance he has upheld in this powerful vintage, which he admits was a challenge to blend. His Special Club philosophy is that it should be more than the sum of its parts, built on old-vine Cramant for structure, balanced with the silkiness of Chouilly, Mont Aigu and Cuis. He has captured a purity and a graceful line that transcend the natural concentration and formidable structure of the season. Elegant white summer fruits, apple and pear are refined by tightly honed lemon fruit of airy delicacy. Wonderful layers of dazzling, fine-strung mineral chalk build a deep, enduring and all-pervading structure that propagates through a finish of unmitigated persistence. A thrilling champagne by any standard, a triumph of 2005, a true prestige cuvée — and preposterously affordable.

PIERRE GIMONNET & FILS CUVÉE PARADOXE 1ER CRU BRUT 2006 • $$

94 points • DISGORGED JULY 2010 • TASTED IN BRISBANE

66% pinot noir (35% Aÿ, 31% Mareuil-sur-Aÿ), 34% chardonnay (9% Mareuil-sur-Aÿ, 5.5% Cuis, 10% Cramant, 7.5% Chouilly, 2% Oger); full malolactic fermentation; aged on lees in stainless steel vats for 6 months and in bottle for 4 years; 7g/L dosage; 7700 bottles

The paradox is that Gimonnet has allowed a red grape into his white cellar, and it's testimony to his dexterity that this outstanding vintage has retained impressive stamina three years on from its disgorgement. The fresh strawberries, red berries, vibrant lemon and grapefruit of its youth are still out to play, maintaining elegant fruit flow of even line and wonderful persistence, ever supported by finely chalky mineral texture. This may not be the ultimate Paradoxe, but it certainly ranks among the best. One bottle opened was oxidised and prematurely developed.

PIERRE GIMONNET & FILS EXTRA BRUT CUVÉE OENOPHILE 1ER CRU BLANC DE BLANCS NON DOSÉ 2005 • $$

90 points • TASTED IN CUIS

2005 Fleuron without dosage; 45% Chouilly, 24% Cuis, 23% Cramant, 8% Oger; aged in bottle more than 6 years; zero dosage; 13,000 bottles

Didier Gimonnet's sincerity is refreshing. 'I am not a lover of champagne without dosage, as dosage is part of the tradition of our region, and even 4–5g/L rounds out the wine. Wine without dosage is interesting when it's recently disgorged, but when I pull them out of the cellar 18 months later I always prefer the same wine with a little dosage to add complexity and balance.' Nonetheless, sales of his zero-dosage Oenophile are on the rise. This is not a dedicated blend, but chosen from the cellar each year according to which cuvée has the natural balance to stand best without dosage. The rounded nature of Fleuron works well in 2005, leading out honed and refreshing, with building complexity of toast, roast nuts, vanilla and nutmeg. It finishes taut, dry and slightly astringent, with good persistence and pronounced salty mineral texture.

PIERRE GIMONNET & FILS MILLESIME DE COLLECTION BLANC DE BLANCS 2005 • $$$

96 points • DISGORGED NOVEMBER 2012 • TASTED IN CUIS

Same as Special Club 2005, bottled in magnum for a later release

Gimonnet says his wines always appear more elegant from magnum and retain their freshness more evenly as they mature. Bottled on the same day as Special Club 2005, but with less oxygen transfer per unit volume, the Blanc de Blancs expresses a more reductive personality of struck-flint aroma, despite his best efforts to aerate the still wine in tank prior to bottling. This reductive character is endearing, emphasising spicy grapefruit notes, making the palate more expressive and more pronounced in its minerality.

PIERRE PÉTERS

(Pee-yair Peh-tair)

9/10

26 RUE DES LOMBARDS 51190 LE MESNIL-SUR-OGER
www.champagne-peters.com

PROPRIÉTAIRE-RÉCOLTANT

Very few champagnes more eloquently articulate their terroirs than those of Pierre Péters. On my first encounter with the young Rodolphe Péters, three hours exploring the fruits of three decades left me mesmerised by the remarkable capacity of the chardonnay vine to extract the salty minerality of the Côte des Blancs' finest grand crus and preserve it in its wines for time eternal. I left with the realisation of another dimension to champagne, one in which minerality assumes a personality all of its own. And I discovered Les Chétillons, the Le Montrachet of Le Mesnil-sur-Oger.

THE PÉTERS FAMILY HAS TENDED ITS VINES IN LE Mesnil-sur-Oger for six generations, and made its own champagne since 1919. Today, the estate is the custodian of just over 18 hectares of well-placed vineyards spanning 63 plots in the finest grand crus of the Côte des Blancs, Oger, Cramant, Avize and, especially, Le Mesnil-sur-Oger.

ATTENTIVE VINEYARD CARE
Rodolphe Péters took control in 2008, but has been helping his father with the blending since 1994, and knows his vines as well as anyone in Champagne. I quickly discovered just how well when I first met him in late July 2011, four weeks before harvest, when he was about to depart for holidays.

'Everyone says I am a crazy man taking holidays until August 19, but I wrote in my book in May that we would begin harvest on August 23, 24 or 25 and I have not revised this since.' A remarkable insight

in one of Champagne's most erratic years, in which others extended their projections by as much as four weeks. 'That's crazy,' he says, 'but I spend more time than any of them in my land.'

Péters' vines are lavished some of the most attentive care in all of Champagne. 'I am reluctant to walk in the vines for fear of crushing the chalk,' he says. I have never heard this from any other grower, but there are few other places that enjoy such ready access to chalk, just 10–30 centimetres below the surface in Le Mesnil-sur-Oger. For this reason, deep roots to access the minerality of the chalk are not the priority for Péters.

'Minerality deep in the chalk is not accessible to the plants, but the interface between the topsoil and the deep soil is where the roots are able to find it,' he explains. The role of micro-organisms and worms in mixing the deeper soils and making this minerality available to the roots is crucial, and he works hard to keep the soil alive with organic material. Grass is acidity.' He considers pH, rather than acidity, to be the best indicator of balance, always aiming for low pH as a sign that he has captured the minerality of the soil.

The racy acidity of Péters' cuvées has traditionally been softened by full malolactic fermentation, but since Rodolphe has been in command, he has selectively blocked malolactic in some tanks.

FORGOTTEN RESERVE

To preserve character and maintain freshness, Péters presses slowly in a modern pneumatic press, protects the juice from oxygen at all times, and ferments in small stainless steel tanks under temperature control.

He considers structure and freshness to be derived from a combination of minerality, acidity and 'pleasant bitterness' derived from lees contact, and hence keeps wines on gross lees for long periods after alcoholic fermentation. The presence of gross lees keeps the wines fresh, permitting a low level of sulphur dioxide as a preservative.

Péters was concerned about the tendency of reserve wines to lose their freshness over time, necessitating use of the best wines as reserves, rather than in vintage and prestige cuvées. This led to a radical reinvention of the non-vintage blend in 1997. Every reserve wine, spanning 1988 to 1996, was blended into a modified solera which became the ongoing reserve, topped up every year, except in 1999 and 2003, which were kept separate to preserve the purity of the reserve. Kept on fine lees in stainless steel tank at 13–14°C, the process of refreshing each year keeps the reserve lively. In 2011, a sample up to and including the 2010 vintage amazed me that a wine of such complexity could still retain such purity of grapefruit and preserved lemon.

This reserve solera embodies Péters' philosophy of keeping the memory of the estate alive in his Cuvée de Réserve Blanc de Blancs Brut NV, which claims a generous 40% reserve wine. His aim is to showcase the terroir of grand cru blanc de blancs, achieved with 60% of the current vintage from 50 plots spanning all of his Côte des Blancs estate vineyards, including Les Chétillons.

'The reserve is the key to the quality, making it easy to maintain consistency,' he says. It's a genius concept, and this cuvée is consistently one of the most precise for its price. Such is the class of the reserve that he has released it as its own cuvée for the first time this year, aptly named La Réserve Oubliée — 'the forgotten reserve'.

Cuvée de Réserve and Péters' vintage blend L'Esprit draw estate chardonnay from across the Côte des Blancs' grand crus. 'I like to think of each of the villages in colours,' Péters explains.

Sunrise at Pierre Péters, one of the most terroir-focused growers in the grand cru of Le Mesnil-sur-Oger.

planted in the mid-rows to provide competition for surface roots, forcing them down to the interface with the chalk.

He is adamant that he cannot keep his soils alive using certified organics. 'My philosophy is to follow the best procedures of the best of all philosophies,' he says, comparing the health of his vines with his own health, treating his allergies with a mixture of conventional medicine, vitamins and homeopathy. 'My first responsibility is to take care of my workers, the first people in contact with the chemicals I use, and by protecting them, I naturally take care of my customers, the vines and the environment.' His soil analyses have revealed high levels of copper sulphate from years of treatment by previous generations, detrimental to the soil but permitted under biodynamics. He instead relies mainly on conventional treatments to protect his vineyards.

A natural balance is achieved in the vineyards, thanks to the regulating effect of old vines (now averaging 30 years of age) and competition from grasses in the mid-rows. 'The fashion now is to say low yields and high maturity, but Champagne was not built on this — it was built on a comfortable balance of production to achieve the correct level of ripeness and

The Champagne Guide

'Le Mesnil-sur-Oger is grey for its chalkiness and stony character, and its strength of less ripe citrus and lack of creaminess. Oger is white for its light, elegant, white citrus blossom, pear, apple and white peach.

'Avize is yellow or orange for its full-bodied ripe citrus of grapefruit, orange, tangerine and apricot: less mineral, stony, chalky and elegant, but more graphite in its structure. Cramant is brown for its complexity of sweet spices, cinnamon, dried flowers and dried tea.

'I have parcels that really express each of these characters and I focus on these for my vintage blend. If a vintage expresses more yellow, orange and brown, it is released as a vintage wine, but if it is more grey and white I blend it as a non-vintage extra brut,' says Péters.

THE LE MONTRACHET OF LE MESNIL

Not far from the village itself, Les Chétillons is one of the finest sites for sparkling winegrowing in Le Mesnil-sur-Oger or, indeed, anywhere on earth. Here the chalk is never more than 10 centimetres from the surface, so the vines are effectively rooted in pure chalk. In slope and exposition, Péters describes it as perfect — not too much and not too little.

The family has nurtured three plots in these calcareous soils since 1930, with vines now an impressive 48 and 69 years old. Each has been vinified separately and blended to produce a single-vintage wine since 1971. This history has created a resource of 'human knowledge' that Péters identifies as the final element of terroir. 'All three plots are planted from our family "seléction massale", a mass selection of clones. Some clones perform better in some seasons than others, so this selection will always produce a wine of balance.'

Péters regards it as his next challenge to identify each of the expressions of his 'seléction massale'. He speaks enthusiastically of the terroirs, vintages and techniques of Burgundy.

'In Burgundy they know much more about their soils than in Champagne, and now they are learning more about their "matériaux végétales" (plant materials). In Champagne we are behind. My family knows our soils, so now we must learn about our matériaux végétales. I think we can achieve the same in Champagne as they have in vineyards like Clos des Lambrays and Clos de Tart in Burgundy,' he aspires.

He speaks of the minerality of Les Chétillons as crushed oyster shells, sea salt, and flavours of the ocean that laid down the chalk millennia ago. 'If you taste a stone in the vineyard, it is salty,' he explains, and it is this that infuses the mineral texture in his wines.

When he produced vintage after vintage from 2012 vins clairs and bottles right back to 1985, a profound picture of the mesmerising minerality of this extraordinary site emerged. Through changes of season and winemaker, flavours evolved, intensity built and bubbles faded, but the minerality remained transfixed. 'It is a stake, it stays for a very long time,' he declares.

Such is the demand for Péters' wines that he is not able to offer every cuvée in every market. He is very concerned that his annual production of 160,000 bottles is no longer able to meet the demand of his loyal customers. 'I try my best to purchase more vineyards and I cross my fingers that I might be able to secure another two hectares in Oger and Avize. But two hectares is nothing in terms of increasing production. And it will cost €3 million.'

PIERRE PÉTERS CUVÉE DE RÉSERVE BLANC DE BLANCS BRUT NV • $$

94 points • 2010 BASE VINTAGE • TASTED IN LE MESNIL-SUR-OGER
95 points • 2009 BASE VINTAGE • TASTED IN ADELAIDE

60% current vintage, 40% reserve solera from 18 vintages; grand cru Côte des Blancs; 6–7g/L dosage; DIAM closure

With all the theatrics of Péters' masterful reserve solera, this is one of the best-value apéritifs in all of Champagne. Effortlessly integrated, ravishingly poised and incisively soil-driven, it's a wine of pronounced minerality and seamless fruit purity. The 2009 base dutifully follows the great 2008 with its pristine lemon and grapefruit, hints of fennel, wonderful mineral precision and crystalline freshness. The 2010 changes down a gear, presenting the more generous pear and apple fruits of the vintage, yet as clean and tight as ever — a grand monument to the signature chalk minerality of the Côte des Blancs.

Pierre Péters Cuvée La Réserve Oubliée Blanc de Blancs Brut NV • $$

95 points • Tasted in Le Mesnil-sur-Oger

Modified solera blend of 18 vintages spanning 1988 through 2007, missing only the inferior 1999 and 2003; dosage from grape juice aged in a small barrel, the only oak in the estate; DIAM closure

Péters is rightly proud of his Réserve Oubliée ('Forgotten Reserve') and offers a taste to visitors to the estate. Forgotten no more, he has bottled it for the first time for the world to admire. Few reserves can boast such ravishing integration, seamless internal harmony and sheer completeness, a credit to both the genius of this modified solera and the painstakingly tended vines that feed it. The contrast of eminent refinement and bewildering complexity is other-worldly, broadcasting lively freshness of pear and apple, set against a layered backdrop of mixed spice and honey. Wonderfully persistent and exquisitely refreshing.

Pierre Péters Cuvée Rosé for Albane Brut NV • $$

95 points • Tasted in Le Mesnil-sur-Oger

7–8g/L dosage; Le Mesnil-sur-Oger chardonnay blended with a saignée of Damery and Cumières pinot meunier; DIAM closure

Eight years ago, Péters discovered a rosé saignée of pinot meunier by a grower in Damery and Cumières, and was intrigued to find it tasted more like pink grapefruit than red berries — a style he felt would marry particularly well with the yellow citrus of a more fruity parcel of his Le Mesnil-sur-Oger chardonnay. It inspired him to create a rosé of deep colour and flavour, rather than a white champagne with colour. His most recent blend meets the brief with breathtaking precision. A bright, medium salmon-pink hue announces euphoric freshness of rose petal, pink pepper and rosehip, underlined by fine, chalky minerality. A delightfully elegant rosé of pinpoint clarity and radiant persistence.

Pierre Péters Cuvée Spéciale Blanc de Blancs Les Chétillons 2006 • $$$

96 points • Disgorged November 2012 • Tasted in Le Mesnil-sur-Oger

100% malolactic fermentation; 4g/L dosage

Tasted just six weeks post-disgorgement, 2006 Les Chétillons won't see the light of day until 2014. A ripe, sunny vintage makes this a generous Les Chétillons, reportedly not a simple wine to blend, with 10–12% rot in the fruit, which Péters says is sometimes good for complexity and sweet spice flavours. At this early age, this is not a wine that reveals itself readily, and it appreciates some time to unravel. When it does, it reveals bold strokes of white peach, pear, apple, fig, even touches of coffee, which Rodolphe says is classic of Le Mesnil. The fine, salty minerality of the site is all-conquering, defining a finish of clean, taut balance.

The Champagne Guide

Pierre Péters Cuvée Spéciale Blanc de Blancs Les Chétillons 2005 • $$$

95 points • Disgorged April 2012 • Tasted in Le Mesnil-sur-Oger

4g/L dosage

True to this warm and ripe vintage, this is an exuberant and earlier-drinking Les Chétillons of generous fruit depth of yellow summer fruits and lemon zest. A dry, structured 2005 vintage finish does little to perturb the bracing mineral fingerprint of this inimitable site, drawing the finish all the way to the horizon.

Pierre Péters Cuvée Spéciale Blanc de Blancs Les Chétillons 2004 • $$$

97 points • Disgorged April 2011 • Tasted in Adelaide

4.5g/L dosage; a large production of 12,000 bottles, but in some years just 4000

Les Chétillons 2004 articulates its mineral birthplace with greater expression than I have tasted anywhere in Champagne outside the thundering single vineyards of Krug itself. Two years after release, perfectly honed lemon zest and preserved lemon are transfixed in time like an ice man, supported by a slowly rising undercurrent of honey, brioche and nougat, accented with notes of gun smoke and oyster shells. Salty, chalky minerality rises like a tidal wave above it all, filling the mouth with strength and texture, but at every moment dizzyingly fine, silky and caressing. This infuses the palate with focused linearity and an inherent internal harmony, lacing everything together with gripping persistence. To achieve such confident fruit persona and mineral expression in a season as high-yielding as this only adds to the intrigue of one of the greatest expressions of 2004 yet released.

Pierre Péters Cuvée Spéciale Blanc de Blancs Les Chétillons 2002

96 points • Disgorged April 2012 • Tasted in Le Mesnil-sur-Oger

2g/L dosage

It was the 2002 that first put Les Chétillons on the world map, and it's even more exhilarating today than the moment it first wowed the world, with an incredible future stretching out long before it. It's surfaced from 13 years under the earth with a glow-in-the-dark brilliance to its pale straw-yellow hue. Taut and refined, and at the same time creamy and succulent, riding the line between great purity of white peach, fig, star fruit and orange and slowly rising complexity of butter, dried peach and truffle. Minerality rises above its fruit, with a silky chalk presence that hovers like a still morning mist over deep-set salty texture.

PIERRE PÉTERS CUVÉE SPÉCIALE BLANC DE BLANCS LES CHÉTILLONS 2000

97 points • DISGORGED IN 2011 • TASTED IN LE MESNIL-SUR-OGER

5g/L dosage

Les Chétillons 2000 seems to transcend the very passage of time itself, evolving in freeze-frame slow motion and consistently trumping the superior season of 2002. A wine of unnerving energy and immaculate poise, projecting an aura of gleaming citrus freshness, becoming preserved lemon and quince. Subtle hints of smoke, coffee, green olives and chocolate are gathering. The inimitable minerality of Les Chétillons is detailed, mouth-embracing, permeating every crevice. This will be the first Les Chétillons to be late-released as an oenothèque, originally due out in 2015, but after the surprise freshness of this bottle, Péters is now considering holding it back longer. When it does finally emerge, be sure to be first in line. I'll see you there.

PIERRE PÉTERS CUVÉE SPÉCIALE BLANC DE BLANCS LES CHÉTILLONS 1996

99 points • DISGORGED IN 2001 • TASTED IN LE MESNIL-SUR-OGER

The enduring ability of the very greatest champagnes to unravel over a lifetime is epitomised in no village more resoundingly than Le Mesnil-sur-Oger, and in no vintage more emphatically than 1996. Even in this inimitable place, few sites are infused with the stamina of Les Chétillons. My first encounter with this wine was such a profound experience of chalk minerality that it became one of the few times that I have ever gone back to retaste a wine obliterated by cork taint, my greatest champagne disappointment of 2011. Peters' policy of never opening a second bottle of a corked wine kept me in suspense for two years. The wine is an epiphany, a monument to the stamina of this cuvée even 12 years after an early disgorgement. It's entered the glorious prime of its life, yet holds a seemingly limitless reserve of energy to thrust it upward for many years yet. Every element is perfectly integrated, like a choral effect in which individual voices are lost. Concentrate hard and you'll hear soprano top notes of fresh lemon and lime, alto tones of preserved lemon and roast almonds, and the rumbling depths of baritone coffee and green olives. Its length is in another league, navigating undeterred for minutes, propelled by chalky minerality that shimmers like jet exhaust.

PIERRE PÉTERS CUVÉE SPÉCIALE BLANC DE BLANCS LES CHÉTILLONS 1986

98 points • DISGORGED IN 1995 • TASTED IN LE MESNIL-SUR-OGER

8g/L dosage

With exotic flavours from a rich, sunny season, Les Chétillons 1986 was overshadowed by 85, 88, 89 and 90, and it was assumed it could not age, so it was disgorged for Rodolphe's wedding in 1995 and 500 bottles were consumed! A few bottles remaining to this day evidence its startling longevity, upholding a core of glacé peach, preserved lemon, lemon tea and honey, overlaid with captivating tertiary development of truffles, smoke, pepper, green olives, coffee and even chocolate. Effortless poise and enduring persistence of lingering fruit is transcendental for a wine of this maturity, eclipsed only by its unrelenting chalk mineral texture. After 27 years the mineral signature of Les Chétillons has all the clarity that it articulates in brand-new vins clairs, permeating the wine with chalky sea salt and oyster shell notes that heave and froth with the waves of the ocean that created this remarkable place 55 million years ago.

PIPER-HEIDSIECK

(Pee-per E-dseek)

5/10

12 Allée du Vignoble 51055 Reims

www.piper-heidsieck.com

first visited Piper-Heidsieck more than a decade ago, and left more than a little bemused by its Disney-like automated tour. Thank goodness it is no more. Piper-Heidsieck has come a long way since then, transformed by champagne genius Daniel Thibault from an austere non-malolactic to a more appealing malolactic style, relying on pinot meunier to bring roundness to the blend, and now on the rise again with increases in quality and price under Thibault's friend and colleague, talented Chef de Cave Régis Camus. Sales of 4.4 million bottles in 2012 elevated Piper to Champagne's eighth largest house and third largest exporter. Created alongside Charles Heidsieck, there is an elegance to Piper's vintage cuvées that distinguishes them from the Charles style (see page 96). Vivacity and tenacity are the goals for Piper's bright, fruity style, though a broad sweep of 11g/L dosage across the range can look a little obvious.

PIPER-HEIDSIECK CUVÉE BRUT NV • $

91 points • TASTED IN BEZANNES, SYDNEY AND BRISBANE

Both 2009 and 2008 base vintages tasted; 55% pinot noir, 30% pinot meunier, 15% chardonnay; 15% reserve wines from 3–4 vintages; 100 villages; matured at least 24 months on lees; 11g/L dosage

Fresh, lively, fruity and precise, Piper is reliable champagne at a great price, making it perfect for weddings, parties, anything. Such is its consistency that I can't pick the 2009 base blend from the 2008. Both are laced with red apple, grapefruit and lemon zest, with notes of toasted almonds. Honeyed dosage, subtle minerality and bright acidity work together in equal measure. A touch of phenolic texture makes for a style to tuck into while it's still young and fresh. Also available in raunchy skin-tight red leather livery, if you're into that kind of thing.

PIPER-HEIDSIECK ROSÉ SAUVAGE BRUT NV • $$

92 points • 2008 BASE VINTAGE • TASTED IN BEZANNES
91 points • 2007 BASE VINTAGE • TASTED IN SYDNEY

Piper-Heidsieck Cuvée Brut with 20% pinot noir red wine; 55% pinot noir, 25% pinot meunier, 20% chardonnay; 15% reserve wines; 11g/L dosage

Piper's gaudy pink label bears no resemblance to the full crimson hue of the wine within. This is an intentionally deep-coloured rosé of well-defined expression of fresh raspberry and strawberry fruit in the 2008 base, and intense blood orange and pomegranate in the 2007. The 2008 is a refreshing and texturally appealing style of fine, soft tannins meshing confidently with soft minerality. The 2007 is bolder in impact, with dosage more apparent on the finish. Both close a little short. Drink them from red wine glasses, as they do at the house.

PIPER-HEIDSIECK CUVÉE SUBLIME DEMI-SEC NV • $$

86 points • TASTED IN BEZANNES

Aged 36 months on lees; 40g/L dosage

A fully sweet demi-sec of candied fruits, honey, a hint of caramel and a note of grapefruit zest. Insufficient acidity to support this level of dosage leaves the finish soft, sweet and simple, with the chewy texture of phenolic grip.

PIPER-HEIDSIECK BRUT VINTAGE 2006 • $$

91 points • DISGORGED SEPTEMBER 2011 • TASTED IN SYDNEY

51% chardonnay, 49% pinot noir from 17 villages; aged more than 6 years on lees; 11g/L dosage

The hot summer of 2006 yielded powerful pinot noir and fruity chardonnay, producing a luscious, rounded, simple and fruity Piper to drink young and fresh. It's a veritable fruit cart of succulent nectarines, white peaches and even blackberries and anise. Just when you fear it's all about to topple, the finish cuts in with citrus zest freshness, finely balanced mineral texture, subtle phenolic structure and honeyed dosage.

The Champagne Guide

PIPER-HEIDSIECK BRUT VINTAGE 2004 • $$

94 points • TASTED IN BEZANNES

60% pinot noir, 40% chardonnay; 11g/L dosage

Evidence of the stamina of 2004, this release is looking even more focused and vivacious than it did on its release two years ago, while showing impressive developed complexity of secondary white peach, baked apple, toast, honey, brioche and a whiff of smoke. The finish retains its composure and persistence, supported by a softly mineral structure. Value.

PIPER-HEIDSIECK RARE MILLÉSIMÉ 2002 • $$$$$

95 points • TASTED IN BEZANNES AND SYDNEY

70% chardonnay from Avize, Vertus and the Montagne de Reims; 30% pinot noir from Aÿ; 11g/L dosage

This is indeed rare, the eighth vintage since 1976. In the years since its release, it's evolved to attain an enticing balance between youthful grapefruit zest, fresh lemons, white peach and crunchy pear, and the depths of toasted cashew nuts, nougat, brioche, nutmeg, crème brûlée and a hint of smoke. A core of concentration and creamy mouthfeel are offset by lively acid and honeyed dosage. It epitomises the gentle, textural minerality, harmonious personality and magnificent persistence of chardonnay in this epic vintage.

PIPER-HEIDSIECK RARE MILLÉSIMÉ 1998

96 points • TASTED IN BEZANNES FROM MAGNUM

60% chardonnay, 40% pinot noir; bottled only in magnums

The endurance of the great 1998 season is proclaimed in large format. A confident chardonnay lead is celebrated in magnificent freshness of lively white peach and wonderful precision of lemon zest, underlined by an expressive mineral chalk texture. Evolution and complexity are understated, in elegant nuances of brioche and anise. A marvellous 1998, with plenty of life still in it.

POL ROGER

(Pol Roh-zheh)

9/10

1 RUE WINSTON CHURCHILL ÉPERNAY 51206
www.polroger.com

CHAMPAGNE

POL ROGER

*S*tepping into Pol Roger's production facility in Épernay is like entering a different world. 'We call this the kitchen,' introduced Laurent d'Harcourt, recently promoted Managing Director of the company. This was not like any kitchen I'd ever seen. Immaculately polished stainless steel tanks perfectly reflected shiny white tiles and snow-white surfaces. It was as if we were entering a brain surgery unit or a NASA assembly room, and I had an uneasy feeling that I might be asked to don a body suit, lest I contaminate this precision machine with a single molecule of foreign material. I have been buying Pol Roger for decades, but it was not until that moment that everything about this celestial estate suddenly snapped into perfect focus. The champagnes that emerge from this extraterrestrial building are as desperately precise, intricately delicate and flawlessly pristine as its polished interior, revealing the manifesto that defines all that lies within.

IT HASN'T ALWAYS BEEN THIS WAY. THE DISORGANISED regime of the 1990s was 'a mess', according to d'Harcourt. The pace of transformation amazes me every time I visit Pol Roger.

Since Chef de Cave Dominique Petit joined the company in 1999, after 24 years at Krug, more than €9 million has been invested in upgrading the winemaking facilities alone.

And it doesn't seem to stop. When I visited four weeks before vintage in 2011, the site was buzzing with activity. There were new cold settling and fermentation halls, six new tiny 2200-litre tanks,

the cellar extended, and the cellar floors concreted to reduce vibrations from electric vehicles. The stainless steel fermentation space was updated in 2001, 2004, 2008, 2010 and 2011, and now provides full capacity to separate parcels. More consistent and more precise disgorgement and dosage machines were installed.

When I returned in 2013, the old concrete tanks had been refreshed, the reception room refurbished around them, and a new cuverie for reserve wines was under construction. Even the address has changed, after the street was renamed last year. Pol Roger now proudly stands at 1 Rue Winston Churchill, although

The Champagne Guide

Pol Roger's illustrious premises on Rue Winston Churchill are home to an immaculate facility making pristine champagnes.

it won't make a big deal about this. 'The street is not that nice!' admits d'Harcourt, who replaced Christian Pol Roger as the face of the company six years ago.

Pol Roger's investment is not to increase production, but to improve quality and consistency. Having already recently grown from 1.5 million to 1.8 million bottles annually, there is no immediate plan to increase further.

'Every year for the past 12 years we have seen results in the consistency of the wines from the work we are doing in the winery,' d'Harcourt explains. 'We have made a solid investment to ensure the family house remains secure in the family's hands into the 21st century.'

EXACTING PRECISION

The rise of Pol Roger is very much a credit to the exacting precision of Dominique Petit, who transformed a disorganised regime with an attention to detail learnt at Krug. The preference of the house for stainless steel over concrete and oak barrels rests on judicious temperature control of its musts during clarification and vinification. Musts undergo a double cold settling process at just 5°C, producing the most pristine juice — a process that Petit's predecessor, James Coffinet, brought to Pol Roger from Billecart-Salmon. Held below 18°C, a cool primary fermentation is drawn out over 15 days, maintaining fruit freshness and aromatic definition.

Secondary fermentation is likewise cool, thanks to Pol Roger's 7.5 kilometres of cellars, which are among the coolest (9–11°C) and deepest (up to 33 metres) in Épernay. Most of the bottles rest in the deepest parts of the cellar. This slow fermentation produces wines of great finesse, fine effervescence and enduring longevity. 'Greater precision in the first and second fermentations have enabled a trend towards lower dosage,' explains d'Harcourt. Pol Roger's vintage wines now receive dosages of 8–10g/litre.

Everything in the cellar is done by hand by a team of no more than 10. Pol Roger boasts four of the remaining 15 riddlers still working in Champagne. Each turning 50,000–60,000 bottles a day, it takes 4–5 weeks to riddle each bottle. Every bottle is stacked in the cellar by hand, including every non-vintage wine — a painstaking process for a company with an incredible 9.5 million bottles in its care. 'Our neighbours think we are strange with such a huge inventory!' d'Harcourt exclaims.

Pol Roger provides for an impressive 51% of this production from 89 hectares of estate vines. 'These holdings allow us to be more consistent over the long term,' clarifies d'Harcourt. The remainder is sourced exclusively from the Marne from long-term contracts under an arrangement that promotes quality. 'Many of the growers from whom we source also care for vineyards that we own ourselves,' he says. 'They cultivate our vineyards, we press all the fruit and then give a portion back to them as payment.'

With such a regime of excellence in the vineyard and winery, under the ownership of the same family since the house was founded in 1849, Pol Roger's success is no surprise. 'We have been selling champagne in all of our markets under allocation in recent years,' d'Harcourt reveals. 'We could sell two or three times the volume in the UK, but we don't want to be too dependent on one market. We've been telling some markets to stop selling because we don't have enough to send! We simply cannot produce more to sell.'

That's a line you don't often hear from any medium-sized wine company in the current climate. And with ever-improving facilities every time I visit, this company is poised for even greater things to come.

It certainly is a different world at Pol Roger.

POL ROGER PURE BRUT NATURE NV • $$

94 points • TASTED IN ÉPERNAY, ADELAIDE AND BRISBANE

2007 base vintage; a blend of the three champagne varieties in roughly equal proportions; a different blend to Brut Réserve, with more floral and less acidic parcels; zero dosage

Pol Roger is one of the few brut nature champagnes consistently more graceful than the dosaged version. The 2007 has been around for a couple of years, and it's as pristine and delightful as ever – quite a feat without the sustaining power of dosage. The quintessential apéritif, as crystal clear as a mountain stream, darting with lemon blossom, lemon zest and crunchy granny smith apples, beginning to build bready, almond nut complexity. A shard of taut acidity meets fine, expressive chalk minerality, holding the finish in razor-aligned precision.

POL ROGER BRUT RÉSERVE NV • $$

93 points • 2008 BASE VINTAGE WITH RESERVES FROM 2007, 2006 AND 2005; DISGORGED NOVEMBER 2012 • TASTED IN ÉPERNAY AND LONDON

93 points • 2007 BASE VINTAGE • TASTED IN ÉPERNAY, ADELAIDE AND BRISBANE

A blend of the three champagne varieties in roughly equal proportions; 20% reserve wines; 150 parcels from 30 crus; 36–48 months on lees in bottle; 9–10g/L dosage; 1.3–1.4 million bottles; bottle code indicates packaging date, with the first digit denoting the year, and next three digits the day of that year

Pol Roger's infamous 'White Foil' is an attractive and refreshing apéritif style, as clean, crisp and well constructed as ever. A sneak preview of the pristine 2008 base on the eve of its release is elegantly refreshing, harmonising lemon, white peach and nectarine of purity and restraint. Hints of apple and nougat glide over an elegant structure of soft, mineral presence. The 2007 base has taken on a nutty, creamy persona, accented by subtle spice, showing a little more richness as it approaches the end of its run, yet retaining all of its fresh citrus energy. While disgorgement dates are not marked on bottles, the packaging date on the carton is about three months after disgorgement.

POL ROGER VINTAGE 2004 • $$$

95 points • DISGORGED MARCH 2013 • TASTED IN ÉPERNAY

60% pinot noir, 40% chardonnay

A classic Pol Roger vintage, without quite the theatrics of 2002, with an effortless purity reminiscent of 1999, and an inherent energy and drive all of its own. There is a calm refinement to 2004, expressed impeccably in almond blossom, fresh lemon, white peach and hints of grapefruit. The slow-motion ageing of Pol Roger's cold cellars is particularly evident in this youthful vintage, only beginning to reveal subtle almond nougat complexity. Its acid line is pristine, underscoring pronounced chalk mineral structure. Another great vintage in the distinguished lineage of Pol Roger.

The Champagne Guide

POL ROGER BRUT VINTAGE 2002 • $$$

96 points • TASTED IN ÉPERNAY, MELBOURNE AND BRISBANE

60% pinot noir, 40% chardonnay; from 20 grand cru and premier cru villages in the Montagne de Reims and Côte des Blancs; full malolactic fermentation; aged 9 years on lees; 8g/L dosage; approximately 250,000 bottles

Long have we awaited the dawning of another grand vintage to follow the legendary 1996 Pol. Now 2002 has arrived, and, my, has it been worth the wait! All the tension of this incredible vintage is on full show, epitomising both the inherent concentration and the scintillating structure of the season. The confidence of pinot noir takes the lead, providing grand red-fruited dimension to the supreme refinement of the Pol Roger house style. Almost a decade in the depths of cold cellars has built ever so subtle toasty complexity, which does nothing to trouble the exacting flow of taut citrus zest, lemon sherbet and yellow mirabelle plum fruit. Its textural presence is pronounced, with driving persistence of finely poised, mouth-embracing chalk minerality that rises and froths on the finish. One bottle tasted was attenuated in persistence and lacking life, presumably due to an inconsistent cork, as four others were sublime.

POL ROGER BLANC DE BLANCS 2002 • $$$

96 points • TASTED IN ÉPERNAY AND BRISBANE

100% Côte des Blancs grand crus: Oiry, Chouilly, Cramant, Avize and Oger; full malolactic fermentation; aged 9 years on lees; 9g/L dosage

For a house once led by pinot noir, Pol Roger is increasingly focusing on chardonnay in its vintage wines, and recent vintages of its Blanc de Blancs demonstrate why. Testimony to the molecular precision of Pol Roger's exacting regime, the propensity of this cuvée to age is astonishing, and the past few vintages seem to escalate every time I come back to them. And 2002 just might prove to be the most enduring of all, charged with the electric energy of the season, perfectly massaged by almost a decade in Pol Roger's deep cellars. Lively lemon blossom, citrus fruits and white peaches abound, touched with brioche, toast and a flattering hint of struck-flint reduction. There's an understated confidence to its fruit power, giving voice to finely poised chalk minerality. Two bottles were faultless and one showed a little more development.

POL ROGER ROSÉ 2004 • $$$

95 points • TASTED IN ÉPERNAY, ADELAIDE AND BRISBANE

50% pinot noir, 35% chardonnay from grand cru and premier cru vineyards of the Montagne de Reims and Côte des Blancs; 15% pinot noir red wine, purchased by the company 'because we are not good at vinifying red wine ourselves'; aged 7 years on lees; 9g/L dosage

Adoring fans of Pol Rosé will immediately spot a change of pace after the slender catwalk curves of 2002 and the elegant finesse of 2000. The most exuberant and vinous Pol Rosé of recent times, 2004 rejoices in pinot noir of black cherry fruit enthusiasm, yet is immaculately constrained within the pristine house style that is Pol Roger. Its full crimson hue is significantly deeper than its predecessors, anticipating great theatrics of strawberry shortcake, red cherries, kirsch, orange zest, even plum pudding, mulled wine spice and an air of smouldering embers. It propagates with great stamina and textural presence, with chalk minerality rising on the finish and soft, fine tannins providing gentle structure. One bottle out of five was a little dried out on the finish.

POL ROGER SIR WINSTON CHURCHILL 2000 • $$$$

97 points • DISGORGED MID-2012 • TASTED IN ÉPERNAY AND BRISBANE

Predominantly pinot noir, with some chardonnay, all from grand cru vineyards under vine at the time of Churchill; cold settled at 6°C; fermented below 18°C; full malolactic fermentation; secondary fermentation in the lowest part of the cellars (9°C); aged 10 years on lees

The blend of Sir Winston Churchill is a closely guarded secret. I ask d'Harcourt every time we taste a new vintage. 'I have not been drunk enough yet to tell you!' he replied this year. I'll keep working on it. Elusive details aside, Sir Winston is looking dignified and refined in 2000, transcending the soft immediacy of the season in an elegant and understated demeanour of tightly wound, super-fine lemon, grapefruit and white peach fruit of pristine focus. This is a cuvée that appreciates plenty of time in a large glass to unravel, and it's just beginning to uncurl to the rhythm of 13 years of age, building subtlety of toasty, buttery complexity, propelled by attentive acid control and an undercurrent of soft, lingering chalk mineral texture. It's making this transition with prowess and effortless grace, with a youthful vigour under that distinguished exterior.

POL ROGER SIR WINSTON CHURCHILL 1999 • $$$$

98 points • DISGORGED IN 2011 • TASTED IN BRISBANE, ADELAIDE AND ÉPERNAY
As above

Dominique Petit's first vintage transformed Churchill from rounded generosity to the classic finesse that defines the face of Pol Roger today. To do so in a vintage as generous as 1999 was an act of genius, and for it to retain such primary focus 14 years later is nothing short of remarkable. It's still shy and introverted, defined by deep-set mineral precision and lingering chalk that penetrates deep into its finish. Lemon zest and yellow summer fruits are only beginning to advance to become roast nuts, fresh almonds and mixed spice. A Churchill of ultra-fine bead, tightly coiled potential and a never-ending story of a finish.

POL ROGER SIR WINSTON CHURCHILL 1998 • $$$$

98 points • TASTED IN ÉPERNAY
As above

One of the great Winstons of the recent era, 1998 is evolving with exacting precision. At 15 years of age, it's attained that magical moment when primary and secondary character marry to create a thrilling accord of stone fruits, citrus, brioche and nougat. Its mineral presence is profound and undeviating, and its freshness is stunning, particularly in magnum. Evidence of the great rewards of cellaring Winston for at least five years after release, and preferably ten.

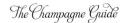
The Champagne Guide

Pommery

(Poh-mer-ee)

5 Place du Général Gouraud 51053 Reims

www.pommery.com

*C*hampagne's seventh largest house has had a rough ride, falling victim to buyout after buyout over recent decades, the most recent in 1996, when it was sold by Moët & Chandon to Belgian entrepreneur Jean-François Vranken, minus its exceptional vineyard holdings of 400 hectares, including more than 300 hectares of glorious grand crus. The inconsistency of its wines, particularly its non-vintage cuvées, is perhaps understandable in the context of this tumultuous history. To its credit, the house has now rebuilt its vineyard holdings to a respectable 255 hectares. Pommery sells close to 5 million bottles each year, and holds some 20 million in 18 kilometres of chalk mines 30 metres under its grand premises in Reims. Pommery is the key house of the Vranken-Pommery group, Champagne's third largest after LVMH and Lanson-BCC.

Pommery Brut Royal NV • $

83 points • Tasted in Brisbane

This might be the first champagne to feature a QR code on the front label as well as the back. Alas, it opens a virtual tour of the cellar and a video of the Chef de Cave, rather than offering insight into the composition of the cuvée. Both bottles I tasted showed reductive savoury character and an awkward, tart, vinegar-like sourness that left them stripped, lifeless and devoid of identifiable fruit definition.

POMMERY GRAND CRU VINTAGE BRUT 2005 • $$

80 points • TASTED IN BRISBANE

A challenging and ripe season in Champagne, 2005 was characterised by phenolic hardness and dryness. This wine takes it to another level of earthy, stale walnuts, finishing short, dried out and stripped.

POMMERY BRUT ROSÉ NV • $$

88 points • TASTED IN REIMS AND BRISBANE

Pommery's rosé is so pale that it could easily be mistaken for a white champagne. It's a soft and fruity style of very pale salmon-copper hue and gentle strawberry, rose water, pink grapefruit and lemon fruit. It finishes short and one-dimensional, with balanced acidity and refreshing dosage. Currently the most balanced of Pommery's cuvées.

POMMERY CUVÉE LOUISE 1999 • $$$$

89 points • TASTED IN BRISBANE

With a fresh cork, this looks like a recent disgorgement, and not nearly as toasty as the bottle I tasted 18 months ago. Its hue is an impressively pale straw for 14 years of age. There's a touch of reductive struck flint over lemon zest and grapefruit on the bouquet. The palate upholds the primary definition of citrus and apple fruit, taking on notes of glacé fig. Sadly, a bitter grapefruit zest tang dominates the finish.

ROLAND CHAMPION

(Roh-lon Shohn-pee-yon)

6/10

16 GRANDE RUE 51530 CHOUILLY
www.champagne-roland-champion.com

CHAMPAGNE

Roland Champion

*T*he Champion family has been growing grapes in Chouilly since the 18th century, and André Champion started making his own champagnes in 1929. His untimely death elevated his eldest son Roland to head of the company at the age of 16, and he went on to expand the estate to 40 plots spanning a respectable 18 hectares, comprising 70% chardonnay in Chouilly, and 22% pinot meunier and 8% pinot noir in Verneuil and neighbouring Vandieres in the Vallée de la Marne. Today, Roland's son François and his daughter Carole sell the majority of their production 'sur latte' to négociants, leaving just 35,000 bottles to sell under their name. All are bottled under reliable DIAM closures. Vinification is conducted in stainless steel tanks, with full malolactic fermentation. The family has skilfully tamed the muscular nature of Chouilly in a characterful set of sensitively styled cuvées.

ROLAND CHAMPION CARTE BLANCHE BLANC DE BLANCS GRAND CRU BRUT NV • $$

93 points • DISGORGED DECEMBER 2012 • TASTED IN BRISBANE

55% 2010, 30% 2009, 15% 2008; 100% Chouilly; aged 26 months on lees; 7g/L dosage; DIAM closure

For bang for your buck, this is a terrific expression of fresh, young blanc de blancs. It wields the concentration of Chouilly in muscular strength of firmly textured mineral expression and powerful white summer fruits, well-defined grapefruit and lemon, and suggestions of buttery almonds. Dosage is subtle, and intricately woven into its seams.

ROLAND CHAMPION BRUT ROSE NV • $$

92 points • DISGORGED DECEMBER 2012 • TASTED IN BRISBANE

85% white wine comprising 35% Chouilly chardonnay 2010, 30% Vandieres pinot meunier 2010 and 35% Verneuil pinot meunier 2009; 15% Vandieres pinot noir red wine 2008; aged 4 years on lees; 7g/L dosage; DIAM closure

There's an appealing restraint to this young yet savoury and nutty rosé of medium salmon-copper hue and subtle pomegranate character. It's not particularly expressive in its fruit presence, but upholds a gentle red berry undercurrent and a softly textural structure, finishing crisp, clean and dry, with well-integrated dosage.

ROLAND CHAMPION CARTE NOIRE BLANC DE BLANCS GRAND CRU MILLÉSIME BRUT 2004 • $$

92 points • DISGORGED DECEMBER 2012 • TASTED IN BRISBANE

100% Chouilly chardonnay; aged 6 years on lees; 6g/L dosage; DIAM closure

Confusingly, the label is black and the name is Noire, but everything else about this blanc de blancs is perfectly white. It's a pale straw hue, with a bouquet laced with grapefruit and lemon zest. There's a core of powerful Chouilly ripeness to the palate, more lemon drops and lemon meringue than fresh lemon fruit. Such is its concentrated breadth and succulent, sweet, ripe fruit that it gives the impression of a higher dosage. Yet just when you fear it's going to meet a sticky demise in a honeypot, it swoops into a clean and taut finish of balanced acidity and soft minerality, making for the ultimate low-sugar wine for lovers of understated sweet.

ROLAND CHAMPION SPECIAL CLUB BLANC DE BLANCS GRAND CRU MILLÉSIME BRUT 2007 • $$$

94 points • DISGORGED DECEMBER 2012 • TASTED IN BRISBANE

100% old-vine Chouilly; aged 4 years on lees; 6g/L dosage; DIAM closure; 6000 bottles

This is quite young for a Special Club, and surprisingly three years younger than Champion's Millésime release, but the power of Chouilly is well suited to an earlier-drinking style. An engaging bouquet sets fragrant delicacy of lemon blossom atop a rich depth of white peach and lemon meringue. The palate is linear and structured, with a firm undercurrent of muscular minerality and great depth of fruit energy. Its power is well toned, creating a sense of linearity rather than breadth, emphasising mineral personality without the distraction of obvious dosage or the cut of tense acidity. This makes it ready to go right away, while refreshing white fruits retain the zing to lift its dry minerality.

RUINART

(Roo-ee-nar)

7/10

4 RUE DES CRAYÈRES 51100 REIMS
www.ruinart.com

THE FIRST ESTABLISHED
CHAMPAGNE HOUSE

Fréderic Panaïotis grew up between his grandparents' chardonnay vines in Champagne, and the variety remains close to his heart, making him very much at home as Chef de Cave at Ruinart since 2007. The longest-established champagne house of all has an affinity with chardonnay's freshness, finesse and elegance, and all of its finest cuvées lead with this variety, even its prestige rosé. Without the might of Moët & Chandon, the brand impact of Veuve Clicquot or the cachet of Krug, Ruinart lurks as the low-profile member of the Louis Vuitton-Moët Hennessy family. On Reim's famed Rue de Crayères, its premises hide behind the grand street presence of Pommery and Veuve Clicquot. Its low profile is just as Panaïotis would have it. 'In France we have a saying, if you live underground, you live happy!' he says. But on its performance, Ruinart has no need to lay low. Its cuvées are currently the most pure and pitch-perfect I've seen from Ruinart.

CHAMPAGNE IS PLANTED TO JUST 28% CHARDONNAY, making this the rarest of the region's three key varieties and the most difficult to source. Ruinart owns just 10% of its vineyards, including longstanding resources of 15 hectares of chardonnay in the grand crus of Sillery and Puisieulx on the eastern slopes of the Montagne de Reims, providing a richer and rounder style than the Côte des Blancs.

Long-term contracts with growers form the vast bulk of Ruinart's supplies, supplemented in recent times through vineyards acquired from Lanson and Joseph Perrier. This has enabled the house to increase its annual production from 1.4 million to 2.5–3 million bottles over the past two decades. 'Ruinart is in demand, so I'm getting all the chardonnay I can find!' Panaïotis exclaims. Annual growth today is under 5%.

To maintain the aromatic freshness and elegance of its fruit, the Ruinart house style is decisively reductive. 'We hate oxygen!' he declares, describing his approach as the antithesis of Bollinger and Krug. A pneumatic press is used in place of a traditional champagne press, to guard the juice against oxidation, and inert nitrogen gas is used to protect the wine at every stage of production. Vinification takes place only in stainless steel. 'We have absolutely no need of oak in any of our wines!' Panaïotis says.

Ruinart's cuvées often carry flattering hints of struck flint or gunpowder, remnants of reductive winemaking. 'My goal is to take reduction even further!' proclaims Panaïotis. 'The stinky white Burgundy thing, I just love it! Like Domaine Roulot, but they use oak. The question is how to do it without oak!'

To soften the austerity of young chardonnay, all cuvées undergo full malolactic fermentation, and non-vintage wines are balanced using respectable quantities of reserve wines. This makes for a style that permits refreshingly low dosages, declining admirably over recent years. The dosage is tweaked for successive disgorgements of Ruinart's prestige Dom Ruinart cuvée, typically lowering as the wine ages.

'For me, it's not a matter of numbers, but of balance,' Panaïotis explains.

Ruinart's distinctive rounded bottles make riddling challenging, and the house relies exclusively on gyropalettes, which Panaïotis claims give a far better result. The clear glass of these bottles renders the wine susceptible to lightstruck degradation, making it vital to store them in the dark.

Ruinart has occupied its premises in Reims since 1768, and was the first in Champagne to use the 3rd century Roman crayères (chalk mines) under the city to age its champagnes.

Its location on top of the hill make its eight kilometres of cellars some of the deepest and most spectacular in the region, plunging to depths of up to 38 metres. These are the only cellars in Champagne classified as a national monument — a distinguished home for such graceful champagnes.

R de Ruinart Brut NV • $$

94 points • Tasted in Reims and Brisbane

75% 2009, 25% 2008 and 2007 reserves; 54% pinot noir, 40% chardonnay, 6% pinot meunier; 8.5g/L dosage; 60% of the production of the house, hence more than 1.5 million bottles

This is the best R de Ruinart of recent times, personifying Panaïotis' vision that purity is the key. 'I joined Ruinart in 2007, it took a couple of years to figure out what was going on, and 2009 was the first year when I said, "Right, we can now start to do things! I don't think there's much I can do with the blanc de blancs or the rosé, but I can do things with R de Ruinart!"' Ruinart's only cuvée to be led by pinot noir kicks off with refined strawberry and red apple fruit, contrasting refreshingly with the lemon pith, pear and finely structured minerality of chardonnay. A suggestion of gunpowder and a hint of balsamic declare its reductive style, with a note of flintiness reinforcing its mineral presence. A youthful and lively apéritif, and as fresh as R de Ruinart has ever been.

Ruinart Blanc de Blancs Brut NV • $$$

95 points • Tasted in Reims, Adelaide, Melbourne and Brisbane

75% 2009, 25% 2008 and 2007 reserves; 80% Côte des Blancs and Montagne de Reims premier crus; 10% Sézanne and 10% St Thierry for approachability and maturity; aged 24–28 months on lees; 8.5g/L dosage

Panaïotis' aim in this young blend is 'to capture the light of Champagne' — the elegance and freshness of chardonnay. The wine articulates its philosophy vividly, singing with delicate citrus blossom, fresh lemon and grapefruit zest. Enticing notes of gunflint and balsamic hark to the reductive nature of the house. A beautifully fresh and electric style with a straight backbone of taut acidity, giving voice to the gentle, elegant minerality of the premier crus of the Côte des Blancs. Older bottles are building nutty development, but are blessed with the energy and structure to confidently retain purity and fruit drive. The first bottle opened for me by the house was lightstruck, having been left in an office for a few days — a pertinent reminder to keep this clear bottle in the dark until the moment it's poured.

The Champagne Guide

RUINART BRUT ROSÉ NV • $$$

95 points • TASTED IN REIMS AND BRISBANE

2010 base vintage and 20–25% reserves from 2009 and 2008; 45% chardonnay from the Côte des Blancs and Montagne de Reims, 36% pinot noir from the Montagne de Reims and Vallée de la Marne; 19% pinot noir red wine, with a short maceration of 5 days to extract colour but not tannin structure; 9g/L dosage

Ruinart's rosé is intentionally fresh, fruity, aromatic and approachable, full in colour but light in structure. A large dose of chardonnay defines the house style of restraint and soft, chalky mineral mouthfeel, while a strong inclusion of red wine infuses a youthful, almost luminescent, medium crimson hue and aromas and flavours of all shades of red: wild strawberries, pink pepper, pomegranate, guava, raspberries and red cherries. Subtle struck flint alludes to reductive complexity. Gracious finesse is upheld without sacrificing flavour or fruit definition, with soft tannin texture and well-gauged dosage maintaining a refreshing finish.

DOM RUINART BLANC DE BLANCS 2002 • $$$$$

96 points • TASTED IN REIMS

100% grand cru chardonnay, 72% Côte des Blancs (predominantly Chouilly and Avize), 28% northern Montagne de Reims (predominantly Sillery and Puisieulx); full malolactic fermentation; 6.5g/L dosage

Ruinart's flagship blanc de blancs plays the high strings of the Côte des Blancs to the thick orchestral scoring of Montagne de Reims, filling out chardonnay's citrus melody with layers of creamy generosity. The confidence of 2002 brings great composure and completeness, sustained with long-lingering acidity and the nostalgic timbre of inimitable Côte des Blancs chalk minerality. A decade in Ruinart's ancient chalk mines has deepened its voice with tones of brioche, roast cashew nut, nougat and burnt butter, retaining the signature gunpowder reduction of Ruinart. A masterpiece.

DOM RUINART ROSÉ 1998 • $$$$$

94 points • TASTED IN REIMS

100% grand cru; Dom Ruinart with red wine; 85% chardonnay (66% Côte des Blancs from Avize, Cramant Le Mesnil-sur-Oger; 34% Montagne de Reims from Sillery, Puisieulx and Verzenay); 15% pinot noir red wine from Sillery and Verzenay; full malolactic fermentation; 5g/L dosage

'Time changes everything', says Panaïotis of the wine he calls his 'blanc de blancs rosé'. And so it does. This wine bears little resemblance to the linear precision of its base Dom Ruinart 1998, its pinot noir contribution now quite evolved, defining pronounced tertiary development. Its medium salmon hue has taken on a copper tint, and its aromas resemble mature pinot noir in allusions of dried flowers, leather, game, dried herbs and truffles. The finish pulls in honed and controlled by the definition of chardonnay, sustaining preserved lemon flavours and soft texture on a lingering finish. A remarkably complex rosé of savoury allure.

SALON

(Sah-loh)

10/10

5–7 Rue de la Brèche d'Oger 51190 Le Mesnil-sur-Oger
www.salondelamotte.com

CHAMPAGNE

SALON
Le Mesnil

*There is only one Salon, and there has only ever been one. One wine of one variety from one vintage,
sourced from one region (Côte de Blancs) and one village (Le Mesnil-sur-Oger). The romantic ideal
ends abruptly here, however, because this is not a single-vineyard wine, nor even an estate wine. The fruit of the
single-hectare estate vineyard of Jardin de Salon is currently declassified to its lower-tier sister house, Delamotte,
and will for at least the next few years, because the vines are just 12 years old. Salon is sourced from 15 hectares
owned by 19 longstanding growers, all of whom sell their fruit only to Salon. Winemaking is handled by the
owner of both houses, Laurent-Perrier.*

THE MINUTE SCALE OF THIS OPERATION SANK IN AS I absorbed it from the homely tasting room in the house in Le Mesnil-sur-Oger. The windows framed the Jardin vineyard stretching up the gentle slope just outside. Directly below, a decade of future releases lay waiting in the small cellar. There are only 10 employees here: six in the cellar and four in the office. Production is typically about 50,000 bottles, and only in worthy vintages. There is no non-vintage wine, so production is limited to the finest years, of which the current release, 1999, is just the 37th since 1905.

It was in that year that Eugène-Aimé Salon created Champagne's first blanc de blancs, originally only for personal consumption. To this day it remains among the very finest and most expensive. The philosophy from the beginning was to build a champagne that could age, and every element of its production is honed toward this goal. The first pressing is used exclusively, fermented in stainless steel under temperature control.

Its natural acidity is upheld by blocking malolactic fermentation, distinguishing it from Delamotte. Aged for an average of 10 years before release, the timing

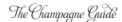

for each vintage is determined according to when it is ready. Riddling is performed by hand, and bottles are disgorged according to when they are released. This usually equates to four to six disgorgements across two years of release. Dosage is tweaked for each disgorgement, typically 5–6g/litre.

Salon is usually the last house to release its vintage wine; even at this age it is far from its peak. 'Whenever I produce a vintage I say, "This is not for me or for my children, but for my grandchildren",' declares Salon Delamotte president Didier Depond, who considers the perfect time to drink Salon to be after 20 years.

'It takes 20 years to truly define a great wine,' he suggests. 'We are always very surprised by the potential of Salons opened from the '70s, '60s and even '50s.'

Laurent-Perrier's vineyard manager Christelle Rinville follows each vineyard throughout the year, and monitors all cultures and treatments that are applied. Depond is afforded the freedom to manage the house independently, and feels no pressure to increase volumes, in spite of limited supply and high demand.

'It's difficult to increase the volume because the vineyards are limited,' he points out. 'And it would be a disaster to increase the number of vintages we release.' A noble stance at a time when some houses appear set on churning out flagship champagnes in lesser seasons.

There will be no 2000 Salon, after mid-August hail devastated the Le Mesnil harvest. The 1999 will be followed by 2002 in early 2014, then 2004, 2006 and 2008 (in magnum only), maintaining Salon's longstanding average of fewer than four vintages each

Jardin de Salon will not be included in Salon for at least five years as the vines are just 12 years old.

decade. To date, no vintages have been produced since 2008. The 1996, 2002 and 2008 are upheld by the house to be the finest vintages for long ageing.

Depond considers 2002 the perfect image of Salon, of blanc de blancs and of Le Mesnil.

SALON CUVÉE S BLANC DE BLANCS 1999 • $$$$$

97 points • DISGORGED DECEMBER 2011 • TASTED IN LE MESNIL-SUR-OGER AND ADELAIDE

The warm and sunny 1999 vintage blesses Salon with a suggestion of generous accessibility, while resolutely upholding its incisive youthfulness, exceedingly backward for its age, even towards the end of its release cycle. It has followed a gentle curve of evolution at the pace of a giant sea turtle since it was first unleashed on the world two years ago, settling comfortably into a place of calm and intricate precision. Delightful lemon freshness is held in suspended animation at a full 14 years of age, only beginning to evolve into preserved lemon and white peach. A youthful whiff of reduction has become a charming note of struck flint. Almond, nougat, vanilla and brioche tell the story of more than a decade in the cellar, with soft suggestions of smoke and dried fig hinting at what is yet to come. Its structure is a revelation, with very fine chalk minerality integrating softly, then rising on the finish to mouth-embracing mineral texture that personifies Le Mesnil. The characteristic poise of Salon triumphs, retaining light-footed restraint and delicacy even in a powerfully concentrated season, promising at least another decade of life.

SÉLÈQUE

(Seh-lek)

(5/10)

10 Rue de l'Égalité 51530 Pierry
www.champagne-seleque.fr

CHAMPAGNE

SÉLÈQUE

———— PROPRIÉTAIRE · RÉCOLTANT ————

H̶enri Sélèque planted his first vines in Pierry, south of Épernay, in 1965 and made his first champagnes in 1976. The estate now comprises 12 hectares across 40 plots in eight villages, with a vine maturity of 18–60 years. Chardonnay defines the house style, comprising 60% of plantings, followed by 30% pinot meunier and 10% pinot noir. Vines are managed with a focus on natural balance, including ploughing by horse, and six hectares are in transition to biodynamic viticulture. The estate's small, far-flung plots necessitate a small press to vinify the juice of each plot separately. Selective oak fermentation was introduced in 2004 to enhance finesse and complexity, and today 30% of parcels are fermented in small, old oak barrels and 2000-litre foudres, with the rest in stainless steel. The estate is managed by Henri's sons Richard and Jean, and their children Nathalie and Jean-Marc. Back labels informatively detail disgorgement date, base vintages, cépage, time on lees and dosage.

SÉLÈQUE CUVÉE SPÉCIALE PREMIER CRU BRUT NV • $

91 points • Disgorged May 2012 • Tasted in Brisbane

60% 2008 base vintage, 40% reserve wines; 60% chardonnay, 30% pinot meunier, 10% pinot noir, from Pierry, Dizy and Vertus; aged 3 years on lees; 7g/L dosage

A vibrant, pale straw hue reflects a strong chardonnay lead, while the bouquet unites apple and pear fruit with the aged complexity of biscuits and honey. The palate celebrates the jubilant 2008 season in its energetic, if slightly hard, acidity, and its grapefruit zest crunch. Some skinsy phenolic texture adds some firmness to the finish, but it retains impeccable freshness and integrated balance.

TAITTINGER

(Tet-ahn-zhay)

(8/10)

9 PLACE SAINT-NICOLAISE 51100 REIMS
www.taittinger.com

CHAMPAGNE
TAITTINGER
Reims

'My grandfather gave me a book when I was five years old,' Pierre-Emmanuel Taittinger recalls. 'In the dedication he wrote, "To my grandson, who will one day be an entrepreneur and be the guardian of the family tradition".' Little did he know how true his prophecy would prove to be, and just what it would take to achieve. In these days of corporate takeovers, it's a gutsy commitment to buy back the family business. When most of the heirs voted to cash in and Taittinger was sold in 2005, Pierre-Emmanuel launched a fierce, year-long buy-back for his branch of the family, to the tune of €550 million, with the help of family friends and French bank Crédit Agricole. The family has since built up its stake in the company to almost half, with the remainder mostly in the hands of its friends. Annual sales of 5.6 million bottles rank Taittinger as Champagne's sixth-largest house.

THE FULFILMENT OF HIS GRANDFATHER'S PREDICTION returned Taittinger to its place among the last big independent, family-owned houses that uphold the family name not only on the label, but in their management. Pierre-Emmanuel remains President of the company, his dynamic son, Clovis, is Export Director, and his delightful daughter, Vitalie, handles the company's artistic vision. The board and family are involved in each cuvée's tastings. 'My father leads the tasting, but it is a collective decision,' says Clovis.

It's a compelling story of fighting for the family business in the middle of one of the biggest corporate jungles anywhere in the wine world. It took Pierre-Emmanuel years to bring his buy-back to fruition, and

it was not until 2008 that it was complete. The wines from this new regime have recently begun to emerge from the hallowed caverns of Taittinger, and its non-vintage wines have never looked more refined.

NATURAL VITICULTURE
Taittinger's 288 hectares of vineyard holdings, predominantly in the Montagne de Reims and Côte des Blancs, provide for half of the company's annual production of 5 million bottles, with recent growth of around 7% each year. Half of its own vines are pinot noir, 35% chardonnay and 15% pinot meunier. Chardonnay plays a significant role in the house style, sourced predominantly from the Côte des Blancs.

An increasingly eco-friendly approach is taken in the vines, with a reduction in the use of pesticides and elimination of herbicides. 'We are aiming to use half the usual dose of chemicals,' outlines Taittinger's young and talented Deputy General Manager, Damien Le Sueur, 'and in 2010 we used less than six treatments across all our vineyards.'

The house is not seeking organic certification, to retain the flexibility to use full doses when difficult seasons dictate. Nonetheless, natural treatments remain the preference, and attention has been given to trellising to provide ventilation to balanced canopies. Grasses are planted in the mid-rows of 80% of estate vineyards, believed to be an unprecedented proportion for an estate of this size, and ploughing is used for weed control, sometimes by horse. Green harvesting to limit yields is only used when necessary, such as in the high-yielding year of 2004, when as much as 40% of fruit was dropped in some vineyards.

ATTENTIVE VINIFICATION

At the time of the family buy-back, the decision was made to work only with the finest juices, using less than 10% of the tailles in the Brut Réserve NV and Brut Prestige Rosé NV, and only the first pressing in the other cuvées. 'We only use the tailles from chardonnay because the tailles of the black grapes are too heavy,' Le Sueur explains. 'Too much of the tailles in the blend makes them too strong and mature, but we want to produce very fine and accurate wines.' Excess tailles are exchanged for the cuvées of other houses.

In the winery, fermentation is conducted in tanks below 18°C to preserve freshness. Malolactic fermentation is allowed to complete on all cuvées, crucial for softening these chardonnay-led styles. 'I say we work with four varieties: chardonnay, pinot noir, pinot meunier and time!' says Le Sueur, emphasising the importance of maturity in allowing these nervy styles to develop. Non-vintage wines are aged on lees for at least three years, Prélude Grand Crus Brut NV for a minimum of five years, vintage wines for longer again, and the flagship Comtes de Champagne eight years or more (the current vintage is 2004).

Such long ageing necessitates large cellar stocks. Taittinger ages all of its vintage wines alongside 3 million bottles of Comtes de Champagne at 9–10°C in its breathtaking four kilometres of galleries under its headquarters in Reims, including a section of 4th century Roman crayères. Some 19 million bottles of non-vintage wine are kept in a facility in town.

The 1734 Château de la Marquetterie in Pierry, near Épernay, is today a reception house for Champagne's sixth largest house, Taittinger.

The Champagne Guide

Taittinger bottles under natural cork, since it hasn't found its cuvées to evolve in the same way under DIAM, which is unfortunate. A disproportionate number of bottles opened for me by the house were cork-tainted this year. Taittinger is introducing a label code that will reveal the base vintage of non-vintage cuvées.

COMTES DE CHAMPAGNE

Taittinger's flagship Comtes de Champagne holds an enviable position among the very finest blanc de blancs. It is sourced principally from Avize and Le Mesnil-sur-Oger, and to a lesser extent from Oger, Chouilly, Cramant, Vertus and Bergères-lès-Vertus.

'We are lucky to work with a huge quantity of wines from the Côte des Blancs, allowing us to choose the best samples for Comtes de Champagne each year,' explains cellar master Loïc Dupont. 'We look for the vats that represent the typicity of each cru, to build the expression of the vintage. Avize brings elegance, finesse and balance, Le Mesnil-sur-Oger contributes body and a subtle reduction akin to grilled bread, Chouilly delivers roundness, Cramant grilled almonds and Oger elegant citrus.' Just 5% is aged for four months in oak barrels, one-third new, and up to four years old — not for strength, but to bring subtle notes of toast and brioche to the delicacy of chardonnay.

Taittinger's depth of reach into the Côte des Blancs grand crus has made Comtes de Champagne one of Champagne's most consistent blanc de blancs, and every even vintage since 1996 has been nothing short of transcendental.

The Taittinger family tradition remains as alive and well as ever, in the capable hands of Pierre-Emmanuel, his children and their loyal team.

TAITTINGER CUVÉE BRUT RÉSERVE NV • $$

93 points • DISGORGED DECEMBER 2011 • TASTED IN REIMS, SYDNEY AND MELBOURNE

70% 2008, 14% 2007, 14% 2006 and 2% 2005; 40% chardonnay, 35% pinot noir, 25% pinot meunier; from 40 crus in the Marne, Sézanne and the Aube; aged 3 years on lees; 9g/L dosage; more than 4 million bottles

Taittinger always prepares its Brut Réserve blend first, and only if the vintage is deemed of sufficient quality are its other cuvées assembled. Accurate precision of lemon zest and stone fruits are supported by the gentle complexity of toast, roast nuts and honey. A generous expression of Taittinger, balanced by the bright, lively mood of 2008. A refreshing apéritif of crisp freshness and lingering persistence.

TAITTINGER CUVÉE NOCTURNE NV • $$

88 points • TASTED IN REIMS

60% pinot noir, 40% chardonnay; 17.5g/L dosage from cane sugar

Taittinger has pimped Nocturne into what it calls a 'disco version', doubling production and decorating it in a shiny iridescent purple disco ball. From a small base, it's now the fastest-growing cuvée in the range. It tastes like candied citrus zest and honey, lacking vibrancy and finishing with an earthy dryness. If mature chamber music isn't your vibe, turn down the lights, crank up the volume and give this a swing.

TAITTINGER LES FOLIES DE LA MARQUETTERIE NV • $$

92 points • DISGORGED JANUARY 2012 • TASTED IN REIMS

100% 2005, though not declared as a vintage; 55% pinot noir, 45% chardonnay

Taittinger's first single-estate wine is blended from parcels surrounding its Château de la Marquetterie in Pierry, just south of Épernay. The typicity of the site is emphasised using viticulture to drop yields to around half of Champagne's average, through green harvest and elimination of soil supplements. The objective is to use no chaptalisation. Some parcels are vinified in large, 10-year-old, 4000-litre foudres to provide subtle oxygenation without oak character.

A distinctive and fruit-packed champagne of grapefruit, golden delicious apple and custard apple, spiced up with notes of almonds and vanilla. It's creamy and soft, with hints of candied sweetness and a tangy, bitter grapefruit pith texture. A dried-apricot note characterises the ripeness of its fruit and the generous character of Pierry.

TAITTINGER CUVÉE BRUT PRESTIGE ROSÉ NV • $$$

93 points • DISGORGED JANUARY 2012 • TASTED IN REIMS AND SYDNEY

2009 base vintage with reserves from 2008 and 2007; 16% pinot noir red wine from Ambonnay, Bouzy and Les Riceys; 9g/L dosage

The successor to the exceedingly sophisticated 2008 base vintage doesn't capture quite the same delicate enchantment, but nonetheless presents an elegant take on gentle, rounded red cherry, plum and red berry fruits. A long, soft, comfortable ride over a smooth, well-defined mineral surface.

TAITTINGER CUVÉE PRÉLUDE GRAND CRUS BRUT NV • $$$

89 points • DISGORGED JANUARY 2012 • TASTED IN REIMS

100% 2005, though not declared as a vintage; 50% Côte des Blancs chardonnay, 50% Montagne de Reims pinot noir; grand cru parcels selected to show the characters of their crus, rather than the mood of the vintage; 9g/L dosage

From medium straw-yellow hue to generous bouquet and palate, this is a deep and expressive declaration of ripe yellow fruits. A hard dryness and hazelnut bitterness characterises this ripe season, making for a lesser Prélude that does not communicate the tightrope tension between power and precision that typically characterises this label. Its idealistic aspiration to communicate place over time can never silence the voice of the season, and a vintage declaration would be helpful, even on the back label. The first bottle opened was corked.

The Champagne Guide

Taittinger Cuvée Brut Millésime 2006 • $$$

94 points • Disgorged January 2012 • Tasted in Reims

50% chardonnay, 50% pinot noir; grand cru and premier cru parcels selected for their vintage typicity; 9g/L dosage

Taittinger's vintage cuvées unashamedly proclaim the personality of the year. The 2006 is a focused and complex vintage that unites youthful apple, stone fruits and citrus with the complexity of brioche and roast cashew nuts derived from six years of bottle age. It finishes with lingering persistence, its soft minerality well balanced with gentle dosage.

Taittinger Cuvée Brut Millésime 2005 • $$$

91 points • Disgorged January 2012 • Tasted in Reims and Sydney

As above

True to the brief, this is a correct representation of 2005, honeyed and rich in its delivery of ripe peach, golden delicious apple and pear fruit. Soft acidity and fine mineral definition dissolve into a finish of gingernut biscuit and dry, nutty texture.

Taittinger Cuvée Brut Millésime 2004 • $$$

95 points • Tasted in Reims

50% chardonnay, 47% pinot noir, 3% pinot meunier

For Taittinger, 2004 was a magnificent vintage, pristinely elegant on release three years ago, and shedding none of its lily blossom air and high-strung white citrus tension since. Chardonnay leads confidently with lively precision and chalk mineral texture, while the intensity of mature pinot noir brings a honeyed fullness to the back palate. A vintage of gracious refinement, with many years before it. The first bottle opened was corked.

Taittinger Comtes de Champagne Blanc de Blancs 2005 • $$$$$

93 points • Disgorged February 2012 • Tasted in Reims

Avize, Le Mesnil-sur-Oger, Chouilly, Cramant, Oger, Bergères-lès-Vertus and Vertus; 5% aged in oak barrels; 9g/L dosage

'It was harder to make Comtes de Champagne in 2005, as the still wines were more mature and more dried-out right from the start, and these are the same characters we see in the wine now,' responded Damien Le Sueur, when I queried the decision to release Comtes in this challenging season. The result is a lesser vintage for Comtes, as it is for Champagne as a whole. It has good fruit expression, excellent length and roast cashew nut complexity, but the character of 2005 speaks loudly, with ripe fruit lending a bitter hazelnut note. Firm phenolic texture tussles with fine minerality.

TAITTINGER COMTES DE CHAMPAGNE BLANC DE BLANCS 2004 • $$$$$

98 points • DISGORGED FEBRUARY 2012 • TASTED IN REIMS

As for Comtes de Champagne Blanc de Blancs 2005

The 2004 Comtes brings back all the innocence of a joyful childhood, of scaling lemon and lime trees to plunder their tangy fruits, of a free-as-air dash through fields of daisies in endless blue daylight, of freshly roasted cashew nuts mounded in market baskets, and of a breathless plunge into an icy mountain rock pool. Then, nougat, pepper, gunflint and rising minerality of iceberg proportions. Such is the nervous tension, racy endurance and sheer stature of 2004 that it best be left until it at least attains adolescence. Do you really want to live forever, forever, forever?

TAITTINGER COMTES DE CHAMPAGNE BLANC DE BLANCS 2002 • $$$$$

98 points • DISGORGED FEBRUARY 2012 • TASTED IN REIMS, ADELAIDE, SYDNEY AND BRISBANE

As for Comtes de Champagne Blanc de Blancs 2005

Comtes de Champagne tames the high-tensile and energetic paradox of the splendid 2002 vintage like no other blanc de blancs in all of Champagne, upholding the essence of the season in tremendous concentration and bracing structure. After more than a decade in Taittinger's cold chalk pits, it retains an icy brightness to its pale hue, dazzling purity of lemon and lime blossom, and stunning, beach-fresh acidity. Great concentration of white peach and yellow mirabelle plums meet suggestions of nougat, roast almonds, vanilla pod and gunpowder. Surging chalk minerality erupts from its core in all-pervading texture of sea salt and oyster shell. Seamless line and enduring perseverance declare a very long future for the most arresting Comtes since 1996.

Taittinger's Deputy General Manager, Damien Le Sueur (right), oversees the company's cellars, including 4th century Roman crayères and the 13th century cellars of the Abbey of Saint-Nicaise (left).

Taittinger Comtes de Champagne Blanc de Blancs 2000 • $$$$

98 points • Tasted in Reims and Sydney

As for Comtes de Champagne Blanc de Blancs 2005

For all its irresistible intensity of white summer fruits, 2000 Comtes has retained an integrity far exceeding expectation, not budging a millimetre since it first emerged two years ago. Its core remains inimitable Comtes: a revelation of intricately, epically spun minerality that bores to the very core of the finest chalkfields of the Côte des Blancs, blessing it with an all-embracing texture of silky softness, yet crystalline assertiveness. Reductive complexity hovers in enchanting wisps of gunsmoke, flint and white pepper, holding mesmeric persistence and laser linearity. Comtes 2000 transcends its vintage, promising baffling longevity.

Taittinger Comtes de Champagne Rosé 2005 • $$$$$

95 points • Disgorged February 2012 • Tasted in Reims

58% pinot noir from Verzenay and Mailly-Champagne; 30% grand cru Côte des Blancs chardonnay; 12% Bouzy pinot noir red wine; no oak

Taittinger has responded to the ripe 2005 season with an intentionally rich and vinous rosé, textural and complex from the outset, with a body that cleverly juxtaposes the dry savouriness of the season. This is a rosé to catch young, while its delectable pomegranate, strawberry and red berry compote fruits are still singing. It's laced with enchanting complexity of anise and fennel, with an underlying backdrop of mouth-filling, chalky acidity, melding seamlessly with the soft tannin texture of 2005.

Taittinger Comtes de Champagne Rosé 2004 • $$$$$

96 points • Disgorged February 2012 • Tasted in Reims

70% grand cru pinot noir; 30% Côte des Blancs grand cru chardonnay; 12% Bouzy pinot noir red wine; no oak

If the philosophy of Comtes de Champagne is that of restraint, the aim of its extroverted Rosé sister is of aromatic explosiveness and energy. In 2004 she meets her brief with particular finesse and grace, holding her head high in the two years since her release. Youthful musk has evolved into an ethereal air of pomegranate, red cherry, pink pepper, strawberry and hints of vanilla and truffles. The palate achieves that elusive ideal of elegance with strength and coiled-up concentration. Lingering kirsch joins allusions of cherry kernel, nougat and almond, with an ever-present theme of expressive chalk minerality. The finish holds long, fresh and picture-perfect.

Tarlant

(Tahr-lohn)

(6/10)

Rue de la Cooperative, Oeuilly 51480
www.tarlant.com

'*Our goal is to express the personality of our unique place,' declares young Benoît Tarlant, and there are few in Champagne who have gone to greater lengths to do so. Within six years of taking the lead at his family estate in 1999, he had eliminated dosage in 80% of his annual production of 120,000–130,000 bottles, no mean feat in a house that preserves tension with malic acidity. 'I am not a cane sugar or beet sugar maker, I produce grapes!' he declares. His is an intuitive and sensitive approach that dares to ride the cutting edge of practice in the vineyard and the winery. 'There are no rules — it depends on the grapes!' he exclaims. A unique display of dried herbs in a corner of the winery celebrates a regime of cover crops and treatments that he dubs 'herbal therapy'. Fermentation is conducted mostly in barrels, some tanks and even small clay amphorae. 'The goal is not the method, the goal is to make great wine,' he sums up, exemplified in a large range of champagnes energised by malic acidity and characterised by the creamy generosity of ripe fruit, barrel fermentation, liberal use of reserve wines and long ageing. Tarlant's Zero is one of champagne's best brut natures.*

Benoît Tarlant's family has tended its vines in the Vallée de la Marne since 1687, made its own wine since the 1870s, and champagne since 1929. Today, the family is one of the most distinguished growers in its village of Oeuilly.

'Our priority is to take care of the vines and make our wines,' says Benoît, who has relished the opportunity to mark his own print on the estate while working alongside his grandfather Georges, his parents Jean-Mary and Micheline, and his sister Mélanie.

HERBAL THERAPY

Mostly on the southern side of the river, Tarlant's north-facing sites require meticulous attention, even use of a tractor winch to haul equipment up the rows of the steepest vineyards in the village. North- and east-facing slopes are prized for retention of acidity, particularly in pinot meunier.

Benoît took me to the edge of the vines on the eastern side of the village. 'The Marne Valley is defined by the river, cutting like a knife and making many soil types,' he explained, pointing out six different soil varities between us and the river, less than 800 metres away. 'Our job is to keep the character of each vineyard.' Tarlant's 14 hectares are spread across 57 plots, each of which are vinified separately. An extensive range of 2012 vins clairs exemplifies the distinctiveness of mineral expression and flavour profile of each plot.

Most of these vineyards were planted by his family and boast an average age of 34 years. The estate has had opportunity to increase slightly as contracts end on his grandfather's vineyards contracted to others, though only one hectare has been gained in this way in the past four years. Benoît credits chalk in the soil for a diversity of grape selection.

'This area is best suited to black grapes, as chardonnay is quite rustic,' he points out, explaining his breakdown of 50% pinot noir, 30% chardonnay, 18% pinot meunier and 2% petit meslier, arbane and pinot blanc.

Benoît prizes the diversity of his many plots, but admits it's a challenge to manage so many distinct sites using techniques sympathetic to organic practices. Three hectares are managed biodynamically, some organically, neither certified, and the remainder rely on his ingenious regime of 'herbal therapy'. A wide range of herbs are planted in the vineyards, including oregano, which he harvests for pizzas and salads. Small concoctions are made from the plants and sprayed on the vines to protect against fungus attacks. He says 2012 was a good year to practise. 'We only lost 30% of fruit in our vineyards with herbal therapy, but 40% with organics and 50% with biodynamics.'

INTUITIVE WINEMAKING

The goal is to harvest ripe, tasty grapes with balanced acidity. To this end, malolactic fermentation is completely blocked. 'I think malolactic is an industry mistake from the 1960s and 1970s,' Benoît suggests. 'Traditionally, the majority of champagne was without malolactic fermentation. It makes sense to me to show the wine naturally, with its natural acidity.'

Intensity, precision and presence of texture are Benoît's priorities. Every transfer in the winery is performed by gravity. The traditional champagne pressing regime is taken one step further, by carefully splitting the juice from the first pressing into two separate components, and the tailles into two components. 'I hate pre-blending, so we vinify every parcel separately,' he explains. 'We should respect the origin of the place here in Champagne as much as they do in Burgundy.'

Two-thirds of the harvest is barrel fermented using wild yeast, without additions of enzymes or bentonite for clarification or stabilisation. The remainder is tank fermented in temperature-controlled stainless steel to preserve vitality. Inspired by friends in Italy, Benoît experimented with ageing in four 200-litre clay amphorae in 2012, for greater oxygen exchange than in barrels, though he's quick to point out he doesn't

The spectacular Château de Boursault overlooks the pinot meunier vines of the southern slopes of the Vallée de la Marne.

want to make orange wines. The plan is to ferment in these for the first time in 2013.

Barrels are always purchased new and maintained until they are up to 30 years of age. 'I'm not a big fan of new barrels, but as a non-malolactic cellar, I don't want to bring the wolf into the sheep pen!' Benoît exclaims, in reference to the risk of introducing brettanomyces from used barrels. Parcels fermented in new barrels are always blended. 'I prefer older barrels, but after long ageing of 7–10 years, the impact of a well-managed new barrel is not so scary!'

Bâtonnage is used to help to finish fermentation and to build texture. 'I love working with barrels, so the wines can breathe and not look so monolithic,' he says. Reserve wines are aged in oak casks, and he incorporates at least three vintages in his Zero Brut, which he considers crucial for this style. Long bottle ageing is also critical in this process. Non-vintage wines are typically matured at least 3.5 years in bottle, and vintage wines typically 10 years.

'When I was young, I wanted to hurry the disgorgement, but my grandfather taught me to wait six years by showing me the profound texture and character that developed as the wine breathed over time. I don't want to show a wine until it reveals its personality.'

Zero dosage

Benoît's ultimate goal is to make zero-dosage champagne. 'We don't need to add sugar to Chablis, so why do we need to do it with champagne?' He aims to pick grapes ripe when he can. 'We must always reach the prettiest maturity, not the highest maturity, so adding sugar should not be a question.' The point is not zero dosage, but to create wine of flavour and atmosphere. He chaptalises when he has to (none was necessary in 2012) and uses low dosages of less than 6g/L in cuvées that require it, though he doesn't enjoy adding dosage.

Benoît's father has been making Zero Brut since the early 1980s, long before zero dosage was the rage in Champagne. 'Back then you could count on one hand all the people making this style in Champagne,' Benoît points out. 'I'm scared that it's becoming trendy now.'

It took him six years to build Tarlant Zero to the major cuvée of the estate, now representing around 100,000 bottles annually — a monumental feat for one of Champagne's better composed examples of this challenging style. He has also elevated Rosé Zero to the main rosé of the house.

'There are perhaps four or five zero-dosage rosés now, but when I began in 2000 it was a no-man's land, and I had no one else's wines to look at,' he says. He made six trials of pinot noir and pinot meunier, each with skin contact, blended from red and white wines and blended with chardonnay. 'The question with zero-dosage rosé was how to get acid and tannin to live together. I found the skin contact wines too angular in their tannin expression, so I prefer to blend.' Benoît chose chardonnay blended with pinot noir red wine, but the evolution continues. The current dilemma is an attempt to build greater persistence using white wine from black grapes — a challenge because even white pinot noir contributes tannins.

Benoît is preparing to release his first series of single-vineyard wines. 'I'm not here to make single vineyards, but sometimes the taste of the samples makes it irresistible!' he exclaims. 'The first year I experienced real taste, explosiveness and length in single parcels was 2003.'

He is about to add a new building to extend the winery, not to increase production but to provide space to work with his 57 plots and a portfolio now spanning 13 cuvées. All have boasted informative back labels since 2000, detailing terroirs, cépages, vintages, disgorgement date and dosage.

Tarlant Brut Reserve NV • $

93 points • Disgorged June 2010 • Tasted in Oeuilly

Zero Brut with dosage; 2006 base vintage; one-third each of chardonnay, pinot noir and pinor meunier; no malolactic fermentation; 6g/L dosage

Tarlant once created Zero Brut by omitting dosage from Brut Reserve, in the pattern of most houses, but Benoît turned the tables and now creates a little Brut Reserve from Zero Brut. The dosage is well integrated and nicely balanced with its acidity, accenting notes of succulent white peach, nectarine and honey. Vibrant lemon zest remains the theme, with toasty roast nut complexity welling up in the background. Well made and wallet-friendly, though Zero Brut has the edge.

The Champagne Guide

TARLANT ZERO BRUT NATURE NV • $

94 points • 55% 2007, 15% 2006, 15% 2005 AND 15% 2004 • DISGORGED JULY 2012
• TASTED IN OEUILLY
94 points • 60% 2006, 13% 2005, 13% 2004 AND 13% 2002 • DISGORGED JANUARY 2011
• TASTED IN OEUILLY AND BRISBANE

One-third each of chardonnay, pinot noir and pinor meunier; vines more than 25 years of age; fermented in stainless steel tanks; reserves aged in oak barrels; no malolactic fermentation; aged 4 years on lees; zero dosage; 100,000 bottles

Benoît Tarlant has sensitively honed every stage of viticulture and production to foster balance in his Zero Brut, aiming for an accuracy, purity and directness that he likens to playing darts. Flavour, not austerity, is a priority here, with ripe fruit, three reserve vintages and long bottle ageing creating balance and presence. The high acid 2007 season was not an easy base on which to build this style, calling for some chaptalisation, though the result is impressive. A fresh, lively and textural apéritif of generous yellow mirabelle plum fruit, pulled in tight by grapefruit and lime juice, emphasising chalk minerality on a crisp finish. The 2006 vintage was an easier season for a friendly and approachable Zero Brut, with its succulent white stone fruits, building generosity of toast, honey, gingernut biscuits, even a hint of dark chocolate. It's at once creamy and tense, with an electric zap of malic acidity energising softly chalky minerality.

TARLANT ROSÉ ZERO BRUT NATURE NV • $$

93 points • DISGORGED APRIL 2012 • TASTED IN OEUILLY

2008 base vintage with 2007 reserves; 85% chardonnay, 15% pinot noir red wine; fermented in stainless steel tanks and oak barrels; reserves aged in oak barrels; no malolactic fermentation; zero dosage

A medium to full salmon-crimson hue is quite bold for such a subtle, elegant and crisp rosé. Precise strawberry hull, pomegranate and lifted rose petal notes are underlined by fine-spun chalk mineral texture and soft, fine tannins. Benoît describes its light and refreshing finish as 'thin and short', but he's a bit harsh. I quite like it.

TARLANT BRUT PRESTIGE EXTRA BRUT 2000 • $$

94 points • DISGORGED DECEMBER 2011 • TASTED IN OEUILLY

90% chardonnay, 10% pinot noir from five vineyards; fermented in stainless steel tanks and oak barrels; no malolactic fermentation; 5g/L dosage

Benoît's second vintage was a tricky one, sustaining significant damage from two hail storms, but the season finished confidently, with chardonnay the star. His philosophy is to draw out the character of the season, varying the blend substantially each year, before ageing the wine a minimum of 10 years. The result will go down among Champagne's longer-lived 2000s. At 13 years of age, it's backward and honed, with tense, fresh malic acidity drawing out grapefruit and preserved lemon flavours, accenting vivid chalk texture. It's developed some hazelnut and toast complexity, but is only halfway through its development, screaming out for more time.

TARLANT BRUT PRESTIGE ROSÉ EXTRA BRUT 2003 • $$

93 points • DISGORGED OCTOBER 2012 • TASTED IN OEUILLY

88% chardonnay, 12% pinot noir red wine; fermented in stainless steel tanks and oak barrels; no malolactic fermentation; 3g/L dosage

'There are no rules for this wine. It could be made by skin contact or blending — it depends on my mood and the grapes!' Benoît exclaims. His aspirations are potential to age, and character of the year. The strength of 2003 was too much for skin contact, so he blended to produce a medium salmon hue. The generosity of the season is declared in ripe yellow plums and gentle white cherries, becoming softly toasty, toned by the lively freshness of malic acidity. A long, generous finish of elegant cherry fruit is balanced with a subtle touch of finely textured grip.

TARLANT BAM NV • $$$$

84 points • TASTED IN OEUILLY

50% 2008, 50% 2007; 66% petit meslier, 17% arbane, 17% pinot blanc; no malolactic fermentation

A new single-vineyard blend was codenamed 'BAM' in the cellar, and it stuck. Benoît admits it's a young release for young vines, and confesses its acidity may never disappear. He's still learning how to handle these varieties. 'Arbane and I have difficulties understanding each other!' he divulges. There's an uncomfortable feeling of unripeness in spicy notes of green herbs, cloves, grapefruit and loquat. Taut malic acidity and firm phenolic grip build an assertive, robust style with a firm, callow finish. Unique, characterful, and more than challenging.

TARLANT LA VIGNE D'OR BLANC DE MEUNIERS EXTRA BRUT 2003 • $$

93 points • DISGORGED JULY 2012 • TASTED IN OEUILLY

Single-vineyard Oeuilly pinot meunier; vines more than 50 years old; vinified in old oak barrels with regular bâtonnage; no malolactic fermentation; 2g/L dosage

The rounded, succulent, fruit-stuffed generosity of pinot meunier is proclaimed in yellow mirabelle plums, dried pear and honey, while a decade in confinement has drawn out complexity of Christmas cake, marzipan and roast almonds. Tarlant's old vines on chalk-clay subsoils retain sufficient acidity to hold this warm season in stead, maintaining the freshness to counter subtle dry bitterness on the finish.

TARLANT LA VIGNE ROYALE BLANC DE NOIRS EXTRA BRUT 2003 • $$$$

92 points • TASTED IN OEUILLY

Single-vineyard pinot noir from the steepest site in Oeuilly; no malolactic fermentation; 1g/L dosage

Powerful, rich and bombastic, this is a pinot noir crammed with succulent, cooked yellow summer fruits, baked apples, cinnamon and nutmeg. Its juicy, rounded, bouncy front end pulls into a finish refreshened by lively malic acidity. The muscular, phenolic texture characteristic of the warm 2003 season makes its mark, though its fruit ultimately retains balanced composure.

TARLANT LA VIGNE D'ANTAN CHARDONNAY 2002 • $$$

Single-vineyard Oeuilly ungrafted chardonnay; vinified in old barrels with bâtonnage; no malolactic fermentation; dosage yet to be determined

Tarlant's 'Vines of Yesteryear' showcases ungrafted chardonnay on an ancient terroir. It's an assertive style of taut grapefruit zest and wood spice, with malic acidity sharp enough to cut paper, yet upholding inherent balance, poise and great persistence. Oak provides strong support without asserting itself too much. At 11 years of age, it screams out for as long again before approaching. Disgorged on the spot without dosage, I can't commit to a score, but given sufficient time this could become one of the highlights of Tarlant.

TARLANT CUVÉE LOUIS NV • $$

95 points • DISGORGED EARLY 2012 • TASTED IN OEUILLY

80% 1998, 20% 1997 and 1996; 50% chardonnay, 50% pinot noir; single vineyard; 64-year-old vines; vinified in old oak barrels with regular bâtonnage; no malolactic fermentation; 3g/L dosage

Tarlant's original and chalkiest vineyard 'Les Crayons' is closest to the cooling influence of the Marne, the quintessential expression of Oeuilly. The wine rises to its grand credentials, with tremendous maturity bringing gentle calm to dynamic malic acidity and great complexity. Tangy grapefruit and ripe stone fruits retain succulent composure, against a backdrop of ever-rising detail of coconut marshmallow, roast almonds and mixed spice. Softly chalky minerality remains an ever-present theme to an energetic and enduring finish, promising a very long future. The high-flying 1996 base vintage is yet to be released, surpassing 1998 in structure, focus and depth. The lesser 1999 is coming next, a taut release that needs more time.

Aspect is critical in Champagne, and these south-facing slopes of Mareuil-sur-Aÿ are a contrast to the north-facing sites of Oeuilly.

TSARINE

(Tsah-reen)

ALLÉE DU VIGNOBLE 51100 REIMS

www.tsarine.com

*T*sarine is a brand of the house of Chanoine Frères, founded in 1730, the second-oldest house in Champagne. Owned by the giant Lanson-BCC group, the house produces 500,000 bottles under the Tsarine brand. Its fresh, fruity and inexpensive champagnes are blended from equal thirds of chardonnay, pinot noir and pinor meunier and carry an air of simplicity.

TSARINE CUVÉE PREMIUM BRUT NV • $$

89 points • DISGORGED APRIL 2012 • TASTED IN BRISBANE

67% 2008, 33% 2007; 34% chardonnay, 33% pinot noir, 33% pinot meunier from the Sézannais, Avize, Écueil, Les Riceys and the Vallée de la Marne; 10.3g/L dosage

An appealing, fruit-focused and fresh style showcasing the robust and slightly rustic richness of pinots in luscious stone fruit, apple, pear and honey. The youthfulness of the blend is announced in quite firm acidity, rounded a little on the finish by honeyed dosage, yet finishing with good tension. The bead is a little large, but it nonetheless represents a value-for-money style — clean, refreshing, primary and well made.

TSARINE ROSÉ BRUT NV • $$

90 points • DISGORGED APRIL 2012 • TASTED IN BRISBANE

70% 2008, 30% 2007; 34% chardonnay, 33% pinot noir, 33% pinot meunier from the Sézannais, Avize, Écueil, Les Riceys and the Vallée de la Marne; 11g/L dosage

A medium-blush crimson hue announces a youthful and flamboyant rosé of elementary rose petal, strawberry and red cherry fruit. There's little depth to carry it through to the finish, which ultimately closes short and simple. Nonetheless, clean, refreshing and well made, with dosage matched to taut, primary acidity.

ULYSSE COLLIN

(Oo-lees Kohl-la)

7/10

---

21 RUE DES VIGNERONS 51270 CONGY

CHAMPAGNE
Ulysse Collin

O livier Collin is a young face on the rise among Champagne's growers, inspired after working with Anselme Selosse to reclaim a portion of his family's vines in Congy in the Sézannais to produce his first vintage in 2004. He has since re-established the family winery and cellar and reclaimed a total of 8.7 hectares in the village, neighbouring Vert La Gravelle and nearby Barbonne-Fayel, planted to chardonnay and pinot noir. His vines are largely aged 30–60 years and are tended using a combination of organic and conventional practices, applying organic compost, ploughing and avoiding pesticides. He is experimenting with biodynamics and aims to convert to organics in the coming years. Winemaking is likewise natural, relying on wild yeasts to complete very long fermentations in predominantly five-year-old and 15% new barriques. All cuvées to date have been single-vineyard blanc de blancs or blanc de noirs, showcasing the grainy minerality and power of the Sézannais. Back labels declare base vintages and disgorgement dates.

ULYSSE COLLIN LES PIERRIÉRES BLANC DE BLANCS EXTRA BRUT NV • $$$

94 points • DISGORGED OCTOBER 2012 • TASTED IN BRISBANE

100% 2008; 1.7g/L dosage

From Collin's 1.2 hectare vineyard of 30-year-old vines on chalk in Vert La Gravelle, this is a vintage of real concentration, fit for main-course game bird fare. A powerful wine from the outset, with a deep hue with gold tints and a voluptuous character of golden delicious apple, brioche, burnt butter, roast nuts, dried fig, even hints of charcuterie. Persistence is profound, framed in taut, lively acidity and grainy minerality.

VAZART-COQUART ET FILS

(Vah-zah Kho-khar e Feess)

6/10

---

6 RUE DES PARTELAINES 51530 CHOUILLY
www.champagnevazartcoquart.com

*T*he Vazart family has tended vines in the Côte des Blancs grand cru of Chouilly for generations. Today it crafts a ripe fruit style exclusively from 30 estate parcels spread over 11 hectares. Vines averaging 30 years of age are limited in yield by green harvesting. Reserve wines are stored as a perpetual blend, dating back to 1982. Each year, 25–30% is taken for Brut Réserve NV and replenished with the current harvest. Sensitive craftsmanship captures the mineral expression and robust character of Chouilly, softened with malolactic fermentation and lees ageing.

VAZART-COQUART & FILS BRUT RÉSERVE BLANC DE BLANCS NV • $$

93 points • DISGORGED JUNE 2012 • TASTED IN BRISBANE

60% 2009 base vintage, 40% reserve solera back to 1982; 100% Chouilly chardonnay; full malolactic fermentation; 8g/L dosage

Impeccably crafted and uncomplicated, this is a quintessential apéritif champagne that declares the signature of Chouilly and the precision of blanc de blancs. The bouquet dances with lifted lemon blossom, pure grapefruit, almost-ripe pear, lemon zest and a hint of struck flint. The intensity of Chouilly is reflected in back palate depth of white peach and grapefruit, sitting within a honed, precise, crisp and crunchy style. The finish is tightly strung.

VAZART-COQUART & FILS GRAND BOUQUET 2006 • $$

93 points • DISGORGED MAY 2012 • TASTED IN BRISBANE

100% Chouilly chardonnay; full malolactic fermentation; 6g/L dosage

The robust personality of Chouilly is on full display here, yet handled with sensitivity and skill. Honed tension juxtaposes expressive generosity as layers of crunchy grapefruit zest, lemon juice and white peach build with considerable weight on the palate. A powerful structure is underlined with well-judged phenolic grip that leaves the finish textural and strong, dodging any sense of dryness or distraction from its even fruit flow and fine, creamy bead. An impeccably handled wine that leaves a subtle trail of nutmeg, spice and salty minerality in the mouth.

VEUVE CLICQUOT

(Verv Khlee-kho)

7/10

1 PLACE DES DROITS DE L'HOMME 51100 REIMS
www.veuve-clicquot.com

Veuve Clicquot

■ REIMS FRANCE ■

*D*ramatic developments are underway in the bellows of Veuve Clicquot that are only just beginning to bubble to the surface. Its characterful, full-bodied, pinot-focused wines are more refined every time I look, an astounding feat for a house with a dizzying annual production of 18 million bottles, ranking a confident number two by volume behind Moët & Chandon in Louis Vuitton-Moët Hennessy's champagne kingdom. Even Clicquot's conspicuous 'Yellow Label' non-vintage, in its inimitable, trademark, mango-orange livery, is looking trim and fit today, having lost its curvaceous sweetness — quite a workout for a cuvée that alone accounts for a whopping 15 million bottles every year. Its vintage wines are where Veuve Clicquot really steps up, and La Grande Dame has entered a new age of dashing, mineral-infused refinement. For an operation of such a grand scale, the consistency of Veuve Clicquot is unrivalled in all of Champagne.

'VEUVE CLICQUOT IS A BIG HOUSE WHERE WE HAVE A big responsibility to maintain the style, but every day we work to improve the quality,' Chef de Cave Dominique Demarville explains as he shows me through one of his two expansive wineries in Reims. With a glimmer in his eye he announces, 'The winery is like a kitchen where we can experiment!'

Then he thrusts open a gigantic door to reveal a grand spectacle of proportions I have never witnessed anywhere in Champagne. Oak barrels. Huge oak barrels. New foudres of 5000 litres and 7500 litres. Lots of them. I know of winemakers proud to show off just one of these beauties. And here, hidden in an enormous warehouse somewhere in the depths of Veuve Clicquot, are 30 of them, lined up in all of their towering magnificence of intricately crafted French oak, perfectly interconnected with arteries of polished stainless steel.

These 200,000 litres of oak-fermented wine — a tiny drop in the ocean of Clicquot — will become just 5–10% of its vintage wines, and a smaller proportion of non-vintage reserves. Leading me around the room to sample from his battalion of barrels, Demarville is as excited as a kid with a room full of new toys. 'Sometimes my team tells me I'm too involved in what I'm doing, but I work with my heart and not my head,' he confesses as he pours me an Oger chardonnay of which he's particularly proud. 'Barrel fermentation offers the chance to improve without changing the Clicquot style,' he explains. 'To add some spice!'

PROGRESSIVE TRANSFORMATION

It's a subtle twist for the company, but it typifies the evolution that is slowly transforming one of Champagne's biggest players, leaving no stage of production untouched. Clicquot is in motion in its vineyards, vinification, and most notably its regimes of malolactic fermentation, reserves and dosage. 'The Veuve Clicquot style is about richness, but also about brightness; strong and full-bodied and at the same time fresh,' Demarville clarifies. It's in brightness and freshness that he has most demonstrably refined these wines since taking the helm in 2006, at just 39 years of age.

This has not been an easy time to drive such evolution. 'With climate change, we are seeing vintages which are more and more diverse,' he reveals. Since 2000, the house has declared just five vintages: 2002, 2004, 2006, 2008 and 2012 (and no Vintage Brut in 2006 or La Grande Dame in 2002).

Demarville remains upbeat. 'I am very confident about the future. So many things have happened in Champagne over the past century, and we will adapt again. We will adjust our winegrowing and our winemaking to ensure that we can continue to make champagnes of elegance and minerality.'

PRIVILEGED VINEYARD RESOURCES

This begins in a substantial and enviably positioned vineyard resource. Clicquot is privileged to a respectable estate of 382 hectares, including a wealth of grand crus, providing for just one-quarter of its needs, with a further 125 hectares supplied by LVMH vineyards, boosting the total to 30%. The remainder is sourced from 1200 growers with an average of less than one hectare each.

'Our smallest contract is for 93 square metres of vines,' Demarville told me when we first met in the small dining room of Montrachet restaurant in Brisbane some years ago. 'That's less than the size of this room!' Many of Clicquot's growers have supplied fruit to no other company for a number of generations.

The estate is planted to almost 50% chardonnay — a high proportion in Champagne, particularly for a house in which every cuvée is led by pinot noir. The Montagne de Reims has been the focus for Clicquot historically, and it is the proud custodian of some of the finest sites for pinot noir in Verzy, Verzenay and Bouzy. These form the core of La Grande Dame.

The house also sources 15% of its needs from the Côte des Bar. 'I have a dream,' Demarville announces. 'I hope that one day in Champagne we will pay for grapes according to quality, not according to volume and vineyard designation.'

Clicquot is working to enhance quality by planting grasses in the mid-rows of its vineyards to encourage deeper roots. This assists with retaining acidity in the wines in warmer vintages, since the vines have more consistent access to water. It also reduces the impact of vintage rains. 'Surface roots pump more water and produce dilution in the fruit when it rains,' Demarville explains. 'Hence, we are able to achieve more consistency in erratic seasons by encouraging deeper roots.'

He is also trialling earlier harvesting in an attempt to retain acidity. 'We have been very happy with the wines from 2009, but not sufficient to become a vintage for us. I think we picked a little too early,' he admits. 'It was not a warm year, but we had a difference between phenolic maturity and sugar maturity. Even at high sugar ripeness, there were green characters which will remain in the wines.'

EVOLUTIONARY WINEMAKING

Veuve Clicquot is investigating other means of retaining acidity. 'In the wake of climate change we must manage not only what happens in the vineyards, but also the winery,' Demarville clarifies. The house has traditionally allowed every parcel to complete malolactic fermentation, but since 2007 has experimented with blocking malolactic in some parcels destined for its reserves and vintage cuvées. This has created a dilemma in maintaining consistency, since malolactic fermentation also contributes texture to the wines.

The introduction of Demarville's prized foudres in 2007 may prove to be the answer, providing barrel fermentation texture without oak flavour to a house style that has traditionally relied on stainless steel tanks. He stepped up the regime in 2012 — a vintage of 'amazing acidity' — by blocking malolactic fermentation in half of the foudres. These vins clairs looked quite incredible at just a few months of age, but the real proof will not come until the 2008 vintage is released in 2015.

The threat of more extreme vintages in the wake of climate change has also bolstered Demarville's resolve to increase his stocks of reserve wines. 'Look at the last four harvests — 2008 was exceptional, with high acidity and lots of structure; 2009 was ripe, with low acidity; 2010 was dilute, and 2011 was very inconsistent. If you don't have sufficient stocks of reserve wines, you can't make great non-vintage champagne,' Demarville points out. On average, Yellow Label Brut Non-Vintage receives 35% reserve wines, increasing every year, with 42% in 2011.

'Our style of lots of body, complexity and richness needs a lot of reserve wines,' he explains. Clicquot claims to hold the biggest collection of reserve wines in Champagne besides Krug. 'We have at our disposal 17 years of reserves, from 2011 back to 1988.' These are amazing wines, and at a full quarter-century of maturity, a 1988 Cramant was ravishingly concentrated and complex, with allusions of chocolate. Clicquot holds the equivalent of an entire year of production in more than 400 different reserve wines, each of which is tasted twice every year, to allocate them before they begin to decline. All are kept on lees without filtration in tanks cooled to below 14°C to retain freshness.

Demarville points out that it's easier to control and refine wine in stainless steel tanks with temperature control, than it was under oak without temperature control. 'We are able to be more precise with our blending now than we were, which has enabled us to reduce levels of dosage,' he explains. 'We are not reducing dosage due to climate change, but because we have better control in the winery. Over the past 40 years we have been able to build greater purity and precision and so reduce dosage gradually.'

It's a flattering trend for Clicquot, embodied most emphatically in Yellow Label Brut Non-Vintage, which was candied and sweet with 12g/L dosage five years ago, now much more refreshing at 9g/L. Veuve Clicquot has resisted the 'low-dosage lobby', as Demarville calls it. 'We have a different vision in that the final sensation of sugar is affected not only by quantity, but also by the time in the cellar after dosage. Our vintage wine is released a year after disgorgement, so the impact of the sugar is diminished.'

Rosé is an increasingly important style for Clicquot, representing 5–6% of sales, and Demarville forecasts that this will double. 'Our demand for rosé has been amazing!' he exclaims. 'It's growing as a category so much faster than white champagne, fuelled by incredible improvements in the style over the past five or six years.'

Three hectares of estate pinot noir vines are allocated to red wine production for rosé, green harvested to reduce yields to 30–40% less than normal, and picked at high maturity. Clicquot also sources from 'top' growers in Bouzy and Ambonnay, and in 2012 for the first time, signed a contract with direct suppliers dedicated to red wines, in the hope of growing production. The house operates a winery dedicated to red wine production in Bouzy, and Demarville has created a new room for red wine storage in Reims. Here he showed me samples of 2012 wines of breathtaking violet and rose petal aromatics, culminating in the most profound Champagne red wine I have ever tasted. From the earth-shaking Clos Colin parcel on the mid-slope of Bouzy, there is complexity and depth that I have only ever seen in grand cru red Burgundy. It's fittingly reserved for La Grande Dame Rosé.

There is talk of printing the disgorgement date and dosage on the back label of vintage wines in the future, and I hope this will be extended to non-vintage cuvées, where it is even more pertinent. Last year, the house could not tell me with certainty the base vintages of the non-vintage cuvées I tasted in Australia. Demarville expresses concern about a disgorgement date being confused with a use-by date, but admits that the biggest challenge lies in managing the logistics on the labelling line. If Lanson and Ayala can do it, surely Clicquot can, too.

'I'm all for transparency, and if I can put the disgorgement date on the label I will do it,' he says. 'We are working on it, and I cross my fingers that we will have it in the next few years.' In the meantime, the three-digit number on the cork is the disgorgement date. The first two digits are the year, and the third digit is the bimester (e.g. 114 is July/August 2011).

In my tastings this year, two out of nine bottles of Veuve Clicquot that I have opened myself have been corked. I also encountered higher than average cork taint in these wines last year. I was impressed with Demarville's openness, explaining that he tests 200 corks from every shipment of 400,000–500,000, and if three are badly tainted or seven have minor taint, the batch is rejected. This should therefore equate to less than 3.5% taint — a tiny fraction of the level I've encountered. Something doesn't add up here. As always, return a corked bottle for replacement.

The lack of pretence and big-company 'spin' of Dominique Demarville and his offsider, Cyril Brun, are refreshing in the world of corporate champagne. 'I love tasting great wine, even if it only costs seven or eight euros!' Demarville remarks.

Over many tastings in Reims and several meetings in Australia, I have come to a high respect for what this man has achieved in his short time at Veuve Clicquot. There are few in Champagne who could seamlessly refine a house as large as this. The 2008 base Yellow Label was his first blend, and the finest I have seen.

'It is because 2008 is an amazing year!' Demarville responds, in unassuming humility. 'And I am very fortunate to have a talented and passionate team.'

Veuve Clicquot Brut Yellow Label NV • $$

91 points • 2009 base vintage with 35% reserves; 9g/L dosage • Tasted in Brisbane and Reims

92 points • 2008 base vintage • Disgorged early 2012; 10g/L dosage • Tasted in Reims and Brisbane

92 points • 2007 base vintage with 29% reserve wines from 2006, 2005 and 2004 • Disgorged early 2011; 10g/L dosage • Tasted in Sydney

50–53% pinot noir, 28–30% chardonnay, 18–20% pinot meunier; from 50–60 villages; 15 million bottles

Yellow Label is on a gentle trajectory of refinement, attaining something of a crescendo in the great 2008 vintage. Led by the crunchy red apples, white peach and generous spice of pinot noir, the subtle sweetness of the 2007 base is trumped by 2008, with its vibrant energy and refined lemon blossom, a wonderful marriage of volume and finesse. At the beginning of its release cycle, the 2009 base is as crunchy and zesty as I have seen Yellow Label, with a harmonious tension of lively acid drive. It seems the honeyed dosage that once left Yellow Label a little candied is a thing of the past.

Veuve Clicquot Rosé NV • $$

90 points • Disgorged July 2011 • Tasted in Sydney, Brisbane and Reims

2007 base vintage; 25–40% reserve wines; 50–55% pinot noir, 28–33% chardonnay, 15–20% pinot meunier; Brut Yellow Label with 12% red wines from the villages that Demarville upholds as Champagne's best for red wine production: Bouzy, Ambonnay, Verzy, Verzenay, Dizy, Aÿ, Cumières and Les Riceys; 10g/L dosage; 1.4 million bottles annually

This is not a rosé that appreciates time in bottle — the fresh redcurrants, strawberries and raspberries that it exuded a year after disgorgement have already faded in every bottle tasted just six months later. A pale crimson hue has deepened to a medium salmon-orange, announcing a softer, more rounded style, beginning to dry out and take on notes of forest floor. Acidity remains vibrant, finishing with a lively tang that perfectly balances its dosage. I would suggest holding out for the 2008 base vintage but, without the benefit of disgorgement dates on back labels, there's no way of identifying fresh stock.

Veuve Clicquot Vintage Brut 2004 • $$$

94 points • Disgorged late 2009 • Tasted in Sydney, Melbourne and Brisbane

62% pinot noir, 30% chardonnay, 8% pinot meunier; 20 grand cru and premier cru Marne villages; 7g/L dosage; next Vintage Brut will be 2008, a noble quality commitment in reducing vintages

For a pinot-led wine in the full-bodied style of Clicquot, this is a tightly wound interpretation of 2004. On release 18 months ago, it looked like it needed some time to unravel, and it's held exactly true to this since. Great fruit intensity of fleshy white peach, white currants and citrus zest is captured with awesome poise, personifying 2004, vivid and bright, yet wonderfully concentrated. The elegance of 2004 prompted one of the lowest dosages ever for a Clicquot vintage, gracefully setting off a fine, creamy bead, penetrating acid line and great chalk mineral depth. The first bottle I opened was cork-tainted, as was the first last year — a disturbing trend.

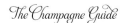

VEUVE CLICQUOT VINTAGE ROSÉ 2004 • $$$

94 points • DISGORGED LATE 2008 • TASTED IN REIMS, SYDNEY AND BRISBANE

Vintage Brut 2004 with red wine; 62% pinot noir, 30% chardonnay, 8% pinot meunier; 15% red wine from Bouzy; 9g/L dosage

Clicquot's Vintage Rosé philosophy is to blend its Vintage Brut with red wines of structure and tannin to create more character. Aged under cork a year after disgorgement, this vintage has already been in the market three years, initially flattering in its pretty red fruits and gradually mellowing to a more juicy demeanour, now much more toasty and savoury, touched with nuances of flinty reduction. An upwelling of forest floor maturity envelops intense red cherries and red berries of all kinds, with a lingering cherry kernel finish. Nuances of wood spice, green coffee beans and roast hazelnuts are supported by a great undercurrent of chalk mineral texture. The 2008 disgorgements I tasted in France and Australia in 2013 are coming to the end of their life, though I am told 2010 disgorgements are still current in France.

VEUVE CLICQUOT LA GRANDE DAME BRUT 2004 • $$$$

97 points • TASTED IN SYDNEY, ADELAIDE, BRISBANE AND REIMS

61% pinot noir from Verzenay, Verzy, Bouzy, Ambonnay and Aÿ; 39% chardonnay from Avize, Oger and Le Mesnil-sur-Oger; 70–75% estate vines; 100% malolactic fermentation; 7g/L dosage

The 2004 is the first La Grande Dame since 1998, an aeon in the modern era of champagne releases. Vintage 2002 was deemed too bold and insufficiently mineral for La Grande Dame, and a small production of 25,000 bottles of 2000 was written off by cork taint. The 2004 ushers in a new age, disarmingly youthful, dramatically high-pitched and as glittering as fresh powder snow in full sun. Its minerality shimmers with ethereal chalk dust and sea-salt texture, penetrating deep into the mouth, illuminated by dazzling acidity. It launches with euphoric lemon zest, grapefruit and cut red apple, slowly morphing into white peach and dried pear, with flickers of honey, toast, cloves, dried lavender and beeswax, tightly contained within a delicate shell. Chalk minerality glimmers and dances long and enduring on an awe-inspiring finish. An introverted Grande Dame of concealed power and breathtakingly youthful demeanour hitherto unknown for Clicquot. Barely beginning its life at almost a decade of age, it has a magnificent life before it. Hold off at least another five years before diving in. One bottle opened was corked.

VEUVE CLICQUOT LA GRANDE DAME ROSÉ 2004 • $$$$$

97 points • DISGORGED LATE 2010 • TASTED IN REIMS

61% pinot noir from Verzy, Verzenay and Aÿ; 39% chardonnay from Le Mesnil-sur-Oger; 15% red wines from Veuve Clicquot's Clos Colin vineyard in Bouzy

The Vintage Rosé's ideal is for the grapes to speak, and La Grande Dame Rosé's ideal is for the soil to speak. And speak it does, with an avalanche of tumbling fury of chalk minerality from the five loftiest grand crus of the Montagne de Reims and Côte des Blancs. Clos Colin delivers a red wine of folkloric magnificence, building a medium salmon hue and orange tint. It swoops and dives with red cherry and raspberry freshness, and acrobatics of truffles, orange rind, anise, vanilla and kirsch. Delivering such formidable power while sustaining arresting finesse is one of Champagne's highest arts, captured here in a melodramatic juxtaposition of complexity and freshness.

Veuve Clicquot Cave Privée Brut 1990 • $$$$$

97 points • Disgorged October 2008 (on back label) • Tasted in Brisbane

56% pinot noir, 33% chardonnay, 11% pinot meunier; 4g/L dosage; 16,388 bottles

Veuve Clicquot has the resourcefulness to set aside a respectable allocation of every vintage release for its late-disgorged Cave Privée. A bold venture, not least because vintages that don't age well will never surface. Future releases are yet to be determined, with 1979, 1982, 1995 and 1996 all in the running, and 1999 in doubt. Twenty-three years post-vintage and five years post-disgorgement, 1990 is a grand testimony to the enduring power of a vintage that has not diminished one bit since I first encountered it four years ago. The bouquet is a mesmerising, inviting, golden sunset, swept with vivid brushstrokes of honey, buttered toast, crème brûlée, toasted almonds and Parisian baguette. The palate is a revelation of silken complexity of such creamy smoothness it's almost impossible to separate its multi-faceted intricacy. Stare hard enough and you might make out shapes of baked peach, lemon butter, dried pear and wisps of pipe smoke. The spectacle lingers for minutes amidst a grainy backdrop of dry, chalky minerality. Find yourself a lofty post and bask in its radiant glow.

Veuve Clicquot Cave Privée 1989 • $$$$$

95 points • Disgorged May 2010 • Tasted in Reims

67% pinot noir, 33% chardonnay; 4g/L dosage

A handsome expression of the secondary development of champagne, full of roast almonds and honey, upholding a gorgeous core of succulent pear, baked white peach and preserved lemon, finishing with a flourish of mixed spice, fennel, fig and a wisp of warm hearth. It's creamy and caressing, contrasting soft, dry, mineral structure with a silky, buttery flow, just beginning to show signs of drying out and fading on the finish, though its fruit holds out for now. If 1989 was your year, this wine is set for release just in time for your 25th, but don't save it for your 30th.

Veuve Clicquot Cave Privée 1982 • $$$$$

96 points • Disgorged June 2010 • Tasted in Reims

66% pinot noir, 34% chardonnay; 4g/L dosage

Here's evidence that high-yielding Champagne vintages are capable of soaring beyond 30 years with effortless grace. Attaining a calm confidence in its old age, upholding delightful intensity of secondary stone fruits and grilled pineapple, it proudly bears the laughter lines of roast nuts, burnt toffee, sautéed mushrooms, even Vegemite and a suggestion of antique sofa. An undented fruit core holds out amidst drying structure — its magnificent peak coinciding with its 2014 release, and every sign it will hold for at least a few years beyond.

Veuve Clicquot Cave Privée Rosé 1990 • $$$$$

96 points • Disgorged May 2011 • Tasted in Reims

56% pinot noir, 33% chardonay, 11% pinot meunier; 17% Bouzy red wine; 4g/L dosage

Enchanting aromas of all manner of goodies fresh from grandma's kitchen: honey biscuits, candied almonds, glacé figs and a hint of last night's poached cherries. It's come to that place of tertiary complexity and deep savoury character, conjuring memories of pine nettles, sweet pipe smoke and the warm glow of smouldering embers. Seamless, silky generosity culminates in the subtle grip of finely structured texture. The impeccable balance and lively acidity of 1990 still sing, amplified by the richness of Bouzy rouge. Just beginning to dry on the finish, this is a vintage to be celebrated on its release in 2014.

Veuve Clicquot Cave Privée Brut Rosé 1989 • $$$$$

95 points • Disgorged October 2008 (on back label) • Tasted in Brisbane

Two-thirds pinot noir and one-third chardonnay, blended with pinot noir red wine; 4g/L dosage; 24,825 bottles

A warm glow of early morning sunrise radiates from the glass. Inhale, and you step out of a cool, damp morning in a towering pine forest, into an old hunting lodge, with pine sap sizzling from logs in a dusty stone fireplace. Sip, and you meet the most enchanting air of leathery old grand cru red Burgundy, with all of its truffles, 'sous bois' (forest undergrowth) and mushrooms. It has ventured to that remote place where tertiary development has fully taken over, yet a core of fig admirably maintains life and persistence amid a dry structure. I first tasted this grand old thing a year after disgorgement, and its light has slowly dimmed since, but it still represents an enchanting old rosé, now in the twilight of its life. Reserve it for long, melancholy nights before glowing embers in faraway places.

Veuve Clicquot Cave Privée Rosé 1979 • $$$$$

97 points • Disgorged in 2011 • Tasted in Reims

61% pinot noir, 33% chardonnay, 6% pinot meunier; 4g/L dosage

Due for release in 2014 at no less than 35 years of age, this is testimony to the mesmeric longevity of 1979. Its primary definition is a revelation, expressing its pinot noir core in blackcurrants, cherry liqueur and anise, with a lifetime gathering complexity of forest floor, leather and game, akin to old red Burgundy. Truffles, roast tomatoes, burnt butter, pipe smoke and Vegemite join the spectacle amidst a silky mouthfeel of great persistence. A towering monument to magnificent old rosé, with no hint of crumbling on any side.

Veuve Clicquot Bouzy Rouge 1955

97 points • Tasted in Reims

Veuve Clicquot today is privileged to some of Bouzy's finest red wines, and I include this rare bottle here as evidence that this is nothing new. After more than half a century, there's still a vibrancy to its red hue and a core of secondary red cherry fruit, encased in truffles, mushrooms and dank cellar notes. Beautifully focused acidity and silky tannins proclaim the breathtaking longevity of Champagne's greatest reds. Remarkable.

VEUVE FOURNY & FILS

(Verv Fawny e Feess)

7/10

5 RUE DU MESNIL BP 12 51130 VERTUS
www.champagne-veuve-fourny.com

CHAMPAGNE
Vᵛᵉ FOURNY & FILS
une Famille, un Clos, un Premier Cru

*W*hen a tiny plot on pure chalk in the coveted 'Le Mont Ferré' hillsides of the northern end of Vertus towards Le Mesnil-sur-Oger came up for sale in the summer of 2011, offers poured in from big houses, but the grower chose the brothers Emmanuel and Charles-Henry Fourny as its new custodians. The offer was indicative of the respect with which the young fifth-generation growers manage some of the finest terroirs in Vertus. Their location on Rue du Mesnil on the northern edge of Vertus is a clue to their success, with vineyards capturing the more mineral side of the premier cru village neighbouring the grand cru of Le Mesnil-sur-Oger itself.

WHEN I FIRST VISITED JUST FOUR WEEKS BEFORE THE scheduled start of vintage 2011, Rue du Mesnil was completely closed off. Veuve Fourny's winery was totally gutted and swarming with construction workers. Emmanuel Fourny emerged from an early-morning meeting with his builders.

'We are grateful for the cooler weather,' he said, 'because there's no chance our new winery would be ready for an early vintage!'

It was the beginning of a grand new era for a family who has tended vineyards at the southern end of the Côte des Blancs since 1856 and made its own champagne since 1931. Theirs is one of the most expressive champagnes of the character of their beloved village of Vertus.

VINEYARD FOCUS

Veuve Fourny's focus remains resolutely and exclusively on Vertus, apart from a small parcel in Cramant. 'I like to express the terroir of Vertus and show that you can have a lot of expression with just one village,' says Emmanuel, who has a self-confessed obsession with purity and precision.

There's no better place in the Côte des Blancs than the sunny, south-east-oriented slopes of Vertus for him to bottle his vision. 'Vertus gives us better expression of fruit than the neighbouring grand crus of Le Mesnil-sur-Oger and Oger,' he explains. 'The chardonnay here has more of a pinot noir richness to it, which enables us to create blends exclusively from chardonnay that can be complete.'

The east-facing slopes of the village nurture chardonnay of fresh definition, while its warmer south-facing aspects are among the only vineyards of the Côte des Blancs planted to pinot noir. The brothers own 8.7 hectares, predominantly on the mineral hillside of 'Le Mont Ferré' towards Le Mesnil-sur-Oger, where thin soils bless vines with easy access to chalk, and a south-east aspect imparts greater fruit expression than the more rounded style of south-facing slopes.

They manage a further 3.6 hectares of family vines now owned by their cousins, supplemented with almost eight hectares managed according to an organic philosophy, most of which were originally part of the family estate. The Fournys work closely with their growers, whom they describe as 'small, serious and interested in separation of plots for precision winemaking.' These are mostly young growers and friends, who are invited back to taste their plots after vinification. In all, the brothers manage the vineyards and harvests for a sizeable 60% of the grapes they purchase. A total of 20 hectares provides for an annual production of 200,000 bottles.

Estate vines now average a hefty 45 years of age. 'Vines over 30 years transform the minerality of the chalk into the salty minerality of the wine, which we feel is very important,' Emmanuel explains. Such old vines ensure that yields are very low for Champagne, averaging below 60hL/hectare, less than two-thirds of Champagne's average, 'to produce a balance in our wines'. Green harvests are conducted in high-yielding years like 2004, when 30% of the crop was dropped.

Veuve Fourny balances a resolute commitment to the environment with a realistic awareness of the limitations of viticulture in a climate as marginal as this. Vineyard practice is essentially organic, with the exception of sprays, which are used when necessary. Grasses are cultivated in the mid-rows of one-third of vineyards, another third is cultivated to bare soil, and a further third without herbicide, with a goal to eliminate herbicide across all vineyards. Insect breeding is controlled using pheromones, canopy management is used instead of chemicals to control botrytis, and composting is used in place of fertiliser.

A normal spray regime is used to manage mildew, particularly in years like 2012, when it saved the crop. 'We like the organic philosophy, but we don't want to sacrifice our grapes to mildew,' Emmanuel says, referring to a trial the brothers conducted shortly after returning to the family estate in the mid-90s. Synthetic chemicals were forsaken in two parcels, but the wild spread of mildew necessitated weekly sprayings with copper sulphate — permitted under biodynamics

despite its toxicity and detrimental effect on the soil and vine growth. Much of the crop was lost and they returned to non-toxic synthetic products.

On the same site as the house on Rue du Mesnil, Clos Faubourg Notre-Dame was purchased by the brothers' grandfather in 1920, but it was only in 1990 that Emmanuel and Charles-Henry proposed to their mother that it be bottled separately.

With just 40 centimetres of soil before the chalk, they consider it a good plot, 'not better, but different, holding its freshness as a long-ageing style'. Its microclimate is protected by the enclosure. This plot is the source of their flagship cuvée. The brothers' grandmother built a house on part of the clos in 1965, which they removed in 2012 after she passed away. They have replanted this part of the vineyard to chardonnay, though won't use the fruit in this wine until the vines have reached 12 years of age.

MINIMAL INTERVENTION WINEMAKING

The brothers are excited about the potential of their new winemaking facility to capture greater detail from every parcel. Previously, the press house was in a different location to the winery. Tanks and winemaking equipment that had gradually amassed over the years were not well suited to small-batch winemaking, so they boldly decided to sell it all and create the new winery from scratch. A huge investment for a small company, and all the more impressive with no imperative to increase production.

Charles-Henry was initially sceptical about the outlay, preferring to see the investment poured into more vineyards. When I met him in Brisbane a few months later, I asked whether they had completed the facility in time for vintage. 'Not quite,' he said. 'It was very distressing! But we managed, and we really needed it this year because it allowed us to separate every single parcel for the first time. The new winery is completely adaptive to the size of the plots, giving us greater precision in the details. It will help us make a more precise expression of each place, so you can expect our wines to be finer in three years' time!'

The 60 plots from which the bothers source are quite distinct, and a year later he showed me 2012 vins clairs that revealed that even parcels just 150 metres apart can show significant diversity. These can now be kept separate for the first time, thanks to a small press that runs 24 hours a day during vintage, and tanks to keep 20 blends, compared with just 12 previously.

Fourny's philosophy of respect and minimal intervention in the vineyards applies equally in the winery, an insulated building built from stone from northern

Burgundy and wood from the nearby Vosges. Glass is utilised to capture natural light, all waste water is recycled on the gardens, and a natural cooling system pulls air in when it's cooler outside.

To preserve purity, only the first pressings are used, and the tailles are sold. Minimal sulphur is used as a preservative, but never so low that wines are at risk from oxidation. Malolactic fermentation is used selectively, so as to maintain tension in each cuvée, with an average of about three-quarters of parcels completing malolactic. Wines are aged on lees with bâtonnage for 6–8 months after primary fermentation, and aged in bottle between 2.5 and 9 years. The purity of the house style permits refreshingly low dosages, never more than 6g/L, from grape liqueur rather than sugar.

Emmanuel learnt the craft of barrel fermentation with bâtonnage in Burgundy, and this has been a key element of the house style since he commenced in 1990. 'I don't like oxidative champagne, so I don't want to be extremist with wood,' he says. The goal is not to impart the taste of wood, but rather to create fresh, focused and textured wines. 'Micro-oxygenation in barrels enhances the minerality of the soil,' Emmanuel explains.

New barrels are purchased from Burgundy and used for ageing a rich resource of some 200 reserve wines. A preference is given to small, 208-litre barrels to keep small plots separate and provide a balance of surface area and volume. Across the estate, 25% of parcels are fermented in old barrels aged 5–15 years, and most cuvées are blended with more citrus-accented parcels from tanks.

This thoughtful approach produces wines that display sensitive oak influence, imparting great resilience and long-ageing potential.

Since 2006, all Veuve Fourny wines have been sealed with Mytik DIAM closures. A five-year trial of DIAM and natural cork revealed DIAM-sealed bottles to be consistent and fresh, with pure fruit, while those under natural cork were more evolved, and 'each bottle had its own personality'. The letter of reply when a corked bottle is returned has not been sent out once since the change was made. Emmanuel refers to natural cork as 'Russian Roulette' and regards DIAM as a revolution, crucial for upholding the freshness and purity of the house.

Disgorgement dates are printed on back labels for markets that request this, including the US, Japan, Australia and China. 'More and more people consider champagne like they do table wine,' Charles-Henry explains. 'Our customers keep champagne in their cellars and need to keep track of it.'

Demand for Veuve Fourny has put supply on allocation in every market, with Cuvée R and Rosé sold out for six months of 2013. The hope is to increase the bottle age of Grande Réserve and Blanc de Blancs from 2.5 years to 3–4 years, but this will take time to achieve, as these cuvées comprise 60% of production.

There is no goal to increase production in spite of these imperatives, even with the new cuverie operational and increased vineyard resources from the 2011 acquisition. 'Our goal is to grow the quality, not the volume, continuing to focus on the vineyards and the winery,' says Emmanuel. 'It depends on whether your goal in life is money or pleasure. My goal is to be able to host tastings and dinners in Japan and Australia and for people to say, "Your wines are wonderful!" That's the goal for me.'

It's a goal the brothers are capably translating into the bottle. The pristine champagnes of Veuve Fourny look more pure, precise and fresh with every release.

VEUVE FOURNY & FILS CUVÉE GRANDE RÉSERVE PREMIER CRU VERTUS BRUT NV • $$

94 points • DISGORGED MAY 2012 • TASTED IN VERTUS AND BRISBANE

60% 2009, 40% 2008 and 2007; 80% chardonnay, 20% pinot noir; average vine age 42 years; 75% malolactic fermentation; reserve wines aged in small oak barrels aged 4–15 years; aged in bottle at least 2.5 years; 6g/L dosage; DIAM closure

Fourny captures the soft voice of the wonderfully textured, frothy, salty minerality of Vertus from its very first cuvée, a beach-fresh apéritif of high-noon brightness. A lively lift of lemon blossom and concentrated drive of lemon, grapefruit and pristine white peach declare the chardonnay signature of the house. Pinot noir brings up the rear with its expansive depth of tangy white cherries and figs, while barrel-aged reserves contribute a spicy, toasty dimension.

The Champagne Guide

VEUVE FOURNY & FILS CUVÉE BLANC DE BLANCS VERTUS PREMIER CRU NV • $$

94 points • DISGORGED JUNE 2012 • TASTED IN VERTUS AND BRISBANE

80% 2009, 20% 2008 and 2007; 100% Vertus; majority from 'Le Mont-Ferré' vineyard; average vine age 42 years; reserve wines aged in small oak barrels aged 4–15 years; 75% malolactic fermentation; aged in bottle at least 2.5 years; 6g/L dosage; DIAM closure

Fourny's mandate of purity and precision shimmers in lemon zest, grapefruit pith, fresh pear, crunchy white peach and granny smith apple of soap-powder brightness. Pristine fruit expression, wonderful concentration and refinement are upheld at every moment, propelled by the texture and depth of barrel-aged reserves, adding hints of roast nuts and a suggestion of anise. A long, soft, salty mineral finish speaks clearly of the terroir of Vertus.

VEUVE FOURNY & FILS CUVÉE BLANC DE BLANCS VERTUS PREMIER CRU BRUT NATURE NV • $$

94 points • DISGORGED JANUARY 2012 • TASTED IN VERTUS

80% 2009, 20% 2008 and 2007; low-yielding vines of 50–56hL/ha, about half of Champagne's average; predominantly from 1950s vines in Le Mont-Ferré; harvested later and with higher concentration; vinified and aged in tanks and oak barrels on lees; zero dosage; DIAM closure

Under the command of old vines, the chalk soils of Le Mont-Ferré hark more to the thundering grand crus to their north than to the more fruity premier crus around them, and without the interruption of dosage, the strength of strong, salt-infused mineral texture is pronounced. Fourny's fanatical attention to ripe fruit from low-yielding old vines is declared in soaring precision of fresh lemons, crunchy nashi pears and a note of honey. A subtle tweak of barrel-aged reserves adds complexity of gingernut biscuits and brioche, culminating in a crescendo of mineral texture, resonating with great soils tapped by deep roots. If only every brut nature were as purposefully crafted in the vineyard as this.

VEUVE FOURNY & FILS ROSÉ VERTUS PREMIER CRU BRUT NV • $$

92 points • TASTED IN VERTUS

100% 2009; 71% chardonnay, 20% blanc de noirs, 9% red wine from long-macerated, ripe Vertus pinot noir; 70–80% malolactic fermentation; 6g/L dosage; DIAM closure

Fourny's rosé philosophy is to retain the structure, finesse and tension of the house in a wine of rounded fruit by tweaking blanc de blancs with just a touch of pinot noir red wine. In an attempt to link the two, a little blanc de noirs has been introduced for the first time this year. The result is not as beguiling as the 2008, but nonetheless a soft, elegant, complex and balanced rosé of medium salmon-crimson hue, with gentle red berry fruits, notes of tangelo and wood spice, a soft, creamy mouthfeel and long finish.

Veuve Fourny & Fils Cuvée Blanc de Blancs Vertus Premier Cru Vintage Extra Brut 2006 • $$

95 points • Disgorged January 2012 • Tasted in Vertus and Brisbane

Always the same single-plot Les Barilliers, in the heart of Vertus near Le Mesnil-sur-Oger; vinified in tanks; 75% malolactic fermentation; aged 6 years in bottle; 4g/L dosage; DIAM closure

An invigorating vintage Fourny that brilliantly contrasts zesty tension, generous expression and awe-inspiring persistence. Purity is retained in glorious grapefruit, white peach and lemon, with oak sitting neatly in the background, drawing out suggestions of gingernut biscuits and mixed spice, propelling fruit upwards and driving all-pervading mineral texture long into the finish, flickering with intriguing notes of licorice, which the Fournys say are characteristic of the chalk minerality of Vertus as it ages. These will build as it matures over many years to come.

Veuve Fourny & Fils Cuvée R de Vve Fourny & Fils Vertus Extra Brut NV • $$

95 points • Disgorged April 2012 • Tasted in Vertus and Brisbane

2008 (aged 1 year in old oak) and 2007 (aged 2 years in old oak); 90% chardonnay, 10% pinot noir; predominantly from Les Barilliers, in the heart of Vertus; average vine age 42 years; fully fermented in small oak barrels aged 4-15 years; bâtonnage; aged 4 years in bottle; 3g/L dosage; DIAM closure

The honed restraint of Fourny's pristine fruit, meeting the ravishing complexity of old oak and swirling, tossing minerality makes for a thrilling display. Fermentation in old oak barrels amplifies salty minerality drawn from the thin soils of the north of Vertus near Le Mesnil-sur-Oger by grand old vines. The exemplary freshness of 2008 overlays its textural backbone with pitch-perfect lemon, grapefruit and golden delicious apple. It's at once creamy and taut, with high-tensile acidity contrasting low dosage and the softening influence of barrel maturation. Carefully crafted old oak cranks things up a notch from Fourny's other non-vintage cuvées, building a gentle, buttery smoothness to the palate, and depth of custard apple, toast, even hints of pine nettles. Give it time for oak and acidity to relax.

Veuve Fourny & Fils Cuvée du Clos Fg Notre Dame Premier Cru Vertus Extra Brut 2002 • $$$$

95 points • Disgorged March 2012 • Tasted in Vertus and Brisbane

100% chardonnay; 100% vinified and aged for 9 months on lees in oak barrels aged 5-6 years; full malolactic fermentation; 3g/L dosage; DIAM closure; just 1604 bottles

Lock up the cellar and throw away the key: Clos Faubourg Notre Dame always needs a very long time to come together, and the outstanding 2002 takes this imperative to new extremes. Its acidity is unnerving, its salty chalk mineral structure well scaffolded, its oak support confident and its persistence disarming. In energy, drive and sheer fruit presence, this wine's dimensions transcend even its season, elevated to extremes rarely seen in Champagne outside vintages of veritable 1996 proportions. Honed, taut lemon zest and pure white peach unravel to powerful depths of fig, wild honey and more than a decade of toast, butter and roast nuts. It needs years to uncoil and when it does finally emerge, drink it slowly from large glasses at white wine temperature. In such limited supply, it sold out from the estate in less than two months.

The Champagne Guide

VILMART & CIE

(Viil-mar e See)

6/10

4 RUE DE LA RÉPUBLIQUE 51500 RILLY-LA-MONTAGNE
www.champagnevilmart.com

CHAMPAGNE

Depuis 1890

In the heart of the village of Rilly-la-Montagne, a stained-glass window handcrafted by René Champs hangs proud in the reception room of Vilmart & Cie. In five scenes of vivid colour and geometric intricacy, the hands-on attention to detail of Vilmart is depicted in hand pruning, tilling the soil with a hoe, hand picking, pressing, and vinification in large and small oak barrels. It's a fitting tribute to the champagnes of this lauded grower, which faithfully reflect every element of their painstaking production in seamlessly interlocking detail and slightly larger-than-life colour.

'MY PHILOSOPHY IS TO MAKE WINE FIRST AND BUBBLES and effervescence second,' Laurent Champs explained on the two occasions I have visited the fifth-generation grower.

On the northern slopes of the Montagne de Reims, the leading grower of Rilly-la-Montagne has set a pace since followed by eco-friendly growers everywhere. Painstakingly tended family vineyards, confident but masterful use of oak and an absence of malolactic fermentation make for full and vinous wines that uphold great purity and fine-drawn detail.

The Vilmarts have tended vines in the premier cru village of Rilly-la-Montagne since 1890, and their wines today are sourced exclusively from 11 hectares of family-owned vines in the village and nearby Villers-Allerand. Averaging 30 years of age, these are planted almost exclusively to chardonnay (60%) and pinot noir (37%), with just 3% pinot meunier. Such a high representation of chardonnay is rare in a village famous for pinot noir, and it's Vilmart's chardonnay-led cuvées that shine brightest.

A pioneer of eco-friendly viticulture, Vilmart's 12 plots have been organic since 1968, with grasses cultivated in mid-rows. Such is the attention to detail here that soils between the rows of vines have been tilled with a hand hoe for five generations, and no chemical fertilisers, herbicides or pesticides are used.

Since his arrival in 1990, Laurent Champs, grandson of the founder of the estate, Désiré Vilmart, has carefully honed the use of oak to lift the fruit in his wines. All are fermented and aged in oak for 10 months, non-vintage wines in foudres of 2200–5000 litres, and vintage wines in 225-litre Burgundy barrels and 600-litre 'demi-muids'. Barrels are purchased from Burgundy after just one use and recycled until they are six years old. Malolactic fermentation is completely blocked in all cuvées.

Of champagne's practitioners who make full use of oak without malolactic fermentation, the wines of Laurent Champs are among the most well integrated. These are wines of freshness, elegance and richness, with a creamy texture derived from oak fermentation rather than malolactic fermentation. A seamless integration finely interweaves taut malic acid, oak, the succulent stone fruits of pinot noir, and zesty citrus rind of chardonnay.

Vilmart & Cie Grande Reserve Brut Premier Cru NV • $$

88 points • Disgorged June 2012 • Tasted in Rilly-la-Montagne

2010 base vintage with 2009 reserves; 70% pinot noir, 30% chardonnay; fermented and matured for 10 months in large oak foudres; no malolactic fermentation; 10g/L dosage

In a bizarre twist for the pinot noir village of Rilly-la-Montagne, Vilmart's lesser cuvées this year are the two led by pinot noir. This is a young, savoury and complex blend with notes of wet wood and a touch of mushroom over a backbone of bruised apple, pear and spice, finishing with primary malic acidity of taut definition. It's a world away from the immaculate, vinous style of the 2008 base of a couple of years ago.

Vilmart & Cie Grand Cellier Brut Premier Cru NV • $$

94 points • Disgorged February 2012 • Tasted in Rilly-la-Montagne

2009 base vintage with 2008 and 2007 reserves; 70% chardonnay, 30% pinot noir; fermented and matured for 10 months in large oak foudres; no malolactic fermentation; 9g/L dosage

Laurent describes Grand Cellier as 'audacious and elegant' and praises the three vintages in this blend for their exceptional quality and maturity. It rises to the expectation, confidently chardonnay-led in its impressive purity of lemon rind, apple and mixed spice. A creamy bead integrates handsomely with the freshness of lemon juice malic acidity, finishing balanced and complete, soaring with zesty freshness and lingering persistence.

Vilmart & Cie Grand Cellier d'Or Brut Premier Cru 2007 • $$$

95 points • Disgorged December 2011 • Tasted in Rilly-la-Montagne

80% chardonnay, 20% pinot noir; fermented and matured for 10 months in small oak barrels; no malolactic fermentation; 8–9g/L dosage

Young chardonnay with full malic acidity, vinified entirely in oak, can be a formidable combination, and the seamless harmony in this wine is testimony to Laurent Champs' sensitivity and skill. The piercing zesty freshness of malic acidity contrasts comfortably with the creamy smoothness of barrel fermentation, as if the wood somehow intricately weaves every element together. Powerful complexity of deep, succulent white peach and white nectarine juxtaposes chardonnay's crunchy lemon zest and hint of fennel. Soft, savoury mineral texture lingers with undeviating line and outstanding length.

The Champagne Guide

VILMART & CIE COEUR DE CUVÉE PREMIER CRU 2004 • $$$$

94 points • DISGORGED NOVEMBER 2011 • TASTED IN RILLY-LA-MONTAGNE

80% chardonnay, 20% pinot noir; from vines over 50 years of age yielding under 45hL/ha, less than half of Champagne's average; only the heart of the pressing; fermented and matured for 10 months in small oak barrels; no malolactic fermentation; 8–9g/L dosage

Such is the prominence of aromas of wood spice and vanilla from very classy barrels that one braces for a thud of oak stave impact on the palate. Thankfully, no such blow is delivered, its oak instead furnishing surprisingly nutty, creamy, buttery smoothness and enticing nuances of coffee, chocolate and mixed spice, without a hint of interruption to its generous fruit flow. Lavish yellow plum, succulent white peach and fig contrast with the zesty cut of lemons and the crunchy vitality of malic acidity. Don't drink it too soon, too cold or from narrow flutes.

VILMART & CIE COEUR DE CUVÉE PREMIER CRU 2002 • $$$$

96 points • DISGORGED MAY 2010 • TASTED IN RILLY-LA-MONTAGNE

80% chardonnay, 20% pinot noir; from vines over 50 years of age, yielding under 45hL/ha, less than half of Champagne's average; only the heart of the pressing; fermented and matured for 10 months in small oak barrels; no malolactic fermentation; 8–9g/L dosage

Vilmart's top cuvée in a vintage that Champs describes as 'close to perfect' is a dazzling display of consummate precision and main-course-ready concentration. Such is its enduring longevity that it's barely budged in two years since it first burst into the world. Grand complexity is on parade, with fruit and oak cartwheeling in perfect unison in a fanfare of fleshy yellow mirabelle plums, ripe pears, figs and mixed spice, slowly building character of baked apple and wood smoke. Alluring creaminess of texture contrasts perfectly integrated malic acidity, finishing with energetic drive, untiring persistence and pinpoint control.

VILMART & CIE GRAND CELLIER RUBIS PREMIER CRU BRUT 2006 • $$$$

92 points • DISGORGED SEPTEMBER 2011 • TASTED IN RILLY-LA-MONTAGNE

60% pinot noir, 40% chardonnay; from vines over 50 years of age; saignée of pinot noir maceration blended just before bottling with chardonnay for finesse and elegance; no malolactic fermentation

A pale salmon hue does little to anticipate the depth of savoury complexity entwined within Vilmart's rosé. Exotic spice, dried herbs and roast tomatoes find something of a savoury synergy with toasty oak and the secondary development of red berry fruits. It's all flawlessly integrated with creamy texture, supportive acidity and lingering persistence.

EPILOGUE
The real magic of champagne

I'M FREQUENTLY ASKED WHY I WRITE MORE ABOUT champagne than anything else. It goes without saying that I love the wine, the place and its people. I am thrilled by the challenge of unravelling what is probably the most complex wine style in the world, and I love the chase of discovering the real story behind the wines of its most guarded brands.

Of all the world's most famous and celebrated wines, less is written about champagne than any other. There is no beverage that speaks of celebration more universally than champagne, traversing cultures and languages to toast everything from christenings to coronations. Of Europe's most highly prized benchmarks, none is more readily available and more affordable across the globe than champagne. There is much to celebrate, much that champagne's eager drinkers are thirsty to learn, and I count it a great privilege to bring the real stories of this enchanting place to the world. But there's more to my love of champagne than this.

My final meal in Champagne this year was my most memorable. On a fortuitous cancellation of a meeting in Paris, Dom Pérignon Chef de Cave Richard Geoffroy invited me to lunch at Patrick Michelon's Michelin-starred Les Berceaux in Épernay. There is probably no higher position in Champagne than Chef de Cave of Dom Pérignon, and Richard Geoffroy has held the honour for 23 years. If anyone has earned the right to be egotistical or snobbish about champagne, surely it's Richard Geoffroy. But that day I saw a different side to the corporate world of big-brand champagne. A great many things were memorable of that lunch and his champagnes, but after three hours of intensive conversation, painstakingly recorded in more than 4500 words in my notes, one thing stayed with me above everything else. 'It's about the people,' Geoffroy declared. 'That is what wine should be about. There are too many egos and too much snobbism in the wine world. But wine should be about bringing people together. Maybe that's the real magic of champagne.'

Every year I gather my eight dearest friends for a champagne dinner to share nine of the highest-rated wines in this guide. I always introduce the event in the same way: 'Tonight is not a celebration of champagne. It's a celebration of friends. As remarkable as these champagnes may be, they merely form the footnotes to mark our own victories and defeats this year. It is to these that we raise our glasses tonight.' Throughout the evening, each guest claims a wine and shares a story of their own success or defeat that year. Above each champagne on our tasting sheet is a space, not for tasting notes, but to remember each other's stories.

Ultimately, it's not about the champagne. It's about the people. And that's worth celebrating more than anything else. My hope for this book is that it might guide you to make opportunities to raise a glass to celebrate someone special in your life.

Maybe that's the real magic of champagne.

SANTÉ!

INDEX
Rise to the Top

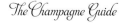

Billecart-Salmon Brut NV, $$, 79
Billecart-Salmon Demi-Sec NV, $$, 80
Bollinger La Côte aux Enfants Coteaux Champenois 2009, $$$$
Canard-Duchêne Charles VII Grande Cuvée des Lys Blanc de Noirs Brut NV, $$, 93
Chaîne d'Étoiles Brut Reserve NV, $, 95
Charles Heidsieck Rosé Réserve NV, $$$, 98
Claude Carré et Fils Blanc de Blancs Brut NV, $$, 104
D de Devaux La Cuvée Brut NV, $$, 118
Delamotte Rosé NV, $$$, 111
Deutz Amour de Deutz Blanc de Blancs Brut Millésime 2003, $$$$, 115
Devaux Cuvée Rosée Brut NV, $$, 118
Devaux Grande Réserve Brut NV, $$, 117
Dosnon & LeRecolte Blanche Blanc de Blancs NV, $$, 127
Duval-Leroy Clos des Bouveries 2005, $$$$, 131
Duval-Leroy Fleur de Champagne Premier Cru NV, $$, 130
Eric Rodez Cuvée des Crayères NV, $$, 139
Fleury Père & Fils Sonate No 9 Extra Brut NV, 146
Gaston Chiquet Special Club Brut Millésimé 2005, $$, 155
Gatinois Coteaux Champenois Grand Cru Aÿ Rouge 2004, $$, 158
Geoffroy Purete Brut Zero NV, $$, 161
Georges Laval Cumières Premier Cru Brut Nature NV, $$, 166
Godmé Père & Fils Blanc de Noirs Brut NV, $$, 168
H. Billiot Fils Cuvée Tradition Brut NV, $$, 174
Henri Giraud Cuvée Hommage Brut NV, $$, 176
Henriot Brut Rosé NV, $$$, 180
Henriot Brut Souverain NV, $$, 179
J. Dumangin Fils Vintage Brut 2003, $$, 183
J. Lassalle Brut Préférence Premier Cru NV, $, 186
J.L. Vergnon Conversation Blanc de Blancs Brut NV, $, 189
J.L. Vergnon Résonance Extra Brut 2006, $$, 189
Jacques Picard Brut Rosé NV, $$, 193
Jérôme Prévost La Closerie les Béguines 2010, $$$, 206
Laherte Frères Blanc de Blancs Brut Nature NV, $$, 221
Laherte Frères La Troisieme Vie Coteaux Champenois, $$, 223
Laherte Frères Les 7 NV, $$, 222
Lanson Noble Cuvée Blanc de Blancs 2000, $$$$, 230

Lenoble Cuvée Riche Demi-Sec NV, $$, 248
Lenoble Grand Cru Blanc de Blancs Chouilly Brut NV, $$, 248
Lenoble Rosé Terroirs Brut 2006, $$, 250
Lombard & Cie Brut Rosé Premier Cru NV, $$, 251
Louis Roederer Blanc de Blancs 2006, $$$, 254
Mailly Grand Cru Les Échansons Millesime Brut 2000, $$$$, 260
Napoléon Tradition Brut NV, $$, 267
Pascal Doquet Horizon Blanc de Blancs NV, $$, 271
Philipponnat Clos des Goisses 2003, $$$$$, 285
Philipponnat Réserve Millésimée 2003, $$$, 284
Piper-Heidsieck Rosé Sauvage Brut NV, $$, 300
Roland Champion Brut Rose NV, $$, 310
Roland Champion Carte Noire Blanc de Blancs Grand Cru Millesime Brut 2004, $$, 310
Taittinger Les Folies de la Marquetterie NV, $$, 320
Tarlant La Vigne Royale Blanc de Noirs Extra Brut 2003, $$$$, 328
Veuve Fourny & Fils Rosé Vertus Premier Cru Brut NV, $$, 343
Vilmart & Cie Grand Cellier Rubis Premier Cru Brut 2006, $$$$, 347
Zoémie De Sousa Brut Merville NV, $$, 107

91 POINTS

Agrapart & Fils Complantée Grand Cru Extra Brut 2008, $$, 56
Alfred Gratien Cuvée Paradis Brut NV, $$$$, 60
Bérêche et Fils Coteaux Champenois 2011, $$, 74
Bérêche et Fils Le Cran Ludes Premier Cru 2005, $$$$, 75
Cattier Brut Premier Cru NV, $, 94
Chartogne-Taillet Heurtebise Extra Brut 2008, $$, 103
Chartogne-Taillet Les Alliées Extra Brut 2007, $$, 103
D de Devaux Ultra Extra Brut NV, $$, 119
Devaux Blanc de Noirs NV, $$, 118
Dom Pérignon 2003, $$$$$, 124
Drappier Signature Blanc de Blancs Brut NV, $, 128
Duval-Leroy Brut NV, $$, 130
Fleury Père & Fils Notes Blanches Brut Nature NV, 145
G.H. Mumm Cordon Rouge Brut Millésimé 2004, $$, 152

G.H. Mumm Cuvée R. Lalou Brut 1999, $$$$$, 152
Geoffroy Blanc de Rosé Extra Brut NV, $$$$, 162
Geoffroy Brut Premier Cru Volupté 2006, $$$, 162
Henriot Blanc de Blancs NV, $$, 180
J. Dumangin Fils Premium Blanc de Blancs Single Vineyard Dessus le Mont NV, $$, 184
J.L. Vergnon Blanc de Blancs Confidence Brut Nature Millésime 2007, $$$, 190
Jacquart Brut Rosé NV, $$
Janisson-Baradon Sélection Brut NV, $, 203
L. Bénard-Pitois Brut Carte Blanche NV, $, 216
Lallier Grand Cru Blanc de Blancs NV, $$$, 225
Lallier Grand Cru Zero Dosage NV, $$$$, 225
Laurent-Perrier L-P Brut NV, $$, 238
Laurent-Perrier L-P Ultra Brut NV, $$$, 238
Nicolas Feuillatte Grand Cru Blanc de Noirs 2002, $$, 269
Nicolas Feuillatte Palmes d'Or Vintage Brut 1999, $$$$, 269
Perrier-Jouët Grand Brut NV, $$, 281
Philipponnat Clos des Goisses 2001, $$$$$
Philipponnat Clos des Goisses 2002, $$$$$, 285
Pierre Gimonnet & Fils Cuvée Paradoxe 1er Cru 2007, $$, 291
Piper-Heidsieck Brut Vintage 2006, $$, 300
Piper-Heidsieck Cuvée Brut NV, $, 299
Sélèque Cuvée Spéciale Premier Cru Brut NV, $, 316
Taittinger Cuvée Brut Millésime 2005, $$$, 320
Veuve Clicquot Brut Yellow Label NV, $$, 336
Zoémie De Sousa Brut Précieuse NV, $$, 106

90 POINTS

Alain Thiénot Brut Rosé NV, $$$, 58
Ayala Brut Nature Zero Dosage NV, $$, 67
Barons de Rothschild Rosé NV, $$$, 69
Boizel Brut Réserve NV, $$, 85
Fleury Père & Fils Bolero Extra Brut 2004, 147
Fleury Père & Fils Cépages Blancs Extra Brut 2005, $$, 147
G.H. Mumm Cordon Rouge Brut NV, $$, 151
Geoffroy Rosé de Saignée Brut NV, $$, 162
Jacquart Brut Mosaïque NV, $$, 191

GLOSSARY

ACIDITY A crucial element that gives champagne its tangy freshness, vitality and life, and a sharp, clean taste on the finish.

AGRAFE A large metal 'staple' to secure the cork during second fermentation and bottle ageing. Historically, used prior to the invention of capsules, and retained today by some houses and growers.

APÉRITIF A drink used to get the taste buds humming before a meal (champagne, naturally!).

ASSEMBLAGE The process of blending a wine (see page 24).

AUTOLYSIS The breakdown of dead yeast cells during ageing on lees, improving mouthfeel and contributing biscuity, bready characters (see page 25).

BALTHAZAR 12-litre bottle (usually filled with champagne fermented in standard bottles or magnums). Be sure to have help on hand to pour it (and drink it!).

BARRIQUE Small oak barrel of 225-litre capacity.

BÂTONNAGE Stirring of the lees in barrel or tank.

BEAD Bubbles. The best champagne always has tiny bubbles, the product of the finest juice fermented in cold cellars.

BIODYNAMICS An intensive viticultural regime of extreme organics, eschewing chemical treatments and seeking a harmonious ecosystem.

BLANC DE BLANCS Literally 'white from white'. White champagne made exclusively from white grapes, usually chardonnay, but also include arbane, petit meslier and/or pinot blanc.

BLANC DE NOIRS Literally 'white from black'. White champagne made exclusively from the dark-skinned grapes pinot noir and/or pinot meunier. This is achieved by gentle pressing removing the juice from the skins before any colour leaches out.

BRETTANOMYCES 'Brett' is a barrel yeast infection, considered a spoilage character in champagne. It may develop further in bottle, manifesting itself as characters of boiled hot dog, antiseptic, horse stable, barnyard, animal or sweaty saddle, adding a metallic bite to the palate and contracting the finish.

BRUT Raw/dry, containing less than 12g/L sugar (formerly less than 15g/L sugar).

BRUT NATURE OR BRUT ZÉRO No added sugar (less than 3g/L sugar).

CAPSULE Crown cap.

CARBON DIOXIDE The gaseous by-product of fermentation that is responsible for the bubbles in sparkling wine.

CAVE Cellar.

CÉPAGE Grape variety or blend of varieties.

CHAMPAGNE Wine from the region of the same name in north-east France. Champagne with a capital 'C' refers to the region; with a lower-case 'c' to the wine. French law prohibits the name for sparkling wines grown elsewhere.

CHAPTALISATION The addition of sugar (yes, this is legal in France) or concentrated grape juice to increase the alcohol strength of the wine (see page 24).

CHEF DE CAVE The 'chief' or 'chef' in the cellar (champagne winemaker).

CIVC The 'Comité Interprofessionnel du vin de Champagne', a semi-public agency of the French government to represent the growers and houses in overseeing the production, distribution, promotion and research of the wines of Champagne.

CLOS Historically a walled vineyard, though the walls may no longer exist.

COOPÉRATIVE DE MANIPULATION (CM) A co-op of growers who produce champagne under their own brand.

COEUR DE LA CUVÉE 'Heart of the cuvée', the middle of the pressing, yielding the best juice.

CORKED Cork taint is an all too common wine fault resulting from the presence of 2,4,6 trichloroanisole (TCA) in natural cork. It imparts an off-putting, mouldy, 'wet cardboard' or 'wet dog' character, suppressing fruit and shortening the length of finish (see page 38).

CORK TAINT See 'corked'.

COTEAUX CHAMPENOIS Champagne released as still wine, mostly red; typically made in tiny quantities, and mostly by smaller producers.

CRAYÈRES Roman chalk pits, now gloriously atmospheric cellars under Reims.

CRÉMANT Formerly used to describe slightly less fizzy champagnes (2–3 atmospheres of pressure) but no longer permitted on champagne, and instead often used for French sparkling wines produced outside of Champagne. Not to be confused with the village of Cramant in the Côte des Blancs. Mumm's de Cramant cuvée is both crémant (in the traditional sense) and exclusively sourced from Cramant.

CROWN CAP A metal seal like a beer cap, used to seal a champagne bottle during second fermentation and lees ageing.

CRU A commune, village, vineyard or officially classified 'growth'.

CUVÉE The first pressing of the grapes (2050 litres from 4000 kilograms of grapes), yielding the best juice. Also refers to an individual blend or style.

CUVERIE Tank room.

DÉBOURBAGE Settling of the solids from the must prior to fermentation (see page 24).

DÉBOURBAGE À FROID Cold settling to clarify the juice, as practised by Billecart-Salmon, Pol Roger and others.

DÉGORGEMENT Disgorgement.

DEMI-MUID Large oak barrel of 500–600-litre capacity.

DEMI-SEC Half-dry or medium-dry (32–50 g/L sugar).

DIAM Mytik DIAM is a brand of champagne closure made by Oeneo, moulded from fragments of cork which have been treated to extract cork taint. Its reliable performance has made it an increasingly popular choice for champagne in recent years (see page 39).

DISGORGEMENT The removal of a frozen plug of sediment from the neck of the bottle (see pages 25 and 42).

DOSAGE The final addition to top up the bottle, usually a mixture of wine and sugar syrup called 'liqueur d'expédition' or 'liqueur de dosage'. A dosage of 10–12g/L of sugar is typical in champagne (see pages 25 and 47).

DOUX Sweet (50+ g/L sugar; Coca-Cola is 150g/L).

ÉCHELLE DES CRUS 'Ladder of growths', Champagne's crude classification of vineyards by village, expressed as a percentage (see page 37).

ÉLEVAGE The process of 'bringing up' a wine, encompassing all cellar operations between fermentation and bottling.

EXTRA BRUT Extra raw/dry (less than 6g/L sugar).

EXTRA DRY OR EXTRA SEC Off dry (12–17g/L sugar).

FERMENTATION The conversion of sugar to alcohol by the action of yeasts. Carbonic gas is produced as a by-product.

FLUTE Narrow champagne glass.

FOUDRE Very large oak cask, typically with a capacity between 2000 litres and 12,000 litres.

GRAND CRU The highest vineyard classification. In Champagne, a classification is crudely applied to a village and all the vineyards within its bounds acquire the same classification. Seventeen villages are classified as grand cru.

GRANDES MARQUES An obsolete, self-imposed term for the big champagne brands. Still used informally.

GREY IMPORTS See 'Parallel imports'.

GROWER PRODUCER A champagne producer who makes wines from fruit only from his or her own vineyards; 5% of fruit is permitted to be purchased.

GYROPALETTE A large mechanised crate to automatically riddle champagne bottles.

INOCULATE To seed a ferment with yeast.

JEROBOAM A 3-litre bottle, previously typically filled with champagne fermented in standard bottles or magnums. However, this is now illegal and it must be made in this format from first bottling.

LATE DISGORGEMENT A champagne that has been matured on its lees for an extended period.

LEES Sediment that settles in the bottom of a tank, barrel or bottle, comprised primarily of dead yeast cells.

LIEU-DIT Individually named plot or vineyard site.

LIGHTSTRUCK The degradation of wine exposed to ultraviolet light. Sparkling wines in clear bottles are most susceptible (see page 44).

LIQUEUR DE DOSAGE See 'Liqueur d'expédition'.

LIQUEUR D'EXPÉDITION The final addition to top up the bottle, usually a mixture of wine and sugar syrup.

LIQUEUR DE TIRAGE A mixture of sugar and wine or concentrated grape juice added immediately prior to bottling, to produce the secondary fermentation in bottle (see page 25).

LUTTE RAISONNÉE Literally 'reasoned struggle', a middle ground between conventional viticulture and organic farming, reducing the use of herbicides and pesticides while retaining the right to employ them in times of need. Often a sensible approach in Champagne's erratic climate.

MAGNUM 1.5-litre bottle. According to the Champenois, the perfect size for two, when one is not drinking.

MACERATION Soaking of red grape skins in their juice in the production of red or rosé wine (see page 26).

MAISON House.

MALIC ACID A naturally occurring acid in grapes and other fruits, notably green apples. It is most pronounced in grapes in cold climates and is responsible for champagne's searing acidity, usually softened through malolactic fermentation.

MALOLACTIC FERMENTATION 'Malo' is the conversion of stronger malic (green apple) acid to softer lactic (dairy) acid (see page 24).

MARQUE D'ACHETEUR (MA) Buyer's own brand. An 'own label' owned by a supermarket or merchant.

MÉTHODE CHAMPENOISE An obsolete term for the traditional method of sparkling winemaking, now 'Méthode Traditionnelle' or 'Méthode Classique' (see page 24).

MÉTHODE TRADITIONNELLE The official name for the traditional method of sparkling winemaking, in which the second fermentation occurs in the bottle in which the wine is sold.

METHUSELAH A 6-litre bottle, usually filled with champagne fermented in standard bottles or magnums.

MILLÉSIME Vintage.

MINERALITY The texture and mouthfeel of a wine derived from its soil (see page 28).

MOUSSE See 'Bead'.

MUSELET Wire cage to hold a champagne cork in the bottle.

NEBUCHADNEZZAR A 15 litre bottle, usually filled with champagne fermented in standard bottles or magnums. Do not attempt while home alone!

NÉGOCIANT-MANIPULANT (NM) Champagne producer who purchases grapes and/or unfinished wines. A négociant may also include up to 95% estate grown fruit.

NON-VINTAGE (NV) A champagne containing wine from more than one vintage.

OENOTHÈQUE Literally a wine library or shop. Sometimes used to refer to bottles held back for extended ageing (such as Dom Pérignon Oenothèque).

OÏDIUM Powdery mildew, a fungal disease which can have a devastating effect on grape crops.

ORGANICS A viticultural regime that avoids the use of any synthetic pesticides, herbicides, fungicides or other treatments. Copper is permitted, though criticised for a toxicity higher than that of some synthetic products.

OXIDISED A wine that has reacted with oxygen. At its most extreme, oxidation can produce browning in colour, loss of primary fruit, a general flattening of flavours, a shortening of the length of finish, or even a vinegar or bitter taste.

PARALLEL IMPORTS Champagne brought into a country by parties other than the usual agent, typically via a third-party country. Good for keeping pricing competitive, but can become problematic if transportation or storage are compromised (see page 49).

PH The level of acid strength of a wine expressed as a number. Low pH equates to high acidity; 7 is neutral.

PHENOLICS A grape compound responsible for astringency and

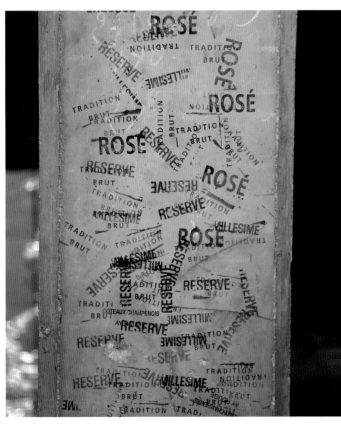

A pillar in the packing room at Gatinois in Aÿ.

The Champagne Guide

bitterness in the back palate. It is particularly rich in stems, seeds and skins, and especially prevalent in champagnes from warm vintages such as 2003 and 2005.

PIÈCE Small oak barrel of 205 litre capacity in Champagne (228 litre in Burgundy).

POIGNETTAGE The vigorous shaking of the bottle after corking to mix the wine and liquor. It can also refer to the old practice of shaking the bottle by hand to stir up the lees and enhance autolytic flavours, rarely used today. Small growers, including De Sousa and J. Dumangin Fils, maintain the tradition.

PREMIER CRU The second highest vineyard classification, awarded to 41 villages. In Champagne, a classification is crudely applied to a village, and all the vineyards within its bounds acquire the same classification.

PRESTIGE CUVÉE The flagship champagne or champagnes of a brand, typically the most expensive.

PRISE DE MOUSSE The second fermentation that creates the bubbles (see page 25).

PUPITRE Hand riddling rack.

RÉCOLTANT-COOPÉRATEUR (RC) Champagne grower selling wine under his/her own brand made by his/her cooperative.

RÉCOLTANT-MANIPULANT (RM) Champagne grower who makes wine from estate fruit; 5% of grapes may also be purchased to supplement production.

REDUCTIVE A wine made or aged with limited contact with oxygen may develop reductive characters, hydrogen sulphide notes akin to struck flint, burnt match and gunpowder. At their extreme, these can manifest themselves as objectionable

characters of rubber, rotten eggs, garlic, onion and cooked cabbage.

REHOBOAM A 4.5-litre bottle, usually filled with champagne fermented in standard bottles or magnums.

REMUAGE The riddling process (see page 25).

RESERVE WINES Wines held in the cellar for future blending in a non-vintage cuvée (see page 25). Usually aged in tanks, although sometimes kept in barrels or bottles.

RIDDLING The process of moving the lees sediment into the neck of the bottle prior to disgorgement, either by hand or by gyropalette (see page 25).

SABRAGE A technique for opening a champagne bottle with a sabre. Practice is recommended prior to attempting this in public. I tried it once with vague success, but I was picking up splinters of glass for days!

SAIGNÉE A technique in which rosé is made by 'bleeding' off juice from just-crushed pinot noir or pinot meunier grapes after a short maceration (soaking) on skins prior to fermentation (see page 26).

SALMANAZAR A 9-litre bottle, usually filled with champagne fermented in standard bottles or magnums.

SEC Dryish (17–32 g/L sugar).

SOLERA A system of fractional blending through a system of wines of different ages, with the bottled wine drawn from the last stage. Also used in Champagne to refer to a less complex system of perpetual blending, in which successive vintages are added to a single tank.

STALE Lacking in fruit freshness.

SUR LATTES See 'vins sur lattes'.

SUR POINTE The storing of bottles neck down, between riddling and disgorgement. Sometimes also used for long-term storage of undisgorged bottles. With the lees settled in the neck, it is believed the wine stays fresher for longer.

TAILLES Coarser, inferior juice that flows last from the press.

TCA See 'Corked'.

TERROIR A catch-all term for anything that defines the character of a vineyard — soil, microclimate, altitude, aspect, exposure, slope, drainage, and perhaps even the hands that tend it.

TIRAGE Bottling of the blended wine with an addition of sugar and yeast, so as to provoke the second fermentation in bottle (see page 25).

TUN Large oak barrel, typically around 1000 litres in volume.

VENDANGE Vintage or harvest.

VIEILLES VIGNES Old vines.

VIGNERON Vine grower.

VIN CLAIR Still base wine that has undergone its primary fermentation and (potentially) malolactic fermentation, but not its secondary fermentation.

VINS SUR LATTES Champagne bottles laid on their side having undergone second fermentation but yet to be riddled. The term has also come to refer to the legal but shady practice by which champagne houses purchase finished but yet to be disgorged champagne made by another producer, to then market it under their own label.

VINTAGE Wine from a single year.

ZERO DOSAGE No sweetness is added during the final addition to top up the bottle (see page 47).